Spanish for Communication
LEVEL ONE

William E. Bull

Laurel A. Briscoe

Enrique E. Lamadrid

Carl Dellaccio

Margaret J. Brown

Editorial Advisor

George E. Smith

Houghton Mifflin Company / Boston

Spanish for Communication

LEVEL ONE

New York / Atlanta / Geneva, Illinois / Dallas / Palo Alto

Acknowledgments

The development and pre-publication classroom testing of SPANISH FOR COM-MUNICATION has involved a great many different individuals. We are grateful to all those who have assisted us.

In particular we are indebted to the teachers and students of the public schools of Scottsdale, Arizona and Tacoma, Washington for their cooperation in the final stages of the classroom testing, to Mrs. Lola Mackey of Arizona State University at Tempe and formerly with the Scottsdale Public Schools, and to Mrs. Mary Hoskins formerly of the Hawthorne California Public Schools.

Library of Congress Catalog Card Number: 76–177296

ISBN: 0-395-12448-4

About the Authors

William E. Bull teaches Spanish, theoretical and applied linguistics, and foreign language teaching methodology at the University of California in Los Angeles. Dr. Bull has also taught at the University of Wisconsin, Iowa, Washington University and, in special teacher-training institutes, at the University of Michigan, New Mexico, Puget Sound, and New York (Buffalo). He has served as a consultant to the U.S. Department of State, the Foreign Service Institute, the Department of Health, Education, and Welfare, the Peace Corps, the Modern Language Association of America, and numerous public school systems throughout the United States. A specialist in linguistics and the training of foreign language teachers, he is the author of *Spanish for Teachers: Applied Linguistics*.

Laurel A. Briscoe teaches Curriculum and Instruction at the University of Texas in Austin. Dr. Briscoe received his graduate degrees in Spanish, linguistics, and education from UCLA, where he served as Coordinator of Teacher Training in Foreign Languages. He has also taught Spanish in both junior and senior high schools in Los Angeles and as a demonstration teacher in several summer institutes. He has served as consultant to state, county, and city school districts.

Enrique E. Lamadrid teaches Spanish, applied linguistics, and teaching methodology at the University of New Mexico where he also directs the lower division courses and the training program for graduate and teaching assistants. Professor Lamadrid has taught Spanish in both junior and senior high schools in New Mexico and Colorado and as a demonstration teacher in special summer and year-long institutes.

Carl Dellaccio is Director of Foreign Languages for the Tacoma, Washington Public Schools. Formerly a teacher of Spanish and later Chairman of the Department of Foreign Languages at the Lakewood High School in Long Beach, California, Mr. Dellaccio has participated in a number of summer institutes. He has served in various capacities in state and regional foreign language organizations and has been a consultant to numerous state and city foreign language programs. He has served as a member of the Committee on Organization of the American Council on the Teaching of Foreign Languages and of the Executive Council of the American Association of Teachers of Spanish and Portuguese.

Margaret J. Brown is a clinical educationist at the University Elementary School at UCLA. She has participated in NDEA institutes in the United States and Spain. She has taught in the San Diego public schools and at the University of New Mexico Peace Corps project, and is the author of numerous articles on FLES (foreign language in the elementary school).

Editorial Advisor

George E. Smith, Vice-Chancellor of the University of California at Santa Barbara, was formerly State Supervisor of Foreign Languages in Indiana and Director of the Indiana Language Program at Indiana University. Dr. Smith taught at Wright Junior College, Purdue University, and Indiana University. He is the author of textbooks and motion pictures for secondary schools and for college courses in foreign language education.

PREFACE

Why are you taking a course in Spanish?

It may be that you cannot answer that question. For that matter, you may not be certain why you should study any foreign language. Possibly you want to meet a college entrance requirement. Maybe your family originally came from a Spanish-speaking area. Perhaps you have already traveled in Spanish-speaking countries or have plans to do so. It could be that you live in an area in which Spanish is spoken. Whatever reasons you have for taking Spanish, we believe that when you have finished this first-level course, you will have another: to be able to communicate in Spanish. That is why this course is called SPANISH FOR COMMUNICATION.

To communicate in any language means more than trying to talk to someone. Communication involves understanding—not only of words, but of customs, interpersonal relationships (family, friends, acquaintances), life style (hours, meals, school, work), relationships to the environment (climate, geography, rural and urban locations), and the influence of history (past and recent).

Spanish is one of the most widely used languages in the world. It is the principal means of communication in the western hemisphere, in Spain, in parts of the Philippines, and in those areas of Africa where Spain has had or still has colonies or possessions. In parts of the United States, Spanish is rapidly becoming a second language.

Today many speakers of Spanish differ from one another as much as do peoples who have neither a language nor a cultural heritage in common. The faces of speakers of Spanish in the western hemisphere reveal a complex mixing of peoples. Most "Latin Americans" trace their ancestry to the Spanish settlers or the Indian civilizations, but for many the words "Northern European" or "African" are more appropriate than "Latin."

Andean Indians of Peru or Bolivia, fair-haired Chileans with German and Irish family names, Blacks from the coastal areas and the Islands of the Caribbean, Americans of Mexican origin whose families settled the South West of the United States when it was still a part of Mexico, and recent arrivals from Mexico, Cuba, the Commonwealth of Puerto Rico, the Dominican Republic, and elsewhere all communicate using the same tool—Spanish. A knowledge of Spanish is your key to understanding them and to making yourself understood by them.

How do you learn Spanish?

There is nothing difficult, complicated, or mysterious about learning Spanish—or any other "foreign" language for that matter. Indeed, learning a language is one of the processes that is least "foreign" to human beings. Whenever we have to make ourselves understood in order to express our needs, we find a way of doing it. History is full of stories of missionaries, shipwrecked sailors, and lost explorers who all became fluent in languages they never even knew existed.

Learning a language in a classroom is, of course, quite different and much less dramatic. It involves working with a teacher, your classmates, and a series of instructional materials—primarily books and recordings. Time in class is also limited, and the number of classes is determined by the length of the school year. This does not mean that you cannot learn well and efficiently. It does mean that you have to go about learning in a more structured way. SPANISH FOR COMMUNICATION will provide that framework. In a few months you will come to see that because of the way in which this course is organized, you will be able to learn almost as much of a "foreign" language in about 100 hours of work as you did of your native language in the first six years of your life.

How does SPANISH FOR COMMUNICATION work?

Learning Spanish in school is basically a cooperative effort between you and your teacher. Each of you has certain specific tasks and specialized materials to work with. At times, principally during the class session, you need to work together. At other times, primarily in order to prepare for the class, you work independently and at your own pace. Practice in speaking Spanish and drill work are mostly reserved for the class session. Explanations of how Spanish is organized and how it functions are provided as part of the individualized work.

SPANISH FOR COMMUNICATION is an integrated system of language learning materials. Each part of the program has a specific role to play. You will work most closely with this textbook. A CUADERNO (Workbook) for additional individualized practice is also available. Your teacher will use a series of DAILY LESSON PLANS (which are like scripts for each lesson); a set of posters called the VISUAL GRAMMAR OF SPANISH; a set of FLASH CARDS with pictures, words, and numbers; and a series of VERB CHARTS. RECORDINGS are also available.

How is SPANISH FOR COMMUNICATION organized?

SPANISH FOR COMMUNICATION is divided into a number of phases of instruction called *Etapas*. Each *Etapa* consists of fifteen to twenty *Programs* and a series of *Exercises*. The *Program* is the individualized work which helps you prepare for a class. It is self-correcting and, with few exceptions, will require only fifteen to twenty minutes of concentrated work. If you complete these *Programs* carefully prior to each lesson, you will be as well prepared for class as any of your classmates. The *Etapas* include brief notes contrasting life in most of the United States with life in Spanish-speaking areas. The *Exercises* in each *Etapa* are usually done in class. There are also a series of *Appendices* which include cultural notes, a listing of proverbs and social customs, and a complete Spanish–English and English–Spanish vocabulary.

SPANISH FOR COMMUNICATION is designed to help you to understand, to speak, to read, and to write Spanish as it is used today throughout the Spanish-speaking world. Your teacher and this text and, if available in your school, the supplementary workbook and recordings will help you achieve the long range goal of communication in Spanish. How well you do, of course, depends for the most part on you—your determination, your interest, and your willingness to try something new. We think you can reach the goal that has been set, and that you will find communication in Spanish well worth the effort.

CONTENTS

Etapa Uno

PROGRAM 1

Learning to Do Programs

There are two kinds of assignments which you already know very well. One kind gives you more practice in doing something you have already learned to do in class. For example, in math class you learn to solve certain problems and then you are given problems to do after class. The other kind of assignment gets you ready to participate in class. You read about geography or history before class so you can take part in discussions.

When you hand in written work or answer questions in class, your teacher judges your performance. The written work is a kind of test to see if you can do by yourself what you have already learned to do in class. Class participation is also a test. You prove to your teacher that you can learn something by reading on your own.

In this Spanish class we will not follow either approach. Your outside work will have a very different purpose: to get you ready to understand what you are going to learn to do in class. In many ways this will be like learning the rules of a new game before you start to play it. To learn these "rules" you need to read very carefully and follow instructions. When you do this you will find that it is very hard to make a mistake. If you do make one, you will know it right away, and you can correct it before you go on. This makes it possible for you to come to class just as well prepared as anyone.

The purpose of this course is to teach you Spanish. However, you already know English and this knowledge, when it is properly used, can make learning Spanish much easier. As a result, some of your outside work will show how understanding English can get you ready to learn Spanish much faster and more easily.

These lessons are based on a way of teaching called *programing*. A Program is made up of little sections called *frames*. A frame always has two parts. The first part asks you to do something, and the second part always gives you the correct answer. Here is an example of a frame.

1 When the teacher calls roll in English, you answer by saying "here" or "present." When the roll is called in Spanish, you say (a) *presente* (b) present. •
presente ("Present" is English; *presente* is Spanish.)

It is extremely important for you to understand that you cannot find out how much you know, what you need to learn, or how well you are learning if you see the answer *before* you solve the problem given to you in the first part of each frame. The answer, as a result, must be kept covered until you have done what you are instructed to do in the first part of the frame. Notice the bullet in the margin on the right which signals the end of the first part and asks you to stop. Here is how you work with a Program.

Step 1: Get a sheet of paper on which to write your answers. One with lines is better.

Step 2: Write 1 at the left edge of the first line.

Step 3: Cover the first page of the Program with a thick piece of blank paper (the cover sheet).

Step 4: Slide the cover sheet down until you come to the bullet in the right-hand margin.

Step 5: Read carefully and do what you are asked to do.

Step 6: Slide the cover sheet down to the answer which begins in the left-hand margin.

Step 7: If your answer is correct, write the number of the next frame on your work sheet, and follow instructions. If you made a mistake, draw a *circle* around the number for the frame on your answer sheet. This is what you will need to review in order to be completely ready for what is going to happen in your next class.

Step 8: When you have finished the Program, review the frames in which you made an error.

It is very important for you to remember that the prime purpose of a Program is to get you ready for what is going to happen in class. What you are supposed to learn outside of class will not be taught again in class. You should be prepared to hand in your work sheet every day. If you are absent, you will have to make up any Programs missed.

You will not be graded on how many frames you get right or wrong in a Program. You can make several mistakes and still learn what you need to know. What really counts is how much you know *after* you have finished a Program. You will be tested on this in all major exams and in frequent quizzes. Your teacher will not tell you when there is to be a quiz, but if you do the Programs thoroughly, you will be prepared for a quiz whenever one is given.

When you have finished a Program, count the number of frames you have missed. Missing more than five frames almost always means you are not working properly. You may not be reading carefully, you may not be following instructions, or you may be trying to get the answer before you have thought enough.

Of course, you cannot find out how well you are *really* doing if you look at the answer before trying to solve the problem. Keep in mind that the Program is to help you get ready for your next class. Be sure you do it before class.

A practice Program follows. Write the number 1 on your answer sheet. Position your cover sheet. Now you are ready to begin. Remember to try to solve the problem before looking at the answer.

1 The Spanish word for "flower" is *flor*. The name of one of the southern states comes from and begins with *flor*. This state is ⁓⁓⁓. •

Florida (*Florida* describes a place that has many flowers.) If you missed this, circle the number 1 and go on.

2 The Spanish verb *nevar* translates "to snow." One of our western states was described by the early Spaniards as "a place covered with snow." The name of this state is *Neva* ⁓⁓⁓. •

Did you write number 2 and *da* on your answer sheet?

3 The Spanish word for "color" is *color*. The name of what state begins with *Color* ⁓⁓⁓? •

Colorado (Colorado has many red rocks. In Spanish *colorado* may mean "red.")

4 *Florida*, *Nevada* and *Colorado* are words borrowed from Spanish. Many English and Spanish words come from Latin. English "student" and Spanish *estudiante* both came from Latin. These look-alikes are called **cognates**. The Spanish cognate of "mountain" is the name of one of our western states. This state is ——.

Montana (Spanish *montaña* means "mountain.")

To get a perfect score on these four practice frames, you had to know the names of four states: Florida, Nevada, Colorado, and Montana. Let us pretend that you missed all of them. The answers told you what you needed to learn. If you learned from your mistakes, you can go to class tomorrow knowing as much as any other student about this practice lesson. With Program learning, you find out *before* you go to class what you still have to learn. You can always be perfect, if you really want to.

How long it will take you to do each Program depends on you. How fast you go depends on how fast you can read, how much you already know, your study habits, and many other things; you should take as much time as you need. Some students may finish a Program in less than fifteen minutes; other students may take five or ten minutes more. With practice, no Program should take you more than 20 minutes of real work. Most of them should take less time. Take the time *you* need to do each Program well. In that way, you will keep up with the best in your class.

The following frames will give you more practice in working with Programs and, at the same time, will teach you some facts about learning a new language. Before you start, use your cover sheet and write a new number 1 on your work sheet.

1 There are two ways of sending messages by using words. One way is by speaking, the other is by ——. (Write the missing word on your answer sheet.)

writing (We speak words and we write words.)

2 Speech and writing are not alike. The front part of a ship is called its *bow*. Say *bow* like *how*. You shoot an arrow with a *bow*. Now, say *bow* and *arrow* aloud. Does the written word, by itself, tell us how to say *bow?* (Write "yes" or "no" on your answer sheet.)

no

3 The capital of Spain is written *Madrid*. Is it likely that the spelling *Madrid* suggests one pronunciation to a Spanish speaker and another to you? (Write "yes" or "no" on your answer sheet.)

yes (Spanish speakers do not say *Madrid* the same way as speakers of English.)

4 The following words are all Spanish words: *general, rodeo, metal, gas*. Can the same letters, arranged in the same order, stand for the different sounds of two different languages?

yes (What you see in writing or print does not always tell you what language the words belong to.)

5 A female deer is called a *doe*. Bread is made out of *dough*. Does what you hear always tell you what to write?

no

6 One learns to spell *dough* from (a) hearing the word (b) seeing it written. (Write (a) or (b) after the frame number on your answer sheet.)

seeing it written or hearing it spelled aloud (When you hear *dough*, all by itself, you do not know whether to write *dough* or *doe*.)

7 The Spanish word for "foot" is *pie*, and the Spanish word for "bread" is *pan*. Can you tell from what is written (*pie*, *pan*) how the Spanish speaker says these words?

no (To speakers of English *pan* is a dish in which one bakes a *pie*.)

8 To learn to speak a new language, one must first (a) see the written words (b) hear the spoken words. (Write the letter of your choice on the answer sheet.)

hear the spoken words (Hearing must come before speaking.)

9 If you see a Spanish word before you hear it, will you pronounce it (a) like a Spanish speaker? (b) like a speaker of English?

like a speaker of English

10 Do you now understand better why you still have not seen any written words in your Spanish class?

Just in case your answer is "no," in your next class your teacher will help you learn to say *pie*—"foot" and *pan*—"bread" in Spanish.

If you missed any frame in this Program, go back and read it again. You will then be certain that you know just as much as everyone else in your class. Remember to take your answer sheet to class.

Everyone knows that the Japanese, Africans, and the Hindus have cultures and ways of life that are very different from the American. There are, however, so many Hispanic people living in the United States that it is frequently assumed that the only major difference between the Spanish speaker and the American is the language that they speak. There are, in fact, hundreds of different ways in which the two cultures are not alike and, as a result, great misunderstandings can be created if you and the Spanish speaker do not realize how and why you are different. To help you understand the Spanish speaker better, you will find hereafter short descriptions of some significant difference between Hispanic and American culture. Read these carefully and eventually you will have a deeper understanding of how you and the Spanish speaker differ. Here is an example.

The Spanish speaker has a very different attitude towards animals than most Americans. The American may keep almost any type of animal as a pet. Many people keep dogs and cats as household companions, and each animal is generally given a name, the way the human members of the family are. There are, in addition, pet stores, animal hospitals, pet beauty salons, and even special graveyards for pets. The Spanish speaker, in sharp contrast, has no word at all for *pet* and frequently does not even give names to animals. Moreover, he carefully keeps animals and people clearly separated in his mind, and it is generally considered improper to describe human speech with verbs used to describe animal noises, such as *growl, bellow, roar,* and *hiss.* As a result, few words in the Spanish vocabulary can be used as impolite substitutes for "to say." In the same way Spanish has two words for "foot," one for people (*pie*) and another for animals (*pata*), and when a person sticks his nose (*nariz*) into someone else's business the word used is *hocico*, the equivalent of "snout." In general it is considered derogatory to use animal terms to describe people.

PROGRAM 2

Some Facts about Speech Sounds

1 The first few frames of this Program are to remind you of the way to do a Program properly. You begin each Program with a clean sheet of paper. You write your name in the upper right-hand corner. At the top left-side you write the number ——.

1 (Before you go on, write 2 below this number for the next frame.)

2 If you miss the answer to a frame, you draw a —— around the frame number.

circle

3 A mark like this —— tells you to write the missing part on your answer sheet. When you are given a choice, shown by (a) and (b), you only write the —— for the correct choice.

letter

4 When there is a single question, you write either —— or ——.

yes or no

5 When you look at the answer part of the frame before you try to get the answer, you are —— yourself.

cheating (Perhaps you had to look to get the right answer to this frame. The important thing is, did you try hard first? The next frame will start your class preparation. Before you begin, you need to know the meaning of certain marks used in writing about sounds and letters. To keep from confusing a letter of the alphabet with the sound represented by that letter in actual speech, the letter is always printed in italics. So you will see: "In our written alphabet *b* is the second letter." In contrast, when a statement is made about the sound made in speech, the letter appears in brackets. So you will see things like this: The [b] of *boy* is very much like the Spanish [b].)

6 Cut a piece of thin paper (an old newspaper will do) into a strip about an inch wide and three inches long. Grasp one end of the strip and hold the flat side of the other end about one-half inch from your lips. Now say *pay* quite loudly and <u>watch</u> the strip. Did the strip (a) stay still? (b) jump?

jump (Let's find out why.)

7 Watch the strip of paper and say *may*. Did the strip (a) stay still? (b) jump?

stay still (*Pay* and *may* begin with different sounds.)

8 Hold the strip of paper in the same position and say *pay* and *may* several times. Watch the paper. Which word begins with a puff sound that makes the paper jump? (a) pay (b) may

pay (The [p] of *pay* is followed by a sharp puff. This makes the paper jump.)

9 Now watch the strip of paper and say English *pie* and *spy* quite loudly several times. The paper jumps when you say (a) pie (b) spy.

pie (There is no puff after [p] in *spy*.)

10 There is a puff after [p] in *pie* and *pay*. In these words the letter *p* actually stands for a [p] that is made with a following ——.

puff (Linguists say this [p] is *aspirated*—made *with* a puff.)

11 Hold the strip of paper before your lips again and say the following pairs of words together. Watch the paper carefully: *pin-spin*, *pat-spat*, *pot-spot*. The paper does not jump when [p] comes right after the sound ⌒⌒⌒.

[s] ([p] has no puff after [s]. It is *unaspirated*—made *without* a puff.)

12 The [p] of *pin*, *pat*, and *pot* is aspirated (made with a puff). The [p] of *spin*, *spat*, and *spot* is unaspirated (made without a puff). Does the letter *p*, in English, stand for (a) just one sound? (b) two slightly different sounds?

two slightly different sounds (one *with* a puff; one *without* a puff)

13 There is no Spanish word in which the sound [p] is ever made with a puff. The Spanish [p] is always (a) unaspirated (b) aspirated.

unaspirated   **14** The Spanish letter *p* stands for (a) one sound (b) two sounds.

one sound (Only the unaspirated [p]: the one *without* a puff.)

There is no [p] with a puff in any Spanish word. However, you have been making this puff sound at the beginning of words starting with *p* all your life. This English habit has to be broken or you will have an accent in Spanish. In your next class your teacher will start some special drills which will help you learn to hear the two English [p] sounds and get you started on the Spanish habit: no puff with [p].

15 In the experiments you just tried, you found that *p* stands for two sounds in English. Most speakers of English do not hear this difference because we are trained to "tune out" sound differences which do not change meaning. To learn Spanish, you must learn to "tune in" sounds you do not listen to in English. It is a lot easier to do this when you know something about how sounds are made.

The sounds we make in speaking are made by forcing air out of our lungs up through the throat and out through either the mouth or nose. Here is a way to prove this. Say *hum* rather loudly and hold the [m] sound for a second. Say *hum* again and watch what you are doing with your lips. Are they (a) closed? (b) open?

closed (You cannot say the sound [m] with your mouth open.)

16 Say *hum* again, hold the [m] sound, and while you are doing this, pinch your nose tightly closed with your fingers. Did the sound (a) stop? (b) go on?

the sound stopped (Your lips were closed and the air was coming out your nose. With your nose closed, you cannot say the [m] sound.)

17 Hold your nose closed and say *ah* the way you do when the doctor wants to look down your throat. The air comes out (a) your nose (b) your mouth.

your mouth   **18** Say the name for the letter *e* and the sound *ah*. Say *e-ah* several times. Watch what your jaws are doing. When you go from the sound of *e* to *ah*, do you (a) open your mouth wider? (b) close your mouth more?

open your mouth wider (If you got the wrong answer, say *e-ah* in front of a mirror. You will see that different sounds are made by changing the shape of the passageway through which the air comes out.)

19 Here is another way of making sounds different. Cup your hands and hold them tightly over your ears. Say *fuzz* and *fuss* real loud. Try this again and hold the last sound of each word for a second. Which word makes a buzzing sound?

fuzz   **20** Take a tight hold of your Adam's apple in your throat. Now say the [ss] of *fuss* and the [zz] of *fuzz*, hold the sounds, and feel the difference. Which sound makes your throat vibrate?

[zz] (When you say *fuzz* the edges of two muscles in your throat—the vocal cords—vibrate to make the buzzing sound.)

21 A sound made with the vocal cords vibrating is said to be *voiced*. A sound made without the vocal cords vibrating is said to be *unvoiced*. Say *sue* and *zoo* aloud. Which word begins with a voiced sound?

zoo (If you got the wrong answer, cup your hands over your ears and say *zoo*. You can hear the buzz, if you say it correctly.)

22 Say *resin*, *resident*, and *president* aloud until you make the same sound [s] for all three. Is this [s] sound (a) voiced? (b) unvoiced?

It is voiced. (The vocal cords vibrate.)

23 In English you may answer roll call by saying *present*. Say *present* aloud several times and listen to the [s] sound. Is it (a) unvoiced? (no buzz) (b) voiced?

voiced **24** In answering roll call, you have already learned to say the Spanish for "present." It is *presente*. Say *presente* and, then, *sente* aloud several times. Is the [s] for *sente* (a) voiced? (b) unvoiced?

unvoiced: no buzz (Spanish, unlike English, never has a voiced [s] sound before a vowel, that is, before *a, e, i, o,* or *u*.)

25 Say *hat* aloud several times, and each time hold the tip of your tongue in the position it has when you finish saying the sound [t]. When you say the sound [t], the tip of your tongue touches (a) the back of your upper front teeth (b) the gum ridge right above the back of your upper front teeth.

the gum ridge (When a Spanish speaker makes a [t] sound, his tongue always touches the back of his upper front teeth, not the gum ridge.)

26 You have just discovered that in Spanish the letters *p, s,* and *t* do not stand for the same sounds in *presente* as they do in "present." Do you remember the difference? The Spanish [p] sound is (a) like the [p] of *pie* (made with a puff) (b) like the [p] of *spy* (made without a puff)

like the [p] of *spy* (It is unaspirated: made without a puff.)

27 The Spanish [s] sound, in front of any vowel, is not like English. It is always (a) voiced (buzzed) (b) unvoiced (no buzz).

unvoiced (The [s] of *presente* does not have the [z] sound of "present." If you missed this frame, go back to Frame 24 and re-read the answer.)

28 When the Spanish speaker makes the sound [t], the tip of his tongue touches (a) the back of his upper front teeth (b) the gum ridge above the back of his upper front teeth.

the back of the teeth ("Dentists" work on teeth. The Spanish [t] is said to be *dental* because the tongue tip touches the teeth.)

29 People learn and work better when they know the names of things they use in learning or working. You have learned the meaning of several technical words in this Program. They will be useful in talking about the new sounds you are going to learn in Spanish. Can you remember their meanings? *Voiced* means that the vocal cords (a) vibrate (b) do not vibrate.

vibrate (They make a buzzing sound.)

30 *Unaspirated* means there is (a) a puff after a sound (b) no puff after a sound.

no puff **31** *Unvoiced* means that the vocal cords ———— vibrate.

do not **32** *Aspirated* means there is a ———— after a sound.

puff **33** *Dental* is an adjective which refers to (a) the tongue (b) the teeth.

the teeth (The Spanish [t] sound is dental.)

It is customary to think of the United States as the great melting pot of the Americas because many people came here from England, Ireland, Sweden, Norway, Africa, Germany, Poland, Italy, China and other countries. In addition, there are a great many speakers of Spanish in the southwestern part of the country, in Florida, in New York City, and other urban areas. In contrast with the United States, there is no Spanish speaking country which has a large number of citizens who speak English. There are a few small colonies of English-speaking Mennonites in Mexico, Central America, and Bolivia. Nevertheless, Latin America is a melting pot like the United States. There are many Negroes in all the countries around the Caribbean Sea, many Germans in southern Chile and southern Brazil, Italians in Argentina, Orientals in most countries, and a considerable number of people who fled from the Turkish Empire after World War I (Syrians, Lebanese, Armenians). There are also considerable numbers of Irishmen who are descendants of the Irish who immigrated to Spain during the great potato famine of the nineteenth century. A glance through the telephone directory of any big city will reveal names like Eduardo O'Higgins, Manuela MacGregor, Rosa Kestleman, or José Stein. Contrary to the general American notion, a person who speaks only Spanish may be black, white, Indian, Oriental, or Irish; and he may very well be blond or even redheaded.

A Linguistic Game

You now know that the sound of Spanish [p] is always unaspirated (made without a puff). You can easily learn to make the Spanish [p] sound by learning to talk English with a Spanish accent. Try this experiment.

Look into a mirror and say English *pie* and *pan* aloud. Notice that at the beginning of each word your lips are pressed tightly together. The puff that follows the English [p] is caused by air pressure built up behind your closed lips. When you open them quickly, the air escapes with a little puff sound.

Now, hold the strip of paper a half inch from your lips. Start to say *pie* or *pan*, but open your lips before any air pressure builds up behind them. When you do this soon enough, the strip of paper will not jump, and you will be speaking English with a true Spanish accent.

Here is another way to find out if you are making [p] with a puff. Hold the back of your hand very close to your lips and say *paper*. You will feel the puff of air after the [p] sound.

PROGRAM 3

A Difference Between English and Spanish Sounds, and Review

Part 1: The English Sound *Schwa*

1 Most spoken words are made up of a series of different sounds. When we write words, these sounds are represented by the ～～ of the alphabet.

letters   **2** Most words are also made up of little parts which may have several sounds, usually represented by two or more letters in writing. The word *important* has three of these pieces. They are called ～～.

syllables   **3** Say *important* aloud. The first syllable is (a) imp (b) im.

im   **4** Say *im-portant* aloud again. Which way will you divide the second part into syllables? (a) port-ant (b) por-tant

por-tant   **5** Divide *important* into syllables.

im-por-tant   **6** Divide these words in the same way: student, mention, pencil, multiply.

stu-dent, men-tion, pen-cil, mul-ti-ply

7 When a word has two or more syllables, one of these syllables is always spoken a little louder than the others. In the word *mention*, the syllable *men* is louder than the syllable *tion*. This louder syllable is said to be (a) stressed (b) unstressed.

stressed   **8** Say the following words aloud, copy them, and underline the stressed syllable in each: gen-er-al, pen-cil, im-por-tant.

gen-er-al, **pen**-cil, im-**por**-tant (If you made a mistake, say the word again and make the stressed syllable very loud.)

9 If one syllable in a word is louder than the others, then the less loud syllables must be unstressed. Copy the following words and underline the unstressed syllable in each: pen-cil, pis-tol, to-tal, fruit-ful, can-cel.

pen-**cil**, pis-**tol**, to-**tal**, fruit-**ful**, can-**cel**

10 The two unstressed syllables in *im-por-tant* are ～～.

im-por-**tant**   **11** Say "It's not important" aloud several times. Try to say this in a way that says you really don't care. Listen carefully to see if you can hear how you pronounce the *a* of *tant*. Is the sound of *a* in *tant* more like (a) the *a* of *tan* or (b) the *u* of *tun?*

the *u* of *tun*   **12** If *important* were spelled the way it is pronounced, it would be written ⁓⁓⁓.

important   **13** Say *fruitful* and *total* aloud several times, one after the other. The sound of *al* in *total* is (a) very much like the *ul* of *fruitful* (b) very different from the *ul* of *fruitful.*

al is very much like *ul*

14 Say *total*, *pencil*, *cancel*, and *pistol* aloud several times. In these words, the sounds of *al*, *il*, *el*, and *ol* are (a) alike (b) very different.

For most speakers of English, these sounds are alike.

15 Look at these words. They are divided into syllables, and the unstressed syllable is indicated: pen-**cil**, to-**tal**, can-**cel**, pis-**tol**. The letters standing for the vowels in the unstressed syllables are ⁓⁓⁓.

i, a, e, o   **16** The last two sounds of *to-tal*, *pen-cil*, *can-cel*, and *pis-tol* are in an unstressed syllable. Say these words aloud again and listen to what you do with *al*, *il*, *el*, and *ol*. In these words, the letters *a*, *i*, *e*, and *o*, stand for sounds which are (a) alike (b) different.

alike (In some unstressed syllables *a, e, i, o,* and *u* may stand for the same
sound. This sound is called *schwa.*)

17 The following words are divided into syllables. Say them aloud, copy them, and underline the letter which may stand for the schwa sound in each. Remember, it must be in the unstressed syllable: trail-er, sail-or, cri-sis, mi-nus, dol-lar, at-las.

trail-**e**r, sail-**o**r, cri-s**i**s, mi-n**u**s, dol-l**a**r, at-l**a**s

18 In spelling, the difference between *pistol* and *total* is shown in two ways. The first syllables are different, *pis* and *to*. In the second syllable, *tol* and *tal*, there is a contrast between *o* and *a* in spelling. However, the difference between the *o* of *tol* and the *a* of *tal* is lost in speech. In speech the vowel of the second (unstressed) syllable is schwa in both words. So the difference, in speech, between the two words is marked only by the stressed syllables ⁓⁓⁓.

pis; to   **19** In English speech, the vowels in unstressed syllables are frequently not used to mark a difference between words. Spanish is very different from English. The two following Spanish words are divided into syllables. The stressed syllable of each is indicated: **ca**-sa (house), **co**-sa (thing). In both English and Spanish, the difference between two words may be marked by a contrast between vowels in (a) a stressed syllable (b) an unstressed syllable.

stressed syllable

20 These Spanish words are divided into syllables. The unstressed syllables are indicated: ca-**sa** (house), ca-**si** (almost). In Spanish, unlike English, the difference between two words may be marked by a contrast between vowels in (a) stressed syllables (b) unstressed syllables.

unstressed syllables

21 If Spanish speakers pronounced *casa* and *casi* with the schwa sound in the unstressed syllables *sa* and *si*, would they be able to tell the difference between these two words?

no (They would sound exactly alike.)

22 The difference between *cosa* (thing) and *casa* (house) is marked by *o* and *a* in the stressed syllables *co-sa* and *ca-sa*. The difference between *caso* (case) and *casa* (house) is also shown by *o* and *a*, but in the unstressed syllables *ca-so* and *ca-sa*. The vowels *o* and *a* mark a difference in meaning (a) in both stressed and unstressed syllables (b) only in unstressed syllables.

in both stressed and unstressed syllables

23 Since *o* and *a*, in Spanish, show a difference in meaning in either stressed or unstressed syllables, must each be pronounced the same all the time?

yes (Spanish vowel sounds are the same in either stressed or unstressed syllables. *Spanish has no schwa sound.*)

As a speaker of English, you have the habit of using the schwa sound in many unstressed syllables. To speak Spanish properly, you must now break this habit. In your next class, your teacher will begin a series of drills which will help you get the Spanish habit.

Part 2: A Review of What You Have Been Learning

You are going to study many things in this course. Some of these things you will learn and remember from seeing, hearing, or doing them just once. However, you will keep on forgetting other things until you have seen them, heard them, or done them many times. You can speed up your learning and improve your memory by discovering what you, as an individual, must pay more attention to in learning. Let's see where your trouble spots are so far.

1 An aspirated [p] in English is made (a) with a puff (b) without a puff.

with a puff
2 The sound [p] in English *put* or *pet* is (a) aspirated (b) unaspirated.

aspirated
3 Does English also have a [p] sound which is unaspirated? (Remember: you write "yes" or "no" on your answer sheet when there is a yes-no question.)

yes (English [p] is not aspirated after [s]: spit, spot, *etc.*)

4 In writing, the letter *p* can stand for two different sounds in English. (a) true (b) false

true
5 Does Spanish have an aspirated [p] sound?

no
6 In Spanish the letter *p* stands for (a) two sounds (b) only one sound.

only one sound, the unaspirated [p]

7 When a sound is voiced, the vocal cords (a) vibrate (b) do not vibrate.

vibrate
8 The [s] of Spanish *presente* is (a) voiced (b) unvoiced.

unvoiced (The *s* before vowels—*a, e, i, o, u*—never has a [z] sound in Spanish.)

9 Spanish speakers and speakers of English do not make the [t] sound in the same way. When a Spanish speaker makes a [t] sound, the tip of the tongue touches ⌒⌒⌒.

the back of the upper front teeth

10 The doctors who take care of teeth are called ⌒⌒⌒.

dentists
11 Because of the tongue position, the Spanish [t] is called a ⌒⌒⌒ [t].

dental (This is really a "tooth [t].")

12 When you say the sound [m], the air comes out (a) your nose (b) your mouth.

your nose
13 When you say any vowel sound (a, e, i, o, u), the air comes out your ⌒⌒⌒.
mouth

14 The schwa sound appears only in (a) stressed syllables (b) unstressed syllables.

unstressed syllables (If you missed this, you were not concentrating when you did Part 1 of this Program.)

15 Spanish, like English, has a schwa sound. (a) true (b) false

false   **16** A "floral" display is made up of "flowers." The Spaniards named one of our states *Florida* because it has many flowers. The Spanish noun *flor* is translated into English by ⁓⁓⁓.

flower (The name for these look-alike words is *cognate*.)

17 Can you tell from looking at *pie* and *pan* what language to use in saying them aloud?

no (*Pie* is a pastry in English; "foot" in Spanish.)

Check the frames that you missed. This will show you the kinds of things you tend to forget. Once you know this, you can watch out for these things and your memory will get better.

PROGRAM **4**

The Pieces and Parts of Words: Morphology

1 You already know that in speaking, words are made up of sounds which in writing, are represented by letters. You also know that words can be broken up into syllables. How many syllables are there in the word *Spanish?*

two   **2** Divide *Spanish* into two syllables.

Span-ish   **3** Does the syllable *ish* have any meaning by itself?

no (In many words the syllables, all by themselves, have no meaning. Put together, they do.)

4 How many syllables are there in *untie?*

two   **5** Divide *untie* into two syllables.

un-tie   **6** Does the part *tie* in *Untie it!* deal with something we can do with a string or ribbon?

yes   **7** *Untie* means (a) to make a knot (b) to take a knot apart.

to take a knot apart

8 If *tie* means "to make a bow or knot," then the *un* of *untie* must mean to do (a) the same thing (b) the opposite.

the opposite (You *untie* what has been *tied*.)

9 You can *tie* and *untie* a knot. Does each part of *untie* have a meaning of its own?

yes   **10** Is the *un* of *untie* like the *un* of *undo?*

yes (You *tie* and *untie*; you *do* and *undo* something.)

11 The word *under*, as in "It is under the table," has two syllables: *un-der*. Does the *un* of *under*, like the *un* of *undo* or *untie*, have a meaning of its own?

no (The *un* of *under* is a syllable, but it has no meaning of its own. It is like the *ish* of *Spanish*.)

12 Does a syllable always have a meaning of its own?

no

13 The opposite of *tie* is *untie*. The opposite of *appear* is *disappear*. Does the *dis* of *disappear* have about the same meaning as the *un* of *untie*?

yes

14 The *un* and *dis* of *untie* and *disappear* have meaning. Are they words?

no (These parts are never used alone. They may be put in front of certain words to change the meaning. Because they are attached to the front of words, they are called *prefixes*.)

15 Copy these words and underline the prefixes: retread, misjudge, malformed, discontented.

retread, **mis**judge, **mal**formed, **dis**contented

16 Compare *actor* and *actress*. The part which is the same in both words is ——.

act

17 What part of *actor* and *actress* tells us that the person has a role in a play or movie?

act (The *act* tells us what the person does. An *actor* acts.)

18 What part of *actress* says the person is a girl?

ress (The *dis* of *disappear* is called a "prefix." The parts added to *act* in *actor* (man) and *actress* (woman) are *suffixes* which tell us that the person acting is male or female.)

19 There are many kinds of suffixes. There is, believe it or not, a suffix in the word *this*. Here is how you can prove it. Compare *this book* and *that book*. If you are speaking and also pointing to one of the two books, which is closer to you? (a) this book (b) that book

this book

20 What part of *this* and *that* is the same?

th (This part, the *th*, tells us we are pointing something out. For this reason words like "this" and "that" are called *demonstratives*, from the verb *demonstrate*,—to show.)

21 The *th* is the same in both *this* and *that*. *This book*, however, is closer to the speaker than *that book*. Now, stop and think. What part of *this* must say "close"? (a) th (b) is

is (Remember: the *th* is the pointing-out part: the demonstrative.)

22 The demonstrative *that* points something out and says that it is not close: *that book over there*. What part of *that* says "not close"?

at

23 How many syllables are there in *this* or *that*? Say each word before you decide.

one (The demonstratives *this* and *that* have only one syllable each, but both have two meaningful parts. The *th* points something out. The *is* says that it is close. The *at* says it is farther away.)

24 May a word have more meaningful parts than syllables?

yes (The meaningful parts of a word may be the same as syllables: *un-tie, re-tread, mal-formed*. The meaningful parts of a word may also be pieces of the same syllable: *this, that*.)

25 What part of *this* and *these* is the same?

th (The *th* is called the *stem*.)

26 The part of a word which is added to the end of a stem is called a "suffix." Copy the suffixes of *this, these, that, those.*

is, ese, at, ose   **27** The demonstrative *this* combines with *dog: this dog.* Is it proper to say *this dogs?*

no   **28** You say *this dog* but not *this dogs.* When you have the plural form *dogs,* you change *this* to 〜〜〜.

these (*This dog* becomes *these dogs.*)   **29** The suffix *ese* of *these* matches the *s* of *dogs.* It is (a) singular (b) plural.

plural   **30** The demonstrative *that* has a stem, *th,* and a singular suffix *at: that dog.* To make the plural form which combines with *dogs,* the suffix *at* must be replaced by 〜〜〜.

ose (*That dog* becomes *those dogs.*)   **31** Does *those* point out things that are (a) near? (b) far away?

far away   **32** The suffix *ese* of *these* goes with the *s* of *dogs.* In addition to saying "plural," this suffix also says the dogs are (a) far away (b) close.

close   **33** The suffix of *these* says "close" and "plural." (a) true (b) false

true   **34** Now be careful, and remember that *these* is a demonstrative. It points out something. How many pieces of information does the whole word *these* give you? 1, 2, 3

3 (It **points out** something that is **close** and **plural**.)   **35** Compare *dog, dogs.* How many pieces of information are there in *dogs?*

two   **36** Both *dogs* and *these* have two parts: a stem and a plural suffix. The stems are 〜〜〜.

dog; th   **37** May a stem be a word by itself?

yes   **38** Are all stems words?

no (Stems like *th* must be a part of a word. They are used only when a suffix is added.)   **39** What part of *remake* is the stem?

make   **40** What part of *churches* is the suffix?

es (The singular is *church.*)   **41** What part of *impossible* is the prefix?

im   **42** You make the opposite of *please* by adding the negative prefix 〜〜〜.

dis (Does that *please* you or *displease* you?)   **43** Does *That is not possible* say the same thing as *That is impossible?*

yes   **44** The *dis* of *displease* and the *im* of *impossible* are like *not.* They are negating prefixes. What does the *re* of *remake* or *redo* tell you? (a) not (b) again

to make or do again   **45** Can you really understand the meaning of *remake* if you do not pay attention to the meaning of both parts, the prefix and the stem?

no (If you wrote "yes," think of the difference between *remake* and *unmake.*)

Spanish words have the same kinds of pieces and parts as English. They have stems, prefixes, and suffixes. To understand or speak Spanish well, you must learn the meaning of these parts just as you have done in English. In your next class, your teacher will begin to teach you some of the parts of Spanish words.

The study of the pieces and parts of words is called *morphology.* The *morph* part of *morphology* comes from the Greek meaning "shape" or "form." The parts of words which have meaning (prefixes, stems, suffixes) are also called *morphemes* (meaningful forms).

From the point of view of the average American, one of the outstanding characteristics of the average Latin is his excessive politeness. Many, in fact, seem to be so polite that they make Americans uncomfortable. It is most interesting, in view of these attitudes, to hear reports from visiting Latins that they frequently find themselves in an embarrassing situation because they have not said "Thank you." Social etiquette requires the American to say thank you in many situations in which Hispanic custom requires no response at all.

When receiving gifts or favors from friends or relatives, for example, though real appreciation may be felt, Latins frequently will not say *gracias.* The average Latin feels that Americans overdo the saying of "thank you."

Street beggars, older persons, and people in rural areas often show their appreciation by saying *Que Dios se lo pague* ("May God reward you") rather than *gracias.* Another variant is *Le estoy muy agradecido* ("I am very grateful to you").

PROGRAM 5

tú versus *usted*: a Spanish Social Custom

1 When we have a conversation, there must be a speaker, the person spoken to, and, very often, the person or thing spoken about. The speaker is called *first person*. The person spoken to is *second person*. The person or thing spoken about is the *third person*. The subject pronoun which stands for the speaker is the singular *I*. The plural of *I* is a completely different word, ⟿.

we (*I* am learning Spanish. *We* are learning Spanish.)

2 When we talk about a third person, that person must be either male or female. The subject pronoun for a third person male is *he*. For a third person female it is ⟿.

she (*She* is playing ping-pong. *He* is polishing the car.)

3 The subject pronouns *he* and *she* are singular. The plural for either one or both is ⟿.

they (*They* are eating candy.)

4 The subject pronoun which stands for the person spoken to, the second person, is ⟿.

you (*You* are right.)

5 In the King James translation of the Bible one of the Ten Commandments says, "Thou shalt not kill." This is old English. In modern English *shalt* becomes *shall* and *thou* is replaced by ⟿.

you (*You shall* not kill.)

6 There is a church hymn which has the line "Come all ye faithful." In this line the second person pronoun *ye* stands for (a) one person (b) many people. ●

many people (*All ye* is like *you all.*)

7 In speaking of subject pronouns, "singular" means one; "plural" means more than one (two, several, many, *etc.*). Which pronoun, *thou* or *ye*, is plural? ●

ye (*Thou* stands for one person.)

8 The second person pronouns, *thou* and *ye*, are no longer used in ordinary conversations by most speakers of English. Some religious groups, however, still use *thou* and *ye* (also *thee*) when talking to members of their families or to members of their church. They usually use *you* when speaking to strangers and to people who are not members of their church. Does the kind of social relationship between the speaker and the person spoken to tell these people when it is proper to use *thou* or *you?* ●

yes (There is a different social relationship between friends than between strangers.)

9 In both English and Spanish there are many little things in speech which clearly show different kinds of social relationships between people speaking to each other. For example, when you speak to your mother, which is the least familiar and most formal? (a) Mommy (b) Mom (c) Mother ●

Mother

10 Do most children address their parents or their teachers by their first names? ●

no (To do so is generally considered to be disrespectful or improper.)

11 Is it improper or disrespectful for parents or teachers to call children by their first names? ●

no (It is considered proper for older people to call children by their first names.)

12 Is it disrespectful for you to call your brother or sister by his or her first name? ●

no (It is generally proper for equals to call each other by their first names.)

13 The president of a large corporation, Peter R. Hollister, addresses his private secretary as *Betty*. She should call him (a) Pete (b) Peter (c) Mr. Hollister. ●

Mr. Hollister

14 When a private in the Army answers a general, he says: (a) Yup (b) Yeah (c) Yes (d) Yes, sir. ●

Yes, sir.

15 The words *sir* and *mister* are most often used in speaking to persons of (a) lower rank (b) equal rank (c) higher rank. ●

higher rank

16 Which of the following shows the greatest respect? (a) Kathy (b) Kathleen (c) Kathleen Durand (d) Mrs. Durand ●

Mrs. Durand (A title of address is a mark of respect.)

17 A child is being naughty. Which of the following, spoken by his mother, is more stern and authoritative? (a) Johnnie, come here! (b) John Harrington Smith, come here! ●

John Harrington Smith, come here! (The full name is more formal than a nickname.)

18 Which form is more likely to be used by a very close friend? (a) Maggie (b) Margaret ●

Maggie

19 Titles are not generally used with nicknames. Which is the proper way to address a letter? (a) Mr. Bill Hammond (b) Mr. William Hammond ●

Mr. William Hammond

20 When one small child asks another his name, the second may reply, "My name's Billy." Is it proper for a lawyer in court to answer the judge by saying, "My name's Billy"? ●

no (Adults do not usually introduce themselves with their nicknames, and especially in a very formal situation. They give their first and last name.)

21 A judge and a lawyer are very close friends. When they go fishing together they call each other *Ed* and *Walt*. When the lawyer is before the court, how does he address the judge? (a) Walt (b) Your honor

Your honor (The formality of a situation determines the form of address.)

22 Your father may call your mother *honey* or *sweetheart*. Is it common for people who have just met to use these terms to address each other?

no (Terms of endearment are usually used only between persons who are very intimate.)

23 When English was still using *thou* and *ye* in contrast with *you*, it was possible to indicate different social relationships or different degrees of formality by choosing between these forms. Today all second persons are addressed as *you*, but differences in rank, degrees of intimacy, familiarity, or formality are still shown by differences in the use of many other words.

Modern Spanish, like old English, still uses pronouns and verb forms which reveal the speaker's social relationship to the person spoken to. The modern Spanish form which is like old English "thou" is *tú*. Will a Spanish speaker normally use *tú* in speaking to a stranger?

no (*Tú*, like "thou," indicates a close social relationship.)

24 The pronoun *usted*, which also translates "you," is a contraction of an older form *vuestra merced*, which meant "your grace." *Vuestra merced* was used as a title of respect in speaking to noblemen. In modern Spanish *señor*, *señora*, *señorita*, *doctor*, *etc.* are still titles of respect. When a Spanish speaker uses a title in speaking to a person, he also uses (a) *tú* (b) *usted*.

usted (*Tú* is not used with titles. The abbreviated forms of *usted, ustedes,* are *Ud., Uds.,* or *Vd., Vds.* SPANISH FOR COMMUNICATION will use *Vd., Vds.* most frequently).

25 Which form, *tú* (thou) or *usted* (your grace) indicates the greatest respect and the highest degree of formality?

usted

26 The kinds of social relationships which exist between Spanish speakers are basically the same as those between speakers of English. The difference between the two cultures lies in the fact that Spanish must use pronouns and verb forms to indicate these relationships. *Usted* is more formal (¿*Cómo está usted?*) and more respectful than *tú* (¿*Cómo estás tú?*).

From what you now know about *tú* and *usted* and about English and Spanish social customs, can you decide which form will be used in the following situations? You are speaking to your teacher. (a) *tú* (b) *usted*

usted (You show respect by using *usted*. *Tú* would be insulting.)

27 You are in grade or high school. Your teacher addresses you. (a) *tú* (b) *usted*

tú (Older persons regularly speak to young people in *tú*. College professors, however, address their students with *usted*.)

28 You are speaking to a person of higher rank, greater authority, or more social prestige. (a) *tú* (b) *usted*

usted

29 You address a person using Mr., Mrs., or Miss and his or her last name. (a) *tú* (b) *usted*

usted

30 You are talking to another student in your class (a) *tú* (b) *usted*

tú (If you use a title and the last name, however, you use *usted*.)

31 You are talking to a dog or cat. (a) *tú* (b) *usted*

tú (Animals have a lower rank than people and are addressed with *tú*.)

32 You are at home talking to a brother, sister, cousin. (a) *tú* (b) *usted*

tú

33 A man addresses a girl friend as *Lolita*, the nickname for Dolores.

tú (People rarely use nicknames unless they are intimate enough to use *tú*.)
Did you remember to write the accent mark (´) over *ú*?)

                   34 You are speaking to a clergyman.

usted   **35** You are asking a police officer for information.

usted   **36** Two very intimate friends are members of a government committee discussing grave, diplomatic problems. They speak to each other as part of the proceedings.

usted (The situation is very formal. It is improper to let personal relationships
show.)   **37** Two people are in love.

tú (People in love talk to each other in *tú*.)

                   38 A Christian is praying to God or to some Saint. (This one will catch you if you don't watch it.)

tú (Christians feel very close to their God and their Saints. The Lord's Prayer
addresses God in the familiar: who art, thy will be done, *etc.*)

                   39 A man is very angry at a strange motorist who is blocking traffic. He wants to insult him.

tú (Using *tú* to an adult stranger suggests that he is an inferior or in the class
of animals.)   **40** At a point in an argument, a man and wife become very angry with each other. There is a temporary breakdown in their normal, intimate relationship. They shift from ⌇⌇⌇ to ⌇⌇⌇.

tú to *usted* (As they get angry, they become more formal. They may behave
like strangers.)   **41** The pronouns *tú* and *usted* must combine with different forms of the verb. *Tú* goes with (a) *¿Cómo estás?* (b) *¿Cómo está?*

with *¿Cómo estás?* (Remember the dialog line: *Y tú, ¿cómo estás?*)

                   42 When a Spanish speaker addresses a person, he must use either a pronoun or a verb (often both). Must he always indicate his social relationship to the person spoken to?

yes (He cannot escape this because both the subject pronoun and the verb
suffix indicate social relationship.)

                   43 The Spanish speaker divides the whole world into two big groups: the people he knows and ⌇⌇⌇.

strangers   **44** When he is being polite, he always speaks to adult strangers with ⌇⌇⌇.

usted   **45** Titles of respect and last names go with (a) *tú* (b) *usted*.

usted (In special situations, like the Army, where only last names are regularly used, *tú* may be used with them.)

                   46 The nickname for *José* is *Pepe* (Joe). A Spanish speaker can, consequently, address another in three ways: *Pepe, José, Martínez*. The nickname goes with ⌇⌇⌇.

tú   **47** The nickname goes with *tú;* a title and the last name with *usted*. Is the following statement a logical conclusion? Either *tú* or *usted* may be used when only the first or last name is used. (a) yes (b) no

yes (The first and last name are neutral, though *usted* is used with the last
name more often than is *tú*. The choice of *tú* or *usted* depends on the formality
of the situation, the age and rank of the people talking, the intimacy of the
social relationship, the speaker's politeness, and the degree of respect
shown.)   **48** When you are in doubt about which form of address to use, which is almost certain to be the right choice?

usted

Forms of the Articles; Plurals; More on Speech Sounds and a Review

Part 1: Forms of the Articles and Plurals

1 The sounds represented by the letters *a, e, i, o,* and *u* are called (a) consonants (b) vowels.

vowels

2 All the other letters, such as *p, c, b, g, m, etc.,* stand for sounds which are called ⌒⌒⌒.

consonants

3 All English words must begin either with a vowel or a consonant sound. This tells us when we must use *a* or *an,* the two forms of the indefinite article. Look at these two columns of words and notice the sound with which each noun begins.

a pen	an apple
a book	an eagle
a cow	an iceberg
a girl	an ocean
a man	an umbrella

The indefinite article form *a* goes with words which begin with a ⌒⌒⌒ sound; *an* goes with words which begin with a ⌒⌒⌒ sound.

a goes with consonant sounds; *an* with vowel sounds. (When a consonant letter is not spoken, you use *an*: an hour.)

4 Do *a* and *an,* in *a pen* and *an apple,* have different meanings?

no (Two forms having the same function may have the same meaning.)

5 Spanish, like English, has two forms of the indefinite article. You have already learned them. They are *un* and *una.* But Spanish is just the opposite of English. The last sound of a word (with very few exceptions) tells the Spanish speaker when to use *un* or *una.* Look at these two columns of words and notice the last sound of each noun.

un libro	una mesa
un rodeo	una silla
un santo	una casa

The indefinite article form *un* goes with nouns which end in the vowel ⌒⌒⌒; *una* goes with nouns ending in the vowel ⌒⌒⌒.

un with *o; una* with *a* (The few exceptions have to be memorized.)

6 English has two forms of the indefinite article, "a" and "an." It has only one form of the definite article: "the." Spanish has four forms of the definite article. You have already learned two of them: *el* and *la.* In almost every case, the last sound of a word tells the Spanish speaker to use *el* or *la.* Compare:

el libro	la mesa
el rodeo	la silla
el santo	la casa

The form *el* goes with the vowel ⁓⁓⁓ ; *la* with the vowel ⁓⁓⁓ .   •
el with *o; la* with *a* (The exceptions have to be memorized.)

7 Look at the form of the two articles and the last sound of the word with which they combine.

un libro	una mesa
el libro	la mesa
un rodeo	una silla
el rodeo	la silla

The forms *un* and *el* combine with words ending in the vowel ⁓⁓⁓ ; the forms *una* and *la* combine with words ending in the vowel ⁓⁓⁓ .
•
un and *el* with *o; una* and *la* with *a*

8 If *un* combines with a sound, will *el* also combine with that same sound?   •
yes (If *una* combines with one sound, *la* will also go with it.)

9 There are several forms of the plural suffix in English which are added to singular noun forms. The singular form *cat* takes an *s* in the plural: *cats*. The plural of *ox* is *oxen*. The plural of *church* is ⁓⁓⁓ .   •
churches (The most common plural suffixes, however, are *s* and *es*.)

10 Spanish, like English, has only two common forms of the plural suffix. They are also *s* and *es*. The difference between vowels and consonants, at the end of words, tells the Spanish speaker when to use *s* or *es*. Look at each of the following words and notice the sound (vowel or consonant) that comes right <u>before</u> the plural suffix *s* or *es; libros, mesas, papeles, señores*. The plural suffix *s* follows a ⁓⁓⁓ ; the plural suffix *es* follows a ⁓⁓⁓ .   •
s after a vowel; *es* after a consonant (The few exceptions have to be
memorized.)   **11** You have already learned that the demonstratives *these* and *those* carry three pieces of information. *These* and *those* are used when you point (a) to one thing (b) to more than one thing.   •
to more than one thing (these scooters; those cars)

12 Are the forms *these* and *those* (a) singular? (b) plural?   •
plural   **13** *This* and *that* are (a) singular (b) plural.   •
singular   **14** Which word, *this* or *these*, goes with each of the following: ox, oxen, churches, cat, cats?   •
this ox, these oxen, these churches, this cat, these cats

15 The plural suffix of *these* (ese) matches the plural suffix of *oxen* (en), *cats* (s), and *churches* (es). This matching is called **agreement**.

The demonstratives (this, that, these, those) are the only English adjectives whose suffixes match the suffixes of the nouns they go with. In Spanish all adjectives agree with (match) their nouns in number (singular or plural). As a result, to make *la mesa* plural, the Spanish speaker must add the plural suffix ⁓⁓⁓ to both *la* and *mesa*.   •
s: las mesas (Remember: *s* is added to vowels.)

16 What is the plural of *la silla?*   •
las sillas

17 The singular form *el* changes to *lo* when the plural suffix *s* is added. So the singular *el papel* becomes the plural *los papeles*. The plural of *el rodeo* is ⁓.

los rodeos

18 The indefinite article *un* and the definite article *el* combine with words ending in *o; un libro, el libro.* They also go with *papel: un papel, el papel. Un* and *el* may combine with words which end in the consonant ⁓.

l

In the suburbs of American cities the people sometimes band together and hire a private guard who patrols the streets at night. This custom is much more prevalent in the Hispanic world where this guard is called *el sereno.* In the old days the *sereno* used to call out the hour and describe the weather. Today he commonly blows a whistle to let the people and prowlers know he is on the job.

Part 2: More on Speech Sounds

1 You have already learned that [p] in *pat* is aspirated (followed by a puff of air). Say *pat* several times and watch what your lips are doing at the start of the word. Are they (a) open? (b) closed?

closed (The lips are closed, air pressure is built up behind them, then they are opened very quickly, and the air comes out with a little explosion or puff.)

2 Do Spanish speakers make the sound [p] with a puff?

no (They open their lips before enough air pressure builds up to make a puff.)

3 Say *boy* and *bat* several times. At the start of these words are your lips (a) tightly closed? (b) open?

tightly closed (Because your closed lips stop the air from coming out, these sounds are said to be *stops.* The [b] sound of *boy* is a "stop [b].")

4 Say *bun* and *fun*. Watch what you do with your lips. When you say the first sound of *fun*, are your lips (a) closed tightly? (b) opened a little? •

opened a little (Some consonants are made by closing the air passageway until the air comes out with a little friction noise. For this reason, these sounds are called *fricatives*.)

5 Say *dough* and *though* several times. Which of these two words starts with your tongue between your teeth? (a) dough (b) though •

though **6** Can you start to say *though* and hold the [th] sound? •

yes (The air keeps coming out between your tongue and teeth.)

7 Is the sound [th] in *though* (a) a stop? (b) a fricative? •

a fricative (The air escapes causing friction.)

8 Can you start to say *dough* and hold the [d] sound? If you are not certain, try it. •

no (A stop is like a little explosion of air. You cannot keep an explosion going. It must come to an end.)

9 Say *Buenos días* (Good morning) aloud and pay attention to what your tongue is doing when you say the [d] sound. Is the [d] sound more like (a) the [d] of "dough" (b) the [th] of "though"? •

the [th] of "though" (This [d] is a fricative.)

10 The word for 2 is *dos*. Say *dos* aloud and note what your tongue is doing when you say the sound [d]. (a) Is your tongue between your teeth? (b) Does it touch the back of your upper front teeth? •

It touches the back of your upper front teeth.

11 When you say *dos* and your tongue touches your teeth, does the tongue block the air passage for a split second? •

yes **12** When you say *dos* by itself, is the sound [d] (a) a stop? (b) a fricative? •

a stop (All stops are made by blocking the air passage in some way.)

13 In *Buenos días* the [d] is a fricative. However, when you say *días* all by itself, the [d] is a stop. The Spanish *d* stands for two sounds just as English *p* stands for two sounds. Does *días*, said with a fricative [d], have the same meaning as *días*, said with a stop [d]? •

yes **14** There must be some signal that tells the Spanish speaker when to say *días* with a stop or fricative [d]. Before you try to find out, let's first look at similar signals in English: You say "an apple," but "a man" in English. What signals you to choose *an* or *a*: the sound that (a) precedes? (b) follows? •

follows (*An* before vowels; *a* before consonants.)

15 The plural of *pat* is *pats*. Say *pats* aloud and listen to the sound [s]. Is it like the (a) [ss] of *miss* (b) [zz] of *fuzz*? •

the [ss] of *miss* (It is unvoiced; the vocal cords do not vibrate.)

16 The plural of *pad* is *pads*. Say *pads* aloud and listen to the sound [s]. Is it like the (a) [ss] of *miss*? (b) [zz] of *buzz*? •

the [zz] of *buzz* (It is voiced; the vocal cords vibrate.)

17 The plural suffix *s* stands for two different sounds in English. What tells you when to say [ss] or [zz]? Here is how you can find out. Cup your hands tightly over your ears and say *pat* and *pad* several times. Which word ends in a buzzing sound? •

pad **18** The [t] of *pat* is unvoiced. The [s] of *pats* is unvoiced. The [d] of *pad* is voiced. The [s] of *pads* is voiced. What tells you when the plural suffix *s* is to be said like [ss] or [zz]? (a) the sound that follows it (b) the sound that precedes it.

the sound that precedes it

    19 The sound that follows either the stop or fricative [d] of *días* is always the same. It is the vowel [i]. What, then, must tell the Spanish speaker when to say the stop or the fricative: (a) what follows [d]? (b) what comes before [d]?

what comes before (Your teacher will tell you more about this in your next class.)

Part 3: Review

Do you want to discover how well your memory is doing? Try the following frames.

    1 The subject pronoun that goes with *estás* is ⁓⁓⁓.

tú (Did you write the accent mark?)

    2 The second person subject pronoun in modern English is ⁓⁓⁓.

you   **3** *Tú* translates "you." Another translation is ⁓⁓⁓.

usted   **4** When a Spanish noun ends in *o*, it combines with the indefinite article form (a) *una* (b) *un*.

un (*Un libro,* but *una mesa.*)

    5 The English cognate of *montaña* is ⁓⁓⁓.

mountain   **6** The demonstrative *these* combines with a noun that is (a) singular (b) plural.

plural (*These words,* not *these word.*)

    7 *These* is made up of two morphemes (meaningful parts): the stem ⁓⁓⁓ and the suffix ⁓⁓⁓.

stem *th* and the suffix *ese*

    8 In English, the letters *a, e, i, o,* and *u* can all stand for the schwa sound, in an unstressed syllable. (a) true (b) false

true   **9** Is there a schwa sound in Spanish?

no   **10** The plural suffix to be added to *papel* is (a) *s* (b) *es.*

es (You add *es* to consonants; *s* to vowels.)

PROGRAM 7

Review of Dialog 1: Getting Ready for a Quiz

    Many students do not do well on quizzes in class simply because they do not understand precisely what they are supposed to do. Consequently, before every major test in this course you will have a Program to help you get ready for it. The Program, however, will not do you much good if you cheat yourself. **Use your cover sheet** and do not peek at the answers.

In your next class you will be evaluated (graded) on how well you can say the dialog between *Tomás* and *Luisa*. Saying the whole dialog from memory will not be the basis for evaluation. Your teacher is going to assume that everybody in the class can do this. The evaluation will be based only on how close you come to sounding like a native speaker of Spanish.

This Program will help you get ready for the quiz by pointing out what your teacher is going to watch for in giving you a grade.

1 The Spanish and English sound [t] are exactly alike. (a) true (b) false

false   **2** When you make the English [t] sound, the tip of your tongue touches (a) your upper front teeth (b) the gum ridge above them.

gum ridge above the upper front teeth

3 When you make the Spanish [t] sound, the tip of your tongue touches the ⁓⁓.

back of the upper front teeth (Spanish [t] is dental. Remember: dentist.)

4 These dialog words have the [t] sound. Say them aloud carefully with the Spanish dental [t]: *tal, bastante, tú, estás, estoy, Tomás, hasta, pronto.*

5 Now say these same words over again just as fast as you can: *pronto, tal, hasta, bastante, tú, Tomás, estás, estoy.*

6 Here is the whole dialog. The [t] sounds are indicated. Say the whole dialog aloud and be careful to make each [t] dental.

Tomás y Luisa

Tomás: ¡Hola, Luisa! ¿Qué tal?

Luisa: Bastante bien. Y tú, ¿cómo estás?

Tomás: Estoy muy bien, gracias.

Luisa: ¿A dónde vas, Tomás? ¿A clase?

Tomás: No, voy a la oficina.

Luisa: Bueno, adiós. Hasta luego.

Tomás: Adiós, Luisa. Hasta pronto.

7 Any English vowel (a, e, i, o, u), when in an unstressed syllable, may be replaced by a single sound called ⁓⁓.

schwa   **8** Does Spanish have a schwa sound?

no   **9** Speakers of English very often substitute schwa for the indicated vowels in the following words. Say them aloud and be very careful to give the proper Spanish vowel sound for each indicated letter: *hola, Luisa, bastante, gracias, donde, clase, oficina, hasta.*

10 Say the same words over again just as fast as you can. Now say them again but start with the last word. Watch for that schwa.

11 Recite the whole dialog from memory and listen for schwas as you do it. If you catch yourself using a schwa, say the word again carefully.

12 The Spanish [p] sound is (a) aspirated (b) unaspirated.

unaspirated (Say *pronto* without a puff after the [p] sound. Remember, you can check whether you have a puff by holding the back of your hand close to your lips. If you puff, you will feel the air coming out.)

13 In Spanish, the letter *d* can stand for two sounds, a fricative and a ⁓⁓.

stop

14 In *¿A dónde vas?* the first [d] sound is like (a) the [d] of "dough" (b) the [th] of "though."

the [th] of "though" (This [d] is fricative. The air escapes with friction.)

15 Is the second [d] in *¿A dónde vas?* (a) a fricative? (b) a stop?

a stop (After the [n] sound [d] is always a stop in Spanish.)

16 The *a* before the first *d* in *¿A dónde vas?* tells you to use a fricative. Is the [d] of *adiós* (a) a stop? (b) a fricative?

a fricative (It is like the [th] of "though.")

17 Say *¿A dónde vas, Tomás?* and *Adiós, Luisa* several times. Be careful with the [d] sounds.

18 The English words "honor" and "hour" begin with the letter *h*. Does the *h* stand for a sound in these words?

no

19 Does the letter *h* stand for a sound in *hola* and *hasta?*

no (The letter *h* never stands for a sound in Spanish.)

20 Keep in mind how you learned the dialog in class. Do you say *¿A dónde vas?* (a) with a little pause between each word? (b) as though all three words were run together in one long word?

as though all three words were run together in one long word: *¿Adóndevas?*

21 Here are all the phrases in the dialog which are spoken as though they were one long word. In the left column is what you see in writing or print. In the right column is what you say in speech. Practice saying the right column aloud several times.

¿Qué tal?	¿Quétal?
Bastante bien	Bastantebien
Y tú	Ytú
¿cómo estás?	¿cómoestás?
Estoy muy bien	Estoymuybien
¿A dónde vas?	¿Adóndevas?
¿A clase?	¿Aclase?
Hasta luego	Hastaluego
Hasta pronto	Hastapronto

22 Now say the whole dialog from memory again, and be sure you do not put pauses where they do not belong. Watch the stresses and the intonation pattern.

23 To sound like a native, you have to be able to talk at the speed of a native. Here is how you can find out whether you are talking at a natural native speed. Get a watch with a second hand. Say the dialog aloud, and time yourself. Keep doing this until you can say the whole dialog, without hesitation, in 11 seconds. When you can do this, you are ready for the test. If you happen to have a tape recorder at home, you will find it fun to tape yourself and hear how you are doing.

24 Say English [e] and hold the sound a moment. Now say *day* and stretch out the last sound. Does it sound like [e]?

yes (*Day* has two vowel sounds that are run together: [a] and [e].)

25 Say English "day" and Spanish *de*. If they sound alike, you have a strong English accent. The *e* of *bastante*, *dónde*, and *clase* stands for a single vowel sound in Spanish. Practice saying these words without making two vowel sounds for the *e*.

26 The Quiz: Your teacher will ask you and someone else to stand in front of the class and act out the dialog. You will use your Spanish first name in place of *Tomás* or *Luisa*. Here are the things your teacher will be watching for:

(1) Do you talk at the speed of a native?

(2) Do you put little pauses in phrases that should be run together?

(3) Are all your [t] sounds dental?

(4) Do you change a Spanish vowel sound to English schwa?

(5) Do you know when to make [d] a fricative or a stop?

(6) Do you say [p] with a puff (aspirated)?

(7) Do you make a sound for *h*?

(8) Do you make two vowel sounds for a single Spanish vowel at the end of a word?

PROGRAM 8

Learning to Read and Write Spanish: I

Part 1: Sounds and Spelling

Before you can learn to write what you hear in Spanish and to say aloud what you see, you must first understand that the relationship between speech sounds and the letters of the alphabet is not exactly the same in English and Spanish.

1 Here are some examples that show this difference. The name of a well-known American game is spelled *béisbol* in Spanish. In English you spell it ⁓. •

baseball

2 A Spanish speaker who knew no English, wrote down the name of a famous president of the United States. He wrote *Guásinton*. You spell his name ⁓. •

Washington

3 When a baseball player knocks a ball out of the park, he gets a *jonrón* in Spanish. In English he gets a ⁓. •

homerun

4 Here's a tougher one to figure out. In Panama when several people get mixed up in a fight, a real melee, they call the fight a *friferol*. Say this word aloud. Can you guess what it came from in English? •

free-for-all

5 Are you ready for one more? The Spanish speaker writes the name of a large American city this way: *Filadelfia*. This city is in the state of ⁓. •

Pennsylvania (And is spelled "Philadelphia.")

6 Let's turn, now, to the more precise differences between English and Spanish. Does *h* stand for a sound in *has* and *happy*? •

yes (But not in *honor, honest,* or *hour*.)

7 Does *h* ever stand for a sound in Spanish? •

no (So you have to write it in when you do not hear it, and leave it out when you see it in reading aloud.)

8 There is no Spanish word that has the spelling sequence *th* in it. When you hear a Spanish sound like [th], as in "though," you must write ～～～ in Spanish. •

d   **9** The Spanish speaker makes two [d] sounds, a fricative and a stop. Must you write *d* for both sounds? •

yes   **10** The Spanish speaker may say *días* with a stop [d], or *buenos días* with a fricative [d]. Does *días* mean "days" no matter how you say it? •

yes   **11** These same two sounds appear in "dough" (stop) and "though" (fricative) in English. Do these words have the same meaning? •

no (For you these sounds are different in English; they mark a contrast in meaning. For the Spanish speaker, however, they are the same: they mark no contrast in meaning.)

12 Say the English name for the letter *a*. Now say *pa*, *pe* in Spanish. Stop and think. If you asked a Spanish speaker (who knew no English) to write the letter for the sound of the name for *a*, would he write either *a* or *e*? •

e (As in *de* or *pe*.)

13 Say the English name for the letter *e*. Now say the Spanish *pe*, *pi*. When you say English [e], the Spanish speaker thinks you are saying Spanish ～～～. •

[i] (As in *si* or *ti*.)

14 Say "pot" and "hot" in English slowly and *pa* in Spanish. Say them again, and listen to the vowel sound. Can the English letter *o* and the Spanish *a* stand for essentially the same vowel sound? •

yes   **15** When you hear a schwa in a word in English, you must choose, in writing, between five letters (*a, e, i, o, u*) in order to spell the word correctly. Spanish has no schwa, and each vowel is clearly pronounced. When you have learned the Spanish system of spelling, will the Spanish vowel sounds always tell you what letter to write? •

yes   **16** There is a [w] sound in Spanish, but Spanish uses the letter *w* only in words of foreign origin. Say [bweno] aloud. The Spanish speaker writes ～～～ when he says the [w] sound. •

u (*bueno, luego, etc.*)

17 Do you pronounce Spanish *tú* as [tw]? •

no   **18** Must you conclude, then, that Spanish *u* stands for two very different sounds? •
yes (The vowel sound [u] and the consonant sound [w].)

19 Say this word aloud in Spanish: *ate*. Do you make a sound for both vowel letters? •

yes   **20** Now, say "ate" in English. Do you make a sound for the *e*? •
no (Spanish, with just one exception, does not write a vowel letter unless it stands for a spoken sound.)

21 Let's look at this problem in another way. Say *sa-le* in Spanish and "sail" in English. Now say "sale" in English. Do "sail" and "sale" sound exactly alike in English? •

yes (English may write the same vowel sounds in two ways. Spanish is neater. A difference in spelling almost always shows some difference in pronunciation of vowel sounds.)

22 You have just learned a lot of new facts about the relationship between speech sounds and letters. Let's review these before you have time to forget them. When you hear a Spanish sound that sounds like the English name for the letter *a*, you are going to write the letter ~~~.

e (As in *tepe* or *Pepe*.)

23 When you hear a Spanish sound that sounds like the English name for the letter *e*, you are going to write the letter ~~~.

i (As in *si* or *ti*.)

24 The letter *o* can stand for several sounds in English: the schwa of "pistol," the [ah] of "hot," or the [oh] of "moment." Does *o* stand for several vowel sounds in Spanish?

no

25 The letter *u*, unlike *o*, may stand for two quite different sounds in Spanish: the vowel sound of *tú*, and the consonant sound ~~~.

[w]

26 Here is a new use of *u*. When you say *¿ Qué tal?* the first word sounds very much like the English name for *k*. One does not say [kue] or [kwe]. Does the *u* of *qué* stand for a vowel sound?

no (Spanish uses the letter *k* only in words borrowed from other languages, such as *kilo, kilómetro, etc*. In native words, the [k] sound is spelled *qu* before *e* or *i*: *que, qui*.)

27 Spanish, like English, has another way of writing the [k] sound. Look at "cent, cinder" and "sent, sinner." English can write the [s] sound before *e* or *i* either with a *c* or an *s*. When *c* comes before *a* (can), *o* (control), or *u* (cunning), it almost always stands for the [k] sound. Spanish also uses *c* for the [k] sound before *a*, *o*, or *u*. So the translation of "how" in "How are you?" is written *¿ ~~~ estás?*

Cómo

You already know that the Latin's sense of human dignity does not normally allow him to use words for animal sounds to describe human speech. This same sense of dignity has prevented the development of certain figures of speech which are common in English. As a result, Spanish has no literal equivalents of *buckteeth, frog-voiced, weasle-eyed, bullnecked, bullheaded,* or *dog-tired. Buckteeth* comes out as *dientes salientes* (projecting teeth); *bullheaded* is *obstinado,* and *dog-tired* is *cansadísimo.* What English considers as picturesque speech, Spanish sometimes treats as undignified.

Part 2: Reading Aloud What is Written

When you write what you hear, you have to learn one set of facts to get what is said on paper correctly. When you read aloud, you have to learn another set of facts to make what you say correct. The Spanish writing system helps you in reading aloud a little more than the English.

1 Compare these sentences in English and Spanish: "Where are you going, Thomas?" *¿A dónde vas, Tomás?* Which language tells you, right at the beginning of the written sentence, that you are to use a question intonation?

Spanish

2 Spanish ends a question with the same punctuation mark as English (?). It begins every question, in contrast, with an upside down or *inverted* question mark. Have you noticed the real difference between these two marks? Look carefully: ¿—? The open part of the regular question mark faces the *left* side of the page (?). The inverted question mark has the open part facing the ⌇⌇⌇ side of the page.

right (Practice writing ¿ until you can do it easily. You may begin with the dot and go down, or at the bottom and go up.)

3 Here is another way that Spanish is different from English in punctuation. Look at this sentence from Dialog 1: *Y tú, ¿cómo estás?* The inverted question mark comes (a) before the whole sentence (b) before just the part which is the question.

just before the question part

4 Spanish also has an inverted exclamation mark (¡) which tells you right at the beginning of the sentence what intonation pattern to use. Write the translation of "Hi, Louise!"

¡Hola, Luisa! **5** The comma (,) and period (.) in Spanish tell you almost the same thing about reading aloud as they do in English. The period marks the end of an utterance. The comma signals a pause within the utterance. Do these two sentences say the same thing? (1) Can you see George? (2) Can you see, George?

no (In the first sentence, George is the person to be seen. In the second, George is the person trying to see. The pause and a change in intonation, marked by the comma, tell you how to say the second sentence so it does not have the same meaning as the first.)

6 In Spanish *No voy a la oficina* says "I'm not going to the office." In contrast, *No, voy a la oficina* translates ⌇⌇⌇.

No, I'm going to the office.

7 Are punctuation marks part of (a) spelling or (b) writing?

writing (They mark intonation patterns. Spelling deals only with words.)

8 The accent mark is a feature of word spelling in Spanish and, from the Spanish speaker's point of view, leaving off an accent mark is a spelling error. You will learn, in a later Program, what the accent mark tells you to do in reading aloud. For the moment let's see what you have observed. The Spanish accent mark is written (a) like this (ˋ) (b) like this (ˊ).

like this (ˊ) (As in *tú*.)

9 Have you noticed this fact? The accent mark is written only over (a) vowels (b) consonants.

only over vowels

10 Copy and add the accent marks to the following: *Y tu, ¿como estas?*

Y tú, ¿cómo estás?

11 Here is the dialog between *Tomás* and *Luisa*. Read it aloud.

Tomás: ¡Hola, Luisa! ¿Qué tal?
 Luisa: Bastante bien. Y tú, ¿cómo estás?
Tomás: Estoy muy bien, gracias.
 Luisa: ¿A dónde vas, Tomás? ¿A clase?
Tomás: No, voy a la oficina.
 Luisa: Bueno, adiós. Hasta luego.
Tomás: Adiós, Luisa. Hasta pronto.

Stop now, and think very carefully. Did the printed dialog tell you precisely what to say and how to say it?

no (If you answered "yes," the next frames will change your mind.)

12 Did the printed dialog tell you what words to say and the order in which to say them?

yes

13 You probably said all the words having accent marks correctly. How did this happen? (a) because you already understand what these marks signal you to do (b) because you memorized the dialog by imitating your teacher *before* you saw it in print

because you have the dialog memorized.

14 This may surprise you a little. You still do not really know how to read Spanish aloud. You have not been taught enough as yet to do this. Are you doubtful? Let's prove it. Can you "read" the difference between *estás* and *estas?*

not unless you have had Spanish before (The verb *estás* has the stress on the second syllable: *es-**tás***. The demonstrative *estas* (these) has the stress on the first syllable: ***es**-tas.*)

15 Here is something else you probably have not observed. The first letters of *Bastante bien* and *Voy a la oficina* are *B* and *V*, but both stand for exactly the same sound. Let's see, now, whether you can discover two more letters in the phrase above, which also stand for the same sound. Don't look at the answer until you have tried hard. These two letters are ⌇⌇⌇⌇.

The *s* of *bastante* and the *c* of *oficina* both stand for an unvoiced [s] sound.

Up until now these letters have not been really telling you what sounds to make when reading aloud. You have made the right sounds because you learned, by imitation, to say the dialog before you tried to read it aloud.

When you try to read aloud something you have never heard before, you have to know exactly what the letters, the accent marks, and the punctuation tell you to say. These facts are not hard to learn, but it will take several more Programs to tell you all about them and more class practice before you can read aloud the way you do in English.

PROGRAM **9**

Learning to Write and to Read Spanish Aloud: II

Part 1: Sounds and Spelling

1 You will learn to speak and read Spanish with less work and more fun if you first understand more about what you really have to do. A Spanish baby has to learn *how* to make *every* Spanish sound. Do you have to go through the same process?

no (Many English and Spanish sounds are exactly alike.)

2 The [s] sound of *clase* is exactly like the [s] of English "say." (a) true (b) false

true (Both words have an unvoiced [s] sound.)

3 The [s] sound of *presente* is not like the [s] of English "present." This Spanish [s] is (a) voiced (b) unvoiced.

unvoiced

4 Does this mean you have to learn how to say the Spanish unvoiced [s] sound? Before you answer, say "sent" aloud in English.

no (You only have to learn to use the unvoiced [s] where English uses the voiced [s] or [z] sound.)

5 You have had to practice saying *pronto* in order to get the proper [p] sound. Does this mean that there is no English [p] sound that is exactly like Spanish?

no   **6** Why, then, have you had to practice *pronto*? Because you have the English habit of starting a word with a [p] sound that is (a) aspirated (puff) (b) unaspirated (no puff).

aspirated (You do not have to learn how to make an unaspirated [p], you just have to learn to make it in a different place.)

7 Does Spanish have an aspirated [p] sound?

no (So you must also learn that English has an extra sound which you cannot use in Spanish.)

8 When two languages have the same two sounds, but between, before, or after different sounds in words, linguists say the sounds have a different *distribution*. It is most important, consequently, for you to know whether you are practicing a different distribution of a sound you can already make or whether you are trying to learn a sound we do not have in English.

Look at the first *t* of "estate" and the *t* of *estás*. Do these *t*'s have the same distribution?

yes (They are preceded and followed by the same sounds.)

9 Are the [t] sounds of Spanish and English exactly alike?

no   **10** The Spanish [t] is dental, the tongue tip touches the ⌒⌒⌒.

back of the upper front teeth

11 To learn to say a proper Spanish [t], you must practice saying [t] with your tongue (a) in the same place as in English (b) in a different position.

in a different position

12 The first syllable of *bastante* and the verb form *vas* sound exactly alike when each word is said by itself. (a) true (b) false

true   **13** The first sound of English "boy" and Spanish *voy* are alike when each word is said by itself. (a) true (b) false

true   **14** Do you have to learn to make a new sound to say the first sound of *voy* in Spanish?

no   **15** Nevertheless, it takes practice to learn to read *voy* aloud correctly. There are two reasons. Look at "ban" and "van" in English. Do *b* and *v* stand for the same sound?

no (So you have been trained, in English, to make two different sounds when you see *b* and *v*.)

16 May *b* and *v* stand for the same sound in Spanish?

yes   **17** Since English also has this same sound, you will get into trouble only when you are (a) imitating Spanish (b) reading aloud.

reading aloud (Your English habit keeps suggesting that *v* should not sound like *b*.)

18 The second reason you may have trouble with *bastante*, *vas*, and *voy* is that they may, in different distributions, begin with slightly different sounds. When you say these words all by themselves, they all begin with the same sound. This sound is almost exactly like the English [b] of "boy." It is a (a) fricative (b) stop.

a stop (Your lips press together, air pressure builds up, and when you open
the lips, there is a tiny explosion. The "bang" in Spanish is not quite as loud
as in English.) **19** To say the [v] sound in *¿A dónde vas, Tomás?* you have to learn how to make
a sound you do not use in English. You do this in just the same way you learned
how to change an English [t] into a Spanish [t], only this time you change an
English stop [b] into a Spanish fricative [b]. When you make a fricative [b],
the lips are (a) closed (b) opened just enough to cause friction as the air escapes.

open to cause friction

20 When you change a stop [b] to a fricative [b], have you made a totally
different sound?

no (The basic sound is the same. It is just made in a slightly different way.)

21 You have discovered, now, that you have one kind of problem when you
imitate spoken Spanish and another when you read aloud. You will have a
third when you try to write down what you hear. What tells you to write *hola*
and *hasta* with an *h*? (a) what you have heard (b) what you have seen

only what you have seen (Just as in English, you must learn which words
can be spelled "by ear" and which ones must be spelled "by eye." Remember:
sale, sail; there, their; to, two, too.)

22 Will what you hear tell you whether to write *b* or *v* in Spanish?

no (You must learn to spell all words having these letters by seeing them.
Spanish speakers have the same problem, and when they hear a new word,
they may ask if it is spelled with *b de burro* (burro) or *v de vaca* (cow). When
they ask, they say *b* and *v* exactly alike.)

23 Learning to write what you hear is going to be a lot easier if you divide all
the Spanish sounds into two classes: the ones that always or almost always tell
you what letter to write, and those that tell you the choice must be learned
from looking at the written word.

Say these vowel sounds aloud in Spanish: *a, e, i, o, u.* Does each sound tell
the Spanish speaker what letter to write?

yes (When there is only one vowel in a syllable you can spell by ear. But
notice this single exception: the translation of "and" is *y.*)

24 There are two [d] sounds in Spanish, a stop and a fricative. Will either one
tell you to write *d*?

yes (One letter stands for both sounds. So your ear will tell you what to
write, but your eye will not tell you what to say.)

25 In English you write the [f] sound several ways: **Ph**il, **f**ill, o**ff**er, lau**gh**.
Except for foreign words, Spanish uses only *f* for this sound. The cognate of
"office" is ——. (Remember the dialog line: *No, voy a la* ——.)

oficina (With one *f*. Spanish does not write double letters unless both stand
for a sound.) **26** Remember *Filadelfia?* You spell it —— in English.

Philadelphia **27** Say *clase* and *gracias* aloud. Do the *s* of *clase* and the *c* of *gracias* stand for
the same sound?

yes (The letters *s* and *c* stand for the same sound before *e* and *i.*)

28 Will the [s] sound in Spanish always be written *s*?

no (It is *c* in *gracias.*)

29 Will the [k] sound, by itself, tell you what letter to write?

no (You write *qu* in *¿Qué tal?*, but *c* in *¿Cómo estás?*)

30 Spanish uses *w* only in foreign words. When you hear a [w] sound, you write ⌒⌒⌒.

u (As in *bueno, luego.*)

31 Say this aloud: *¡Hola, Luisa! ¿Qué tal?* Will your ear tell you to write *e* in *qué?*

yes (You can always trust the [e] sound to tell you what to write.)

32 Unlike English, the Spanish [t] sound is a dental. Does this change the spelling?

no (So you can also trust the [t] sound.)

33 Now, be careful. You hear the question word *dónde*. Will what you hear tell you how to write the word?

no (Hearing does not tell you the word has a written accent. When the word is not used in a question it is spelled *donde*.)

The great development of industry and commerce in the U.S. makes American culture different from Hispanic culture in many ways. One of these differences is seen in what is taught in the schools. Most American schools offer courses designed to prepare one for making a living. In many high schools there are courses in machine shop, woodwork, economics, typing, bookkeeping, etc. In college there are frequently courses given in business management, computers, marketing, advertising, etc. Courses such as these are not taught in the equivalent schools in Latin America, but rather in specialized trade and business schools. Latin American universities generally offer only courses in the humanities, and the three practical courses most commonly found are law, medicine, and engineering.

Part 2: Writing Practice

1 The accent mark is put only over (a) consonants (b) vowels.

vowels

2 Copy these words and add the accent mark: *que, tu, donde, Tomas, como, estas, adios.*

qué, tú, dónde, Tomás, cómo, estás, adiós

3 Here are some other words you have had which you have to see in order to learn to spell them. Say each aloud, cover it with your finger, and then write it from memory. Check to be sure you have spelled it correctly: *hola, bastante, bueno, vas, gracias, voy, hasta.*

4 Copy the following and add the punctuation marks. ... *Hola Luisa* ... ... *Qué tal* ...

¡Hola, Luisa! ¿Qué tal? (If you missed this you have not been seeing what

you read.)   **5** Copy and add all the marks not used in English. *Y tu, como estas?*

Y tú, ¿cómo estás?

6 You hear a Spanish speaker say a word that sounds like English "boy". You write ⌢⌢⌢ .

voy

7 Copy this line carefully: *Estoy muy bien, gracias.*

Estoy muy bien, gracias. (Now check to see if you got the *i* before the *e* in *bien*.)

8 The Spanish question word for "where" is ⌢⌢⌢ .

¿dónde? (Did you get the accent mark?)

9 Copy this word and correct the error: *tomás.*

Tomás (Spanish proper names are capitalized as in English.)

Part 3: The Accent Mark and Reading Aloud

The accent mark, as you will learn later, tells the Spanish speaker many things. One of the things it tells him is what syllable to stress when he reads a word aloud. Here is how it works.

1 The words *estás* and *Tomás* have two syllables: *es-tás* and *To-más*. Say them aloud. Which syllable is spoken louder (stressed)? (a) the first (b) the last

the last (The one with the accent mark.)

2 The word *gracias* also has two syllables: *gra-cias*. Say it aloud. Which syllable is stressed (spoken louder)? (a) the first (b) the last

the first

3 The words *estás* and *gracias* both end with the sound (consonant) ⌢⌢⌢ .

s

4 *Gracias* has two syllables. It ends in *s*, but has no written accent mark. The stressed syllable is (a) *gra* (b) *cias*.

gra

5 When the last syllable of a word ends in *s*, but has no written accent mark, the stress falls on the syllable just before it. (a) true (b) false

true (You say **gra**cias, not gra**cias**.)

6 The verb form *estás* has two syllables: *es-tás*. The last syllable ends in *s* and has an accent mark. Which syllable is stressed? (a) *es* (b) *tás*

tás

7 When the last syllable of a word ends in *s* and has an accent mark, this syllable is stressed (spoken louder). (a) true (b) false

true

8 Copy each word, say it aloud, and be careful to stress the last syllable: *es-tás, To-más, a-diós.*

Doers and Their Actions: Subject Pronouns and Verb Forms

Part 1: Subject Pronouns and Verb Forms

1 When people talk, in any language, they have to talk about something. They talk about other people, animals, things like cars, dolls, or law, religion, and democracy. Almost anything we talk about can be thought of as a doer. A doer is somebody or something that acts or does something. In the sentence, *Dogs bark*, the word which tells what the doer **does** is ⌢⌢⌢. •

bark   **2** In *Dogs bark*, the subject (doer) is ⌢⌢⌢ and the verb (action) is ⌢⌢⌢. •
the subject is *dogs*; the verb is *bark*

3 The subject *dogs* does not go with *bites*. *Dogs bites* sounds very odd. What part of *bites* must you drop to make it go with **dogs?** •
s (*Dogs bite*, not *Dogs bites*.)

4 Compare *bark* and *barks*. Which verb form has two parts? •

barks   **5** What part of *barks* is the stem? The suffix? •
bark is the stem; *s* is the suffix

6 Copy the suffix in each verb form: *burns, burned, burning*. •

s, ed, ing   **7** Which is standard English? (a) It burns easily. (b) It burn easily.
It burns easily.   **8** Which is standard English? If you are not sure, say each sentence aloud. (a) We burns easily. (b) We burn easily. (c) She burns easily. (d) She burn easily. •
We burn easily; She burns easily.

9 The pronouns *he*, *she*, and *it* go with (a) burn easily (b) burns easily. •
he burns, she burns, it burns easily

10 The subject pronouns *I, we, you*, and *they* combine with (a) burns easily (b) burn easily. •
I burn, we burn, you burn, they burn easily

11 Are *he, she*, and *it* (a) singular? (b) plural?

singular   **12** Copy the subject pronouns which are plural: *I, we, she, they, he*. •
we; they (*I, she*, and *he* can only stand for one person.)

13 In *I see you*, who is the speaker? The person spoken to? •
I is the speaker; *you* is the person spoken to

14 Who does *they* stand for in *They are home?* (a) the speaker (b) the persons spoken to (c) the persons spoken about •
the persons spoken about

15 When we have a conversation, the speaker is called "first person." The person spoken to is "second person," and the person or thing spoken about is "third person." In the following sentence there are three pronouns: *I* see *you* have *it*. Copy the pronouns, and write either 1, 2, or 3 after each to show which is first, second, and third person. •
I—1, you—2, it—3

16 In *I want a Coca Cola*, the speaker is one person (singular). A speaker may talk for several persons. When this happens, *I* is replaced by ⁓⁓.

we (We want a Coca Cola.)

17 In *We want a Coca Cola*, *we* is first person plural. What person and number is *they* in *They want a Coca Cola?*

third person plural

18 The singular of *they* may be *he* or *she*. What person and number is *she* in *She wants a new car?*

third person singular

19 Here are all the regularly used subject pronouns in English. Copy those which are third person, *I, they, we, she, you, he, it.*

they, she, he, it

20 The third person singular pronouns are *she, he, it.* There is only one English third person plural pronoun. It is ⁓⁓.

they (You will soon learn that there are two in Spanish.)

21 Which subject pronoun, *she* or *they*, goes with each of the following? (1) ⁓⁓ talk a lot. (2) ⁓⁓ talks a lot.

They talk a lot; *She* talks a lot. (This is another kind of "agreement." The *s* of *talks* goes with *he, she,* and *it,* but not with *I, we, you,* or *they.* In English and Spanish the subject matches or agrees with the verb suffix.)

22 The verb form *talks* has a stem (*talk*) and a suffix (*s*). The form *talk* (a) has a suffix (b) has no suffix.

has no suffix (Another way of saying this is that *talk* has a *zero suffix.*)

23 Does the zero suffix of *talk* tell us as much about agreement as the *s* suffix of talks?

yes (*He talk Spanish* sounds strange. *Talk* does not agree with *he.*)

24 Copy the pronouns which match a zero suffix. As a guide for choosing, say each pronoun with ⁓⁓ *talk too much: I, he, we, it, you, she, they.*

I, we, you, they talk too much. (But he, she, it *talks* too much.)

25 All third person pronouns may stand for or be used in place of a noun. *They* may stand for *dogs.* Will *they* and *dogs* agree with the same verb suffix?

yes (*Dogs bark* too much; *They bark* too much.)

26 *They* may stand for proper names, for example, *Linda and Paul.* Which of the following is standard English? (a) Linda and Paul works after school. (b) Linda and Paul work after school.

Linda and Paul work after school.

27 Nouns can only be replaced by the subject pronouns *he, she, it,* or *they.* What person must all subject nouns be? (a) first (b) second (c) third

third

28 The subject pronouns in both English and Spanish agree with the verb suffix and tell us the person of the subject (first, second, third). In both languages they also give us some special information. For example, does *he* refer to (a) a boy? (b) a girl?

a boy

29 *He* and *she* indicate male and female. Does *they* indicate sex?

no (It just says "third person plural.")

30 May *they* stand for boys, for girls, or for boys and girls?

yes

31 Modern English has only one second person subject pronoun. It is ⁓⁓.

you

32 Can *you* be used to speak either to one or to several persons?

yes (Some Southerners say "you all" when talking to several people.)

33 The Spanish words for "you" always indicate whether the subject is singular or plural. The formal form *usted* is singular. It ends in a consonant. It is made plural by adding (a) *s* (b) *es*.

es (*Ustedes* is like *papeles* or *señores*.)

34 The Spanish word for "she" is *ella*. It ends in a vowel. It is made plural by adding ⁓⁓⁓.

s (*Ellas* is like *plumas* or *sillas*.)

35 *Ellas*, the plural of *ella*, means (a) they (all boys) (b) they (all girls).

they (all girls) **36** Compared to English "they," Spanish *ellas* gives us (a) less information (b) more information.

more information (English "they" does not tell us the sex of the subject.)

37 When you ask, in Spanish, *¿Cómo está usted?*, are you speaking (a) to one person? (b) to more than one person?

to one person (The subject, *usted*, and the verb, *está*, are singular.)

38 Look carefully at the two indicated verb forms in these two questions.

*¿Cómo **está** usted?*	How **are** you?
*¿Cómo **están** ustedes?*	How **are** you?

What has been added to the second Spanish verb form to make it agree with the plural *ustedes?*

n (*n* is a mark of the plural when added to a verb form.)

39 Look carefully at the indicated suffixes of both the verb forms and the pronouns in:

¿Cómo están ustedes?	How are you?
¿Cómo están ellas?	How are they?

Does the plural suffix *n* agree with the suffix of *ustedes* and *ellas?*

yes (*n* is a plural suffix of verbs; *es* and *s* are plural suffixes of pronouns and nouns.)

40 Think about this carefully: *ustedes* is second person; *ellas* is third person. Both are plural. Both combine with *están*. What does the *n* of *están* tell us?

(a) the person of the subject (first, second, third) (b) just that the subject is plural

just that the subject is plural (*n* goes with either second person, *ustedes*, or third person, *ellas*.)

41 Look carefully at the indicated verb forms in both Spanish and English.

*¿Cómo **está** usted?*	How **are** you?
*¿Cómo **están** ustedes?*	How **are** you?

In which language does the verb form carry the most information?

Spanish ("Are" does not tell whether the subject is singular or plural.)

Part 2: What's Your Name?

1 Everyone in our culture has several names: a regular name like *Mark* or *Mary* and several pronoun names used in conversations. What's your pronoun name in English when you are the speaker? (The doer and subject of a sentence.)

I (*I* am speaking.)

2 What's your pronoun name when you are spoken to?

you

My Land
Your Land
Our Land

The history of the United States is a history of immigration. Speakers of Spanish have been part of that immigration since the beginning, and in certain parts of the country Spanish, not English, is the basic means of communication. Specialized organizations assist newcomers to make a home and earn a living. Bilingual classes help students communicate and share different cultural heritages.

Regardless of their surroundings, Mexican children celebrate their old Christmas traditions.

Through advertisements, merchandise, and signs, stores cater to their bilingual clientele.

Music and art know no language barriers. An artist and a music teacher from Cuba continue their work in their new homeland.

In the mountains of New Mexico the Spanish-style of this adobe church recalls the time when this area belonged to Mexico.

The Idaho grasslands are a long way from the Pyrenees mountains in Spain, but the Basque shepherd is just as much at home.

3 You are a girl. What's your pronoun name when someone talks **about** you?
~~~~ *has a new dress.* •

She   **4** You are a boy. What's your name when someone talks **to** you? **About** you? •
you; he   **5** You are the speaker for a group. What's the name for all of you? •
we   **6** Someone talks to you and all your group at once. What's your name? •
you   **7** You are outside a friend's house making a noise. The people inside do not
know what is making the noise: a person, an animal, the wind. Fill in your
name. ~~~~ *is making a noise again.* •

It   **8** You already know that when you are talked to in Spanish you may have two
different pronoun names. They are ~~~~. •

tú; usted (You will soon discover that you are going to have more pronoun
names in Spanish than in English.)

In most American buildings the first floor is the ground or street floor. In contrast, the *primer piso* (first floor) in Hispanic buildings is regularly the equivalent of the American second floor. The ground floor is the *piso bajo* (low floor), and the top floor is the *piso alto* (high floor).

PROGRAM 11

The Difference Between Speech and Writing: Learning to Spell

This Program begins with a linguistic puzzle or experiment. If you follow each step carefully, you will have some fun, perhaps you will be surprised, and, at the end, you will learn something important about the difference between speech and writing which will make learning Spanish easier for you. You will need an adult to help you when you get to Frame 4. However, do not look ahead at any frame. If you do, you will spoil the experiment and miss the fun.

1 Here is a perfectly good English sentence which is made up of four clauses: *Ifurightwriteriteukanreedhwatuwrightbuttifuritewrightrongukanknot* Can you read it aloud? Do you know what it means? Why can't you read it aloud? (a) because there are no punctuation marks (b) because the words are not spelled correctly (c) because there are no spaces between the words •

You probably decided that the reason you cannot read the sentence is because there are no spaces between the words. Let's see how important this really is.

2 Here is the same sentence with spaces between the "words." Look at it, but do not *say* the words aloud or to yourself:
If u right write rite u kan reed hwat u right butt if u rite wright rong u kan knot.

You now have the spaces between the words. Why is the sentence still hard to understand? (a) because the words are not spelled correctly (b) because there are no punctuation marks

Let's wait and see. You may want to change your mind about the answer.

3 Here is the sentence with all the proper punctuation marks. This time read all the "words" aloud, one after the other, and listen carefully to what you are saying. Remember to pause just a little at each punctuation mark:

> *If u right "write" rite, u kan reed hwat u wright: butt if u rite "wright" rong, u kan knot.*

Does the sentence mean more to you now? Have the punctuation marks helped you understand what it means?

Let's test your answer by the following experiment.

4 Step 1: Get a pencil and a piece of blank paper.

Step 2: Ask an adult to help you.

Step 3: Tell this person. "I'm going to read an English sentence aloud, and I want you to write it down just as you hear it."

Step 4: Read the following aloud, and remember to pause just a little bit at each punctuation mark:

> *If u right "write" rite, u kan reed hwat u wright: butt if u rite "wright" rong, u kan knot.*

Wait for your helper to write.

Step 5: Read the sentence once more so the person taking it down will get it correct.

Step 6: Read what was written.

With the exception of the words in quotation marks, what was written should be very close to or exactly like the following: *If you write "rite" right, you can read what you write; but if you write "wright" wrong, you cannot.*

5 Now, let's see how this experiment proves that speech and writing are very different. What told the person who wrote down the sentence what to write? (a) what *you saw* in writing (print) (b) what *you* actually *said*

what you actually said

6 Has the experiment proven that what you say can be written in several different ways?

yes

7 If the same sentence can be written in different ways, what tells you what the sentence means? (a) the way the words are spelled (b) the sounds they stand for

the sounds they stand for (*kan* and *can* stand for the same sounds.)

8 Here is a question which will catch you, if you don't watch out. Do you always say *reed* and *read* exactly alike?

no (If you wrote "yes," you will see why you are wrong in the next frame.)

9 Say this question aloud: *Did you read what you wrote?* Now this answer. *Yes, I read it.* In which sentence must *read* be spoken like "red"? (a) first (b) second

the second: *Yes, I read it.* (You are talking about the past and what you say is like "Yes, I red it.")

10 Say this question aloud: *Do you read Spanish?* Now this answer: *Yes, I read it.* This time you said *read* like "reed," not like "red." What tells you to say *read* in two different ways? (a) spelling (b) meaning

meaning

11 Does what you *see* in print or writing always tell you what to say?

no (You see *read* and say either "reed" or "red.")

12 Say these words aloud: *right, write, rite, wright.* Are they exactly alike when spoken?

yes
13 What tells us how to spell words like *right, write, rite,* and *wright?* (a) the sounds they stand for (b) their meaning

their meaning (To learn to spell them, you also have to see them. This is "eye" spelling.)

14 Do the sounds of a word always tell us what to write?

no
15 Can we write things we cannot say?

yes (You cannot say the difference between *right, write, rite,* and *wright.* Neither can you say the difference between *not* and *knot* or *doe* and *dough.*)

16 Can we say things we cannot write? Stop and think before you answer.

yes (If you answered "no," the next frame may surprise you.)

17 These three words in English are spoken exactly alike: *to, two, too.* Can you fill in the space in this sentence? "There are three ⁓⁓⁓s in English."

no (You can say it, but you cannot write it.)

18 You have now learned the following facts: (1) You can write what you say in different ways (*doe, dough*). (2) You can say what you write in different ways (*read*). (3) You can write things you cannot say (*rite, right*). (4) You can say things you cannot write. Is writing an accurate way of representing what we actually say?

no (If you answered "yes," the following frames may change your mind.)

19 We write most words in just one way, but there are many words which we say in several different ways. For example, the form *going* is made up of the stem *go* and the suffix *ing.* Say the suffix *ing* aloud and, then, say *going* very carefully. Do this until you can hear precisely what you are saying. (a) Did you say the last [g] sound of *going?* (b) Did you leave it off?

You said the last [g] sound if you pronounced *going* carefully. (When a word is said all by itself it is called a *citation form.*)

20 Read this sentence aloud very carefully: *I am going to Madrid.* Did you say the last [g] sound of *going?* Did you pronounce *to* with a schwa?

You said the last [g] and you did not use the schwa.

21 Which of the following pairs do you say in an ordinary conversation with a friend? You can't be sure until you say them aloud.

> I'm going to Madrid.   I'm gointuh Madrid.
> I'm going to make it.   I'm gonna maykit.

(a) the first pair (b) the second pair

the second pair (All educated speakers of American English, even teachers of English, regularly say the second pair in relaxed conversation.)

22 Do we pronounce the same word in the same way when we give a citation form, read aloud, or just talk?

no
23 How many different ways may we pronounce *going?* (a) one (b) two (c) three If you are uncertain, look at Frame 21 again.

three (We say *going,* with the last [g] sound, *goin,* without the last [g] sound, and *gon,* as in *gonna.*)

24 Does what we write always represent what we say?

no (Let's prove this once more in the next frame.)

25 We say this very frequently: *Shur, aikinduit.* Say it aloud and, then, rewrite it with standard spelling and word spacing.

Sure, I can do it. **26** You have now learned that there are three different ways of saying many words: (1) the way we pronounce isolated words or citation forms (*going*), (2) the way we say words when we read aloud (*goin*), (3) the way we say the same words when we just talk (*gonna*). What is standard spelling most like? (a) the pronunciation of citation forms (b) the reading pronunciation (c) the way we talk

the pronunciation of citation forms

27 The difference between plain talk, reading aloud, and writing is just about the same in Spanish as in English. The word which most Spanish speakers say for clock is [reló]. This word is spelled ~~~~~.

reloj

28 Are *sent* and *cent* pronounced exactly alike?

yes

29 Does *c* stand for the same sound in *cent* and *cinder*?

yes

30 Does *c* stand for the same sound in *can't* and *cent*?

no (*c* stands for the [k] sound in *can't*.)

31 Look at the vowel which follows *c* in these sets of words and say them aloud: cat, cot, cut, center, cinder, cent. The *c* stands for a [k] sound when it is followed by the vowels ~~~~~; the *c* stands for an unvoiced [s] sound when it is followed by ~~~~~.

c for [k] before *a, o,* and *u*; *c* for [s] before *i* and *e* (with a few minor exceptions)

32 In Spanish the letter *c* stands for the [k] sound before *a, o, u* and the unvoiced [s] sound before *e* and *i* just as in English. Which *c* of *cinco* stands for the [k] sound? (a) *ci* (b) *co*

co (You are really saying [sinko].)

33 Which *c* of *catorce* stands for the unvoiced [s] sound? (a) *ca* (b) *ce*

ce (You say [katorse].)

34 What sound does the *c* of *oficina* stand for, [k] or [s]?

[s]

35 Copy each word carefully and underline every letter that stands for an unvoiced [s] sound. Say each word aloud before you decide: *mesa, gracias, tiza, lápiz, tres, cinco, luz.*

*me**s**a, gra**c**ia**s**, ti**z**a, láp**iz**, tre**s**, **c**inco, lu**z***

36 Spanish (except for the Castilian dialect) has three letters which stand for the unvoiced [s]. They are ~~~~~.

s, c, z

37 How are you going to learn to spell Spanish words which have an [s] sound? (a) by hearing them (b) by reading and writing them

by reading and writing them

38 Here are 10 Spanish words which you know that have an [s] sound in them. Say each aloud and copy it. Then cover the Spanish and write the translation for each English word from memory. Check your spelling.

lápiz	pencil	*tiza*	chalk
silla	chair	*gracias*	thanks
mesa	table	*luz*	light
pizarra	chalkboard	*está*	is, are
oficina	office	*cinco*	five

If you misspelled any word, write it again twice.

39 The Spanish letter *r* stands for two sounds: a single [r] and a double [rr]. The *r* stands for a double [rr] sound at the beginning of words. Say these words aloud and copy them: *reloj, regla*.

40 The *r* stands for a single [r] sound in these words. Say them aloud and copy them: *cuaderno, libro, pupitre, puerta*. Check your spelling.

41 Say *libro* and *ventana* aloud. Does what you hear tell you when to write *b* or *v*? •

no (You have to see words with *b* and *v* in them to learn how to spell them. You do not, however, write *v* before a consonant in Spanish.)

42 Say *papel* and *pluma* aloud. Does what you hear tell you how to spell these words? •

yes (The sounds of *p, l, m* and the vowels always tell you what to write.)

In both cultures there are social rules which govern who may and may not use diminutives. People of all ages and both sexes may use the diminutives of given names to show friendliness or affection (*Pancho > Panchito, Ana > Anita, John > Johnny, Juan > Juanito*). A child or a woman may say *horsie,* but a grown male, and especially a cowboy, is not likely to use the word. This would be childish. Similarly, women may say *dearie,* but men use it less. In Latin America the diminutives are used much more frequently by women and children than by men. From the point of view of the Peninsular Spaniards, however, the Latin Americans overwork the diminutives, and there are quite a few which are not used in Spain at all; for example, *adiosito* (bye-bye) and *nadita* (hardly nothing), which are largely confined to Mexico.

Review: *tú* and *usted; ustedes* for the familiar plural

1 When "you" (singular) or "you" (plural) are spoken to in Spanish you may have two pronoun names. *Tú* and *usted* are (a) singular (b) plural. •

singular   **2** Add the plural suffix to *usted*. •

ustedes   **3** In Spain the plural of *tú* is *vosotros* or *vosotras*. These forms are not used in Latin America, and you will, consequently, only have to learn to read them or understand them when you hear them. Since there is no special plural form for *tú* in common use in Latin America, when you talk, you will have to use ⌇⌇⌇⌇ as the plural of *tú*. •

ustedes   **4** When you address your teacher, which subject pronoun do you use? (a) *tú* (b) *usted* •

usted   **5** When adult strangers meet, they speak to each other with (a) *tú* (b) *usted*. •

usted   **6** Children usually talk to each other with ⌇⌇⌇⌇. •

tú (There is even a verb for this: *tutear,* "to talk with *tú*.")

    7 Which pronoun is used most frequently when you address a person by his or her last name? •

usted   **8** Very intimate friends usually talk to each other with ⌇⌇⌇⌇. •

tú   **9** When you talk to animals, you use ⌇⌇⌇⌇. •

tú

Morphemes and the Pieces and Parts of Verbs, and More about Speech and Writing

Part 1: Morphemes and the Pieces and Parts of Verbs

1 You already know that words may be divided into either syllables or meaningful parts. The syllables of *important* are *im-por-tant*. Does each of these syllables have a meaning of its own?

no

2 The meaningful parts of words are called *morphemes*, pronounced [morefeems]. This word comes from the Greek *morph* (shape), and *eme* (meaningful). How many morphemes (meaningful parts) are there in the verb form *walking*?
(a) one (b) two

two (The stem *walk* and the suffix *ing*.)

3 The Spanish noun *libro* ends in a vowel. To make it plural, you add the suffix ~~~~.

s

4 The noun *papel* ends in a consonant. To make it plural, you add the suffix ~~~~.

es

5 Do the two plural suffix forms, *s* and *es*, tell the Spanish speaker the same thing?

yes

6 Do the *s* of *dogs* and the *es* of *churches* tell you the same thing?

yes

7 When two forms (parts), like *s* and *es*, have the same meaning, each is called an *allomorph* (other shape) of the same morpheme. So linguists say that in both English and Spanish the *s* and *es* are allomorphs of the plural morpheme. There is another allomorph of the English plural morpheme in *oxen*. It is ~~~~.

en (The singular is *ox*.)

8 The definite article in English has only one form, *the*. In contrast, the indefinite article has two allomorphs. Write them on your answer sheet: (1) It is ~~~~ man. (2) It is ~~~~ apple.

a man; **an** apple

9 The allomorphs of a morpheme can never be used in the same combination. You use *a* before consonants in English and *an* before ~~~~.

vowels

10 In Spanish, you add the plural allomorph *s* to nouns ending in a vowel (*libros, mesas*). When a noun ends in a consonant, you add the plural allomorph ~~~~.

es (*papeles, señores*)

11 Pay special attention to the meaning and the suffix of the indicated words in these sentences: (1) He builds *churches*. (2) He *teaches* Spanish. Does the *es* of *churches* have the same meaning as the *es* of *teaches*?

no (*Church* stands for a building; *teach* for an action.)

12 When *es* is added to a *noun stem* like *church*, it indicates (a) plural (b) present tense.

plural (One does not say, "He churches.")

13 When *es* is added to a *verb stem* like *teach*, it indicates (a) past tense (b) present tense.

present tense   **14** The *s* of *hats* and the *es* of *churches* are allomorphs of the English plural morpheme. Look at the suffixes of the indicated verb forms in these sentences: (1) She *talks* to him in Spanish. (2) She *teaches* him Spanish. Are the *s* of *talks* and the *es* of *teaches* allomorphs of the same morpheme?

yes (Both indicate present tense.)

15 The difference in meaning of the following sentences is shown by the contrast between just two morphemes: (1) She talks to him in Spanish. (2) She talked to him in Spanish. The two morphemes are ⸺.

s; ed   **16** The morpheme in *talked* which tells us the action is past is (a) talk (b) ed.

the suffix ed   **17** The *s* of *talks* and the *es* of *teaches* say the action is present or current. Compare the verb forms of these sentences. (1) They talk to him in Spanish. (2) They talked to him in Spanish. Does the zero suffix of *talk* indicate (a) past action? (b) present action?

present action   **18** The zero suffix of *talk* and the *s* of *talks* indicate the same tense. (a) true (b) false

true (They *talk* Spanish. She *talks* Spanish.)

19 Are the *s* of *talks* and the zero suffix of *talk* allomorphs of the same morpheme?

yes (Both are markers of present tense.)

20 Which form describes an action that may be going on right now? (a) walked (b) walking

walking (She is *walking* in the park.)

21 The verb form *walking* has two morphemes, a stem and a suffix. Which morpheme says the action may be going on now?

ing   **22** The suffix morphemes of *jumps*, *jumped*, and *jumping* are ⸺.

s, ed, ing   **23** How many morphemes are there in each of these verb forms: calls, called, calling?

two (The stem *call* and the suffixes *s, ed, ing*.)

24 The stem (*call*) is the same in *calls*, *called*, and *calling*. Does this stem have the same meaning in all three forms?

yes (The verb stem always tells us what action is being talked about.)

25 Most English verb forms are made up of just two morphemes: the stem and one suffix. Almost all Spanish verb forms have three morphemes: the stem and two suffixes. The stem of *estoy*, *estás*, and *están* is the part that is the same in all three forms. It is ⸺.

est   **26** What immediately follows the stem of *estoy*, *estás*, and *están*? (a) a vowel (b) a consonant

a vowel (All regular Spanish verb forms, in all tenses, always have a vowel right after the stem.)

27 The suffix *n* of *están* agrees with the *es* of *ustedes* in *¿Cómo están ustedes?* There are three morphemes in *están:* the stem ⸺, the first suffix ⸺, and the second suffix ⸺.

est, á, n   **28** If the *n* of *están* agrees with the plural suffix *es* of *ustedes*, then *n* is also a plural marker. (a) true (b) false

true

29 Which suffix of *están*, *á* or *n*, tells the Spanish speaker that the form is present tense?

á (The first suffix after the stem indicates tense.)

30 The subject pronoun that goes with *estás* is (a) *yo* (b) *usted* (c) *tú*.

tú

31 Which form is plural? (a) *usted* (b) *ustedes*

ustedes

32 *Tú* stands for (a) one person (b) more than one.

one person (*Tú* is singular.)

33 The *s* of *estás* agrees with *tú*. The *n* of *están* agrees with *ustedes*. The second suffix of a Spanish verb indicates (a) tense (b) whether the subject is singular or plural.

whether the subject is singular or plural (And sometimes the person.)

34 In Spanish, as in English, there can be three persons in a conversation: first, second and third. The *s* of *estás* agrees in number and person with *tú*. Both *s* and *tú* indicate ～～～ person.

second (The person spoken to.)

35 In which sentence do both the subject pronoun and the verb have a zero suffix which indicates singular? (a) *¿Cómo está usted?* (b) *¿Cómo están ustedes?*

¿Cómo está usted? (Spanish, like English, uses zero to indicate meaning.)

35 What subject pronoun goes with *estoy* and *voy*?

yo

36 *Están* is plural, but *yo estoy* and *yo voy* are ～～～.

singular

37 Which person are *estoy* and *voy*? (a) first (b) second (c) third

first (*Yo* stands for the speaker.)

38 The forms *am*, *is*, *are*, *was* and *were* all belong to the same verb in English. There is another form. Can you write it? "Are you going to ～～～ at home tonight?"

be

39 When we have to talk about all these forms, we need to pick one as the name of the verb. So we say that *am*, *is*, *are*, *was*, and *were* are all forms of the verb "to ～～～."

be

40 Forms like *to be*, *to sing*, *to play*, or *to learn* are called *infinitives*. This is the name form for the verb. The infinitive for *found*, as in "He found the money," is ～～～.

to find

41 English infinitives are made up of two words, "to" and the verb form: to eat, to run, to be. The mark of all Spanish infinitives is the suffix *r*. The infinitive form of *estoy*, *estás*, or *están* is *estar*. The vowel which follows the stem of *estar* is ～～～.

a

42 The vowel between the stem and the *r* mark of the infinitive determines the verb set. So *estar* is said to be an *a*-verb. There are just two more verb sets in Spanish: *e*- and *i*-verbs. In your next class session you will learn all of the present tense forms of a regular *a*-verb. Its infinitive form is *hablar*, meaning "to speak" or "to talk."

Part 2: More about Speech and Writing

1 In writing we make marks on paper. There are three different kinds of marks used in Spanish: letters of the alphabet, accent marks, and punctuation marks. Most letters of the alphabet stand for a ～～～.

sound

	2 Does the written accent mark in *estás* stand for a sound?
no	**3** When a word has more than one syllable, the written accent mark tells which syllable to ———.
stress	**4** Punctuation marks tell you two things. When you see a comma (,), a semicolon (;), or a colon (:), in reading aloud, (a) you keep right on going (b) you pause for a split second.
you pause	**5** The period, question mark, and exclamation mark indicate the intonation pattern for a sentence or utterance. Below is a sentence without punctuation marks. Say it aloud as instructed and, then, write the punctuation mark for each example. (a) You are making a statement of fact. *Henry is sick* (b) You want to check what you just heard. *Henry is sick* (c) You are astonished at what you heard. *Henry is sick*

(a) Henry is sick. (statement) (b) Henry is sick? (question) (c) Henry is sick!

(exclamation)	**6** Spanish written questions and exclamations, unlike English, must ———— and end with the question or exclamation mark.
begin	**7** The English noun *résumé* (pronounced [rez-zoom-máy]) means "a summary" or "a condensed statement." The verb *resume* (pronounced [re-zoom]) means "to take up again." Are the accent marks necessary to spell *résumé* correctly?

yes (If you leave them off, you get *resume*, a different word.)

	8 When you leave off an accent mark in Spanish, do you make a mistake in spelling?
yes	**9** Do all the letters of Spanish always stand for a speech sound?

no (You hear *ola, asta,* and *reló,* but must write *hola, hasta,* and *reloj.*)

Optional Writing Practice

Here are some Spanish words you have to see and hear in order to learn to spell them. Say each aloud and copy very carefully. The indicated part is the one that may cause errors. Check it carefully.

cuaderno	*notebook*
silla	*chair*
ventana	*window*
puerta	*door*
pizarra	*chalkboard*
verdad	*true (really)*
regla	*ruler*
lápiz	*pencil*
relo**j**	*clock*
tiza	*chalk*
luz	*light*
mesa	*table*
ofi**c**ina	*office*
gracias	*thanks*

When a person does not know the name of a shoemaker or a carpenter, it is socially acceptable in English culture to address him as Mr. carpenter or Mr. shoemaker. It is this custom which accounts for the fact that *mason, baker, cook,* and many more words like them may be found in both the dictionary and the telephone directory. In the Hispanic world it is also proper to address a man as *Sr. carpintero,* but the translations of the above English name words (*carpintero, zapatero, albañil, panadero, cocinero*) are not used as proper names as frequently as in English. The phonemic structure of Spanish words, however, makes it possible to do something in Spanish which is impossible in English. When it is customary for only men to follow a given trade or occupation, words like *carpintera* and *zapatera* translate as *the wife of the carpintero, the wife of the shoemaker.* The use of these forms, once universal, is today largely restricted to small towns in the rural areas.

PROGRAM 13

Review of Subject Pronouns and Verb Forms

1 Most English verb forms have just two parts, a stem and one suffix. The present tense forms of a Spanish verb, in contrast, are made up of a stem and ⁓ suffixes.

two (So Spanish verbs have three parts.)

2 To make *habla* agree with *nosotros* you must add the suffix ⁓.

mos (*Nosotros hablamos inglés.*)

3 The word *hablamos* may be divided in two ways. To pronounce it properly, we must divide it into syllables. To understand what it means, we divide it into meaningful parts or morphemes: the stem and the two suffixes. Which of the following is divided into syllables? You can tell by picking the one you have learned to say aloud: (a) *ha-bla-mos* (b) *habl-a-mos*.

ha-bla-mos (*Habl-a-mos* shows the three morphemes.)

4 The stem of *hablamos* is not the same as the first syllable. It is ――――.

habl

5 The morpheme in *habl-a-mos* which indicates present tense is ――――.

a

6 The present tense morpheme of regular *a*-verbs has two allomorphs. One is *a* as in *tú habl-a-s* or *nosotros habl-a-mos*. The other goes with *yo* and is *habl-*――――.

o (*Yo hablo inglés.*)

7 The second suffix of a Spanish verb form sometimes indicates person (first, second, third). It always indicates the number (singular, plural) of the subject. (a) true (b) false

true

8 The subject pronouns *él* (he) and *ella* (she) indicate number (singular), person (third), and sex (male or female). Both combine with the same form, *habla: él habla, ella habla.* Does any part of *habla* tell you whether the subject is male or female?

no (The sex of a subject is shown by some pronouns but never by any part of a Spanish or English verb form.)

9 Here are the common English subject pronouns. Which ones tell us the subject is either male or female: *I, we, you, he, she, it, they?*

he, she

10 Which pronouns tell us the subject is plural: *I, we, you, he, she, it, they?*

we, they (*You* may be either.)

11 Spanish subject pronouns give us more information about the number and the sex of the subject than English pronouns. To do this they have to have (a) fewer meaningful parts than English (b) more meaningful parts.

more meaningful parts

12 The pronouns *ellos* and *ellas* are made up of three parts (morphemes): *ell-o-s* and *ell-a-s.* The stem is ――――.

ell (This says third person.)

13 The final *s* tells us the subject is (a) singular (b) plural.

plural

14 The *a* of *ellas* says the subject is (a) all boys (b) all girls.

all girls

15 The translation of *ellas* (all girls) is "they." The translation of *ellos* is also "they." Spanish has no other word for "they"; as a result, the form *ellos* may stand for either all boys or a group made up of boys and girls. (a) true (b) false

true (*Ellas* clearly says "all girls," but *ellos,* like English "they," is ambiguous.)

16 Which form, *nosotros* or *nosotras,* is used when the group is all boys?

nosotros

17 When a pronoun has two forms, the *a*-form stands only for all ――――.

girls

18 When a pronoun has two forms, the *o*-form may stand for either all boys or ――――.

boys and girls

19 A pronoun has to have two forms to show the difference between male and female. (a) true (b) false

true

20 Do *usted* and *ustedes* show the difference between male and female?

no (They show only singular and plural.)

21 Does *yo* tell whether the speaker is male or female?

no (Either a girl or a boy may say *Yo hablo inglés.*)

22 Here are all the subject pronouns you are going to learn to use. Which ones clearly indicate the subject is female: *yo, nosotros, nosotras, usted, ustedes, él, ellos, ella, ellas, tú?*

nosotras, ella, ellas

23 Look at these pronouns and translate them: *yo, nosotros, usted, ustedes, él, ellos, tú.* There is only one that clearly says the subject is male. It is ‿‿‿.

él (Remember: *nosotros* and *ellos* can stand for all males or males and

females.)　**24** A plural noun or pronoun in Spanish must have a plural suffix: *s* or *es.* Which of these pronouns tell you the subject is plural: *yo, nosotros, nosotras, usted, ustedes, él, ellas, ella, ellas, tú?*

nosotros, nosotras, ustedes, ellos, ellas

25 The singular form of *ellas* (they) is ‿‿‿ (she).

ella　**26** The stem of *ella* is ‿‿‿.

ell　**27** The *a*-suffix of *ella* says female. When the *a* is dropped, the zero suffix should stand for the opposite or ‿‿‿.

male　**28** In modern spelling one *l* of *ell* has been dropped. The form *el* translates "the." To make it stand for "he" in writing, you must add what?

an accent mark: *él*

29 To make *ella* plural you just add *s* (*ellas*). To make *él* plural, you drop the accent mark, change *el* to the stem ‿‿‿, and add *os*.

ell (*él; ellos*)　**30** "You" in English may be either singular or plural. The Spanish equivalents used among strangers are ‿‿‿ (singular) and ‿‿‿ (plural).

usted; ustedes　**31** The plural of the English subject pronoun "I" is ‿‿‿.

we (This form indicates person and number but not sex.)

32 The plural of Spanish *yo* has two forms based on the stem *nosotr.* Both show sex. They are ‿‿‿.

nosotros; nosotras

33 When you speak in private to a very close friend, you address that friend with the subject pronoun ‿‿‿.

tú　**34** When we talk about a verb and all its forms, we use the name form or infinitive. Thus, we say, "*Spoke* is a form of *to speak.*" The Spanish equivalent of the "to" in "to speak" is the last suffix of any Spanish infinitive. It is ‿‿‿.

r: hablar (The stem *habl-* labels the action. The first suffix is *a*, the set vowel, and the second suffix, *r*, marks the form as the infinitive.)

35 To make *hablar* agree with *tú*, the *r* is replaced by the person-number suffix ‿‿‿.

s (*Tú hablas* has the same second suffix as *tú estás.*)

36 The second suffix *s* of *hablas* agrees with *tú.* To change *hablas* so it agrees with *ustedes*, the *s* is replaced by the plural suffix ‿‿‿.

n (*ustedes hablan*)

37 Make *ustedes hablan* singular by dropping the plural suffix of both the pronoun and the verb. The result is ‿‿‿.

usted habla (You dropped the *es* of *ustedes* and the *n* of *hablan.*)

38 Both the subject pronoun and the verb in *ella habla* are singular. To make these forms plural, you add the plural suffixes: *ella ... habla ... .*

*ella**s** habla**n***　**39** The second suffix of the singular form *habla* is zero. What suffix must be added to *habla* to make it agree with either *nosotros* or *nosotras?*

mos (*nosotros hablamos*)

40 When *yo* is the subject of a regular verb form, the first suffix in the present tense is the vowel ⁓⁓⁓.

o

41 When there is no suffix after *o* or *a*, we know the subject of the verb is (a) plural (b) singular.

singular (*yo hablo ; usted habla*)

42 The *s* of *hablas* matches *tú* and gives us the same three pieces of information as the subject pronoun: person, number, and social relationship. Select the right combination for meaning of both *tú* and the suffix *s*: (a) second person, singular, friend (b) second person, plural, stranger (c) second person, plural, friend (d) second person, singular, stranger

second person, singular, friend

43 Compare "you speak" and *habla, hablas*. Do Spanish verb forms give us more information than English verb forms?

yes (So you have to pay attention to more facts in order to speak Spanish.)

44 To learn all the present tense forms of *hablar*, you must learn first, the stem, which is ⁓⁓⁓.

habl (This gives the meaning of the verb.)

45 The first suffix of *hablar* is *a*. It marks the verb set and is used, with one exception, in all forms of the present tense. The single exception is the form that goes with *yo*. It is ⁓⁓⁓.

*yo habl***o**

46 The second suffix may be zero or an actual form: *mos, n,* or *s*. Which suffix goes with these subject pronouns?

nosotros nosotras	habla⁓⁓⁓.
ustedes ellos ellas	habla⁓⁓⁓.
tú	habla⁓⁓⁓.

nosotros—mos, tú—s, and *n* matches the plural suffix *es* and *s* of
ustedes, ellos, and *ellas*

47 The present tense of all regular *a*-verbs in Spanish is made up just like *hablar*. To get all the present tense forms of *llamar* you simply replace the stem *habl* with ⁓⁓⁓.

llam

48 You will learn how to make up regular verb forms faster and with less work if you remember these facts. The stem of the verb is the same in all forms. (a) true (b) false

true

49 The first suffix of *a*-verbs in the present tense is either *a* or ⁓⁓⁓.

o (*o* only with *yo.*)

50 The second suffix is either zero or ⁓⁓⁓.

mos, n, or *s*

51 The *o* of *hablo* and the *a* of *habla* are allomorphs of the same morpheme. Both indicate that the forms are (a) past tense (b) present tense.

present tense

PROGRAM **14**

What Have You Learned? How Much Do You Remember? A Test

Part 1: What Have You Learned?

1 Here are ten facts about English which have been talked about in your Programs. Check those which you really knew for sure *before* you began this class.

    (1) Most English verb forms are made up of two meaningful parts (morphemes).

    (2) The demonstratives *this*, *that*, *these*, and *those* have a stem and a suffix.

    (3) The demonstratives agree in number with the nouns they combine with.

    (4) The *s* of *talks* indicates present tense.

    (5) A zero suffix can have meaning.

    (6) The letter *p* stands for two different English sounds.

    (7) The air comes out your nose when you say [m].

    (8) The first sound of a noun tells us when to say *a* or *an*.

    (9) Any English vowel may become schwa in an unstressed syllable.

    (10) The [s] of *present* is voiced.

If you were consciously aware of three or more of these facts before you began this course, you already had unusual training in the nature of English.

2 You learned to talk English as a small child without being consciously aware of any of these facts. Yet you do make demonstratives agree with their nouns and you do use *a*, instead of *an*, before a noun that begins with a consonant. Let's see how you learned this. Can you remember ever hearing *an cat*?

no   **3** Do you learn to imitate something you never hear?

no   **4** So you learned to say *those cats* and *a cat* (a) because someone said you should (b) because you only heard and imitated *those cats* or *a cat*.

because you never heard *that cats* or *an cat*, and you only heard and imitated *those cats*, and *a cat*

5 When you say *an apple*, (a) do you stop to think about choosing between *a* and *an*? (b) do you just say the right one out of habit?

you say the right one out of habit without thinking about the choice

6 When you were learning to write, did someone have to tell you how to make certain letters or to use a capital letter to begin a name?

yes (You were told to do these things. Today you do them without thinking, just out of habit.)

7 You have two sets of language habits or skills. One set you learned all by yourself without being aware of what you were learning. The other set was taught to you. Let's see which way of learning will be the fastest in learning Spanish. Which is the fastest way to learn to swim? (a) by just watching and imitating others (b) by taking lessons in which you are told precisely what to do with your arms and legs

by taking lessons

52   Etapa Uno

8 Which is the fastest way to learn to use a typewriter? (a) you poke the keys and figure out for yourself which finger to use for each key (b) a teacher tells you how the touch system works

a teacher tells you

9 Can an Olympic champion win a swimming race if he has to think about what the coach taught him every time he takes a stroke?

no

10 To become a champion swimmer one must turn consciously learned knowledge into a set of automatic habits. (a) true (b) false

true (The swimmer swims without thinking of what to do with his arms and legs. A typist types without thinking about what finger to use to strike the key for the letter *a*.)

11 Let's apply this logic to learning Spanish. Which is the fastest way for a speaker of English to learn how to say *Buenos días* without using the English schwa? (a) by just listening to and imitating a native (b) by first learning that there is a schwa in English, but none in Spanish, and, then, practicing how to say *Buenos días* without a schwa

by first learning about the schwa and how to get rid of the English habit

12 Native children take several years to learn when to use *tú* or *usted* correctly. You learned this in one Program. However, will you ever learn to speak Spanish well if you have to stop and think about which pronoun to use every time you speak to someone?

no (What you are now learning to do must become an unconscious habit before you can talk Spanish well.)

13 Where do you first learn the most facts about the Spanish language? (a) in the Programs (b) in class

in the Programs

14 What, then, is the purpose of most of the classroom activity? (a) to teach you new facts (b) to practice what you already know until it becomes a habit

to practice

15 Long before you began this course you had already learned, by imitating older people, to make English demonstratives agree in number with their nouns. You said "those cats," not "those cat," without even thinking about the fact that *those* has a stem and a plural suffix. Does knowing what form to use mean you are consciously aware of what you are doing?

no (Chances are that you did not consciously know that the demonstratives have number suffixes before you started this course.)

16 Knowing what to do or say, without being consciously aware of what you are actually doing, is called *intuitive knowledge*. You have a "feel" for what is right. Will having a feel for what is right in English help you learn what is right in Spanish?

no (What you are not aware of will not help you learn something you need to understand.)

17 To make your intuitive knowledge of English be a help in learning Spanish, the intuitive knowledge must be changed to conscious knowledge (something you are aware of and understand). (a) true (b) false

true (What you *feel* must become what you *understand* consciously.)

18 Does the discovery that English verbs have a stem and a suffix make it easier to deal with and learn the stem and suffixes of Spanish verbs?

yes (You do not have to learn so much.)

19 When you were very small and were first learning English, you knew so few words no one could talk to you about what you were learning. Your parents could not, for example, say to you, "Say 'pistol' with an aspirated [p] and with a schwa in the unstressed syllable." Which way will you learn Spanish easier and faster? (a) neither your teacher nor your textbook explains what you are learning or why; you just imitate (b) you are told precisely what you are to do or learn, why you must do it, and how to do it; then you imitate and practice •

you are told what you are to do, *etc.*

20 Is it necessary to learn some technical terms in order to be able to talk intelligently about learning a second language? •

yes (Your teacher cannot help you get rid of the schwa in Spanish unless it is possible to name it and talk to you about it.)

In both English and Spanish there are common adjectives which are also used as last or surnames. Some are the same, *Brown* (*Moreno*), *White* (*Blanco*), but many do not match. Spanish does not generally use *Black* or *Green*, while English does not use Rojo (red), Rubio (blond), Bello (beautiful), Caro (expensive) or Calvo (bald).

Most American girls called *Dolores* probably do not know that the word comes from Our Lady of Sorrows (*Nuestra Señora de los Dolores*) and the majority of *Lindas* are probably unaware of the adjectival meaning "pretty." In Spanish there are many first names which would sound extremely strange in English. Boys, for example, may be named *Severo* (severe), *Modesto* (modest), *Justo* (just), *Cándido* (candid), or *Amado* (loving). Girls may be called *Dulce* (sweet), *Pura* (pure), *Clara* (clear), *Bárbara* (barbaric), *Blanca* (white), *Celeste* (heavenly), or *Modesta* and *Cándida*. When an adjective has two forms (*Modesto, Modesta*), the form ending in *o* is a boy's name; the form ending in *a* is a girl's name. The name, like a common adjective, agrees with the sex of the person bearing it. Diminutives may also be used as a first name: *Blanquita* (from *blanca*).

Part 2: How Much Do You Remember? A Test

You are going to have a major classroom test very soon. This practice test is to help you get ready for it. Do the following Program to find out what you still have not mastered.

Do this test as fast as you can. Remember that if you have to stop to think very long, what you know will not be much help in speaking a language.

Do not cheat yourself. If you peek at the answers before you solve the problem, you will not really discover how well you are doing or what you still have to learn.

If you make a mistake, circle the number for that frame. At the end of the test, you will be told how to evaluate your score.

1 Look-alike words such as "mountain" and *montaña* are called cognates.

Look at the first part of "library" (libr) and think of what you will find on the shelves in a library. The Spanish cognate of "library" that you already know is the noun ⁓.

libro (Both cognates come from the Latin stem *libr.*)

2 The two standard ways of sending messages (communicating) are ⁓.

speech and writing

3 There are four language skills: reading, speaking, writing, and hearing. Can you learn to imitate in speech something you have never heard?

no

4 Must you learn to hear Spanish before you can learn to speak it?

yes

5 Can you learn to write *hola* and *hasta* with an *h* from just hearing *ola* and *asta?*

no

6 Must you see some written Spanish before you start learning how to write it?

yes (If you have not seen *hasta* and have only heard *asta,* you will not know that what you say and what you see are the same word.)

7 Review the last 4 frames before you try to do this one. In what order should the four language skills be learned? (1) ... (2) ... (3) ... (4) ...

hearing, speaking, reading, writing

8 When we say that the [p] of English *pie* is aspirated, we mean that the sound is followed by a little ⁓ of air.

puff

9 All Spanish [p] sounds are (a) aspirated (b) unaspirated.

unaspirated (There is no puff of air.)

10 The English letter *p* stands for two sounds: the aspirated [p] of *pie* and the unaspirated [p] of *spy.* Spanish letter *p* stands for only ⁓ sound.

one

11 The [s] sound of "present" is not like the [s] sound of *presente.* This English [s] is voiced (the vocal cords vibrate). The Spanish [s] before a vowel is (a) voiced (b) unvoiced.

unvoiced (The vocal cords do not vibrate.)

12 The sounds of English and Spanish [t] are (a) exactly alike (b) somewhat different.

different (The Spanish [t] is dental.)

13 When you make a Spanish [t] sound, the tip of the tongue touches ⁓.

the back of the upper front teeth.

14 Does a letter of the alphabet always represent a sound in a word?

no

15 The *h* stands for no sound in *honor* or *hour.* It never stands for a sound in Spanish. Write one Spanish word having an *h.*

(You know two!) *hola; hasta*

16 When one syllable of a word is spoken louder than the others, it is said to be (a) stressed (b) unstressed.

stressed (Most English words have no written mark to show this.)

17 Spanish can show which syllable of a word is stressed by using ⁓ in writing.

the written accent mark (ʹ)

18 The first syllable of English *total* is stressed: *to-tal.* Which syllable normally has a schwa sound?

tal (We normally say something like [totul].)

19 The schwa appears in unstressed syllables and may be substituted for any English vowel. As a result, in relaxed speech you do not hear the difference between *vender* and *vendor.* Spanish has no schwa. Can the vowel in unstressed

syllables be used in Spanish to show that two words have different meanings? •

yes. (Spanish *libro* is "book"; *libre* translates "free.")

20 The stem of *estar* is ~~~~. •

est   **21** A *suffix* is a part of a word which comes (a) before the stem (b) after the stem. •

after the stem (*Prefixes* come before.)

22 The meaningful parts of words have a technical name which comes from the Greek meaning "meaningful shape." This word is ~~~~. •

morpheme (Don't take off for misspelling.)

23 Morphemes and syllables are not always identical. (a) true (b) false •

true (*Ha-bla-mos* shows the syllables while *habl-a-mos* shows the morphemes.)   **24** The four English demonstratives are ~~~~. •

this, that, these, those

25 The suffixes of *this*, *that*, and *those* are the parts which are different, or ~~~~. •

is, at, ose   **26** Look at the difference between the suffixes of both words in this pair of phrases: *this hat: these hats.* English demonstrative adjectives agree in ~~~~ with their nouns. •

number   **27** Do all Spanish adjectives agree in number with their nouns? •

yes   **28** Which word has a zero suffix? (a) *mesas* (b) *mesa* •

mesa   **29** In English may a stem sometimes be a word by itself? •

yes (*Talk* is the stem of *talked.*)

30 The first part of *morpheme* is like the first part of *morphology*. Morphology is (a) the study of speech sounds (b) the study of the pieces and parts of words, or morphemes. •

the study of the pieces and parts of words

31 *Tú* is used when you address a person with a title of respect (*señor, señorita,* etc.). (a) true (b) false •

false (The use of a title of respect requires *usted.*)

32 You should always use *usted* when you address a person by his first name. (a) true (b) false •

false (The choice between *tú* and *usted* depends on how intimate the speakers are.)   **33** Is it disrespectful for an older person to use *tú* in talking to a child? •

no   **34** When you speak to adult strangers, you use (a) *tú* (b) *usted.* •

usted   **35** When sweethearts talk to each other, they use (a) *tú* (b) *usted.* •

tú   **36** What tells you to use *a* or *an* with a noun in English? (a) the first sound in the noun (b) the last sound •

the first sound (*an egg,* but *a leg*)

37 What tells you to match *la* with *mesa* and *el* with *papel* in Spanish? (a) The first sound in the noun (b) the last sound •

the last (*a* with *a ; l* with *l*)

38 When a noun ends in *a*, the form of the Spanish indefinite article to be used is almost always (a) *una* (b) *un.* •

una   **39** If *un* agrees with a noun (*un libro*), the definite article form *el* will also agree with that same noun. (a) true (b) false •

true (*un libro ; el libro*)

40 Spanish has two allomorphs of the plural noun suffix. They are ~~~~. If you are not sure, make *usted* and *libro* plural before you give the answers. •

s ; es

41 Which plural suffix follows (a) a consonant? (b) a vowel?

es after a consonant; *s* after a vowel

42 When the air passage is closed in making a sound, that sound is called a ~~~~.

stop

43 The stops in *¿Dónde?* are ~~~~.

the two [d]'s

44 When a sound is made with friction, it is called a ~~~~.

fricative

45 Say this aloud: *¿A dónde vas?* The two fricatives are ~~~~.

first [d] of *dónde* and [v]

46 What tells you that the first [d] is a stop in *¿Dónde?* but a fricative in *¿A dónde vas?* (a) what comes before (b) what follows

what comes before

47 There are spaces between the words of *¿A dónde vas?* Do you say the sentence (a) with a pause for each space? (b) like this: *¿Adóndevas?*

like one, big word

48 Does writing represent exactly what we say?

no

49 The two Spanish punctuation marks which begin a sentence (or phrase), and are not used in English, are ~~~~.

¡ and *¿*

50 The subject in *Pedro habla español* is ~~~~.

Pedro

51 The precise meaning of *Me llamo Pablo* is not the common translation "My name is Pablo." To the Spanish speaker the meaning is "I ~~~~ myself Pablo."

call

52 The verb form in *Me llamo Pablo* is ~~~~.

llamo

53 The English subject pronouns which indicate sex are ~~~~.

he; she

54 Copy the six Spanish subject pronouns which indicate sex: *yo, nosotros, nosotras, usted, ustedes, él, ella, ellos, ellas, tú.*

nosotros, nosotras, él, ella, ellos, ellas

55 There are three persons: first, second, and third. Which person is each of the following: *yo* ~~~~, *tú* ~~~~, *ellos* ~~~~?

yo, first; *tú*, second; *ellos*, third

56 English verb forms have ~~~~ parts. Spanish verb forms have ~~~~ parts.

two; three

57 The infinitive or name form of *hablas* has ~~~~ in place of the final *s*.

r (hablar)

58 Which two morphemes in the following phrase show agreement: *ustedes hablan?*

ustedes hablan (Both are plural markers.)

59 The second suffix of a Spanish verb form indicates (a) tense (b) person and number.

person and number

60 What part of *estoy* is irregular?

oy

61 The form *hablas* has two syllables (*ha-blas*) but three meaningful parts: a stem and two suffixes. Write *hablas* indicating the morphemes.

habl-a-s

62 The stem *habl* labels the action. The *s* agrees with *tú*. The first suffix *a* gives the verb set and also tells us the verb is ~~~~ tense.

present

63 Write *ellas* indicating the morphemes.

ell-a-s (The *a* marks sex, female, and the *s* is the plural suffix.)

64 Rewrite and make both forms singular: *ustedes hablan.*

usted habla
él

65 The singular of *ellos* is ~~~~.

What Your Score Means

Count the frames in which you made a mistake.

0 to 3 mistakes	outstanding	10 to 12 mistakes	good
4 to 6	excellent	13 to 15	average
7 to 9	very good		

If you do not like your score, study the frames in which you made a mistake.

PROGRAM 15

Matching Sounds and Suffixes: Nouns, Adjectives, and Pronouns

1 The English indefinite article has two allomorphs, *a* and *an*, which are matched with the first sound of the adjective or noun following immediately. For example: ... cowboy, ... Indian, ... able man, ... thin sheet.

a cowboy, *an* Indian, *an* able man, *a* thin sheet

2 The demonstratives *this* and *these* have a stem, and a suffix which indicates number. What parts of *these dogs* match? (a) the stems (b) the suffixes

the suffixes (You do not say *these dog* or *this dogs*.)

3 The English definite article has only one form, *the*. You say *the cowboy, the Indian, the dog,* and *the dogs.* Does *the* match anything in these words?

no (A form which combines with everything matches nothing.)

4 Matching is possible only when a word has at least ——— different forms or a stem has at least ——— suffixes.

two forms (a, an) or two suffixes (th-is, th-ese)

5 The definite article forms *los* and *las* have a matching sound (*o* or *a*) and a matching plural suffix (*s*). Copy the following pairs of words and underline the matching plural suffixes of each pair: *los papeles, los señores, los libros.*

lo-s, papel-es, lo-s señor-es, lo-s libro-s

6 Now, draw a circle around the letter which comes *right before* the plural suffix of each word. This is the word's *matching sound.*

l(o)-s pape(l)-es, l(o)-s seño(r)-es, l(o)-s libr(o)-s

7 The *o* of *los* matches the ——— of *papeles,* the ——— of *señores,* and the ——— of *libros.*

o matches *l, r, o*

8 Write the singular of *los papeles, los señores, los libros.*

el papel, el señor, el libro (The final sound of each noun is its matching sound.)

9 The notion of singular is shown by a zero suffix. The *l* of the definite article form *el* matches the final sounds ——— of *papel, señor,* and *libro.*

l matches *l, r, o*

10 The indefinite article has two allomorphs, *un* and *una*. Which one may replace *el* in *el papel*, *el señor*, or *el libro*?

un (The *n* is the matching sound of this allomorph.)

11 Does the *n* of *un* match the same sounds as the *o* of *los* and the *l* of *el*?

yes (*un libro, el libro, los libros*)

12 *Un*, *el*, and *los* each have a matching sound. They are ⁓⁓⁓.

n, l, o   **13** *Un* does not combine with *mesa*, *señora*, or *puerta*. It is replaced by ⁓⁓⁓.

una (*una mesa, una señora, una puerta*)

14 Look for the matching sounds in these words:

una mesa	una señora	una puerta
la mesa	la señora	la puerta
las mesas	las señoras	las puertas

In all these examples, the ⁓⁓⁓ of the article matches the ⁓⁓⁓ of the nouns.

the *a* of the article matches the *a* of the nouns

15 The *a* of *la* and *las* matches the *a* of *mesa* and *mesas*. Must you pay attention to the plural suffixes when matching the sounds of the articles and their nouns?

no (The plural suffixes come after the matching sounds.)

16 There are six forms of the articles: *un*, *una*, *el*, *la*, *los*, and *las*. They are divided into two matching sound sets. Every member of one set has the matching vowel sound ⁓⁓⁓.

a: *unà, la, las* (This is the *a*-set, and the nouns they combine with are

a-nouns.)   **17** The second set of article forms is made up of ⁓⁓⁓.

un, el, los (Because *los* has an *o*, this is called the *o*-set, and the nouns they combine with are called *o*-nouns.)

18 Which set combines with *muchacho* or *libro*? (a) *o*-set (b) *a*-set

o-set (*los muchachos, los libros, un muchacho, un libro, etc.*)

19 Which set combines with *muchacha* or *mesa*? (a) *o*-set (b) *a*-set

a-set (*una muchacha, una mesa, la muchacha, las muchachas*)

20 Which set combines with *señor* and *papel*? (a) *o*-set (b) *a*-set (If you are not sure, translate "the men" first.)

o-set (*un señor, los papeles, el señor, etc.*)

21 When one member of an article set combines with a matching noun sound, then all other members of that set may also combine with the same noun. (a) true (b) false

true (If the *n* of *un* matches the *r* of señor, you know you can say *el señor* or

los señores.)   **22** The articles are also adjectives. There are many other Spanish adjectives which have two forms and two matching sounds. The matching sound of one of these forms is always *a*, as in *una* or *la*. The most common contrasting sound is *o*. The two forms for "Chilean" are *chilena* and *chileno*. Which form goes with *señora* or *mesa*?

chilena (*a* matches *a*.)

23 The form *chilena* belongs to which set of adjectives? (a) *o*-set (b) *a*-set

a-set (*una chilena, la chilena, las chilenas*)

24 When two or more adjectives combine with a noun, all must be of the same

set. Which of the following shows the proper matching of sounds? Look carefully or you will make a mistake. (a) *una muchacho chileno* (b) *una muchacho chilena* (c) *un muchacho chileno*

un muchacho chileno (All three words belong to the *o-set*.)

25 When an adjective has two forms, the final sound of the singular form is the matching sound. When the form is plural, there are two kinds of agreement: sound matching and number agreement. Add what is necessary to *chilen* to make it match the noun and its article: *un libro chilen* ⎯⎯, *los libros chilen* ⎯⎯.

un libro chileno, los libros chilenos

26 Try this again: *una señora chilen* ⎯⎯, *el señor chilen* ⎯⎯.

una señora chilena, el señor chileno

27 Once more: *los papeles chilen* ⎯⎯, *las mesas chilen* ⎯⎯.

los papeles chilenos, las mesas chilenas

28 Spanish has another kind of agreement. María and Pilar are girls. Neither noun combines with *muchacho*. María and Pilar combine with *muchacha*: *María es una muchacha; Pilar es una muchacha; María y Pilar son muchachas.* Pilar is from Chile, so we may say "Pilar is Chilean." Can you guess which of these two sentences translates this? (a) *Pilar es chilena.* (b) *Pilar es chileno.*

Pilar es chilena. (*Pilar es una muchacha chilena.*)

29 Which is correct? (a) *José es una muchacha.* (b) *José es un muchacho.*

José es un muchacho.

30 You must say *María es chilena.* What will you say? (a) *José es chileno.* (b) *José es chilena.*

José es chileno. (*José es un muchacho chileno.*)

31 *José y María son muchachos.* Which is correct? (a) *José y María son chilenas.* (b) *José y María son chilenos.*

José y María son chilenos. (*Son muchachos chilenos.*)

32 The four forms of the definite article, *el, los, la, las*, all came from the same Latin word (*ille*) as the four forms of the third person pronouns. This can be easily seen by writing the subject pronouns this way: *él, el-los, el-la, el-las.* Which set of adjectives will combine with *ella* and *ellas*? (a) the *o*-set (b) the *a*-set

the *a*-set   **33** Write the matching sound. *José es chileno. Él es chilen* ⎯⎯.

Él es chileno.   **34** Write the matching sound. *María es chilena. Ella es chilen* ⎯⎯.

Ella es chilena.   **35** Add what is needed to make the adjective agree with the subject pronoun. *Ellos son chilen ... ; Ellas son chilen ... .*

Ellos son chilenos; Ellas son chilenas.

36 You use *tú, usted*, or *ustedes* in talking to either boys or girls. Suppose you are talking to a boy. Which question is correct? (a) *¿Es usted chilena?* (b) *¿Es usted chileno?*

¿Es usted chileno?

37 You are talking to several girls. Which question is correct? (a) *¿Son ustedes chilenos?* (b) *¿Son ustedes chilenas?*

¿Son ustedes chilenas?

38 The first person plural subject pronouns *nosotros* and *nosotras* have the *o* and *a* matching sounds. Which translation of "We are Chilean" is correct? (a) *Nosotros somos chilenas.* (b) *Nosotros somos chilenos.*

Nosotros somos chilenos. (*o* matches *o*. The *o* of *mos* does not agree.)

39 This question may catch you if you don't watch out. "You" want to say, "I am Chilean." What do you say? (a) *Soy chileno.* (b) *Soy chilena.*

Are "you" a boy or a girl? A boy says, *Soy chileno.* A girl says, *Soy chilena.*

There are, in all of Spanish, a very few exceptions to the rules of agreement which you have just learned. One that you already know is *Buenos días.* The noun *día* ends in *a*, but it combines, nevertheless, only with the *o*-set of adjectives (*un día, el día, los días*). These exceptions have to be memorized.

There are still many ways of writing numbers in the world today, but the one used by mathematicians everywhere came to Europe from India after the Arabs conquered most of the Spanish Peninsula in 711 A.D. Since the Arabs introduced their way of writing the Hindu numbers into Europe, we still speak of these numbers as Arabic numbers. Some of the Arab mathematicians tried to make each number have the same number of angles as the number itself. So 3, which originally was the written form ≡ , took the shape of

with three angles as numbered above. To make 7 have seven angles it was necessary to use two bars, one through the middle 7 and another at the bottom 7 . Part of this old Arabic symbol is still conserved in Spanish writing today, that is, the seven is still written with a bar: 7 . What Americans write as a seven (7), consequently, is frequently read as a 1 by a Spanish speaker, and great care is needed, for example, when writing checks.

PROGRAM **16**

More about the Differences Between English and Spanish Sounds, and a Review

This Program is a linguistic game. You are going to play two parts. In your first role, you are a linguistic "criminal." In your second role, you are a linguistic "detective" who is supposed to prevent "crime."

Why are you a linguistic "criminal"? Because you speak English, you want to "steal" English sounds and put them in place of Spanish sounds. Let's see if you can catch yourself doing this *before* you do the answer part of each of the following frames. It's easy to be a "criminal," but hard to be a good detective. So, be on your toes.

1 Say the following aloud very carefully in Spanish. Pay attention to the position of the tip of your tongue as you make the first sound of each word: *ta, te, ti, to, tu.* When you made the sound of [t], the tip of your tongue touched ⁓⁓⁓.

Were you "stealing" this sound from English? The tip of your tongue should have touched the back of your upper front teeth, not the gum ridge above them. Spanish [t] is dental.

2 Now, watch your tongue tip again and say in Spanish: *da, de, di, do, du.* When you made the sound [d], the tip of your tongue touched ⁓⁓⁓.

the back of your upper front teeth (Not the roof of your mouth. Spanish [d] is also dental.) **3** Hold the back of your hand about one-half inch from your lips. Now say "too" and "two" real loud. Did you feel a puff of air on your hand?

yes **4** Put your hand in the same place and say Spanish *tú* several times. Did you feel the same puff of air?

If you wrote "no" on your answer sheet, go on to Frame 5. If you wrote "yes," you are a good detective and a linguistic criminal. Why? Because English [t] is aspirated (made with a puff) while Spanish [t] is not.

If you said *tú* with a puff, hold the back of your hand close to your lips again and practice *tú* until there is no puff. You get rid of the puff by pulling your tongue away from the teeth before air pressure builds up. When you can say *tú* without a puff, try saying *ta, te, ti, to, tu* again. Remember: no puff, and the tongue tip touches the teeth, not the gum ridge as in English.

5 Say English *see* aloud. Say *see* aloud again and try to say it with your lips very close together. Now, try this. Say *see,* and as you make the [ee] sound try to open your mouth as much as possible. Experiment until you can end the word with your jaws wide open.

Here's the question. No matter how wide you opened your mouth, did you still hear *see?*

yes (You are just more emphatic when you open your mouth wider.)

6 Now, polish your wits and your detective badge, and say Spanish *sí* aloud several times. Watch what you are doing with your jaws as you say the vowel sound [i]. (a) Do you move your jaws? (b) Do you hold them in the same place?

If you moved them, you did not say *sí.* You said "see," and were talking English not Spanish. Write what you said (*sí* or "see") on your answer sheet. Here's how to say *sí* properly in Spanish. Put one finger of each hand in a corner of your lips. Pull each corner back sharply. Hold your jaws and lips still and say *sí.* **7** Say *bueno* aloud twice. Now say it without the [b] sound: *ueno.* When you say *ueno,* is the first sound (a) a vowel? (b) a consonant?

This one may have trapped you if you looked at *u* instead of listening to the sound [u]. Spanish uses *w* only in a few foreign words. Spanish speakers write the sound [w] as *u* before a vowel. Practice saying these words aloud:

| Luisa | bueno | luego | muy | cuaderno | puerta |

Now say them without the first sound and with *w* in place of *u.*

| wisa | weno | wego | wy | waderno | werta |

Now put the first sound back and say:

| Lwisa | bweno | lwego | mwy | cwaderno | pwerta |

Now you should have much less of an English accent.

8 Say the name for the English letter *k* as in *KK*. Does this name end in a vowel sound?

yes (It's like the name for the English letter *a*.)

9 Now say the name for the letter *k* and add the name for the letter *a*. Try this again and run the two names together. You have just said the name of one of the knights of King Arthur's Round Table. His name is Sir ⁓⁓.

Kay (Don't worry if you missed this one.)

10 You made up the name *Kay* by adding the name for *a* to the name for the letter *k*. How many vowel sounds are there in *Kay*? (a) one (b) two (If you're not sure, read frames 8 and 9 again before you answer.)

two (Some linguists call this a "complex vowel.")

11 Say *¿Qué tal?* aloud and, then, *qué*. How many vowel sounds are there in *qué*? (a) one (b) two

If you marked two, your detective work is slipping. If you said *qué* with two vowel sounds, you really said "Kay," not *qué*. Spanish *qué* sounds like the name for "k" when you say "KK" very quickly. Practice this several times.

12 Say Spanish *de* and English "day." Do they sound exactly alike?

Not if you said each properly. "Day," like "Kay," has two vowel sounds (a complex vowel); *de* has only one (a simple or pure vowel). You change your tongue position as you say "day." Nothing changes position as you say the [e] sound of *de*.

13 A *ventana* is something the wind or air may come through. One English cognate of *ventana* is the verb "ventilate" (to let or force air in). Do you say the *ven* of both words in precisely the same way?

no (If you wrote "yes," be very careful with the next four frames. You're about to be fired from the police force.)

14 The first syllable of *ventana* is *ven*. When you say this in Spanish it sounds like the nickname for a very famous, early American inventor and diplomat called Benjamin Franklin. His nickname is spelled ⁓⁓.

Ben

15 Say *ventana* and *la ventana*. Did you say the syllable *ven* the same way both times?

If you said "yes," you've been caught again.

16 When you say *ventana* all by itself, the first sound is (a) a stop (b) a fricative.

a stop

17 When you say *la ventana*, the sound [v] is (a) a stop (b) a fricative.

a fricative

18 Here is a frame which will really test your detective powers. Say *ventana*, *la ventana*, and English "ventilate." Say them again and watch what your lower lip is doing as you say the [v] sound in each. In which word does your lower lip touch your upper front teeth as you make the [v] sound?

ventilate (No sound of Spanish *v* or *b* is normally made in this way.)

19 If you wrote *ventana* as *bentana*, would you pronounce it differently?

no

20 If you wrote *la ventana* as *la bentana*, would you pronounce it differently in Spanish?

no (*b* and *v* always stand for the same sounds in standard Spanish.)

21 Say *Buenas noches* aloud. The last syllable of *noches* is *ches*. It is pronounced (a) like the last syllable of English "notches" (b) like the English word "chase."

like "chase" ("Notches" has a schwa sound in *ches*.)

22 This frame is to find out whether those who missed Frame 13 must now turn in their detective badges. Be careful. The verb form *voy*, when spoken by itself, sounds (a) like the English "boy" (b) like the first part of "voyage."

like "boy" (If you marked "voyage," say "voyage" and "boyage" until you hear the difference.)

23 Say "no" in English emphatically. Now say it in Spanish. In which language is the sound [o] the longest?

English (Spanish cuts the sound short even when emphatic.)

24 Say *señor* aloud and pay special attention to how you make the [r] sound. Say English "for" and *señor* one after the other. Now say "ladder" and *señor* together, and pay special attention to the sound you make for [dd]. The [r] sound of *señor* is (a) like the [r] of "for" (b) like the [dd] of "ladder"

like the [dd] of "ladder"

25 The tongue position for Spanish [r] and English [dd] is almost the same. You can check your pronunciation of Spanish [r] by saying "lad" or "had." Hold your tongue in position as you finish the word. That is where your tongue should be when you finish *señor*.

Have you been a good linguistic detective? Don't worry too much if you missed several frames. There has not been enough class time as yet to tell you about every Spanish sound. As a result, this Program has dealt mostly with sounds that you have been trying to learn only by imitation.

Do you believe that you will hear them better and imitate them better now that you know more about them?

yes (It is always easier to practice what you know than to imitate something you really don't understand.)

Review: How sharp have you been?

You may be surprised to discover that you have been learning a lot of Spanish and a lot about Spanish in your class sessions without really being aware of it. Have you noticed the following facts about the words used in talking about the days of the week?

1 The translation of the greeting *Buenos días* is ⌒⌒.

Good morning. **2** The translation of *día* in the question ¿ *Qué día es mañana?* is ⌒⌒.

day **3** Now be careful. The Spanish speaker says *Buenos días* when we say "Good morning." Does this translation give the real meaning of *días?*

no (The Spanish greeting is a shortened form of something like "May you have good days.")

4 There are two English translations for *día* but, for the Spanish speaker, only one meaning. (a) true (b) false

true **5** A week is divided into seven 24-hour intervals. Are you aware of the fact that you already know five different ways of naming each of these seven 24-hour intervals? Let's prove this. Do *día* and *hoy* both stand for a 24-hour interval in ¿ *Qué día es hoy?*

yes **6** If the answer to ¿ *Qué día es hoy?* is *Hoy es martes*, do *día, hoy,* and *martes* all stand for a 24-hour interval of time?

yes

7 *Martes* comes before *miércoles* in the days of the week. Suppose *hoy* is *miércoles;* then another name for *martes* could be of the same set as *hoy,* or ~~~~~~.

ayer (*Ayer fue martes.*)

8 Suppose *hoy* is *lunes,* then another name for *martes* is ~~~~~.

mañana (*Mañana es martes.* So now you have the five labels you have already learned for any one of the 24-hour divisions of the week: *día, ayer, hoy, mañana* plus the calendar name for each day of the week: *lunes, martes, etc.*)

9 Have you also noticed that the verb form *es* in *¿Qué día es hoy?* is (a) present tense? (b) past tense?

present tense **10** Is *es* also present tense in *¿Qué día es mañana?*

yes **11** What tense, then, is *fue* in *Y ayer, ¿qué día fue?*

past **12** "Is" and "was" are irregular forms of "to be." Is it logical to suppose that their translation, *es* and *fue,* are forms of the same verb in Spanish?

yes (The Spanish infinitive for *es* and *fue* is *ser.*)

13 Have you really been paying attention to all the facts taken up in the last 12 frames? Probably not, and that is why they are here: to show you that you are learning a lot more than you think.

PROGRAM 17

Getting Ready for a Classroom Test

The time has come for your teacher to find out exactly how well you manage certain language skills. In order to help you to continue to progress, a test is necessary. However, your teacher can't get very precise information about your language ability if you make mechanical errors or mistakes simply because you don't know how to handle the test. This Program describes the test and is designed to help you avoid mistakes that don't show how much Spanish you actually know. Go through it carefully. You will be much better prepared for all your tests if you always use your cover sheet as suggested.

1 Part A of the test is to find out how well you understand *spoken* Spanish. What will you do? (a) listen (b) read (c) write

listen, paying attention to the meaning of what you hear

2 You will have an answer sheet. For Part A the answer sheet will have a column of 10 numbers each followed by a b c. For example: 1. a b c The same letters will be on the board so your teacher can point to them. The test will be given by your teacher. A recording may or may not be used. Either way the test will begin with a sentence in Spanish. For example, *¿A dónde vas, Tomás?* This means, in English, ⁓.

Where are you going, Thomas?

3 After you hear *¿A dónde vas, Tomás?*, your teacher will point to a b c on the board and, for each letter, you will hear something else in Spanish. For example: a. *Estoy muy bien.* b. *De Bogotá.* c. *A la oficina.* After you hear what goes with c, you are to draw a circle around the letter which goes with the sentence that is the best or most logical reply to *¿A dónde vas, Tomás?* In this example, the letter is ⁓.

c (*A la oficina* is the most likely answer to *¿A dónde vas, Tomás?*)

4 Here is another example to practice. You hear *¿Cómo se llama él?* Your teacher next points to *a* on the board and you hear, *Estoy bien, gracias.* Do you draw a circle around *a*?

no ("I'm fine, thank you" is not a proper reply to "What's his name?")

5 Teacher now points to b and you hear *Se llama Luisa.* This sounds a lot like *¿Cómo se llama él?* Why is it a wrong answer?

because *él* stands for a boy and *Luisa* is a girl

6 Teacher now points to c and you hear *Se llama Tomás.* Can *Tomás* and *él* stand for the same person?

yes

7 So you draw a circle around ⁓.

c

8 Here is another model and three test sentences for you to practice. Model: *El libro está en la mesa.* a. *Dos y dos son cuatro.* b. *No habla inglés muy bien.* c. *¿Es bueno?* Which letter will you draw a circle around?

c ("Is it good?" is the only sentence that can apply to *libro*.)

9 Part B of the test is to find out whether you have learned enough about Spanish sounds to know what is *right* or *wrong*. On your answer sheet *R* will stand for "right," and *W* will stand for ⁓.

wrong

10 You will hear five sentences, some spoken correctly and some with errors in pronunciation. If you hear, for example, a [p] with a puff after it, you will draw a circle around (a) W (b) R.

W (Spanish [p] is not aspirated.)

11 Your teacher says *Dos y dos son cuatro* with two stop [d] sounds. You draw a circle around ⁓.

W (The second [d] should be fricative.)

12 Part C is to find out whether you know the Spanish words for the Arabic numbers: 1, 4, 9, 14, *etc.* Your teacher may say *quince*. What Arabic number do you write on your answer sheet?

15

13 Part D is like Part C, but it deals with addition and subtraction, and you are to write in Arabic numbers the entire problem. Your teacher may say, *Cuatro y cuatro son ocho.* What will you write on your answer sheet?

$4 + 4 = 8$ (Don't forget the plus, minus, and equals signs.)

14 Your answer sheet for Part E will have a column of 8 numbers, each followed by the forms of the indefinite article, *un una.* You must circle the form that goes with the word your teacher says. If the word is *señorita*, you draw a circle around (a) *un* (b) *una*.

una (*Una señorita*, not *un señorita*.)

15 Part F will have a column of 8 numbers followed by the forms of the definite article: *el, la, los, las.* Your teacher will say a noun and you must circle the form

that goes with it. If the noun is *escuela*, you circle: *el la los las.*
la (The *a* of *la* matches the *a* of *escuela*.)

16 Part G is to find out how well you know your verb forms. It is like a pattern drill. You will hear a model and, then, a different subject. If the model is *Yo hablo español* and the new subject is *tú*, which of the following forms will you circle? *hablamos hablan hablas habla*

hablas (The *s* of *hablas* agrees with *tú*.)

17 Part H will just have a column of 10 numbers. There will be several flash cards on the board with a capital letter under each one. You will hear ten sentences. If a sentence names anything in a picture or talks about a picture in a logical way, you write the letter of the picture on your answer sheet. So, if you see and hear *Ella es de Chile*, you write the letter ~~~~.

A　　　　　B　　　　　C

B (Picture B is the only one with a girl. *Ella* stands for a girl.)

18 Part I is to discover whether you can spot the signals which tell you when to use a fricative or stop [d] sound. There will be six sentences on the answer sheet. You are to <u>underline</u> each fricative [d] and <u>circle</u> each stop [d]. Copy the following example and make the marks. *¿Dónde está Dorotea Aldeano?*

¿ Ⓓó n ⓓe e s t á D o r o t e a A l ⓓe a n o ?

Additional Practice for the Test

1 The signal or cue for the use of the right allophone of /d/ is (a) what comes directly before the [d] sound (b) what comes directly after.

what comes directly before the [d] sound

2 When [n] or [l] comes directly before the [d] sound, you use (a) a stop (b) a fricative.

a stop

3 Silence comes before a [d] sound whenever you start a new sentence or when you pause or hesitate in the middle of a sentence you have already started.

a stop [d]　After silence you use (a) a fricative [d] (b) a stop [d].

[n] or [l]　**4** You always use a fricative [d] except after silence and after the sounds ~~~~.

5 The form of the definite article that goes with *mesa* and *puerta* is ~~~~.

la　**6** The form of the indefinite article which goes with *día* and *lápiz* is ~~~~.

un　**7** The Arabic numbers for *Nueve menos tres son seis* are ~~~~.

9 − 3 = 6　**8** Which is the most logical (best) reply to the model *La oficina está allí?* (a) *¿Qué es?* (b) *Gracias.* (c) *¡Hola, Luisa!*

Gracias.　**9** Copy and circle the stop [d] sounds in the following: *Dos y dos y seis son diez.*

Ⓓo s y d o s y s e i s s o n ⓓi e z.

10 What does *¿Me llamo Paco?* actually mean to a Spanish speaker? (a) My name is Paco. (b) I call myself Paco.

I call myself Paco. (The common translation, however, is "My name is Paco.")

11 The [s] of *presente* is (a) voiced (b) unvoiced.

unvoiced   **12** Spanish [t] is dental (a) true (b) false

true   **13** Which numbers between 1 and 20 are made up of *y* and two number words in speech?

dieciséis, diecisiete, dieciocho, diecinueve (These words, which are really made up of three words, *diez, y, seis, etc.*, can also be spelled this way: *diez y seis, diez y siete, etc.* SFC uses the one word form. Notice that *dieciséis, veintidós, veintitrés* and *veintiséis* require a written accent mark.)

14 When you add numbers in Spanish, you use (a) *son* (b) *es.*

son *(Cuatro y cuatro son ocho.)*

15 When you subtract numbers, you use (a) *son* (b) *es.*

son *(Diez menos tres son siete.)*

16 When you change the subject of a verb, which suffix do you also change? (a) the first (b) the second

the second   **17** You hear *Hablamos español* and the cue *usted.* Which form do you circle on the answer sheet: *hablo, hablan, habla, hablas?*

habla   **18** You see a picture of: A. a cat, B. a car, C. a snow-covered mountain. You hear the sentence *Está en Ecuador.* Which letter do you write on your sheet?

C

¡No!
No!
(a negative response)

Wave index finger of either hand from left to right at just below shoulder height, pivoting at the elbow and/or wrist.

¡Ojo!
Look out! Be careful!

Touch index finger of right hand to cheek directly below right eye, pointing up toward it.

¡Piensa!
Think! Use your head!

Place index finger of right hand over the nose so that the tip touches the center of the forehead.

Un momentito.
Just a moment.

Hold hand in front with thumb and index finger about one-half inch apart as if showing the thickness of a book.

Etapa Dos

Words for Time Intervals and Their Spelling

You already know how to say all the words in this Program. You can also read them. The purpose of this Program is to tell you more about these words and to help you find out which ones you need to practice spelling and writing. You will be asked to write the words from memory in several frames. If you write a word correctly, go on to the next frame. If you make a mistake, copy the correct spelling twice on your answer sheet. Check what you are doing very carefully.

1 Time is divided, in both English and Spanish, into two sets of segments or intervals. One set is made up of words for clock time. The other set is made up of words for calendar time. The English word for the interval of clock time made up of 60 minutes is ~~~~.

hour (The Spanish word is *hora*. Copy it twice. Note: The *h* stands for no sound in either language.)

2 24 *horas* make up an interval of calendar time called *un* ~~~~.

día (Copy *día* twice if you made a mistake.)

3 Spanish speakers divide each *día* into three parts or calendar intervals. The interval of time from midnight to noon is spelled exactly like their word for tomorrow. It is ~~~~.

mañana (Did you remember the little wiggle over the *n*? It is called a *tilde*, and was once a tiny *n*. Although it is now a single letter, *ñ* stands for two sounds, [n] plus [y].)

4 The interval of time between noon and sunset is called ~~~~.

tarde (This is the late part of the day. When you are late to class, your teacher uses a cognate to say you are "tardy.")

5 The time between sunset and midnight is called ~~~~.

noche **6** One of the three parts of the 24-hour *día* is an interval made up of half darkness and half light. Its name is ~~~~.

mañana (This *mañana* is *la mañana*.)

7 The word *día*, like English "day," has two meanings. It stands for the astronomical day, an interval of 24 ~~~~. (Use Spanish word.)

horas **8** *Día* also stands for that part of the 24-hour astronomical day during which the sun shines and there is ~~~~.

luz (light) **9** *Noche* also has two meanings. It labels the dark part of the astronomical day. It also stands for the part of the *día* that comes between ~~~~. (Use Spanish words.)

tarde and *mañana*

10 The number of *días* that there are in a week (*semana*) comes from the Bible. According to Scriptures, six days were allotted for work, "but the seventh day is the day of the Lord Thy God; in it thou shalt not do any work." The Latin word for Lord is *dominus*. The Spanish word for the Lord's day is ~~~~.

domingo (If you misspelled it, copy it correctly.)

11 Look very carefully at the spelling of *domingo* and of its translation: "Sunday." What difference in spelling habits do you see?

Spanish names for the days of the week do not begin with a capital letter.
Copy *domingo* again.

12 The Hebrew name for the seventh day of the week is *shabbath*. In English this is "Sabbath." The Spanish cognate of "Sabbath" is ———.

sábado (Did you remember the accent mark?)

13 Although Spanish *sábado* is a cognate of "Sabbath," it is translated into English as ———.

Saturday　　**14** The English word "Sabbath" means the day dedicated to God, that is, "Sunday." The Spanish translation of "Sunday" is ———.

domingo (No capital letter.)

15 Spanish calendars often do not agree with the Bible. They frequently put *domingo* as the last day of the week, not *sábado*. The first day on such a calendar is ———.

lunes　　**16** According to the Bible, the seventh day of the week is the day dedicated to the Lord. English calendars put this day first, so, on the English calendar, the first day of the week is ———. (Use Spanish word.)

domingo (Are you confused? So are both cultures. You'll see why in the following frames.)

17 You have learned that the Spanish name for one day of the week comes from the Christian religion (*domingo*) and one comes from the Jewish religion (*sábado*). All the other Spanish names for days of the week come from the gods or goddesses of the ancient Roman religion. One day of the week was dedicated to the goddess of the moon. The Spanish word for moon is *luna*. This day is ———.

lunes ("Monday" also used to mean "Moon's day.") Copy *lunes*.

18 One Roman day was dedicated to the god of war, *Mars*. This day is ———.

martes　　**19** *Martes* is translated by ———.

Tuesday (Which used to be "Tiw's day," after *Tiw*, the god of war in ancient England.)　　**20** The next day was devoted to the god of commerce and the messenger of the other gods, *Mercury*. The modern Spanish name for this day is ———.

miércoles (Check your spelling carefully.)

21 The following Roman day was named after the greatest god of all, *Jove*. (Also called *Jupiter*.) It is ———.

jueves　　**22** The English translation of *jueves* is ———.

Thursday (Which means "Thor's day," the day of the God of Thunder. *Thor* was to the Anglo-Saxons what *Jove* was to the Romans.)

23 One Roman day was set aside to worship the goddess of love, *Venus*. This day is ———.

viernes　　**24** The translation of *viernes* is ———.

Friday (This is "Frigg's day," from "Fria's day," the old Germanic goddess of love, and the wife of the god *Woden*, whose English day is "Woden's day" or "Wednesday.")

25 The first day of the week in the Roman calendar was *Dies solis*, day of the Sun (*sol*) or "Sun's day." Spanish speakers replaced this with ———.

domingo (Remember: no capital letter.)

26 The last day of the week in both the Roman and English calendar is "Saturn's day," the day of the god of sowing or seed. Spanish speakers replaced this with a word that came from Hebrew. It is ⁓⁓⁓.

sábado (Are you still forgetting the accent mark?)

27 Here are the original meanings of the Spanish names of the days of the week. Can you give the modern Spanish for each? Watch your spelling: *Moon's day, Mars' day, Mercury's day, Jove's day, Venus' day, Lord's day* (Jewish), *Lord's day* (Christian).

28 Here are the Spanish names for the days of the week. Copy each one you misspelled above. Remember: no capital letters, and *domingo* comes last on calendars: *domingo, lunes, martes, miércoles, jueves, viernes, sábado.*

29 Each day of the week has a fixed position in a series. When the days are put on a line, as in a Spanish calendar, the series goes from left to right, like this:

| lunes | martes | miércoles | jueves | viernes | sábado | domingo |

Both English and Spanish have another way of naming days, and a different way of putting them in a calendar series. You cannot do or say anything in a past day or a future day. You can only do something in a present day, that is, this day right now. The English name for the day that is always the present day, this day in which you are doing this Program is ⁓⁓⁓.

today
hoy

30 The Spanish translation of "today" is ⁓⁓⁓.

31 The name for the day in which you always find yourself is "today" or *hoy.* This day is the central or axis day of a series which goes in two directions, like this

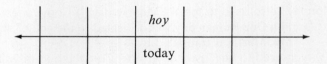

The English name for the day that always comes *before* today is ⁓⁓⁓.

yesterday
ayer (Copy it if you made a mistake.)

32 The Spanish *día* that always comes before *hoy* is (a) *ayer* (b) *mañana.*

33 The *día* that always follows *hoy* is ⁓⁓⁓.

mañana (This is *el mañana,* "tomorrow," not *la mañana,* "morning.")

34 The word *ante* is translated as "before." The day that comes before *ayer* is ⁓⁓⁓.

anteayer
day before yesterday

35 The translation of *anteayer* is ⁓⁓⁓.

36 The word *pasado* is an adjective which means "passed" or "gone by." After *mañana* has passed or gone by, you come to the day called ⁓⁓⁓.

pasado mañana (Notice that the *o* of *pasado* matches the *l* of *el* (*el mañana*), not the *a* of *mañana.* This is an exception to your rule on matching the last sounds of nouns and adjectives.)

37 Here are the English and Spanish words arranged in the two-directional series. One series goes toward the left of the central or axis day. The other series goes toward the right of the axis day. Copy the Spanish names carefully.

day before yesterday	yesterday	today	tomorrow	day after tomorrow
anteayer	*ayer*	*hoy*	*mañana*	*pasado mañana*

38 Copy, punctuate, and add the accent marks: *Que dia fue anteayer.*
¿ Qué día fue anteayer? (Copy again.)

39 Copy, punctuate, and add the accent marks: *Y pasado mañana que dia es.*
Y pasado mañana, ¿qué día es? Copy again.

Optional Study

In Ancient England, each day of the week was dedicated to a pagan god. Here is what our modern names used to mean. Write the Spanish translation for each: Sun's day, Moon's day, Tiw's day, Woden's day, Thor's day, Frigg's day, Saturn's day.
Check your spelling: *domingo, lunes, martes, miércoles, jueves, viernes, sábado.* If you are still making a mistake on a word, copy it several times. Remember: no capital letters for Spanish days of the week.

PROGRAM **19**

Numbers, and Plural of Nouns; Review

Part 1: Numbers, and More About Words and Their Spelling

1 The Latin words *undecim* and *duodecim* mean *1 + decem* and *2 + decem* or *1 + 10* and *2 + 10*. Look at the end of these Spanish number words: *once, doce, trece, catorce, quince.* Which part of each word is what is now left from the Latin *decim*, "ten"?
ce (Are you remembering to circle the frame number you miss?)

2 When you take the *ce* away from the words above, you have something left that looks somewhat like the modern Spanish number word that is added to 10. Write this modern Spanish word for each of the following: *on-ce, do-ce, tre-ce, cator-ce, quin-ce.*
uno, dos, tres, cuatro, cinco

3 *Trece* is actually *tre* (three) plus *ce* (ten). The number *dieciséis* is translated as ⌇⌇⌇.
sixteen

4 Does "sixteen" mean "six + ten"?
yes

5 What is the word-for-word translation of *dieciséis*, which may also be written *diez y seis?*
ten and six, or 10 + 6

6 The base of the Spanish number system is zero and nine numbers: 1, 2, 3, 4, 5, 6, 7, 8, 9. *Ten* is made by combining 1 and 0: 10. Write the Spanish number words for the Arabic numbers from 0 through 10.

cero, uno, dos, tres, cuatro, cinco, seis, siete, ocho, nueve, diez (Check your spelling by copying each word again. Copying is a dull activity, but you need the practice.)

7 The next five numbers are made up of a different form of the first five digits (*uno, dos, tres, cuatro, cinco*) and *ce*, the leftover of the Latin *decim*, "ten." Write the number words for: 11, 12, 13, 14, 15.

once, doce, trece, catorce, quince (Copy any word you misspelled.)

8 The next four numbers are actually made up of three separate words. The word for "ten," *diez* (to be written *diec*), plus the word *y* (to be written *i*), and the number to be added to ten. Write the number words for: 10 + 6, 10 + 7, 10 + 8, 10 + 9.

dieciséis, diecisiete, dieciocho, diecinueve (Copy any word you misspelled.)

9 The number word for 20 is ⁓.

veinte (Did you write the *e* before the *i*?)

10 You now know enough to make up the number words from 21 through 29. You just add the digit number words to *veinte* using the plus word *y* just as you did for 16, which is 10 + 6 or *dieciséis*. (You drop, however, the final *e* of *veinte*.) The number word for 21 is ⁓.

veintiuno = 20 + 1

11 Write the number words for the following:

22 = (20 + 2)	24 = (20 + 4)	26 = (20 + 6)	28 = (20 + 8)
23 = (20 + 3)	25 = (20 + 5)	27 = (20 + 7)	29 = (20 + 9)

veintidós   *veinticuatro*   *veintiséis*   *veintiocho*
veintitrés   *veinticinco*   *veintisiete*   *veintinueve*

Part 2: The Plural of Nouns

In each of the following 8 frames you will see a small picture of an object which you have seen on some flash card. Write the singular and plural form of the noun that stands for the object.

1

libro ; libros   **2**

reloj ; relojes   **3**

regla ; reglas

4

pluma; plumas

5

silla; sillas

6

puerta; puertas

7

muchacho; muchachos

8

muchacha; muchachas

9 The noun *lápiz* and all other nouns ending in *z* have a special change when the plural suffix *es* is added to them. The *z* is replaced by *c*. Copy *lápiz* and *lápices*, and do not forget the written accent.

10 Write the plural for *luz*.

luces

11 Copy the following and make them plural: *el cuaderno, la ventana, la mesa, la pizarra, el pupitre, la tiza.*

los cuadernos, las ventanas, las mesas, las pizarras, los pupitres, las tizas

Part 3: Pronouns and Verb Forms

1 Write the plural form for each of the following pronouns: *yo, tú, él, ella, usted.*

nosotros or *nosotras, ustedes, ellos, ellas, ustedes*

2 Write the form of *hablar, desear,* and *estudiar* which goes with *tú, él, nosotros.*

tú hablas, deseas, estudias; él habla, desea, estudia; nosotros hablamos, deseamos, estudiamos

3 There are three different subject pronouns which may combine with the verb form *desean*. They are ⁓⁓⁓ .

ellos, ellas, ustedes

Part 4: Question Words

1 The question word in "What is this?" is ——.

What   **2** The Spanish equivalent of "what" is ——.

qué (With an accent mark.)

3 Write the missing question word: ¿ —— *son siete menos tres?* (It asks for an amount and is plural.)

Cuántos (With capital *C* and accent mark.)

4 When you want a place or destination as an answer, you use the question word ——.

dónde   **5** Now look at *qué*, *cuántos*, and *dónde*. What do they all have in common?

an accent mark (When a question word is used in a question, it *always* has an accent mark in writing.)

6 When you ask about a person's health, the question word is ——.

cómo (*¿Cómo está Vd.?*)

Among the superstitious people of the United States, Friday is considered to be an unlucky day, and Friday the thirteenth is the unluckiest day of all. In the Hispanic world the unlucky day of the week is Tuesday. Superstitious people feel that one should not undertake major enterprises on Tuesday. This belief is expressed in a well known saying, *En martes, ni te cases ni te embarques.* The translation is *On Tuesday don't get married or start a trip.*

Part 5: A Self-test

Let's find out how much you have really learned from doing this Program. Do the following frames, and at the end, you can give yourself a grade. Don't forget your cover sheet.

1 English "fourteen" is really "four + ten." Spanish uses Latin *ce* for 10 and its word for 14 is ——.

catorce   **2** Spanish spells the word for 4 ——.

cuatro   **3** A teenager is a person whose age is given as a number plus ten (teen): thirteen through nineteen. "Six + ten" (sixteen) becomes 10 + 6 in Spanish or ——.

dieciséis   **4** The order of the vowel letters in certain numbers causes spelling problems. Be careful with this. Write the Spanish word for these numbers: 6, 7, 20, 9, 10.

seis, siete, veinte, nueve, diez

5 The hyphen in "twenty-two" is translated into Spanish by ——.

i(y) : veintidós   **6** Say [rreló] aloud. Now write the word as it is normally spelled.

reloj   **7** The written form *reloj* ends in a consonant. This tells you the plural is ——.

relojes   **8** Write the plural of *luz* and *lápiz*.

luces ; lápices (The *z* of the singular form becomes *c* before *es*.)

9 Copy the following but leave out *muchacho*. What must you do to *el*: *¿ Está el muchacho allí?*

¿ Está él allí? (You need an accent mark on *él*.)

10 Change *estudiar* so it agrees with *nosotras*.

estudiamos

11 What special feature do all question words have in common?

an accent mark 12 English uses "How much" in asking about either addition or subtraction. Spanish usage frequently parallels this form. It is ⁓⁓.

cuántos 13 The question word for place, origin, or destination is ⁓⁓.
dónde

Count the number of circled frame numbers. Your grade is:

1 error	A+	5 errors	C+
2 errors	A−	6 errors	C−
3 errors	B+	7 errors	D+
4 errors	B−	8 errors	D−

Write your grade in a large letter at the end of your worksheet.

PROGRAM 20

More Practice in Writing

1 *Writing down* what you hear becomes a lot easier to do when you clearly understand what tasks you have to perform. There are three basic things to which you must pay attention. One is intonation. You hear a spoken sentence and its intonation tells you how to ⁓⁓ it in writing.

punctuate 2 In speech all the words of a phrase are run together as though they were one long word. Do you write the phrase down exactly the way you hear it?

no (You take it apart and put spaces between most words in writing.)

3 You hear ¿Adóndevas? Rewrite this with proper spacing.

¿A dónde vas? 4 After you have figured out where the spaces go, you have to spell each word. There are four different kinds of cues that tell you how to spell what you hear. One is meaning. Here is an English example. Which spelling, *weighs* or *ways*, is proper in this sentence: "She ⁓⁓ 87 pounds."?

weighs (In this case, there are two *ways* of writing what you hear.)

5 When two different words sound exactly alike only the meaning tells you what to write. Spanish *el* and *él* sound exactly alike. Which spelling goes in the blanks below? ⁓⁓ muchacho está allí; ⁓⁓ está allí.

El (the definite article); él (the subject pronoun)

6 Most words have a distinct shape of their own. For example, *papel* does not sound like *tarde*. In cases like these, what you hear tells you what to write. (a) true (b) false

true 7 Spanish, like English, has a lot of tricky words. You can understand them; you can tell their shape, but what you hear does not tell you how to spell them.

You have to see them in print to learn how they are spelled. For example, you hear [yama] in the question *¿Cómo se [yama] él?*, but you write ～～.

llama **8** You hear [senyor], but you write ～～.

señor **9** You hear [ke], but you write ～～.

que or *qué* (If you misspelled [yama], [senyor], or [ke], you have proof that you have not been paying enough attention to the relationship between what you *hear* and what you *see* in print.)

10 The four cues for spelling are (1) meaning, (2) what you hear, (3) what you see in print, and (4) rules. Which three of these must you memorize?

meaning, what you see in print, and the rules

11 The words you will have to practice most in order to learn to spell them correctly are those that have letters or marks not used in English. Copy these words and add the tilde: *espanol, senor, manana, Espana, senorita.*

español, señor, mañana, España, señorita

12 The written accent mark is placed over (a) consonants (b) vowels.

vowels **13** When a word has only one syllable, the meaning, not what you hear, tells you that it has an accent mark in writing. Copy these words and add the accent mark: *tu, el, si, que.*

tú, él, sí, qué **14** Question words always have an accent mark on the stressed syllable. The following are divided into syllables. Copy them the way they are normally written and add the accent mark. *¿Co-mo? ¿Don-de? ¿Cuan-tos?*

¿Cómo? ¿Dónde? ¿Cuántos?

15 The accent mark on all other words indicates the syllable to be stressed in speech. Copy the following words the way they are normally written and add the accent mark: *di-as, a-lli, a-dios, a-qui, es-tas, per-don, in-gles, la-piz.*

días, allí, adiós, aquí, estás, perdón, inglés, lápiz

16 What you see below represents what you actually hear. Say these aloud, then spell them correctly: [ay], [oy], [asta], [ola], [ora].

hay, hoy, hasta, hola, hora

17 When you say the Spanish word for "watch," you say [rreló]. You spell this word ～～.

reloj **18** How does Spanish differ from English in writing the days of the week? (Think of what happens to the first letter of each word.)

no capital letter

19 Write the Spanish for "Wednesday, Thursday, Friday, Saturday."

miércoles, jueves, viernes, sábado

20 Copy and underline the letter(s) that stand(s) for the [k] sound: *aquí, cinco, poquito, escuela, catorce, qué.*

*a*qu*í, cin*c*o, po*qu*ito, es*c*uela, *c*atorce, *qu*é*

21 Look at the vowel that follows each [k] sound. The [k] sound is written ～～ before *i* and *e*.

qu **22** The [k] sound is written ～～ before *a, o,* and *u.*

c (With these two rules you can spell the [k] sound before a vowel from what you hear.) **23** Let's test you. You hear [keso]. What will you write?

queso **24** You hear [kosa]. What will you write?

cosa **25** The words for "I" and "call" begin with the same sound in Spanish. Write "I call myself Pancho" and be careful with the spelling.

Yo me llamo Pancho.

26 Learning to spell requires practice in copying words accurately. Also practice in how they may be changed. Copy the following and make them stand for females: *señor, profesor, muchacho, nosotros, alumno.*

señora, profesora, muchacha, nosotras, alumna

27 Copy and make plural: *señor, reloj, lápiz, mes, luz, usted.*

señores, relojes, lápices, meses, luces, ustedes

28 Copy and make plural: *tarde, noche, oficina, tiza, ojo, cuaderno.*

tardes, noches, oficinas, tizas, ojos, cuadernos

29 What is the rule for making words plural? You add *es* to ～～～ and *s* to ～～～.

es to consonants; *s* to vowels

30 The four forms of the definite article (the) are ～～～.

el, los, la, las　**31** The two forms of the indefinite article (a, an) are ～～～.

un, una　**32** Write the five number words that end in *ce.*

once, doce, trece, catorce, quince

33 When you write the number word for 20, which letter, *i* or *e*, comes first in the first syllable?

e : veinte (Copy if you were wrong.)

34 Here are some infinitives of verbs you know. Copy the stems and add the suffix that goes with *yo: estar, hablar, necesitar, estudiar, desear.*

estoy, hablo, necesito, estudio, deseo

35 Rewrite these forms so they will agree with *nosotros.* You replace the first suffix and add the second: *trabajo, estoy, llamo, estudio.*

trabajamos, estamos, llamamos, estudiamos

36 Write out in number words: $7 - 2 = 5.$

Siete menos dos son cinco.

37 Write out in number words: $4 + 9 = 13.$

Cuatro y nueve son trece.

38 What tells you when to write *b* or *v*? (a) what you hear (b) what you have seen

what you have seen

39 In this and the next frame, say the Spanish for each word aloud, then write it: window, twenty, well, enough.

ventana, veinte, bien, bastante

40 Translate and write the following: Isn't it?, good, I speak, Come!

¿Verdad?, bueno, hablo, ¡Venga!

41 In this and the next four frames there are some words that are often misspelled. Write the Spanish equivalents and check your spelling very carefully: lights, pencils, I am going.

luces, lápices, Voy

42 professor, notebook, school

profesor, cuaderno, escuela

43 desk, chair, blackboard

pupitre, silla, pizarra

44 I am (*ser*), See you later, there

Soy, Hasta luego, allí

45 Wednesday, Thursday, Friday, Saturday

miércoles, jueves, viernes, sábado

Getting Ready for a Speaking Quiz on Dialog II

You are going to get a grade on how well you can say Dialog II. Your grade will *not* depend on the fact that you know it by heart but on how much you sound like a native Spanish speaker. This Program deals with the things you should watch out for.

1 When the letter *n* is followed by *p*, as in *un poquito*, it does not stand for an [n] sound. It stands for the sound [   ].

[m] (Say [umpoquito] aloud several times.)

2 The following words have spaces between them when written. However, when you say them, they sound like one long word. Practice saying them aloud:

hablausted	esusted	denada	estudiaringlés
quédesea	deespaña	dedónde	muyamable
conel	soyde	delaescuela	soydeChile

3 Here is the whole dialog. The words which are run together are joined with a hyphen (-). Practice saying the dialog aloud *without any pause or hesitation* between these words.

El nuevo alumno

Pablo: Perdón, señorita, ¿habla-usted-español?
Linda: Sí, un-poquito, ¿Qué-desea?
Pablo: Tengo-que-hablar con-el-director-de-la-escuela.
Linda: ¿De-dónde-es-usted? ¿De-España?
Pablo: No, soy-de-Chile. Necesito-estudiar-inglés.
Linda: Venga-conmigo. Yo-trabajo-en-la-oficina.
Pablo: Es-usted-muy-amable. Muchas-gracias.
Linda: De-nada. Sígame, por-favor.

4 The Spanish [p] and [t] are not aspirated (no puff). Put the back of your hand near your lips and practice saying the words below without a puff. If you feel the air, you have a puff. You can get rid of it by pulling your tongue away from the teeth or separating your lips before pressure builds up: *papel, perdón, por, poquito, tú, tiza, señorita, director, tal.*

5 The Spanish phoneme /d/ has two allophones (two different sounds), a stop and a fricative. Say all of the following with a fricative: *perdón, usted, ¿Qué desea?, soy de Chile, estudiar.*

6 These phrases have a stop and a fricative [d]. Copy and underline the stops: *el director de la escuela, ¿De dónde es usted?, De nada.*

el **d**irector de la escuela, ¿**D**e dón**d**e es usted? **D**e nada. Now say them aloud.

7 Say "had" and hold the tongue in position as you finish the word. This is where the tongue flaps when you say Spanish [r]. Here are all the words with [r] in them. Practice saying them aloud, and be sure your tongue flaps against the roof of your mouth each time: *perdón, señorita, hablar, director, estudiar, trabajo, gracias, por, favor.*

8 Using the schwa in talking Spanish gives a very bad accent. Here is the whole dialog again. The vowels that you are likely to replace with schwa are indicated. Practice saying the dialog twice and be careful not to use the schwa.

El nuevo alumno

Pablo: Perdón, señorita, ¿habla usted español?
Linda: Sí, un poquito. ¿Qué desea?
Pablo: Tengo que hablar con el director de la escuela.
Linda: ¿De dónde es usted? ¿De España?
Pablo: No, soy de Chile. Necesito estudiar inglés.
Linda: Venga conmigo. Yo trabajo en la oficina.
Pablo: Es usted muy amable. Muchas gracias.
Linda: De nada. Sígame, por favor.

9 Say the words *hat* and *had* aloud several times. In which one is the vowel sound longer?

had | **10** Cup your hands tightly over your ears, say *had*, and listen to the sound of [d]. The [d] sound is (a) voiced (b) unvoiced.

voiced (If you got this wrong, say *had* again, and listen for the buzz sound.)

11 The [t] sound of *hat* is unvoiced (the vocal cords do not vibrate). The [d] sound of *had* is voiced. In English a vowel sound is longer when it is followed by a voiced consonant. (a) true (b) false

true | **12** In Spanish a vowel sound has the same length before either a voiced or an unvoiced consonant. Say the following aloud without lengthening the indicated vowel as you do in English: *perdón, usted, hablar, conmigo, señorita, ¿Qué desea? director, favor.*

13 These words are divided into syllables. Say them aloud, copy them, and underline the stressed syllable: *se-ño-ri-ta, po-qui-to, de-se-a, Chi-le.*

*se-ño-**ri**-ta, po-**qui**-to, de-**se**-a, **Chi**-le* (Notice that all these words end in a vowel sound: *a, o, e.*)

14 When a word of two or more syllables ends in a vowel which has no accent mark, the stress falls on this vowel. (a) true (b) false

false (The stress is put on the first vowel before it: *se-ño-**ri**-ta, po-**qui**-to, etc.*)

15 Say each word aloud, copy it, and underline the stressed syllable: *us-ted, es-pa-ñol, ha-blar, fa-vor.*

*us-**ted**, es-pa-**ñol**, ha-**blar**, fa-**vor*** (Notice that all these words end in a consonant: *d, l, r.*)

16 When a word ends in a consonant, the stress is usually on the last vowel. (a) true (b) false

true | **17** There are three exceptions to the above rules. Let's see if you can discover them by yourself. Say *hablas* with the stress on the first syllable, **ha**-blas, and, again, with the stress now on the second syllable, *ha-**blas***. Which is correct? (a) first syllable stress (b) second syllable stress

first syllable stress

18 Words which end in *s*, like words ending in a vowel, have the stress on the next-to-last vowel. (a) true (b) false

true

19 Now say *ha-blan* and *ha-blan*. Which is correct? (a) first syllable stress (b) second syllable stress

first syllable stress

20 Words which end in *n*, like words ending in *s* or a vowel, have the stress on the next-to-last vowel. (a) true (b) false

true

21 The new rule, then, is this: words which end in a vowel or *n* or *s* have the stress on the next-to-last vowel. Now, watch out. Copy the following and underline the stressed syllable: *per-dón, in-glés, a-quí.*

*per-**dón**, in-**glés**, a-**quí***

22 The written accent mark tells you, when reading aloud, that the rule in Frame 21 does not apply to these words. (a) true (b) false

true

23 A large part of your grade is going to depend on whether you make the stop and fricative sounds of [b] and [d] in the right place. Here is the dialog again. The stops are circled, the fricatives are underlined. Practice until you feel certain you can pick the right allophone without thinking about it.

El nuevo alumno

Pablo: Perdón, señorita, habla usted español?
Linda: Sí, un poquito. ¿Qué desea?
Pablo: Tengo que hablar con el ⓓirector de la escuela.
Linda: ¿Ⓓe dónⓓe es usted? ¿Ⓓe España?
Pablo: No, soy de Chile. Necesito estudiar inglés.
Linda: Ⓥenga conmigo. Yo trabajo en la oficina.
Pablo: Es usted muy amable. Muchas gracias.
Linda: Ⓓe nada. Sígame, por favor.

24 Everyone is more likely to have an accent when speaking Spanish words that have English cognates. Look-alikes are traps because they invite us to put English sounds in place of Spanish sounds. When you say "director" in English, it sounds something like this: [die-wreck-ter]. The stress is on the ⁓⁓⁓ syllable.

second

25 When you say *di-rec-tor* in Spanish, the stress is on the ⁓⁓⁓ syllable.

last (The word ends in a consonant other than *n* or *s*.)

26 When you say "office" in English, the first vowel sounds like (1) [aw] of "saw" (2) [oe] of "toe."

like [aw] of "saw" (Now, say *oficina* with an English accent: [awficina]. Now say it in Spanish: *oficina*.)

27 The [chi] of Spanish *Chile* is (a) like the [chi] of English "children" (b) more like the [chea] of "cheap."

more like the [chea] in "cheap" (Say *Chile* aloud in Spanish.)

28 Speakers of English often make four mistakes in saying Spanish *favor*. First, they forget that the [a] has a different sound in Spanish. (a) It is something like the [ay] of "say." (b) It is more like the [a] of *fa* in *do, re, mi, fa*.

more like *fa* (Say *favor* aloud in Spanish.)

29 The second mistake is to use the English sound [v]. Say "favor" aloud in English and watch, as you say the [v] sound, what happens to your lower lip and upper front teeth? (a) They touch. (b) They do not touch.

They touch. (Linguists say this is a "lip-tooth" sound, but they use a big word to say it: *labiodental*. The Spanish word for "lip" is *labio*.)

30 Now say *vo* with a stop [b] sound and *avo* with a fricative [b] sound. Say *vo—avo* again and watch what your lips do. (a) Your lower lip touches your upper front teeth. (b) Your lips touch each other for the stop *vo* and come very close together for the fricative *avo*.

Lips touch for stop; close together for fricatives. (This is called a "two-lip fricative" or, in big words, a *bilabial fricative*.)

31 Say *favor* in Spanish and be sure the [v] is a two-lip fricative, not a lip-tooth sound.

32 Say "favor" once more in English. Which vowel is a schwa?

the second (The *o* stands for schwa.)

33 Say "favor" again in English. Do you flap the [r]?

no (But you do in Spanish.)

34 The four common mistakes in saying *favor* in Spanish are: [ay] for [a], lip-tooth sound for *v*, schwa for *o*, and no flapped [r]. Say *favor* aloud several times in Spanish.

35 Say "pan" in English. This is what speakers of English want to put into *español*. Say *español* aloud without using English "pan."

36 Here are all the cognates in the dialog. Practice them carefully in Spanish. Notice that the English cognate is not always a good translation. These are called *deceptive cognates*.

Spanish	English
perdón	pardon (Pardon me)
español	Spanish
desear	to desire (to want)
director	director
escuela	school
España	Spain
Chile	Chile
necesitar	to necessitate (to need)
estudiar	to study
inglés	English
oficina	office
amable	amiable (nice)
gracias	gracious (thanks)
favor	favor

37 Your teacher, in the coming quiz, is going to pay a great deal of attention to the speed with which you say the dialog. Get a watch with a second hand and time yourself as you say the dialog aloud. You will be doing fine when you can say the whole dialog in 17 seconds.

The vocabulary of a culture often influences the way people think and behave. In recent years the words *colored, black,* and *negro* have created many debates in the United States which cannot be duplicated in Spanish because *negro* stands for both *negro* and *black,* and the cognate of *colored* is *colorado,* which translates *dyed, red,* or *reddish.*

Writing Dialog II and Some Facts about Translation

1 Here are all the words in the dialog which have special marks (˜ or ´) not used in English. Copy them and add the missing mark: *perdon, senorita, que, si, espanol, donde, Espana, ingles, Sigame.*

perdón, señorita, qué, sí, español, dónde, España, inglés, Sígame

2 Punctuate the following to make them questions. (1) *Habla usted español* (2) *Qué desea* (3) *De España*

¿ Habla usted español ? ¿ Qué desea ? ¿ De España ?

3 In this frame and the next 8 there are parts of the dialog in which the verb is in the infinitive. Copy what you see, but change the verb to the form used in the dialog. Be sure to check your spelling carefully.

¿ Hablar usted español?

¿ Habla usted español ?

4 Tener que hablar con el director.

(Are you copying exactly ? Check.) *Tengo que hablar con el director.*

5 ¿ De dónde ser usted?

¿ De dónde es usted ?

6 Ser de Chile.

Soy de Chile.   **7** Necesitar estudiar inglés. (*Which verb gets changed ? Be careful.*)

Necesito estudiar inglés.

8 Venir conmigo. (*This is the command form. Be careful.*)

Venga conmigo. (Did you write *n* plus *m* in *conmigo ?*)

9 Yo trabajar en la oficina.

Yo trabajo en la oficina.

10 Ser usted muy amable.

Es usted muy amable.

11 Seguirme, por favor. *Seguir* changes to something that hardly looks like it: ———.

Sígame, por favor (Did you remember the accent mark ?)

12 A native may say the following the way you see it written. Rewrite it with the proper spaces: *Tengoquehablarconeldirectordelaescuela.*

Tengo que hablar con el director de la escuela.

13 In this frame and the next 7 you will see the first word of each sentence of the dialog. Complete the sentences. Be sure to check your spelling and punctuation.

Perdón, ———.

Perdón, señorita, ¿ habla usted español ?

14 Sí, ———. ¿ Qué ———?

Sí, un poquito. ¿ Qué desea ?

15 Tengo ———.

Tengo que hablar con el director de la escuela.

16 ¿ De ⎯⎯? ¿ De ⎯⎯? (Watch those marks.)
¿ De dónde es usted? ¿ De España?

17 No, ⎯⎯. Necesito ⎯⎯.
No, soy de Chile. Necesito estudiar inglés.

18 Venga ⎯⎯. Yo ⎯⎯.
Venga conmigo. Yo trabajo en la oficina.

19 Es ⎯⎯. Muchas ⎯⎯.
Es usted muy amable. Muchas gracias.

20 De ⎯⎯. Sígame, ⎯⎯.
De nada. Sígame, por favor.

21 Do you capitalize the names of languages in Spanish?

no   **22** Write the translation of *Spanish* and *English*.

español; inglés

23 Do you capitalize the names of countries in Spanish?

yes   **24** Write the Spanish for *Spain* and *Chile*.

España; Chile   **25** Write the translation of "I."

yo (Remember: You capitalize *yo* only at the beginning of a sentence.)

26 Do you capitalize titles like "Miss" in Spanish?

no (Only at the beginning of a sentence or when abbreviated.)

27 Do you capitalize names of people in Spanish?

yes (All proper names are capitalized as in English.)

28 The English translations of the dialog lines which you have learned are merely equivalents, not word for word translations. Here is a word for word translation. Put it back into Spanish: "From where is you?"

¿ De dónde es usted? (English uses "are" to translate both the singular *es*
(is) and the plural *son* (are).

29 Give a word-for-word translation of *Es usted muy amable.*

Is you very kind. (This is the meaning to the Spanish speaker. The English
translation is "You are very kind.")

30 In standard English we say "you are." To make English like Spanish we have to have another form "you is." The following two sentences are like Spanish. Translate them and make the Spanish verb (*ser*) agree in number with the English forms. The "you" will have two forms in Spanish, singular and plural. (1) From where is you? (2) From where are you?

The subject of the first sentence is singular: *¿ De dónde es usted?* The subject
of the second sentence is plural: *¿ De dónde son ustedes?*

31 When you translate from one language to another, do you translate the actual meaning of each word?

no (English does not use "you is," so we translate "you are.")

32 The Spanish *¿ De dónde es usted?* and *¿ De dónde son ustedes?* are both translated by "Where are you from?" Do you add or do you subtract information when you translate these questions into English?

You subtract. (The English does not tell us whether the subject is singular or
plural. Spanish, in this instance, gives more information.)

33 Look at the words in these two sentences and notice the difference in word order: "Where are you from?" *¿ De dónde es usted?* The order is the same except for ⎯⎯.

de and "from"

34 Which of the following do you say in English? (a) To where are you going? (b) Where are you going to?

Where are you going to? (But we often leave off the "to.")

35 Now translate "Where are you going?" into Spanish. Remember it is like "To where go you?" (Use *tú*-form.)

¿A dónde vas? (You may add the *tú*.)

36 Look at the indicated words in these two questions and their translations: (1) *¿De dónde es usted?* "**Where** are you **from?**" (2) *¿A dónde vas?* "**Where** are you going (**to**)?" Now look at these answers. (1) *Soy de Chile.* "I am **from Chile.**" (2) *Voy a la oficina.* "I'm going **to the office.**" English and Spanish word order may be alike in statements but not in questions. (a) true (b) false

true (Spanish puts *de* and *a* in front of question words. English puts "from" and "to" only in front of answer words.)

37 These two sentences, <u>when spoken</u>, have just one word which is alike. Copy that word. (1) *¿Qué desea?* (2) *Tengo que hablar con el director.*

In speech *qué* is stressed and *que* is not. Otherwise they sound exactly alike.

38 Now look at the punctuation of the two sentences in Frame 37. *Qué* has a written accent only when it is used in a 〰.

question

39 What do all the question words have in common in writing?

a written accent mark

In the United States the majority of people who are well-to-do live in the cities. About two million of these people have a second home in the country which is used for week-ends and vacations. In Latin America the rich are mostly owners of great estates or *haciendas*. A great many of these people have a second home in the nearest big city or the capital of the country. In the United States people want to escape from the big cities to the country. In Latin America they want to escape from the country to the cities.

How Much Are You Learning? A Self-test

Your parents did not teach you English. You learned it *from* them. This book cannot teach you Spanish. You have to learn from it. Here is a test to help you find out how much you are learning from it.

Part 1 : Writing Dialog II

1 Here is Dialog II. Read it aloud *three* times. (You can do this in less than one minute.)

El nuevo alumno

Pablo: Perdón, señorita, ¿habla usted español?
Linda: Sí, un poquito. ¿Qué desea?
Pablo: Tengo que hablar con el director de la escuela.
Linda: ¿De dónde es usted? ¿De España?
Pablo: No, soy de Chile. Necesito estudiar inglés.
Linda: Venga conmigo. Yo trabajo en la oficina.
Pablo: Es usted muy amable. Muchas gracias.
Linda: De nada. Sígame, por favor.

2 Get a sheet of paper and copy the dialog with very great care. As you do this, underline every word which has a mark not used in English. Draw a circle around each punctuation mark not used in English. When you have finished, check again to be certain you have underlined and circled everything that is not used in English. You are now ready for Part 1 of the test.

3 In this frame and in the following seven, you will find the English translation of a line of the dialog. Write the Spanish. Don't forget the accents, tilde, and the punctuation marks.

Pardon me, Miss, do you speak Spanish?

Perdón, señorita, ¿ habla usted español? Check what you wrote carefully and draw a circle around each error. Notice especially what is indicated in the sentence above: accent, tilde, and the inverted question mark. Count your errors and write the number in the left-hand margin.

4 Yes, a little. What can I do for you?

Sí, un poquito. ¿ Qué desea?

5 I have to speak with the principal of the school.

Tengo que hablar con el director de la escuela. (Circle and count your errors, and put the number in the margin.)

6 Where are you from? Spain?

¿ De dónde es usted? ¿ De España?

7 No, I'm from Chile. I need to study English.

No, soy de Chile. Necesito estudiar inglés.

8 Come with me. I work in the office.
Venga conmigo. Yo trabajo en la oficina.

9 You are very kind. Thank you very much.
Es usted muy amable. Muchas gracias.

10 You're welcome. Follow me, please.
De nada. Sígame, por favor.

11 Add up the number of errors. Your grade is: 0–2 errors = A, 3 = B, 4 = C, 5 = D, 6 = F.

If you do not like your grade, copy the lines in which you made an error again. Only *you* can practice until you are perfect. Nobody can do this for you.

Part 2: Vocabulary Test

In the following frames, you will find a Spanish sentence with a blank in it. The blank may stand for a whole word or just a suffix. When it stands for a whole word, what you are to write is described in English. If you use a wrong suffix or word, write 2 in the left margin. If you have the right answer, but misspell it, write 1 in the margin.

1 *Necesito una ———.* (You use it to measure and draw straight lines.)

regla   *¿ De ——— es usted?* (A question word which asks about a place or country.)
dónde (Take off one point if you forgot the accent mark.)

3 *Yo ——— llamo Carlos Pinel.* (A pronoun that matches *yo*.)

me   **4** *Allí hay tres ———.* (Pieces of furniture you sit on.)
sillas (Did you make it plural to agree with *tres*?)

5 *¿ ——— dónde vas?* (A relator indicating direction of movement. The function of relators is to establish a relationship between two entities, two events, or an entity and an event.)

A (You use a capital *A* to begin a sentence.)

6 *Yo ——— español.* (The action that leads to learning.)

estudio   **7** *No tengo ———.* (What this is printed on.)
papel   **8** *¿ Cómo estás ———?* (The name for the present day: the one between *ayer* and *mañana*.

hoy   **9** *¿ Que desea ——— ustedes?* (Add plural suffix that matches *ustedes*.)
n   **10** *La ——— está allí.* (The room at school in which the principal works.)
oficina   **11** *¿ Qué hablan ———?* (A third person subject pronoun that stands for girls.)
ellas (Be sure it has *a*, not *o*.)

12 *Ayer fue ———.* (The day dedicated to Mars, the god of war.)
martes (Take off a point if you used a capital letter.)

13 *Son de ———.* (Its capital city is Madrid.)
España (Take off a point if you forgot the tilde.)

14 *Adiós, hasta ———.* (The day that comes after *hoy*.)
mañana (No tilde? One more point off.)

15 *¿ Qué es María? ¿ Un muchacho? No, es ———.*

una muchacha **16** *¿ ——— son tres y cinco?* (A question word asking about the total you get when adding numbers.)

Cuántos (Did you use a capital, the accent, and the plural suffix?)

17 *Buenas noches, ———.* (A title for a young woman, unmarried.)
señorita (No capital letter, and a tilde.)

18 *Venga* —— *migo.* (A relator indicating togetherness.)
con (It is attached, in writing, to *migo: conmigo.*)

19 ¿ *Qué* —— *es mañana?* (A time interval of 24 hours.)
día (One point off if you forgot the accent mark.)

20 *Hay dos* —— *aquí.* (You sharpen them and write with them.)
lápices (Did you remember *c* before *es?* The accent mark?)

21 ¿ *No hay* —— *en la escuela?* (They shine and illuminate building interiors.)
luces (Did you change *z* to *c* this time?)

22 *Es de Chile, ¿*——*?* (A word asking for a "yes" answer.)
verdad

23 *Ocho* —— *tres son cinco.*
menos

24 *Luisa es una alumna* ——. (She's only been at this school a very few days.)
nueva (Did you match *nueva* with *alumna?*)

25 ——, *hasta pronto.* (You say this as you take leave of someone.)
Adiós (Capital letter and accent mark.)

26 Add up the number of errors. Your grade is: 0–3 errors = A, 4–6 = B, 7–9 = C, 10–12 = D.

If you do not like your grade, you may want to study the following vocabulary list. It contains all the words you are supposed to know up to this point. Make yourself a list of the ones you are not sure about writing. Then copy them again. Words which have marks not used in English are indicated by italics.

Subject Pronouns
yo I
nosotros we, us
nosotras we, us (*fem.*)
usted you
ustedes you (*pl.*)
él he, him
ellos they, them
ella she, her
ellas they, them (*fem.*)
tú you

Verbs
desea (desear) to desire, wish
estoy, *está, están* **(estar)** to be
hay (haber) there is, there are; to have, to be
hablar to speak
voy, vas (ir) to go, to come
me llamo, se llama (llamar) to call, to name
necesito (necesitar) to need
soy, es, son, fue (ser) to be; being

siga (seguir) to continue, follow
tengo (tener) to have, possess
trabajo (trabajar) to work (*not* to function)
venga (venir) to come

Adverbs
allí there
aquí here
ayer yesterday
bastante enough, quite, fairly
bien well
hoy today
luego then, later
mañana morning, tomorrow
menos minus, less
muy very
no no, not
pronto soon, fast
sí yes

Nouns

alumno pupil, student
alumna pupil, student (*fem.*)
Chile Chile
clase class, kind, (type); classroom
cuaderno notebook
día day
director principal, director
escuela school
España Spain
español Spanish, Spaniard
gracias thanks
inglés English
lápiz (lápices) pencil
libro book
luz (luces) light
mesa table
momentito moment, minute
oficina office
ojo eye
papel paper
pizarra blackboard
pluma pen, feather
poquito a little bit
profesora teacher (*fem.*)
profesor teacher, professor
pupitre desk
regla ruler (for measuring)
reloj clock, watch
señora Mrs., lady, wife
señorita Miss, young lady
señor Mr., sir, man, gentleman
silla chair
tiza chalk
ventana window
verdad truth

Days of the Week

domingo Sunday
lunes Monday
martes Tuesday
miércoles Wednesday
jueves Thursday
viernes Friday
sábado Saturday

Adjectives

bueno good, O.K.
el the
la the
las the
los the
nuevo new
presente present
una a, an, one (*fem.*)
un a, an, one

Numbers

uno one
dos two
tres three
cuatro four
cinco five
seis six
siete seven
ocho eight
nueve nine
diez ten
once eleven
doce twelve
trece thirteen
catorce fourteen
quince fifteen
dieciséis sixteen
diecisiete seventeen
dieciocho eighteen
diecinueve nineteen
veinte twenty

Relators

a at, by, from, on, to
de of, from, about
con with
en in, on, at, into
hasta until; even

Conjunctions

y and

Interjections

adiós good-bye
hola hi!, hello
perdón Pardon me! Excuse me!

Question Words	Fixed Phrases
¿Cómo? What? How?	**Buenos** *días* Good morning.
¿Cuánto? How much?	**Buenas tardes** Good afternoon.
¿Cuántos? How many?	**Buenas noches** Good evening; Good night.
¿Dónde? Where?	*¡Qué* **tal!** Hi!; What's new?
¿Qué? What? How?	**tengo que** I have to

PROGRAM 24

Learning How to Read for Meaning

1 Here is a sentence you have never seen. It has three words you do not know. Read it aloud in Spanish. Remember to use what you know about Spanish pronunciation: *Esas camas cuestan mucho.*

You have just proved an important point about reading. You can read aloud something you do not understand.

2 There is a very great difference between reading aloud and reading for meaning. Do you have to say words aloud when you read for meaning?

no (Most people read silently.)

3 When you read for meaning, it is what you see that counts, not the sounds. Look at this sentence (do not say the words aloud), copy and underline all the words you have studied so far: *El primer presidente de los Estados Unidos fue Jorge Washington.*

El primer presidente **de los** Estados Unidos **fue** Jorge Washington.

4 The verb *fue* translates (a) is (b) was (c) will be.

was

5 Which word in the sentence describes what George Washington was?

presidente

6 Remember that in Spanish only proper names are capitalized. Look at the word *Unidos* in *los Estados Unidos.* It has an English cognate. Think a minute about this. Now translate the following into English: *Jorge Washington fue el presidente de los Estados Unidos.*

George Washington was the president of the United States.

7 There is now only one word in the original sentence that you do not know. Let's see if you can guess its meaning: *El primer presidente de los Estados Unidos fue Jorge Washington.* The translation of the adjective *primer* is ⌐⌐⌐.

first (The book used to teach *first* graders to read is called a "primer.")

8 When you read for meaning, you begin with what you know and, then, go on to what you do not know. If you think carefully, you can often make out the meaning of words you have never seen before. Let's try this again: *Hay siete días en una semana.* The noun *semana* is translated as ⌐⌐⌐.

week (This is the most likely answer.)

9 An unknown word is like a blank which you have to fill in. There is a blank at the end of this sentence. Figure out the meaning of what you see, then select the most logical English word to complete the sentence. This word will be the name of a holiday. *El día veinticinco de diciembre es* ⁓.

Christmas   **10** You did not know the word *cama* in Frame 1. Let's put more context with it and see if that helps you figure out its meaning. *Pedro necesita un doctor. Tiene un virus. No va a clase hoy. Está en cama.* The translation of *cama* is ⁓.

bed (People who have a virus and need a doctor are usually in bed.)

11 Let's see how you can figure out the entire meaning of *Esas camas cuestan mucho.* You begin with what you know. You know *mucho* in the plural as in *muchas gracias.* The translation of *muchas* is ⁓.

many   **12** Is many (a) singular? (b) plural?

plural   **13** Look at *mucho.* It looks a lot like its English cognate, which is ⁓.

much   **14** You know that subjects agree with their verbs in Spanish. Write the word which has a verb suffix which matches the plural suffix of *camas: Esas camas cuestan mucho.*

cuestan   **15** The verb *cuestan* says something about *camas* (beds). The stem of *cuestan* is ⁓.

cuest   **16** Now think of "beds" and the word "much." One meaning of "much" is "a lot." The verb *cuestan* says something about beds which goes with "a lot." The stem of *cuestan, cuest,* has an English cognate which begins with *c* and ends with *st.* Let's put a blank in place of *ue* and see if you can fill it in: "Beds c...st a lot."

Beds cost a lot.

17 There is now only one word in *Esas camas cuestan mucho* that you do not know. It is *esas.* The *a* and *s* of *esas* match the *a* and *s* of ⁓.

camas   **18** What is *esas?* (a) a noun (b) a verb (c) an adjective

an adjective (It agrees with the noun *camas.*)

19 The adjective *esas* says something about *camas* that cost a lot. There isn't enough context to help you figure out the meaning of *esas.* However, instead of adding context this time, let's put the statement into a live situation.

You are in a furniture store. A salesman points toward some beds which are on the other side of the store and says, *Esas camas cuestan mucho.* The adjective *esas* is a pointer word used to describe something that is not close to you. Its translation is ⁓.

those (You can figure out the meaning of many new words by paying attention to the situation in which they are used.)

20 You have just learned that each word in a sentence helps you figure out the meaning of the others. Words combine in a logical fashion, and each one carries signals that tell you what it may combine with. To learn to read for meaning, you must learn to spot these signals and to find out what they are telling you. Let's practice this.

You know the sentence is talking about a person. The unknown words combine with *una: una mujer.* The article *una* tells you the person is (a) a man (b) a woman.

a woman   **21** The sentence begins with *El muchacho se llama* . . . What is most likely to follow? (a) another verb (b) a name

a name (*El muchacho se llama Jorge.*)

22 The question word *dónde* asks about (a) a place (b) a person.

a place (*¿De dónde es usted? ¿De España?*)

23 When *dónde* combines with *de* (*de dónde*), the question is about (a) where something is (b) where it is from (c) where it is going.

where it is from (*¿De dónde es José?*)

24 When *dónde* combines with *a* (*a dónde*), the question is about (a) where something is (b) where it is going (c) where it is from.

where it is going (*¿A dónde vas?*)

25 The phrase *de dónde* signals origin (place from): *¿De dónde es usted?* In contrast, *a dónde* indicates destination (place to): *¿A dónde vas?* When *dónde* is used <u>without</u> a relator in front of it, the question is about (a) where something is from (b) where it is going (c) where it is in space.

where it is in space (*¿Dónde esta Jóse?*)

26 Is it logical to assume that either *está* or *vas* will combine with *de dónde*?

no (The *de* signals origin, not location or destination.)

27 A word can tell you what will go with it. It can also tell you which meaning another word will have. You see the name of a person, a city, and a country in *José es de Santiago, Chile*. This tells you that *de* means ⁓⁓⁓.

from

28 Does *de* have the same meaning in *El señor Moreno es el director de la escuela?*

no (Mr. Moreno is the principal *of* the school.)

29 What a word combines with usually signals its meaning. When you say, *Sí, señor*, the word *señor* is a title of respect which is translated as ⁓⁓⁓.

sir

30 When *señor* combines with a proper name, *Sí, señor Moreno*, it is still a title of respect, but now it is translated by ⁓⁓⁓.

Mister

31 When *señor* is used as a common noun and combines with an article, *Es un señor muy amable*, it has a third meaning. It now stands for a person who is male and is translated ⁓⁓⁓.

man or gentleman

32 The little words of a sentence almost always carry big signals. Look at this: *En la . . . de la escuela.* The definite article *la* tells you that the blank must be filled with (a) a verb (b) a noun (c) a relator.

a noun

33 The same article, *la*, tells you the noun must be (a) plural (b) singular.

singular

34 *La* also tells you that the noun is likely to end in the sound of *o*, *l*, or *a*.

a (*En la oficina de la escuela.*)

35 With one exception, the *en* of *En la oficina* tells you something very important about any verb that may combine with the phrase. When you combine *en* and *la oficina*, the verb must describe either an action that can take place <u>in</u> the office (*Trabaja en la oficina.*), or it must say that someone or something ⁓⁓⁓ <u>in</u> the office.

is; is located (*José está en la oficina.*)

36 Let's see, now, how much you have really learned from the last several frames. Which relator goes with movement in the direction toward some place: *de, a, en, con*?

a (*¿Vas a la oficina?*)

37 Which relator goes with the city or country from which one comes (origin): *de, a, en, con*?

de (*¿De dónde es usted? ¿De España?*)

38 What relator goes with the place where something is located: *de, a, en, con?*
en (*María está **en** la oficina.*)

39 When *a* indicates direction toward something, you know that the verb which goes with it must also stand (a) for location (b) for movement.
for movement (You move *toward* something.)

40 To be able to talk about what you read, you need to learn to spot the key words in statements, questions, and answers. Many key words simply show a different way of talking about the same thing. The verb *desea* in *¿ Qué desea José?* is replaced by what phrase in *José tiene que hablar con el director?* (a) *tiene que hablar* (b) *con el director*
tiene que hablar (*José desea hablar* is like *José tiene que hablar.*)

41 A key word may tell you the meaning of its substitute. For example: *María habla dos lenguas, el inglés y el español.* The translation of *lenguas* is ⌒⌒⌒.
languages

42 *El señor Prieto es de México.* (a) *¿ Es mexicano?* (b) *¿ Es chileno?*
Es mexicano.

43 All question words are key words. *Cómo* asks for what in *¿ Cómo se llama él?*
a name (*Se llama Miguel.*)

44 *Cómo* asks about what in *¿ Cómo estás?* (Think of how you would answer this question before you decide what is being asked about.)
health or state of being (*Estoy bien.*)

45 In your answer to *¿ Qué es esto?* you will replace *qué* with what kind of word?
the name for the thing: *tiza, lápiz, etc.* (*Es un lápiz.*)

46 *Qué* asks about what in *¿ Qué estudia usted?*
a lesson, a language, some school subject, *etc.* (*Estudio español.*)

47 *Cuánto* and *cuántos* always ask about ⌒⌒⌒.
amount (How much, how many.)

48 If you pay attention to key words, the context, and cognates, you will be surprised at just how much Spanish you are already prepared to read and understand. Look at the following sentence carefully and then translate it mentally: *Cristóbal Colón descubrió las Américas en 1492.*
Christopher Columbus discovered America in 1492.

49 Want to try another? *El presidente Kennedy fue asesinado en Dallas, Tejas.*
President Kennedy was assassinated in Dallas, Texas.

In most of the United States when a person becomes very ill he goes to see a doctor and when he is seriously ill, he goes to a hospital. In a great many parts of Latin America there are neither doctors nor hospitals and, as a result, when a person becomes sick he goes to see the *curandero*. A *curandero* has no formal education or training in medicine and is sometimes very much like a witch doctor. Occasionally a *curandero* discovers from experience real cures for certain diseases and modern drug companies will often send out expeditions to find out what *curanderos* use for medicine. The ancient Indian *curanderos* discovered that *digitalis* is good for heart trouble and that quinine will cure malaria and reduce fevers. Most of their "prescriptions", however, are useless, but the patient often feels better and even gets well simply because of the attention paid to him.

PROGRAM **25**

Estar, and More on Writing and Spelling

Part 1: The Forms of *estar*

1 A verb is said to be regular when the stem is the same in all forms and when the morphemes of the first and second suffixes are those used by the vast majority of the verbs of that set. Thus, *hablar*, *estudiar*, and *necesitar* are regular *a*-verbs. The first suffix of the present tense of a regular *a*-verb that agrees with *yo* is ~~~~.

o (*yo hablo, yo estudio, yo deseo*)

2 The form of *estar* that goes with *yo* is ~~~~.

estoy

3 The form *estoy* has the suffix *oy* instead of *o*. Is *estoy* regular?

no (It is irregular. This means that it does not follow the pattern of the vast majority of *a*-verbs.)

4 The *oy* of *estoy* is the only irregularity in the slot for the first suffix. All the other present tense forms have the vowel ~~~~ in this slot.

a (*estamos, está, están, estás*)

5 The present tense of *estar* has another irregularity. Let's see if you can discover it. Below is the present tense of the regular verb *hablar* and the irregular verb *estar*. The forms are divided into syllables. The stressed syllables are indicated. In what way is *estar* irregular?

> *ha-blo, ha-bla-mos, ha-blas, ha-bla, ha-blan*
> *es-toy, es-ta-mos, es-tás, es-tá, es-tán*

The stress is on the second syllable of <u>all</u> the *estar* forms.

6 You already know that when a word ends in a vowel or *n* or *s* stress falls on the next-to-last syllable. Do both *ha-bla-mos* and *es-ta-mos* follow this rule?

yes

7 Are *es-tás*, *es-tá*, and *es-tán* exceptions to this rule?

yes

8 What in writing tells you they are exceptions?

the written accent mark

9 The other rule about stress says that a word ending in a consonant (except *n* or *s*) has the stress on the last vowel (syllable). The form *estoy* has the stress on *toy*. Is it logical to assume that Spanish speakers consider a final *y* to be a consonant?

yes

10 Does this explain why *estoy* has no written accent mark?

yes

11 The stem of *estar* is ~~~~.

est

12 The second suffix of a verb form that goes with the *s* of *ellos* and the *es* of *ustedes* is ~~~~.

n

13 Write the form of *estar* that goes with *ellos* and *ustedes*.

están (Did you remember the accent mark?)

14 To make *están* agree with *él* and *usted*, you take off the ~~~~.

n (*él está; usted está*)

15 To make *está* agree with *tú*, you add the second suffix form ⌢⌢.
s (*tú estás*)   16 The form of *estar* that goes with *nosotros* is ⌢⌢.
estamos   17 What other form of *estar* has no accent mark?
estoy

Part 2: More on Writing

1 When you learn any language, you learn patterns. *¿ Habla usted español?* is a question pattern. A pattern, like the forms of a verb, is made up of a series of slots. You can keep the pattern, but change the message, by putting different words in each slot. What word do you know that you could put in place of *español* in the question given above?

inglés (*¿Habla usted inglés?*)

2 The pattern *¿Habla usted inglés?* is the same as *¿Habla usted español?*. The message, however, is different. Only words of a certain kind can go in a given slot of a pattern. Let's put *lápiz* in place of *inglés: ¿Habla usted lápiz?* Does this make sense?

no (You can say *lápiz*, but you cannot talk *lápiz*.)

3 In the pattern *¿Habla usted español?*, the noun *español* can be replaced only by the name of another ⌢⌢.

language (These names make up a set: *español, francés, italiano, ruso, etc.*)

4 If one member of a set goes in a slot, then all members of the same set may also go in that slot. (a) true (b) false

true (Any language can go in place of *español* in *¿Habla usted español?*)

5 The action of speaking (*hablar*) belongs to a set which combines with languages. What other action could replace *hablar* in the pattern *¿ Habla usted español?* Think of what you are doing right now.

estudia (*Hablar* and *estudiar* belong to the same set.)

6 Does *trabajar* belong to the same set as *hablar* and *estudiar?*

no ("Do you work Spanish?" does not make much sense.)

7 Can a noun replace *usted* in the pattern *Usted habla inglés?*

yes (*El muchacho habla inglés.*)

8 Does *¿Habla la mesa español?* make sense?

no (Tables cannot talk and, therefore, cannot combine with *habla* and *español*.)

9 To be able to speak or write a language you must know all its basic patterns and the sets that go into each slot. Here is another pattern: *Yo trabajo en la oficina.* Here is a list of verb forms. Copy those that can logically replace *trabajo: estudio, tengo, necesito, estoy.*

estudio; estoy   10 The verb forms *necesito* and *tengo* cannot replace *trabajo* in *Yo trabajo en la oficina* because they have to have an object, something that is acted on. When you say, "I have" or "I need," you have to add something: "I have a book"; "I need a book." Put any Spanish word that makes sense in the following sentence: *Yo tengo un* ⌢⌢ *en la oficina.*

libro, lápiz, reloj, etc. (The noun must agree with *un*.)

11 There are three basic ways of changing a pattern to send a different message. First, you may keep all the same stems and just change the suffixes. Rewrite the

following pattern and change the suffix of the indicated words: *Yo tengo **las plumas** en la oficina.*

*Yo tengo **la pluma** en la oficina.*

12 When the suffix of one word matches the suffix of another word in the pattern, you cannot change one without changing the other. Rewrite the following pattern by changing *habla* to *hablan* and by making whatever other change is needed: *¿ Habla usted inglés?*

*¿ Hablan usted**es** inglés?*

13 The second way of changing a pattern is to keep the same suffixes and to replace the stems. Rewrite the following and put the stem of *estudiar* in place of *habl: ¿ **Habl**an ustedes inglés?*

*¿**Estudi**an ustedes inglés?*

14 The third way to change a pattern is to replace whole words. You still have the same basic pattern, but now you may have a very great change in the message. The message of the following pattern deals with movement toward a destination: *¿A dónde **va** usted?* Rewrite this and replace the indicated words so that the message deals with the origin of the subject.

*¿**De** dónde **es** usted?*

Part 3: Spelling

1 When you hear [rregla], you write ⁓.

regla (The *r* at the beginning of a word stands for [rr] in speech.)

2 The Spanish word for "ouch" is *ay*. The translation of "there is" sounds exactly like it, but is written ⁓.

hay

3 What tells you not to write *ojo* with an *h*? (a) what you hear (b) what you see in print

what you see in print

4 You hear [abla] and [asta], but you write ⁓.

habla; hasta **5** Translate: hello; today.

hola; hoy **6** English writes the [s] sound with either an *s* (sent) or a *c* (cent). Spanish also writes it with a *z*. You hear [los], and you write ⁓.

los **7** You hear [lus], and you write ⁓.

luz **8** Write the plural of *luz*.

luces **9** You hear [tisa], but you write ⁓.

tiza **10** Write the plural of *tiza*.

tizas **11** You hear [dies] and [lápis], but you write ⁓.

diez; lápiz **12** Write the plural of *lápiz*.

lápices **13** Does what you hear tell you to change *z* to *c* in *lápices*?

no (You only learn this from seeing the two spellings in print or from a rule.)

14 Which *c* of *cinco* stands for the [s] sound? (a) first, (b) second

first **15** The *c* before *o* stands for the sound [   ].

[k] You learn a new language by memorizing patterns and the sets of stems, suffixes, and words which can logically go into each slot. One purpose of the pattern drills which you have in class is to teach you to replace parts of the patterns without having to stop to think about the mechanics of the pattern.

There are many types of shops in the United States which sell only one class of items: shoes, dresses, hats, lampshades, etc. It is hard, however, to find a drugstore that sells only drugs, a grocery store that sells nothing but food, or a fruit shop that sells only one kind of fruit. In the Hispanic world the shops and stalls in the markets tend to be more specialized. Drugstores tend to sell only drugs, a hat shop may sell only one type of hat, and in the public markets each stall keeper usually sells only one type of item. This is especially true in the sidewalk markets because the sales person is often the one who has produced the item being sold.

PROGRAM 26

More on the Spanish *r*'s; Writing Geographic Names

Part 1: More on the Spanish *r*'s

1 Do the *qu* of *qué* and the *c* of *cómo* stand for the same sound?

yes (the [k] sound)

2 The *qu* is not treated as part of the Spanish alphabet. Spanish does, however, have three letters in its alphabet which, in fact, are actually made up of two letters. They are called "digraphs" (two graphs). These three digraphs are *ch*, *ll*, and ⁓.

ñ

3 It is important for you to know when a digraph stands for one or two sounds. How many sounds does *qu* stand for? (Just think of the answer; you do not need to write it.)

one

4 Say the noun *silla* aloud. The *ll* stands for (a) one sound (b) two sounds.

one sound

5 Say *muchacha* in Spanish and "cha-cha" in English. Does the *ch* stand for the same sound in both English and Spanish?

yes

6 Say [senyor] aloud in Spanish. Did you say something very much like *señor?*

yes (The digraph *ñ* stands for the sounds [n] plus [y].)

7 The letter *ll* stands for just one sound in the Spanish-American dialects. The letters *ch* and *ñ* each stand for two different sounds. Do the letters *rr* in *pizarra* stand (a) for two <u>different</u> sounds? (b) for two or more repetitions of the <u>same</u> sound?

for two or more repetitions of the same sound

8 Say *latter* and *ladder* aloud several times and watch what your tongue is doing. Now say them slowly with this syllabication: *lat-ter, lad-der.* Is your tongue in the same position when you say [t] and [d]?

yes (The only difference between the two sounds is that [d] is voiced, [t] is
unvoiced.)

9 Say *lat-ter* and *lad-der* aloud again. Now say *lat* and *lad.* When you make the [t] and [d] sounds, your tongue touches (a) the back of your upper front teeth (b) the gum ridge above the front teeth.

the gum ridge

10 When the Spaniard makes the sound for [r] or [rr], his tongue is in almost the same position as yours when you say the sound of [t] or [d]. Say *feed* and *fear* and watch where your tongue is when you say the [d] and the [r]. The tongue position is (a) the same (b) different.

different (English [r] is not like Spanish [r].)

11 Say *feed* and *fear* again. Your tongue touches the gum ridge above the front teeth when you say (a) the [d] of *feed* (b) the [r] of *fear.*

the [d] of *feed* (This is the tongue position for Spanish [r].)

12 If you say the Spanish adjective *todo* with an English stop [d], you have the right tongue position for Spanish [r] and many natives will mistake *todo* (all) for *toro* (bull). However, they never mistake *de*, said with a stop [d], for *re*. What does this tell you? Stop and think. The tongue positions for [d] of *de* and [r] of *re* are the same. Are these sounds made in exactly the same way?

no (The next frames will tell you more precisely how to learn to say Spanish [r]
correctly.)

13 You can say English *hot* in two different ways. Say *hot* and be very careful *to hold the tongue position at the end of the word.* This [t] sound is a stop. (a) It is aspirated (is followed by a puff of air). (b) It is unaspirated (is not followed by a puff of air).

It is unaspirated. (You held your tongue position and no air could escape.)

14 Say, very emphatically, *Boy is it hot!* To be emphatic, you let out a big puff of air at the end of *hot.* Now say, very fast, *hot-hot-hot-hot.* Now watch how long your tongue stays on the gum ridge as you say the [t] of *hot* and the [tt] of *tottle.* Go very fast: *hot-hot-hot-hot; tottle-tottle-tottle-tottle.* In which word does your tongue stay on the gum ridge longer?

hot

15 When you say *tottle* very fast, the tongue tip snaps or flaps very hard against the gum ridge for just a very tiny fraction of a second. Is it there long enough to build up enough air pressure to make a real stop sound?

no

16 Say this nonsense word aloud until you can say it very fast: *poddle*. Now be very careful. Say *poddle* several times and, then, at the end, leave off the sound of *le*. Try this again several times. If you do this right, you are saying the Spanish noun *par* (pair) with a very good Spanish accent.

17 This frame is a test to find out whether you have trained your tongue to make and your ear to hear the Spanish [r] sound. Say English "ear," and Spanish *ir*. Did you flap your tongue against the gum ridge when you said *ir*?

If you did not, tell your teacher about this in your next class. You need more practice.

18 When you are learning about anything new, it is better to learn some things by figuring them out for yourself, as in this Program. Other things, however, are learned much faster by simply memorizing facts. Here are some facts about the letters *r* and *rr* and their sounds which you are to memorize.

(1) The [rr] sound is simply a series of flaps made so fast that the sound becomes a trill.

(2) The letters *rr* are written only between vowels (*a, e, i, o, u*): *pizarra*.

(3) The letters *rr* always stand for a trilled or multiple flap sound.

(4) The letter *r* regularly stands for a single flap sound only when it is between vowels: *señora*.

(5) The letter *r* always stands for a multiple flap sound at the beginning of any word: *regla, reloj*, and immediately after *n, s,* or *l* in a word: *Enrique, alrededor, Israel*.

Part 2: Writing Geographic Names

1 You already know how to write all the letters of the Spanish alphabet. As a result, the real purpose of a Spanish writing exercise is (a) to improve your handwriting (b) to teach you to spell Spanish words.

to teach you to spell

2 Here is a list of the names of the countries you have already learned to say in Spanish. Copy the two which are spelled differently in English: *Argentina, Bolivia, Brasil, Chile, Colombia, Ecuador, Paraguay, Perú, Uruguay, Venezuela.*

Perú has a written accent; in Spanish "Brazil" is spelled with an *s*, not a *z*.

3 Write *Perú* and *Brasil* again.

4 A boy from Chile is called a *chileno*. A boy from Colombia is called a ──────.

colombiano (Adjectives of nationality are not capitalized in Spanish.)

5 Are names of countries and cities capitalized in Spanish?

yes

6 *Bolívar* is considered the George Washington of South America. He was a famous general in the War of Independence (1810). The country named after him is ──────.

Bolivia (Check your spelling.)

7 In 1499 Alonso de Ojeda discovered an Indian village built on piles in a large lake called Maracaibo. He called the town "little Venice." The country which took this name is ──────.

Venezuela (Write this again and check your spelling.)

The Land:
Colombia, Ecuador,
Venezuela

Colombia's rivers cut deeply into the Andean valleys. Bogota, the capital, lies high in the mountains, well over a mile above sea-level.

In Colombia's rich agricultural zone around Cali, fishing and farm work are major sources of income.

Quito, the capital of Ecuador, lies on the equator at 9,000 feet above sea-level. Houses on the outskirts of the city adjust to the surrounding higher mountains.

The skyline along the Venezuelan coast
is marked by oil wells and refineries.
Venezuela is one of the world's major
producers of petroleum.

SOUTH AMERICA
Countries & Capitals

b

10

•a

9

•d

8

7

1

•e

•c

6

•f

5

4

•g

3

2

•i

•j

h

8 There is one country in South America that is bigger than the United States. It is ⁓.

Brasil (Remember, it has a *z* in English: Brazil.)

9 Buenos Aires is the capital of ⁓.

Argentina (If you misspelled it, write it again.)

10 In between Argentina and Brasil are two countries with rather similar names. They are ⁓.

Paraguay; Uruguay

11 One country is located on the equator and is named after it. This country is ⁓.

Ecuador

12 The narrowest and longest country of South America is ⁓.

Chile (If you missed, your mistake is in geography, not Spanish.)

13 Bogotá is the capital of ⁓.

Colombia (With two *o*'s, not an *o* and a *u* as in "Columbus.")

14 You have written the names of *Perú*, *Brasil*, *Uruguay*, *Paraguay*, *Argentina*, *Bolivia*, *Ecuador*, *Colombia*, *Venezuela* and *Chile*. Here is an interesting bit of information. Bolivia is the only country in South America that has two capital cities. One is Sucre, the other is ⁓.

La Paz

15 Here is a list of the South American capital cities that you have studied: *Brasilia, Caracas, Bogotá, Lima, La Paz, Quito, Santiago, Asunción, Montevideo, Buenos Aires*. This frame and the next 9 are testing your knowledge of geography and your spelling.

The capital of Argentina is ⁓.

Buenos Aires (The literal meaning is "Good Airs.")

16 The capital of Bolivia is ⁓.

La Paz (The translation is "The Peace.")

17 The capital of Paraguay is ⁓.

Asunción (Named after the day of the Assumption of the Virgin Mary.)

18 The capital of Chile is ⁓.

Santiago (Saint James)

19 The capital of Brazil is ⁓.

Brasilia (A city built specifically to be the federal capital and dedicated in 1960.)

20 The capital of Colombia is ⁓.

Bogotá (Full name: *Santa Fe de Bogotá*)

21 The capital of Ecuador is ⁓.

Quito (The name of the Indian tribe that lived there.)

22 The capital of Venezuela is ⁓.

Caracas (Named by Diego de Losada in 1567 after the Indians of the area and the patron saint Santiago de León. Full name is *Santiago de León de Caracas*.)

23 The capital of Uruguay is ⁓.

Montevideo (From Latin *video*—"I see" and *monte*—"mount.")

24 The capital of Perú is ⁓.

Lima (Corruption of the name for the river Rimac. Was once written *Limac*.)

25 On page 103 you will find a blank map with the outlines of the South American countries. Circles show the location of the capital cities. Trace a copy of this map and write in the names of the countries and their capitals. Be prepared to hand this in to your teacher.

Part 3: How Good is Your Memory?

1 Between two vowels the letter *r* always stands for (a) a single flap sound (b) a multiple flap.

a single flap   **2** At the beginning of words the letter *r* always stands for (a) a single flap (b) multiple flaps.

multiple flaps   **3** The letters *rr* appear only ～～～.
between vowels

   4 The letters for the Spanish vowel sounds are ～～～.

a, e, i, o, u   **5** The letter *r* stands for two phonemes: /r/ and /rr/. The digraph *rr* stands for only one phoneme, the sound [rr]. (a) true (b) false

true

New Vocabulary

Begin a separate page in your notebook entitled *Vocabulary*. Draw a line down the middle of the page. Write the Spanish words on the left half of the page and the English equivalents on the right half. From now on when you have new vocabulary introduced in class, it is included in a short list at the end of each Program. Always add these words to your vocabulary list. The amount of vocabulary that is being presented to you is increasing at a pace that will make it difficult for you to learn well all new words without keeping a vocabulary list and studying it regularly. Most students can learn vocabulary thoroughly by studying their list for about four minutes each day. Cover the Spanish column, look at the English equivalents and see if you can remember the Spanish. Make a light check mark opposite the words that you don't remember. Return to them several times during the four minutes until they are learned well.

mina	mine	**ciudad (la)**	city
capital (la)	capital	**gaucho**	gaucho
rodeo	rodeo	**tigre (el)**	tiger, cougar, mountain lion
corral (el)	corral	**elefante (el)**	elephant
jardín (el)	garden	**animal (el)**	animal
¡Espera!	Wait!		

In the United States almost no one believes that it is dangerous to go out at night. In most of the Hispanic world there are people who believe that the night air, *el sereno,* is harmful to one's health. *El sereno* is believed to damage the lungs and to cause a variety of illnesses. As a result, many people will go out at night only in an emergency while others cover their nose and mouth with a handkerchief until their system gets used to *el sereno.*

Some Differences between *ser, haber*, and *estar*

Part 1: Location versus Origin: *estar* and *ser*

1 You have already learned three Spanish verbs which are all translated into English by "to be." You know forms like *soy, estamos,* and *hay.* The infinitive form of *hay* is *haber.* The infinitives for *soy* and *estamos* are ‿‿‿.

ser; estar
2 Can the English translation of these verbs tell you which one to use in Spanish?

no (Since the translation is the same for all, it cannot cue a choice.)

3 The cues that tell you when to use *ser, estar,* or *haber* are to be found in the context, that is, in the forms and especially the meaning of the sentence. Is there a real difference between saying where a person is from (origin) and where a person is (location)?

yes (A gaucho *from* Argentina may be *in* New York.)

4 Chile, Bogotá, Ecuador, and Chicago belong to a set of words that label geographic entities (countries or cities). A person or thing may be located in a country or may be from a country or city. In *Pablo está en Chile*, the relator *en* tells you Pablo is (a) *in* Chile (b) *from* Chile.

in Chile
5 In *Pablo es de Chile*, the relator *de* tells you Pablo is (a) *in* Chile (b) *from* Chile.

from Chile
6 The irregular forms *soy* and *es* have the same infinitive. It is ‿‿‿.

ser
7 Now, compare these sentences: (1) *Pablo está en Chile.* (2) *Pablo es de Chile.* Here is one rule for choice: when you locate a person in a place, the use of *en* cues the choice of (a) *ser* (b) *estar.*

estar
8 Here is the second rule for choice: when you say where a person or thing is from, the use of *de* cues the choice of ‿‿‿.

ser
9 Here is a way to summarize this: person + location + *en* = ‿‿‿ (*ser, estar*); person + origin + *de* = ‿‿‿ (*ser, estar*).

person + location + *en* = estar; person + origin + *de* = ser

Part 2: *Estar* versus *haber* for Location

1 Does *Buenos Aires está en Argentina* give us the same kind of information as *Pablo está en Chile?*

yes (Both sentences locate the subject: tell us where it is.)

2 Does *El libro está en la mesa* also give you the location of *libro,* that is, tell you where it is?

yes
3 Does *Hay un libro en la mesa* also give the location of *libro?*

yes
4 When a Spanish speaker locates something, may he choose between two verbs, *haber* and *estar?*

yes
5 The Spanish speaker, however, does not use *haber* or *estar* for location just when it strikes his fancy. There are easily recognized cues or signals which always tell him which verb to use. Let's see whether you can discover these cues.

Copy the following questions, compare them word for word, then underline those words which are exactly the same in both: (1) *¿ Hay un libro en la mesa?* (2) *¿ Está el libro en la mesa?*

(1) *¿ Hay un **libro en la mesa**?* (2) *¿ Está el **libro en la mesa**?*

6 Will the parts that are exactly alike cue the choice between *hay* (*haber*) and *está* (*estar*)?

no

7 Remember, you are looking for the cues that tell when to use *hay* or *está*. These cues must be in the context. There must be one for *hay* and another for *está*. These cues are the words ⁓.

un; el

8 You now have all the information you need to figure out the rule for choosing between *haber* and *estar* for location. For each choice there are actually two cues. The first is the location of something in space (on a table, in Santiago, at the door, south of the Equator, *etc.*). The second is the article (definite or indefinite) used with the noun standing for the thing (entity) to be located. Look at these sentences carefully: (1) *¿ Hay un libro en la mesa?* (2) *¿ Está el libro en la mesa?* Here's the first rule: when something is to be located, the Spanish speaker uses *hay* when the noun combines with ⁓.

un

9 The summary of this rule is: entity + location + *un* cues the use of ⁓.

haber (There is only one present tense form of *haber* for location; it is *hay*.)

10 Here's the second rule: when something is to be located, the Spanish speaker uses *estar* when the noun combines with ⁓.

el

11 The summary of this rule is: entity + location + *el* = ⁓.

estar

12 Let's see, now, if you have all the facts straight. Will the notion of location, all by itself, tell you when to use *haber* or *estar* for location?

no (You need a second cue: the definite or indefinite article.)

13 In *Hay un muchacho en Montevideo* the cues for the choice of *haber* are *muchacho, en Montevideo,* and ⁓.

un

14 In *El muchacho está en Montevideo,* the change that cues the choice of *estar* is ⁓.

el

15 Now, let's expand these two rules. If you can say, *Hay un libro allí,* is it logical to assume that you can also say, *Hay una pluma allí?*

yes (Either form of the indefinite article, *un* or *una,* cues the choice of *haber* for location.)

16 The answer to the question *¿ Hay una pluma allí?* may be *Sí, hay una allí.* Translate the answer.

Yes, there is one there.

17 You have made a linguistic discovery. The word *una* has two English translations: "one" and ⁓.

a (The indefinite article forms "a" and "an" once also meant "one" in English.)

18 Spanish has three number words for the Arabic numeral 1: they are *un, una,* and ⁓.

uno (This form is the one you use in counting: *uno, dos, tres, etc.*)

19 Do *un, una, uno, dos, tres, etc.* all belong to the same set?

yes

20 Is it now logical to assume that all numbers will cue the choice of *haber* for location?

yes

21 Write the missing verb form: ⁓ *tres plumas allí.*

Hay

22 Your expanded rule is now: the indefinite article forms *un* or *una* and all other numbers cue the choice of ⁓ for location.

haber (Do not mark this frame wrong if you wrote *hay*.)

23 Numbers like 5, 10, 20, *etc.* are called *public numbers* because they stand for precise amounts understood by everyone. In contrast, words like *some, few, many, a lot, etc.* are called *private numbers* because they stand in place of different public numbers. Each of us may, consequently, have a different answer to "How many is some?"

A person has 10 close friends. Does he have (a) some friends? (b) a few friends? (c) many friends?

It depends entirely on you. To some people 10 is a lot; to others 10 is a few.
That is why these words are called private numbers.

24 *Un libro* is singular and stands for *1 libro.* Can you tell the number that the plural suffix of *libros* stands for?

no (The plural suffix *s* is like a private number word: it can stand for any
number over 1.) **25** Think of what you just learned and, then, answer this question. Which verb form will you use? (a) *Están* (b) *Hay . . . libros en la mesa.*

Hay (A private number, like any other, cues the use of *haber* for location.)

26 A plural noun all by itself may cue the choice of *haber* for location. (a) true (b) false

true **27** Here is a summary of the cues for choosing *haber* for location:

*Hay **un** libro en la mesa.*　　　　(Indefinite article = "a" or "one.")
*Hay **diez** libros en la mesa.*　　　(Public number + plural suffix.)
*Hay **muchos** libros en la mesa.*　　(Private number + plural suffix.)
Hay libros en la mesa.　　　　　　(‿‿‿ all by itself.)

plural suffix (*s* or *es*)

28 We now have to expand the rule for choosing *estar* for location. If you can say, *La muchacha está en Quito, Ecuador*, is it logical to assume that you can also say, *Las muchachas están en Quito, Ecuador?*

yes (All four forms of the definite article—*el, los, la, las*—cue *estar* for location.)

29 The subject pronoun which can replace *la muchacha* is ‿‿‿.

ella **30** So you can say, *Ella está en Quito.* Remember, now, that if one member of a set cues *estar* for location, then all members of that set will also cue the same choice. So, is this true? All subject pronouns cue the choice of *estar* for location.

yes **31** The pronouns *él, ellos, ella*, and *ellas* stand for people. People have names. What kind of an educated guess can you now make? Which form will you use? (a) *Hay* (b) *Está ¿* ‿‿‿ *Pedro en La Paz, Bolivia?*

Está **32** A proper name all by itself cues *estar* for location. Now be very careful. Which form will you use? (a) *Hay* (b) *Está ¿* ‿‿‿ *un Pedro en la clase?*

Hay (This is just like *Hay un muchacho en clase.*)

33 Here is a summary of the cues for choosing *estar* for location:

Santiago está en Chile.　　　　(A proper name all by itself.)
Pedro está en Chile.

Él está en Chile.　　　　　　(Any subject pronoun.)
Yo estoy en Chile.

El libro está en la mesa.
Los libros están en la mesa.　　(All forms of the ‿‿‿ article.)
La pluma está en la mesa.
Las plumas están en la mesa.

definite

Part 3: The Equals Sign in Math and Speech: *ser*

1 When you say *4 + 4 = 8* in Spanish, the word for = is 〜〜〜. •

son

2 When you say *8 − 4 = 4* in Spanish, the word for = is 〜〜〜. •

son

3 Compare these sentences: (1) *Cuatro y cuatro son ocho.* (2) *Ocho menos cuatro son cuatro.* Do the words on either side of the verb stand for the same amount? •

yes

4 Do *Martínez* and *profesor* stand for the same person in *Martínez es profesor?* •

yes

5 When you want to say that two numbers are equal or that two words stand for the same person or thing, you use the verb (a) *haber* (b) *ser* (c) *estar.* •

ser

Part 4: A Test on What You Have Learned

Before you start the test, study the following summary carefully. It gives you all the rules on the choice of *haber*, *ser*, and *estar* that you have had so far.

The cues to use *ser* are:
  (1) *de* plus a place name (origin)
      Soy de Uruguay.
  (2) equations (the equals sign)
      Dos y dos son cuatro.
      Cuatro menos tres son uno.
      Buenos Aires es una ciudad.
The cues to use *estar* for location are:
  (1) entity + location + definite article (*el, los, la, las*)
      El tigre está en el corral.
      Los tigres están en el corral.
      La pluma está en el pupitre.
      Las plumas están en el pupitre.
  (2) location + any unmodified proper name
      José está en Lima.
      Asunción está en Paraguay.
  (3) location + any subject pronoun
      Ella está en Bolivia.
The cues to use *haber* for location are:
  (1) entity + location + indefinite article (*un, una*)
      Hay un tigre en el corral.
      Hay una pluma en el pupitre.
      Hay un Sánchez en la clase.
  (2) entity + location + any public or private number
      Hay treinta muchachos aquí.
      Hay muchos muchachos aquí.
  (3) location + unmodified plural noun
      Hay tigres en el corral.
Here are ten frames covering what you have just studied. Let's see if you can recognize all the cues for choosing *ser*, *estar*, and *haber*. Think of the choice before you check the answer. Circle the number of any missed frame. To get a grade, take 10 points from 100 for each mistake. Don't forget your cover sheet.

1 Pilar and María *are* girls. Which verb do you use?

ser (Pilar + María = girls. *Pilar y María son muchachas.*)

2 Miguel *is in* Caracas.

estar (Proper name + location: *Miguel está en Caracas.*)

3 The book *is under* the table.

estar (Definite article + location cues *estar*: *El libro está debajo de la mesa.*)

4 Rosario *is from* Lima, Perú.

ser (Origin or place from cues *ser*: *Rosario es de Lima, Perú.*)

5 *Near here is a* volcano called Paricutín.

haber (Indefinite article + location cues *haber*.)

6 4 = 4

ser (The equals sign is *ser*.)

7 What *is* this?

ser (What = this?)

8 *Is* there *a* Mr. Machado *in* this office?

haber (Indefinite article + location cues *haber*.)

9 They *are from* La Paz, Bolivia.

ser (Origin cues *ser*.)

10 They *are in* La Paz, Bolivia.

estar (All subject pronouns cue *estar* for location.)

If you missed two or more frames you need to go through this Program again. The verbs *ser*, *estar*, and *haber* are used more frequently than any other verb in Spanish. To use one of these verbs in the wrong place is a glaring mistake much like saying in English "Is you there?"

New Vocabulary

Remember to add the following words to your vocabulary list and to spend four minutes studying your entire list.

argentino	Argentinian	**paraguayo**	Paraguayan
boliviano	Bolivian	**chileno**	Chilean
uruguayo	Uruguayan	**si**	if

PROGRAM **28**

ser, and More about Adjectives; practice for a Quiz

Part 1: The Present Tense Forms of *ser*

The Spanish you are learning is a modern dialect of ancient Latin, the language spoken by the Romans who invaded Spain and made it a province of the Roman Empire. While Latin was slowly changing into Spanish, the people got mixed up about the meaning of the Latin verbs *sedere* (to sit) and *esse* (to be). Gradually they came to believe that the different forms of these two verbs actually belonged to the same verb. As a result, the modern verb *ser* has forms which come from both Latin verbs. It is very irregular, and its forms have to be learned one by one. English "to be" is also very irregular: am, are, is, was, were, be.

1 The *yo*-form of *ser* has the same ending as the *yo*-form of *estar*. The whole form is written ———.

soy

2 The *nosotros*-form, like all regular verbs, ends in the suffix *mos*. The stem and first suffix is *so*. The whole form is written ———.

somos

3 In regular verbs the second suffix *s* tells you that the subject is ———.

tú (Did you forget the accent mark?)

4 The present tense of *ser* has two forms which end in *s*. The form that goes with *tú* is *eres*. The form *es* goes with *usted*, *él*, and *ella*. Copy *tú eres* and *él es*. Notice that *él es* is translated "he is" and *usted es* means "you is" but is translated "you ———."

you are

5 The form which combines with *ustedes*, *ellos*, and *ellas* ends, like regular verbs, in *n*. It has the same stem as *somos* and is written ———.

son (Here are all the present tense forms of *ser*.

yo soy	usted		ustedes	
nosotros somos	él	es	ellos	son
tú eres	ella		ellas	

Say these aloud twice, then go on to Frame 6.)

6 In this and the next eight frames, you are to write the proper form of *ser*. Nosotros ——— de Asunción, Paraguay.

somos

7 Usted ——— muy amable.

es

8 Tú ——— muy amable.

eres

9 María y Linda ——— muchachas.

son

10 ¿——— ustedes de Venezuela?

Son (Did you use a capital letter?)

11 Él ——— profesor.

es

12 José y yo ——— alumnos.

somos

13 Ellas ——— chilenas.

son

14 Yo ——— Pilar.

soy

15 Write the form of *ser* that goes with each of the following subject pronouns: *tú* ———, *usted* ———, *yo* ———, *nosotros* ———, *ustedes* ———.

tú eres, usted es, yo soy, nosotros somos, ustedes son

16 The subject pronouns *él*, *ella*, and *usted* all combine with the form ———.

es

17 The subject pronouns *ellos*, *ellas*, and *ustedes* all combine with ———.

son

18 To learn all the present tense forms of *ser*, you really have to learn only five forms. They are: *es, son,* ———.

soy, somos, eres

Part 2: *ser* and Adjectives of Nationality

1 Adjectives of nationality have two forms. The singular forms you have learned so far end in either the vowel ———.

o or *a* (*chileno, chilena, etc.*)

2 When you are talking about people, the forms ending in *o* are used to describe (a) males (b) females.

males (*Manuel es chileno.*)

3 If you change *Manuel* to *Manuela*, you must change *chileno* to ~~~~.

chilena (Remember: you do not capitalize adjectives of nationality in Spanish.)

4 Adjectives of nationality, like all other Spanish adjectives, agree in number with the object or objects being described. When the singular form of an adjective ends in a vowel, it is made plural by adding ~~~~.

s (*chileno, chilenos; chilena, chilenas*)

5 Adjectives which have two forms, behave like nouns which have two forms. What do you say? *José es un* (a) *muchacho* (b) *muchacha.*

muchacho   **6** What do you say? *José es un muchacho* (a) *argentino* (b) *argentina.*

argentino (The *o* of *argentino* matches the *o* of *muchacho.*)

7 What do you say? *Josefa es una* (a) *muchacho argentino* (b) *muchacha argentina.*

muchacha argentina

8 Now be careful. What do you say? *José y Josefa son* ~~~~. (Argentine children)

muchachos argentinos (When you talk of a boy and a girl, you use the *o*-form
of the noun and the *o*-form of the adjective in the plural.)

9 To learn to use adjectives in Spanish, you have to learn to react to cues to which you pay no attention in English. For example, you are a girl. What do you say? (a) *Soy uruguayo.* (b) *Soy uruguaya.*

Soy uruguaya. (Remember that the *a*-form of adjectives is used to describe
females.)   **10** You are a girl and are talking for a group made up of boys and girls. What do you say? (a) *Somos paraguayos.* (b) *Somos paraguayas.*

Even though you are a girl, you are describing a mixed group and must say,
Somos paraguayos.

11 You are a boy talking to a girl. What do you say? (a) *Pancho y tú son chilenas.* (b) *Pancho y tú son chilenos.*

Tú is a girl; Pancho is a boy. You must use *chilenos.*

12 You are a girl talking to a girl. You must say, (a) *No somos argentinos.* (b) *No somos argentinas.*

The adjective describes only girls and must be *argentinas.*

13 You are a boy talking to a girl. You must say, (a) *No somos bolivianos.* (b) *No somos bolivianas.*

No somos bolivianos.

14 Will the pronoun forms *usted, ustedes,* and *tú* tell you whether to use an *o*- or *a*-form adjective?

no (Only the sex of the person you are speaking to gives you the cue. The
subject pronouns *yo, tú, usted,* and *ustedes* have no mark to indicate sex.)

15 There are four subject pronoun forms that have an *o* and *a* contrast which does indicate sex. They are ~~~~.

nosotros, nosotras, ellos, ellas

16 The form *ella* contrasts with ~~~~ to indicate sex.

él   **17** Can a male ever speak for a group and use *nosotras?*

no (Since he is one of the group he must use *nosotros.* Only girls have to
worry about choosing between *nosotros* and *nosotras.*)

In most American stores everything for sale has the price marked on it. Except during sales, this price is fixed and the customer does not argue over it. In the large stores and supermarkets of Latin America the prices are also fixed. However, in small shops and the market place, the prices are rarely fixed. The buyer must haggle with the seller. The seller usually begins by setting a price according to what he thinks the customer can afford. After that, the bargaining becomes a kind of a game of wits and patience to see who gives up first. Many American tourists do not understand the unwritten rules of this game and, as a result, they often settle for a price that may be many times higher than a native would pay for the same article. One knowledgeable tourist once bought an ashtray from an Indian craftsman for 50 cents. His friend happily paid two dollars for the same article.

The word for this bargaining process is *regateo*. The verb is *regatear*.

Part 3: Review of Uses of *ser*, *estar*, and *haber*

1 When you ask about a person's health, you use ⌇⌇⌇. (Think of the infinitive.)

estar (¿Cómo está usted?)

2 The origin of a person or thing cues ⌇⌇⌇.

ser (¿De dónde es usted? ¿De España?)

3 To state a person's nationality. (He is Bolivian), you use ⌇⌇⌇.

ser (Es boliviano.)

4 Any one of the four forms of the definite article cues the use of ⁓⁓ for location.

estar (*Los libros están en el pupitre.*)

      5 To say that two things are equal or the same, you use ⁓⁓.

ser (*Panchito es un elefante.*)

      6 Any form of the indefinite article or any number (public or private) cues the use of ⁓⁓ for location.

haber (*Hay un tigre en el corral; Hay dos tigres en el corral.*)

      7 An unmodified plural noun cues the use of ⁓⁓ for location.

haber (*Hay gauchos en el rodeo.*)

      8 An unmodified proper name cues the use of ⁓⁓ for location.

estar (*Pedro está en Paraguay.*)

      9 The subject pronouns cue the use of ⁓⁓ for location.

estar (*Ellos están en Bolivia.*)

      10 When a proper name is combined with *un* or *una*, you use ⁓⁓ for location.

haber (*Hay un Francisco en la clase.*)

      11 *Hay* may be used to locate either a singular or a plural entity. (a) true (b) false

true (*Hay* comes from the Latin *ille habet ibi*—"he has there" and does not agree in number with its object. He can "have one there" or "have two there".)

Part 4: Practice for a Quiz

In your next class session you will have a quiz on the South American countries and capitals that you have studied. You will be graded on two things. (1) Can you understand what you hear? (2) Have you learned your geography? Do these ten frames to see whether you need to study some more. 1 mistake = A, 2 = B, 3 = C, 4 = D, 5 = F.

      1 In this and the next 9 frames, answer *sí* or *no* mentally.
      Una de las capitales de Bolivia es Sucre.

sí (The other is La Paz.)

      2 Montevideo no es una ciudad, es un país.

no   **3** Lima está en Paraguay.

no   **4** Santiago es una ciudad de Chile.

sí   **5** La capital de Venezuela es Caracas.

sí   **6** Asunción y Paraguay son países.

no (Asunción es la capital de Paraguay.)

      7 Brasilia es un país de Sudamérica.

no (Brasilia es la capital de Brasil.)

      8 Quito no está en Ecuador.

no   **9** Buenos Aires está en Argentina.

sí   **10** Una de las ciudades de Colombia es Bogotá.

sí

New Vocabulary

Hace calor.	It is hot.	**Hace viento.**	It is windy.
Hace frío.	It is cold.	**Hace buen tiempo.**	It is good weather.
Hace fresco.	It is cool.	**Hace mal tiempo.**	It is bad weather.

haber	to be, have	ecuatoriano	Ecuadorean
ser	to be	peruano	Peruvian
brasileño	Brazilian	venezolano	Venezuelan
colombiano	Colombian		

PROGRAM 29

Word Sets and Using a Dictionary

1 The words *trabajar*, *necesitar* and *esperar* are members of the *a*-set. Do they have the same meaning?

no
2 Do the words standing for the members of the same set have to have the same meaning?

no
3 Is *ser* a member of the *a*-set?

no (It has *e* before the infinitive marker.)
4 To be a member of a set, a form, a word, or a thing must have something in common with all other members of that set. (a) true (b) false

true
5 Is it logical to say that dogs, Chinese, bolts, and wars are members of the same set?

no (They have nothing significant in common.)
6 Are oranges, apples, peaches, and pears members of the same set?

yes (They are all fruits that grow on trees.)
7 Do *martes,* *viernes*, and *domingo* belong to the same set?

yes (They are all days of the week.)
8 It is important for you to know about sets in learning Spanish. Let's see why. Are the four forms of the definite article (*el*, *los*, *la*, *las*) members of the same set?

yes
9 Do all members of this set cue the use of *estar* for location?

yes
10 It would be a great waste of time for you if you had to learn four separate rules just to discover that all four forms of the definite article set cue the use of *estar* for location. What we do instead is to make a generalization and say, if one member of a set cues the use of *estar*, then all members of that set will also cue the use of *estar* for location.

Neither you nor a native child can learn Spanish without learning to deal with sets. You may not be aware of it, because you learned English when you were very little, but you have a tremendous amount of information in your head about sets and English usage. Let's prove this by having you discover a generalization which foreigners learning English have great trouble with.

You can count apples, pigs, cars, and telephones. Do you (a) *count* or (b) *measure* water?

You measure water.

11 Can you count either dust or milk?

no

12 Now, copy the words which stand for entities which belong to the same set as water, dust, and milk: *hat, mud, ink, pen, flour, butter, boy*.

mud, ink, flour, butter

13 The words in the above answer are members of the same set as water, H_2O. They stand for a set made up of measure entities, things that cannot be counted. Which would you say: (a) What are waters? (b) What is water?

What is water?

14 We do not make *water* plural when we are talking about H_2O. Do you say "Pass the butters, please."?

no

15 You have proven that you can identify the members of the set made up of measure entities and that you know their labels do not take a plural suffix without changing the meaning. Let's see how much more you really know about this set. Write the number for the sentences which are *not* proper English answers to the question, *What's that on the table?* (1) It's a bug. (2) It's a milk. (3) It's a pencil. (4) It's a dust. (5) It's a bottle.

You wrote the number for *It's a milk* and *It's a dust* because milk and dust are measure entities, and you do not use the indefinite article *a* with measure entities.

16 Is this a logical generalization? If *a* is not used with *milk*, a measure entity, then *a* will not be used with any other word which belongs to the same set as *milk*. (a) logical (b) not logical

logical

17 You know *by feel* how to deal with a very large number of sets in English. You learned this by imitation, by trial and error. Why do you *not* say, "I want some milks."? (a) because somebody told you not to (b) because you never heard anyone say it

because you never heard it said

18 It took you many years to learn to deal with English sets by feel or intuition. You do not have time to learn Spanish in this way. You need to learn to deal with sets consciously, that is, by actually *knowing* what they are and what they can tell you about Spanish usage.

You have already learned some set rules. Do you remember this one? The forms of the indefinite article (*un* and *una*) and all private and public numbers belong to the same set. They all cue the use of (a) *haber* (b) *estar* for location.

haber

19 Here's another set rule: all nouns that end in a consonant belong to the same set. Any final consonant cues you to add ⁓⁓⁓ to make the noun plural.

es (*papel, papeles*)

20 Let's see if you can discover two important Spanish sets and what they tell you about usage. A Spanish speaker may ask, *¿Dónde está el libro?* The answer might be: (1) *El libro está en la mesa.* (2) *Está en la mesa.* He may ask, *¿Dónde está José?* The answer may be: (1) *José está en clase.* (2) *Él está en clase.* (3) *Está en clase.*

Do *libro* and *José* belong to the same set?

no

21 *José* is a living being. Is *libro* a living being?

no (*Libro* belongs to the set of inanimate or non-living entities.)

22 *José*, a name for a living being, can be replaced by the subject pronoun *él* (he). *José está en clase* can be changed to *Él está en clase. Libro*, a word for an inanimate entity, cannot be replaced by *él*. Is this generalization logical? *Libro* belongs to the set of inanimate entities. *Libro* cannot be replaced by *él*. No noun standing for an inanimate entity may be replaced by *él*, a pronoun that stands for a male. (a) logical (b) not logical

logical (Spanish has *no* subject pronoun for inanimate entities, that is, no word to translate "it". You use zero and the verb.)

23 Read the explanation above carefully. Now translate: It is on the table.

Está en la mesa.

24 Let's take another step just to see how sets and logic can make learning Spanish easier. The singular form *libro* cannot be replaced by *él*. Do you expect, consequently, that the plural form *libros* can be replaced by *ellos*?

no (Making the form plural does not change the set.)

25 Spanish has no word to translate "they" when this subject pronoun stands for inanimate entities. Translate: They are on the table.

Están en la mesa.

26 Sets are very important in learning the meaning of words. When you meet a new Spanish word you must assign what it stands for to a set. You know, for example, the word *mesa*. The set it belongs to is called ～～～.

furniture (table, chair, desk, stool, *etc.*)

27 There are many words which can stand for things belonging to different sets. Words of this kind have (a) just one meaning (b) more than one meaning.

more than one meaning (If you got this wrong, pay special attention to the next frame.)

28 A Spanish speaker may say, "I bought that ranch up on the *mesa*." Can *mesa*, in this sentence, be standing for a piece of furniture?

no (A *ranch* cannot be on a *table*.)

29 When logic tells you that a word you have learned cannot stand for the set you have assigned it to, you have been signaled that it has another meaning. When a ranch is on a *mesa, mesa* must stand for ～～～.

a tableland, a geographic shape, an upland (If you got the general idea, you're doing fine.)

30 Now, let's turn this around. Suppose you do not know the Spanish word for "magazine." You want to look it up in an English-Spanish dictionary. You will find *revista, almacén, cámara,* and *santabárbara.* All of these translate "magazine," but each one stands for something belonging to a different set. Can you decide which one to pick before you decide the set you want "magazine" to stand for?

no

31 Suppose you want "magazine" to stand for the set composed of newspapers, pamphlets, periodicals, and reviews. You have a better chance of picking the right translation now if you use your head. How? By looking for a cognate. Copy the word in this list which looks like it might be a cognate of "review": *almacén, cámara, revista, santabárbara.*

Revista is the word, and it translates "magazine" when you are talking about periodicals.

32 Let's try this again. You want a different meaning for "magazine." This time you are talking about a gun. You put bullets in the magazine. "Magazine" now stands for something that belongs to the set of things in which other things are put, held, or stored. Another name for the magazine of a gun is its "chamber." Copy the word which looks like it might be a cognate of "chamber": *almacén, cámara, revista, santabárbara.*

Cámara is the only one beginning with *c*. It is the Spanish word for the chamber or magazine of a gun.

33 You are learning to use what you know to guess intelligently. Let's try this once more. A Spanish speaker says, "Our house has a kitchen, dining-room, parlor, two baths, and *tres cámaras*." The set he is talking about is ――――.

rooms of a house

34 Does *cámara*, in this context, logically stand for the magazine of a gun?

no

35 It stands for ――――. (Before you answer reread the quoted sentence in Frame 33.)

bedroom

36 Now let's see how knowing about sets helps you solve this problem. Think carefully. People who are interested in hunting, "read" gun "magazines." Which word would you pick for magazine? (a) *cámara* (b) *revista*

revista (People don't "read" bullet chambers.)

37 The verb "read" in "People read gun magazines" helps you define the set to which "magazine" belongs.

Let's see how watching other words in a sentence helps you discover the set of an unknown word and, in the process, its meaning. You have not had the word *cuchara*. What set does it belong to in this sentence? "He brought a knife, a fork, and *una cuchara*."

silverware (or tableware)

38 The translation of *cuchara*, a member of the silverware set, is ――――.

spoon

39 Here are more examples of the importance of sets in learning Spanish. To choose between *haber* and *estar* for location you must be able to recognize the set of relator words used in locating entities. Copy the words not used in talking about locating something in space: *in, under, over, from, near, on, for.*

from; for

40 Question words all belong to the same set. What they have in common *in writing* in Spanish is an ――――.

accent mark

41 The adjectives of nationality belong to the same set. In writing they differ from English in that they do not begin with a ――――.

capital letter

42 All plants and all inanimate entities belong to the same set. When English uses *it* as a subject pronoun to talk about these things (*It is in the garden.*) Spanish uses no ―――― pronoun.

subject (*Está en el jardín.*)

The gun has played a very different role in the history of the Hispanic world and the United States and there are variations in the development of the vocabulary of the two languages. In Latin America, excepting the periods of Conquest and Independence movements, guns played a fairly minor role and most people never even owned one. In contrast, during the settling of most of the United States the possession and use of firearms was widespread. As a consequence, there are in American English many "gun" words which have no equivalent in Spanish. When something goes wrong in a shop the boss sends for a "trouble shooter." If he is a very important person, he is a "big shot," but if he fails, he is a "dud." If he is honest, he is a "straight shooter" who sometimes tells the workers that they need to "raise their sights." If the troubleshooter is very successful, the company buys his suggestions "lock, stock and barrel." You could probably think of many other examples of this type of "gun" vocabulary if you tried. It would probably be almost impossible for a Spanish speaker to come up with even one.

Optional Practice: *ser, haber,* and *estar*

Write the form of the verb you would use to translate "to be" in each example. Use your cover sheet.

1	How *are* you? (*tú*)	*estás*
2	Where *are* you (*usted*) from?	*es*
3	Brasilia *is* in the interior of Brazil.	*está*
4	There's a fly on your ear.	*Hay*
5	Dogs *are* animals.	*son*
6	6 minus 2 *is* 4.	*son*
7	6 plus 2 *is* 8.	*son*
8	We *are* from Colombia.	*somos*
9	Raúl *is* in Perú.	*está*
10	Near here *is* a large lake.	*hay*

New Vocabulary

Remember to add the following word to your list and to spend four minutes studying the entire list. By now you probably know the first group of words so well that you can check through them in just a few seconds to see if you have forgotten any. Some lessons do not include new vocabulary; however, even when this is the case, still spend three or four minutes reviewing your entire list. This will enable you to know all your vocabulary well.

perfecto   perfect

PROGRAM 30

Practice in Writing *ser* and *estar,* and Adjectival Agreement

The three verbs which translate "to be," *ser, estar,* and *haber,* are used more often than any other verb in the Spanish language. As a result, you will give natives a bad impression if you make mistakes in spelling, writing, or using these forms. Treat this Program as a self-test to find out what you still have to learn to reach perfection.

1 You have learned, so far, only one form of *haber.* It is ———.

hay

2 Translate the indicated part of each sentence: (1) *There is* a book on the table. (2) *There are* two books on the table.

Hay un libro en la mesa; *Hay* dos libros en la mesa.

3 Does the form *hay* agree in number with what is being located?

no (You just used *hay* with *un libro* and *dos libros.*)

4 The cue to say *hay* for location is (a) the definite article (b) the indefinite article, any number, or a plural noun.

the indefinite article, any number, or a plural noun

5 Translate the verb form only: Near our house *is* a large tree.

*hay (Cerca de nuestra casa **hay** un árbol grande.)*

6 *Hay* translates "there is," "there are," or simply "is" or "are." (a) true (b) false

true (Actually the word "there" disappears in the Spanish translation.)

7 The *yo*-form of *estar* is irregular. It is ⟿.

estoy

8 The forms *está* and *están* are irregular because they ⟿. (Before you answer think of *habla* and *hablan*.)

have the stress on the first suffix (This is shown by the written accent marks.)

9 Change *estoy* so it will match *nosotros*.

estamos (Estoy and *estamos* are the only present tense forms of *estar* that do not have a written accent mark.)

10 Make *ellas están* singular.

ella está

11 What form of *estar* goes with *tú?*

estás

12 The plural of *tú estás* is ⟿.

ustedes están (There are forms for a plural of *tú: vosotros estáis, etc.* These are not part of the ordinary speech in Latin America. You will learn to read and understand these later on.)

13 All of these subject pronouns, *usted*, *él*, and *ella*, combine with the same form of *estar*. It is ⟿.

está

14 All these pronouns, *ustedes*, *ellos*, and *ellas*, combine with ⟿.

están

15 A proper name cues the use of ⟿ for location.

estar

16 Translate the indicated part: Miguel *is in* Santiago.

*Miguel **está en** Santiago.*

17 Translate the indicated part: Santiago *is in* Chile.

*Santiago **está en** Chile.*

18 The (a) definite (b) indefinite article is the cue to use *estar* for location.

definite

19 Translate: The pen is on the table.

La pluma está en la mesa.

20 All subject pronouns cue the use of ⟿ for location.

estar

21 Translate: We are in the class.

Nosotros estamos en la clase.

22 There are two verbs in Spanish that are used to locate entities in space. They are ⟿.

estar; haber (When you talk about a verb in a general sense, you use the infinitive form as its name.)

23 Is *estar* also used to talk about a person's health or state of being?

yes

24 Translate, using the *tú*-form: How are you?

¿Cómo estás? (Did you remember the inverted question mark and the accent mark over *cómo?)*

25 Translate: I'm fine, thank you.

Estoy bien, gracias.

26 In this and the next 3 frames translate the indicated words.
They (girls) *are in* Argentina.

Ellas están en (Did you remember the accent mark?)

27 *I am in* Asunción, Paraguay.

Yo estoy en   **28** *Are* you *in* Chile? (*tú*)

¿Estás en (You need the inverted question mark. You may omit the *tú*.)

29 *How are you?* (*ustedes*)

¿Cómo están ustedes?

30 *Haber* and *estar* are used for location. Is the verb *ser* ever used to locate an entity in space?

no   **31** When the relator *de* combines with the name of a place, it is translated by ~~~~~.

from   **32** Translate: Carlos is from Lima.

Carlos es de Lima.

33 The origin of a person or thing is indicated by the verb ~~~~~ and *de*.

ser   **34** The equals sign (=) is translated into a word by ~~~~~.

ser   **35** Do "we" and "students" stand for the same persons in "We are students?"

yes   **36** Translate the verb form in "We are students."

somos   **37** *Ser* is used to say that numbers equal numbers or that words equal words. (a) true (b) false

true (*Dos y dos son cuatro; María es alumna.*)

38 Is *ser* also used with adjectives of nationality?

yes   **39** *Josefina y Teresa son de Argentina. ¿Qué son?* The answer is the translation of "They are Argentines."

Son argentinas. (You may omit *ellas* in this context. Did you make *argentinas* agree? Plural and *a*.)

40 In this frame and the next six each sentence translates "You are Brazilian." Be careful with the verb form and the spelling of "Brazilian." *Tú* (boy) ~~~~~.

Tú eres brasileño. (The adjective has no capital letter, it ends in *o*, it is written with *s*, and has a tilde over the *ñ*.)

41 *Tú* (girl) ~~~~~.

Tú eres brasileña. (*a* for girl.)

42 *Usted* (boy) ~~~~~.

Usted es brasileño. (*o* for boy.)

43 *Usted* (girl) ~~~~~.

Usted es brasileña. (*a* for girl.)

44 *Ustedes* (girls) ~~~~~.

Ustedes son brasileñas. (*s* for plural; *a* for girls.)

45 *Ustedes* (boys) ~~~~~.

Ustedes son brasileños. (*s* for plural; *o* for boys.)

46 *Ustedes* (any combination of boys and girls as: boys and girls; boys and girl; boy and girls; boy and girl) ~~~~~.

Ustedes son brasileños. (*s* for plural; *o* for boys and girls or any combination of the two.)   **47** Translate: We are from Bogotá.

Somos de Bogotá. (You may omit the *nosotros*.)

48 The present tense forms of *ser* are very irregular. Let's see if you now know them all. The subject pronouns *usted*, *él*, and *ella* combine with ~~~~~.

es   **49** *Ustedes*, *ellos*, and *ellas* combine with ~~~~~.

son   **50** The forms that go with *yo* and *nosotros* are ~~~~~.

soy; somos   **51** *Tú* combines with ~~~~~.

eres

New Vocabulary

Study all of your adjectives of nationality changing the final *o* to *a*, the form used when referring to a girl or lady from that country.

malo   bad

When the Spanish speakers came to their part of the New World, they came as conquering armies. For a long time no Spanish women came to the New World and, as a result, the soldiers who stayed often married Indian women and their children had a mixture of Spanish and Indian blood. In many countries of Latin America today the majority of the people have some Indian blood.

   In contrast, when the early settlers came to the United States they brought their families with them and, as you already know, they drove the Indians off their lands. Because the Indians continued to fight the settlers until late in the 19th century there was almost no intermarriage between the two groups until the present century.

PROGRAM **31**

e-Verbs and Learning by Sets

Part 1: A New Verb Form

1 Spanish verb forms are made up of three parts or morphemes: the *stem* and two ⌇⌇⌇⌇.

suffixes

2 Which part gives the meaning of the verb, tells *what* the action is?

the stem

3 The first suffix tells ⌇⌇⌇⌇ the action takes place.

when (present or past)

4 The second suffix tells *who*, that is, it indicates either the person or ⌇⌇⌇⌇ of the subject.

number (The second suffix always shows number, singular or plural, but not always the person.)

5 The three sets of verbs in Spanish are shown by the vowel which comes before the infinitive marker *r*. These vowels are ⌇⌇⌇⌇.

a, e, i

6 In the infinitive forms, the set markers *a*, *e*, and *i* (a) have meaning of their own (b) have no meaning by themselves.

have no meaning by themselves (These are just forms inherited from Latin.)

7 The forms of the second suffix are the same for the present tense of all regular verbs. (a) true (b) false

true

8 The first suffix of the present tense of *a*-verbs (*trabajar*, *hablar*) has only two forms. They are the vowels ⌇⌇⌇⌇.

o; a

9 The stem of *leer* (to read) is *le*. To what verb set does *leer* belong?

e-set

10 The *yo*-form of the present tense of all regular verbs of all sets ends in *o*. The first suffix of the present tense of *e*-verbs has two forms or morphemes. They are ⌇⌇⌇⌇.

o; e

11 Copy and add the first suffix to these forms: *yo le ...*, *usted le ...*, *él le ...*, *ella le ...* .

yo leo, usted lee, él lee, ella lee

12 Copy and add the first and second suffix to these forms: *nosotros le ...*, *ustedes le ...*, *ellos le ...*, *ellas le ...* .

nosotros leemos, ustedes leen, ellos leen, ellas leen

13 Let's see exactly how much you have had to learn to know all the forms of a new verb set. You learned the meaning of *leer*. It is "to ⌇⌇⌇⌇."

read

14 The stem is ⌇⌇⌇⌇.

le

15 The first suffix is *o* from the *yo*-form and ⌇⌇⌇⌇ for all the rest of the forms.

e (And that is all you have had to learn because the second suffixes are the same as those used with *a*-verbs.)

16 You are now going to learn another *e*-verb. It is *comer* (to eat). The cognate is "comestible" (edible). Say it aloud: *co-mer*. The stem of *leer* is *le*. The stem of *comer* is ⌇⌇⌇⌇.

com

17 To change *leemos* (we read) to "we eat" you replace the stem *le* with ⌇⌇⌇⌇ and you have ⌇⌇⌇⌇.

com and you have *comemos*

18 Change *leen* to "they eat."

comen (*Ellos* may be omitted in speech when the subject is already known.)

19 Change *leo* to "I eat."

como

20 You already know that the way a verb form is divided into morphemes is not the way it is divided into syllables in speech. Here are the present tense forms of *comer* divided into syllables. The indicated syllable is stressed. Say them aloud and, remember, no schwa sound. Notice that the forms in the first column have no second suffix.

yo *co*-mo	tú *co*-mes
usted *co*-me	nosotros co-*me*-mos
él *co*-me	nosotras co-*me*-mos
ella *co*-me	ustedes *co*-men
	ellos *co*-men
	ellas *co*-men

Part 2: Learning by Sets

1 You have just learned that all regular *e*-verbs belong to a set which has the same forms (morphemes) for the first and second suffix in the present tense. Because all members of a set behave alike, you can now make up the present tense forms for all the regular *e*-verbs in the entire Spanish language. Let's see how this works. Here is another regular *e*-verb, *vender*, "to sell." Its stem is ⁓.

vend

2 Write the forms for "I sell" and "we sell."

vendo; vendemos

3 The verb *temer* is regular and translates "to fear." The stem is ⁓.

tem

4 Write the form that goes with *ustedes*.

temen

5 Change *temen* so it agrees with *tú*.

temes

6 "To drink" is translated by the regular *e*-verb *beber*. Write the form that agrees with *yo*.

bebo

7 There are five different forms in the present tense of every regular *e*-verb. If you learn 100 new *e*-verbs and all their forms *one by one*, how many separate forms must you learn? ⁓

500

8 Which is harder? (a) to learn *how* to make the forms for the whole set (b) to learn 500 forms *one by one*

to learn 500 forms one by one

9 You know all the subject pronouns. You also know all the forms of both the first and second suffix of the present tense of *e*-verbs. To learn a new *e*-verb you only have to learn the ⁓ and its meaning.

stem

10 The stem of the *e*-verb *correr* is ⁓.

corr

11 The stem *corr* describes the action of using one's feet to move very rapidly from one place to another. How do you say "we run" in Spanish?

corremos

12 Everything you learn is learned more easily and remembered longer when you know the set to which it belongs. Here is a different kind of set for you to practice on. When we say, "He eats too much," does *too much* describe (a) the *manner* of eating? (b) the *amount* of food eaten?

the amount of food eaten

13 Look at the indicated parts of these sentences: (1) He eats *too much*. (2) He eats *too rapidly*. Do these two adverbs belong to the same set?

no (*Too much* deals with amount; *too rapidly* describes speed.)

14 The notion of "amount" covers many different degrees of amount. Do *too much*, *a lot*, *very little*, and *a little* belong to the same set?

yes (They all describe different degrees of amount.)

15 The notion of amount covers a scale in which every specific amount must either be smaller or larger than any other specific amount. Which is larger? (a) too much (b) a lot

too much (He eats *a lot*, but not *too much*.)

16 On the amount scale, what is the opposite of *a little*?

a lot   **17** Which is smaller? (a) a little (b) very little

very little (He reads *a little*; He reads *very little*.)

18 When you know what a set deals with, you understand the meaning of the words which belong to that set better. (a) true (b) false

true   **19** Here are three Spanish words that deal with amount. They are arranged in their degree order, that is, from small to large: *poco*, *mucho*, *demasiado*. Match them with: a little, a lot, too much.

a little—*poco*, a lot—*mucho*, too much—*demasiado*

20 Does knowing what the set deals with make learning the Spanish words for the set easier?

yes (You really do not know the meaning of a word until you know the set to which it belongs.)

21 Translate: She eats too much.

(*Ella*) *come demasiado*.

22 Which sentence describes a person who does <u>not</u> read a great deal? (a) *Lee demasiado*. (b) *Lee mucho*. (c) *Lee poco*.

Lee poco.   **23** Do *poco* and *mucho* belong to the same set as *bien* and *mal*?

no   **24** Which sentence describes the <u>manner</u> in which the action is performed? (a) *José lee poco*. (b) *José lee bien*.

José lee bien tells you <u>how</u> he reads. *José lee poco* tells you <u>how much</u> he reads.   **25** The opposite of *bien* is ⌇⌇⌇.

mal   **26** *Bien* and *mal* stand for degrees on a scale. The adverb *bastante* is used to increase the degree of either *bien* or *mal*. It is put just before these words. Translate: *José* reads quite well.

José lee bastante bien.

27 The opposite of *José lee bastante bien* is *José lee* ⌇⌇⌇.

bastante mal   **28** Every word belongs to two very different kinds of sets. One set deals with what the word stands for. The other set deals with the linguistic class of the word. Copy the words which belong to the set that stands for <u>actions</u>. *José lee bastante bien; Tú comes mucho*.

lee; comes   **29** Do these two words belong to the linguistic set called "verbs"?

yes   **30** The words *leer* and *comer* belong to two sets. One set deals with reality and actions. The other set deals with the form and function of the word. (a) true (b) false

true

31 The words *leer* and *comer* actually belong to three sets: (1) They stand for actions, (2) they have suffixes which classify them as verbs, and (3) they belong to a special set of verbs (a sub-set) whose first suffix in the present tense can only be the morphemes (vowels) ⌇⌇⌇.

o or *e*

No new vocabulary.

PROGRAM 32

Preparing for an Oral Reading Quiz

In your next class session you are going to have a reading quiz. The purpose of this Program is to remind you of all those things you need to remember in order to read aloud like a Spanish speaker.

1 First, let's answer the question, "Why should you learn to read aloud in Spanish?" Do you spend very much time reading aloud in English?

no (So why spend a lot of time learning to do this in Spanish?)

2 Wouldn't it be considered peculiar if you could not read this sentence aloud in English?

yes (One mark of the educated and literate person is the ability to read aloud in any language he can speak.)

3 Think of the number of minutes you spend in your Spanish class each week. Now make a guess about how many Spanish words you have learned so far. 100? 200? 300? 400? 500?

So far you have been taught about 235 words and forms. Now consider this.
It took about 100 different words just to write this Program up to the end of the last sentence.

4 Before you can learn to talk in Spanish about all the things you talk about in English, you will have to learn *many thousands* of Spanish words. Will there be enough time to hear, learn, and practice all these words in class?

no (So the time must come when you will have to learn a lot of new words by reading outside of class.)

5 Let us suppose you are reading Spanish and you come across the word *ejercicio*. You do not know what it means. So you look it up in the dictionary and get its translation: "exercise." Can you now make *ejercicio* part of your speaking vocabulary if you cannot read it aloud?

no (Now you know why you are practicing how to read aloud in Spanish.
So you can very soon learn to say new words that you have not heard before.)

6 Your teacher cannot help you learn to say new words correctly without knowing what kinds of mistakes you are still making. The purpose of the quiz you are going to have is to discover these mistakes. You will be asked to read aloud something you have never seen or heard before. However, this time there will be no new words, no new forms, and no old verbs with new meanings. Will you be able to understand what you read?

yes **7** You have never heard or seen this sentence. Read it aloud and then translate it mentally: *Miguel es de Buenos Aires, pero hoy está en Montevideo.*

Miguel is from Buenos Aires, but today he is in Montevideo.

8 There are spaces between the words in the clause *Miguel es de Buenos Aires.* Should there be any pauses between these words when you read the clause aloud?

no (You read it like one long word: *Miguelesdebuenosaires.*)

9 Here is the way *Buenos Aires* is divided into syllables when you read it aloud. The stressed syllable is indicated. Read this aloud: *Bue-no-sai-res.* The *s* of *Buenos* goes with the *ai* of *aires.*

10 This is the way to say *Miguel es de: Mi-gue-les-de.* Say this aloud. The *l* of *Miguel* goes with the verb *es.*

11 Now practice saying the following until it all comes out as one long word: *Mi-gue-les-de-bue-no-sai-res.*

12 Say "red ants" in English. Can we run these words together the way Spanish words are run together? Say *redants.* Does this sound like "red ants"?

no (We sometimes run words together; for example, *gonna.*)

13 Say *Whatchaduin?* until you understand it. Then write it out the standard way.

What are you doing?

14 Spanish, unlike English, always runs the words of a phrase or breath group together in one long word. So *¿Es él un alumno?* is resyllabicated in speech as *¿E-se-lu-na-lum-no?* Now say this aloud: *¿Eselunalumno?*

15 The way words are spaced in writing does not tell you how they are said in speech. Do the letters in the words always tell you what sound to make?

no (If you wrote "yes" on your answer sheet, say this word aloud: [rreló]. It is spelled *reloj*.)

16 Does the letter *r* at the beginning of a word always stand for the sound [rr]?

yes **17** You see the letter *h* in a Spanish word. Do you make a sound for it?

no **18** The word "honor" is spelled and means the same in both English and Spanish. Say it in English and Spanish. Now say: *hola, hasta, hoy, hora.*

19 You see the letter *d* in a word. Will it tell you, all by itself, what sound to make?

no (If you wrote "yes," study the next frames very carefully.)

20 When the difference between *two words* having *two different meanings* is marked only by a contrast between *two sounds*, these contrasting sounds are called *phonemes* (sounds that mark meaning).

The two contrasting phonemes of *dos* and *los* are written ⌣⌣⌣.

d; l **21** In "telephone" and "phoneme" the part *phone* is the Greek for "sound." The *eme* of phon*eme* is the Greek for "meaning." Does the word *dos* have the same meaning for a Spanish speaker in these two utterances? (1) *¡Dos libros!* (2) *¡Los dos libros!*

yes **22** Is the [d] sound of *¡Dos libros!* a (a) stop or a (b) fricative?

a stop (Because it comes after silence.)

23 Is the [d] sound of *¡Los dos libros!* also a stop?

no (Except after *n* or *l*, it is always a fricative inside a word.)

24 Does *dos*, spoken with a fricative [d], and *dos*, spoken with a stop [d], signal the same meaning in Spanish?

yes   **25** Can two different sounds mark the same meaning in the same word?

yes   **26** When a phoneme has two different sounds, these sounds are said to be *allophones* (other sounds) of that phoneme. The Spanish phoneme /d/ has two allophones, a stop and a fricative. Does the letter *d* stand for either allophone?

yes   **27** The letter *d* stands for two allophones. Will this letter, all by itself, tell you what sound to make when you read aloud?

no   **28** What will tell you which allophone to make? What comes ﹏﹏ the [d] sound.

before   **29** Say ¿*De España?* aloud. When a pause (silence) comes before the phoneme /d/, the allophone you say is (a) a stop (b) a fricative.

a stop   **30** Say *el día* and *en dónde* aloud. When the sound [l] or [n] comes before the phoneme /d/, the allophone you make is (a) a stop (b) a fricative.

a stop   **31** When the phoneme /d/ does not follow silence, [n] or [l], you always make the ﹏﹏ allophone.

fricative   **32** Copy and underline the two fricative [d]'s: *Donaldo, ¿cuándo va usted? ¿Los domingos?*

*Donaldo, ¿ cuándo va uste**d**? ¿ Los **d**omingos?*

33 Does the Spanish phoneme /p/ have two allophones?

no   **34** Hold the back of your hand near your lips and say "paper." Do you feel the puff of the aspirated [p]?

yes   **35** Test yourself now. Can you say *papel* with no puff at all? Practice until you feel no puff. Remember: Spanish [p] is always unaspirated.

36 Do the letters *b* and *v* stand for two different phonemes in Spanish?

no (They stand for the same phoneme in standard Spanish.)

37 Now be careful. Do both *b* and *v* stand for two different sounds in Spanish?

yes (For two allophones of the same phoneme /b/.)

38 Say *ventana* and *Bolivia* aloud. After a pause or silence, either *v* or *b* stands for the same sound. This allophone is (a) a stop (b) a fricative.

a stop   **39** You say *Bolivia* and *en Bolivia* with a stop [b]. What happens when you say *de Bolivia* or *una ventana?* Both sounds are now ﹏﹏.

fricatives (When any phoneme, except /n/ or /m/, comes before *b* or *v*, they stand for the fricative allophone.)

40 Say these two questions aloud: (*v* is fricative) ¿*A dónde vas?*; (*v* is a stop) ¿*Vas a dónde?*

41 Speakers of English frequently make two kinds of mistakes in saying Spanish vowels. When the vowel is in an unstressed syllable, they often substitute a sound called ﹏﹏.

schwa (Say *buenos días* without schwa.)

42 When a vowel is the last sound in a word, as in *de*, English speakers tend to substitute two sounds (a complex vowel) and make *de* sound like English ﹏﹏.

day   **43** Say English "to" and Spanish *tú* until you are certain you can hear the difference and can say *tú* with just one vowel sound.

44 You have never read these sentences before. Say them aloud. They are like the ones you will read for the test.

Roberto le dice buenas noches a Pilar.

El número de días en una semana es siete.

En un mes hay cuatro semanas.

Hay veinte sillas en la clase.

¿Cuántas horas hay en un día?

Brasilia y Asunción son ciudades.

Si yo soy de Chile, ¿qué soy?

44 If you want to practice more for the test, read aloud everything you have already read in your Programs and *Ejercicios*.

No new vocabulary.

A major difference between Hispanic and American culture developed from the fact that the Indians in Latin America were mostly farmers who lived in one place while almost all the Indians in the United States were hunters who moved about in search of game. When the early Americans came, they drove the Indians from their lands so that they could be farmed; and after the Indian wars of the last century, most of the tribes were forced to live on reservations. Today there are still many tribes which live on reservations and have a culture which is still Indian, not modern American.

PROGRAM **33**

Getting Ready for a Test

Many students think a test is just a means of helping the teacher make out a grade. In a programed course of study tests are designed primarily to help the teacher find out how to make learning less confusing for you. Every major exam in this course actually tests you, your teacher, and the course program. In other words, a test shows (1) how much *you* have learned *by your own efforts*, (2) how well *you are being taught* in the class, and (3) *the efficiency* of the course materials (your Programs, *etc.*).

Since tests are designed to discover what needs to be changed (your study habits, classroom procedures, or the course materials), the test results will be useless if you make mechanical errors, if you fail to understand what you are to do, or if you do not prepare yourself properly for the test.

You can help yourself by helping your teacher. Do this Program carefully. Be sure you do *not* look at the answers *before* you have tried to think of them. If you make a mistake, study the frame carefully. This Program reviews *everything* you are going to have on the test.

1 Part A: On your answer sheet you will find a column of spaces numbered 1 to 10. For each number you will hear a statement in Spanish. For example: *Los* *gauchos son de Argentina.* You will then be asked a question in English. "Where are gauchos from?" Write your answer, in English, in three words or less.

Either "from Argentina" or "Argentina" is correct.

2 Here is another example: *Ayer fue lunes.* What day is today? (You answer with the day after *lunes.*)

Tuesday

3 Part B is labeled, on your answer sheet, *Numbers.* There are five blank spaces numbered 11 to 15. You will hear a number. You write the Arabic numeral for it. For example: *once* ⁓⁓⁓ ; *trece* ⁓⁓⁓ .

11; 13

4 Part C is labeled *Math Problems.* You will hear an equation: *Veinte menos siete son trece.* You write this in Arabic numbers: ⁓⁓⁓ .

$20 - 7 = 13$

5 In English equations you use "is" or "are." In Spanish you are to use ⁓⁓⁓ .

son

6 When you add, the question word is (a) *¿Cuánto son dos y tres?* (b) *¿Cuántos son dos y tres?*

Cuántos

7 What do you put in place of *y* to change this to subtraction? *¿Cuántos son siete y cuatro?*

menos (*¿Cuántos son nueve* **menos** *siete?*)

8 What words in equations, except *cuántos,* cue subtraction and addition?

subtraction: *menos* (minus); addition: *y* (plus)

9 Part D is labeled *Matching words and pictures* on your answer sheet. There will be some pictures on the board with a capital letter under each. You will hear a statement or a question once. You are to match what you hear with the picture that is *most* logically related.

For example, you see a lake, a dark cloud, and a pencil, lettered A, B, and C respectively. You will hear: "It is broken." You write the letter ⁓⁓⁓ after the question number.

C for pencil (Pencils get broken; lakes and clouds do not.)

10 You see a car, a pig, and an apple, lettered A, B, and C. You hear: "Do you need gasoline?" You write the letter ⁓⁓⁓ after the question number.

A (Pigs and apples are not logically associated with gasoline.)

11 Now try this in Spanish. You see *una puerta,* *una pluma,* and *una muchacha* lettered A, B, and C. You hear: *Ella es de Perú.* You write the letter ⁓⁓⁓ after the question number.

C (Because subject pronouns can only stand for people.)

12 In Part E there are 12 numbers each followed by the letters a, b, and c. These letters will also be on the board. You will hear a question and then, as the teacher points to the letters, you will hear three answers. You wait until you have heard the entire problem twice and, then, draw a circle around the letter for the best or most logical answer. For example:

Question: *¿De dónde son los elefantes?*
Answers: **a** *Son de la escuela.*
           b *Son de California.*
           c *Son de India.*
You circle ⁓⁓⁓ .

ⓒ

13 Question: *¿Quién está en la clase?*
Answers: **a** *El tigre.*   **b** *El gaucho.*   **c** *La profesora.*
You circle ⁓⁓⁓ .

ⓒ

14 Part F deals with adjective and noun agreement. You will see six sentences with a blank space at the end of the adjective. For example: *Son chilen* . . . You will hear: *María y José son de Chile* and the question: *¿Qué son?* You fill in the blank with ――.

os (*Son chilenos*. You use the *o*-form for a boy and a girl.)

15 When you talk about people, adjectives of nationality and nouns agree in ―― and gender.

number

16 When you talk about people, the phoneme /o/ stands for ――; /a/ stands for ――.

/o/ for males; /a/ for females

17 Rewrite this sentence so it talks about females: *Ellos son bolivianos.*

Ellas son bolivianas.

18 Part G deals with verb forms. Here are the verbs for which you should know all present tense forms. See *Ejercicios* 69–72 for a model of all the forms.

estar	hablar	necesitar	trabajar	leer
ser	desear	estudiar	esperar	comer

Here are single forms you should know.

vas	tengo	hay	piensa	dice	siga
voy	fue	venga	tienes	hace	

This part of the test is like a pattern drill. You will hear a model: *María está en la clase.* Then a new subject: *Tú.* You circle the form that matches the new subject: *estoy, están, estás, estamos.*

(estás)

19 Part H will test your ability to spot the cues which tell you to use *haber, ser,* or *estar.* This and the next six frames review the cues. Origin is expressed by *de,* the name of a place, and the verb ――.

ser (*Jesús es de Quito.*)

20 When you talk of a person's state of health or well being, you use an adverb (*bien, mal, etc.*) and ――.

estar (*Estoy bien, gracias.*)

21 To say that two numbers or two things are equal, you use ――.

ser (*José es un alumno; Dos y dos son cuatro.*)

22 The indefinite article, public and private numbers, and a plural noun suffix make up a set that cues the use of ―― for location.

haber (*Hay un libro en la mesa; Hay libros en la mesa; Hay dos libros en la mesa.*)

23 Is *ser* used to locate an entity?

no

24 The definite article, unmodified proper names, and the subject pronouns cue the use of ―― for location.

estar

25 When the subject is described by an adjective of nationality, you use ――.

ser (*Malvina es ecuatoriana.*)

26 In the part of the test on *haber, ser,* and *estar,* there are ten numbers each followed by *hay es está.* You will hear a sentence in English using some form of "to be"; for example: "Leonor is a teacher." You circle ―― to show which verb to use.

(es)

27 Part I is to discover whether you recognize the written cues which tell you to say [r], a single flap, or [rr], a multiple flap. The letter *r* always stands for a multiple flap when it ―― a word.

begins (*reloj, regla, etc.*)

28 When *r* comes between vowels, it always stands for (a) a single flap (b) a multiple flap.

a single flap **29** Copy and underline the *r*'s which stand for [rr] and circle those which stand for [r]: *El señor Rodín es un hombre rico.*

El seño(r) Rodín es un homb(r)e ̲rico.

30 In Part J you must recognize the written cues for stop and fricative [b] sounds (written *b* or *v*). After a pause or silence you say a (a) stop (b) fricative.

stop (*¿Vas a la clase?*) **31** On your test there will be a sentence in Spanish. You are to circle the stop [b]'s and underline the fricative [b]'s. The letter you see may be *b* or *v*. Here's an example for you to practice: *Hay veinte hombres que también saben hacerlo. ¿Verdad?*

Hay ̲veinte hom(b)res que tam(b)ién sa̲ben hacerlo. ¿(V)erdad?

32 After /n/ or /m/ you say a (a) stop (b) fricative.

stop (After all other phonemes you say a fricative.) **33** Part K will test your ability to read for meaning. On your answer sheet there are five incomplete sentences and for each, four choices to complete them. You are to pick the best and *most logical* choice. For example:

En la clase hay . . .
a cuatro tigres.
b una montaña.
c treinta alumnos.
d dos países.
You circle letter ⁓⁓.

ⓒ (*En la clase hay treinta alumnos.*) **34** Part L, the final section, also deals with reading for meaning. You are to match a statement or question with its most sensible or logical reaction. For example:

¿Necesita usted un lápiz?
a Sí, soy de La Paz.
b Sí, tengo que comer.
c No, hablo español.
d Sí, gracias.
You circle letter ⁓⁓.

ⓓ

New Vocabulary

leer	to read	**mucho**	a lot
comer	to eat	**poco**	a little
demasiado	too much	**bastante**	enough
bastante bien	pretty well	**bastante mal**	pretty poorly

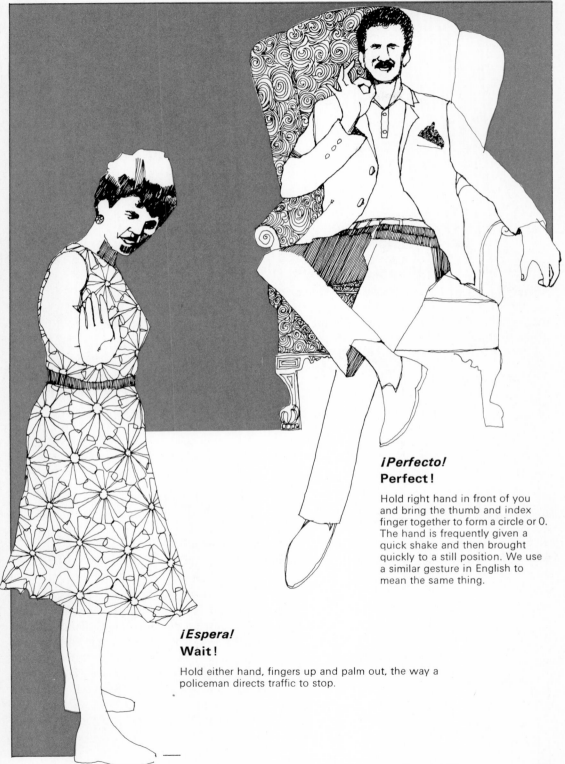

¡Perfecto!
Perfect!

Hold right hand in front of you and bring the thumb and index finger together to form a circle or 0. The hand is frequently given a quick shake and then brought quickly to a still position. We use a similar gesture in English to mean the same thing.

¡Espera!
Wait!

Hold either hand, fingers up and palm out, the way a policeman directs traffic to stop.

Ejercicios

Ejercicio 1 | Stop [b] and Fricative [b̞]: Reading Aloud

1 va / iba		**6** bien / Estoy bien.
2 be / ive		**7** bien / Muy bien.
3 vi / ibi		**8** ventana / una ventana
4 bo / ivo		**9** ventana / la ventana
5 vu / ibu		**10** veinte / las veinte ventanas

Ejercicio 2 | [r] and [rr]: Reading Aloud

Remember always to *try* to make these sounds no matter how unsuccessful you are. At least you will be getting practice in the right direction. *Never* substitute the English sound that these letters represent or you will never learn proper pronunciation.

1 puerta / tres	**7** rosa / zorra	**13** ere / erre
2 árbol / Brasil	**8** roca / corra	**14** era / erra
3 Vargas / gracias	**9** rana / narra	**15** pero / perro
4 tarde / grande	**10** ropa / porra	**16** pera / perra
5 martes / frío	**11** roba / borra	**17** caro / carro
6 miércoles / creo	**12** rabo / barro	**18** fiero / fierro

Ejercicio 3 | Reading Aloud

Always remember to use the pronunciation that you have been learning. It is easy to forget and let your English habits interfere.

En la oficina

(1) En la oficina de la escuela hay dos alumnos: un muchacho y una muchacha. (2) El muchacho se llama José y es de Santiago de Chile. (3) Él habla español y desea estudiar inglés. (4) La muchacha se llama Luisa y trabaja en la oficina del director. (5) Ella habla inglés y un poquito de español. (6) Estudia español en la clase de la señora Navarro que es una profesora muy buena. (7) José tiene que hablar con el señor Moreno, el director de la escuela. (8) El señor Moreno es de California y habla inglés y español muy bien. (9) Él es un director muy bueno y un señor muy amable. (10) Luisa y José están en la oficina; necesitan hablar con el señor Moreno.

Ejercicio 4 | Reading Cues for Stop and Fricative [d] and [b]

Number a column from 1 to 22. Write *f* (for fricative) or *s* (stop) after each number to identify the sound represented by *d* or *b*.

          1   **2**
En la oficina de la escuela hay dos alumnos: un muchacho y una muchacha.
                  3   **4**   **5**
El muchacho se llama José y es de Santiago de Chile. Él habla español y desea
  6   **7**   **8 9**
estudiar inglés. La muchacha se llama Luisa y trabaja en la oficina del director.
             10   **11**
Ella habla inglés y un poquito de español. Estudia español en la clase de la
      12   **13**   **14**
señora Navarro que es una profesora muy buena. José tiene que hablar con el
     15   **16**   **17**
señor Moreno, el director de la escuela. El señor Moreno es de California y
  18   **19**   **20**   **21**
habla inglés y español muy bien. Él es un director muy bueno y un señor muy
  22
amable.

Ejercicio 5 | Reading Aloud

Don't forget to use your new Spanish habits, forget your old English ones.

1 Hay treinta pupitres y tres pizarras en la clase.
2 Una señorita amable dice perdón y gracias.
3 Hoy es viernes y anteayer fue miércoles.
4 Deseo hablar con la profesora y con el director.
5 El nuevo alumno tiene un libro muy bueno.
6 ¿De dónde son ustedes? ¿De Bolivia?
7 Margarita, dile buenos días a Roberto.

Ejercicio 6 | Reading Cues for *d, b, r, rr,* and Vowels

boda / una boda   debe / rumbo
burro / un burro   adobe / ronda
broma / una broma   roba / Dora
duro / un duro   borra / beber
drama / un drama   red / dudar
¿Dónde vive el burro?   Donaldo tiene un cuaderno y un libro.

Ejercicio 7 | Noun and Verb Agreement

Your teacher will give you four numbers, corresponding to an item from each column. Write out each sentence making all the necessary agreements.

Ejemplo: 2314 = La señora trabaja aquí.

1 El	**1** muchach-	**1** trabaj-	**1** en la clase.
2 La	**2** alumn-	**2** estudi-	**2** en la escuela.
3 Los	**3** señor-	**3** habl-	**3** allí.
4 Las	**4** profesor-		**4** aquí.

Ejercicio 8 | Noun and Verb Agreement

Write out the combinations your teacher gives you. Don't forget the accent marks in certain forms of *estar*.

Ejemplo: 4212 = Las alumnas están en la escuela.

1 El	**1** muchach-	**1** est-	**1** en la clase.
2 La	**2** alumn-	**2** trabaj-	**2** en la escuela.
3 Los	**3** señor-	**3** estudi-	**3** allí.
4 Las	**4** profesor-	**4** habl-	**4** aquí.

Ejercicio 9 | Location, Identification and Spelling of South American Cities and Countries

Use the map on page 103.

On a separate sheet of paper, number a column from **1** to **10**. Follow this by a second column lettered from **a** through **j**. Write the names of countries after the numbers and their capitals after the letters as indicated on the map.

Ejemplo: **1** Brasil   **a** Brasilia

Ejercicio 10 | *Ser* and Adjectives of Nationality

There are several things for you to remember in this exercise. Be sure to use the correct form of the verb *ser*. Make all adjectives of nationality agree with the subject, and don't forget that when you use *Yo* the adjective will end in *a* if you are a girl and end in *o* if you are a boy.

Write out the combinations as your teacher gives them.

Ejemplo: 32 = Enrique y tú son argentinos.

1 Paco		**1** bolivian-
2 Él y yo		**2** argentin-
3 Enrique y tú		**3** chilen-
4 Yo	ser	**4** uruguay-
5 María y Alicia		**5** ecuatorian-
6 Tú (*f*)		**6** venezolan-

Ejercicio 11 | Translating "to be": *haber* and *estar* for Location

a It is necessary to learn when to use *haber* and *estar*, otherwise, you may send a message you don't intend to send. They are both used in sentences that locate things and people. For example:

Hay una silla (señorita) aquí.
La silla (señorita) está aquí.

b *Hay* is from *haber*. It is frequently translated "is, are, there is, there are." It always is used in the third person. The label for what is being located normally follows the verb.

Hay un gaucho en el rodeo.
Hay gauchos en el rodeo.

c *Haber* (*hay*) is used to locate entities that combine with:

1 *un* or *una:*
Hay un muchacho en la oficina.
Hay una muchacha en la oficina.
2 nothing (zero):
Hay muchachos en la oficina.
Hay papel en la mesa.
3 public and private numbers:
Hay tres ventanas allí.
Hay muchas ventanas allí.

d *Estar* is used to locate entities when they are expressed by:

1 a proper noun:
María está en España.
Pancho está en la escuela.
2 nouns that combine with *el*, *los*, *la*, and *las:*
El señor está en Chile.
Las plumas están allí.
3 subject pronouns:
Yo estoy en Ecuador.
Ellos están en Paraguay.

e You will find some combinations between **c** and **d** above, in which case the articles (*un, una, el, los, la, las*), and zero (with plural proper nouns) take precedence. For example:

1 *Hay tres lápices en el pupitre.*
But: *Los tres lápices están en el pupitre.*
2 *María está en la oficina.*
But: *Hay una María en la oficina.*
¿Hay Marías en está clase?

Practice

A Cover the answers on the right. Check your answers immediately after working each problem.

1 What two Spanish verbs are used to locate things and people? *estar, haber*
2 Which verb is translated frequently by "there is" and "there are," *hay* or *está?* *hay*
3 Which verb combines with the indefinite article (*un* or *una*) and numbers? *haber*
4 Which verb combines with the definite article (*el*, *los*, *la*, and *las*)? *estar*
5 When both the definite article and a number combine with a noun, which verb is used for location? *estar*
6 Which verb combines with an unmodified proper noun? *estar*
7 If a proper noun is preceded by *un* or *una* or if it is plural, which verb is used for location? *haber*
8 Which verb combines with subject pronouns? *estar*
9 Which verb combines with zero? *haber*
10 Does *hay* usually precede or follow its object? precede

B Choose *hay*, *está* or *están* for the following blanks:

1 Ella . . . en Ecuador. está
2 Pancho y María . . . en España. están
3 . . . cinco profesores en la familia. Hay
4 ¿. . . el profesor en la oficina? Está
5 ¿. . . una señorita en la oficina? Hay
6 ¿. . . Pancho en la escuela? Está
7 Sí, . . . tres Panchos en la escuela. hay
8 En la clase . . . un profesor. hay
9 El radio . . . en la mesa. está
10 ¿. . . diez papeles aquí? Hay
11 Sí, los diez papeles . . . allí en el pupitre. están
12 Ellas no . . . aquí hoy. están
13 . . . muchos libros en la cafetería. Hay
14 Los tres Panchos . . . en la clase de inglés. están

C Choose *un*, *una*, *el*, *los*, *la*, *las* or zero for the following blanks:

1 Hay . . . lápiz allí. un
2 . . . oficina y . . . clase están allí. La, la
3 Hay . . . pizarras en la oficina también. zero
4 ¿Está . . . señor en la capital? el
5 . . . reloj está en la mesa de la cafetería. El
6 ¿Hay . . . papel en esta mesa? un (*or* zero)
7 ¿Dónde hay . . . plumas? zero
8 ¿Dónde están . . . papeles? los

Ejercicio 12 | Translating "to be": *estar* for Health; *ser* for Origin and Equation

a Review the uses of *estar* and *haber* in Ejercicio 11. More practice is included here.

b *Estar* is used in sentences that talk about one's state of health. For example:
¿Cómo estás, Paco?
Yo estoy bien, gracias.

c *Ser* is used in sentences that tell where someone or something comes from (origin). For example:
El libro es de España.
¿De dónde es usted?
Yo soy de Chile.

d *Ser* is used in sentences as a link between two items to show that they are equal. For example:
Esta es una luz. (*Esta = luz*)
Cuatro y dos son seis. (4 + 2 = 6)
Ella es alumna. (*Ella = alumna*)

Practice

Cover the answers on the right. Check your answer immediately after working each problem.

A Which verb is used:

1 in sentences that locate things and people?	estar *or* haber
2 to make equations?	ser
3 when discussing one's state of health?	estar
4 when locating something that combines with the indefinite article?	haber
5 when indicating the origin of someone?	ser
6 in a sentence locating a person labeled by a subject pronoun?	estar
7 in addition and subtraction problems?	ser

B Choose *es, son, está,* or *están* for the following blanks:

1 La señorita . . . de Ecuador.	es
2 Las dos reglas . . . en el pupitre.	están
3 Este . . . el señor López.	es
4 Cinco y cinco . . . diez.	son
5 El alumno no . . . bien, hoy.	está
6 El alumno no . . . en la escuela hoy.	está
7 El alumno . . . de Argentina.	es
8 ¿Qué . . . esto?	es
9 . . . un reloj.	Es
10 Ellas . . . muy bien.	están

c Give in Spanish the infinitive of the verb that would be used in sentences pertaining to the following:

1 location with numbers	haber
2 location with "zero"	haber
3 equations	ser
4 one's state of health	estar
5 origin	ser
6 location of an entity with *el*	estar

D Choose the appropriate form of *ser*, *haber*, or *estar* according to the nature of the sentence:

1 Yo . . . muy bien, gracias.	estoy
2 ¿ . . . usted de Colombia?	Es
3 No, yo . . . de Brasil, pero . . . aquí ahora.	soy, estoy
4 ¿ . . . muchachos de Ecuador aquí? (*Be careful.*)	Hay
5 ¿ . . . aquí el muchacho de Ecuador?	Está
6 ¿ . . . usted de Ecuador?	Es
7 Yo . . . el nuevo profesor.	soy
8 ¿Cuánto . . . cinco menos tres?	son
9 ¿Cuántos diálogos . . . en este libro?	hay
10 . . . pocos diálogos en este libro.	Hay
11 ¿Dónde . . . María y José?	están
12 En la mesa . . . tiza.	hay
13 —¿El profesor ausente? —Sí, no . . . bien hoy.	está
14 Ella . . . una señora muy amable.	es

Ejercicio 13 | Reading Aloud

Remember what you have learned about the pronunciation of the sounds represented by *p*, *d*, *b*, *r*, and *rr*.

1 Hoy es miércoles y hace mucho viento.
2 Pancho va a trabajar en la mina hoy.
3 La mina donde trabaja Pancho es bastante nueva.
4 Él va a la oficina antes de ir a trabajar.
5 El director de la mina está allí en una silla.
6 Los dos señores hablan en español un rato (a while).
7 Pancho le pregunta dónde va a trabajar hoy.
8 El director le contesta que debe preguntarle al señor Romero.
9 Pancho pregunta dónde está ese señor.
10 El director no contesta nada; va a la puerta.
11 Pancho y el director van a donde está Pedro Romero.
12 Pancho es boliviano y su señora es paraguaya.
13 Los dos viven en La Paz, capital de Bolivia.
14 La señora de Pancho se llama Dolores y le dicen Lola.

Ejercicio 14 | Reading Aloud

1 Roberto le dice buenos días a Bárbara.
2 —Buenos días— le dice Bárbara a Roberto.
3 El nombre de esta señorita es Bárbara Delgado.
4 El muchacho se llama Roberto Ramos.
5 Los dos son alumnos de una escuela venezolana.
6 Roberto es de La Paz, Bolivia, pero vive en Caracas.
7 Cuando no hay clases, Roberto va a La Paz.
8 Bárbara es venezolana; es de Caracas.
9 Los dos alumnos estudian inglés en su escuela.
10 Es jueves y hace bastante calor.
11 En la clase donde estudian hay treinta y nueve pupitres.
12 En la clase hay nueve ventanas y dos puertas.
13 La escuela es nueva y el director es un señor muy amable.
14 La escuela está en el centro de la capital de Venezuela.
15 Roberto y Bárbara son muy buenos alumnos. Hablan inglés bastante bien.

Etapa Tres

PROGRAM 34

Telling Time in Spanish

By now you are well aware of the fact that you learn faster, understand better, and remember longer when you know exactly what you are doing while you are learning something new. Let's begin, then, by talking about what you are actually doing when you tell time in English. Knowing this will make learning how to tell time in Spanish a lot easier.

1 A day is a unit or interval of time in our calendar system. Seven days make up a calendar interval called a ⌇⌇.

week (In Spanish: *una semana.*)

2 A day is a fraction ($\frac{1}{7}$) of a week. A week is a fraction ($\frac{1}{4}$) of a ⌇⌇.

month (*un mes*)

3 A month is a fraction ($\frac{1}{12}$) of a larger calendar interval called a ⌇⌇.

year (*un año*)

4 A week is 7 days. A month is 4 weeks or 30 days. A year is 12 months, 52 weeks, or 365 days. In a calendar system each interval of time is a multiple of a smaller interval and, also, a fraction of a larger interval. (a) true (b) false

true

5 The ancient people of Europe learned to make calendars when they discovered that the sun, the moon, and the seasons are like hands on a great, cosmic clock. So they called the time between two full moons a "moon" and the word they used gradually changed until it became "month" in English and *mes* in Spanish. The time between seeing the sun in the same position <u>twice</u> is equal to the time it takes the earth to revolve <u>once</u> on its axis. This calendar interval is a ⌇⌇.

day (*un día*—The word ends in *a* but, as an exception to standard agreement, takes *un* or *el*.)

6 A day, like a month or a year, may be divided into smaller intervals. Three positions of the sun are used to measure these intervals: (1) sunrise, (2) the point at which the sun is highest in the sky, and (3) sunset. The interval between sunset and sunrise is called ⌇⌇.

night (*noche*—the dark part of the day)

7 The point at which the sun is highest in the sky is called ⌇⌇.

noon (*mediodía*—mid-day)

8 The interval between midnight and noon is called ⌇⌇.

morning (*mañana*—This interval is half dark and half light.)

9 The interval between noon and sunset is called ⌇⌇.

afternoon (*tarde*—This interval is all light.)

10 The length of an interval in a calendar is the time *between* two natural or cosmic events. (a) true (b) false

true

11 The words *morning, afternoon, day, week, month,* etc., stand for intervals of calendar time, the time between natural events. There are no easily observed natural events which can be used to divide morning or afternoon into smaller time intervals. To make smaller divisions, man had to invent mechanical substitutes for natural events. The most widely used mechanical substitute for natural events is a ⌇⌇.

clock or watch

12 A clock, like natural events, divides time into fixed intervals. The three common clock intervals are *second*, ―――― and ―――――.

minute; hour **13** Every day, month, and year in a calendar has a special name which indicates its position in a series: *Monday, Tuesday; January, February; 1912, 1960*, etc. Is there a special name for the interval between 2 and 3 o'clock?

no (We simply say that it is an hour.) **14** In a calendar system, each time interval has a special name. In a clock system the intervals do not have special names. Now, be careful. In the sentence, *It is three o'clock*, the number *three* stands for (a) an interval of time (b) a point in time.

a point in time **15** The numbers on the face of a clock stand for the points at which each hour (a) begins (b) ends.

begins **16** We are "lost" in time if we do not know the calendar interval <u>in which</u> we happen to be and the time point <u>at which</u> we are. When we say, *It is three o'clock in the morning*, we use both clock point (three) and calendar interval (morning) to locate ourselves in time. (a) true (b) false

true **17** We can locate ourselves in terms of a clock point in just three ways. We can say we are *at* a point (It is two o'clock), *before* a point (It is fifteen minutes before two), or *after* a point (It is fifteen minutes after two). Look at these sentences:

> It is fifteen minutes to two.　　It is fifteen minutes of two.
> It is fifteen minutes before two.　　It is one forty-five.

Are they all talking about the same clock point?

yes **18** The twelve numbers on the face of the clock mark the beginning of the hours. When we say, *It is one forty-five*, you are (a) adding minutes to the hour (b) subtracting minutes from the hour.

adding minutes (It is 1 plus 45 minutes.) **19** *It is ten minutes to five* subtracts ten from five. How do you say this by adding?

It is four fifty. **20** In *It is four fifty*, the number ―――― stands for the hour point and the number ―――― stands for the minutes.

four for the hour; *fifty* for the minutes **21** Change *It is three forty* to the subtraction equivalent.

"It is 20 minutes to four" or "It is 20 minutes before four." **22** The 12 numbers on a clock mark the points at which each hour begins. When we want to know what hour it is by the clock, we ask, "What ―――― is it?"

time **23** The Spanish speaker, however, asks, *¿Qué hora es?* The noun *hora* is a cognate of the English word ――――.

hour (So the Spanish speaker asks, "What hour is it?") **24** Spanish *hora* ends in the phoneme /a/. What form of the definite and indefinite article will go with it?

la; una **25** The Spanish speaker uses *hora* when he asks, "What time is it?" *¿Qué hora es?* Hundreds of years ago the answer might have been *Es la hora una*. Today the Spanish speaker always drops *hora* in the answer and simply says, *Es la una*. This is translated into English by ――――.

It is one o'clock.

26 In *Es la una* the verb *ser* is third person singular and the form agrees with *una*, a singular number. The third person plural form of *ser* is ⸺.

son

27 Look at *Es la una* (It is one o'clock.). If a Spanish speaker wants to say, "It is two o'clock," he must change *una* to ⸺.

dos

28 To make everything agree in number with *dos* he must also change *Es la una* to ⸺ *dos*.

Son las dos.

29 *Es la una* translates "It is one o'clock." Translate: It is two o'clock.

Son las dos. (*Dos* is a plural number; *son* and *las* agree with it.)

30 English uses only one present tense form of "to be" in telling time. "What time *is* it? It *is* one o'clock. It *is* two o'clock." In Spanish *ser* always agrees in number with the hour. To ask "What hour is it?" the Spanish speaker uses the verb form ⸺.

es (*¿Qué hora es?*)

31 To answer the question *¿Qué hora es?* the Spanish speaker may use either the singular number *una* or 11 other plural numbers: *dos, tres, cuatro, cinco, etc*. With any plural number the form of *ser* is ⸺.

son (*Son las dos, tres, cuatro, etc.*)

32 As in English, the Spanish speaker adds and subtracts minutes in telling time. The Spanish word for the plus sign (+) is ⸺.

y

33 The word for the minus sign (−) is the cognate ⸺.

menos

34 A Spanish speaker has been asked the time. He answers: *Es la una y diez.* Translate his answer.

"It is 1 + 10" or "It is ten minutes after one." (The plus sign *y* is translated as "after.")

35 In English we subtract ten minutes from the following hour (one) in "It is ten to one." We can give the same time by adding 50 minutes to the previous hour (twelve). This gives "It is ⸺."

It is twelve fifty.

36 The Spanish speakers also add minutes to the previous hour and subtract minutes from the following hour but, unlike the English, most Spanish speakers add *only up to 30 minutes*. After the half hour they *subtract* from the following hour. There is, as a result, only one standard Spanish translation for "It is ten to one. It is twelve fifty." The translation subtracts ten from one. It is *Es la una* ⸺ *diez*.

Es la una **menos** diez.

37 The two English translations for *Son las ocho menos veinte* are ⸺.

It is twenty to eight; It is seven forty.

38 One of the most commonly used translations of "It is fifteen to four" and "It is three forty-five" is ⸺.

Son las cuatro **menos** quince.

39 In English you may add 59 minutes to the previous hour (It is ten fifty-nine). In Spanish you may add only ⸺ minutes to the previous hour.

30

40 To translate "It is ten fifty-nine" into Spanish you must change it to "It is one to eleven" and subtract one from eleven. What you get is: *Son las once* ⸺ *uno*.

menos

41 To translate "It is two thirty" you add thirty to two: *Son las dos* ⸺ *treinta*.

Son las dos **y** treinta.

Review: How Much Did You Really Learn?

1 An interval of calendar time has two names. One name gives its position in the calendar series; the other name gives its length. One 24-hour division of the week is called *domingo*. The word in Spanish for the <u>length</u> of this interval is ⁓⁓⁓.

día

2 Do intervals of clock time have two names?

no

3 The numbers on a clock mark points in time. Each of the 12 numbers stands for the point at which the hour (a) begins (b) ends.

begins

4 To tell time we must give the hour number. If the time is not exactly on the hour, we must either ⁓⁓⁓ or ⁓⁓⁓ minutes.

add or subtract

5 English does this with "after" and "before." Spanish does this with the math words

y; menos

6 English asks for the "time." Spanish asks for the ⁓⁓⁓. (Write the Spanish word.)

hora

7 Which form of *ser* do you use in asking for the *hora?*

es (¿Qué hora es?)

8 To say it is 2:50 in Spanish you ⁓⁓⁓ 10 from 3.

subtract *(Son las tres menos diez.)*

9 To say it is 2:10 in Spanish you ⁓⁓⁓ 10 to 2.

add *(Son las dos y diez.)*

10 After what number of minutes do you stop adding and start subtracting from the next hour in Spanish?

30

If you missed more than two of these 10 frames, you have evidence that you are not studying carefully enough.

No new vocabulary.

PROGRAM 35

Regular *i*-Verbs, and Present of *ir*

1 How many parts or morphemes are there in the present tense forms of all verbs?

three

2 The morpheme that stands for the action or state is the ⁓⁓⁓.

stem

3 The infinitive form of a verb always ends in the suffix ⁓⁓⁓.

r

4 The vowel that precedes the infinitive suffix has no meaning. It only marks the ⁓⁓⁓ of the verb.

set (The class or category to which the verb belongs: *a, e,* or *i.*)

5 The set marker (*a, e,* or *i*) tells us what morphemes make up (a) the first suffix (b) the second suffix.

the first suffix

6 Are the second suffix forms the same for *all* sets of verbs?

yes (The *mos, n, s,* and "zero" are the same for all classes of verbs and, with one exception, all tenses.)

7 To learn the forms for a new verb set, you have only to learn the stem and the morphemes of the ⁓⁓⁓ suffix.

first

8 In the present tense all regular *a*-verbs have only two morphemes for the first suffix. They are ⁓⁓⁓.

o; a

9 The two morphemes of the first suffix of regular *e*-verbs are ⁓⁓⁓.

o; e

10 The first suffix of regular *i*-verbs has three morphemes in the present tense. They are *o, e,* and *i.* The *o*-suffix of any verb in the present tense always goes with the subject pronoun ⁓⁓⁓.

yo

11 The infinitive *vivir* is translated by "to live." The stem is *viv.* How do you say "I live in Madrid"? (Before you answer, reread Frame 10.)

Yo vivo en Madrid.

12 The *i*-suffix appears in only one form, the one that goes with *nosotros.* How do you say "We live in Madrid"?

Nosotros vivimos en Madrid. (You may omit *nosotros.*)

13 The *i*-verbs in the present tense have *o* for *yo* and *i* for *nosotros.* All other forms are like *e*-verbs and have *e* for the second suffix. The form that goes with *tú* is ⁓⁓⁓.

vives

14 The form that goes with *él, ella,* and *usted* is ⁓⁓⁓.

vive

15 The form that goes with *ustedes, ellos,* and *ellas* is ⁓⁓⁓.

viven

16 You can now make up all the present tense forms of all the regular *i*-verbs in the Spanish language. You know the second suffix. You must, of course, learn the infinitive and its meaning. You know that the *yo*-form of all regular verbs has *o* for the first suffix. What do you have left to remember? Just *i* for *nosotros* and ⁓⁓⁓ for all other forms.

e

17 Here is an *i*-verb which is an obvious cognate: *admitir.* The stem is ⁓⁓⁓.

admit (The Spanish stem is one form of the English verb.)

18 Copy and add the suffixes. Say the forms aloud in Spanish: *yo admit* ... , *nosotros admit* ... , *ustedes admit* ... .

*yo admit**o**, nosotros admit**imos**, ustedes admit**en***

19 The *i*-verb which translates "to go" is very irregular in Spanish. The infinitive is *ir.* Does *ir* have a stem?

no

20 When an infinitive has no stem, one has to be made up. When the ancient Spaniards did this hundreds of years ago they became confused and mixed up Latin *ire* (to go) and *vadere* (to go quickly), and so today *ir* is treated as though the infinitive were *var,* and the present tense forms of *ir* are like those of *estar.* The form of *estar* that goes with *yo* is ⁓⁓⁓.

estoy

21 The present tense stem of *ir* is *v.* The form that goes with *yo* is ⁓⁓⁓.

voy (All by itself it sounds almost like English "boy.")

22 All other forms of *ir* are also said to be irregular because they take the same first suffix as *a*-verbs. The form that goes with *nosotros* is ⁓⁓⁓.

vamos (Like *estamos.*)

23 To make *vamos* agree with *tú* you replace *mos* with ⁓⁓⁓ and you get *tú* ⁓⁓⁓.

s; vas

24 The form that goes with *usted, él,* and *ella* is ⁓⁓⁓.

va

25 To get the form that goes with *ustedes, ellos,* and *ellas* you add ⌇⌇⌇⌇ to *va*.

n (Ustedes van.)

26 You will have less trouble learning Spanish if you check each new word you meet for "trouble spots" in pronunciation. Which letter in *vas* stands for a "trouble" sound?

v (It stands for a phoneme which has two allophones: a stop and a fricative.)

27 If you say *voy* emphatically, it sounds almost like English "boy." The sound of *v* is a (a) stop (b) fricative.

a stop (When you are not emphatic, the stop is less explosive than the [b] sound of "boy.")

28 Is the sound of *v* also a stop when you say *yo voy* or *tú vas?*

no

29 The stop allophone of /b/ (spelled *b* or *v*) appears only after silence and [m], spelled *n* or *m*. The subject pronouns end in the phonemes /o/, /u/, /l/, /d/, and /s/. When you use the subject pronouns with the forms of *ir*, the sound of *v* will always be a ⌇⌇⌇⌇.

fricative

30 Will what you hear tell you how to spell the present tense forms?

no (Remember: *b* and *v* stand for the same phoneme: You learn to spell words having a *b* of a *v* only by seeing them.)

31 It does not make much sense to learn to say "go" in Spanish unless you also learn more words for places to which people actually go. The words of this set will replace which word in the answer to the question *¿A dónde vas?*

dónde (This is the question word for place. "(To) where are you going?")

32 Here is a word that will replace *dónde*. It is *cine*, a shortened form of the cognate "cinema." Most people no longer say that they are going to the cinema. They say, instead, that they are going to the ⌇⌇⌇⌇.

movies

33 In Program 1 you learned that *montaña* gave us the state name "Montana." The common noun English cognate of *montaña* is ⌇⌇⌇⌇.

mountain

34 Translate: "I am going to the mountains" as the answer to *¿A dónde vas?*

(Yo) voy a las montañas. (You may omit *yo*.)

35 Spanish often writes *qu* where we write *k*. Hence, the cognate of *parque* is ⌇⌇⌇⌇.

park

36 Translate: *¿Vas tú al parque?*

Are you going to the park? or Do you go to the park?

37 The land area in between cities and towns is called *el campo* in Spanish. The English word for this area is ⌇⌇⌇⌇.

country (He lives in the country.)

38 You have been practicing reading aloud so you can learn to say new words that you have never heard before. Have you been trying to say these words aloud in Spanish? Let's try. The words are divided into syllables and the stressed syllable is indicated:

    ci-ne (The *c* stands for an [s] sound.)

    mon-ta-ña (You say [ny] for *ñ*: [mon-ta-nya].)

    par-que (Flap the [r].)

    cam-po (The [p] has no puff. Two English cognates are "camp" and "campus.")

39 A sandy place at the edge of an ocean, lake, or river is a *playa*. Translate "They are going to the beach" as the answer to *¿A dónde van ellos?*

Van a la playa. (Now say it aloud.)

40 Spanish uses the same word for either "house" or "home"; it is *casa*. How do they know which is which? From the context. Look at these two sentences.

I'm going home.	*Voy a casa.*
I'm going to the house.	*Voy a la casa.*

Which word in the context tells you that *casa* has the meaning of "house"?
la (Notice that there is no article before either "home" or *casa.*)

41 "I'm going" is the shortened form of ~~~~.

I am going   **42** The form *voy* all by itself tells you the subject is ~~~~.
yo (So you actually say **yo** *voy* only when you want to be emphatic or to call special attention to what you are doing: *Tú vas a casa, pero* **yo** *voy al parque.*)

43 Which sentence describes what you do regularly or habitually? (a) I am going to the movies. (b) I go to the movies.
I go to the movies. (You could add "regularly" or "very often.")

44 Which sentence is the most likely answer to "What are you doing tomorrow?" (a) I go to the movies tomorrow. (b) I'm going to the movies tomorrow.
I'm going to the movies tomorrow.

45 Does "I am going to the movies tomorrow" say what you are planning to do?
yes   **46** You are riding a bus. Someone asks, "Where are you going?" Which sentence describes what you are actually in the process of doing? (a) I go to the movies. (b) I am going to the movies.
I am going to the movies.

47 Does "I am going to the movies" have two different meanings in English?
yes (If you missed this, reread Frames 45 and 46.)

48 Spanish is more economical in speech than English. *Voy al cine* is the standard translation for both meanings, "I am going to the movies" and "I go to the movies." Must the Spanish speaker pay more attention to context to get the right meaning every time?

yes

New Vocabulary

hora	hour, time	**medio**	half
cuarto	quarter	**tacaño**	stingy, skinflint

PROGRAM 36

Writing Practice with *ser, estar,* and *haber*

1 The only form of *haber* that you have learned so far is ~~~~.

hay   **2** Copy the parts of these two sentences which are translated by *hay:* (1) There is a book on the table. (2) There are books on the table.
There is a book on the table; **There are** books on the table. (Now look at the forms of the verb and the object being located.)

3 In English, does "to be" agree in number with the entity (or entities) being located?

yes   **4** The translations of the two sentences in Frame 2 are: *Hay un libro en la mesa* and *Hay libros en la mesa*. In Spanish *hay* (a) agrees (b) does not agree in number with what is being located.

does not agree (Remember, *hay* comes from the Latin "he has there."
Spanish verbs agree with their subject, not their object.)

5 The indefinite article or any number (public or private) cues you to use ~~~~ for location.

hay   **6** There is another cue for the use of *hay* for location in this sentence: *Hay libros en la mesa*. It is the noun suffix ~~~~.

s (The s-suffix means plural and plural means "more than 1," a number notion.)

7 What will you use to translate "is" in "Near Naples is a volcano called Vesuvius"?

hay   **8** Does *hay* translate both "there is; there are," and "is, are"?

yes   **9** Translate: On the table is a book.

En la mesa hay un libro.

10 Now translate: The book is on the table.

El libro está en la mesa.

11 Copy and fill in the blanks with *pluma* and the right cue: *Hay* ~~~~ *en la mesa;* ~~~~ *está en la mesa.*

*Hay **una pluma** en la mesa; **La pluma** está en la mesa.*

12 The stress falls on *ha* in *ha-blas*. It falls on ~~~~ in *es-tás*.

tás   **13** There are two present tense forms of *estar* that do not have a written accent on the first suffix. They are ~~~~.

estoy; estamos   **14** Write the forms that go with *usted, ellos,* and *tú.*

usted está, ellos están, tú estás (If you left off the written accent, write the forms of *estar* that go with *él, ellas,* and *ustedes.*)

él está, ellos están, ustedes están

15 The present tense of *estar* has two irregularities: the stress on the first suffix and the use of ~~~~ instead of *o* for the *yo*-form.

oy   **16** You know two other verb forms that take *oy* for the *yo*-form. They are ~~~~.

soy; voy   **17** The infinitive of *soy* is ~~~~; the infinitive of *voy* is ~~~~.

soy, **ser;** voy, **ir**

18 When you make up the present tense of *ser*, you add what to *tú er* ... , *nosotros so* ... , *ustedes s* ... ?

tú er**es**, nosotros so**mos**, ustedes s**on**

19 The present tense form of *ser* that goes with *usted, él,* and *ella* is ~~~~.

es   **20** Now be careful. Copy and fill in the blanks with the proper choice of *ser* or *estar: Yo* ~~~~ *en Madrid; Yo* ~~~~ *de Madrid.*

*Yo **estoy** en Madrid; Yo **soy** de Madrid.*

21 *Estar en* plus a place noun gives the ~~~~ of the subject.

location   **22** Translate: They (females) are in Caracas.

Ellas están en Caracas.

23 *Ser de* plus a place noun tells us the ~~~~ of the subject.

origin   **24** Translate: We are from Colombia.

Somos de Colombia. (You may omit the *nosotros.*)

25 Write out this equation: *Nosotros = alumnos.*

Nosotros somos alumnos.

26 Write out this equation: *Dos + dos = cuatro.*

Dos y dos son cuatro.

27 To say that two words stand for the same thing or that numbers are equal, you use the verb ———.

ser (When you talk about a verb in general, you always use the infinitive form.)

28 *Yo (una muchacha) soy de Argentina. ¿Qué soy? Tú eres* ———.

Tú eres argentina.

29 Adjectives of nationality cue you to use ———.

ser   **30** What form of *ser* do you use when you add numbers?

son   **31** Write out: 3 + 6 = 9.

Tres y seis son nueve. (Check your spelling.)

32 What form of *ser* do you use when you subtract numbers?

son (*Tres menos tres son cero.*)

33 Write out: 8 − 5 = 3.

Ocho menos cinco son tres.

34 Translate: "What time is it?" Watch your punctuation.

¿Qué hora es? **35** When the hour is 1 (1:00 o'clock), you answer ———.

Es la una.   **36** For all other hours you must use the verb form ———.

son (*Son las dos, tres, cuatro, etc.*)

37 In this and the following frames, you will find a statement about cues for choice of *ser*, *estar*, or *haber* and a sentence to be translated. Write the infinitive and translate the sentence with the proper form of the verb. Any subject pronoun cues the choice of ——— for location: They are in Bogotá.

estar (*Están en Bogotá.*)

38 The relator *de* plus a place name cues the choice of ——— for origin: We are from Lima.

ser (*Somos de Lima.*)

39 An unmodified plural noun cues the choice of ——— for location: Are there pens on the table?

haber (*¿Hay plumas en la mesa?*)

40 A proper name, all by itself, cues the choice of ——— for location: Santiago is in Chile.

estar (*Santiago está en Chile.*)

41 The combination *un señor Abreu* cues the choice of ——— for location: There's a mister Abreu here.

haber (*Hay un señor Abreu aquí.*)

42 Any kind of equals sign cues the use of ———: She is the professor.

ser (*Ella es la profesora.*)

43 The definite article cues ——— for location: The girl is here.

estar (*La muchacha está aquí.*)

44 When an adjective of nationality describes the subject, you use ———: He is Bolivian.

ser (*Él es boliviano* (No capital *B.*))

45 Any number cues the choice of ——— for location: There are ten girls in the class.

haber (*Hay diez muchachas en la clase.*)

46 In telling time you use ——: What time is it?

ser (¿Qué hora es?)

47 The number word for 1 is *uno*. This is replaced by *un* or *una* when in combination with a noun. All number words cue the use of —— for location: There is one man here.

haber (Hay un señor aquí.)

In the United States only the very wealthy can afford to have full-time household servants and chauffeurs. In Latin America there are more people than there are jobs and, as a result, wages are generally very low. Many people take jobs as servants because this gives them their food and a place to stay. Because servants are paid very little, people with modest incomes can afford to hire them. It is not uncommon for young teenagers to work as servants while they are still going to school. This helps their parents because they do not have to pay for their board, room, and clothing.

In the United States even the poor often feel that is is undignified to be a household servant. In the Hispanic world this feeling is by no means so common.

Review

Here are the generalizations you have learned so far about the uses of *haber*, *estar*, and *ser*. Study them carefully.

Haber and *estar*, but never *ser*, are used to locate entities (people, animals, things, cities, *etc.*)

The cues to choose *haber* for location are:
- (1) entity + location + indefinite article
  Hay un tigre en el corral.
  Hay una pluma en el pupitre.
- (2) entity + location + any public or private number
  Hay treinta muchachos aquí.
  Hay muchos muchachos aquí.
- (3) location + unmodified plural noun
  Hay tigres en el corral.

The cues to choose *estar* for location are:
- (1) entity + location + definite article (all four forms)
  El tigre está en el corral.
  Los tigres están en el corral.
  La pluma está en el pupitre.
  Las plumas están en el pupitre.
- (2) location + any unmodified proper name
  Rosario está en Quito.
  Asunción está en Paraguay.
- (3) location + any subject pronoun
  Yo estoy en La Paz, Bolivia.

Estar is used to talk about a person's health or state of being.
  ¿Cómo estás? Estoy bien, gracias.

The cues to use *ser* are:
- (1) *de* plus a place noun (origin)
  Soy de Uruguay.
- (2) equations
  Dos y dos son cuatro.
  Cuatro menos uno son tres.
  Buenos Aires es una ciudad.
- (3) telling time
  ¿Qué hora es? Son las tres.
- (4) with adjectives of nationality
  Pedro es venezolano.

New Vocabulary

casa	house	**montañas**	mountains
cine	movies	**vivir**	to live
parque	park	**a**	to
playa	beach	**al (a + el)**	to the
campo	country		

PROGRAM 37

On Using AM and PM, and Learning How to Reason Linguistically

Everyone who is allowed to go to school has already learned one language pretty well. Anyone who can learn one language can also learn another. Nevertheless, many people try to learn a second language in school and fail. Why? When you learn a language as a little child you learn by imitation and *without* having to think about what you are doing. You learned, for example, when to use a schwa without even knowing it was there. There is not enough time in school to learn another language just by imitation. You have to be shown short-cuts, and you have to learn to think logically about what you are learning. Experts who are trained to reason linguistically can learn to speak and read a new language in a few months. From now on some Programs will have a section which will teach you some of the expert's learning tricks.

1 One of the "tricks" you need to learn is that the meaning or form of one word often tells you something about the meaning or form of another. For example, when the number *dos* stands before a common noun, that noun will end with the ⁓⁓⁓ suffix.

plural (Either *s* or *es*.)

2 The meaning and form of a word may tell you what something unknown is. The following sentence begins with an abbreviation for a "subject" pronoun: *Vds. son alumnos. Vds.* stands for the full form ⁓⁓⁓. •

ustedes (Did you miss? If you did, you were not careful. Because there is only one subject pronoun that has a *d* in it and ends in the plural *s* that matches *son*.)

3 The abbreviations *Sra.* and *Srta.* stand for the titles of address ⁓⁓⁓. •

señora; señorita

4 Are you *thinking* about what you are learning? Want to test yourself? Aside from the contraction, there is a spelling difference between the above abbreviations and their long forms. What is it?

The abbreviations are capitalized: *Vds., Sra., Srta.;* the long forms are not: *ustedes, señora, etc.*

5 Let's try another problem. The English abbreviations **AM** and **PM** are the first letters for the Latin words *ante meridiem* and *post meridiem*. We use **AM** and **PM** in telling time. The *ante* means "before"; the *post* means ⁓⁓⁓. •

after

6 Remember, now, we are talking about clock time. If *ante* means "before" and *post* means "after," then *meridiem* must stand for (a) an interval of time (b) a point in time. •

a point in time

7 Let's look at *meridiem* again. It came from an earlier Latin combination of an adjective, *medius*, and a noun, *dies*. As Latin became Spanish *medius dies* changed to *mediodía*. The second part of this compound word is the modern Spanish for ⁓⁓⁓. •

day (*día*)

8 Latin *meridiem* and Spanish *mediodía* are the name for a point in the calendar interval of time called *día* or "day." Their English translation is ⸺.

noon (The point at which the sun is highest in the sky.)

9 Why do we have to use AM and PM to tell time? There are 24 hours in a day. The highest number on standard clocks is ⸺.

12

10 Every number on the clock stands for (a) one point in a day (b) two points in a day.

two points in a day

11 Since every number on the clock stands for two points in the day, can we be sure what time we are talking about when we say, "I'll see you tomorrow at ten o'clock"?

no

12 "Tomorrow at ten o'clock" can stand for either 10 AM or 10 PM, that is, 10 *before* noon (*ante meridiem*) or 10 *after* noon (*post meridiem*). What part of the day does *10 after noon* fall in? (a) morning (b) afternoon (c) night

night (Did you get caught? *After noon* (PM) is not the same as *afternoon*. You also forgot that there is no 10 in the afternoon.)

13 The AM hours stop at 12 o'clock noon. When do the PM hours stop?

at 12 o'clock midnight

14 Now let's see how your linguistic reasoning is getting on. The Spanish cognate of *mid*, as in "mid-night," appears in *mediodía*—"mid-day" or "noon." It is the adjective ⸺.

medio

15 The Spanish word for "night" is *noche*. This noun ends in the phoneme /e/, but the definite article form that goes with it is ⸺.

la (Most /e/-ending nouns take *el*, but, remember, you say, Buen**a**s noch**e**s.)

16 If "mid-day" in Spanish is *mediodía*, then it is logical that "mid-night" should be ⸺.

Did your logic fail you? Did you remember that *el día* takes *medio* but *la noche* takes *media*? Copy, if you made a mistake: *el mediodía, la medianoche.*

17 Spanish speakers do not use AM and PM when they tell time. They say, rather, that each hour point belongs to <u>two</u> of the <u>three</u> parts of the day. In what part of the day does a Spanish speaker say *Buenas tardes?* (a) morning (b) afternoon (c) night

afternoon

18 When the Spanish speaker says, *Son las dos de la tarde* he means (a) it is 2 AM. (b) It is 2 PM.

It is 2 PM. (Two o'clock in the afternoon: *post meridiem.*)

19 In the Spanish speaker's way of organizing the world, the hour point labeled "2" belongs to the afternoon (*tarde*) and, also, to another part of the day. When he says, "2 AM," this hour point belongs to (a) *la tarde* (b) *la noche* (c) *la mañana.*

la mañana (2 AM is "2 in the morning": *Son las dos de la mañana.*)

20 In clock time all AM numbers in English fall in (a) the morning (b) the afternoon (c) the night.

the morning (We say either "at 1 in the morning" or "at 11 in the morning.")

21 In Spanish all English AM numbers become *mañana* numbers. (a) true (b) false

true

22 The Spanish speaker says *Son las dos de la mañana* and *Son las once de la mañana.* Now watch your logic. All AM numbers become *mañana* numbers. Will all PM numbers become *tarde* numbers?

no

23 If you wrote *yes*, you forgot that the Spanish speaker divides the day into three parts. They are *mañana*, ⁓ and ⁓.

tarde ; noche   **24** All AM numbers become *mañana* numbers. PM numbers, in contrast, become either *tarde* or *noche* numbers. 11 PM is a ⁓ number.

noche (Son las once de la noche.)

25 3 PM is a ⁓ number.

tarde (Son las tres de la tarde.)

26 Let's stop for a moment to see how your linguistic reasoning is doing. Have you overlooked this important fact? When a Spanish speaker tells time, does *noche* stand for the entire dark part of the day?

no (Only for the interval between sunset and midnight.)

27 You are now reaching a point in your learning of Spanish where it is impossible to tell you everything which would make learning easier for you. Your teacher does not have enough class time for this and to put everything in your textbooks would require hundreds more pages. As a result, you have to learn some things all by yourself. Let's see if there are some things that you might have learned in this Program that you did not. Memory experts know that we remember new words better if we tie them to something we already know very well. Say *tarde* aloud. Does it remind you of a word that is used when you are late for class? The word is ⁓.

tardy (*Mañana* is the early part of the day; *tarde* is the late part of the day.)

28 *Tarde* and "tardy" both come from the same Latin word. They are called ⁓.

cognates   **29** The number of cognates that you can discover as memory helpers depends, of course, on how many English words you already know. You might have recognized this one. Wild animals that sleep during the day and prowl at night are called "nocturnal" animals. The Spanish cognate of "nocturnal" is ⁓.

noche   **30** Do you recognize cognates (a) by the way they are pronounced? (b) by matching spelling?

by matching spelling

31 Here is something else you should have noticed in this Program. Look at these two sentences: (1) *Son **de** Venezuela.* (2) *Son las diez **de** la noche.* Does *de* have the same meaning in both sentences?

no   **32** Are *Venezuela* and *noche* members of the same set?

no   **33** *De* is a relator which describes the relationship between people and place in *Son de Venezuela.* Can the same relationship exist between *horas* and *noche*?

no (So *de* must have another meaning.)

34 Can you discover the meaning of *de* from its translation? Let's see. Which is the best translation of *Son las diez de la noche*? (a) It is ten o'clock *in the night*. (b) It is ten o'clock *at night*.

at night (So *de* = "at.")

35 Now, which is the best translation of *Son las diez de la mañana?* (a) It is ten o'clock *in the morning*. (b) It is ten o'clock *at the morning*.

in the morning (So *de* = "in.")

36 Look at the translation of *de* in these sentences: (1) *Las muchachas son de Lima.* (from) (2) *Son las diez de la noche.* (at) (3) *Son las diez de la mañana.* (in) Is it logical to suppose that *de* means "from," "at," and "in" to Spanish speakers?

no

37 Should we say, instead, that there are several English translations of *de*?

yes

38 To the Spanish speaker the *de* in *Es la una de la tarde* has the same meaning as the *de* in *Es el director de la escuela.* If English were exactly like Spanish, both would be translated by the relator ⁓.

of

39 The only translation of "Pilar's house" is *la casa de Pilar.* Does *de* here have the meaning of "belonging to"?

yes

40 So the Spanish speaker says there is an *una* that belongs to the *tarde* (*Es la una de la tarde.*) and another *una* that belongs to (a) *la noche* (b) *la mañana.*

La una comes after *medianoche,* so for most people it belongs to *la mañana* in telling time: *Es la una de la mañana.* (*La una* can, however, be used with *noche* in a statement like "You don't call people up *a la una de la noche* just to say hello.")

41 May you translate an AM number by *de la mañana?*

yes

42 You translate PM in two ways. Before sunset you use *de la* ⁓.

tarde

43 After dark you use ⁓.

de la noche

44 You have now learned that there is a great difference between meaning and translation. Let's think about this some more. The Spanish word for a 24 hour interval of time is ⁓.

día

45 The common translation of *días* is ⁓.

days

46 The common translation of *bueno* is ⁓.

good

47 Now, watch out. The greeting *Buenos días* is not translated as "Good days," but as ⁓.

Good morning.

48 Does *días* in Spanish also mean "morning"?

no (The greeting *Buenos días* means something like "may all your days be good.")

49 When we translate from one language to another, we do not translate the individual words, we find equivalent meanings. (a) true (b) false

true

50 *Yo me llamo Juan Saucedo* means in Spanish "I call myself Juan Saucedo." The common English equivalent is ⁓.

My name is Juan Saucedo.

51 Here is a nice example of translating meaning, not words. We say in English, "You can't have your cake and eat it too." The best Spanish translation of this says, "You can't walk in the parade and ring the bell in the church steeple." The Russians say, "You can't take a bath and have a dry skin."

All of these say the same thing with very different words. Do you really know what they mean? You won't be testing your linguistic reasoning powers if you peek at the answer *before* you try to find it. Think about this for a while, then look at the answer.

They all mean that there are some actions which one person cannot perform at the same time. They also mean that the person who tries to do this really wants the impossible.

52 Are you certain of what you learned about the divisions of the 24-hour day? Want to check? Below are two clocks. One represents the dark half of the day; one the light half. ◄── 1 ──►◄──────── 2 ────────►◄─── 3 ──►

The names for the intervals marked 1, 2, and 3 are ⁓.

noche, mañana, tarde

New Vocabulary

centro	downtown	**iglesia**	church
café	restaurant	**tienda**	store
correo	post office	**lugar**	place
banco	bank	**escribir**	to write

PROGRAM 38

Writing Practice: Adjectives of Nationality, Weather, and Adverbs

Part 1: Adjectives of Nationality

1 Because you already know how to read and write one language and because the Spanish and English alphabets are almost identical, writing practice at this stage in learning Spanish is primarily an exercise in ⁓⁓⁓.

spelling (This is what you are to be careful with in this Program.)

2 Write the name of the largest country in South America in English and Spanish.

(English) Bra**z**il; (Spanish) Bra**s**il

3 Going from north to south the earth is divided into halves: the northern hemisphere and the southern hemisphere. The great circle or line between them is called, in English, the ⁓⁓⁓.

equator 4 Change "equator" into the name of a South American country.

Ecuador (The equator runs through it. Many people still call it el Ecuador, "the Equator.")

5 Why do Spanish speakers write c before ua instead of q? Here's why. Say ¿Qué tal? aloud. Does qué stand for something like (a) [kay] or (b) [kway]?

like [kay] 6 The digraph qu stands for (a) one sound (b) two sounds.

one sound: the one represented by k in English.

7 By some historical accident qu was not included in the Spanish alphabet along with the other digraphs ll, ch, and ñ. Because it always stands for one sound, that of [k], can the Spanish speaker use it when u actually stands for a sound?

no 8 When ua stands for the sounds [wa], the [k] sound is spelled ⁓⁓⁓.

c (So [ekwador] is written Ecuador.)

9 The country named after Simón Bolívar, the hero of the 1810 War of Independence, is ⁓⁓⁓.

Bolivia (Check your spelling.)

10 The country called "Little Venice" is ⁓⁓⁓.

Venezuela (Check your spelling.)

11 Buenos Aires está en ⁓⁓⁓.

Argentina

12 Men from Argentina are called, in Spanish, ⎯⎯.

argentinos (No capital letter for adjectives of nationality.)

13 *Santiago es la capital de* ⎯⎯.

Chile   **14** Can you figure this out? Read frame 12 again first: *Los hombres de Chile se llaman chilenos.* The noun *hombres* means ⎯⎯.

men (Men from Chile call themselves *chilenos.*)

15 All of the adjectives of nationality you have learned so far have two forms. When they describe a male, they end in the phoneme / /; when they describe a female, they end in / /.

/o/ for males; /a/ for females

16 The stems of the adjectives *chileno* and *boliviano* are ⎯⎯.

Chile; Bolivia (The names of the countries.)

17 To change *Bolivia*, *Colombia*, and *Chile* into adjectives you use a small letter and add the suffix ⎯⎯.

no or *na*   **18** Copy these three adjective forms: *boliviano, colombiano, chileno.*

19 To convert *Paraguay* and *Uruguay* to adjectives, you add either ⎯⎯.

o or *a*   **20** Change *Perú* into an adjective describing a girl.

peruana (Small letter, no accent mark, and the suffix *ana.*)

21 Change *Brasil* into an adjective describing boys.

brasileños (Did you remember the tilde over the *n*?)

22 The *a*-form of one adjective of nationality is spelled almost exactly like the name of the country. This adjective is ⎯⎯.

argentina (It is not exactly like *Argentina* because it does not begin with a

capital letter.)   **23** You know two adjectives of nationality whose stem is not spelled exactly like the name of the country. To write the adjective for *Ecuador*, you must change *d* to ⎯⎯.

t   **24** Write the *o*-form.

ecuatoriano (This spelling is more like "equator.")

25 When you write the adjective for Venezuela, you must change *ue* to ⎯⎯.

o   **26** Write the plural *o*-form.

venezolanos **27** Let's stop and learn something about these changes in spelling in Spanish and the difference between English and Spanish spelling habits. These words are divided into syllables and the stressed syllable is indicated: *Ve-ne-zue-la, ve-ne-zo-la-nos.* When Latin *o* was stressed it sometimes changed to ⎯⎯ in Spanish.

ue (So many related Spanish words have two different spellings.)

Part 2: Weather

1 When the Spanish speaker describes the weather, as in "It is hot, cold," *etc.*, he uses the verb ⎯⎯. (Write the infinitive.)

hacer   **2** To describe present weather he uses only one form. It is ⎯⎯.

hace   **3** The translation of *Hace calor* is ⎯⎯.

It is hot.   **4** Does *hace* mean "It is" to a Spanish speaker?

no (The English translation does not give the Spanish meaning.)

5 To a Spanish speaker the meaning of *hace* in *Hace calor* is ⎯⎯.

makes (There is no logical subject for *hace* in weather expressions.)

6 Both "to make" and *hacer* cannot stand by themselves. When you make, you must make something. This something is the object of the verb (the done-to) and the word for it is always a noun. The Spanish noun which is a cognate of "fresh" is ⁓⁓⁓. •

fresco (Copy: *Hace fresco.*)

7 The Spanish noun which is a cognate of "frigid" is ⁓⁓⁓. •

frío (Copy: *Hace frío.*)

8 A house that is well "ventilated" has lots of air moving through it. The stem *vent* is like the Spanish cognate ⁓⁓⁓. •

viento (Did you put the *i* before the *e* ?)

9 Translate; It is windy. •

Hace viento. **10** The Spanish word for "weather" is ⁓⁓⁓. •

tiempo (Our English cognate does not mean "weather" but a storm. It is "tempest.") **11** There are two other forms of *bueno*. They are *buena* and ⁓⁓⁓. •

buen (This is the form used directly in front of any noun that also takes *un*. *Uno* becomes *un*; *bueno* becomes *buen*.)

12 Translate: It is nice weather. •

Hace buen tiempo. (If you made any spelling mistake, copy the whole sentence.) **13** Any noun that takes *el* also combines with *un*, not *uno*. Directly in front of these nouns *bueno* becomes *buen* and *malo* becomes ⁓⁓⁓. •

mal **14** Translate: The weather is bad. •

Hace mal tiempo.

15 The word that comes after *hace* in all these examples is always a noun: *calor, viento, tiempo, etc.* The English noun for *calor* is not "hot," but ⁓⁓⁓. •

heat (So *Hace calor* means "Makes heat.")

16 The translation of *Hace calor* is ⁓⁓⁓. •

It is hot. **17** "Hot" is (a) a noun (b) an adjective. •

an adjective **18** In English we say "It is very hot, very cold, very windy" because "hot," "cold," and "windy" are used as adjectives. The Spanish speaker cannot use *muy* in his translation of these weather expressions because *muy* is an adverb and cannot combine with a noun (*calor, viento, frío, etc.*). He cannot say, "Makes very heat," he must say, *Hace* ⁓⁓⁓ *calor*. •

Hace mucho calor. (Makes much heat.)

19 Does what you say in English tell you very much about what words and forms you will use to give the same meaning in Spanish? •

no (You keep the meaning but change the words and forms.)

20 Will you ever learn to understand Spanish like a native speaker if you really believe that *Hace mucho viento* means "It is very windy"? •

no (Because, to a Spanish speaker, it means "Makes much wind.")

Part 3: Adverbs and Adjectives

1 Many words in both English and Spanish have multiple functions. Thus in "a slow train" the word "slow" is an adjective, but in "go slow" it is an adverb. The following words may be used either as adjectives or adverbs: *mucho, poco, mal, demasiado, bastante.* In this and the next three frames, give the Spanish and, then, the English translation. "Makes much wind." •

Hace mucho viento. It's very windy.

2 Makes enough wind.

Hace bastante viento. It's quite windy.

3 Makes too much wind.

Hace demasiado viento. It's too windy.

4 Makes little wind.

Hace poco viento. It's not very windy.

5 In this and the next four frames, copy the verb and translate the adverb. Check your spelling.

Habla ～～～ (too much).

Habla demasiado.

6 *Come* ～～～ (enough).

Come bastante.

7 *Lee* ～～～ (badly).

Lee mal. **8** *Trabaja* ～～～ (a lot).

Trabaja mucho. **9** *Estudia* ～～～ (very little).

Estudia muy poco.

10 The adjective *bueno* has a companion form which is used only as an adverb. It is ～～～.

bien **11** Copy and fill in the blanks: *Hace* ～～～ *tiempo* (good); *Miguel trabaja* ～～～ (well).

Hace buen tiempo; Miguel trabaja bien.

New Vocabulary

cantar	to sing	**todo el día**	all day
todo, -a	all	**todos los días**	every day
todos, -as	every		

The United States has been characterized as an extremely mobile society. There are highways and roads that lead just about everywhere, and every day thousands of people use cars, buses, trains and planes to move about. Communications media are also very highly developed, and the gradual result of all this is a breakdown in regional loyalties and differences.

In many parts of Latin America, however, communications are not so highly developed and transportation is still a major problem. This is in part due to local geography and climate, and many millions of people rarely if ever travel very far from their homes. The frequent result of this is a strong sense of regional identification; historically, this in part explains the formation of so many small countries, each with their fixed prejudices against people of other regions. There are often great differences in customs, social mores and even dialects. In fact, linguists have discovered areas where people on opposite sides of the same town exhibit noticeable differences in speech. An expression exists in Spanish, *la patria chica*, "the little home-country," which defines the area in which one is born and to which one owes the greatest emotional attachment. This expression in Spanish is more like "home is where your heart is" than is the contrasting English expression "home is where you hang your hat."

Negative Words, and How to Learn a Dialog

Part 1: Positive and Negative Sentences

There are lots of words which do not mean very much until you know their opposites. *Up* really has little meaning until you know it is the opposite of *down*. *Before* becomes more meaningful when paired with *after*.

In this Program you are going to learn the most common Spanish negative words and their positive opposites. Many frames will also test your linguistic logic. There are two things to be learned: first, what the negative-positive words are and, second, how they are used.

1 The English opposite of "no" is "yes." The Spanish opposite of *no* is ⌒⌒⌒. •

sí
       2 You know what these paired words mean. Now let's see how they are used. Make "I have some money" negative. •

I have *no* money.
       3 Do *some* and *no* both modify *money?* •

yes (Both *some* and *no* are adjectives in English.)
       4 These two sentences translate each other. Look at them carefully: "I speak no Spanish." *Yo no hablo español.* In English the "no" modifies the noun "Spanish." In Spanish the *no* modifies the ⌒⌒⌒. •

verb *hablo*
       5 You have just observed an important difference between English and Spanish. English "no" modifies (negates) nouns. Spanish *no* negates ⌒⌒⌒. •

verbs (Spanish *no* does not combine with nouns.)
       6 There is another English way of saying "I speak no Spanish." It is: "I ⌒⌒ speak Spanish." •

I **do not** speak Spanish.
       7 We often contract "do not" to "don't." Which form does the *not* negate? (a) do (b) speak •

do
       8 There is only one possible Spanish translation for either "I speak no Spanish" or "I do not speak Spanish." It is: *Yo no hablo español.* Does Spanish have an equivalent of "do not"? •

no
       9 Change "He speaks Spanish" to a question. •

Does he speak Spanish?
       10 Make the question into a negative statement.

He does not speak Spanish.
       11 Now look at these sentences and their translations: •

He speaks Spanish.	*Él habla español.*
Does he speak Spanish?	*¿Habla él español?*
He does not speak Spanish.	*Él no habla español.*

English uses the helping verb "do" in questions and negative statements. Spanish has no helping verb like "do." To make a question, Spanish puts the subject 〜〜〜 the verb.

after (And changes to the question intonation.)

12 To make a negative statement, Spanish puts *no* 〜〜〜 the verb.

before (between the subject and the verb)

13 Do you remember the difference between meaning and translation? Make a literal translation of *Él no habla español* to show its real meaning.

He no speaks Spanish. (This is closer to "He speaks no Spanish" than to "He does not speak Spanish.")

14 Have you ever observed something peculiar about the spelling of most negative words? Notice: *negate, negative, never, no, none, not, nothing, nobody*. What do they have in common?

All begin with *n*. **15** Do these two sentences say the same thing? (1) He never speaks Spanish (2) He does not ever speak Spanish.

yes (Now you have discovered that *never* is a contraction of an old negative prefix (*ne + ever*) which becomes *not ever* in modern English.)

16 The opposite of "He *never* speaks Spanish" is 〜〜〜.

He *always* speaks Spanish.

17 Here is the translation of the two opposites given above: *Él nunca habla español; Él siempre habla español*. Which word translates "always"?

siempre **18** The opposite of *siempre* is 〜〜〜.

nunca (Notice it begins with an *n* also.)

19 Here are some practice frames on what you have learned so far. Translate: "Pablo reads no Spanish" and "Pablo does not read Spanish." There is only one translation for both sentences.

Pablo no lee español.

20 Translate: Do you (*usted*) read Spanish?

¿Lee usted español? (Read you Spanish?)

21 Translate: You do not read Spanish.

Usted no lee español.

22 Rewrite this last sentence with the Spanish for "never."

Usted nunca lee español.

23 What is the negative opposite of "somebody"?

nobody **24** Does "body" mean "person"?

yes ("Somebody left this here" is the same as "Some person left this here." The fact that "some" is attached to "body" in "Somebody" is just a writing convention.) **25** The opposite of "nothing" is 〜〜〜.

something (These are just "no thing" and "some thing" run together.)

26 Let's test your logic: *No hay nada en la mesa; Hay algo en la mesa*. Which word translates "nothing"?

nada **27** The translation of *algo* is 〜〜〜.

something **28** Want to try again? *No hay nadie en la oficina; Hay alguien en la oficina*. Which word translates "somebody"?

alguien **29** The translation of *nadie* is 〜〜〜.

nobody (Have you noticed that *nadie* and *nada* begin with an *n*?)

30 You will remember these four new words much better if you say them aloud and write them. Do this: nothing—*nada*; nobody—*nadie*; something—*algo*; somebody—*alguien*. (Say *gu* as [g].)

31 Some people say, "He doesn't do nothing." It's more standard English to say ‿‿‿.

He doesn't do anything.

32 Standard English permits two negative words in a sentence only when they cancel each other and produce a positive. The two negative opposites of "possible" are ‿‿‿.

*im*possible; *not* possible

33 "That is *not im*possible" means "That is ‿‿‿."

possible

34 Spanish uses the <u>double negative</u> in the same way. *Eso no es imposible* means *Eso es posible*. But Spanish also uses <u>two negative words</u> where standard English permits only one. Translate this sentence word for word: *Pedro nunca lee nada.*

Pedro never reads nothing.

35 In standard English "nothing" is replaced by ‿‿‿.

anything (Pedro never reads anything.)

36 Watch your logic and translate the meaning of *Pedro no lee nada.*

Pedro no reads nothing.

37 Now put this into standard English.

Pedro does not read anything.

38 When "anything" combines with a negative in English, its Spanish translation is ‿‿‿.

nada

39 What can you generalize from this? The Spanish equivalent of "anybody" in "I do *not* see *anybody*" is ‿‿‿.

nadie

40 To translate "There isn't anybody in the office," you will use *No hay* ‿‿‿ *en la oficina.*

nadie

41 The opposite of "Somebody is talking" is ‿‿‿.

Nobody is talking.

42 "Somebody is talking" becomes *Alguien habla* in Spanish. Because Spanish can have two negative words together, there are two possible opposites of *Alguien habla.* One is like English: *Nadie habla.* The other is like non-standard English: ‿‿‿.

No habla nadie.

43 Look at these pairs:

*Pedro **nunca** habla.*	*Pedro **no** habla **nunca**.*
***Nadie** habla.*	***No** habla **nadie**.*
***Nada** hay en la mesa.*	***No** hay **nada** en la mesa.*

When a negative word <u>follows</u> the verb in Spanish, you must put ‿‿‿ in front of the verb.

no

Part 2: How to Learn a Dialog

In your last class, you began to learn three lines of a new dialog. Let's see if you can learn some more lines all by yourself.

1 When you meet something new in print, what do you do first? (a) read it aloud (b) try to find out what it is saying

try to find out what it is saying

2 How do you find out what it is all about? By first looking at (a) the words you know (b) the words you don't know.

the words you know (They will help you figure out the others.)

3 What should you do first when you meet a word you do not know? You can find out what it is doing in the sentence *without* knowing what it means. Let's experiment. Roberto and Miguel are at Roberto's house. Roberto complains about the heat. Miguel agrees and suggests they go outside. Roberto says it's harder to study out there. Miguel looks at his watch and says, *¡Caray! Ya son las cinco y media.* Now be logical. What is Miguel talking about?

the time of day (*Son las cinco y media.*)

4 There are two words in the line that say something additional about the time of day. They are *caray* and *ya*. Look at the punctuation of *¡Caray!* The punctuation tells you that Miguel is exclaiming about (a) the weather (b) what he sees on his watch.

what he sees on his watch

5 Must *ya* be saying something about what he sees?

yes

6 Miguel looks at his watch. It is five-thirty. This surprises him, and he shows his surprise by exclaiming: *¡Caray!* There are only two possible conclusions. It is either ⁓⁓⁓ than he thought or ⁓⁓⁓ than he thought.

earlier or later

7 Now, let's go around on this again. Miguel is a guest in Roberto's house. They are studying together. Miguel looks at his watch and is surprised at what time it is. What is most likely to surprise him? (a) It is early. (b) It is late.

It is late.

8 *Ya* says something about five-thirty being late. Is this (a) a good guess? (b) a poor guess?

a good guess

9 What do you say when five-thirty is later than you expected? "Golly! It's ⁓⁓⁓ five-thirty."

already (This is like saying "It is late.")

10 Roberto now replies to this by saying, *Todavía es temprano.* Roberto is talking about Miguel's surprise that it is already five-thirty. He can only be saying one of two things: He agrees that it is late. He thinks it is still early. Now, let's go back and look at something you probably missed. Miguel said, **Ya son las cinco y media.** Roberto changes *son* to *es* and replaces *ya* with *todavía.* What is he most likely to be saying? (a) the same thing as Miguel (b) something different

something different

11 Roberto is saying, (a) I agree with you, it's late. (b) It is still early.

It is still early. (*Temprano* is the opposite of *tarde.*)

12 Here are the first five lines of the dialog, *En casa de Roberto.* Practice reading them aloud at least five times.

En casa de Roberto

Roberto: ¡Caramba! ¡Qué calor hace!
Miguel: ¡Terrible! Creo que hace más fresco afuera.
Roberto: Es verdad, pero es muy difícil estudiar allí.
Miguel: ¡Caray! Ya son las cinco y media.
Roberto: Todavía es temprano. ¿A qué hora comen en tu casa?

The Land: Peru, Bolivia

High on the Andean plateau or altiplano, the Inca ancestors of this Peruvian shepherd built a royal city, Machu Picchu, rediscovered only in this century.

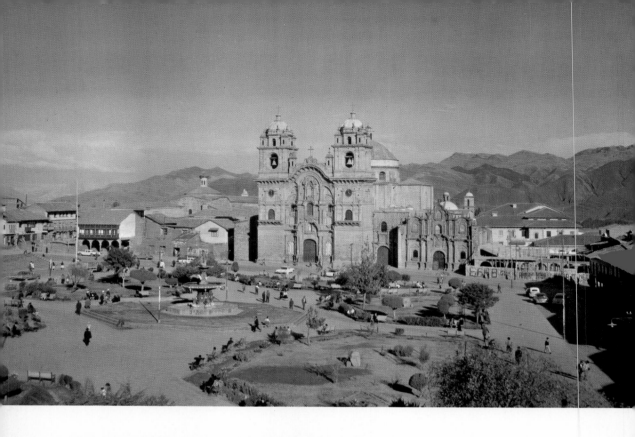

The church in modern Cuzco is three hundred years old. The Inca wall, also in Cuzco, dates from a time when the use of the wheel was yet unknown.

Skills and handicrafts, forgotten in many cultures, continue to play an important part in the everyday life of the Andean Indian.

The market in Cochabamba, Bolivia is a place to visit, buy, and eat.

Titicaca, the world's highest lake, provides landlocked Bolivia with its only shoreline.

In La Paz, cultural capital of Bolivia, Indian and European life-styles meet and blend.

New Vocabulary

creer que	to believe that	**terrible**	terrible
difícil	difficult	**más**	more
afuera	outside	**Vamos a**	Let's
pero	but	**de la mañana**	AM
de la tarde	PM	**de la noche**	PM

PROGRAM 40

A Review: Spelling, Vocabulary, and Usage

Part 1: Spelling and Vocabulary

1 Copy and underline the letters standing for the sound [ss] in "miss": *clase, tiza, catorce.*

clase, tiza, catorce

2 Except in some of the dialects of Spain, the letters *s*, *z*, and *c* stand for the same sound. Will you learn to spell words having these letters (a) by hearing them? (b) by reading and writing them?

only by reading and writing them

3 Here are all the words you have had in which *z* and *c* stand for the [s] sound. Say them aloud and copy them carefully. Pay special attention to the indicated letter in each: *gracias, cinco, oficina, lápiz, diez, once, tiza, Asunción, La Paz, venezolano, centro, doce, trece, catorce, quince, pizarra, luz, necesitar, ciudad, Venezuela, cine.*

4 Copy and underline the letters which stand for the [k] sound: *casa, parque, cual, colombiano, quien.*

casa, parque, cual, colombiano, quien

5 Look at the phonemes that follow the [k] sound. The [k] sound is written *c* when it is followed by the three phonemes / /.

/a/, /o/, /u/

6 The [k] sound is written *qu* when it is followed by the two phonemes / /.

/e/; /i/

7 Copy these words: *cuaderno, poquito, aquí, quince, cuando, cuánto, escuela, Ecuador, parque, porque.*

8 Copy and underline the letters that stand for the sound [g] as in "ago": *algo, alguien.*

algo, alguien

9 Sounds, like everything else, fall into sets, and the cues for spelling the members of a set are the same. The Spanish [g] sound is the voiced equivalent of the unvoiced [k] sound. The digraph *qu* stands for the [k] sound before the vowels *e* and *i*. The digraph *gu* stands for the [g] sound before *e* and *i*. You will write *g* before the vowels ⁓.

a, o, u

10 Copy the following: *sígame, tengo, uruguayo.*

11 Here are some words that need a tilde over the *n*. Copy them and write it in: *manana, Espana, brasilena, senorita.*

mañana, España, brasileña, señorita

12 Here are some words that need a written accent mark. Copy them and write it in: *frio, sabado, Bogota, Peru, lapiz, estan.*

frío, sábado, Bogotá, Perú, lápiz, están

13 Here are some cognates that are spelled differently in Spanish. Write the Spanish: present, professor, pardon, minus, Brazil, park.

presente, profesor, perdón, menos, Brasil, parque

Part 2: A Self-test

Here are 25 facts you should know very well by now. Except for mechanical errors and slips, you should get close to a perfect score on this test. You won't be testing yourself if you peek at the answers. Be sure to circle the number of any frame missed.

1 The four forms of the definite article are ‿‿‿‿.

el, la, los, las **2** In writing, the infinitive form of a verb always ends in the letter ‿‿‿‿.

r **3** The plural noun suffix in Spanish has two forms. After a vowel it is ‿‿‿‿. After a consonant it is ‿‿‿‿.

vowel + *s*; consonant + *es*

4 The only present tense form of an *i*-verb which has the *i* as the first suffix is the form that goes with the subject pronoun ‿‿‿‿.

nosotros (*vivimos*)

5 The definite article, the subject pronouns, and an unmodified proper noun cue the choice of the verb ‿‿‿‿ for location.

estar **6** When you make a Spanish [t] or stop [d] sound, your tongue touches ‿‿‿‿.

the back of the upper front teeth

7 When you describe the weather, you use the verb ‿‿‿‿.

hacer (If you wrote *hace*, do not mark this frame wrong.)

8 When you tell time, what cues the use of *son?*

any plural number for a clock point

9 You put the tip of your first finger just below your eye. This gesture means ‿‿‿‿.

Watch out! Be careful!

10 The four vowels which appear as the first suffix of present tense forms are ‿‿‿‿.

o, a, e, i **11** In telling time in Spanish, you can add how many minutes to the previous hour?

only 30 **12** When you add or subtract numbers the form of *ser* is ‿‿‿‿.

son **13** Adjectives of nationality are capitalized in Spanish. (a) true (b) false

false **14** The first suffix of the present tense form for *yo* for all regular verbs is ‿‿‿‿ for all three verb sets.

o **15** Silence, /n/, or /l/ cue you to use which allophone of /d/?

the stop **16** Why do English "day" and Spanish *de* not sound alike?

The [e] of *de* is one pure vowel; the [ay] of "day" is two vowels. (If you got this general idea, do not mark this frame wrong.)

17 Why must you use *mucho* (the adjective), not *muy* (the adverb), to say *Hace mucho calor?* Because *calor* is a ⁓⁓⁓. •

noun (In English you say "It is very hot" because "hot" is an adjective.)

18 The letter *r* at the beginning of a word always stands for (a) a single flap (b) a multiple flap. •

a multiple flap **19** The number *dieciséis* is really made up of three words. They are ⁓⁓⁓. •

diez y seis **20** The plural noun *muchachos* stands for all boys or ⁓⁓⁓. •

boys and girls **21** The relator *de* plus a place name cues the verb ⁓⁓⁓ to express origin. •

ser **22** If a noun takes *el* or *un*, it will also take adjective forms ending in ⁓⁓⁓. •

o **23** The two second verb suffixes indicating a plural number are ⁓⁓⁓. •

n ; mos **24** Are the names for the days of the week capitalized in Spanish? •

no **25** There are five Spanish digraphs. They are: *gu, qu, ñ,* and ⁓⁓⁓. •

ch, ll

If you did this test without peeking, and if you missed more than seven frames, it would be wise to ask your teacher for help in improving your study habits.

The capital of the state of Alaska, Juneau, can be reached in only two practical ways: by plane or by boat. It is impossible to get to Juneau by road because no road leads to Juneau. This seems strange to most Americans because almost every town and village in the continental United States can be reached by car. Latin America, like parts of Alaska, has many towns that can be reached only by boat or plane and a great many villages which can be reached only by foot or horseback. Many people in these villages live their whole lives without ever being farther away from home than a long day's walk.

New Vocabulary

mes	month	**alguien**	someone
año	year	**nadie**	no one
enero	January	**algo**	something
febrero	February	**nada**	nothing
marzo	March	**tu**	your
abril	April	**siempre**	always
mayo	May	**nunca**	never
junio	June	**ya**	already
todavía	still, yet	**temprano**	early
lejos	far (away)	**¡Caray!**	Gosh! Wow!

PROGRAM 41

More on Learning Dialog III

1 What is the purpose in memorizing a dialog? (a) to remember what is said (b) to remember the basic patterns and vocabulary

What is said in many practice dialogs is hardly worth remembering. The patterns and the vocabulary, however, are basic Spanish which no native ever forgets.

2 Line 1 of Dialog III goes like this: *¡Caramba! ¡Qué calor hace!* What is this line teaching you to talk about?

the weather **3** When you talk about the weather in Spanish, the verb is ⁓.

hacer (Remember, when you talk in general about a verb, you use the infinitive as its name.)

4 To talk about the weather, you use *hacer* plus a noun. In exclamations, the noun precedes the verb: *¡Qué calor hace!* This is the exclamation pattern. Change this into a statement of fact.

Hace calor. (This is the statement pattern.)

5 A pattern can be thought of as a series of slots. In *Hace calor* the noun *calor* occupies a slot. Can any noun belonging to the same set as *calor* be used in this slot?

yes (If it cannot replace *calor*, it does not belong to the same set.)

6 One opposite of *Hace calor* is *No hace calor*. Another way of getting the opposite is to replace *calor* with ⁓.

frío (*Hace frío.*)

7 To learn to talk about the weather in Spanish, you have to learn two things. First, the basic pattern: *hacer* plus a noun. Second, the complete set of weather nouns that combine with *hacer*. Which noun says it is neither hot nor cold?

fresco (*Hace fresco.*)

8 Line 2 of the Dialog goes like this: *Creo que hace más fresco afuera.* Which word can be replaced by *en el patio?*

afuera (Both talk about <u>where</u> it may be cooler.)

9 Here is a verb you have never seen: *dudo.* Look at its form very carefully. Now, try an educated guess, and copy the verb it might most logically replace in: *Creo que hace más fresco afuera.*

Creo   **10** The verb *dudo* is the opposite of *creo.* So *dudo* in *Dudo que hace más fresco afuera* may be translated by ⁓.

"I doubt" is the opposite of "I believe."

11 Compare these two sentences: (1) *Creo que hace más fresco afuera.* (2) *Dudo que hace menos calor en el patio.* Do both have the same basic pattern?

yes (They just have different words in the same slots.)

12 Once you have learned a pattern and the word sets that go into each slot, you can frequently make up again a line in a dialog which you may have forgotten. For example, you remember the temperature is 103. Roberto exclaims about the weather. What is he likely to say?

¡Qué calor hace!

13 You will always learn a dialog faster and remember it longer if you pay attention to two things: (1) What, in general, is being talked about (the subject of discourse), and (2) the basic patterns being used. What is being talked about in this line? *Ya son las cinco y media.*

the time of day   **14** When you give the time of day you may, in the present tense, use only two forms of *ser.* They are *son* and ⁓.

es   **15** In the basic time-telling pattern there are three slots. One is for a form of *ser,* one is for a number from 1 to 12, and the third can be filled with only one of two forms. They are ⁓.

la or *las* (*Es la una; Son las dos.*)

16 Look at the indicated words in this sentence: *Ya son **las** cinco y **media.*** Both have *a* which matches the omitted noun ⁓.

hora   **17** Here is what you have to remember about telling time:

    (1) You may use two forms of *ser: es* or *son.*

    (2) You use the numbers 1 to 12.

    (3) Adjectives that have two forms (*o* or *a*), take *a* to match *hora* (*la hora, media hora*).

    (4) The verb *ser* and the adjectives agree in number with the number of the ⁓.

hora (*Es la **una.** Son las **dos**.*)

18 Translate this dialog line: "Wow! It's already five-thirty."

¡Caray! Ya son las cinco y media.

19 Very few people remember conversations word for word, but most of us remember the basic message. The basic message in *¡Caramba! ¡Qué calor hace!* is an exclamation about the high temperature. Let's see how close you can get to the basic message in Miguel's response to the line above: *Terrible! Creo que hace más fresco afuera.* Miguel agrees by saying ⁓.

¡Terrible! (This adjective describes *calor. Hace un calor terrible.*)

20 Miguel does not say so in precise words, but he suggests that they go outside, because it is likely to be ⁓.

más fresco afuera

21 In line 3, Roberto agrees by saying *Es verdad.* Do you remember what comes after *Es verdad, pero es* ⁓?

muy difícil estudiar allí.

22 Roberto has an objection to going outside. The fact that he objects is shown by the conjunction (connecting word) ⁓⁓⁓.

pero   **23** So the basic message in *Es verdad, pero* is agreement about one fact (*Hace fresco afuera*) and objection to Miguel's suggestion. Copy the part which gives Roberto's reason for his objection: *Es verdad, pero es muy difícil estudiar allí.*

es muy difícil estudiar allí.

24 In this last sentence, which word belongs to the same set as *afuera?*

allí   **25** What is the basic message in *¡Caray! Ya son las cinco y media?*

It's late.   **26** Roberto now says, *Todavía es temprano.* Is he (a) agreeing? (b) disagreeing with Miguel?

disagreeing (He is saying, "It's not late; it's still early.")

27 Miguel says it's late and Roberto says it's early. Can they be thinking about precisely the same thing?

no   **28** So Roberto asks, *¿A qué hora comen en tú casa?* And Miguel answers, *A las seis.* He still has a half hour; it's only five-thirty. Why does Miguel think it's late? He says this with, *Pero vivo muy lejos de aquí.* It's late because he has ⁓⁓⁓.

a long way to go.

29 Here are the lines of Dialog 3 that you have studied so far. Read them carefully and be sure you know what each means.

En casa de Roberto

(1) Roberto: ¡Caramba! ¡Qué calor hace!
(2) Miguel: ¡Terrible! Creo que hace más fresco afuera.
(3) Roberto: Es verdad, pero es muy difícil estudiar allí.
(4) Miguel: ¡Caray! Ya son las cinco y media.
(5) Roberto: Todavía es temprano. ¿A qué hora comen en tu casa?
(6) Miguel: A las seis, pero vivo muy lejos de aquí.
(7) Roberto: Espera, hombre. Vamos a terminar la lección.

In line 8 Miguel says, *No puedo* (I cannot). Can this mean either "I cannot wait" or "I cannot finish the lesson"?

yes   **30** So Miguel explains by saying, *Estoy cansado de leer.* Let's put this all together and see if you can make an educated guess about the meaning of *cansado.* Roberto and Miguel are at Roberto's house. They have been studying together after school. It is now late, that is, five-thirty. Miguel says, *No puedo terminar la lección* because "I am ⁓⁓⁓ of reading," *Estoy cansado de leer.* A likely translation of *cansado* is ⁓⁓⁓.

tired   **31** Say the whole line aloud twice: *No puedo. Estoy cansado de leer.* All the [d] sounds are (a) stops (b) fricatives.

fricatives   **32** Say the English translation: *No puedo. Estoy cansado de leer.*

I can't. I'm tired of reading.

33 The word "reading" is the noun form of the verb "to read." Copy the noun form of the equivalent verb in Spanish: *Estoy cansado de leer.*

leer (This is the infinitive: the form that follows a relator.)

34 In line 8, Miguel says, *No puedo. Estoy cansado de leer.* Roberto, in line 9, says he is too, and, besides, he is hungry. Here are his exact words: *Bueno, yo también. Además, tengo mucha hambre.* You have learned one meaning of *bueno,* "good." Is *Estoy cansado de leer* a very logical response to *No puedo terminar la lección*?

no   **35** Try another guess. Miguel says, *No puedo. Estoy cansado de leer.* Roberto replies, *"Bueno,* I am too." Is he (a) agreeing? (b) disagreeing with Miguel?

agreeing   **36** Is he agreeing that it is time to stop studying?

yes   **37** There are two English letters (sounds) which indicate agreement. They make the best translation of *bueno* in this line. They are ~~~~.

OK   **38** Finally, Roberto adds, *Además* (besides), *tengo mucha hambre.* Now, be careful, and look at these two sentences: (1) *Hace mucho calor.* (2) *Tengo mucha hambre.* The Spanish meaning of number 1 is "Makes much heat." The Spanish meaning of number 2 is ~~~~.

I have much hunger. (The English translation is "I'm very hungry.")

39 Here are the last three lines of the dialog. Say them aloud until you are certain you know them and will be able to recite them in your next class.

Roberto: Espera, hombre. Vamos a terminar la lección.
Miguel: No puedo. Estoy cansado de leer.
Roberto: Bueno, yo también. Además, tengo mucha hambre.

40 Did you notice that *hambre* takes *mucha*, not *mucho*? If you did not, you are still not using your linguistic reasoning power as well as you should.

New Vocabulary

julio	July	**terminar**	to finish
agosto	August	**fácil**	easy
septiembre	September	**adentro**	inside
octubre	October	**tarde**	late
noviembre	November	**cerca**	near (by)
diciembre	December	**hombre (el)**	man
lección (la)	lesson	**¿cuándo?**	when?
padre	father		

PROGRAM 42

Months of the Year

1 Hundreds of years ago, long before the modern languages of Western Europe came into being, ancient people watched the changes in the moon and discovered that they could be used to measure the time intervals between earthly events. As a result, they called the moon something equivalent to the "Measurer." The stem of the word they used was probably *ma* or *me*, and from this came the Latin verb *metiri*, "to measure," the noun *mensura*, "a measure," and the participle *mensus*, "measured."

Is it logical to assume that English "measure" and Latin *mensura* are cognates?

yes   **2** Look at these three Latin words: *mensus, mensis, mensa*. Do they appear to have the same stem?

yes   **3** The noun *mensis* is the Latin word for "moon," the "Measurer" of the ancient people. This word gradually changed until it became modern Spanish for an interval of calendar time. This word is ～～～.

mes   **4** Now, let's see how your linguistic logic is working. When *mensis* became *mes*, the *n* disappeared. What other modern Spanish word comes from *mensa*?

mesa (In ancient Roman markets a "table" was used in measuring goods.)

     5 The old Romans also used their hands to measure goods. They sold things by the handfuls. Their word for "hand" was *manus*, which became Spanish *mano*. Is it a good guess that *manus* and *mano* came from the same ancient stem as *mensis* and *mes*?

yes (The hand was once also called something like the "Measurer.")

     6 The old English word for "moon" was *mona*. The old German word was *mano*. The modern English words "moon" and "month" appear to have come from the same ancient stem as *mes*, *mesa*, and *mano*. (a) logical (b) not logical

logical (English, German, Latin, and Spanish belong to the same family of languages, and many of their words come from the same ancient stems. This family is called the Indo-European languages.)

     7 The ancient 'Measurer" could not help the people keep track of events, holidays, *etc.*, until each moon period or interval was given a name. When this happened, they had the beginnings of a calendar. About 2,300 years ago the old Romans had named only ten of the 12 lunar months in the year. They called the last month of their year *December*. The *ber* part of this word comes from the verb *fer*, "to bear" or "carry." *December*, then, is the month that bears the number ～～～.

10   **8** Latin *decem* became Spanish ～～～.

diez   **9** What Spanish number words are suggested by these names: *septiembre, octubre, noviembre?*

siete, ocho, nueve

     10 The last four months of the ancient Roman calendar were the months that bore the numbers 7, 8, 9, and 10. Their Latin and English names are *September, October, November*, and *December*. Now, be careful, and count back from December to get your answer. In the old Roman calendar the first month of their ten-month calendar was ～～～.

March   **11** English "March" and Spanish *marzo* and *martes* are cognates. The month and the day are named after the Roman god of war, ～～～.

Mars (Mars was also the god of vegetation. In ancient Rome, warfare and planting were undertaken in this month.)

     12 In the ten-month calendar there were no names for two lunar months, and the first month of the calendar year was March. It was a religious custom in those days to get ready for the new year by performing ceremonies of purification. Gradually the un-named month before the new year came to be called the month of *purification*. The Latin verb for "to purify" is *februare*. The month is ～～～.

February (In Spanish *febrero.*)

13 The old Romans now had one un-named lunar month. They named it after the god *Janus*, the god of "beginnings," and because this was the month when new government officers *began* their term of office, in 153 B.C., they changed their calendar and made this month the beginning month of the new year. It is ‿‿‿. •

January (Spanish *enero.*)

14 When the month of Janus became the first month of the new calendar, the number-bearing month names no longer described their serial position in the calendar.   (a) true (b) false •

true   **15** To get the right month number today, you have to add ‿‿‿ to the numbers in *septiembre*, *octubre*, *noviembre*, and *diciembre*. •

2 (The old Latin tenth month, *December*, is now our 12th month.)

16 Julius Caesar was born in the month of *Quintilis*. To honor him after his death this month was renamed ‿‿‿. •

July   **17** Now, watch your spelling carefully or you will make a mistake. Write the Spanish for "Julius" and "July." •

Julio, julio (You capitalize the person's name, *Julio,* but not the name of the

month, *julio.*)   **18** In the spring the buds unfold and the blossoms open up. The Latin verb *aperire*, "to open," describes this and provides the base for the name of the month ‿‿‿. •

April   **19** "To open" is *abrir*. The Spanish name of this month is ‿‿‿. •

abril   **20** Begin with March, the first month of the old calendar, and count to the sixth month. This month was called *Sextilis* until 8 B.C., when it was renamed to honor the Roman Emperor. It is now ‿‿‿. •

August (From *Augustus,* which became *agosto* in Spanish.)

21 There are two months which got their names so long ago that no one knows for sure where they came from. Some people say one of these was named after the goddess *Juno*, the wife of Jupiter. This month is ‿‿‿. •

June (Some say it was the month dedicated to the young or *juniors.*)

22 The Spanish month-name cognate of "junior" is ‿‿‿. •

junio   **23** The other month whose name is in doubt may have been dedicated to old people (*maiores*) or to the goddess *Maia*. This month is ‿‿‿. •

May   **24** You add ‿‿‿ to "May" to get the Spanish word. •

o: mayo (And remember: no capital letter for the name of the month in

Spanish.)   **25** The Spanish for "September" is *septiembre*. Does the *p* in this word stand for a sound in ordinary speech? •

no (You say [setiembre]. It may also be spelled *setiembre*.)

26 Here are all the Latin number-bearing months and their Spanish equivalents. Copy and underline the parts of the Spanish words not spelled like Latin and English. You will have to look closely or you will miss something. •

September	October	November	December
septiembre	*octubre*	*noviembre*	*diciembre*

septiembre, octubre, noviembre, diciembre

27 The verb part (*ber*) of the Latin month names regularly becomes ‿‿‿ in Spanish.

bre

28 Say these words aloud and, then, copy them: *septiembre, octubre, noviembre, diciembre.*

Did you remember not to say the *p* in *septiembre?*

29 Say these aloud and copy them carefully: *enero, febrero, marzo, mayo, junio, julio, agosto.*

Did you notice they all end in *o?*

30 There is only one Spanish month name that ends in a consonant. It is ‿‿‿.

abril

Certain people in the United States have been struggling with the problem of who is a Black. The question, you should notice, is never "Who is white?" because from the first, popular opinion considered anyone with any black ancestry to be a Black.

In Latin America there were never any laws prohibiting marriage between the Spanish and the Indians and there are, as a result, millions of people who have Indian ancestry. The Latins, nevertheless, are preoccupied with who is and who is not an Indian. Strange as it may seem, in Latin America a person who has an absolutely pure Indian ancestry may not be an Indian at all. In Bolivia a pure Indian may be classified as white when he acquires a certain level of education and economic status. The same is true for Mexico where the shift may be accomplished by shifting from Indian costume to store-bought clothes. One Mexican once jokingly defined the difference between Indian and white by saying, "Anyone who wears shoes is *not* an Indian."

Review

Write in Spanish.

1 The two months named after Roman emperors are ‿‿‿.

julio; agosto **2** The month bearing the number 7 in the old calendar is ‿‿‿.

septiembre (Did you get the *i* before the *e*?)

3 The three other number-bearing months are ‿‿‿.

octubre, noviembre, diciembre (Check your spelling carefully.)

4 The day of the week named after Mars is ‿‿‿. The month named after him is ‿‿‿.

martes, marzo **5** The verb *abrir* and the month ‿‿‿ come from the same Latin verb.

abril **6** The month of the "juniors" is ‿‿‿.

junio **7** The month of purification is ‿‿‿.

febrero (The Romans had a great feast of purification during this month called

Februa.) **8** There are two months you have not written. One follows *abril* and is ‿‿‿; the other is named for the god of "beginning" and is ‿‿‿.

mayo; enero

New Vocabulary

tener hambre	to be hungry	beber	to drink
tener sed	to be thirsty	empezar (ie)	to begin
luna	moon	subir	to go up
gente (la)	people	entrar	to enter
niño	child	deber	ought, must (*infinitive*)
también	also	correr	to run
rápido	fast	además	besides
cansado	tired	despacio	slow

PROGRAM 43

Writing Dialog III

1 The written accent is placed (a) over consonants (b) over vowels.

over vowels   **2** Copy and add the accent to these words: *todavia, dificil, aqui, leccion, ademas, alli.*

todavía, difícil, aquí, lección, además, allí

3 The accent mark on the words above tells you which syllable to stress when you read aloud. Does it give you the same information in the word *qué* in *¿A qué hora comen en tu casa?*

no (Question words have an accent just to show they are stressed in speech.)

4 Look at *que* in these two sentences. Which *que* needs an accent mark? (1) *¡Que calor hace!* (2) *Creo que hace más fresco afuera.*

When *que* combines with a noun in an exclamation, it is written *qué* to show that the word is stressed.

5 In English we say "It is *very* hard to study out there" and "I'm *very* hungry." You use two different Spanish words to translate "very." They are: ⁓ *difícil* and ⁓ *hambre.*

muy difícil; mucha hambre

6 The part of speech (noun or adjective) gives the cue to use *muy* or *mucho* in Spanish. You use *muy* with ⁓ and *mucho* with ⁓.

muy with adjectives; *mucho* with nouns (Did you ever notice this before? When you talk about a word that has two forms (*mucho, mucha*) you use the o-form.)

7 A "calorie" in English is a unit of heat. The Spanish cognate used in the dialog is ⁓.

calor   **8** Write the infinitive cognate of "to terminate."

terminar   **9** You do not translate *terminar* as "terminate" in *Vamos a terminar la lección.* You use the more common verb ⁓.

finish   **10** Which is more common? (a) at the end of the semester (b) at the termination of the semester

end

11 Both English and Spanish use verb forms as nouns. English uses the *-ing* form as a noun. Translate Miguel's words: "I am tired of reading."

Estoy cansado de leer. (If you missed this it suggests that you have not been paying attention to the meaning of the dialog lines when they are practiced in class.)

12 The equivalent of "reading" in Spanish is ∼∼∼.

leer

13 A *creed* in English is something a religious group *believes*. How do you say "I believe" in Spanish?

creo

14 The infinitive for *creo* is ∼∼∼.

creer (You can see the stem in "credit." Your credit is no good if people do not believe in your word.)

15 The infinitive *ir* has no stem. In the present tense forms *voy* and *vas* the stem is ∼∼∼.

v

16 Translate the dialog line: Let's finish the lesson.

Vamos a terminar la lección.

17 Write the missing adjective used in the dialog: *Además, tengo* ∼∼∼ *hambre.*

mucha (Not *mucho*, because *hambre* is an *a*-noun. The Spanish meaning is "much hunger.")

18 Say the proper form of *ser*: *Ya* ∼∼∼ *las cinco y media.*

son (Plural to agree with *las horas.*)

19 The English "That's true," translates the Spanish "Is truth." How do you say this?

Es verdad.

20 Write the Spanish for: outside, there, here, still, besides.

afuera, allí, aquí, todavía, además (Write any word you missed a second time. This will help your memory.)

21 Here is the whole dialog. The indicated words are the ones you are most likely to spell wrong. Read the dialog once silently and stop to look carefully at the spelling of the indicated words. Then read it aloud at the regular speed of speech.

En casa de Roberto

Roberto: ¡Caramba! *¡Qué* calor *hace!*
Miguel: ¡Terrible! Creo *que hace más* fresco *afuera.*
Roberto: Es verdad, pero es muy *difícil estudiar allí.*
Miguel: *¡Caray!* Ya son las *cinco* y *media.*
Roberto: *Todavía* es *temprano.* ¿A *qué hora* comen en *tu* casa?
Miguel: A las *seis*, pero *vivo* muy *lejos* de *aquí.*
Roberto: Espera, *hombre. Vamos* a terminar la *lección.*
Miguel: No *puedo. Estoy* cansado de *leer.*
Roberto: *Bueno*, yo *también. Además*, tengo *mucha hambre.*

22 Write the infinitive for *estoy, creo, es, vivo, tengo,* and *voy.*

estar, creer, ser, vivir, tener, ir

23 The adverb form of *bueno* is ∼∼∼.

bien

24 The word *también* is really *tan bien* (as well) run together. However, you translate *Bueno, yo también* as ∼∼∼. Before you answer reread the last three lines of the dialog above.

OK, I am too.

25 In this and the next 8 frames, you are to write the missing words of each dialog line. Check your spelling carefully.

¡ ... ! ¡ ... *calor* ... !

¡Caramba! ¡Qué calor hace!

26 ¡ ... ! ... *que hace* ... .

¡Terrible! Creo que hace más fresco afuera.

27 *Es* ... , *pero es muy* ... .

Es verdad, pero es muy difícil estudiar allí.

28 ¡ ... ! *Ya son las* ... .

¡Caray! Ya son las cinco y media.

29 ... *es temprano. ¿A* ... *comen en* ...?

Todavía es temprano. ¿A qué hora comen en tu casa?

30 *A las* ... , *pero* ... *muy* ... .

A las seis, pero vivo muy lejos de aquí.

31 ... , *hombre.* ... *terminar la* ... .

Espera, hombre. Vamos a terminar la lección.

32 *No* ... . *Estoy* ... *de* ... .

No puedo. Estoy cansado de leer.

33 ... , *yo* ... . , *tengo* ... .

Bueno, yo también. Además, tengo mucha hambre.

No new vocabulary.

PROGRAM 44

More Practice in Learning to Spell

1 When you hear *Whatchaduin?*, you write (a) what you have heard (b) what you have seen.

what you have seen (You write "What are you doing?")

2 When linguists write what is said, they put brackets [ ] around the words to show they are talking about sound, not spelling. How do you spell the word [ke] in Spanish?

que　　　　　**3** Write the spelling for these words: [sine], [sentro], [sinko].

cine, centro, cinco

4 There are many cues in Spanish which tell you how to spell words. The vowels are the best signals. The sound [s] may be spelled *c*, *s*, or *z* only before the vowels ⁓⁓.

e ; i (There are extremely few Spanish words which have *z* before *e* or *i*.)

5 The sound [s] may be spelled *s* or *z*, but not *c*, before the vowels ⁓⁓.

a, o, u (You have to see these words to learn to spell them.)

6 When *c* comes before *a*, *o*, or *u* it stands for the sound [   ].

[k] (*casa, como, cuando*)

7 There are two cueing sets of vowels. One is made up of *i* and *e*; the other of *a*, *o*, and *u*. Let's see all the things they tell you about spelling. The sound [k] is a voiceless stop. The only letter, besides *k*, which can stand for [k] before *a*, *o* and *u* is ⁓⁓⁓.

c

8 Before *e* and *i* you write [k] with the digraph ⁓⁓⁓.

qu (*que, quien*)

9 The sound [g], as in *tengo*, is the voiced equivalent of the voiceless [k]. The only letter that can stand for [g] before *a*, *o*, and *u* is ⁓⁓⁓.

g (*venga, algo, Paraguay*)

10 Now, remember that the only difference between [k] and [g] is the difference between *voiceless* and *voiced*. You write [k] with the digraph *qu* before *e* and *i*. What digraph would you expect to be used for [g] before *e* and *i*?

gu (If you got this right, your linguistic logic is doing just fine, because you have not, up to this point, seen very many words with *gu* in them. *Alguien* is one.)

11 The [k] is a stop. Its fricative equivalent is the *jota* sound which linguists write as [x]. The only letter which can stand for [x] before *a*, *o*, or *u* is ⁓⁓⁓.

j (*trabaja, ojo, junio*)

12 Before *e* or *i* the [x] may be spelled either ⁓⁓⁓.

j or *g* (You have to see these words to learn to spell them.)

13 Write the spelling equivalents of the following: [arxentino], [trabaxo], [páxina], [xulio].

argentino, trabajo, página, julio

14 Now, let's put all you have just learned into a chart so you can remember it better.

You write [k]: *ca   co   cu   que   qui*
You write [g]: *ga   go   gu   gue   gui*
You write [x]: *ja   jo   ju* | je | ji |
                                | ge | gi |

You write [s]: | sa | so | su | se | si |
                 | za | zo | zu | ce | ci |
                 | | | | ze | zi |

Can you learn to spell all the italicized combinations above by *hearing* the word in which they appear and by *watching* the cues?

yes (You can learn to spell these combinations by rule.)

15 Must you learn to spell the boxed sequences by *seeing* the words in which they are used?

yes

16 You have never seen this word: [keso]. Say it aloud in Spanish. Now write it.

queso (This is Spanish for "cheese.")

17 The Spanish word for "lame" is [koxo]. It is spelled ⁓⁓⁓.

cojo (Only *c* for [k] before [o]; only *j* for [x] before [o])

18 The letter *g* may stand for [g] before *a*, *o*, or *u*, and for [x] before *e* or *i*. Which sound does it always stand for before another consonant?

[g] (*gracias, inglés*)

19 The letter *z* comes before *e* or *i* mostly in words borrowed from other languages. When Spanish words ending in *z* are made plural, *z* changes to _____. •

c (luz, luces; lápiz, lápices)

20 The two words below have one sound that is alike, but it is spelled in two ways. Say them aloud and, then, copy and underline the two letters which stand for the same sound: *playa, allí*. •

playa, allí (Some poorly educated natives write *llo* instead of *yo*. You have to see these words to learn to spell them.)

21 Can you tell from what you hear when to write *n* or *ñ*? •

yes   **22** Say *montañas* aloud and then copy it. The wiggle over the *n* is called a _____. •

tilde   **23** Can you tell how to spell *Roberto* from hearing it? •

no   **24** The sound does not cue you how to spell the first *r* or the _____. •

b (You never write *rr* for [rr] at the beginning of a word, and *v* might be used in place of *b*.)   **25** In this and the next 10 frames write the *Spanish* word that makes the most sense for the blank.

Priests usually perform their ceremonies in *una* _____. •

iglesia   **26** *El edificio en que un hombre vive es su* _____. •

casa (You really don't need to know every word to get the general meaning.)

27 When you send a letter, you take it to *el* _____. •

correo   **28** *Comemos en casa y, también, en* _____. •

cafés (The word for "coffee" is also *café*.)

29 *Los Andes de Sudamérica son* _____. •

montañas   **30** If you want to save money, you put it in *un* _____. •

banco   **31** *Buenos Aires y Lima son ciudades. La parte central de una ciudad es el* _____. •

centro   **32** A Spanish cognate of "camping" is _____. •

campo (This is the "country" between cities and towns. The name for a "country" like Argentina is *país*.)

33 Spanish shortens "cinema" to _____. •

cine   **34** The spelling of [parke] is _____. •

parque   **35** A sandy place along a river or ocean is *una* _____. •

playa   **36** In this and the next five frames, there is a word you do not know and have not heard. If you say each right and remember the spelling cues, you can write all of them correctly. Watch the first sound. [kiso] •

quiso (He wished.)

37 [kola] •

cola (tail)   **38** [xamón] •

jamón ("Ham" for eating.)

39 [kinto] •

quinto (fifth)   **40** [kulebra] •

culebra (snake) ([b] + consonant is always spelled *b*, not *v*.)

New Vocabulary

primero	first	**primavera**	spring
segundo	second	**verano**	summer
tercero	third	**otoño**	autumn
cuarto	fourth	**invierno**	winter
		estaciones (las)	seasons

Thousands of Words for Free: Cognates

Because Spanish is a modern dialect of Latin and because English borrowed tens of thousands of words from Latin, there are a great many Spanish words which you can easily learn to recognize the first time you hear or see them.

Let's begin with a guessing game which will show you something about how many words you already know. In the first 10 frames you will find some Spanish you have never seen or heard. Do *not* try to read it aloud. Read it for meaning, and when you think you understand what it says, look at the answer frame.

1 Abrahán Lincoln fue asesinado por un actor llamado John Wilkes Booth.
Abraham Lincoln was assassinated by an actor called John Wilkes Booth.

2 Bermuda está en el Océano Atlántico; Hawaii está en el Océano Pacífico.
Bermuda is in the Atlantic Ocean; Hawaii is in the Pacific Ocean.

3 Julio César era cónsul de Roma en el año 45 antes de Cristo.
Julius Caesar was consul of Rome in the year 45 B.C.

4 Cuba, Puerto Rico y Trinidad son islas.
Cuba, Puerto Rico and Trinidad are islands.

5 El primer presidente de los Estados Unidos fue Jorge Washington.
The first president of the United States was George Washington.

6 La penicilina y la quinina son medicinas.
Penicillin and quinine are medicines.

7 Un millonario es un hombre que tiene un millón de dólares.
A millionaire is a man who has a million dollars.

8 Los Estados Unidos están divididos en cincuenta partes o estados. En España las partes o divisiones se llaman provincias.
The United States is divided into fifty parts or states. In Spain the parts or divisions are called provinces.

9 La primera letra del alfabeto es *A* y la última es *Z*. El alfabeto español tiene tres letras que no tenemos en inglés. Son, en realidad, letras dobles. Una de estas letras tiene una historia muy interesante.
The first letter of the alphabet is *A* and the last is *Z*. The Spanish alphabet has three letters that we do not have in English. They are, in reality, double letters. One of these letters has a very interesting history.

10 Es evidente que ya tiene usted un vocabulario bastante grande en español. Usted puede leer y comprender mucho. ¿Está usted contento?
It is evident that you already have a quite large vocabulary in Spanish. You can read and understand a lot. Are you content (happy)?

11 You can learn to recognize thousands of cognates by yourself. However, you will learn a lot more if you know how to go about it in a scientific fashion. Look at these Spanish infinitives and copy their stems: *presentar, consultar, armar, importar.*
present, consult, arm, import (Spanish keeps the verb suffixes of Latin; English borrowed only the stems.)

12 Copy and leave off the part of these words which English did not borrow from Latin: *instante, grande, evidente, importante.*

instant, grand, evident, important (Spanish has no words that end in *nd* or *nt*. English has many, so the final vowel can be left off.)

13 You already know that many Spanish nouns and adjectives have two forms, an *o*-form and an *a*-form. Spanish adjectives can also be made plural. Look at these:

perfecto	colombiano	contento
perfecta	colombiana	contenta
perfectos	colombianos	contentos
perfectas	colombianas	contentas

English borrowed only the stems. (a) true (b) false

true (perfect, Colombian, content)

14 Look at these words: *defensivo, defectivo, expansivo, activo.* To get the English, you change *o* to 〰.

e (defensive, defective, expansive, active)

15 How do you change these words to make them English: *condición, perfección, conversación?*

Final *c* becomes *t:* condition, perfection, conversation.

16 Look at these words: *Filadelfia, elefante, alfabeto, filosofía.* Spanish writes *f* where English writes 〰.

ph (Philadelphia, elephant, alphabet, philosophy)

17 When you learn to pronounce cognates in Spanish, you must pay attention to differences in spelling. In learning to hear or see them as cognates, you must discover what differences are not important. Except for the digraph *ll*, and the combinations *cc, nn,* and *rr,* Spanish does not follow the English custom of doubling consonants in the middle of words: bb, cc, dd, ff, gg, ll, mm, nn, pp, ss, tt. Write the English for the following: *profesor, gramatical, suficiente, inteligente, posible.*

profe**ss**or, gra**mm**atical, su**ff**icient, inte**ll**igent, po**ss**ible

18 In most cases it is the first part of the word (the stem) that tells you it is a cognate. The suffixes may be very different in the two languages. Here are some Spanish nouns and verbs. The stems are indicated.

comunicación	*complicación*	*concentración*
comunicar	*complicar*	*concentrar*

To get the English verbs you change *ar* to 〰.

ate (communicate, complicate, concentrate)

19 The noun-forming suffixes are frequently not alike in the two languages. Spanish speakers add *idad* to many adjectives to make nouns: *real-idad, inferior-idad, mental-idad.* English adds the *i* but changes the rest of the suffix to 〰.

ty (real-ity, inferior-ity, mental-ity)

20 Write the English cognate for these words: *historia, miseria, vocabulario.*

You drop the final vowel and change *i* to *y:* history, misery, vocabulary.

21 There are many Spanish nouns which end with the suffixes *ismo* and *ista:* *comun-ismo, comun-ista.* The equivalent English suffixes are ‿‿‿.

ism; ist (communism, communist)

22 To change the nouns *literatura, miniatura, ventura* into English, you replace the final *a* with ‿‿‿.

e (literature, miniature, venture)

23 You will increase your vocabulary very rapidly by learning how Spanish builds words by adding different suffixes to the same stem. Look at these:

1	2	3
geografía	geográfico	geógrafo
geología	geológico	geólogo
biología	biológico	biólogo

Column number ‿‿‿ stands for the sciences; column number ‿‿‿ for scientists.

1 for sciences: geography, geology, biology; 3 for scientists: geographer, geologist, biologist

24 The *ico* words above are (a) nouns (b) verbs (c) adjectives.

adjectives

25 Many suffixes carry very useful information about what the word stands for. Some always tell you its part of speech. This is very helpful when English also has several cognates based on the same stem. Let's see how this information can help you. The suffix of *coleccionar* tells you it is a (a) noun (b) verb (c) adjective.

verb

26 You cannot make *coleccionar* into an English verb by changing *ar* to "ate." There is no "coleccionate" in English. So, let's look at the stem again. The suffix on *colección* tells you that this form is (a) a noun (b) an adjective.

noun

27 Write the English for *colección*.

collection (As in a "coin collection.")

28 Now you can pick the right cognate for *coleccionar*. The English verb that goes with "collection" is "to ‿‿‿."

to collect (He collects coins.)

29 A person who collects coins is called a coin ‿‿‿.

collector (The *tor* on many English words tells us the word stands for the doer.)

30 What is the most logical cognate translation for *un coleccionista?* (a) collect (b) collection (c) collector

collector

31 Now, let's try something a little harder. Many times you can figure out an English cognate which will give you the general meaning, but it will have to be replaced by another word to get the right translation. Look at the indicated word in this sentence: *Una persona que colecciona* **monedas** *se llama un coleccionista.* One English cognate of *moneda* is ‿‿‿.

money

32 Is a person who collects money really a coin collector?

no

33 So, to get the right translation for *moneda* you replace the cognate "money" with ‿‿‿.

coins (The Spanish word for "money" is *dinero.*)

34 Here are some facts for you to remember. These suffixes indicate a noun: *ción, dad, ismo, ía, ura* (*perfección, realidad, comunismo, geología, literatura*). The *ista* marks a noun and a person (*socialista*) or an adjective (*una idea socialista*). The *dor* most commonly marks the doer or an adjective: *hablar* (to talk),

hablador (talker); *un hombre hablador* (a talkative man = gossip). The *dor-*
forms may have an added *a* as noun or adjective: *una persona habladora.*

35 You will learn much more about cognates in future Programs. Now, a word
of warning. The fact that English and Spanish do have so many recognizable
cognates can be a trap that will catch you. Very few share all the same meanings,
and some are real deceptive demons. For example, *papa* looks like it is the
identical cognate of _____.

papa (But *papa* means either "potato" (*una papa*) or "pope" (*un papa*) in
Spanish. The Spanish equivalent of "papa" is *papá.*

36 In this and the next ten frames, rewrite the Spanish word with English
spelling.

positivo   •

positive (You change final *o* to *e.*)

37 *imposible*   •

impossible (You double the *s.*)

38 *acción*   •

action (The *c* of *ción* becomes *t.*)

39 *eternidad*   •

eternity (*dad* becomes *ty.*)

40 *banco*   •

bank   **41** *centro*   •

center **42** *latín*   •

Latin (Capital letter and drop the accent mark.)

43 *defender* (an *e*-verb)   •

defend **44** *admitir* (an *i*-verb)   •

admit   **45** *preparar* (an *a*-verb)   •

prepare

In your next class, you will have a dictation quiz. Do you want to review the
spelling of the [k] sound and the *jota?* See your *Cuaderno.*

New Vocabulary

verdad	truth (true)	**morir**	to die
mentira	lie (false)	**descansado**	rested
mujer (la)	woman, wife	**magnífico**	magnificent

In the United States it is often said that "time is money." A great many Americans feel that time should not be wasted and that things should get done as soon as possible and, moreover, with as much dispatch as possible. This attitude produces a style of life very different from that in the Hispanic world.

Almost all human affairs in the Hispanic culture are conducted with more ceremony than in America. Introductions and farewells are more elaborate. The Spanish speaker very frequently uses more words to say the same thing as an American. Ordinary meals are frequently like dinner parties in America. The signatures to formal letters are often elaborate and, by American standard, stilted and over-done. There are more rituals to be observed in almost all social situations. In business it takes longer to get to the point. For the American who is not accustomed to all this the Latin seems to lack directness and, often, normal behavior is interpreted as a sign of insincerity. The Latin appears to be putting things off.

PROGRAM 46

Spelling Review, and Getting Ready to Recite Dialog III

Part 1: Spelling

1 Can the letters *ll*, *y* and *i* stand for sounds that are very much alike?
yes (In most Latin-American dialects.)
2 Look at the spelling of these cognates:

type	mystery	symphony
tipo	*misterio*	*sinfonía*

Spanish never writes a *y* next to another consonant. (a) true (b) false
true (You write only *i* in Spanish immediately before or after a consonant.)
3 In Castilian, which sets the standard for spelling, the digraph *ll* stands for a consonant. Do you think it will be used for [i] when this sound is word final or in between two other consonants?
no (The letter *ll* can come only before a vowel at the beginning of a word or syllable. It is not used as the last letter of a word.)
4 Here are all the words you have had which have *ll* in them. Say them aloud: *llamar, silla, allí, ella, ellos, ellas.*
5 The *y* is used to begin a syllable (before a vowel) and to end a word (after a vowel). There are extremely few Spanish words which end in *i* after a vowel. The Spanish for these words or phrases has a *y* in them. Write the Spanish for: I am (two verbs), I go, today.
yo estoy, soy, voy, hoy
6 Write the Spanish for: very, yesterday, there are, and.
muy, ayer, hay, y

7 Spanish never writes a *v* immediately before or after another consonant in the same syllable. You have to learn when to use *b* or *v* only when a vowel follows. Here are some words that may give you trouble. Copy and add the missing letter: *...ueno, ...ien, ...i...ir, ...entana, ...enga.*

bueno, bien, vivir, ventana, venga

8 Copy and add the missing letter, *v* or *b*: *...astante, ...iernes, ...erdad, sá...ado, ...olivia.*

bastante, viernes, verdad, sábado, Bolivia

9 Copy and add the missing letter, *v* or *b*: *...iento, ...amos, toda...ía, ...alcón, ...e...er.*

viento, vamos, todavía, balcón, beber

10 Here are all the words you have had that you must see in order to learn to write *g* or *j* for [x]. Copy and add the missing letter: *pá...ina, ar...entino, relo..., ...ente.*

página, argentino, reloj, gente

11 The letter *c* cannot stand for [s] at the end of a word or syllable or before *a, o,* or *u.* The letter *z* rarely comes before *e* or *i.* *S* comes before all vowels. Here are some words you have to see to spell [s] correctly. Write the Spanish translation: five, pencil, chalk, blackboard, Brazil.

cinco, lápiz, tiza, pizarra, Brasil

12 Copy and put the tilde on these words, and say them aloud: *nino, manana, brasileno, senorita.*

niño, mañana, brasileño, señorita

13 There are two letters missing in these words. Copy and fill them in: *t...nes, v...nto, dic...mbre, v...nte.*

*tie*nes, *vie*nto, dic*ie*mbre, *vei*nte (Did you get the *e* before the *i* in *veinte?*)

14 Write the Spanish for: hour, hello, until, to speak, Thursday.

hora, hola, hasta, hablar, jueves (Did you remember not to use a capital letter for *jueves?*)

Part 2: Dialog III

In your next class, you will recite Dialog III for a grade. Your teacher will assume that you know it by heart, so you will get a grade *only* for how much you sound like a native.

1 Here are the phrases in which *b* and *v* stand for a stop. Say them aloud: *¡Caramba! Espera, hombre; Vamos a terminar; Bueno, yo también; Tengo mucha hambre.*

2 The *v* in these phrases stands for a fricative. Say them aloud: *Es verdad; Todavía es temprano; Pero vivo muy lejos.*

3 The *d* in these phrases stands for a fricative. Say them aloud: *Es verdad; Es muy difícil estudiar; lejos de aquí; las cinco y media; todavía; no puedo; cansado de leer; además.*

4 To talk Spanish well, you run the words together. Say these aloud several times, as fast as you can: *¡qué-ca-lo-rhace! es-tu-dia-ra-llí; co-me-nen-tu-casa; va-mo-sa-terminar; tengo-mu-chaham-bre.*

5 Here is the whole dialog. Get a watch with a second hand and see how long it takes you to say it. Practice until you can do it in 20 seconds. Don't let speed spoil your pronunciation. Watch the schwas.

En casa de Roberto

Roberto: ¡Caramba! ¡Qué calor hace!
Miguel: ¡Terrible! Creo que hace más fresco afuera.
Roberto: Es verdad, pero es muy difícil estudiar allí.
Miguel: ¡Caray! Ya son las cinco y media.
Roberto: Todavía es temprano. ¿A qué hora comen en tu casa?
Miguel: A las seis, pero vivo muy lejos de aquí.
Roberto: Espera, hombre. Vamos a terminar la lección.
Miguel: No puedo. Estoy cansado de leer.
Roberto: Bueno, yo también. Además, tengo mucha hambre.

Part 3: More Spelling Review

Here are some words which are frequently misspelled. Write the translation and check your spelling carefully.

1 Wednesday
miércoles (Remember: no capital letter for days of the week.)
2 Thursday
jueves   **3** twenty
veinte (The *e* comes before the *i*.)
4 church
iglesia   **5** someone
alguien   **6** September
septiembre, also spelled *setiembre* (No capital letter for months of the year.)
7 still
todavía   **8** too (also)
también   **9** difficult
difícil   **10** January
enero

New Vocabulary

norte	north	**mar**	sea
sur	south	**océano**	ocean
este	east	**oeste**	west

PROGRAM 47

More on Cognates

There are cognates that look exactly alike and many that are so different that the average person cannot recognize them at all. You have to be a specialist in the history of words (a philologist) to discover that *buitre* is a cognate of "vulture." In between *doctor* and *buitre* there are many cognates which hardly look alike but which you can learn to recognize if you pay careful attention to the context and make educated guesses.

1 You know the meaning of *Hablan español en España*. Translate the last word of: *Hablan inglés en Inglaterra*.

England
Ireland

2 Translate the last word of: *Dublín es la capital de Irlanda*.

3 You can also learn to recognize thousands of cognates very easily when you understand what happened to Latin words as they became Spanish and English. Look at this difference:

estado	*España*	*español*
state	Spain	Spanish

When an English word begins with an *s* plus another consonant, the Spanish cognate begins with ⁓.

e (As a result, when Spanish speakers try to learn English they say *Espain*, *espinach*, and *estand*.)

4 Let's put what you have just learned in the last three frames together and see if it helps you understand the following: *Hoy vamos de Nueva York a Filadelfia. Hay tres maneras de ir: por automóvil, por tren, y por avión. Vamos por tren y estamos en la estación central del ferrocarril.*

5 The three ways of going from New York to Philadelphia are by automobile, ⁓.

train, and plane (Did *avión* suggest "aviator" or "aviation"?)

6 You certainly got the meaning of *en la estación central* (the central station). We are going by <u>train</u>. We are in the <u>central station</u>. Logic should now tell you that *ferrocarril* translates ⁓ in *la estación del ferrocarril*.

railroad (The literal meaning of *ferro-carril* is "iron road.")

7 You have already learned that "December" becomes *diciembre* in Spanish. Here is why. The stressed syllable of Latin *De-cem-ber* is ⁓.

cem

8 An *e* in a stressed syllable in thousands of Latin words became *ie* in Spanish. Once you know this, *sentimiento* looks more like ⁓.

sentiment

9 You can now use this knowledge to figure out strange words. Remember *Inglaterra*? The modern Spanish word *tierra* translates ⁓.

land (Another cognate is "territory.")

10 English did not change *e* to *ie* when it borrowed Latin words. The English cognate stem of *viento*, consequently, is ⁓.

vent (Something through which air passes to "ventilate" a building.)

11 The word for a huge fire (and Hell) in Spanish is *infierno*. In English you spell this ⌇⌇⌇.

inferno

12 "Petroleum" means "rock oil;" "petrify" means "to turn to stone." Spanish *piedra* translates either ⌇⌇⌇.

rock or stone (Latin *t* became Spanish *d.*)

13 The cognate *diente* will certainly mean nothing to you all by itself. Changing it to *dente*, however, may suggest it belongs to the same family as *dentista* and *dental*. Now you can say that the stem of "dentist," "dentistry," and "dental" means ⌇⌇⌇.

tooth (A "dent" is a tooth only in special machinery in English. Old English already had a good word in "tooth" so "dent" became a technical term.)

14 Here is another example of this. Write the missing word:

mental	*mentalidad*	*mente*
mental	mentality	⌇⌇⌇

mind

15 Here is another common difference in spelling. A "portal" in English is an entrance. The Spanish cognate you know is ⌇⌇⌇.

puerta

16 The stress is on *tal* in the Spanish word *por-tal* but on *puer* in **puer**-ta. A stressed Latin *o* may change to ⌇⌇⌇ in Spanish.

ue

17 What does *fuerte* suggest to you in the context "The soldiers defended *el fuerte*"?

fort (As an adjective *fuerte* can also mean "strong.")

18 What does *fuerza* suggest to you in *Habla con mucha fuerza?* The word you want is like *forz.*

force

19 English translates *muerte* with an Anglo-Saxon word, not a Latin cognate. You can guess its meaning, however, from its stem. Write the missing word.

mortal	*mortalidad*	*muerte*
mortal	mortality	⌇⌇⌇

death (If you missed, you probably forgot sentences like "The mortality rate from accidents is very high on long weekends." This means the "death rate.")

20 Let's review what you have learned. You should now be able to understand: *En un huracán hay vientos tropicales muy fuertes.* When you think you understand this, look at the translation.

In a hurricane there are very strong tropical winds.

21 Use your linguistic logic and you will understand this: *Los Estados Unidos no es un país tropical. En unas regiones tenemos huracanes; también tenemos, en otras regiones, vientos muy fuertes y destructivos que se llaman "tornados" o "ciclones."* (Read this again before you look.)

The United States is not a tropical country. In some regions we have hurricanes; we also have, in other regions, very strong and destructive winds which are called "tornados" or "cyclones."

22 Remember that context and logic can tell you the meaning of a strange word. See what you can make out of this: *La palabra "cansado" termina en o, pero la palabra "cansada" termina en a.* The translation of *palabra* and *termina* are ⌇⌇⌇.

word and ends (Think of "palaver" and "terminate.")

23 Una puerta es la entrada de una casa. La traducción de la palabra "puerta" es *door*. Un puerto es una entrada también. San Francisco y Nueva York son puertos importantes. La traducción de "puerto" no es *door*, es ———.

port (*Puerto Rico*—"rich port.")

24 En todos los puertos importantes siempre hay muchos barcos. El cognado inglés de "barco" es *bark*. La traducción de "barco" no es *bark*, es ———.

ship

25 You are learning how to recognize and understand cognates when you see or hear them. They cannot, however, become part of your speaking vocabulary until you can say them aloud in Spanish without a heavy accent. Three things will tend to give you an accent. First, because the words look a lot like English you may let the letters suggest English instead of Spanish sounds. Second, the Spanish cognates will not be divided into syllables in the same way as in English. Third, the stress is very often on a different syllable.

These cognates are divided into syllables and the stressed syllable is indicated. Say the English; shift your phonetic gears into Spanish, and, then, say the Spanish: *per*-fect—*per-**fec**-to;* class—**cla**-se; i-**dea**—i-de-a.

26 English often uses the same word for several functions. Say "May I present my friend?" aloud. Which pronunciation did you use for "present?" (a) *pres*-ent (b) pre-*sent*.

pre-*sent* (This is the verb which describes the act of introducing a person.)

27 On birthdays most people get a present. Which pronunciation do you use now? (1) *pres*-ent (2) pre-*sent*

pres-ent

28 Is this the same pronunciation you use in answering roll call in English?

yes

29 You now have three separate meanings for "present." Two of these have Spanish cognates. The Spanish for "*pres*-ent" to answer roll call is ———.

presente

30 This word is divided *pre-sen-te*. Copy and underline the stressed syllable.

pre-**sen**-te

31 The verb for "pre-*sent*" is *pre-sen-**tar***. The form that goes with *nosotros* is *pre-sen-t-...* .

pre-sen-ta-mos

32 The stress is now on the syllable ———.

ta

33 Will English stress patterns tell you what to do in Spanish?

no

34 The third meaning of "present" is something that is given to you, a ———.

gift

35 Suppose one says, "May I present you with this gift (present)?", would you expect "present" and "gift" to be translated by the same cognate word in Spanish?

no

36 The word for "present" = "gift" is *regalo*. This is an example of a very important point in dealing with cognates. You cannot expect all cognates to have the same meanings in both languages. Some are very misleading. What does *un vapor* suggest as its translation?

a vapor

37 Let's put this in context: *Vamos a Europa en el vapor Queen Mary*. The translation of *vapor* is now ———.

steamship (A standard meaning of *vapor* is "steam." Spanish just leaves off the "ship.")

38 Until you have learned a lot more Spanish, you should not try to make up Spanish words from English words borrowed from Latin. This can be *embarrassing*. Look at the italicized cognate and this statement by a woman: *Estoy embarazada*. This could be translated as ———.

I am embarrassed. (Its more common meaning, however, is: "I am pregnant.")

39 Translating Spanish cognates into English can also trap you. Here's a real

deceptive demon. *Estoy constipado* looks very much like "I'm constipated."
Can you guess its real meaning?

no (It means "My nose is plugged; I have a cold.")

No new vocabulary.

PROGRAM 48

Paired Words, and a Review of Phonetics, Phonemics, and Graphemics

Part 1: Paired Words

1 Synonyms are words which have (a) similar (b) different meanings.

similar meanings (No two words ever have completely identical meanings.)

2 Words which have opposite meanings are called "antonyms." The *onym* part of these words comes from the Greek for "name," so *ant-onym* is an "anti-name," an opposite name. *Syn-onym* means roughly "same name." The antonym of *malo* is ———.

bueno

3 There are many words which are neither synonyms nor antonyms. Yet we regularly associate them with each other. Fill in the missing word: hunger and ———, shoes and ———, bread and ———.

Most people would say: hunger and thirst, shoes and socks (stockings), bread and butter.

4 You are beginning to discover that learning words in pairs helps you remember them. In this frame and the next seven, you will find one word of a pair. Write the other. Watch your spelling.

algo

nada (This pair deals with things or actions.)

5 *alguien*

nadie (This pair deals with people.)

6 *nunca*

siempre (This pair deals with the frequency of an action.)

7 *fuera*

dentro (This pair deals with position in terms of an enclosure.)

8 *fácil*

difícil (This pair describes the amount of trouble it takes to do something.)

9 *tarde*

temprano (This pair describes relationships to a point in time.)

10 *cerca*

lejos (These words describe the distance from a point in space. They are antonyms.) **11** *sed*

hambre **12** Are *sed* and *hambre* synonyms?

no

13 Are *sed* and *hambre* antonyms?

no (They are just words that are frequently associated with each other, that is,
one frequently suggests the other.)

14 The antonym of *empezar* is ——.

terminar   **15** A verb frequently associated with *comer* is ——.

beber   **16** Let's reverse the process. Write the antonyms for the following: *nada,*
nadie, siempre.

algo, alguien, nunca

17 Write the antonyms for *dentro* and *lejos.*

fuera; cerca   **18** Paired words very frequently go in the same pattern slot and combine with
other words in the same way. Translate: "I am hungry and thirsty." Stop and
think of the special verb used to translate "I am" in this context.

Tengo hambre y sed.

19 The Latin word *multo* produced two modern Spanish words: *mucho* and
muy. Which one do you use in: *Hace* —— *viento; Tengo* —— *hambre?*

Hace mucho viento; Tengo mucha hambre. (Mucho is the adjective form
which combines with nouns.)

20 Translate: "It is very far." *Está* ——; "It is very easy." *Es* ——.

Está muy lejos; Es muy fácil. (Muy combines with adverbs and adjectives.)

21 The translation of "I am very thirsty" is *Tengo mucha sed.* Its meaning to a
Spanish speaker is ——.

I have much thirst.

22 Let's go back, again, to the paired words and your spelling. Write the paired
word for: *difícil, temprano, empezar, beber.*

fácil, tarde, terminar, comer

23 "Circle" and "circus" are cognates of the Spanish word for "near," that is,
——.

cerca (Circus in Latin is a "ring": a "three-ring" circus. Anyone in the same
ring or circle with you is *cerca.*)

24 One of the paired words is a cognate of "time" or "temporal." It is ——.

temprano ("Time" comes from the same Latin word as *tiempo: tempus.*)

25 How's your logic? Try this one. If you want to *comer* in Spanish, you must
buy things at a *tienda de* **comestibles**. Can you guess the translation?

grocery store (Things that are edible in English may be called "comestibles.")

Part 2: Phonemics and Graphemics

1 It is very hard to write about sounds without confusing people. Consequently
linguists use special signs to keep things straight. They write, for example,
that the Spanish phoneme /b/ has two allophones, [b] and [b̶] which may be
written by the graphemes *b* or *v.* "Grapheme" is just a technical word for ——.

letter (*graph* = letter; *eme* = meaningful, so (#) and (+) are not
graphemes.)

2 You already know that /b/ and /d/ have two allophones in Spanish, a stop and
a fricative. Linguists show this by putting a bar through the letter standing for
the fricative, like this [b̶], [d̶]. With these marks one can show more precisely
how to say *vivir,* that is, [b i b̶ i r]. Spanish letters tell you what phoneme to say
but not which allophone. (a) true (b) false

true

3 When you say *vivir* all by itself (a citation form), you say [biβir]. When you say *Vamos a vivir*, you say [bamosaβiβir]. Are [biβir] and [biβir] the same word?

yes   **4** Linguists say that when two sounds are phonetically different, but do not change the meaning of a word, they belong to the same phoneme. So the two allophones [s] and [z] make up the phoneme /s/. Now, think carefully. Can anyone actually say the phoneme /s/?

no (You cannot say two sounds *at the same time.* When you talk, you say allophones, not phonemes.)

5 In phonetic symbols the English words "den" and "then" are written [den] and [ðen]. Would a Spanish speaker who does not know English hear them as the same word?

yes (Because, for him, [d] and [ð] are just allophones of /d/.)

6 Aside from the fact that Spanish has a few phonemes that are not found in English, the biggest difference between the two languages comes from only slight changes in how allophones are made. The English phonemes /p/, /t/, and /k/ all have an aspirated or "puff" allophone. Do these same phonemes in Spanish have an aspirated allophone?

no   **7** The Spanish [t] has no after-puff (aspiration). It differs from English in another way. When you say [t] in Spanish, the tip of your tongue touches (a) the gum ridge (b) the back of the upper front teeth.

the teeth for Spanish, the gum ridge for English

8 Remember *diente, dentista, dental?* Write the missing word. *La* [t] *española es* ⁓⁓⁓.

La [t] *española es dental.*

9 The phoneme /g/ is the *voiced* equivalent of /k/. The *fricative* equivalent of /k/ is the phoneme that can be written either ⁓⁓⁓.

j or *g* (before *i* or *e*)

10 The Spanish [l] is very different from the English [l]. Let's see if you have learned to say the Spanish sound. Say Spanish [i] and [o] several times and watch carefully what your tongue is doing. Your tongue is closer to the roof of your mouth when you say ⁓⁓⁓.

[i]   **11** Now say Spanish *los* and English "loss" several times and watch your tongue. Say them until you are sure you know what your tongue is doing when you make the two [l] sounds. Now look at the answer.

You have learned to say Spanish [l] if your tongue is as close to the roof of your mouth as when you say Spanish [i].

12 Here are the graphemes which signal you to make different allophones of the same phoneme: *b, v, d, m, n, r, s.* What tells you when *r* stands for [rr]?

the letter begins a word

13 What tells you which allophone of /b/ or /d/ you are to say? What comes (a) before (b) after.

before   **14** After silence you always use (a) a stop (b) a fricative.

a stop   **15** Which allophone, [b] or [b], do you say for *b* in *también?*

the stop [b] (You will soon learn that /m/ may also be written *n: tan bien* and *también* sound exactly alike.)

	16 Which allophone of /d/ do you use after /n/ or /l/? Do you use [d] or [đ]? •
the stop [d]	**17** When two letters (*ll, ch, qu, gu, ñ*) are treated as single letters they are called *dígrafos*. The English cognate is 〰〰. •
·digraph	**18** The *h* does not stand for a sound in Spanish. Do the *j* of *reloj* and the *p* of *septiembre* stand for a sound in these words? •
no (You say [rreló] and [setiembre].)	

New Vocabulary

desierto	desert	flaco	thin
último	last	feliz	happy
grande	large	triste	sad
pequeño	small	joven	young
gordo	fat	viejo	old

PROGRAM 49

Irregular Verbs, Linear Movement, and Writing Practice

Part 1: What is an Irregular Verb?

	1 You cannot really answer the above question until you know precisely what a regular verb is. To change *She works here* to the past tense, you drop the *s* of *works* and add the suffix 〰〰. •
ed	**2** To change *They talk Spanish* to the past tense, you add 〰〰 to *talk*. •
ed	**3** Is it proper to change *She teaches Spanish* to *She teached Spanish*? •
no (Small children and uneducated people often make this mistake.)	
	4 You must change *teaches* to the irregular form 〰〰. •
taught	**5** There are many irregular verb forms in English. The past of *run* is *ran*. The present form *speaks* becomes the past *spoke*, and the past of *sing* is 〰〰. •
sang	**6** Spanish, like English, has many common verbs which have irregular forms. To learn to deal with these forms you first need to know in what way they are irregular. *Hablar* is a regular *a*-verb. The present tense form that goes with *yo* is 〰〰. •
hablo	**7** *Estar* is an irregular *a*-verb. If it were regular, the form that would go with *yo* would be *esto*. This is not so. The form that actually goes with *yo* is 〰〰. •
estoy (There is an added *y*.)	

8 Which part of *estoy* is irregular? (a) the stem (b) the first suffix

the first suffix (The stem *est* is the same in all tenses.)

9 The infinitive form that gives *voy* is ———.

ir

10 Are both the stem (*v*) and the first suffix (*oy*) irregular?

yes

11 A verb may be irregular in either its stem, its first suffix, or in both. (a) true (b) false

true (The second suffix, however, is almost never irregular.)

12 The verb *comer* is regular. The verb *tener* is irregular. Can you discover these facts from hearing or seeing the infinitive forms?

no (Somebody has to tell you, or you have to discover this by yourself.)

13 *Comer* and *vivir* are regular. The forms that go with *yo* are ———.

como; vivo

14 The verb *tener* has a regular stem *ten*. This is used to make up the form that goes with *nosotros* which is ———.

tenemos

15 The form of *tener* that goes with *yo* is *tengo*. Is this form regular?

no (To be regular it would have to be *teno*.)

16 The form of *tener* that goes with *ustedes* is *tienen*. Is this form irregular?

yes

17 You have discovered that to use *tener* you have to work with three forms of the stem. They are ***ten*-emos**, ***teng*-o**, and ***tien*-en**. Is it logical to assume that all three stem forms mean the same thing to a Spanish speaker?

yes (The difference is no greater than the difference between "buy" and "bought" in English, both of which describe purchasing.)

18 The stems *ten*, *teng*, and *tien* are like the two forms of the plural noun suffix, *s* and *es*. They all carry the same meaning.

Let's learn the technical names for these multiple forms. You already know that when a phoneme has two or more sounds, these sounds are called *allophones* (other sounds). So, to be scientifically consistent, when a morpheme has two or more forms, they should also be called "other forms" or "...morphs."

allomorphs

19 We can now say that the present tense stem of *tener* is made up of three allomorphs: *ten*, *teng*, and *tien*. Let's see where *tien* came from. Remember English "vent," "ventilate," and the Spanish cognate *ventana*. Which syllable is stressed in *ven-ta-na*?

ta

20 The word for "wind" in Spanish is also a cognate of "vent." It is ———.

viento (With the stress on the first syllable: ***vien**-to.*)

21 When Latin became Spanish, a stressed *e* sometimes changed to ———.

ie (This is how Spanish got the irregular form *tien.*)

22 The stress is on *tie* in *tie-nen*. The stress is not on the stem in the form that goes with *nosotros*. So you have ... ... *emos*.

***ten**-e-mos*

23 What, now, must you remember to make up these irregular *e*-verbs in the present tense? First: the first and second suffixes are the same as those for regular *e*-verbs. Thus the *yo*-form of *tener* ends in ———.

o (The stress, however, is on the *ten* of *tengo*, and to be consistent the form should be *tiengo*. It is in one dialect, but not in the one you are learning.)

24 The *yo*-form has the stem *teng* (*yo tengo*). The infinitive and the *nosotros* forms have the stem ———.

ten

25 <u>All</u> the other forms you are to learn have the stress on the stem. So the allomorph to be used is ———.

tien

26 To make up the form that goes with *él, ella,* and *usted,* you add *e* to the irregular stem allomorph ∿.

tien

27 To make *tiene* agree with *ellos, ellas,* and *ustedes,* you add the second suffix ∿.

n (You have now learned all the present tense forms of *tener.* Say them aloud. The stem allomorphs are indicated.)

yo **teng**o

nosotros **ten**emos

tú **tien**es

usted	e
ustedes	en
él	e
ellos	en

28 You can learn the irregular *i*-verb *venir* (to come) by just learning two facts. First, the *nosotros*-form has *i,* not *e,* as the first suffix (*venimos*). Second, to get all the other present tense forms you change the *t* of the *tener* forms to *v.* So the form that goes with *yo* is ∿.

vengo (Like *tengo.*)

29 The *venir* form that goes with *ellos, ellas,* and *ustedes* is ∿.

vienen (Like *tienen.*)

30 To make *vienen* agree with *él, ella,* and *usted,* you drop the ∿.

n

31 To make *viene* match *tú,* you add the second suffix ∿.

s

32 The *nosotros* form of *i*-verbs differs from *e*-verbs. Write the whole form: *nosotros* ∿.

venimos

33 You now know how to make up the forms of a special set of stem changing *e*- and *i*-verbs. Suppose you meet a new verb in its infinitive form. Will you be able to tell whether its stem has two or more allomorphs?

no (You have to memorize the members of this set. See your *Cuaderno* for a list of these special verbs.)

Part 2: Linear Movement

1 "Linear" is an adjective. Its noun form is the stem ∿.

line (So "linear movement" describes going *from* one place *to* another, as along a *line.*)

2 Do these two sentences give about the same information? (1) *Miguel es de Venezuela.* (2) *Miguel viene de Venezuela.*

yes

3 In terms of linear movement, *venir de* describes movement (a) away from a place (b) to a place.

away from a place

4 What would be the logical opposite of *viene de* in *Miguel viene de Venezuela?* *Miguel* ∿ *Venezuela.* Before you decide, keep in mind that in the logical opposite Miguel must be <u>here</u> and Venezuela is <u>there</u>.

Miguel va a Venezuela.

5 *Ir* and *a* are associated with (a) the origin of movement (b) the destination of the mover.

the destination of the mover

6 In English we may say either "The train is coming!" or "The train is arriving!" What are we talking about? (a) the origin of the train (b) its getting near to its destination

its getting near to its destination

7 In English "to come" can be associated either with the origin of movement or the arrival at the destination. (a) true (b) false

true (He comes from Venezuela; The train is coming.)

8 When arrival at the destination is the really important part of the message, neither English nor Spanish uses a verb associated with the origin of movement. Which sounds better to you? (a) The train comes to the station at six o'clock. (b) The train arrives at the station at six o'clock.

Most people prefer "arrives at."

9 Let's label a square "here" and another one "there." You pretend you are a Spanish speaker standing at "here." This is how you see the world and linear movement.

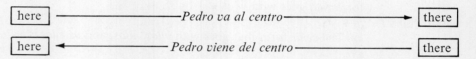

The pronoun *dónde* is the question word for any place that can be named. It combines with either *a* or *de*. Write the proper verb: *¿A dónde ~~~ Pedro? ¿De dónde ~~~ Pedro?* Look at the diagram above before you decide.

¿A dónde **va** *Pedro? ¿De dónde* **viene** *Pedro?*

10 Let's put Pedro in two places. The arrow shows his direction of movement.

Pedro llega al centro.   *Pedro sale del centro.*

Which verb form translates "is leaving"?

sale

"to arrive"

11 The logical opposite of *salir* is *llegar*. It translates "to ~~~ ."

12 So when you say "come" and really mean "arrive at," you will use (a) *venir* (b) *llegar* in Spanish.

llegar

13 *Salir* and *venir* go with *de; ir* and *llegar* go with *a*. With two of these verbs the mover must be close to the place indicated by *de* or *a*. They are ~~~ .

salir; llegar

14 *Salir* can only be used in Spanish to describe this kind of movement.

You are out in the country picnicking with some friends. One of them looks at his watch and says, "It's getting late. I have to leave now." Will *salir* translate "to leave" in this situation? Before you answer, reread the first sentence in this frame.

no (The Spanish speaker will use *ir*. Out in space he does not go from "inside" to "outside.")

15 You have now studied Spanish long enough to begin to be aware of an important fact. To learn to talk like a native speaker, you have to do more than memorize patterns and words. You have to learn to *think* like a Spanish speaker and to *see* and *organize* reality in his way. As a speaker of English you see the world through an English window. When you start to talk Spanish, you need to pull down the shade on that window and pull up the shade on the Spanish window. It may seem a bit strange at first, but there are two different worlds out there. You won't see them, however, unless you look out a different window.

In English a chair and a saddle are two quite different things. The Spanish speaker sees them both as something to sit on, and consequently, calls them both *silla*. In English a table and a chair are two pieces of "furniture." The Spanish speaker sees them as movable property or "movables" and says *Una mesa y una silla son muebles*. It looks like he is saying they are "furnitures." Remember that Latin *o* often became Spanish *ue*. The cognate of *mueble* is "mobile," as in "automobile" (self moving). So to a Spanish speaker pieces of furniture are "mobiles" (*muebles*).

Part 3: Spelling Review

1 There are thousands of English words like *sent, cent; guild, gild; to, too, two;* or *right, rite, write,* and *wright* whose spelling must be learned word by word. This happens because modern English comes from a mixture of three different languages—Old English, Saxon, and French—and also because the language has borrowed thousands of words from many other languages (Greek, Latin, German, Spanish, Italian, Russian, *etc.*) The majority of Spanish words, in contrast, come from a single language, Latin, and the spelling system is better organized than English. As a result, learning to spell Spanish words is made much easier when you study the system instead of the spelling of individual words.

To understand the system you need to know that certain phonemes are closely related to each other and, as a result, are treated in spelling in a similar fashion. For example, there are three Spanish phonemes whose sounds are made at the same place (point of articulation) in the mouth. The back of the tongue arches up toward the roof of the mouth when you make the Spanish sounds for *c* (*nunca*), *g* (*algo*), or *j* (*lejos*). The [k] sound is an unvoiced stop. One allophone of the phoneme /g/ differs from this in only one detail. It is a voiced stop (*tengo*). The other allophone of /g/ is a voiced fricative (*amigo*), and the *jota* (*j* sound) differs from this only in the fact that it is an unvoiced fricative (*trabaja*). Is it logical to assume that sounds so much alike could have become confused as Latin became Spanish?

yes (Latin *catum* became English "cat" but Spanish *gato*.)

2 The unvoiced Latin [k] sound frequently became the voiced Spanish [g] sound. Does this tell you that *c* and *g* will frequently be followed by the same letters in spelling?

yes. Here is a spelling rule whose only exception is found in foreign words. The phoneme /g/ is always spelled *g* when followed by a consonant (only *r* or *l* in the same syllable: *grande, Gloria*) or by *a, o,* or *u* (*amiga, amigo, jaguar.*)

3 Translate and check your spelling: heat, cool, fourth.

calor, fresco, cuarto

4 If Spanish /g/ frequently came from Latin /c/, is it logical to assume that the [k] sound will also be written *c* before *r, l, a, o* and *u*?

yes **5** Translate and check your spelling: class, house, how, notebook, to believe.

clase, casa, cómo, cuaderno, creer

6 Translate and check your spelling: to work, I work, July.

trabajar, trabajo, julio

7 Does this seem to be a logical rule? The *jota* is always written *j* before *a, o,* and *u.*

yes (*j* is not followed by a consonant.)

8 Let's see how carefully you have been reading. What two vowels have not been mentioned so far?

e, i (These are signals for exceptions.)

9 Translate: what? who?

¿qué? ¿quién? **10** Do both of these words begin with the [k] sound?

yes **11** Before the vowels *e* and *i*, the [k] sound is always spelled with the digraph ~~~~.

qu **12** The opposite of *nadie* is ~~~~.

alguien **13** The translation of "Michael" is ~~~~.

Miguel **14** Before the vowels ~~~~, the [g] sound in native Spanish words is always spelled with the digraph *gu.*

e; i **15** Say *mujer* (woman) and *gente* (people) aloud. The *jota* may be spelled either *j* or *g* before the vowel ~~~~.

e (Also before *i.* Words like these have to be memorized.)

New Vocabulary

venir	to come	**alto**	tall
sucio	dirty	**bajo**	short
limpio	clean		

PROGRAM 50

Reading Cognates Aloud and Adjectives with One Form

Part 1: Cognates

You have already been told that there are thousands of Spanish words whose meaning you can recognize at sight. You are discovering in your class that, with practice, you can understand many of them when you first hear them spoken. To make all of these words part of *your* active (usable) vocabulary you have only to do two things: first, discover that they exist and, second, learn to say them aloud *in Spanish*. You can learn to do this much faster and a lot easier by first learning more about the difference between English and Spanish cognates.

1 Say *match* and *church* aloud in English. How many syllables do these words have? (a) one (b) two

one
2 To make *match* and *church* plural, you add the plural allomorph ⌇⌇⌇.

es
3 Now say *matches* and *churches* aloud in English. How many syllables do they now have? (a) one (b) two

two (*match* becomes *mat-ches; church* becomes *chur-ches*)
4 Say the English noun *metal* aloud. How many syllables does it have?

two (It is divided like this: *met-al.*)
5 To make English *metal* plural you add ⌇⌇⌇.

s
6 When you add *es* to *church*, you get another syllable (*chur-ches*). Do you get another syllable when you add *s* to *metal* (*metals*)?

no
7 The noun *ox* is singular. It has one syllable. The plural form is *oxen*. It has ⌇⌇⌇ syllables.

two
8 Now, let's see how your linguistic logic is working. These nouns are plural and have two syllables: *chur-ches, ox-en*. These nouns are plural and have only one syllable: *hats, rods*. To add another syllable to a word, you must have another (a) consonant (b) vowel.

another vowel
[be]
9 Say the English name for the letter *b* aloud. What did you say? [b] or [be]?

10 Say the English name of the letter *n* aloud. Did you say something that sounds very much like the Spanish relator *en*?

yes
11 Say the English name for the letter *s* aloud. Did what you say sound something like the Spanish verb form *es*?

yes
12 Now say the name for *r* and the English verb form *are* aloud. Do they sound exactly alike?

yes
13 You should, by now, have guessed something very important about English speech. Do we have any spoken words which are made up of just a single consonant with no vowel?

no
14 Copy the word in this sentence which is made up of a single vowel.

a
15 A word may be made up of a single vowel but not a single consonant. If we do not say a single consonant by itself, does it follow that every syllable in a word must have at least one vowel? (a) logical (b) not logical

logical
16 The noun "metal" has two vowels and two syllables. The plural form "metals" has two vowels and two syllables. The Spanish word for "metal" is also *metal*. It ends in a consonant, so the plural form is ⌇⌇⌇.

metales
17 *Metales* has three vowels. How many syllables does it have?

three
18 The verb form *habla* has two vowels and two syllables. The form *hablamos* has three vowels and ⌇⌇⌇ syllables.

three
19 The number of single vowels in a Spanish word tells you the number of syllables in that word. (a) true (b) false

true
20 Now, look at these two English words: *hat, hate*. The first has one *vowel letter;* the second has two. Say the two words aloud. Does *hate* have two syllables?

no
21 What tells you how many syllables there are in an English word? What you (a) see (b) hear.

hear
22 Spanish is not like English. With only two exceptions (which you will learn about in Program 56) when you see a vowel letter in a Spanish word, you must

say the vowel sound. Let's look at the difference in the two languages. Say "tile" aloud in English. There are two vowel letters but only ～～ syllable.

one
23 In the English word "reptiles," there are three vowel letters but only ～～ syllables.

two
24 The plural of "reptile" in Spanish is *reptiles*. This noun is now Spanish. It has three vowel letters and, consequently, ～～ syllables.

three (The word is divided like this: *rep-ti-les*. The stressed syllable is *ti*. Say it aloud: *rep-**ti**-les*.)

25 Here is another difference between English and Spanish cognates. English has many words which end in two consonants. For example: "plant, present, grand, palm." Spanish has almost no native words which end in two consonants. As a result, the Spanish equivalents of these words have another vowel added at the end: *planta*, *presente*, *grande*, *palma*. This vowel is always pronounced in Spanish. Do these Spanish words have one more syllable than their English cognates?

yes
26 You know how to say *presente* in Spanish. How do you say it? (a) *pre-sent-e* (b) *pre-sen-te*

pre-sen-te (With the stress on *sen*.)

27 The English noun "plant" has one syllable. The Spanish cognate *planta* has two. Now, make a guess. Will the *t* go with (a) the first syllable? (b) the second?

the second
28 Let's review what you have just learned. In both English and Spanish, a syllable must have at least one vowel. (a) true (b) false

true
29 In English a vowel letter may or may not stand for a sound. (a) true (b) false

true (You do not say the final *e* in "brave, pale, date, save.")

30 When you *see* a vowel letter in a Spanish word, you know you are to pronounce it. (a) true (b) false

true (There is an exception in the digraphs *qu* and *gu*.)

31 When Spanish adds a vowel to a cognate ending in two consonants, the second consonant always goes with the last syllable. (a) true (b) false

true (**plan**-ta, **pal**-ma, **gran**-de)

32 You know that Spanish *presente* has three syllables because it has three ～～.

vowels
33 Here is one more important fact about Spanish words. You know how to say, *Usted habla español*. Let's see if you know what you are really doing when you say these words aloud. Here is the sentence with the words divided into syllables. Copy and underline the stressed syllable in each word: *Us-ted ha-bla es-pa-ñol*.

Us-**ted ha**-bla es-pa-**ñol**.

34 Now, let's put your linguistic logic to work. With very few exceptions, the stressed syllable in a Spanish word can be discovered by looking at the last phoneme. When a word ends in a consonant other than *n* or *s* (and has no written accent mark), you stress (a) the last syllable (b) the next-to-last syllable.

the last syllable
35 When a word ends in a vowel, *n* or *s* (and has no written accent), you stress (a) the last syllable (b) the next-to-last syllable.

the next-to-last syllable

36 You have now been reminded of another big difference between English and Spanish cognates. You stress the first syllable when you say these words in English: "**mo**-tor, **to**-tal, **ca**-pi-tal, **doc**-tor." The last syllable is unstressed and its <u>vowel sound is schwa</u>. These words end in a consonant, so in Spanish the stress is on the last syllable and there is no schwa. Say them aloud in Spanish: *mo-**tor**, to-**tal**, ca-pi-**tal**, doc-**tor**.*

For a very long time the *siesta,* or afternoon nap or rest period, has been a special feature of Hispanic culture, especially in the hotter countries and during the summer. This custom, however, is gradually disappearing. Very few young people take the siesta. In many places, however, the shops still close down between two and five, and as a result, remain open late in the evening. There are other remnants of the custom. In general it is still not considered proper to make social calls during the siesta hours. Many social functions still begin late in the evening, especially formal dinners, and many people still believe that there should be a rest period of some kind during the hot part of the day. Thus in Southern Spain the siesta is considered as something necessary to maintain good health.

Part 2: Adjectives with One Form.

1 Have you ever stopped to think about why some adjectives in both English and Spanish have to agree with their nouns? What makes agreement possible? Remember the English demonstratives *this*, *these*, and *that*, *those*. The stem of all four forms is ⁓⁓⁓.

th (There are two forms for things near you—*this* and *these*—and two forms for things farther away—*that* and *those*.)

2 This same stem appears in the definite article *the*. Now, you say *the book* and *the books*. Does *the* have a suffix that agrees in number with *book* and *books*?

no (*The* has only one form, so it cannot agree with a word that has two forms.)

3 You do say *this book* and *these books*. Think about this fact. Agreement is possible only when an adjective has ⁓⁓⁓ forms.

two forms, that is, two different suffixes

4 Except for the demonstratives, all English adjectives have only one form. All Spanish adjectives, in contrast, have at least two forms. Write the plural of the following: *la idea importante*.

las ideas importantes

5 Do Spanish adjectives have a singular and a plural form?

yes

6 A great many Spanish adjectives have four forms: two singulars and two plurals. The plural forms take the same suffix as the nouns, that is, either *s* or ⁓⁓⁓.

es (*muchachos buenos; papeles españoles*)

7 When an adjective has four forms, one of the singular forms always ends with the phoneme /a/. The contrasting form (with one exception) may end in a consonant or the vowel ⁓⁓⁓.

o

8 When an adjective has four forms, it agrees with nouns in two ways, it must have the same ⁓⁓⁓ suffix as the noun.

number (It must be either singular or plural.)

9 When there are two singular forms (*bueno, buena*), the last phoneme of the adjectival form (with a few predictable exceptions) matches the last phoneme of the noun. (a) true (b) false.

true (*muchacha buena; muchacho bueno*)

10 There are, as in English, a great many Spanish adjectives which have only one singular form. Can these adjectives agree with their nouns in two different ways?

no

11 When there is only one singular form of an adjective, it can agree with its noun only in ⁓⁓⁓.

number (For example: *el profesor importante, los profesores importantes,* and *la profesora importante, las profesoras importantes.*)

12 Now, let's do a little educated guessing. You come across, for the first time, a new adjective which ends in *o*, for example, *bravo*. Will it have a contrasting *a*-form?

yes (Any adjective which has an *o*-form will also have an *a*-form; *bravo, brava.*)

13 Remember, now, that Spanish does not like to end a word with two consonants. So you come across, for the first time, an adjective which has two consonants before a final *a*. For example, *contenta*. Is there likely to be a contrasting *o*-form?

yes (There are some exceptions, mostly words ending in the suffix *ista.*)

Optional Pre-quiz Practice

In your next class session, you are going to read aloud for a grade. The purpose of the quiz is to find out how well you can read aloud some sentences which you have never said before. Here are some points to remember.

1 The phoneme /b/ has two allophones, [b] and [b̵], and may be written either *b* or *v*. Do these letters tell you which allophone you are to say?

no

2 Which allophone of /b/ do you say in *no voy?* (a) stop (b) fricative

fricative

3 If you just say *voy*, you use a ~~~~.

stop

4 Does the phoneme /d/ have two allophones?

yes

5 In *todos* the allophone of /d/ is like the initial sound of English (a) **d**ough (b) **th**ough.

though (It is fricative.)

6 Say *ciudad* aloud. Does the *u* stand for a sound like the one in *tú?*

yes

7 Does the letter *u* stand for the same vowel sound in *nueve?*

no (You do not say [nu-e-ve], you say something very close to [nwe-ve]. The *u* usually stands for a [w] sound immediately before a vowel.)

8 Say these words aloud: *nueve, cuarto, escuela.* Does the *u* stand for a sound in *aquí?*

no (It is part of the digraph *qu* which stands for the [k] sound.)

9 Are all the words of a phrase run together in speaking Spanish?

yes

10 If you run *a las siete* together, will you say two separate [s] sounds?

no (You will get one [s] that is a bit longer than the [s] of *las* said all by itself. Say [alasiete] aloud.)

11 Here is a sentence of the kind you will read aloud: *En el mes de julio no vamos mucho a las montañas.* Copy and write a bar (/) at the end of the first two phrase groups.

En el mes de julio | no vamos mucho | a las montañas. (Now read this aloud without any pauses or hesitation except at the bars.)

New Vocabulary

barco	boat	**bonito**	pretty
tranvía (el)	streetcar	**feo**	ugly
túnel	tunnel	**salir**	to leave; go out
llegar	to arrive		

PROGRAM 51

"to go" and "to come": *ir* versus *venir*

1 If you look up *ir* and *venir* in almost any English-Spanish dictionary, you will discover that *ir* is translated "to go" and that *venir* is translated either by "to go" or by "to come." Does this information tell you when to use *ir* and *venir* in Spanish?

no   **2** You cannot learn what cues you to use *ir* and *venir* in Spanish until you understand that Spanish looks at the actions of going and coming from a different point of view than English. Must you first understand the uses and meanings of "go" and "come" in English before you can learn how Spanish is different?

yes   **3** Let's begin, then, by making certain that you know the difference between "go" and "come" in English.

Mr. Brand phones his wife to tell her his car has broken down. She asks him if he is at the office. He answers, "Yes, I'm *there* now, and I'll be *here* for another hour." How does English logic permit Mr. Brand to be *there* and *here* at the same time? Let's see. Remember that Mrs. Brand is *at home*. From her point of view what is *at the office*? (a) here (b) there

there   **4** Whose point of view does Mr. Brand use when he says, "Yes, I'm *there* now"? (a) his own (b) Mrs. Brand's

Mrs. Brand's   **5** Mr. Brand is in his office. From his point of view, where is he? (a) here (b) there

here   **6** Whose point of view does Mr. Brand use when he says, "and I'll be *here* for another hour"? (a) his own (b) Mrs. Brand's

his own   **7** In English a speaker may use his own point of view or the point of view of the person spoken to in describing his position in space. (a) true (b) false

true   **8** Remember, Mr. Brand's car has broken down. He has called his wife. He wants her to pick him up. He is at his office. Here is a diagram of the situation. The arrow shows the directions of Mrs. Brand's movement from Mr. Brand's point of view.

What will Mr. Brand say, (a) "Will you *go* to the office and pick me up?" (b) "Will you *come* to the office and pick me up?"

Will you *come* to the office?

9 How will Mrs. Brand answer? (a) "I'll *go* and get you." (b) "I'll *come* and get you."

I'll *come* and get you.

10 Mrs. Brand goes to the garage and starts her car. Her son asks, (a) "Where are you *coming*?" (b) "Where are you *going*?"

Where are you *going*?

11 Mrs. Brand answers, (a) "I'm *coming* to the office to get Daddy." (b) "I'm *going* to the office to get Daddy."

I'm *going* to the office to get Daddy.

12 In Frame 9, Mrs. Brand answered her husband by saying, "I'll come and get you." Whose point of view was she using when she picked *come* instead of *go*? (a) her own (b) her husband's

her husband's

13 In Frame 11, Mrs. Brand answered her son by saying, "I'm going to the office to get Daddy." Whose point of view was she using when she picked *going* instead of *coming*? (a) her own (b) her husband's

her own

14 When you are using your own point of view, where must you always be? (a) here (b) there

here

15 When you use your own point of view, and you move from where you are (here) toward where you move (there), what verb describes your movement? (a) I'm going. (b) I'm coming.

I'm going.

16 When you talk to a person who is where you are and you want to say you are departing, what do you say? (a) I'm coming. (b) I'm going.

I'm going.

17 Someone knocks at your door. You are in the kitchen by the sink. You walk away from the sink, you leave the kitchen and move *toward* the door. Are you (a) going to the door? (b) coming to the door?

going to the door

18 Before you get to the door, there is another knock and a call, "Anybody home?" You say, (a) "I'm going." (b) "I'm coming."

I'm coming.

19 In Frame 17, you *were going* to the door. In Frame 18, you said, "I'm coming." Whose point of view were you using when you picked *come* instead of *go* to answer the person at the door? (a) your own (b) the person at the door

the person at the door

20 Let's see, now, why your linguistic intuition tells you to say, "I'm *coming*" when, in fact, you are *going* from the kitchen to the door.

Paul is at a party. It is getting late. He needs to be home soon. What will he say to the host? (a) It's time for me *to go*. (b) It's time for me *to come*.

It's time for me *to go*.

21 If Paul goes, the direction of movement will be (a) toward his host (b) away from his host.

away from his host

22 Before Paul leaves, he calls his home. His mother answers. He says, "I called because it is late. (a) I'm *going* home right away." (b) I'm *coming* home right away."

I'm *coming* home right away.

23 When Paul says, "I'm coming home right away," he is using (a) his point of view (b) his mother's point of view.

his mother's point of view

24 When you talk to a person in English, *go* has the meaning of "to depart" or "to leave," that is, to move away from the person to whom you are talking. *Come* has the meaning of (a) to move away from that person (b) to move *toward* that person.

to move *toward* that person (So you say, "I'm coming" when someone knocks at the door.)

25 The answer to the command, "Come here!" is (a) I'm going. (b) I'm coming.

I'm coming.

26 We use the point of view of the person to whom we are talking when we say, "I'm coming." We use our own point of view when we say, "I'm going." The Spanish speaker, in sharp contrast with English speakers, uses his own point of view in choosing between *ir* and *venir*. When someone knocks at his door, he says, (a) *Ya voy.* (b) *Ya vengo.*

Ya voy. (Literally, "Already I go.")

27 So now you know why "to come" may be translated by either *ir* or *venir*. Let's practice reading the cues for choice. "Come here!" means to move toward me, the speaker, like this:

What verb do you use? (a) *ir* (b) *venir*

venir

28 "Go!" means to move away from me, the speaker. What verb do you use? (a) *ir* (b) *venir*

ir

29 When you reply to the commands "Come here!" or "Go!" in Spanish, you use the same verb. It is (a) *voy* (b) *vengo*

voy

30 *Voy* has two meanings. One is to move <u>toward</u> the person to whom you are speaking. The other is to move <u>away</u> from that person. (a) true (b) false

true

31 Let's review. You are in the kitchen with a relative who is busy making a cake. Someone knocks at the front door. Your relative asks, "Will you go to the door?" Does "go" mean *move* through the house *to* the door?

yes

32 Which verb will you use in Spanish to answer the question "Will you go to the door?" (a) *ir* (b) *venir*

ir

33 You stop to finish a coke. The person at the door knocks again and calls out, "Anybody home?" You now start for the door and answer, (a) "I'm going." (b) "I'm coming."

I'm coming.

34 What will you say in Spanish? Remember, you have to pick your own point of view to make the right choice. (a) *Ya voy.* (b) *Ya vengo.*

Ya voy.

35 Now, let's do this all over again. You are back in the kitchen with your relative. Someone knocks at the front door. Your relative asks, "Will you go to the door?" You stop to finish a coke. Your relative looks at you somewhat annoyed. You get the message, and say, (a) "I'm coming." (b) "I'm going."

I'm going.

36 To the person in the kitchen you said, "I'm going," but to the person at the door you said, "I'm coming." Do both statements describe your moving toward the door?

yes

37 When a person is confused, we often say, "He doesn't know whether he is coming or going." Let's see if you know whether you are coming or going in Spanish.

You are on a hike in a park and everyone is sitting down on the grass resting. One person stands up and says, "Come on; come along." Does this mean, "Let's move on, depart from here"?

yes

38 Which verb will you use in Spanish? Before you answer, remember that the speaker wants them to move away from the place they are at. (a) *ir* (b) *venir*

ir (You translate either "Come on!" or "Come along!" with *¡Vamos!* Literally, "Let's go.")

39 We really don't care whether we are coming or going when we ask either, "Are you going with me to the store?" or, "Are you coming with me to the store?" In this situation, the Spanish speaker also uses either verb: *¿Vas conmigo a la tienda? ¿Vienes conmigo a la tienda?*

Here is a summary of what you have just studied:

(1) When the speaker and the person spoken to are at different positions in space, the English speaker (who is *here*) uses the point of view of the person spoken to in choosing between "come" and "go."

> Are you **coming here** tomorrow?
> Yes, I'm **coming there** tomorrow.

(2) In Spanish, in contrast, each person uses his own point of view. The Spanish speaker, in short, believes you cannot "come" to where you are not. You have to "go" there.

> *¿Vienes aquí mañana?*
> *Sí, voy allí mañana.*

(3) When both persons are at the same place and one begins to move away, this person may urge the other to come along by saying, "Come on! Let's go." Spanish uses only the equivalent of "Let's go": *¡Vamos!*

(4) When both speakers are at the same place both languages use "go" (*ir*) to describe movement to somewhere else.

> **Are** you **going** to the store?   *¿Vas a la tienda?*

(5) When one states that one person will go with the other, both languages may use either verb.

> Are you going with me?   *¿Vas conmigo?*
> Are you coming with me?   *¿Vienes conmigo?*

No new vocabulary.

PROGRAM 52

Predicate Adjectives and Our Organization of Reality

1 Here is a phrase which has a noun and four adjectives: *those two big, black dogs*. The noun is ~~~~.

dogs
    2 Two of the four adjectives paint a kind of word picture of the dogs. They describe the dogs. They are ~~~~.

big; black (These are called *descriptive adjectives*.)
    3 Two of the four adjectives do not really describe the dogs. One points out the distance of the dogs from the speaker. It is ~~~~.

those (*These* would say the dogs are closer.)

4 *These* and *those*, like *this* and *that*, are special kinds of adjectives. They point out the distance that something is away from the speaker. They are called ~~~~~ adjectives.

demonstrative (If you missed this one it may mean you have not been paying careful attention to the words you need to know in order to talk about learning a language.)

5 The adjective *two* does not describe the dogs. It tells us the ~~~~~ of dogs being talked about.

number (Adjectives which point out or give the number are called *limiting adjectives.*)

6 This Program deals only with descriptive adjectives. A descriptive adjective in both English and Spanish may stand next to its noun: "The *big dog* is in the yard." The same adjective may come after the verb: "The dog in the yard *is big*." Does *big* still describe the dog?

yes

7 There are two parts in *The dog is big*. The subject is ~~~~~.

dog

8 The rest of the sentence says something about the subject. The Romans said this part of the sentence "proclaimed" something about the subject, and they used the verb *praedicare* to say this. The English word which comes from *praedicare* is ~~~~~.

predicate (If you missed this, you probably paid no attention to the title of this Program.)

9 The predicate adjective is italicized in this sentence: "The dog is *big*." A predicate adjective is one which describes the subject of the sentence and comes *after* the ~~~~~.

verb (The dog *is* big.)

10 This Program deals only with descriptive adjectives which come *after* the verb *to be*. Sentences like *The dog is big* are our linguistic paint brushes. We use them to organize and describe everything in the world. Let's see how much linguistic logic there is locked up in sentences of this type. Everybody agrees that deserts have certain characteristics. Which single adjective gives the most accurate description of deserts? *Deserts are* ~~~~~.

dry

11 In 1925 it rained so much in the Atacama Desert in Chile that there was a great flood. Was this (a) normal? (b) abnormal?

abnormal

12 The word *normal* has an adjectival suffix. When you remove it, you get the noun form ~~~~~.

norm

13 What is *your norm* for deserts? (a) dry (b) wet

dry

14 What is *your norm* for a tropical jungle? (a) dry (b) wet

wet

15 What single adjective best describes your norm for ice? *Ice is* ~~~~~.

cold

16 *The sun is hot* and *The earth is round* are statements of natural law. (a) true (b) false

true (It would be *abnormal* for the sun to be cool.)

17 Is this a statement of natural law? *Henry is furious*. Let's think through your answer. Is it normal for people to be furious?

no (Being angry is abnormal for most people. It is not natural to be angry.)

18 So *Henry is furious* really says that Henry has changed from the normal, that he *has become furious*. (a) true (b) false

true (Did you ever notice that *become* is *come to be*?)

19 What is the norm for brand new clothes? They are (a) clean (b) dirty.

clean

20 Which sentence is like *Your shirt is dirty*? (a) The sun is hot. (b) Henry is furious.

Henry is furious. (The shirt changed from clean to dirty.)

21 What is the norm for most people? (a) They are healthy. (b) They are sick.
They are healthy.

22 So what does *María is sick* tell you? (a) It is natural for María to be sick. (b) She has changed from the normal.
She has changed from the normal.

23 What is your color norm for grass? *Grass is ———.*

green

24 There has been a long dry spell and the grass in your front yard is now brown. Has the grass changed its color?

yes

25 Perhaps you have never thought about this until now, but you have a norm for almost everything you talk about. What does this sentence talk about? *The sky is red.* (a) norm (b) deviation (change from the norm)
Our color norm for the sky is blue. Red is a change or deviation from that norm.

26 What does this tell you? *Chalk is white.* (a) norm (b) deviation
We do have colored chalk, but that is white chalk which has been changed by adding dyes. Our norm for chalk is white.

27 Now, stop and think. Is it possible for everybody to have exactly the same norm for everything?
no (Some students feel that Spanish *is easy;* others think it *is hard.*)

28 There are a great many norms which we share with most of the speakers of English, but, at the same time, every person also has a large number of private or personal norms of his own. For example, Mildred White, age 10, has a brother, George, age 24. Their father is 55 years old. The father thinks that both George and Mildred *are young*, but Mildred thinks George *is old*. Do Mildred and her father have the same norms for old and young?

no

29 Are Mildred and her father both right?
yes (They are just describing George from different, personal points of view.)

30 You now know that the same sentence pattern ("to be" plus a predicate adjective) can be used to describe a subject in two quite different ways. *The sky is blue* states the color norm for most people. *The sky is red* gives a deviation from that norm. What does this sentence tell you? *Harvey is pale.* (a) norm (b) deviation (c) you can't tell
you can't really tell

31 There are two reasons why you cannot tell precisely what *Harvey is pale* actually means. First, you do not know Harvey, so your logic cannot help you discover the meaning. Second, there is nothing in the forms of the words or their serial arrangement which cues the meaning. Now, watch how your linguistic logic goes to work on this: *Harvey has just seen a terrible accident. Is he pale!* Does Harvey normally have a pale skin?

no

32 There are now two things that tell you that Harvey's paleness is abnormal. First, your logic tells you that seeing the accident *caused* Harvey to change, to turn pale. Second, ———. Before you answer, take a good look at the sentence: *Is he pale!*
the word order of *Is he pale!* (And the exclamation.)

33 Now, let's see how your logic works on these sentences: *The oven is hot; The oven is cold.* Do both of these statements describe a change in the temperature of the oven? Think before you decide.
yes (When the oven is hot, *it has been heated.* When the oven is cold, *it has lost its heat.*)

34 Can a hot dog (wiener) be cold?

yes   **35** Do you have a norm for the temperature of hot dogs?

no   **36** We say "The door is open" and "The door is closed." Does either one of these give a norm?

no   **37** There are some things for which we have no norms. We can say "Steel is hard" and immediately understand that this is a standard characteristic of steel. We really can't say which is normal for doors: being opened or closed. If we have no norm for something, must our description always imply that there has been a change from some previous state?

yes   **38** But you have to be careful. A man buys a cup of coffee in a *café*. He tastes it, turns angrily to the waiter, and says, "This coffee is cold." Does he have a norm for the way coffee ought to be when served?

yes   **39** Does "Cement is hard" state a norm?

yes   **40** Does "You can go there now. *The cement is hard.*" state a norm?

no (It has become hard; it has changed.)

41 The Spanish speaker organizes the world with precisely the same kind of logic as you do. He has norms that are just like yours, and he understands the difference between the normal and the abnormal just the way you do. There is, however, a great big difference between what he says and what you say. The Spanish speaker always tells his hearer whether the predicate adjective describes the norm or some deviation or change from his norm. He does this in a very neat and simple way by using two verbs where you use "to be." These verbs are *ser* and *estar*. You will learn how the Spanish speaker uses them to help his hearers understand him better in the next Program.

No new vocabulary.

PROGRAM **53**

Predicate Adjectives and the Spanish Organization of Reality

1 A predicate adjective must describe the subject of the sentence. Is there a predicate adjective in this sentence? "I want a red car."

no   **2** A predicate adjective may give your norm for the subject (Grass is green) or state that something has happened to the subject, that is, it has ~~~~~

changed (*The grass is brown.*)

3 The Spanish speaker recognizes the same natural laws as you do. For him it is normal for the sun to be hot, for ice to be cold, for the earth to be round, *etc.* Look at these translations:

The sun is hot.	*El sol es caliente.*
Ice is cold.	*El hielo es frío.*
The earth is round.	*La tierra es redonda.*

To state a natural law the Spanish speaker uses the verb ⁓⁓⁓ and a predicate adjective.

ser

4 If the Spanish speaker uses *ser* to state a natural law, is it logical to expect him to use *ser* when the predicate adjective describes his norm for any subject?

yes

5 Do you remember this sentence from Program 52? "Harvey is pale." It has two very different meanings.

(1) Harvey has a light colored skin. He is normally pale.

(2) He has a dark skin. It is abnormal for him to be pale. Here are the two Spanish translations:

Harvey is pale.   *Harvey es pálido.*
Harvey está pálido.

The Spanish speaker indicates the abnormal, a change or deviation from his norm, by using the verb ⁓⁓⁓ and a predicate adjective.

estar (In English you have to figure out the meaning by logic or from the context. The Spanish speaker always tells the hearer what he means.)

6 Mr. Nicanor Salcedo takes a sip of his morning coffee and says to his wife, *Mi café está frío*. Does this tell her that he normally expects his coffee to be hot?

yes (Mr. Salcedo has a norm for good coffee. It should be hot. Being cold is a change from his norm.)

7 Mr. Salcedo is 84 years old. He is the oldest man in the village. Everybody in the village says, (a) *El señor Salcedo es viejo.* (b) *El señor Salcedo está viejo.*

84 meets everyone's norm for old, so they say, *El señor Salcedo es viejo.*

8 Mrs. Salcedo has a reputation throughout the whole village for being a neat and careful housekeeper. "Her house is very clean." When the villagers say this, they use (a) *ser* (b) *estar*.

ser (*Su casa es muy limpia.*)

9 Mr. Salcedo, in spite of his age, is a happy and cheerful man who enjoys life and has fun telling jokes. One day he gets a letter with some terrible news in it. As he walks across the plaza on his way home, he speaks to no one, and people say, "What's the matter with Mr. Salcedo? He is sad!" They say, (a) *¡Es triste!* (b) *¡Está triste!*

¡Está triste! (It is not normal for Mr. Salcedo to be sad.)

10 When the Spanish speaker describes anything with a predicate adjective he has to choose between *ser* and *estar*. Now, suppose a tourist who has just come to the village happens to see Mr. Salcedo as he walks home thinking about that terrible news. Does the tourist have a norm for Mr. Salcedo?

no (He has never seen him before.)

11 Has the tourist any way of knowing that Mr. Salcedo is normally a happy man who has become sad?

no

12 Can the tourist, from experience, classify people as either sad or happy?

yes

13 What is the tourist's first impression of Mr. Salcedo?

sad

14 The tourist can judge only by what he sees and from his own experience of other people. How do you think he will describe Mr. Salcedo? (a) *Es triste.* (b) *Está triste.*

Es triste. (His first impression becomes his norm for Mr. Salcedo.)

15 The villagers say that Mr. Salcedo *está triste*. The tourist says that he *es triste*. Do the villagers and the tourist have really different norms for a sad and happy man?

no (They all belong to the same culture.)

16 Do the villagers and the tourist have very different information with which to judge Mr. Salcedo?

yes (The villagers know that it is abnormal for Mr. Salcedo to be so sad.)

17 Does the tourist, who has just seen Mr. Salcedo for the first time, have any way of knowing that it is abnormal for him to be sad?

no

18 There are two very different and correct answers to this next question. Is the tourist wrong when he says, *Ese señor es triste?* In terms of what the villagers know, the tourist is wrong in using *ser*. However, the tourist is right because ~~~~~~.

From the point of view of what he has seen and his own experience of other people, the tourist can arrive at no other conclusion. He is right in terms of *his* information.

19 Now let's see how Spanish helps the hearer in a way that English does not. The tourist stops to talk with a villager. The villager happens to mention that Mr. Salcedo *está triste*. What does this immediately tell the tourist? That his first impression was (a) right (b) wrong.

wrong (The *estar* tells him instantly that Mr. Salcedo is not normally sad.)

20 What is normal for any individual depends entirely on *his* knowledge and personal experience. In many of the tropical regions of South America (Colombia for example) the heavy rains turn the iron in the rocks to rust and the soil there is red. The color norm for soil for the people of these regions is red, because wherever they go, they see red earth. Would it be logical for them to conclude that red is the natural color of soil all over the earth?

yes (All of their experience points to this conclusion.)

21 In parts of Argentina where there is less rain, the land is covered with thick, natural grass. The roots of the grass rot and become humus, and the soil, as a result, is almost black. Mr. Martín, from the jungles of Colombia, visits Argentina. He looks at the black soil. Does the color fit his color norm for soil?

no (For him, soil should be red.)

22 Mr. Martín is astonished. What do you think he will say? (a) *La tierra es negra.* (b) *La tierra está negra.*

La tierra está negra.

23 To tell someone that what you see does not fit *your* norm, you use ~~~~~.

estar (The soil has not really changed, but its black color is a deviation from Mr. Martín's norm for soil [red].)

24 Mr. Martín goes back home to his jungle with a lot of new information. He now knows that there are different colored soils: black, red, grey, *etc.* Can he any longer have a single color norm for soil?

no (He now has to have a color norm for different regions.)

25 He wants to teach his children about Argentina. What does he now tell them? (a) *La tierra de Argentina es negra.* (b) *La tierra de Argentina está negra.*

One teaches norms, so he says, *La tierra de Argentina es negra.*

26 Now, think about this. Something happens and something changes. Mr. Salcedo, the old villager, gets a letter with some very bad news in it. He becomes sad. He is pretty old and never recovers from the blow. His old happiness does not come back. Will the villagers gradually replace their old norm for him (happy) with a new norm (sad)?

yes 　　　　**27** When this has happened, what do they say? (a) *El señor Salcedo es triste.* (b) *El señor Salcedo está triste.*

They have a new norm, so they say, *es triste.*

28 You have learned that the Spanish speaker sees the world almost exactly like you do but that he has to tell his hearer about this by choosing between *ser* and *estar.* Let's see, now, if you can choose like a Spanish speaker.

Marta has a nice home, kind parents, and many friends. She *is happy.* (a) *ser* (b) *estar.*

ser (Es feliz.) 　　**29** Operating rooms in hospitals have *to be clean.* (a) *ser* (b) *estar*
ser (Is any other norm logical?)

30 You find a white glove lying in the mud. It *is dirty.* (a) *ser* (b) *estar*
estar (Gloves are bought clean. They have *to get dirty.*)

31 Most pigs *are dirty.* (a) *ser* (b) *estar*
ser (Dirt is normal for pigs.)

32 Diamonds *are hard.* (a) *ser* (b) *estar*
ser (Hardness is one of the most outstanding characteristics of diamonds.)

33 Mr. Pimental is sixty-five and has felt fine all his life. He wakes up one morning feeling a bit stiff and not too energetic. Suddenly it dawns on him that his age is catching up with him. He exclaims, "*I'm old!*" (a) *ser* (b) *estar*
estar (He's just become aware of the change. His norm up to now has been that he is not old.)

34 You have washed the dishes, and you say to your mother, "All the dishes *are clean.*" (a) *ser* (b) *estar*
estar (They *got dirty* at the table; they have to *get clean* in the kitchen.)

35 There's a big difference about this restaurant. When they serve you food, the food *is always hot.* (a) *ser* (b) *estar*
ser (This is normal for this restaurant.)

36 Gloria has the flu. She *is very sick.* (a) *ser* (b) *estar*
estar (Está muy enferma.)

37 Fernando has just fallen down the stairs and hurt his leg. He *is lame.* (a) *ser* (b) *estar*
estar (Está cojo.)

38 Panchito, the bootblack, has just been told he has won 10,000 pesos on the lottery. He shouts, "*I'm rich!*" (a) *ser* (b) *estar*
estar (¡Estoy rico!)

39 Let's review the difference between norm and deviation from the norm (abnormal).

Tropical rain forests are hot and damp. (a) norm (b) deviation from the norm

norm 　　　**40** Most Latin Americans are short. (a) norm (b) deviation from the norm
norm 　　　**41** This milk is sour. (a) norm (b) deviation
deviation 　**42** Look out! The rug is wet! (a) norm (b) deviation
deviation 　**43** Most people believe that deserts are hot. (a) norm (b) deviation
norm 　　　**44** Are all tigers ferocious? (a) norm (b) deviation
norm 　　　**45** Most students who study with Programs usually change their mind about learning, because they discover that learning *can be easy.* (a) norm (b) deviation

They discover a new norm.

46 Here is a summary of what you have just studied:

(1) To state a natural law or to give your norm for anything, you use *ser* plus a predicate adjective.

> The earth is round.   *La tierra es redonda.*
> Grass is green.   *La hierba es verde.*

(2) To state that the subject has changed, is deviating from the norm, you use *estar* and the adjective which describes the deviation.

> Harvey is pale.. (norm)   *Harvey es pálido.*
> Is Harvey pale! (deviation)   *¡Harvey está pálido!*

(3) When you meet something for the first time, and can find no evidence that a change has taken place, you state your first impression with *ser*.

> I just met Mrs. Canedo. She is very friendly. *Ella es muy amable.*

(4) Two speakers of Spanish can view the same person or thing from two different points of view. What is normal for one person (*ser*) may be abnormal for the other (*estar*).

> *El señor Salcedo es triste. No, está triste.*

(5) When something or someone changes, there may be no change back. When this happens you gradually get used to the change, you develop a new norm and you now use *ser*.

New Vocabulary

cruel	cruel
enfermo	ill, sick
ecuador	equator
quiero	I want

PROGRAM 54

A Review of the Four Ways of Learning to Spell in Spanish

1 Most people believe that the letters of all words stand for the sounds one makes when the words are said. There is a city in southern Mexico whose name is pronounced [wajaca]. The Mexicans write this word *Oaxaca*. Does this spelling tell you what to say?

no (To learn to spell *Oaxaca* you have to see the word. Let's call this *eye spelling.*) **2** If you hear the word [papel], will you be able to write all the proper letters?

yes (What you hear in this case tells you what to write because each phoneme in the word is always represented by the same grapheme. This is *ear spelling.*)

3 The sound [k] may be spelled *c* or *qu*. Say [sinko] aloud. You write [k] as (a) *c* (b) *qu*.

c   **4** What tells you to write *c*? (a) what you hear (b) what you see (c) a spelling rule and what you hear.

a spelling rule and what you hear (You write [k] as *c* before *a, o,* and *u*. This is *rule spelling.*)   **5** The [s] sound of [sinko] might be written either *c* or *s*. What tells you to write *cinco*? (a) rule spelling (b) ear spelling (c) eye spelling

eye spelling (You have to see *cinco* to find out that it begins with a *c*.)

6 A baker makes a loaf of bread out of *dough* and a female deer is called a *doe*. These words sound exactly alike. What tells you when to write *dough* or *doe*? (a) what you hear (b) the meaning of each word

the meaning of each word (This is *meaning spelling*. What the word stands for tells you which spelling to use. You have, of course, to see each word to learn both spellings.)   **7** Before you spell any word must you decide which spelling cues are to be used in writing the word correctly?

yes   **8** Say [felipe] and [lunes] aloud. Does what you say and hear tell you what to write? You are going to be trapped if you don't write out each word before you answer.

Did you goof? The answer is "no." You capitalize proper names but not the days of the week. Capitalization is part of rule spelling.

9 Does the letter *h* stand for a sound in Spanish?

no (All words with *h* have to be seen before you can learn to spell them.)

10 Does *u* always stand for a sound in Spanish?

no (It is part of a digraph in **qu**é and *Mi***gu**el.)

11 Say *lunes* and *bueno* aloud. Do this again and listen to the sound of *u* in each word. Does the *u* stand for the same sound in both words?

no   **12** In which word does the *u* stand for [w]?

bueno (Pronounced [bweno]. Remember that Spanish has no letter *w* in native words and has to use *u* in its place.)

13 In [lunes] the *u* stands for (a) a pure vowel (b) a consonant.

a pure vowel (When *u* is followed by a consonant, it always stands for a vowel.)

14 Does knowing that *bueno* is pronounced [bweno] help you learn to spell it?

no (Knowing that *u* can stand for [w] helps you read aloud properly.)

15 Do you remember the cognates "cat" and *gato*? This should remind you that [k] is the unvoiced equivalent of what voiced sound?

[g]   **16** A spelling rule tells you that [k] and [g] are spelled *c* and *g* before which three vowels?

a, o, u   **17** What graphemes (letters) are used to spell [k] and [g] before *e* and *i*?

the digraphs *qu* and *gu*

18 Say [ke] aloud. What tells you to write [ke] with or without an accent mark? (a) what you hear (b) a spelling rule (c) meaning

meaning (*Qué* has the accent mark in a question: *¿Qué es esto?*, but no accent in *El hombre que está allí.*)

19 What tells you to write "to, two, too" in English?

the meaning (Plus what you see.)

20 Will your ear tell you how to spell the subject pronoun *tú*?

no (Your ear will tell you to write *t* plus *u*, but not the accent mark. You have to see *tú* (the subject) and *tu* (the possessive adjective) to learn the difference.)

21 Here's a question that lots of people answer wrong. Let's see if you can escape being trapped. Can you write everything you can say?

no (Here is the proof. You can say, "There are two ...s in Spanish (*tú* and *tu*) and three ...s in English (to, too, two)" but no one can write what you say in regular letters.) **22** In this and the following frames you will find a word written in phonetic script. Say the word aloud and write it in regular letters.

[tisa]

tiza (You must remember what you have seen to spell *tiza* correctly.)

23 [siyas]

sillas (In the dialect you are learning, *ll* stands for [y].)

24 [ola]

hola (Only eye spelling tells you to write *h*.)

25 This one has two words in it: [ketal]. And to get it right you have to remember punctuation *and* capitalization.

¿Qué tal? (Did you also remember the accent mark?)

26 [senyor]

señor **27** [mwi]

muy (*u* stands for [w] in speech in this word.)

28 [lwego]

luego **29** [¿donde?]

dónde (This is a question word and so it needs the accent mark on the stressed syllable.) **30** [aki]

aquí ([k] is written *qu* before *i* and *e*.)

New Vocabulary

recto	straight
fecha	date (calendar)
torcido	twisted

PROGRAM 55

More on *ser* and *estar*, and Vocabulary Round-up

Part 1: *ser* versus *estar*

By now you understand pretty well what cues you to choose between *ser* or *estar* with predicate adjectives. However, to learn to talk Spanish like a native, you have to learn to spot the cues and select the verb without really thinking about the process consciously. This takes a lot of practice. Look at each frame below and see how fast you can decide whether you would use *ser* or *estar*. If you do not use your cover sheet, you will spoil your practice and learn very little.

1 The water in the pot *is* now *hot.*
estar (It has been heated and, so, changed.)

2 The White House in Washington *is white.*
ser (That's our color norm for the White House.)

3 All astronomers know that some stars *are red.*
ser (There are, as a part of nature, red and white stars.)

4 Any man who has lived 90 years *is old.*
ser (90 meets our norm for old age.)

5 Charo has just gotten a new car. She *is happy.*
estar (Getting the car made her happy.)

6 Somebody smashed the window. Father *is furious.*
estar (The broken window caused him to become angry, a change.)

7 You can't go yet. The stoplight *is red.*
estar (It always keeps changing so you have no norm for stoplights.)

8 Look at your shoes! They *are dirty!*
estar (You got them dirty.)

9 Snow *is white.*
ser (We would be astonished by green snow.)

10 Mr. Martel is such a nice man. He *is so kind.*
ser (The speaker always sees him this way.)

11 Watch out! The floor *is slick!*
estar (It's dangerous to have slippery floors. This is abnormal.)

12 I haven't seen John in weeks. Look how *thin* he *is* now! (What does the exclamation intonation tell you?)
estar (We usually don't exclaim about what is normal.)

13 Lead *is heavy;* feathers *are light.*
ser (The weight norm for both.)

14 We can't go sailing today. It's storming and the sea *is rough.*
estar (The storm has caused the sea to become rough. Notice that "become" signals a change. It is sometimes the best translation of *estar.*)

15 Lincolns and Cadillacs *are expensive.*
ser (Prestige cars are always expensive.)

16 That's odd. In this light your face *is green.*
estar (Green is not our color norm for human skin.)

17 The pampas of Argentina *are very flat.*
ser (A plain has to be fairly flat.)

18 Grown elephants *are huge.*
ser (We usually think so.)

19 Pygmies *are small.*
ser (It's their nature.)

20 If you got all of these correct, you *are very intelligent.*
ser (You were born that way. You are also pretty smart if you got most of them right.)

Americans, by and large, are slaves to the clock and to unwritten social rules which are tied to the clock. It is expected that you come to class on time. If you don't, you may get a tardy mark. Conductors get annoyed if people come late to concerts. You must get to the doctor's office at the appointed hour or you may miss your turn or upset his schedule. Every effort is made to be certain that trains, buses, and planes leave on time. One must check out of hotels and motels at a certain time of day or pay an extra day's rent. People buy things on a time payment plan. And, in addition, there is an unmentioned but general agreement that the importance of the person with whom you have an appointment determines how much you arrive *ahead of time* to keep the appointment. Because we are afraid of being *late,* we give ourselves more time in proportion to the importance of the person we are to meet. The more insecure a person is, the earlier he arrives. Many people go to the airport an hour before their plane is to leave.

The Latins are much more nonchalant about arriving on time. Millions of them do not even own a watch or clock and many live a life which is almost totally unregulated by clocks.

Guests may arrive for dinner an hour late and no one expects an apology. Teachers are frequently late for classes. Knowledgeable people call the railroad station or airport before going to meet arrivals because trains and planes are often behind schedule.

The following anecdote clearly reveals the difference in attitude toward punctuality. A North American living in a Latin country had a date to go to the theater with a man and his wife. Because of heavy traffic there was a delay, and upon arriving *five* minutes late he found the couple gone. On next meeting they explained their action in this manner, "We are so accustomed to having you arrive *ahead of time,* we just assumed that you couldn't make it. So we left."

Part 2: Vocabulary Round-up

You can know all about the grammar of a language, all of its morphology, its phonemic system, and its syntactic patterns, but you cannot *talk* in the language until you know enough words to say what you want to say. It has taken you quite a few years to learn all the English words you now know. You can't afford to spend that much time learning the vocabulary of a second language. There have to be short-cuts. One of these is to study words with the purpose of remembering them. Just learning lists, however, is a great waste of time. To learn for remembering you need to know the meaning, the form, and the function (how the word is used). Here are some meanings; write the Spanish word which fits the meaning.

vivir
director
frío
campo
país

1 The act of being alive or residing in a given place.
2 The person in charge of a school or institution.
3 Having a very low temperature.
4 The territory or land in between cities and towns.
5 A geographic area governed by a president and a congress.

6 A building in which Christians worship.

iglesia **7** An institution which guards peoples' money.

banco **8** To be lacking something that is needed. (Write the infinitive.)

necesitar **9** A misrepresentation of the facts.

mentira **10** An interval of time made up of 30 days.

mes **11** To move very rapidly on foot (from one place to another).

correr **12** Located at a great distance from a given point.

lejos **13** Being only a few years old. (Write the adjective.)

joven **14** People who herd cattle in Argentina.

gauchos **15** A building where merchandise is sold.

tienda (A long time ago merchants put up tents in the market place to sell things. The Spanish word for "tent" is still *tienda*.)

16 Another way to learn to remember words is to associate them with some other word, especially with one you already know well. Name three places in Spanish you associate with fun or entertainment.

You might have chosen *cine, parque, playa, etc.*

17 Give three verbs that are associated with school and learning.

estudiar, leer, escribir, hablar, etc.

18 Name three things you might associate with *grande, enorme,* or *inmenso.*

elefante, Brasil, océano, montañas, etc.

19 What mechanical thing do you associate with *hora* and *minuto?*

reloj **20** The noun *viento* suggests something that houses have.

ventana **21** Writing is associated with ~~~~.

papel, lápiz, pluma, etc.

22 Learning words along with their opposites makes them easier to remember. Let's see if you have been making this association. The opposite of *ayer* is not *hoy* but ~~~~.

mañana **23** The opposite of *magnífico* is ~~~~.

terrible **24** The opposite of *verano* is ~~~~.

invierno **25** The opposite of *más* is ~~~~.

menos **26** Another important way of improving your memory of words is to write them. Practicing the physical act of making certain sequences of letters establishes memory patterns in your brain. Below are all the common nouns you have had up to a few days ago, arranged in the order you first met them.

Each person has his own personal lag time in learning new words, that is, the amount of time he has to be in contact with a word before he has complete mastery of it. Cover the Spanish column and go down the English list carefully until you find the place where you are no longer certain of the meaning, function, or spelling of quite a few Spanish words. You have discovered, when this happens, your personal lag point. Study *all the rest* of the list carefully and copy every word about which you have the slightest hesitation.

señor	mister, man	**clase**	class
señorita	miss, lady	**mañana**	tomorrow, morning
profesor	professor	**inglés**	English
día	day	**oficina**	office
tarde	afternoon	**libro**	book
noche	night	**cuaderno**	notebook

lápiz	pencil	cuarto	room
reloj	clock	medio	half
momentito	moment	casa	house
papel	paper	cine	movie
pupitre	desk	parque	park
pluma	pen	playa	beach
silla	chair	montaña	mountain
mesa	table	campo	country
ventana	window	centro	center, downtown
puerta	door	café	café, coffee
ojo	eye; Watch out!	correo	mail, post office
pizarra	blackboard	lugar	place
regla	ruler	banco	bank
luz	(a) light	iglesia	church
tiza	chalk	tienda	store
muchacho	boy	mes	month
muchacha	girl	enero	January
diálogo	dialog	febrero	February
lunes	Monday	marzo	March
martes	Tuesday	abril	April
miércoles	Wednesday	mayo	May
jueves	Thursday	junio	June
viernes	Friday	año	year
sábado	Saturday	julio	July
domingo	Sunday	agosto	August
perdón	pardon	septiembre	September
español	Spanish	octubre	October
director	principal	noviembre	November
escuela	school	diciembre	December
alumno	student	lección	lesson
favor	favor	hombre	man
país	country	padre	father
semana	week	hambre	hunger
mina	(a) mine	sed	thirst
capital	capital	luna	moon
gaucho	gaucho	balcón	balcony
elefante	elephant	gente	people
tigre	tiger, jaguar	niño	child
animal	animal	primavera	spring
rodeo	rodeo	verano	summer
jardín	garden	otoño	autumn
corral	corral	invierno	winter
frío	cold	estación	season, station
fresco	cool	verdad	truth
tiempo	time, weather	mentira	(a) lie
calor	heat	mujer	woman
viento	wind	norte	north
hora	hour	este	east

sur	south	desierto	desert
oeste	west	pampa	pampa
océano	ocean	selva	jungle
mar	sea	barco	ship
río	river	tranvía	streetcar
		túnel	tunnel

27 Except for the articles, here are all the adjectives you have had, also arranged in the order you first met them. Find your lag point and study the rest.

presente	present	paraguayo	Paraguayan
bueno	good	uruguayo	Uruguayan
uno	one	fresco	cool
dos	two	frío	cold
tres	three	buen	good
cuatro	four	brasileño	Brazilian
cinco	five	colombiano	Colombian
seis	six	ecuatoriano	Ecuatorian
siete	seven	peruano	Peruvian
ocho	eight	venezolano	Venezuelan
nueve	nine	perfecto	perfect
diez	ten	malo	bad
once	eleven	medio	half
doce	twelve	cuarto	fourth
trece	thirteen	tacaño	stingy
catorce	fourteen	todo	all
quince	fifteen	terrible	terrible
dieciséis	sixteen	difícil	difficult
diecisiete	seventeen	tu	your
dieciocho	eighteen	fácil	easy
diecinueve	nineteen	cansado	tired
veinte	twenty	primero	first
nuevo	new	segundo	second
amable	kind	tercero	third
mucho	much	último	last
ventiuno	twenty-one	magnífico	magnificent
veintidós	twenty-two	descansado	rested
veintitrés	twenty-three	feliz	happy
veinticuatro	twenty-four	triste	sad
veinticinco	twenty-five	grande	big
veintiséis	twenty-six	pequeño	small
veintisiete	twenty-seven	joven	young
veintiocho	twenty-eight	viejo	old
veintinueve	twenty-nine	gordo	fat
treinta	thirty	flaco	thin
argentino	Argentine	alto	tall
boliviano	Bolivian	seco	dry
chileno	Chilean	húmedo	humid

inmenso	immense	**limpio**	clean
bajo	short	**bonito**	pretty
sucio	dirty	**feo**	ugly

28 Here is the list of adverbs you have had, also in the order you have met them. You should know the meaning of all of them by now.

bien	well	**demasiado**	too much
bastante	quite, pretty	**más**	more
muy	very	**afuera**	outside
no	no	**siempre**	always
luego	then	**nunca**	never
pronto	soon	**ya**	already
sí	yes	**todavía**	still
allí	there	**temprano**	early
menos	less	**lejos**	far away
hoy	today	**adentro**	inside
ayer	yesterday	**tarde**	late
mañana	tomorrow	**cerca**	near
aquí	here	**también**	also
anteayer	day-before-yesterday	**además**	besides
nada	nothing	**rápido**	rapidly
mucho	a lot	**despacio**	slowly
poco	a little		

PROGRAM 56

Getting Ready for a Test: How Much Have You Learned?

You are going to have a major test very soon. The purpose of this Program is not to teach you something new but to help you discover what you still have not learned well. As a result, if you make a mistake, stop and think very carefully about what you missed.

Part 1: Verb Forms

1 The three sets of verbs are marked by the vowels ⁓⁓⁓.

a, e, i

2 The set vowel of a verb tells you what morphemes to use for the (a) first (b) second suffix.

first

3 In the present tense of all regular verbs, the *yo*-form always ends in the morpheme ⁓⁓⁓.

o

a	**4** Aside from the *yo*-form, the first suffix of *a*-verbs is always ⌇⌇⌇.
o; e	**5** The regular *e*-verbs have only two morphemes for the first suffix: ⌇⌇⌇.
true	**6** Regular *i*-verbs are almost like *e*-verbs. (a) true (b) false
o, e, i	**7** The *i*-verb forms have three morphemes for the first suffix: ⌇⌇⌇.
nosotros (vivimos)	**8** The *i* always goes with the subject pronoun ⌇⌇⌇.
the subject	**9** The second suffix tells you something about (a) the action (b) the subject.
plural *(ustedes viven, ellos hablan)*	**10** The *n* tells you the subject is either second or third person and ⌇⌇⌇.
	11 There are three suffixes for second person. One is zero *(usted habla)*. The other two are ⌇⌇⌇.
n; s	**12** The *s* always goes with the subject pronoun ⌇⌇⌇.
tú (Did you remember the accent mark? *Tú hablas.*)	**13** The *mos* tells you the subject is ⌇⌇⌇ and plural.
first person *(nosotros)*	**14** A regular verb has only one stem form. (a) true (b) false
true	**15** The stem of the irregular verb *tener* has three allomorphs in the present tense: ⌇⌇⌇.
teng, ten, tien	**16** Complete the form: *yo teng* ... .
yo tengo	**17** Which subject pronoun goes with the stem *ten*?
nosotros tenemos	**18** There are seven different subject pronouns that go with the stem *tien*. Write them down, copy *tien*, and add the matching suffixes.
tú tienes, él tiene, ella tiene, usted tiene, ustedes tienen, ellos tienen, ellas tienen	**19** What verb has the same irregularities as *tener*?
venir (vengo, vienes, venimos)	**20** The verb *estar* has two irregularities. One is in the form that goes with *yo:* ⌇⌇⌇. The other is the stress on the suffix. (a) first (b) second suffix
estoy; the stress on the first suffix	**21** The two present tense forms of *estar* that do not have a written accent are ⌇⌇⌇.
estoy; estamos	**22** The present tense forms of what verb are like *estar*?
ir	**23** Copy and fill in the forms: *yo* ... , *tú* ... , *ellos* ... .
yo voy, tú vas, ellos van	**24** *Ser* is one of the most irregular verbs in the Spanish language. You have to learn most forms one by one. Copy and fill in the blanks: *yo* ... , *nosotros* ...*mos*, *tú* ...*s*, *ustedes* ...*n*.
yo soy, nosotros somos, tú eres, ustedes son	

25 Here are all the verbs you have had to learn up to this point. Do you know their meaning and the present tense forms for all of them? If not, see your *Ejercicios* and *Cuaderno*.

beber	empezar	ir	ser
cantar	entrar	leer	subir
comer	escribir	llamar	tener
correr	estar	llegar	teminar
creer	estudiar	morir	trabajar
deber	haber	necesitar	venir
desear	hablar	salir	vivir

Part 2: Phonetics, Phonemics, and Graphemics

1 The phoneme /d/ has how many allophones?

two   **2** One of its allophones is a ~~~~; the other is a ~~~~.

stop; fricative   **3** The stop [d] is dental. (a) true (b) false

true   **4** The letter or grapheme *d* tells you which allophone to say. (a) true (b) false

false   **5** What tells you which allophone to say? What comes (a) before the *d* (b) after the *d*.

before the *d*   **6** What do you say after silence, /n/, or /l/, the stop [d] or the fricative [đ]?

the stop [d]   **7** The phoneme /s/ has two allophones. It is voiced before a vowel. (a) true (b) false

false (It may be voiced before a following voiced consonant.)   **8** The graphemes *b* and *v* stand for different sounds. (a) true (b) false

false (Some speakers, however, make a different sound for each.)   **9** There are three digraphs which are part of the regular Spanish alphabet. They are *ñ* and ~~~~.

ch; ll   **10** There are two other digraphs which did not get into the alphabet. They appear only before *e* and *i*. They are ~~~~.

qu (que); gu (Miguel)   **11** You can write the phoneme /k/ with two different graphemes. Before *o, a,* and *u* you write ~~~~.

c   **12** What you hear tells you how to write the phoneme /s/. (a) true (b) false

false (You learn to spell /s/ by *seeing* the word it is in.)   **13** Here is the English for twenty words that you have to *see* in order to learn to spell them. Write the Spanish for each and, when you are through, check your spelling word by word.

1 How?	6 How many?	11 wind	16 to live
2 Where?	7 there is	12 well	17 to drink
3 What?	8 thou art	13 difficult	18 winter
4 truth	9 Brazil	14 easy	19 immense
5 very little	10 Who?	15 balcony	20 dirty

1 *¿Cómo?*	6 *¿Cuántos?*	11 *viento*	16 *vivir*
2 *¿Dónde?*	7 *hay*	12 *bien*	17 *beber*
3 *¿Qué?*	8 *tú eres*	13 *difícil*	18 *invierno*
4 *verdad*	9 *Brasil*	14 *fácil*	19 *inmenso*
5 *poquito*	10 *¿Quién?*	15 *balcón*	20 *sucio*

Part 3: Making Choices

1 Match *yo* and *llamo* with the right object pronoun: *Yo* ~~~~ *llamo Alberto.*

me   **2** When you add, what form of *ser* do you use? *Dos y siete* ~~~~ *nueve.*

son   **3** When you subtract, you use ~~~~: *Siete menos dos* ~~~~ *cinco.*

son (*Siete menos dos son cinco.*)   **4** When you address your teacher, you use (a) *tú* (b) *usted.*

usted   **5** When a noun ends in a consonant, you make it plural by adding ~~~~

es   **6** What tells you to use *el* with *libro?*

the final phoneme /o/

7 You want to locate Santiago in Chile. You use the verb ~~~~.

estar (Santiago está en Chile.)

8 You want to locate *una pluma* on the table. You use the verb (a) *haber* (b) *estar* (c) *ser*.

*haber (**Hay** una pluma en la mesa.)*

9 You want to say where someone is from. You use the verb ~~~~.

ser (Es de las Guayanas.)

10 You are a girl speaking for a group of girls. You use the subject pronoun ~~~~.

nosotras   **11** To say a person *is hot*, you use the verb ~~~~.

tener (Tiene calor.)

12 To say the weather *is hot*, you use ~~~~.

hacer (Hace calor.)

13 To change *Hace calor* to the equivalent of "It is very hot," you add (a) *muy* (b) *mucho*.

mucho (Because calor is a noun and muy is an adverb.)

14 With all clock numbers from 2 to 12 you use the verb form ~~~~ in telling time.

son (But Es la una.)

15 In telling time, the hour 2 can be used with two different parts of the day: ~~~~.

mañana; tarde **16** Write the missing relator: *Vamos* ~~~~ *cantar.*

a   **17** You will find it helpful in getting ready for the test to reread the stories you have had in your *Ejercicios*.

No new vocabulary.

PROGRAM **57**

Preparing for a Test

In your next class you are going to have a test which will cover everything you have learned about Spanish except speaking and reading aloud. If you have been doing your Programs carefully and have been doing your work in class, you are ready for the test. The purpose of this Program, consequently, is not to teach you something new or to review what you already know, but rather to make sure you know how to take the test, and to help you avoid mistakes which have nothing to do with how much Spanish you really know.

1 Part A deals with listening comprehension. Can you understand what you hear, and say something that shows that you have? You will hear a sentence *in Spanish* and, then, a question *in English*. You are to write an answer *in English* with a word or phrase which *proves* you understand the Spanish sentence. Here is an example: *María tiene dos hermanos y una hermana*. How many sisters does María have?

one **2** Here is another example: *Miguel escribe en la pizarra*. What is Miguel writing with?

chalk (You normally write on the blackboard with chalk.)

 3 *Carlota está muy triste*. Is this what Carlota is normally like?

no (*Estar* tells you that sadness is not normal for her.)

 4 Part B of the exam also deals with listening comprehension. You will hear a statement or question twice. On your answer sheet, there will be three answers—two wrong and one right—labeled a, b, c. You are to circle the letter that goes with the right answer.

 Here is an example of what you will hear: *Mañana es el 25 de diciembre.* Here are three responses. Which is most likely? (a) *Es un día terrible.* (b) *Estoy muy contento.* (c) *Hace mucho calor en Alaska.*

(b) is the most logical response.

 5 Here's another example: *Mi padre está en la playa.* (a) *Es un día de verano.* (b) *Está lejos del mar.* (c) *Son las tres de la mañana.*

(a) is the most logical next statement.

 6 Can you answer this one? *¿Dónde está Venezuela?* (a) *al sur del ecuador* (b) *en el ecuador* (c) *al norte del ecuador*

al norte del ecuador (The question is about the "equator," not the country, *Ecuador.*) **7** Part C is to find out whether you really understand the relationship between speech and reality. There will be 10 picture posters on the board. You will hear 10 statements or questions. You are to pick the picture which goes most logically with the statement or question. For example, you hear: *Hace frío* and see: (A) palm trees and people swimming (B) a man reading a book (C) a snow-covered mountain.

You pick the snow-covered mountain and write the letter C on your answer sheet. **8** You hear: *José está enfermo.* You see (D) a malted milk (E) a banana (F) a bottle of pills.

Pills are more logically associated with illness than a banana or a malted milk.

 9 You hear: *Mamá está alegre.* You see (G) a car with a flat tire (H) a sink full of dirty dishes (I) a nice, new hat.

Flat tires and dirty dishes do not make most women happy. New hats, however, often do. Remember, these questions test your *logic* as well as your Spanish. **10** Part D is to find out if you know your verb forms. You will hear a model: *Gordo come demasiado* and, then, a cue: *Ustedes . . .* You circle the verb form on your answer sheet that matches *ustedes: como comemos comes comen.*

comen **11** Model: *Ernesto trabaja mucho.* Cue: *José y yo . . . trabajo trabajas trabajamos trabajan*

trabajamos **12** Part E deals with telling time. You will hear a statement, *Son las cuatro y media de la mañana*, and you will write on your answer sheet the Arabic numbers and add either PM or AM.

4:30 AM **13** *Son las diez menos quince de la noche.*

9:45 PM **14** *Es la una y diez de la tarde.*

1:10 PM **15** Part F is to find out whether you can match the right form of an adjective with a noun or pronoun and spell the adjective correctly. You will hear a

sentence which has a predicate adjective: *José es chileno*, and a cue: *Ellas*
... You change *chileno* to ⁓.

chilenas   **16** For Part G there will be three sentences on your answer sheet. You are to
rewrite them and make them negative. So, *Yo tengo algo* becomes ⁓.

Yo no tengo nada.

17 *Juan está en el correo* becomes ⁓.

Juan no está en el correo. (Be careful to copy the words correctly. You don't
want to lose points on spelling errors. Write as neatly as you can.)

18 Your answer sheet for Part H will have two columns of paired words. One
column will have a number before the word and a parenthesis ( ) after it, like
this: **4** *invierno* ( ). The second column will have a letter before each word. You
pick the word which goes with or is the opposite of the numbered word and
write its letter in the parentheses. The opposite of *invierno* is ⁓.

verano   **19** The opposite of *calor* is ⁓.
frío   **20** What do you regularly associate with *papel?*
lápiz or *pluma*   **21** On your answer sheet for Part I, you will find 5 sentences with a blank for
the verb. Each blank is to be filled with the proper verb, *ser (es)* or *estar (está)*.
For example: *La tiza* ⁓ *blanca.*

es   **22** *¿ Dónde* ⁓ *mi reloj?*
está   **23** *¿ De dónde* ⁓ *Carlos?*
es   **24** ⁓ *la una de la mañana.*
Es   **25** Part J is to find out whether you can understand what you read. You will
see on your answer sheet a part of a sentence, for example: *La parte central
de Argentina* ... and four completions, only one of which is logical: (a) *es una
inmensa playa.* (b) *no produce absolutamente nada bueno.* (c) *se llama la pampa.*
(d) *tiene mujeres y niños pero no tiene hombres.*

se llama la pampa

26 *En español las horas de la noche son de* ... (a) *siete a seis.* (b) *una a doce.*
(c) *siete a doce.* (d) *una a siete.*

siete a doce (de la noche)

27 *Cuando tenemos mucha hambre vamos* ... (a) *al teatro.* (b) *a la escuela.*
(c) *al correo.* (d) *a un café.*

a un café   **28** Part K also deals with reading. It is to see whether you can pick a logical
response to a statement or question. There will be a statement or question on
your answer sheet. For example: *El sur de Chile está muy cerca de Antártica.*
There will be four reactions. You pick the most logical. (a) *El Polo Norte está
allí.* (b) *Hay muchos elefantes en esta región.* (c) *Sí, Chile es un país tropical.*
(d) *Nunca hace mucho calor allí.*

(d) is the most logical.

29 *José está muy cansado.* (a) *No tiene hermanos.* (b) *Come mucho.* (c) *Es de las
Guayanas.* (d) *Trabaja demasiado.*

(d) is the most logical response.

30 In this and all the rest of the frames in this Program, you will be given practice that will help you get ready for the test.
Usted escribe con ⁓.

pluma, lápiz, o tiza

31 *El español es un dialecto moderno del latín.* (a) *sí* (b) *no*

sí

	32 ¿En qué parte de Argentina está Buenos Aires? Está en ~~~.
el norte	**33** ¿Cuál es más grande? (a) un mar (b) un océano
un océano	**34** El país más húmedo de Sudamérica es ~~~.
Brasil (con *s* en español; con *z* en inglés)	
	35 Hay dos hemisferios. La línea que divide el globo en hemisferios se llama el ~~~.
ecuador	**36** El tigre es un animal doméstico. (a) *verdad* (b) *mentira*
mentira	**37** ¿Cuántas horas hay en la mañana?
doce	**38** La primera estación del año es la ~~~.
primavera	**39** Veintiocho menos doce son ~~~.
dieciséis	**40** Cuando hablamos de la temperatura de personas usamos el verbo (a) hacer (b) tener.
tener (*Tengo calor, frío, etc.*)	
	41 Con el nombre *ciudades* es necesario usar el adjetivo (a) moderno (b) moderna (c) modernas.
modernas	**42** Si el sujeto del verbo es nosotros, el segundo sufijo siempre es ~~~.
mos	**43** ¿Qué verbo es necesario para completar esta frase? José y Rosario ~~~ de Asunción.
son o vienen	**44** Un alumno que nunca estudia es ~~~. (a) diligente (b) perezoso
perezoso (lazy)	

No new vocabulary.

Tacaño
Stingy, tightwad

Bend elbow of left arm until hand is directly below chin. With right hand sharply pat the end of the left elbow two or three times.

The Land: Chile, Argentina

Both Chile and Argentina have long coastlines. Separated by the Andes and at one time enemies, these two neighbors erected the gigantic Cristo de los Andes as a symbol of peace between them.

The barrenness of the Atacama Desert contrasts with the abundance of goods in the Chilean market.

Where Argentina, Paraguay, and Brazil all meet, the Iguassu river creates a spectacular waterfall.

The modern wheat farmer and the legendary gaucho both claim the immense Argentinean plain, the Pampa, as home.

In the Spanish tradition, Argentineans of northern European descent decorate graves, or nichos, on special holidays.

From the busy harbor of Buenos Aires, Argentinean meat, leather, wool, tea, and agricultural products are shipped throughout the world.

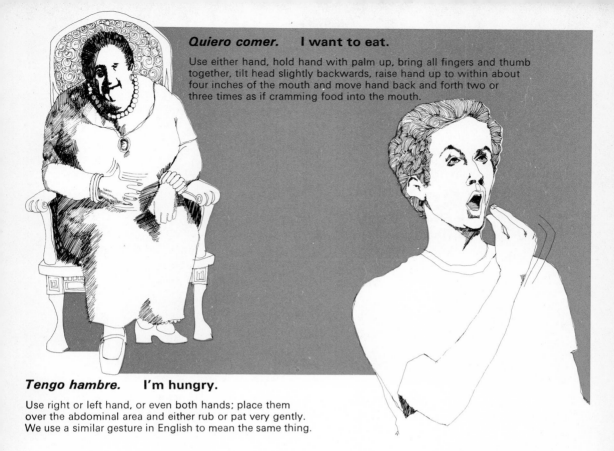

Quiero comer. **I want to eat.**

Use either hand, hold hand with palm up, bring all fingers and thumb together, tilt head slightly backwards, raise hand up to within about four inches of the mouth and move hand back and forth two or three times as if cramming food into the mouth.

Tengo hambre. **I'm hungry.**

Use right or left hand, or even both hands; place them over the abdominal area and either rub or pat very gently. We use a similar gesture in English to mean the same thing.

Ejercicios

Ejercicio 15 | Reading Aloud

Don't forget to use all that you have learned about Spanish pronunciation as you read this.

Panchito, el boliviano

Me llamo Francisco Ramírez Velasco. Pero° en el pueblo° donde vivo todos° me llaman Panchito. El nombre de mi papá también° es Francisco. En el pueblo le llaman Pancho. Yo soy Panchito y él es Pancho. Así° no hay problema con los nombres.

But/village/ they all
also
So

    Soy boliviano, de un lugar muy frío en las montañas de los Andes. En mi pueblo hay muchas minas. Bolivia es un país muy rico° en productos minerales. Mi papá es minero. Trabaja en una mina de lunes a viernes.

rich

    Yo no trabajo en las minas. Yo voy a la escuela con los otros muchachos del pueblo. Allí estudiamos mucho todos los días. La profesora es una señora muy amable. Ella es de la capital, pero ahora vive en el pueblo con nosotros. Tengo muchos amigos en la escuela. Los padres de mis amigos también son mineros.

Mi mamá es de Perú, pero ahora vive en Bolivia. Ella trabaja mucho en la casa. Es una casa de adobe con un jardín muy bonito. También tiene un corral donde hay muchos animales. Mi papá siempre viene° de la mina con mucho apetito. Comemos a las siete y media de la tarde. Papá come mucho porque° trabaja mucho en la mina. Yo también como bastante porque trabajo mucho en la escuela.

°comes

°because

Ejercicio 16 | Reading Aloud

1 Creo que alguien está a la puerta de la casa.
2 Todos los veranos vamos a la playa por la mañana.
3 Venimos de Santiago de Chile y vamos a una ciudad de Alaska.
4 Los pobres niños tienen sed y están muy cansados.
5 Aquí en las montañas hace mucho calor en el mes de julio.
6 Mamá dice que el vicepresidente del club tiene un problema mental.
7 Yo creo que cuando hace fresco estudio más fácilmente.
8 Hoy es jueves, el treinta y uno del mes de octubre.
9 Hoy es un día magnífico y vamos al parque nacional.
10 La última estación del año es el invierno; viene después del otoño.
11 El tigre de las Américas es el jaguar o puma.
12 Lima no es una ciudad muy grande, pero es bastante vieja.
13 Este pobre señor es muy gordo y debe comer menos.
14 No hace demasiado calor allí, pero es tan húmedo que el tiempo es terrible.
15 Ecuador es un país tropical, pero el elefante no es de allí.

Ejercicio 17 | Reading Aloud

1 Ya son las nueve y cuarto; es hora de comer.
2 Es bastante difícil estudiar aquí; hace demasiado calor.
3 Un animal famoso de las Américas es el tigre.
4 Yo leo el español fácilmente, y además lo (it) escribo bastante bien.
5 Ya es muy tarde y todavía no vienen las otras personas.
6 Hoy es miércoles, el veintisiete de noviembre.
7 A esta hora trabajamos todos los días en la escuela.
8 En mi casa comemos cada noche a las siete menos cuarto.
9 En la América del Sur hay nueve países en que hablan español.
10 Brasilia es la capital de Brasil y allí no hablan español.
11 Los gauchos argentinos no viven en la ciudad de Buenos Aires.
12 Un señor muy tacaño trabaja en el banco nacional.
13 Todos los domingos vamos a la iglesia y a la playa.
14 En verano, la estación del calor, no vamos nunca al desierto.

Ejercicio 18 | *ser* versus *estar*

In this exercise you must first decide whether *ser* or *estar* is to be used according to what follows the verb. Then, select the correct form of whichever verb you choose. Remember that there is an adjectival agreement problem with the last two entries in the right column. Write the combinations that your teacher gives you.

1	María			1	bastante bien.
2	Pepe y tú			2	aquí hoy.
3	Yo	estar		3	en la mina.
4	Ustedes	ser		4	de Bolivia.
5	Tú			5	chilen- .
6	Pancho y yo			6	peruan- .

Ejercicio 19 | *ser* versus *estar*

Write the combinations that your teacher gives you.

1	Todos los muchachos			1	bien, gracias.
2	Tú y yo			2	venezolan- .
3	Yo	estar		3	en el campo.
4	Paco y Elena	ser		4	aquí ahora.
5	Tú (*f*)			5	brasileñ- .
6	Usted			6	de Caracas.

Ejercicio 20 | **Adjectival Agreement and** *ser*

Write the combinations that your teacher gives you.

1	Él			1	cruel.
2	Ella	ser		2	amable.
3	Ellos			3	joven.
4	Ellas				

Ejercicio 21 | **Verbs of Motion**

Write the combinations that your teacher gives you.

		1	salir de			
1	Yo	2	venir de		1	(e)l parque.
2	El alumno y yo	3	llegar a		2	las montañas.
3	Tú	4	subir a		3	(e)l café.
		5	correr a		4	la iglesia.
		6	ir a			

Ejercicio 22 | *ser* versus *estar*

First decide whether to use *ser* or *estar*, then write the appropriate form of the verb plus the cue for choosing it.

Ejemplo: ¿ Dónde . . . los alumnos ? (Your answer should be *están*.)

1 ¿ Dónde . . . el papel ?
2 Pancho y Elena . . . de Paraguay.
3 Entonces ellos . . . paraguayos, ¿ verdad ?
4 Sí, pero ahora ellos . . . en Panamá.
5 Yo . . . muy bien, gracias.
6 Este . . . un lápiz muy bueno.
7 ¿ Qué hora . . . ?
8 . . . exactamente las tres y cuarto.
9 Yo . . . de Perú.
10 ¿ De dónde . . . tú ?
11 Yo tengo que . . . en la escuela mañana a las siete.
12 Nosotros . . . argentinos, de la capital.

Ejercicio 23 | *ir* versus *venir*

Choose between the two forms in parentheses.

1 Mañana mi familia y yo . . . (venimos, vamos) a las montañas.
2 Yo creo que ellos . . . (vienen, van) aquí a las dos y cuarto.
3 Mi mamá me llama. —¡ . . . (Vengo, Voy) en un momentito, mamá !
4 El presidente de México . . . (viene, va) a mi casa en mayo.
5 Cuando salimos del cine yo le pregunto a Pepe, —¿ Deseas . . . (venir, ir) aquí también el domingo por la noche ?
6 Dos muchachos hablan en la playa. —Cuando hace calor, mi familia y yo siempre . . . (vamos, venimos) a esta playa.
7 Dos alumnos hablan por teléfono. —¿ No deseas . . . (venir, ir) a mi casa a estudiar conmigo ?
8 —Sí, . . . (voy, vengo) en una hora.

Ejercicio 24 | *ir* versus *venir*

Choose between the two verbs in parentheses.

1 Rosa está en la oficina del director de la escuela. Dice, —Mi papá tiene que hablar con usted. Él desea . . . (ir, venir) a la escuela mañana.
2 El director dice, —No voy a estar aquí mañana. Tengo que . . . (ir, venir) a una reunión de profesores.
3 Juana y Luisa están en casa de Margarita. Margarita dice, —El domingo voy a tener una fiesta aquí. ¿ . . . (Van, Vienen) ustedes a mi fiesta ?

4 Juana dice, —Sí, yo . . . (voy, vengo).

5 Luisa responde que el domingo tiene que . . . (ir, venir) a las montañas con su familia.

6 Es viernes. Luisa y Roberto están en clase. Luisa pregunta, —¿ Roberto, . . . (vas, vienes) a la fiesta en la casa de Margarita el domingo?

7 Roberto responde, —Sí, . . . (voy, vengo).

8 Alguien llama (*knocks*) a la puerta. Pilar responde, —. . . (Voy, Vengo).

9 Ezequiel pregunta, —¿ Vienes a estudiar en mi casa esta noche?— Usted responde, —Sí . . . (voy, vengo).

10 Usted está en casa. Por teléfono habla con el director de la escuela. Él pregunta, —¿ Vienes a la escuela mañana?— Usted responde, —Sí, . . . (voy, vengo).

Ejercicio 25 | Role-Playing the Native: Geography

Try to sound like native speakers of Spanish as you ask and answer these questions.

¿ De dónde eres?

¿ Qué está al norte de tu país?

¿ Qué está al oeste de tu país?

¿ Cuál es la capital de tu país?

¿ En qué parte del país está la capital?

¿ Qué es un señor de tu país? ¿ Es brasileño?

Ejercicio 26 | Role-Playing the Native: Geography

¿ De dónde eres?

¿ Qué está al norte de tu país?

¿ Qué está al sur de tu país?

¿ Qué está al este de tu país?

¿ Qué está al oeste de tu país?

¿ En qué parte del país está la capital?

¿ Qué es un señor de tu país? ¿ Brasileño?

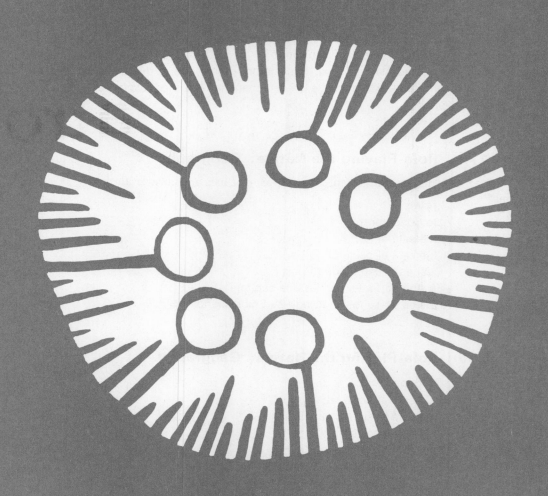

Etapa Cuatro

Dividing Words into Syllables: Syllabication

Part 1: Consonants

You do not need to know how to divide words into syllables as long as you are learning by direct imitation of speech. However, when you begin to read new words aloud without a spoken model, you get into trouble unless you know how to syllabicate and stress them.

1 You remember that Spanish does not like to end words with two consonants. To English cognates that end in two consonants they usually add (a) another consonant (b) a vowel.

a vowel **2** To the English adjective "modern" Spanish adds an *o* and gets *moderno*. There are two vowels in "modern" and ﹏﹏ syllables.

two **3** There are three vowels in *moderno* and, so ﹏﹏ syllables.

three **4** The English adjective is divided into syllables and stressed this way: *mod*-ern. Let's add the Spanish *o*. If we change nothing else, we get **mod**-ern-o. Spanish speakers would never understand this because they divide the word differently and stress a syllable which does not even exist in English. They say *mo-**der**-no*. Here is something like what could happen to a Spanish speaker if you said **mod**-ern-o. Say this aloud in English: [mek-ani-*kal*]. Can you guess the real English word? It is ﹏﹏.

me-*chan*-i-cal

5 Let's figure out how Spanish speakers divide their words. Look at these words which are typical of the whole language: *to-**tal**, **ma**-lo, **bue**-no, **vi**-ven*. The first syllable ends in a ﹏﹏. The second begins with a ﹏﹏.

vowel; consonant

6 Since these words are like all others in the language, is it logical to conclude that a consonant between two vowels always goes with the following syllable?

yes **7** Copy and syllabicate these words: *pálido, feliz, pero, una, fácil.*

pá-li-do, fe-liz, pe-ro, u-na, fá-cil

8 Now divide this one: *Toledo.*

To-le-do **9** Now look at these words carefully: *doc-tor, gor-do, tris-te, lim-pio, rec-to.* The last phoneme of the first syllable and the first phoneme of the second syllable are ﹏﹏.

consonants **10** In these examples when there are two consonants between two vowels, one goes with the first syllable and the other with the ﹏﹏ syllable.

second or next syllable

11 Copy and syllabicate these words: *Atlántico, norte, cerca, tarde.*

At-lán-ti-co, nor-te, cer-ca, tar-de

12 Will the digraphs *ch* and *ll* be divided between two syllables?

no (Because in Spanish each one is a letter in the alphabet and you cannot divide a letter.)

13 Copy and syllabicate these words: *mucho, pizarra, allí, señor.*
mu-cho, pi-za-rra, a-llí, se-ñor

14 There is an exception to the rule on how to divide double consonants. Look what happens to these words: *ha-blar, i-gle-sia, a-le-gre, pa-dre, cen-tro.* When the second of two consonants in a row is either ——, the first goes along with it..
l or *r* (The exceptions to this exception are *s* (*is-la*) and *t* (*at-lán-ti-co*).)

15 Most of the time, when there are two consonants between two vowels, the Spanish speaker divides them between two syllables. Now, remember that Spanish does not like to end a word with two consonants. Is this, then, a logical conclusion: the Spanish speaker, if he can avoid it, generally does not like to end or begin a syllable with two consonants?

yes

16 Here is something interesting about the way Spanish speakers talk which, perhaps, you have forgotten. See how these cognates are different.

Spain	*España*
Spanish	*español*
state	*estado*
school	*escuela*
special	*especial*

The Spanish forms all begin with an added ——.

e

17 The Spanish speaker never begins a native word with *s* plus another consonant. He adds a syllable-forming *e* because, without special practice, it is difficult for a Spanish speaker to say *s* plus another consonant in the same syllable. Think of this fact, then answer this question: how will the Spanish speaker syllabicate *instante?*
ins-tan-te (An *st* sequence does not bother us at all, and we syllabicate the cognate like this: in-stant.)

18 This is the way we syllabicate "con-struc-tor." How will the Spanish speaker do it?

cons-truc-tor **19** Syllabicate these words: *español, estado, estar.*
es-pa-ñol, es-ta-do, es-tar

Part 2: Vowels

1 The letters which may stand for vowel sounds in Spanish are ——.
a, e, i, o, u (*Y* is a true vowel only in the translation of "and.")

2 Say *bueno* aloud. What do you say? (a) [bu-*e*-no] (b)[*bwe*-no]
If you said it correctly, you said [*bwe*-no].

3 The letter *w* in [bwe-no] stands for (a) a vowel (b) a consonant in speech.

a consonant **4** Does Spanish use *w* in writing native words?

no **7** Spanish writes the consonant sound [w] and the vowel sound [u] with the same letter. (a) true (b) false

true **6** So, if you are going to learn to read new words aloud without a model, you must learn when *u* stands for the vowel sound [u] and the consonant [w]. What does *u* stand for in these words? Say them aloud: *u-nos, su-cio, mu-cho, Ra-úl.*
(a) vowel (b) consonant

vowel

7 When the letter *u* is the only vowel letter in a syllable, it stands for the vowel sound. (a) true (b) false

true   **8** The spelling *cuando* stands for (a) [ku-an-do] (b) [kwan-do].

[kwan-do]   **9** How many vowel sounds are there in *cuando?* (a) two (b) three

two (The *u* stands for [w] and, so, there are just two vowels, [a] and [o].)

10 You pronounce *bueno* as [bwe-no]. How do you say *escuela?* (a) [es-ku-e-la] (b) [es-kwe-la]

[es-kwe-la]   **11** You have never seen this word: *cui-da-do*. How do you think the Spanish speaker will pronounce it? Will the *u* stand for (a) [u]? (b) [w]?

for [w]   **12** The Spanish speaker says these words like this: *cuando* [kwan-do], *bueno* [bwe-no], *cuidado* [kwi-da-do]. When the letter *u* comes directly before *a*, *e*, or *i*, it stands for the consonant sound [w]. (a) true (b) false

true   **13** How many vowel sounds are there in *Uruguay?*

three   **14** Can you divide *Uruguay* into syllables?

U-ru-guay   **15** Here's the word for "fire": *fuego*. How many vowel sounds does it have?

two   **16** Copy and syllabicate *fuego*.

fue-go (You pronounce it [fwe-go].)

17 To find out how many syllables there are in a Spanish word, you count (a) the vowel letters (b) the vowel sounds.

the vowel sounds

18 The cognate of "pause" is *pausa*. Spanish speakers pronounce *pausa* like [pow-sa]. But they pronounce the proper name, *Raúl*, like this [rra-úl]. What does the accent mark on the *ú* tell you? To read it aloud as [u] or as [w]?

as [u] (The accent mark, then, is a spelling device to show that *u* really stands for the vowel sound [u], not the consonant [w].)

19 Let's see what this little writing trick tells you about the letter *i*. Say *dí-a* and *me-dia* aloud. What is your educated guess? Do *í* in *dí-a* and *i* in *me-dia* stand for exactly the same sound?

no   **20** The accented *í* stands for the vowel sound [i]. Now say *yo* and *ya* aloud. When you say *me-dia* does it sound a lot like [me-dya]?

yes   **21** The letter *i* has, like *u*, two jobs to do. The Spanish speaker writes *y* only at the beginning of a syllable or at the end of a word. Everywhere else he uses *i* for [y]. So he says these words like this: *media* [me-ɡya], *tiene* [tye-ne], *veinte* [veyn-te], *aire* [ay-re].

What does he do with *ciudad?* He divides it this way: *ciu-dad*. Now, there must be only one vowel in every syllable. The *u* stands for [u], the *i* must stand for (a) the vowel [i] (b) the consonant [y].

[y] (So he says [syu-ɡaɡ].)

22 Let's put all this information together, now, so you will know the right cues for reading aloud. The letters *a*, *o*, and *e* always stand for vowel sounds. Are they always pronounced in Spanish?

yes (Except when run together in rapid speech.)

23 Does what comes before or after them produce different vowel allophones?

no   **24** The letters *u* and *i* may stand for two different sounds, a vowel and another sound which is more like a consonant. (Linguists say it is sometimes a semi-vowel, a semi-consonant, or a consonant. We will say it is not a vowel.) The letters *u* and *i* always stand for the vowel sound when they have an accent mark (*ú*, *í*). (a) true (b) false

true (*frí-o*, *dí-a*, *Ra-úl*)

25 The letters *u* and *i* always stand for the vowel sound when they are the only vowel letter in a syllable. (a) true (b) false

true (**cin**-co, vi-**vi**-mos, **lu**-nes)

26 When *u* has no accent mark and is immediately followed by any vowel letter, it stands for [w]. (a) true (b) false

true (**cuan**-do [kwan-do], **bue**-no [bwe-no], **cui**-da-do [kwi-da-do])

27 When *i* has no accent mark and is immediately followed by any vowel letter, it stands for [y]. (a) true (b) false

true (me-**dia**, **tie**-ne, su-**cio**, **ciu**-dad)

28 In these combinations the second vowel letter always stands for a real vowel. (a) true (b) false

true (This is the one you count in finding out how many syllables there are in a word.)

29 When *i* comes before *u*, the *u* stands for a vowel. Now, *e*, *a*, and *o* must always stand for a vowel. How about an educated guess? When *a*, *e*, or *o* comes immediately before *u* (with no accent mark), the *u* also stands for (a) a vowel (b) a sound like [w].

a sound like [w] (Remember *pausa* which is pronounced [pow-sa].)

30 Want to guess again? When *a*, *e*, *o* comes immediately before *i* (with no accent mark), *i* stands for [i] or [y].

[y] (Compare *hay* and *ai-re*.)

31 One more guess. The number of vowel sounds in a word is always the same as the number of syllables. There can, consequently, never be two vowel sounds in the same syllable. (a) true (b) false

true

32 The English word "triumph" is divided *tri-umph*. Its Spanish cognate is *triunfo*. It has ⎯⎯⎯ pure vowel sounds.

two (If you got it right, it's a triumph for you. The *n* and *f* must go in separate syllables, so *triun* has only one real vowel, *u*. The *i* is pronounced [y].)

Optional Practice

In a few days, you will have a quiz on the uses of *ser* and *estar*. If you are not certain about what cues you to choose these verbs, see Ejercicios 29 and 30 for a review.

No new vocabulary.

The American male takes it for granted that he is a male and he does not feel insecure doing some things that by tradition are usually done by women. The American frequently likes to cook, often does not object to doing the dishes, and carries groceries to the car without giving the matter a second thought. Spanish speakers, in contrast, are *muy macho* (very much a male), and many of them believe it is undignified to do anything that is woman's work. Those who believe this will not carry a baby on the street or even a grocery bag. Many would not ever think of doing the dishes or sweeping the floors. There is, consequently, a sharp contrast between what a man and a woman may do in the Hispanic world.

PROGRAM 59

Word Stress and the Written Accent Mark

1 The smallest possible syllable may be just one phoneme. When a syllable contains just one phoneme it must be (a) a vowel (b) a consonant.

a vowel

2 The way to tell the number of syllables in a Spanish word is to count the number of pure ~~~~~.

vowel sounds

3 The vowel sound is the nucleus or center of a syllable, and in every word with two or more vowel sounds, one is always stressed more than the others. It is common to say, consequently, that the whole syllable is stressed. One way to show where this falls on a word is to put an accent mark over the stressed (a) vowel (b) consonant.

vowel

4 If we are going to talk about stressed syllables, you need to know what makes up a syllable. When there is one consonant between two vowels, the consonant always goes with the second vowel. Copy and syllabicate these words: *vivimos, Caracas, mucho.*

vi-vi-mos, Ca-ra-cas, mu-cho (Did you forget that the digraph *ch* is one letter in Spanish?)

5 When there are two consonants between two vowels, one usually (with two exceptions) goes with the first vowel and one with the second vowel. Copy and syllabicate these words: *marzo, algo, balcón, gente.*

mar-zo, al-go, bal-cón, gen-te

6 When *l* is preceded by any consonant, except *t* and *s*, the two consonants go with the second vowel. Copy and syllabicate *hablo* and *Atlántico.*

ha-blo, At-lán-ti-co

7 When *r* is preceded by any consonant, except *s*, *l*, or *n*, the two consonants go with the second vowel. Copy and syllabicate *padre, alegre, abril.*

pa-dre, a-le-gre, a-bril

8 The *s* never combines with a following consonant in the same syllable because the Spanish speaker cannot readily say this sequence. As a result, when a Spanish speaker first tries to talk English he says [espin] for "spin" and makes two syllables for the word. So the cognate of English "special" becomes *especial* in Spanish. Copy and syllabicate *español* and *especial.* (Remember what happens to *i* without an accent when it comes next to *a*, *o*, or *u*.)

es-pa-ñol, es-pe-cial

9 When *i* has a written accent, it can be the only vowel in a syllable. Copy and syllabicate *frío* and *día.*

frí-o, dí-a

10 There can never be two pure vowel sounds in the same syllable. Copy and syllabicate *leer, oeste,* and *correo.* (Remember what happens to *s* plus another consonant and to *rr*.)

le-er, o-es-te, co-rre-o

11 To be able to read a new word aloud you have to know three facts: (1) which sounds do and do not go together (you say *ha-blar*, not *hab-lar*), (2) how many syllables there are (you say *cuan-do*, not *cu-an-do*), and (3) which syllable is stressed (you say *o-es-te*, not *o-es-te*.)

If a word has a written accent mark, you immediately know which vowel to stress. So to say the word right you only have to be able to break it up into the right syllables. Copy and syllabicate these words, then say them aloud and underline the stressed syllable: *Asunción, último, fácil, diálogo.*

*A-sun-**ción**, **úl**-ti-mo, **fá**-cil, **diá**-lo-go* (*diá* is not like *dí-a.*)

12 Here are two columns with the words divided into syllables. In one column the right syllable is indicated to show stress, in the other column the wrong syllable is indicated. Which column do you say?

A	B
vi-*ves*	*vi*-ves
co-*men*	*co*-men
pa-pe-les	pa-*pe*-les
ha-*blan*	*ha*-blan

Column B

13 Copy and syllabicate *tienen, alumnos, popular, vienes*. Then say each aloud and underline the stressed syllable.

***tie**-nen, a-**lum**-nos, po-pu-**lar**, **vie**-nes*

14 There is a high probability that you did not underline the right syllable of *tienen, popular*, or *vienes* because you didn't pay close attention to what you actually said.

When a word ends in the phoneme /s/ or /n/ (and has no written accent), the stress falls on the next-to-last syllable: *tie-nen, pa-pe-les*. In contrast, when a word ends in a consonant, except *n* or *s* (and has no written accent), the stress falls on the last syllable. Copy, syllabicate, and underline the stressed syllable: *tropical, preguntan, subir, directores.*

*tro-pi-**cal**, pre-**gun**-tan, su-**bir**, di-rec-**to**-res*

15 The prime purpose of the written accent mark is to tell you (when you read a new word aloud) that the stressed syllable does not obey the two rules given above. Thus, when a word ending in *n* or *s* is stressed on the last syllable, it always has a written accent. Copy, syllabicate, write in the accent mark, and underline the stressed syllable: *perdon, estas, jardin, balcon.*

*per-**dón**, es-**tás**, jar-**dín**, bal-**cón***

16 When a word ends in a vowel, the vowel of the preceding syllable is stressed. If the final vowel is stressed, it always has a written accent mark. Copy, syllabicate, add the accent mark, and underline the stressed syllable: *Bogota, esta, aqui, alli.*

*Bo-go-**tá**, es-**tá**, a-**quí**, a-**llí*** (Did you slip on *a-llí?* The digraph *ll* is one letter in the Spanish alphabet.)

17 How's your linguisitc logic doing? Have you noticed that most Spanish words are stressed on either the last or the next-to-last syllable? When a word has the stress on any syllable before the last syllable, it will have a written accent mark. Say these words aloud: *miercoles, rapido, ultimo, lapices*. Now copy, syllabicate them, and add the written accent.

***miér**-co-les, **rá**-pi-do, **úl**-ti-mo, **lá**-pi-ces*

18 Let's test your linguistic logic now. Copy and syllabicate these words and underline the stressed syllable: *como, donde, cuantos, cuales.*

co-mo, **don**-de, **cuan**-tos, **cua**-les

19 When these words are used in questions or exclamations, they always have an accent mark over the stressed vowel: *¿Có-mo? ¿Dón-de? ¿Cuán-tos? ¿Cuá-les?* Is the accent mark needed to tell you what syllable to stress?

no (The accent mark now says the whole word is stressed in asking a question.)

20 There are seven very common words in the Spanish language which are used in asking questions. When they are used in a question sentence or in an exclamation, they have an accent mark on the stressed vowel. Let's see if you remember them and know the type of question in which they are used.

This question word asks about the location, origin, or destination of something. As in *¿De ——— viene? ¿A ——— va? ¿——— está Montevideo?* This question word is ———.

¿Dónde? **21** This question word asks about the amount of something that can be measured. The question word is ———.

¿Cuánto (deseas)? **22** When the question asks about the number of something that can be counted, you add ——— to *cuánto.*

s (¿Cuántos deseas?) **23** This question word asks about the hour or the day when something happens, as in *¿——— vas a la escuela?*

¿Cuándo? **24** This question word asks for a definition (the name) of some object, as in *¿——— es esto?*

¿Qué (es esto)? **25** This question word must be replaced in the answer by the name of a person. *¿——— está en la oficina?* It is *Pablo.*

¿Quién? **26** There are several possible choices. The question word asks you to pick one out of these. *De estos libros, ¿——— desea usted leer?*

¿cuál? **27** This question word asks about the health of someone, the state of something (deviation from the norm), or for a norm. It is ———.

¿Cómo está María? ¿Cómo está la casa? ¿Cómo es? **28** When [ke] is used in exclamations, it may be stressed, and take an accent mark. Punctuate this sentence as an exclamation and write in the accent mark: *Que calor hace.*

¡Qué calor hace!

29 Whether a word should or should not have an accent mark is decided by the members of the Spanish Academy (*Real Academia Española*) in Madrid. Most of these men are writers (poets, novelists, historians, *etc.*), not linguists, and, as a result, the "rules" they invent are not always consistent with linguistic logic. Every once in a while they change their minds and, as a result, you will find, as you read other books, that when the accent mark is not used to tell you what syllable to stress, the same word may or may not have an accent mark. For example, before 1952 all books used an accent mark on the demonstratives when they were not followed by a noun: *éste, ése, ésta, etc.* This is no longer necessary.

Don't be disturbed if you come across a usage different from what you are learning in SFC. You will be right until the Academy changes its mind again.

30 Here are all the words you have had which have the stress on a syllable which is *before* the last two. They must all have a written accent mark. Cover the italicized columns and think of where the accent mark goes on the syllabicated forms. Slide your cover sheet down word by word and check your accuracy.

mier-co-les	*miércoles*	nu-me-ro	*número*
sa-ba-do	*sábado*	o-ce-a-no	*océano*
A-me-ri-ca	*América*	do-mes-ti-co	*doméstico*
ra-pi-do	*rápido*	zo-o-lo-gi-co	*zoológico*
dia-lo-go	*diálogo*	mag-ni-fi-co	*magnífico*
Me-xi-co	*México*	ul-ti-mo	*último*
re-pu-bli-ca	*república*	hu-me-do	*húmedo*
pa-gi-na	*página*	mu-si-ca	*música*
At-lan-ti-co	*Atlántico*	o-lim-pi-co	*olímpico*
Pa-ci-fi-co	*Pacífico*		

31 Here are all the words you have had which end in a consonant but do not have the stress on the last syllable. Cover the right column and write the Spanish equivalents. Slide your cover sheet down word for word to check your accuracy.

pencil	*lá-piz*
difficult	*di-fí-cil*
easy	*fá-cil*
tunnel	*tú-nel*

32 Here are all the words you have had that end in a vowel and are stressed on the last syllable. Cover the right column and write the Spanish equivalents.

there	*a-llí*
here	*a-quí*
he is (here)	*es-tá*
cafe	*ca-fé*

33 Here are all the words you have had which end in *n* or *s* and do have the stress on the last syllable. Cover the italicized column and say the Spanish equivalents aloud one by one.

English	*in-glés*	season	*es-ta-ción*
pardon	*per-dón*	invention	*in-ven-ción*
they are (here)	*es-tán*	television	*te-le-vi-sión*
you are (here)	*es-tás, es-tán*	garden	*jar-dín*
combination	*com-bi-na-ción*	also	*tam-bién*
lesson	*lec-ción*		

New Vocabulary

familia	family	**padre**	father
hijo	son	**madre**	mother
hija	daughter	**hermano**	brother

tío	uncle	hermana	sister
tía	aunt	abuelo	grandfather
sobrino	nephew	abuela	grandmother
sobrina	niece	primo, -a	cousin
apellido	last name	nombre (el)	name

PROGRAM 60

Getting Ready for a Quiz on *ser* and *estar*, and Review of *haber*

Part 1: *ser* and *estar*

There will be a quiz in your next class on the forms and uses of *ser* and *estar*. To choose between these two verbs you must remember two things: how they stand in contrast with each other and what cues the choice.

1 *Estar* is an *a*-verb with two irregularities in its present tense forms. One irregularity is in stress. The stress falls on (a) the stem (b) the first suffix (c) the second suffix.

the first suffix

2 As a result, three forms must have a written accent mark. These forms are ⌇⌇⌇.

está, están, estás

3 The two forms of *estar* which do not need an accent mark are ⌇⌇⌇.

estoy; estamos

4 You have been taught three uses or functions of *estar*. It is used to ⌇⌇⌇ something in space: *Juan está en Granada.*

locate

5 To talk about a person's ⌇⌇⌇: *¿Cómo está usted?*

health

6 To describe the subject with a ⌇⌇⌇ adjective: *María está triste.*

predicate

7 You will understand why *ser* is so irregular if you remember that it got its forms from two Latin verbs, *sedere* (to sit) and *esse* (to be). *Ser* is so irregular that each present tense form has to be learned by itself. Write the forms that go with *yo* ⌇⌇⌇, *él* ⌇⌇⌇, and *tú* ⌇⌇⌇.

yo soy, él es, tú eres

8 Write the forms for *nosotros* and *ellos*.

nosotros somos; ellos son

9 The forms that go with *él* and *ellos* are also used with *usted* and *ustedes*. Write two translations of "you are."

usted es; ustedes son

10 You know that *ser*, *estar*, and *haber* all translate "to be." Which of these verbs has the greatest number of uses or functions?

ser

11 Since *ser* has more functions than either *haber* or *estar*, some of its uses do not stand in contrast with the other two verbs. (a) true (b) false

true

12 The only one of these three verbs used to state the origin of a person or thing is ———.

ser
13 When you give the origin of a person or thing, you use *ser*, the relator ———, and a place name.

de (Yo soy de Argentina.)
14 When a subject noun and a predicate noun stand for the same entity, you say they are equal by using only ———.

ser
15 Is the sentence *Antonio es un alumno* very much like this formula: *Antonio = alumno?* (a) yes (b) no

yes
16 The only verb you use for adding and subtracting is ———.

ser
17 When you add, you use the form ———.

son
18 Write this out: 10 + 11 = 21.

Diez y once son veintiuno.
19 You also use *son* when you subtract. Write out 12 − 3 = 9.

Doce menos tres son nueve.
20 Which verb do you use for telling time?

ser
21 You use two forms of the Present of *ser* in telling time. They are ———.

es; son (The subject is the noun *hora* or *horas* and the forms are third person.)
22 Write this out in Spanish: It's 1:30 A.M.

Es la una y media de la mañana.
23 Write out: It's 2:00 P.M.

Son las dos de la tarde.
24 When you talk about the location of an entity, you must choose between *haber* and ———.

estar
25 An unmodified proper name cues the use of ——— for location.

estar
26 Write a sentence locating Norma in the patio.

Norma está en el patio.
27 Rewrite the sentence using a pronoun for *Norma*.

Ella está en el patio.
28 In speaking of location, the subject pronouns cue the choice of ———.

estar
29 Write the missing verb form: *California ——— cerca del océano.*

está
30 When you describe the subject with a predicate adjective, you must choose between ———.

ser and *estar*
31 The sentence states your norm for the subject. You use ———.

ser
32 Describe Gilda as very friendly according to your experience.

Gilda es muy amable.
33 The sentence states that the subject has undergone some change. You use ———.

estar
34 Write a sentence in which you suggest with the verb chosen that something has caused Jesús to become sad.

Jesús está triste. (Remember *Jesús* is a common name in Spanish.)
35 You discover, frequently to your surprise, that something does not fit your norm or previous experience. You report this by using ———.

estar
36 Michael has thought that choosing between *ser* and *estar*, in his words, *es difícil*. He gets to this point in the Program and suddenly has to change his mind. He exclaims, *¡——— fácil!*

¡Está fácil!
37 By tomorrow he gets used to this and has a new norm. He now says, ——— *fácil.*

Es fácil.

38 You stop at a tourist trading post along the highway. A plain handkerchief costs $5.00; a simple belt $20.00. You say, "Man, the prices *are* high here!" (a) *ser* (b) *estar*

estar　　　　　　**39** Steel *is* harder than iron. (a) *ser* (b) *estar*

ser　　　　　　**40** A huge tank of chemicals catches fire at night. For hours the sky *is* brilliant white. (a) *ser* (b) *estar*

estar　　　　　　**41** It is the first day of the fair in the village. Everybody *is* excited. (a) *ser* (b) *estar*

estar　　　　　　**42** The sun comes up and soon the ground *is* warm. (a) *ser* (b) *estar*
estar (The sun heats up the cold ground; its temperature changes.)

43 It is natural for the water in tropical oceans *to be* warm. (a) *ser* (b) *estar*

ser　　　　　　**44** Everybody knows that lead *is* soft. (a) *ser* (b) *estar*

ser　　　　　　**45** Don't touch it. Your gloves *are* dirty. (a) *ser* (b) *estar*

estar　　　　　　**46** Most of the music written by de Falla *is* very Spanish. (a) *ser* (b) *estar*
ser (After all, de Falla was a Spaniard.)

If you feel you need more review, see Ejercicios 28 and 29.

In many American families the use of familial titles such as aunt, uncle, brother, sister, cousin, etc. is rapidly disappearing. Most people still use grandmother (granma), grandfather (granpa), father (pa, dad), and mother (mom, ma) in addressing their elders, but first names only are commonly used in talking to other members of the family, especially when the age difference is small. This custom upsets many Latin Americans who visit the United States. They feel that this is disrespectful and that American parents are not bringing up their children properly.

Part 2: Review of *haber*

You will not be tested on the uses of *haber* in the upcoming quiz, but, as you noticed in Part 1, you have to know what cues you to choose between *ser, estar,* and *haber* when you translate "to be."

1 The only form of *haber* you have learned so far is ~~~~.

hay
2 You may use *hay* to ~~~~ an entity in space.

locate
3 You may also use *estar* to locate an entity in space. So you must learn what cues the choice between *haber* and *estar*. What will you use to complete this question? ¿~~~~ *un elefante en el jardín?* (a) *Está* (b) *Hay*

¿Hay un elefante en el jardín?
4 The translation of *hay* in this context is ~~~~.

Is there
5 Rewrite the sentence in Frame 3 and change *un* to *tres.*

¿Hay tres elefantes en el jardín? (Did you forget to make *elefante* plural?)
6 Will there be any other change if you put *muchos* in place of *tres?*

no (*¿Hay muchos elefantes en el jardín?*)
7 Will there be any other change if you just use *elefantes?*

no (*¿Hay elefantes en el jardín?*)
8 You should now be able to complete this rule: a simple plural noun or any number adjective with a noun standing for an entity cues the choice of ~~~~ for location.

haber (hay)
9 Write the missing verb form: *Cerca de California* ~~~~ *un océano.*

hay (You will learn more about choosing between *haber* and *estar* in later Programs.)

New Vocabulary

maestro -a	teacher	**contestar**	to answer
chico	boy; small	**lindo**	pretty
estudiante	student	**alegre**	happy
castellano	Castilian, Spanish	**ese**	that
dinero	money	**aquel**	that
responder	to answer		

PROGRAM 61

La familia: Vocabulary Comprehension and Writing Practice

1 Each person in a family tree can have many different relative names. I am the "son" of my father, the "grandson" of my father's mother, the "nephew" of my aunt, and the "cousin" of my uncle's son. These relationship words are really not names for me but for the family relationship between me and other

members of the family. You already know all these facts in English and the set of words to describe the various relationships. The Spanish patterns are just like English so all you need to learn is the spelling and pronunciation of the Spanish words.

Here is the basic difference between two sets of family relationship words. English usually tells the sex of individuals having the same relationship by using paired words that are very different. For example:

mother	daughter	sister	aunt	niece	grandmother
father	son	brother	uncle	nephew	grandfather

English does not distinguish the sex of "cousins." In contrast, Spanish has different paired words for *padre* and *madre* and tells the sex only by the contrast between *o* (masculine) and *a* (feminine) in all other words. For example:

madre	hija	hermana	tía	sobrina	abuela	prima (*cousin*)
padre	hijo	hermano	tío	sobrino	abuelo	primo

Here is one other basic difference. The Spanish cognate of "parents" is *parientes*, but it means "relatives." The word for "parents" is *padres*, which looks exactly like "fathers."

Let's see, now, how well you can understand family relationships in Spanish. Write the missing word and check your spelling: *La hija de mi padre es mi* ——.

hermana   **2** Yo, Pablo, soy el —— de mi hermana.

hermano   **3** Somos los —— de mi padre.

hijos   **4** El hermano de mi madre o de mi padre es mi ——.

tío (Did you remember the accent mark?)

   5 La hermana de mi padre o de mi madre es mi ——.

tía   **6** Mi padre y mi madre son mis ——.

Did you get trapped? Not *parientes* but *padres.*

   7 La madre de mi padre o madre es mi ——.

abuela   **8** El padre de mi madre o de mi padre es mi ——.

abuelo   **9** Los padres de mis padres son mis ——.

abuelos (Just like *muchachos,* boy and girl.)

   10 Yo soy el hijo de mis ——.

padres   **11** Yo soy el sobrino de mis ——.

tíos   **12** La hija de mi hermana es mi ——.

sobrina   **13** Los hijos de mi hermano son mis ——.

sobrinos   **14** María es la hija de mis tíos. ¿Qué es? Es mi ——.

prima   **15** Mi primo, Jorge, es el —— de mis tíos.

hijo   **16** El padre de Jesús y de Remigia es el señor Villarreal. Jesús y Remigia son hijos del señor Villarreal. ¿Qué son también?

hermanos   **17** Mis primos, tíos, y sobrinos son mis ——. (*Remember that deceptive cognate.*)

parientes   **18** Write the Spanish equivalents for: aunt, uncle, aunt and uncle.

tía, tío, tíos   **19** Translate: son, daughter, children.

hijo, hija, hijos

20 One word for "priest" is *padre*. The word for "father" is *padre*. The word
for "parents" is ———.

padres   **21** Paco and Lola are my cousins. The Spanish word is ———.
primos   **22** However, Lola is my ——— in Spanish.
prima

Vocabulary Round-up

1 In a few days you will have a quiz on vocabulary. Which words should you
review most? (a) those you can spell by ear (b) those you must see to learn to
spell
those you must see to spell (You have to hear and see these words.)

2 What tells you to write "elephant" with an *f* in Spanish?
the knowledge that there is no *ph* combination in the Spanish alphabet

3 What tells you to add the *e* to *elefante?*
what you hear

4 To change "perfect" to its Spanish cognate, you add ——— at the end.
o   **5** Do you remember why this happens?
Spanish does not end words in two consonants.

6 In England and Canada "center" is spelled *centre*. In Spanish "tiger" is
spelled ———.

tigre   **7** A stressed Latin *e* often became *ie* in Spanish, but not in English cognates.
Translate "wind" and "weather."
viento, tiempo (Compare "vent" and "temperate.")

8 What tells you to capitalize proper names? (a) what you hear (b) a spelling
rule

a spelling rule   **9** You know the names of 10 South American countries. Write them.
Argentina, Colombia, Paraguay, Uruguay, Bolivia, Chile, Venezuela, Brasil,
Perú, Ecuador (Check your spelling.)

10 The Spanish cognate of "garden" is ———.
jardín   **11** The cognate of "frigid" is ———.
frío   **12** Change the noun "mine" to make it Spanish.
mina   **13** Do you change "animal" (except in pronunciation) to make it Spanish?
no (*Es un animal.*)

14 Write [bwen] with regular spelling.
buen   **15** Check all the following words. You should know the meaning of every one.
If not, look them up in the end vocabulary.

| país | frío | ¡Espera! | ciudad | viento | mal |
| semana | fresco | hace | calor | tiempo | buen |

New Vocabulary

hacer	to make; to do
saber	to know
poner	to put
ver	to see

PROGRAM 62

Possessive Adjectives

1 There is research which indicates that the student who thinks critically and logically about what is being studied actually learns easier, faster, and better than the student who tries to learn without a conscious understanding of what is going on. So let's begin this Program with some logical thinking about what adjectives are and what they tell us.

An adjective tells us something about whatever a noun labels. The plural suffix of the noun *dollars* tells us the number is larger than one. The adjective *ten* in *ten dollars* makes the number precise. The adjective *these* in *these dollars* tells you they are (a) close to the speaker (b) far from the speaker.

close to the speaker (Far from would require *those dollars.*)

2 Do the adjectives *ten* and *these* actually describe what the dollars are like?

no

3 Does the adjective *red* in *a red car* describe a feature of the car?

yes

4 Does the adjective *distant* give an inherent characteristic or a quality of *star* in *a distant star?*

no (It describes the space between the speaker on earth and the star.)

5 Does the adjective *blue* in *a blue star* describe a quality of the star?

yes

6 If I say, *That is my book*, does *my* (a) give a characteristic of the book? (b) tell you who owns it?

my tells you who owns it

7 How's your critical thinking doing? Look at *five sheep*. The adjective, and nothing else, gives you the number of animals that *sheep* stands for. (a) true (b) false

true

8 Look at *those sheep*. Does the adjective *those* give a characteristic or quality of the sheep?

no (If they move up close to you, they suddenly become *these sheep.* The demonstrative (pointing out) adjectives measure the distance between the speaker and the thing being talked about.)

9 Now, watch out. *That is my book* tells you that I own the book. Is this always true?

no

10 Did you get caught? Think of this: *That is my home town.* Do you own the town?

no

11 Does *That is my Spanish class* say that you own the class?

no (Here *my* says you belong to that group: are a member of the class.)

12 What does *That is my uncle* tell you? (a) you own him (b) you both belong to the same family and he is your father's or mother's brother

you both belong to the same family, *etc.*

13 A small child says, *That's my house.* What does this tell you? (a) the house belongs to him (b) he belongs there, *i.e.*, lives there

he belongs there

14 What does *That is my teacher* tell you? (a) the teacher belongs to you (b) you belong to the class she teaches

you belong to the class she teaches

15 You borrow a book from the library and take it to school. Someone picks it up by mistake and starts to carry it off. You say, *That is my book*. What does *my* mean? (a) you own the book (b) you are in temporary possession of it

you are in temporary possession of it

16 Someone says of a table, *Its leg is broken*. What does *its* tell you? (a) the table owns the leg (b) the leg is part of the table, that is, belongs to the table

the leg is part of the table

17 The forms *my*, *your*, *his*, *her*, *our*, *their*, and *its* are called **possessive adjectives.** Does "possession" always mean ownership?

no

18 You already know by feel all the things that possessive adjectives tell you. You will, however, learn to use the Spanish possessive adjectives more easily if you think critically about what the possessive adjectives actually tell you. The possessive adjectives in both English and Spanish are actually pronouns with a possessive suffix. The subject pronoun for *George* is ———.

he

19 If we add the apostrophe *s* to *George* we get *George's* as in *That is George's hat*. So to replace *George's* we need a morpheme for *George* and another for *'s*. The possessive that replaces *George's* is ———.

his (hi + s)

20 The subject pronoun that replaces *George and Mary* is ———.

they

21 If you rewrite *they* as *thei*, what must you add to make the form possessive?

r (their)

22 In addition to indicating possession the form *his* tells you the possessor is (a) a girl (b) a boy.

a boy

23 Rewrite *That is his hat* so that the hat belongs to a girl.

That is *her* hat.

24 The possessive adjectives *his* and *her* tell us the sex of the person to which something belongs. (a) true (b) false

true

25 Rewrite *That is her house* so that the house belongs to a boy and a girl, that is, a brother and sister.

That is *their* house.

26 Does *their* tell you the sex of the possessors?

no

27 Very young boy and girl babies look a lot alike. You frequently can't tell whether one is a boy or a girl. What do people say: (a) What is his or her name? (b) What is its name?

What is its name?

28 When we don't know the sex of a person or animal we use the neuter adjective *its*. (a) true (b) false

true

29 Let's summarize what you already know. In English there are two adjectives that tell us the sex of the possessor. They are ———.

his; her

30 In English there is one possessive adjective which is used when we don't know the sex of the possessor. It is ———.

its

31 Do *my*, *your*, *our*, and *their* indicate the sex of the possessor?

no

32 Have you ever paid any attention to this fact about possessive adjectives? The adjectives *our* and *their* tell you the possessor is (a) singular (b) plural.

plural

33 The adjectives *my*, *his*, *her*, and *its* tell you the possessor is (a) singular (b) plural.

singular

34 The possessive adjective *your* is different. It may tell you the possessor is either singular or ‿‿‿ .

plural (It is like *you* which can be *you*, singular, or *you all*, plural.)

35 When you stop to think critically about possessive adjectives you discover that they give you a lot of information which you have not paid much attention to up to this point in your education. Can you learn how to use the Spanish possessive adjectives if you do not know precisely what information they carry?

no

36 To learn and understand a foreign language in the easiest way, you need to discover how the foreign language differs from your own. Here is a major contrastive difference between English and Spanish. Does *my* agree in number with the noun in *my friend* and *my friends*?

no

37 Contrast these translations:

my friend	*mi amigo*
my friends	*mis amigos*

Do *mi* and *mis* agree in number with their noun?

yes (Spanish possessive adjectives, like all other Spanish adjectives, always agree in number with their nouns.)

38 Do English "my" and Spanish *mi*, *mis* mark the sex of the speaker?

no (There is no need for this. The hearer usually knows who the speaker is.)

39 The forms *mi* and *mis* go with *yo*, the speaker. The *m* is the pronoun stem, the *i* indicates possession, and *s* is the plural suffix. The plural of "my" is ‿‿‿ .

our

40 There are four Spanish forms that translate "our." Two are plural; two are singular, to agree with the noun in number. Look at these translations.

our friend	*nuestro amigo*	our friends	*nuestros amigos*
	nuestra amiga		*nuestras amigas*

The *our*-forms of the Spanish possessive adjectives have *o*- and *a*-forms that match the terminal phoneme of the noun. (a) true (b) false

true

41 Translate: "Our house is here." Look at Frame 40 for the right form for *our*.

Nuestra casa está aquí.

42 Translate: Our houses are here.

Nuestras casas están aquí.

43 Translate: Our books are here.

Nuestros libros están aquí.

44 In speech the possessive adjective that matches the subject pronoun [tu] is [tu]. In writing it has no accent mark: *tu*. You make it plural by adding ‿‿‿ .

s: *tus* (there is no *o-a* agreement.)

45 Translate: your friend; your friends (male).

tu amigo; tus amigos

You now know eight possessive forms and their meanings. Here they are:

			nuestro		
			nuestra		
yo	mi	nosotros		tú	tu
	mis	nosotras			tus
			nuestros		
			nuestras		

All of the other possessive English adjectives—"your" (*usted, ustedes*), "his" (*él*), "her" (*ella*), "their" (*ellos, ellas*), and "its" (*zero*)—are translated by just two forms: the singular *su* and the plural *sus*. How do you suppose the Spanish speaker keeps everything straight? You will find out in your next class session if you listen carefully and use your linguistic logic.

New Vocabulary

fiesta	party	**invitar**	to invite
compleaños (el)	birthday	**después (de)**	after
¿por qué?	why	**porque**	because

PROGRAM 63

Help on Memorizing Dialog IV

1 The purpose in memorizing a new dialog is (a) to remember it forever word for word (b) to learn new patterns and words.

to learn new patterns and words

2 Words are put together in a pattern to send a message. Do you have to remember every word in a sentence to be able to remember the message it carries?

no

3 Here is the first line of Dialog IV: *¿Qué vas a hacer el sábado?* The basic message is carried by only three words. The question word *qué* plus ⁓⁓⁓.

hacer and sábado (These three words would be what you would send in a telegram: ¿ Qué hacer sábado ?)

4 Look at these two sentences: (1) *¿Qué vas a hacer el sábado?* (2) *¿Qué haces el sábado?* Is the message essentially the same in both sentences?

yes

5 The message is the same, but the pattern is different. Translate the indicated part of each sentence: *¿Qué **vas a hacer** el sábado? ¿Qué **haces** el sábado?* Translate *hacer* as "to do," not "to make."

are you going to do; are you doing

6 In both of the sentences above, the present tense of the verb and the phrase *el sábado* tell us Sara is asking a question about the (a) past (b) present (c) future.

future

7 We just said that the message in both sentences is essentially the same. Let's see what happens when we drop *el sábado*. Translate these: *¿Qué vas a hacer? ¿Qué haces?*

What are you going to do ? What are you doing ?

8 The patterns *vas a hacer* and *haces* send essentially the same messages. (a) true (b) false

false

9 Sara's question is about what Carmen is going to do in the future. The notion of future is marked twice in the question. Copy the two parts that indicate future: *¿Qué vas a hacer el sábado?*

vas a ; el sábado

10 You are memorizing this dialog so you can learn to talk Spanish. Is it important that you remember that the verb form used in the dialog is *vas*, not *va?* This one will catch you if you do not stop and think about why you are learning the dialog.

no (Because when you want to ask a question like this, you will have to decide whether to use *tú* or *usted*.)

11 The infinitive form of *vas* is ﹏﹏.

ir

12 If you remember the function of *ir a* plus an infinitive, will you always be able to make up a question in which you talk to a person with *tú?*

yes

13 The most important thing in learning a new dialog is not to be able to remember it forever word for word, but to be able to make up the same or similar messages whenever you want to say something. (a) true (b) false

true

14 You want to remember two things: *what* is said (the message) and *how* to say it (the pattern). Can you learn a new pattern if you do not understand the message?

no (You can, of course, learn it like a parrot, but remember that parrots who talk do not know what they are talking about.)

15 The first thing you want to do when you start to learn a new dialog is to find out *what* is being talked about (the message). Linguists call this "what" *the subject of discourse*. The subject of discourse in Dialog IV is ﹏﹏.

an invitation to a birthday party

16 Now that you know the subject of discourse, there are lots of things you don't have to worry about remembering at all. Why? Because, with a little thought, you can guess what will be talked about. For example, who can come, who will be invited, family and guests, presents, *etc.*

With this information you won't be able to make up the whole dialog word for word, but you do have a big head start on learning it. You know, for example, that the word for "party" is ﹏﹏.

fiesta

17 The word for "to invite" is ﹏﹏.

invitar

18 The English noun form of "invite" is ﹏﹏.

invitation

19 In Spanish cognates the *t* of the suffix *tion* is usually changed to the letter ﹏﹏.

c (And the *o* has an accent mark: *ción*)

20 Write the Spanish cognate of "invitation."

invitación

21 People who are invited to a fiesta are called *invitados*. This is translated into English by ﹏﹏.

guests

22 Spanish guests do not give *presentes* at a birthday party; they give ﹏﹏ to the person whose birthday is being celebrated.

regalos (*Presente* is a deceptive cognate.)

23 Each *invitado* brings a *regalo*. So, many *invitados* means many *regalos*. The word for "many" is ﹏﹏.

muchos (*Muchos invitados, muchos regalos.*)

24 A birthday party usually takes place on your "birth" day, the day on which you have finished another year of living. The verb "to finish" or "fulfill" in Spanish is *cumplir*. The word for "years" is ﹏﹏.

años

25 So *fiesta de cumpleaños* translates ﹏﹏.

birthday party

26 When you have a birthday party, you invite relatives, friends, and often, people who live near your home, that is, in the immediate vicinity of your house.

People who live in the immediate "vicinity" of your house are called *vecinos* in Spanish. This cognate is translated by ⁓.

neighbors

27 When you have a birthday party, you have to tell people you want them to come. Translate: *Quiero invitarte a mi fiesta de cumpleaños.*

I want to invite you to my birthday party. (If you missed this it means you have been practicing the dialog in class without paying attention to meaning.)

28 The person who is invited has to accept the invitation and, to be polite, say "thank you." Translate: *Acepto tu invitación. Un millón de gracias.*

I accept your invitation. Thanks a million.

29 You now have a pretty good idea of what the dialog is about. Now, let's look at what you are supposed to learn from memorizing the dialog.

You get some practice using verbs in a life-like situation, not just in pattern drills. Change the infinitives to present tense forms to match the pronouns: *tú ir, yo saber, tú preguntar, yo decir, quién ir, yo aceptar.*

tú vas, yo sé, tú preguntas, yo digo, quién va, yo acepto

30 You learn some new words. Look at these two sentences: (1) *Lo digo en serio.* (2) *Lo digo en broma.* Now, an educated guess. Which one says something like, "I'm joking," (literally, "I say it in joke.") 1, 2

2

31 Can you guess the translation of the infinitive *bromear?*

to joke

32 Sara tells Carmen a lot of people are going to be at her *fiesta de cumpleaños: ¡Hasta el gato!* When Latin words became Spanish, the phoneme /k/ sometimes changed to /g/. The English cognate of *gato* is ⁓.

cat

33 Carmen teases Sara about all the guests coming to her party, and says, *¡Claro! Muchos invitados, muchos regalos.* The opposite of *claro* is *oscuro.* The English cognate of *oscuro* is "obscure" (dark). The cognate for *claro* is ⁓.

clear

34 Is "clear" a good translation for *claro* in this context?

no

35 How about, "It's all clear to me now?"

yes (A short cut would be "of course.")

36 Sara is a little upset about being teased, and she says to Carmen, *Ay, chica. No seas tonta. No te invito por eso.* The adjective *tonta* translates "silly." You have not had the verb form *seas.* It is the imperative form of a verb you know very well. Its three parts are *se-a-s.* The stem is *se-.* Can you guess its infinitive?

ser

37 So *No seas tonta* translates ⁓.

Don't be silly.

38 The relator *por* appears in three different combinations of the dialog. A word for word translation does not make sense in English. When *por* combines with the question word *qué,* it deals with the cause, reason or motivation for an action. So *por qué* in *¿Por qué preguntas?* is translated simply as ⁓.

why

39 When these same words are used in the answer, they combine into one, *porque,* and the translation still deals with cause. The answer to "Why do you ask?" could be "Cause I want to invite you." However, we usually say ⁓.

because

40 Sara tells Carmen that the reason (cause) she is inviting her is not just to get a present. She says, *No te invito por eso.* Would this be a logical translation? "That's not why I'm inviting you."

yes (So "that" translates *eso* and "why" translates *por.*)

41 You now know everything that is to be found in the new dialog. All you have to memorize is the order in which it is said. Here is the whole dialog. Practice saying it aloud, and remember to pay attention to the meaning as you say it.

Después de clase

Sara: ¿Qué vas a hacer el sábado?
Carmen: No sé; depende. ¿Por qué preguntas?
Sara: Porque quiero invitarte a mi fiesta de cumpleaños.
Carmen: ¡Qué bueno! ¿Quién va a estar allí?
Sara: Todos mis hermanos, mis tíos, vecinos, amigos . . . ¡Hasta el gato!
Carmen: ¡Claro! Muchos invitados, muchos regalos.
Sara: Ay, chica. No seas tonta. No te invito por eso.
Carmen: Lo digo en broma. Acepto tu invitación. Un millón de gracias.

Spelling Review

1 The two words for country are ~~~~. (Check your spelling in each frame.)

país; campo   2 Which word stands for a nation?

país   3 Translate "cold," "cool," and "hot," "heat."

frío, fresco, calor

4 "Good" is translated by two forms (allomorphs) of same word. They are ~~~~.

bueno; buen   5 The form of *malo* that is like *buen* is ~~~~.

mal   6 Write out 22, 27, and 29.

veintidós, veintisiete, veintinueve

7 Translate "There's a tiger in the corral."

Hay un tigre en el corral.

8 The cognate of "ventilation" that you know is ~~~~.

viento

New Vocabulary

vecino	neighbor	**mi**	my
amigo	friend	**su**	your
gato	cat	**nuestro**	our
¿quién?	who		

PROGRAM 64

Adjectival Residuals and Pre-quiz Practice on Cognates

Part 1: Adjectival Residuals

1 If you put ordinary water in a test tube and let it evaporate there will be left a *residue* of salts and minerals in the tube. A residue is something that remains after something else is taken away. *Residue* is a noun. The adjectival form that comes from it is ~~~~.

residual (This form can also be used as a noun: the residual.)

2 George says to Peter, *I need three pencils.* The subject of discourse (what is being talked about) is ~~~~.

pencils   **3** George knows what he is talking about and so does Peter as soon as he hears the sentence. Which of these two sentences is Peter most likely to use in his response? (a) I'll lend you three pencils. (b) I'll lend you three.

I'll lend you three.

4 Peter drops the noun *pencils* because both he and George already know they are talking about pencils and there is no need to say the word again. (a) true (b) false

true   **5** What part of speech is the number *three* in *I need three pencils*? (a) noun (b) verb (c) adjective

adjective   **6** So when Peter leaves out *pencils* in *I'll lend you three*, the word *three* becomes an adjectival ~~~~.

residual (Did you miss this one? If so, you are not paying attention to the subject of discourse of this program: *adjectival residuals.*)

7 Two people are in a museum of modernistic art. One exclaims excitedly, *Look at that painting!* The other does not like the painting and asks in disgust: (a) Do you like that painting? (b) Do you like *that*?

Do you like *that*? (The demonstrative *that* is now an adjectival residual.)

8 The answer to *Do you have some change?* may be *Yes, I have some.* The adjectival residual is ~~~~.

some   **9** In English only the demonstratives and adjectives of number or quantity regularly become adjectival residuals. In Spanish any adjective can become a residual. Rewrite this sentence and leave out the noun: *El hombre está aquí.*

Él está aquí.   **10** Say both of the above sentences aloud. Do you hear the same word at the beginning of each sentence?

yes   **11** Is *Él* in the second sentence an adjectival residual?

yes   **12** Now, let's see the difference between English and Spanish. Translate the two sentences: *El hombre está aquí. Él está aquí.*

The man is here. He is here.

13 The definite article *the* cannot become an adjectival residual in English. When we drop a noun standing for a person, we also have to drop its adjective and replace both with a ~~~~.

pronoun (Latin *pro* means "in place of" so *pro-noun* means "in place of a noun.")

14 If you rewrite *They are going to buy the house* and drop *the house*, what will you replace *the house* with?

it (They are going to buy *it.*)

15 Now, let's look at the Spanish translation of these sentences.

> They are going to buy **the house.**   *Van a comprar **la casa.***
> They are going to buy **it.**   *Van a comprar**la.***

The Spanish speaker just drops the noun and keeps the article, but we have two translations of *la*: ~~~~.

the; it   **16** Now, be careful with your logic. Does *that* change its meaning when you change *Do you like that painting?* to *Do you like that?*

no   **17** From the Spanish speaker's point of view, does *la* change its meaning when he changes *Van a comprar la casa* to *Van a comprarla?*

no   **18** Speakers of English get the feeling that *la* changes meaning only because we cannot use "the" as an adjectival residual and, as a result, have to use two different words to translate *la*. (a) true (b) false

true

19 Let's look at this difference in the two languages again. Translate these two sentences: *Ellos van a comprar las casas. Ellos van a comprarlas.*

They are going to buy the houses. They are going to buy them.

20. English has to replace "the houses" with "them." Spanish just drops *casas* and keeps the adjectival residual ⌒.

las

21 When the subject of discourse is a thing, we have to translate *la* and *las* three different ways. Translate the indicated words: (a) *Van a comprar la casa.* (b) *Van a comprar las casas.* (c) *Van a comprarla.* (d) *Van a comprarlas.*

the; the; it; them

22 Now, let's see what happens when the subject of discourse is a person. Translate the indicated words. Be careful. *Voy a ver a la muchacha. Voy a verla.*

the first *la* is "the"; the second has to be changed in our translation to "her".
(For the Spanish speaker, however, *la* is the same word in both sentences.)

23 Look at the article in *las muchachas*. It is made up of three parts. The plural marker is ⌒.

s

24 The agreement phoneme is ⌒.

a

25 So the stem must be ⌒.

l

26 Now, make *el hombre* plural.

los hombres

27 Does *los*, like *las*, have three parts?

yes (The stem *l*, the agreement phoneme *o*, and the plural suffix *s*.)

28 You can make the plural form *las* singular by just dropping the *s* (*la*). Now, stop and think about this. Would it seem logical to a Spanish speaker that he might also be able to make *los* singular by just dropping the *s* to get *lo*?

yes

29 You will remember that every syllable has to have one vowel in it. The /e/ of *el* is there just to make the stem *l* into something that can be said all by itself. Why does the /e/ disappear when *el* becomes *los*? Because *los* has ⌒.

the syllable-forming /o/ in it: a vowel

30 So the Spanish speaker has two singular forms for *los*. They are ⌒.

el and *lo* (We say, then, that this singular stem has two allomorphs, *el* and *l*.)

31 You already know that when a morpheme has two allomorphs, you find them used in different combinations. You use *teng* with *yo* (*tengo*), but *tien* with *tú* (*tienes*). The same thing happens to *el* and *lo*. Look at these four sentences and the indicated words.

Voy a comprar *los* lápices.   Voy a comprar**los**.
Voy a comprar *el* lápiz.   Voy a comprar**lo**.

The singular of *los* before a noun object is *el*. When the noun object is dropped, the adjectival residual form is ⌒, not *el*.

lo

Part 2: Pre-quiz Practice on Cognates

In your next class, you are going to be quizzed on your ability to hear and understand sentences which have many cognates in them. Your teacher will read 20 statements and you will decide whether each is true or false. Here are some practice sentences. Do not try to say them aloud, just read them silently.

	1 El animal más grande que vive en el océano es el elefante. (a) *verdad* (b) ● *mentira*
mentira	**2** Una persona que tiene tuberculosis o cáncer sufre de una enfermedad. (a) *verdad* (b) *mentira* ●
verdad	**3** Los cristianos creen en Jesucristo. (a) *verdad* (b) *mentira* ●
verdad	**4** Compramos libros en una librería, pero leemos libros en la biblioteca de la escuela. (a) *verdad* (b) *mentira* ●
verdad	**5** El árbol es una planta muy pequeña. (a) *verdad* (b) *mentira* ●
mentira	**6** El oxígeno es un mineral. (a) *verdad* (b) *mentira* ●
mentira	**7** Julio César fue un emperador del imperio romano. (a) *verdad* (b) *mentira* ●
verdad	**8** Un gorila es un animal. Un *guerrilla* en inglés es un hombre. (a) *verdad* (b) *mentira* ●
verdad	**9** La física, la química y la biología son ciencias. (a) *verdad* (b) *mentira* ●
verdad	**10** Arlington es el nombre de un cementerio nacional que está en el estado de Virginia. (a) *verdad* (b) *mentira* ●
verdad	**11** El tigre de Sudamérica es un puma. (a) *verdad* (b) *mentira* ●
verdad	**12** La ciudad de Washington no está en el Distrito de Columbia. (a) *verdad* (b) *mentira* ●
mentira	**13** Stalin fue un dictador de Rusia. (a) *verdad* (b) *mentira* ●
verdad	**14** San Francisco fue un santo y San Francisco es una ciudad de California. (a) *verdad* (b) *mentira* ●
verdad	**15** El estado más grande de los Estados Unidos es Tejas. (a) *verdad* (b) *mentira* ●

mentira (*Es Alaska.* Do not mark this wrong if you just forgot about Alaska but understood the sentence.)

New Vocabulary

invitado	guest	**invitación**	invitation
broma	joke	**tonto**	foolish
millón	million	**cementerio**	cemetery
regalo	gift		

PROGRAM 65

tener versus "to be," and More on Dialog IV

Part 1: *tener* versus "to be"

	1 You already know that Spanish translates "to be" in many ways. You have also learned that there are very clear cues which tell you which verb to use in Spanish. To locate an entity, you use either ⌒⌒⌒. ●
haber or *estar*	**2** To give the origin of someone or something, you use ⌒⌒⌒. ●
ser	

3 When you describe the weather, you use ‿‿‿.

hacer

4 Now, let's look at some other kind of cues which will tell you what verb to choose. Copy and fill in the blanks with *has* or *is:* He ‿‿‿ a fever. He ‿‿‿ feverish.

He has a fever. He is feverish.

5 Do this again: He ‿‿‿ ill. He ‿‿‿ an illness.

He is ill. He has an illness.

6 Copy and fill in the command forms *have* and *be:* ‿‿‿ care! ‿‿‿ careful!

Have care! Be careful!

7 What tells you to choose between *to have* and *to be?* Look at the parts of speech of the words that come after *to have* and *to be:* Have care! Be careful! *Have* is followed by a ‿‿‿.

noun

8 *Be* is followed by an ‿‿‿.

adjective

9 The part of speech which follows the verb tells you which verb to use. (a) true (b) false

true

10 In Spanish, as in English, the part of speech tells you what verb to use. The Spanish translation of "It's wind" is *Es viento.* Spanish also uses the noun *viento* to describe the weather: "It's windy." Can you use *ser* for this, also?

no (You say, *Hace viento,* "makes wind.")

11 The Spanish speaker uses the noun *calor* to describe both the weather and people. Do you think he will say, "I am heat?"

no

12 He does not say "I am heat" for the same reason that you do not say it or "I am a fever." The noun "fever" tells you to say "I have a fever." Now, watch your logic. The noun *calor* tells the Spanish speaker to say: (a) *Yo hago calor.* (b) *Yo tengo calor.*

Yo tengo calor.

13 How will you say, "I am cold?" ‿‿‿ *frío.*

Tengo frío.

14 The Spanish speaker uses *hacer* plus *calor* or *frío* to describe the weather temperature but ‿‿‿ plus *calor* or *frío* to describe the people.

tener

15 What verbs does the Spanish speaker use to describe the temperature of things that have norms or deviate from a norm?

ser and *estar*

16 You use "have" with the noun "care" (Have care!) but "be" with the adjective "careful" (Be careful!). The Spanish speaker always uses the noun *cuidado* to say both. What verb will he choose? (a) *ser* (b) *tener*

tener (And the command form: *¡Tenga cuidado!*)

17 How will you say "I am careful?" ‿‿‿ *cuidado.*

Tengo cuidado.

18 You translate "It is very windy" by *Hace mucho viento.* How will you say "I am very careful?"

Tengo mucho cuidado.

19 We can say in English either "He has a great thirst" or "He is very thirsty." Spanish uses only the noun *sed* to say this. You will use the verb ‿‿‿.

tener (*Tiene sed.*)

20 In learning paired words, you discovered that the noun frequently associated with *sed* is ‿‿‿.

hambre

21 How do you say "I am hungry?" ‿‿‿ *hambre.*

Tengo hambre.

22 The Spanish speaker translates "He is old" as *Es viejo* when this is a norm.

Both "old" and *viejo* are adjectives. Are "year" and *año* adjectives?

no   **23** Does "He is ten years" make sense in English?

no   **24** What do you think *diez años* will cue the Spanish speaker to say? (a) *Es diez años.* (b) *Tiene diez años.*

Tiene diez años.

25 In English we use "right" as an adjective (You are right) or as a noun (You have the right). Spanish uses the noun *razón* (reason) to translate the adjective meaning. How do you say "I am right?" ⁓⁓⁓ *razón.*

Tengo razón.   **26** If *Tengo razón* translates "I am right," then *No tengo razón* must translate "I am ⁓⁓⁓."

wrong

Part 2: More on Dialog IV

This section is to help you memorize the dialog and to give you more practice in saying it aloud. In each frame you will find some blanks. Say the missing part and the rest of the line aloud. Then look at the answer part of the frame to check what you have said.

1 ¿Qué vas a ... ... ?

hacer el sábado (Did you stress **sá**-ba-do ?)

2 No ... ; depende. ¿ ... ... preguntas?

sé ; Por qué

3 Porque ... ... a mi ... ...

quiero invitarte ; fiesta de cumpleaños

4 ¡ ... bueno! ¿Quién ... ... allí?

Qué ; va a estar

5 Todos mis ... , mis ... , ... , amigos . . . ¡ ... el ... !

hermanos ; tíos ; vecinos ; ¡Hasta el gato!

6 ¡Claro! ... invitados, ... regalos.

Muchos ; muchos

7 Ay, ... No ... tonta. No te ... ...

chica ; seas ; invito por eso

8 Lo digo ... . Acepto tu ... . Un ... de gracias.

en broma ; invitación ; millón

9 Here is the whole dialog. Get a watch with a second hand and practice saying the dialog aloud until you can do it in 25 seconds. At this speed, you will be talking at the normal Spanish speech rate.

Después de clase

Sara: ¿Qué vas a hacer el sábado?
Carmen: No sé; depende. ¿Por qué preguntas?
Sara: Porque quiero invitarte a mi fiesta de cumpleaños.
Carmen: ¡Qué bueno! ¿Quién va a estar allí?
Sara: Todos mis hermanos, mis tíos, vecinos, amigos . . . ¡Hasta el gato!
Carmen: ¡Claro! Muchos invitados, muchos regalos.
Sara: Ay, chica. No seas tonta. No te invito por eso.
Carmen: Lo digo en broma. Acepto tu invitación. Un millón de gracias.

No new vocabulary.

PROGRAM 66

Preparing to Read Aloud for a Grade

At the end of this Program you will find a little story entitled *Estudios de verano*. In your next class, you will be asked to read some part of it aloud for a grade. Before you do this part of the Program, turn to the end of the Program, read the story silently and be sure you understand it all.

1 A large part of your grade will depend on whether you can put the stress on the right syllable of a word. In this and the next 9 frames, you will find three words that have been divided into syllables. Copy and underline the stressed syllable, check your accuracy, and, then, say them aloud at least twice.

es-tu-dian-tes, se-cun-da-ria, du-ran-te

*es-tu-**dian**-tes, se-cun-**da**-ria, du-**ran**-te*

2 es-co-lar, a-sis-ten, es-cue-la

*es-co-**lar**, a-**sis**-ten, es-**cue**-la*

3 ve-ra-no, in-te-li-gen-tes, a-pli-ca-dos

*ve-**ra**-no, in-te-li-**gen**-tes, a-pli-**ca**-dos*

4 es-tu-dian, in-te-rés, quie-ren

*es-**tu**-dian, in-te-**rés**, **quie**-ren*

5 gra-duar-se, bas-tan-te, na-cio-nal

*gra-**duar**-se, bas-**tan**-te, na-cio-**nal***

6 bi-ci-cle-ta, mo-to-ci-cle-ta, can-sa-dos

*bi-ci-**cle**-ta, mo-to-ci-**cle**-ta, can-**sa**-dos*

7 pre-pa-rar, lec-cio-nes, si-guien-te

*pre-pa-**rar**, lec-**cio**-nes, si-**guien**-te*

8 in-có-mo-do, pa-tio, a-de-más

*in-**có**-mo-do, **pa**-tio, a-de-**más***

9 a-gra-da-ble, di-fi-cul-tad, con-cen-trar

*a-gra-**da**-ble, di-fi-cul-**tad**, con-cen-**trar***

10 tiem-po, va-ca-cio-nes, mon-ta-ñas

***tiem**-po, va-ca-**cio**-nes, mon-**ta**-ñas*

11 There are two words in the story which you may not know how to read aloud. They are the adverbs *sumamente* and *solamente*. All words like these came from the Latin noun *mente* (mind) and an adjective with the /a/ phoneme of agreement.

A long time ago *Habla claramente* (He speaks clearly) actually meant *Habla con mente clara* (He speaks with a clear mind.) Today the Spanish speaker is no longer aware of this, and the *mente* has no more meaning to him than the English adverbial suffix ~~~~ has to you.

ly (clear, clearly; slow, slowly; quick, quickly)

12 The *mente* today merely says that the adjective to which it is attached describes an action (modifies a verb, not a noun). Nevertheless, the Spanish speaker still has a little memory of how these forms developed and, as a result, he stresses both parts as though they were still two separate words. Copy and underline the stressed syllables: *su-ma-men-te, so-la-men-te.*

su-*ma*-**men**-*te*, *so*-*la*-**men**-*te* (Now, say them aloud.)

13 In Spanish, as in English, every sentence can be divided into phrases, a string of words which must be spoken together. Read this sentence aloud with a pause wherever you see a slant bar (/): *The man who / came to dinner had / a long red / beard.* Sounds kind of silly this way, doesn't it? Now, rewrite it with the pauses where they should be.

The man / who came to dinner / had a long / red beard.

14 You are going to sound kind of odd in Spanish if you read aloud and put pauses where they should not be. Below is the whole passage with the possible pauses marked with a slant bar (/). Practice reading it aloud with pauses only at the bars. You do not, of course, have to pause at the bars. They show you where you may pause. Remember that the pauses must be very short except at periods.

Practice reading the story aloud until you can do the whole thing without a stumble. Don't forget the cues for the right allophones. A native can read the whole passage aloud in one minute and twenty-five seconds and sound as though he is reading slowly.

Estudios de verano

Roberto y Miguel / son estudiantes de secundaria. / Durante el año escolar / asisten a una escuela / muy cerca de su casa. / Este año / ellos van / a la escuela de verano. / Son alumnos inteligentes / y muy aplicados. / Estudian en el verano / porque tienen mucho interés / en terminar pronto / sus estudios. / Quieren graduarse / lo más pronto posible.

En su escuela / no ofrecen / cursos de verano. / Por eso / tienen que ir / a otra escuela / bastante lejos del lugar / donde viven. / Está en el centro de la ciudad / cerca del Banco Nacional. / Roberto va en bicicleta; / Miguel tiene / una motocicleta muy buena. / Todos los días / los muchachos / llegan a la casa / sumamente cansados. / Solamente / tienen clases / por la mañana. / Por la tarde / tienen que preparar las lecciones / para el día siguiente.

Cuando hace mucho calor / es muy incómodo / estar dentro de la casa. / Entonces / Roberto y Miguel / salen a estudiar / al patio. / Allí hace / un poco más fresco. / Además / el patio / es un lugar muy bonito / y agradable. / Pero los muchachos tienen dificultad / en concentrar su interés / en sus estudios. / El verano no es tiempo / de libros y tareas escolares. / Es tiempo / de vacaciones, / de ir a las montañas / y a la playa. / Allí están / sus otros amigos / y compañeros de escuela. / Allí es donde / también / ellos quieren estar.

New Vocabulary

tener sueño	to be sleepy	**inteligente**	intelligent
tener cuidado	to be careful	**bruto**	stupid, ignorant
tener razón	to be right	**enemigo**	enemy
perro	dog	**tener 15 años**	to be 15 years old

Most young people in America feel that when a boyfriend calls on his girl, the parents should allow them to have privacy. In the Hispanic world the tradition of the chaperone is still strong, and it is usually considered improper for a young man and his *novia* to be alone in a room. In certain middle and upper-class families a couple may be engaged for as long as eight years and never be alone. Some older member of the family in either her or his house will always be present to chaperone them.

PROGRAM **67**

Writing Dialog IV

Very soon you are going to have a writing quiz. This Program is designed to help you do well on that quiz. Use your cover sheet and work carefully so you can help yourself do well.

1 By now you should be well aware of the fact that the mere mechanics of writing what you hear depend upon three things: (1) what you hear, (2) rules for spelling, and (3) what you have seen. Write the *yo*-form of the present tense of *saber*.

sé

2 What tells you to put an accent mark on *sé*? (a) what you hear (b) what you have seen

what you have seen

3 The morphemes *por* and *que* combine in two different ways and have two different meanings. In a question, they are written ∼∼∼∼.

por qué (With a space and accent mark.)

4 The best translation of *¿por qué?* is ∼∼∼∼.

why? (The reason or motivation for an action.)

5 In a statement, these same morphemes are written ∼∼∼∼.

porque

6 And the meaning is now ∼∼∼∼.

because

7 All question words are regularly written with an ∼∼∼∼.

accent mark (These same words have the mark in exclamations.)

8 Copy and write in the accent marks for this line: *¿Que vas a hacer el sabado?*

¿Qué vas a hacer el sábado?

9 All words in Spanish ending in *cion* have an accent mark over the ∼∼∼∼.

o (*invitación, condición, acción*)

10 The word *millon* is stressed on the last syllable, *mi-llon*. So you write an accent mark over the ∼∼∼∼.

o (*millón*)

11 Here is what you hear, written in phonetic transcription. Say it aloud and, then, write it in regular spelling: [¿Ke b̸as a aser?].

¿Qué vas a hacer?

12 Try this again. You hear: [¿Kyem ba a estar ayí?]. You write ∼∼∼∼.

¿Quién va a estar allí?

13 Let's try this once more: [Porke kyero imbitarte].

Porque quiero invitarte.

14 The opposite of *Lo digo en serio* is *Lo digo en* ~~~~.

broma

15 The name for people who live in the immediate vicinity of your house is the cognate ~~~~.

vecinos

16 To make the English verb "depend" into its Spanish cognate infinitive, you add the suffixes ~~~~.

er (depender) **17** The Spanish cognate for "to accept" is ~~~~. (Watch the change in spelling.)
aceptar (only one *c*.)

18 You have seen *n* before *v* in *invitar*, *invitados*, and *invitación*. What are you going to hear and say, [n] or [m]?

[m] (And remember, the *v* stands for a stop [b] in speech.)

19 In this and the next several frames, you will find something that suggests a sentence in the dialog. Write the sentence and be careful with your spelling. Have you forgotten that peekers do not learn as much as those who really try before they look at the answer? "Carmen tells Sara she is kidding."

Lo digo en broma.

20 Sara tries to find out if Carmen will be busy this weekend.

¿Qué vas a hacer el sábado? (Check your spelling.)

21 Carmen comes back with a question.

¿Por qué preguntas?

22 Carmen also asks about the guests who will come to the party.

¿Quién va a estar allí? (Are you remembering the *¿ — ?*)

23 Carmen says something about the ratio of guests to presents.

Muchos invitados, muchos regalos.

24 Sara is somewhat upset by this remark and says three short sentences in which she chides her friend and explains her invitation.

Ay, chica. No seas tonta. No te invito por eso.

25 Carmen agrees to come and says something polite.

Acepto tu invitación. Un millón de gracias.

26 Every native speaker of Spanish can speak that language fluently before he or she begins school and learns to read and write. Learning to write, for the native, means little more than learning to spell what he can already say very well.

You have different problems. You are still learning to say what you are trying to write. In addition, you have to be careful not to let your English spelling and writing habits get in your way. Moreover, unlike the native, you are not writing Spanish in all your classes, and you are learning to write and spell at an age when this is no longer a great accomplishment or really much fun. Nevertheless, you do have to practice spelling and writing Spanish to learn to do it. So, let's write the dialog again. In this and each of the following frames, give the Spanish translation. Watch your punctuation and spelling (accent marks, too).

What are you going to do Saturday?

¿Qué vas a hacer el sábado?

27 I don't know. It depends. Why do you ask?

No sé; depende. ¿Por qué preguntas?

28 Because I want to invite you to my birthday party.

Porque quiero invitarte a mi fiesta de cumpleaños.

29 How nice! Who's going to be there?

¡Qué bueno! ¿ Quién va a estar allí?

30 All my brothers, my aunts and uncles, neighbors, friends . . . Even the cat!

Todos mis hermanos, mis tíos, vecinos, amigos . . . ¡Hasta el gato!

31 Of course! Lots of guests, lots of presents.

¡Claro! Muchos invitados, muchos regalos.

32 Oh, come now! Don't be silly. I'm not inviting you for that.

¡Ay, chica! No seas tonta. No te invito por eso.

33 I'm joking. I accept your invitation. Thanks a million.

Lo digo en broma. Acepto tu invitación. Un millón de gracias.

Optional Practice

While two girls, in actual life, would probably take more than 20 seconds to have this conversation, they would say each line at a speed which would add up to only 20 seconds of real talking time. Get a watch and time yourself for native speed.

Después de clase

Sara: ¿Qué vas a hacer el sábado?

Carmen: No sé; depende. ¿Por qué preguntas?

Sara: Porque quiero invitarte a mi fiesta de cumpleaños.

Carmen: ¡Qué bueno! ¿Quién va a estar allí?

Sara: Todos mis hermanos, mis tíos, vecinos, amigos . . . ¡Hasta el gato!

Carmen: ¡Claro! Muchos invitados, muchos regalos.

Sara: Ay, chica. No seas tonta. No te invito por eso.

Carmen: Lo digo en broma. Acepto tu invitación. Un millón de gracias.

No new vocabulary

PROGRAM **68**

Pre-quiz Practice on Dialog IV and More Practice in Situational Discrimination

Part 1: Pre-quiz Practice on Dialog IV

In your next class, you will write Dialog IV from dictation for a grade. In each of the frames below you will find a line of the dialog. The words you are most likely to misspell are left out. Write them and check your spelling carefully.

1 ¿... vas a ... el ... ?

¿ Qué vas a hacer el sábado?

2 No ...; depende. ¿.... ... preguntas?

No sé ; depende. ¿ Por qué preguntas?

3 Porque ... ... a mi ... de ... .
Porque quiero invitarte a mi fiesta de cumpleaños.

4 ¡... bueno! ¿... va a estar ... ?
¡Qué bueno! ¿Quién va a estar allí?

5 Todos mis ... , mis ... , vecinos, amigos . . . ¡... el gato!
Todos mis hermanos, mis tíos, vecinos, amigos . . . ¡Hasta el gato!

6 ¡Claro! ... invitados, muchos ... .
¡Claro! Muchos invitados, muchos regalos.

7 ¡... , chica! No ... . No te ... por eso.
¡Ay, chica! No seas tonta. No te invito por eso.

8 Lo ... en ... . tu ... . Un ... de gracias.
Lo digo en broma. Acepto tu invitación. Un millón de gracias.

In both Hispanic and American culture girls tend to get married at a younger age than men. The Hispanic men, however, rarely marry as young as the average American. There is a strong tradition that a man should not get married until he is thoroughly established in his career. As a result, courtships are frequently long, sometimes lasting several years. The courting process is usually a much more elaborate affair than in America. The man may serenade his girl with a guitar and, sometimes, with an orchestra. In the "proper" families there is always a chaperone present when he comes to visit, and the typical American date is considered in bad taste.

Part 2: Situational Discrimination

1 You already know five common verbs that translate "to be." They are *ser*, *estar*, *haber*, *tener*, and *hacer*. When the Spanish speaker says the equivalent of "I am hungry," he really says, "I have hunger." Translate this into Spanish. ●

Tengo hambre. (He can't say, "I am hunger.")

2 How does the Spanish speaker say, "I am thirsty?" ●

Tengo sed. (He can't say, "I have thirsty.")

3 Translate "I am right." ●

Tengo razón.

4 To use *tener* (to have) the Spanish speaker has to have something. This something is labeled by a noun, the object of the verb. This noun object cues the use of *tener* to translate "to be." Here is the set of nouns that cue this choice. Memorize them.

	calor	*I am hot.*
	frío	*I am cold.*
	hambre	*I am hungry.*
Tengo	sed	*I am thirsty.*
	sueño	*I am sleepy.*
	cuidado	*I am careful.*
	razón	*I am right.*
	15 años	*I am 15 years old.*

5 When the Spanish speaker talks about the weather, he really says that something makes heat, cold, wind, *etc.* We say, "It is hot, cold, windy," *etc.*, but nobody really knows what *it* stands for. What is windy when *it* is windy? What is cold when we say, "*It* is cold today?" In both languages we know what we mean but we cannot explain very well what we actually say. How does the Spanish speaker say, "It is windy?" ●

Hace viento. **6** Translate: It is hot here. ●

Hace calor aquí.

7 Translate: What is the weather like? ●

¿Qué tiempo hace?

8 Translate: The weather is bad (makes bad weather). ●

Hace mal tiempo.

9 You use *tener* to talk of the temperature of people or living creatures (*Tengo frío*) and *hacer* to talk of air temperature (*Hace fresco*). What two verbs do you use in talking about the temperature of things (inanimate objects)? ●

ser or *estar* **10** Which verb will you use? *Los desiertos* ——— *calientes.* (a) *ser* (b) *estar*

ser (The norm for deserts is hot: *Son calientes.*)

11 Which verb will you use? *¡Mamá! ¡Mi sopa* (soup) ——— *fría!* (a) ser (b) *estar*

estar (The exclamation suggests the speaker expects soup to be normally hot.)

12 Your critical analysis of the pattern tells you when to use *tener* or *hacer*. Your analysis of reality tells you when to use *ser* or *estar*. What tells you to use *hay* in *Hay un libro en la mesa?* One fact is location (*en la mesa*); the other is the cue in the language: the use of ———. ●

un (Remember: numbers by themselves cue *haber* for location.)

13 The cues for choice can also be found in the way the Spanish speaker organizes reality. In English someone knocks at the door and we answer, "I'm coming." The Spanish speaker sees the whole situation differently and says, ~~~~~.

Ya voy, or simply *Voy.*

No new vocabulary.

PROGRAM 69

Pre-quiz Practice: Reciting Dialog IV

In your next class, you will recite Dialog IV for a grade. You will get no grade for having it memorized. Your grade will depend entirely on how much you sound like a native. Can you say it without hesitations, with no pauses in the wrong places, with the right allophones of all phonemes, and with the intonation of natural, Spanish speech? Here is a review of all the things you can study by yourself.

1 The English word *den* begins with (a) a stop *d* sound (b) a fricative *d* sound.

a stop *d* (The phonetic symbol for this is [d].)

2 The sound of *th* in *then* is the same as the (a) fricative (b) stop *d* sound in Spanish.

fricative (The phonetic symbol for this is [ð].)

3 The /d/ and /th/ are separate phonemes in English. Are the Spanish [d] and [ð] allophones of the same phoneme?

yes

4 You say the stop allophone [d] in Spanish whenever you start a new sentence or immediately after any pause in a sentence. (a) true (b) false

true

5 You also say the stop [d] when /d/ comes right after the phonemes ~~~~~.

/n/ or /l/

6 You say the fricative [ð] whenever the /d/ is inside a phrase and not after /n/ and /l/. (a) true (b) false

true

7 Here are all the phrases that have a /d/. Practice saying them aloud. Remember plain [d] = stop, and [ð] = fricative.

el sábaðo | muchos invitaðos
depende | Lo ðigo en broma
fiesta ðe cumpleaños | Un millón de gracias
Toðos mis hermanos

8 The phoneme /b/ may be written with either the letter ~~~~~.

b or v

9 How many allophones does /b/ have? (a) one (b) two

two

10 The phoneme /b/, like /d/, has a stop [b] and a fricative [β] allophone. You say the stop [b] when you begin a new sentence, after a pause, and immediately after the phoneme /m/, which may be written either with the letter ~~~~~.

m or n

11 Here are all the phrases that have a /b/. Underline the fricatives, circle the stops.

¿Qué vas a hacer?	quiero invitarte	¡Qué bueno!
¿Quién va a estar allí?	muchos invitados	No te invito por eso.
Lo digo en broma.	Acepto tu invitación.	vecinos

¿ Qué v̲as a hacer?	quiero inⓥitarte	¡ Qué b̲ueno!
¿ Quién ⓥa a estar allí?	muchos inⓥitados	No te inⓥito por eso.
Lo digo en ⓑroma.	Acepto tu inⓥitación	ⓥecinos

Now practice saying the above aloud.

12 The phoneme /m/ may be written either *m* or *n*. In the following words the *n* stands for [m]. Say them aloud and be sure you say [m] and, immediately after it, a stop [b]: *invitar, invitados, invito, invitación, en broma, ¿ Quién va?*

13 Does the letter *u* stand for a vowel sound in the digraph *qu?*

no   **14** Either the digraph *qu* or the letter ——— may stand for the sound [k].

c   **15** The [k] is often strongly aspirated in English (made with a puff). Is it aspirated in Spanish?

no (Some speakers of Spanish give it a very slight aspiration.)

16 Here are all the words with [k] in them. Say them aloud without any aspiration: (Remember how to check for aspiration? Hold the back of your hand close to your lips. If you feel a puff, there is aspiration.) *qué, porque, quiero, cumpleaños, quién, claro, chica.*

17 The letter *c* stands for [k] when it comes before the vowels *a*, *o*, or *u*. It stands for [s] when it comes before ———.

i or *e*   **18** Say these words aloud: *hacer, vecinos, invitación, gracias.*

19 The letter *u* stands for no sound in *que*, for a vowel in *cumpleaños*, and for [ ] in *cuánto*.

[w] ([kwanto])   **20** When *r* is the first letter in a word, does it stand for [r] or [rr]?

[rr] (Say [rregalos] aloud.)   **21** These words have a single flap [r] sound. Say them aloud. Watch for the schwa too: *hacer, por, preguntas, quiero, invitar, estar, broma, gracias.*

22 You already know that in speech words are grouped in phrases. Should you pause in the middle of a phrase?

no (Pauses in the wrong place sound odd.)

23 Copy and put a slant bar (/) where you may pause in this sentence: *Porque quiero invitarte a mi fiesta de cumpleaños.*

Porque quiero invitarte | a mi fiesta de cumpleaños.

24 When you say *por eso* the two words are run together like this: *poreso*. Divide this phrase into syllables as though it were just one word.

po-re-so   **25** The stress is now on the syllable ———.

re   **26** At the end of the question *¿Por qué preguntas?* the pitch (a) goes up (b) down. Before you decide, say the question aloud.

down (In Spanish the pitch goes down at the end of questions asking for information.)

27 The pitch also goes down in these sentences. Practice saying them this way: *¡Claro! ¡Ay, chica! Un millón de gracias.*

28 Here is the whole dialog. The phonemes that may give you trouble are indicated. Slant bars tell you where you may pause within a sentence. The pitch of your voice drops at the end of every sentence. Practice reading the dialog aloud several times, then practice saying it from memory.

Después de clase

¿Qué vas a hacer / el sábado?
No sé; / depende. / ¿Por qué preguntas?
Porque quiero invitarte / a mi fiesta de cumpleaños.
¡Qué bueno! / ¿Quién va a estar allí?
Todos mis hermanos, / mis tíos, / vecinos, / amigos ... / ¡Hasta el gato!
¡Claro! / Muchos invitados, / muchos regalos.
¡Ay, chica! / No seas tonta. No te invito por eso.
Lo digo en broma. / Acepto tu invitación. / Un millón de gracias.

29 In a very few days you will be having another major exam. You need to review the verb forms. Spanish verb forms are made up of three parts: the stem and ⌇⌇⌇ suffixes.

two   **30** The dictionary form of a verb always ends with the suffix ⌇⌇⌇.

r   **31** This form is called the ⌇⌇⌇.

infinitive   **32** Write the infinitive for these forms: *estoy, eres, seas, hay, tengo, salgo.*

estar, ser, ser, haber, tener, salir

33 When a verb has a subject, the *r* of the infinitive is replaced by a person-number marker. The suffix that stands for the first person plural (matches *nosotros*) is ⌇⌇⌇.

mos   **34** The suffix that matches *tú* is ⌇⌇⌇.

s   **35** The plural suffix that matches either *ustedes* or *ellos* is ⌇⌇⌇.

n   **36** Is there anything in the third slot that matches *yo, usted, él,* or *ella?*

no   **37** Write the present tense forms for the following: (*desear*) *yo,* (*vivir*) *usted,* (*beber*) *él,* (*subir*) *ella.*

yo deseo, usted vive, él bebe, ella sube

38 All verbs belong to one of three sets. The verb sets are marked by the vowels ⌇⌇⌇.

a, e, i   **39** The set of a verb tells you what morphemes to use for the (a) first suffix (b) second suffix.

the first suffix (The second suffix is the same for all verb sets.)

40 The present tense suffix which matches *yo* is the same for all regular verbs of all three sets. It is ⌇⌇⌇.

o   **41** Write the *yo* forms for *entrar, deber,* and *subir.*

yo entro, yo debo, yo subo

42 You need to remember the verb set in order to choose the right first suffix for all other forms. The first suffix for *a*-verbs has two forms: *o* and ⌇⌇⌇.

a   **43** Write the correct forms for (*llegar*) *nosotros* and (*entrar*) *ustedes.*

llegamos, entran

44 The first suffix for all regular *e*-verbs has only two forms: ⌇⌇⌇.

o and e   **45** Write the form that goes with either *ustedes* or *ellos: correr, leer, comer.*

corren, leen, comen

46 For regular *i*-verbs, there are three forms of the first suffix. They are *o,* ⌇⌇⌇.

e, i   **47** The *i* appears only in the form that goes with the subject pronoun ⌇⌇⌇.

nosotros   **48** Write the *nosotros* form for *morir, venir,* and *escribir.*

morimos, venimos, escribimos

49 Write the *tú* forms for *subir, vivir,* and *escribir.*

subes, vives, escribes

50 The subject pronouns are really special names for the people taking part in a conversation. The name for each person depends on his role in the conversation. When I am doing the talking, my name is ～～.

yo   **51** When a very close friend is talking to me, my name is ～～.

tú   **52** When a stranger talks to me, my name is ～～.

usted   **53** If I am a male and someone talks about me, my name is now ～～.

él (So I can have four different names in a conversation: yo, tú, usted, él or ella.)

No new vocabulary.

PROGRAM 70

Vocabulary Round-up

This is a review Program of all the words you have spoken, seen, and written: your active vocabulary. It is not expected that you will do every section or every frame in each section today. You may want to put extra time on this Program for several days. Study the sections which deal with the words and forms on which you still need the most practice. If you are not certain what to study, do the first few frames of each section. If you miss several answers, do the whole section. Look each section over to see if there is something you should study. Remember that you cannot review a whole course in one day.

Part 1: Pronouns

1 The six subject pronoun forms which indicate sex are ～～.

nosotros, nosotras, él, ella, ellos, ellas

2 The four subject pronouns that do not indicate sex are ～～.

yo, tú, usted, ustedes

3 Is there a subject pronoun which replaces a noun standing for a thing (non-person)?

no (There is no Spanish equivalent for *it* or its plural, *they*. You just say the verb form all by itself.)

4 Translate: Do you (*usted*) have the book? Yes, it is on the table.

¿Tiene usted el libro? Sí, está en la mesa.

5 The subject pronouns which are made plural simply by adding the plural suffix are ～～.

usted—ustedes; ella—ellas

6 Write the plurals for these pronouns: *tú, él, yo.*

ustedes, ellos, nosotros, nosotras

7 You want to talk about some unknown person. The pronoun you use translates "someone."

alguien   **8** The opposite of this is the negative ～～.

nadie

algo
nada
tú ; él
conmigo

9 You want to talk about some unknown thing. The pronoun you use is ~~~~. •
10 The opposite of this is the negative ~~~~. •
11 The two subject pronouns which have a written accent are ~~~~. •
12 Spanish has a single word for "with me." It is ~~~~. •

In most of the United States teenage girls and women think nothing of going to a store or to a party by themselves after dark. Except for the great metropolitan centers, in most of Latin America a teenage girl does not leave the house after dark unless escorted by a parent and a woman does not go out unless escorted by her husband or a relative. In many places it is considered immoral for a woman to be on the street alone after dark.

Part 2: Question Words

1 All question words have one thing in common *in writing*. They all have a ~~~~. •
written accent mark (Always over the stressed vowel.)

2 The answer to your question will be a number. The question word is ~~~. •
¿Cuántos? (¿Cuántos libros quieres?)

3 You ask to have a person identified by name or occupation. The question word is ~~~~. •
¿Quién? (¿Quién es? Es Pilar. Es la profesora.)

4 The answer to your question will be the name of a place, a region, territory, location, *etc.* The question word is ~~~~. •
¿Dónde? (¿A dónde va? ¿De dónde viene? ¿Dónde está?)

5 This question word asks for a quantity or amount (not a number). •
¿Cuánto? (¿Cuánto deseas? Muy poco.)

6 You want to know the manner or way something is done or the state or characteristics of someone or something. The question word is ~~~~. •
¿Cómo? (¿Cómo se llama? ¿Cómo estás?)

7 You want a thing identified by its label (noun). The question word is ~~~. •
¿Qué? (¿Qué es esto? Es un capibara.)

8 There are several choices and this question word asks you to select a particular one. •
¿Cuál? (¿Cuál de los libros quiere usted?)

9 The plural form is ~~~~. •
¿Cuáles?

10 You ask for the time at which something happens. The question word is ~~~~. •
¿Cuándo? (¿Cuándo comemos?)

Part 3: Relators

There are very few relators in the Spanish language and every one, as a result, has many functions and meanings. Relators establish relationships between entities, between events, or between entities and events. To understand them, you need to know what cues their choice. Here are the ones you know: *a, de, en*, *con*, *hasta*, and *por*. Think of the relator that would be used in the blanks below, then check the answer.

1 *Marcos es* ——— *Venezuela.*

de (The relationship is between a person and his country of birth; *ser* + *de* describes origin.)

2 *Montevideo está* ——— *Uruguay.*

en (*estar* + *en* talks about the location of the subject inside or on something.)

3 ¿——— *qué hora comen en tu casa?*

A (When we talk about clock time, *a* marks the point at which something takes place.)   **4** ¿——— *dónde viene?*

De (*de* + *venir* talks about movement from some place toward here.)

5 *Adiós,* ——— *luego.*

hasta (The translation does not tell you much about *hasta*. One meaning is "until" or "up to" some point in time.)

6 *Venezuela está* ———*l norte de Ecuador.*

a (Here *a* indicates compass direction.)

7 *Vienes* ——— *migo?*

con (This translates "with" in the meaning of "being in the company of someone.")   **8** *Vamos* ——— *trabajar. Vamos* ———*l cine.*

a (Indicates the goal of movement: a place (*cine*) or an action (*trabajar*).)

9 *Tú lápiz está* ——— *el piano.*

en (All this really means is "in contact with the surface of something else.")

10 ¿——— *qué me preguntas?*

Por (One of the common meanings of *por* is "for what reason, cause, motivation.")   **11** The word for "even" or "including" is ———.

hasta (*¡Hasta el gato!*)

Part 4: Adverbs

1 The Spanish equivalent of the English adverbial suffix *ly*, as in "rapidly," is ———.

mente (This is the only Spanish suffix that clearly tells you the word is an adverb.)   **2** An adverb may give the distance of a thing or event from the speaker. You know two adverbs that say something is not far away. They are ———.

aquí; cerca (*Está aquí. Está cerca.*)

3 The opposite of *aquí* is ——— (over there).

allí

4 The opposite of *cerca* is ———.

lejos

5 Here are a dot and a square. What adverbs describe the position of the dot in relation to the square? $\boxed{\cdot}$ $\boxed{}$ •

$\boxed{\cdot}$ *dentro* $\boxed{}$ • *fuera*

6 One adverb states that an event is going to happen in a very little while. It is ———.

pronto (*Viene pronto.*)

7 This adverb says a person is feeling fine (literally "standing up well").

bien (*Estoy bien, gracias.*)

8 The name for any interval of calendar time may be used to say when something takes place. Copy the adverb in *¿Qué vas a hacer el sábado?*

el sábado

9 If today is *viernes*, you could replace *el sábado* with the adverb ———.

mañana **10** The opposite of *mañana* is ———.

ayer **11** The day in between *ayer* and *mañana* is ———.

hoy (¿Qué vas a hacer hoy?)

12 What adverb will make this sentence negative? *Siempre estudia.*

Nunca estudia. **13** A few words can be pronouns and adverbs at the same time. Any word that makes a sentence negative is an adverb. The negative opposite of *Alguien viene* is ———.

Nadie viene. **14** The negative opposite of *algo* is ———.

nada (Nada tengo is like No tengo nada.)

15 If *no* is an adverb, then its opposite, ———, is also an adverb.

sí (Did you remember the accent mark?)

16 There are two adverbs in this sentence: ***Ya es tarde.*** Translate the sentence.

It's already late.

17 The opposite of *tarde* is ———.

temprano **18** The adjective *bueno* has a matching adverbial form *bien*. The adverb form that comes from *malo* is ———.

mal **19** Write the Spanish equivalents: still, also, besides.

todavía, también, además

20 There are three adverbs which may be added to the sentence *Ella habla.* Write the proper adverb for each sentence below. (a) She rarely talks. (b) She talks a lot. (c) She talks too much.

Habla poco. Habla mucho. Habla demasiado.

21 If *Ella habla demasiado*, we might say, *Debe hablar* ——— (less).

menos **22** The opposite of *Debe hablar menos* is *Debe hablar* ———.

más **23** There are a few adverbs which do not describe actions or events. Instead, they change the degree of other adverbs or adjectives. Which ones change the degree of *bien*? (a) High degree: *Trabaja* ——— *bien.* (b) Satisfactory degree: *Trabaja* ——— *bien.*

Trabaja muy bien. Trabaja bastante bien.

24 When you say you'll see someone soon, you may say *Hasta* ———.

luego **25** There are two paired adverbs you have learned which describe the speed of movement. They are *rápido* and ———.

despacio **26** Which one translates "slow?"

despacio **27** "Today" is *hoy.* "Yesterday" is *ayer.* "Day before yesterday" is *anteayer.* *Ante* comes from *antes* (before). The opposite of *antes* translates "after" and is ———.

después

Part 5: Nouns

1 Which sets of nouns do you *not* capitalize in Spanish? (a) days of the week (b) proper names (c) names of languages (d) months of the year

You do not capitalize (except at the beginning of a sentence) the days of the week, the months, or the names of languages.

2 The morpheme of plurality in Spanish has two allomorphs. They are ———.

s; es **3** You add *es* to a noun when it ends in a (a) vowel (b) consonant.

consonant (You add *s* to vowels.)

4 Some Spanish nouns have only one form. Others have two forms. When a noun has two forms, one form may end in a consonant, or either *o* or *e*. The other form must end in ⌇⌇⌇.

a

5 Here are all the nouns you have studied that have two forms. Look at each word and, then, say the opposite form aloud.

señora	directora	chica
muchacha	hermana	vecina
hija	sobrina	amiga
tía	alumna	invitada
abuela	prima	enemiga
maestra	profesora	perra

Except for *señor*, *director* and *profesor*, all take *o* as the opposite of *a*.

6 Here is a way of finding out which nouns you need to study more. Below you will find a list of nouns first in English and then in Spanish. Start with the first column and slide your cover sheet slowly down the list. If you do not *instantly* recall the Spanish equivalent, copy the Spanish word. When you get to the end, you will have a complete list of all the nouns you need to study some more. Study them as much as you need to in order to get the kind of a grade you want. With enough effort, you can be perfect.

The nouns appear in five columns. Look at and work with only one column at a time. The first words you meet are the last ones you studied. The English given is the standard translation used so far.

dog	vecino	niece	fecha	west
perro	birthday	sobrina	equator	oeste
enemy	cumpleaños	grandfather	ecuador	woman
enemigo	party	abuelo	tunnel	mujer
right	fiesta	grandmother	túnel	lie
razón	stingy	abuela	streetcar	mentira
careful	tacaño	aunt	tranvía	truth
cuidado	money	tía	ship	verdad
sleepy	dinero	uncle	barco	season
sueño	Castilian	tío	pampa	estación
million	castellano	brother	pampa	spring
millón	student	hermano	desert	primavera
invitation	estudiante	sister	desierto	summer
invitación	boy	hermana	river	verano
joke	chico, muchacho	son	río	fall
broma	teacher	hijo	sea	otoño
gift (present)	maestro	daughter	mar	winter
regalo	surname	hija	ocean	invierno
guests	apellido	father	océano	child
invitados	name	padre	north	niño
cat	nombre	mother	norte	moon
gato	cousin	madre	east	luna
friend	primo	family	este	people
amigo	nephew	familia	south	gente
neighbor	sobrino	date	sur	balcony

balcón	*lugar*	*animal*	*domingo*	*mesa*
thirst	store	garden	pupil (student)	pen
sed	*tienda*	*jardín*	*alumno*	*pluma*
hunger	church	elephant	school	desk
hambre	*iglesia*	*elefante*	*escuela*	*pupitre*
man	bank	corral	principal	moment
hombre	*banco*	*corral*	*director*	*momentito*
lesson	post office	tiger	Spanish	watch
lección	*correo*	*tigre*	*español*	*reloj*
December	cafe	rodeo	pardon me	pencil
diciembre	*café*	*rodeo*	*perdón*	*lápiz*
November	downtown	gaucho	day	notebook
noviembre	*céntro*	*gaucho*	*día*	*cuaderno*
October	mountain	capital	dialog	book
octubre	*montaña*	*capital*	*diálogo*	*libro*
September	country (side)	city	boy	office
septiembre	*campo*	*ciudad*	*muchacho*	*oficina*
August	beach	mine	girl	English
agosto	*playa*	*mina*	*muchacha*	*inglés*
July	park	week	paper	number
julio	*parque*	*semana*	*papel*	*número*
June	movie	country (nation)	chair	morning
junio	*cine*	*país*	*silla*	*mañana*
May	house (home)	favor	chalk	class
mayo	*casa*	*favor*	*tiza*	*clase*
April	hour	Monday	light	night
abril	*hora*	*lunes*	*luz*	*noche*
March	weather	Tuesday	ruler	afternoon
marzo	*tiempo*	*martes*	*regla*	*tarde*
February	wind	Wednesday	blackboard	teacher
febrero	*viento*	*miércoles*	*pizarra*	*profesor*
January	cool	Thursday	eye	madam
enero	*fresco*	*jueves*	*ojo*	*señora*
year	cold	Friday	door	miss
año	*frío*	*viernes*	*puerta*	*señorita*
month	heat	Saturday	window	mister
mes	*calor*	*sábado*	*ventana*	*señor*
place	animal	Sunday	table	

Part 6: Adjectives

1 Adjectives, like nouns, may or may not have two forms. An adjective which has an *a*-form is very likely to have another form which will end in either a consonant, or ⌐⌐⌐⌐.

o

2 What form of an adjective will you use to match nouns ending in these phonemes: *r, o, l?* (a) *o*-form (b) *a*-form

o-form

3 When adjectives agree in number with their nouns, they have the same number suffix as the noun (a) true (b) false

true

4 Here are the adjectives which have two forms. Look at each word and, then, say aloud the plural, *a*-form.

bueno	cuarto	cuarto	flaco	bonito
el	medio	descansado	alto	feo
un	tacaño	magnífico	seco	recto
nuevo	todo	demasiado	húmedo	torcido
mucho	cansado	último	inmenso	chico
frío	primero	enfermo	bajo	lindo
fresco	segundo	pequeño	sucio	nuestro
perfecto	tercero	viejo	limpio	tonto
malo		gordo		bruto

5 Write the adjective of nationality for these countries, *a*-form: *Venezuela, Brasil, Ecuador, Uruguay, Perú.*

venezolana, brasileña, ecuatoriana, uruguaya, peruana

6 Here are the adjectives which have only one form in the singular. Say them aloud in the plural form.

presente	cruel	joven
terrible	caliente	popular
fácil	amable	alegre
feliz	difícil	excelente
grande	triste	inteligente

7 The adjectives *bueno-buena* and *malo-mala* have special forms which are used before nouns that also combine with *un*. They are ———.

buen; mal (*uno* becomes *un*; *bueno* becomes *buen*; *malo* becomes *mal*)

In the United States there exists a custom which is rarely talked about but which is followed with very considerable consistency. This custom says that a man should be as tall or taller than his wife. A very large majority of Latin men are short and, as a result, many Latin wives are taller than their husbands. It is considered impolite to mention this fact to the individuals concerned.

Part 7: Verb Forms

There are three things you have to remember about each verb: (1) the meaning of its stem, (2) its set, *a*, *e*, or *i*, and (3) whether it is regular or irregular. The system tells you how to get all the forms of regular verbs. You must remember which slot has a special form for irregular verbs.

1 The stem of *tener* has three allomorphs in the present tense: ———.

ten, tien, teng (There are no other irregularities.)

2 *Venir* has the same irregularities as *tener*. (a) true (b) false

true (*ven, vien, veng*)

3 The present tense stem of *ir* is ———.

v (And the forms are like *estar; voy, vamos, etc.*)

4 *Estar* has two irregularities: *estoy* and the stress on the ——— suffix.

first

5 The two forms of *estar* that do not have a written accent are ———.

estoy; estamos

6 *Pensar* and *empezar* have two stem forms. The *nosotros* form is regular (*pens, empez*). All other forms change *e* to ———.

ie (pienso, empieza, etc.)

7 *Salir* is irregular only in the *yo* form ———.

salgo

8 *Hacer* is irregular only in the *yo* form ———.

hago

9 *Morir* and *poder* have two stem forms. The *nosotros* form is regular (*mor, pod*). All other forms change *o* to ———.

ue (puedo, muero, pueden, mueren, etc.)

10 *Ser* is one of the most irregular verbs in the language. Write these forms: *tú ... , yo ... , él ... , ustedes ... , nosotros ... .*

eres, soy, es, son, somos

11 You should be able to make up all the present tense forms of these regular verbs.

llamar	esperar	escribir	deber
hablar	cantar	subir	correr
desear	terminar	leer	responder
necesitar	entrar	comer	contestar
estudiar	llegar	creer	invitar
trabajar	vivir	beber	aceptar

Part 8: Fixed Phrases

Give the Spanish equivalent of the following:

1 How goes it?

¿Qué tal? **2** Please.

Por favor. **3** day after tomorrow

pasado mañana

4 to be hungry

tener hambre **5** It is windy.

Hace viento. **6** Pardon me.

Perdón. **7** See you soon.

Hasta luego or *Hasta pronto.*

8 You're welcome.

De nada. **9** OK

OK or *Bueno.* **10** To be . . . years old.

Tener . . . años.

11 Good morning.

Buenos días. **12** Good afternoon.

Buenas tardes.

13 Good evening, good night.

Buenas noches.

No new vocabulary.

PROGRAM 71

Review 1:

Before all major tests up until now, you have had a special Program that goes over the test in detail. Since your next big exam is going to be like the ones you have already had, there is no longer any need to practice the details. This Program, instead, reviews some important points you should remember.

You have acquired two kinds of knowledge in this course. First, you have learned how to analyze, describe, and talk about language and language learning. This knowledge will help you with your English and many other subjects. It is, however, only a means to an end; that is, learning how to hear, speak, read, and write Spanish. Your next exam will deal only with these four skills: your ability to communicate in Spanish.

Here is a self-test. If you really want to know how you stand in the course, use your cover sheet and do not look at the answer frame until you have done the best you can. Check each frame you miss. At the end you can give yourself a grade.

1 You want to locate an entity modified by the indefinite article or a number. This cues you to use the verb ~~~~.

haber　　2 *El hombre que descubrió el Nuevo Mundo fue italiano.* He was born in ~~~~.

Italy　　3 Speakers of English often replace unstressed Spanish vowels with a special vowel sound called ~~~~.

schwa　　4 To make "He eats too much" negative in English, you must say, "He does not eat too much." Write the translation for both sentences.

Él come demasiado. Él no come demasiado.

5 English /p/ has two allophones. Spanish /p/ has only one allophone. It is never ~~~~.

aspirated (made with a puff)

6 You are talking about a person. What verb do you use with these nouns: *calor, frío, hambre, sed?*

tener　　7 Translate: He is nine years old.

Tiene nueve años.

8 In English we say, "His name is Jorge." The meaning of the Spanish is "He calls himself Jorge." The Spanish is ~~~~.

Se llama Jorge.

9 You are describing the weather. What verb do you use with these nouns: *viento, frío, calor, mal tiempo?*

hacer　　10 Translate: It is very windy.

Hace mucho viento. (You use the adjective *mucho,* not the adverb *muy.*)

11 When you describe the subject with a predicate adjective in Spanish, you must choose between the verbs ~~~~.

ser and *estar*　　12 The norm for the subject takes ~~~~. Any change or deviation from the norm takes ~~~~.

norm takes *ser;* change or deviation takes *estar*

	13 Look! The snow is pink! (a) *ser* (b) *estar*
estar	**14** The second suffix of a verb gives person and number. The plural morphemes are ———.
mos ; n	**15** The suffix that matches *tú* is ———.
s	**16** The stem of *tener* in the present tense has three allomorphs: ———.
teng, ten, tien	**17** Write the form that goes with *ustedes*.
ustedes tienen	**18** Where English uses the possessives *his, her, your, their,* and *its,* Spanish uses only two forms: ———.
su ; sus	**19** English possessive adjectives agree in number with the possessor; Spanish possessive adjectives agree in number with the noun they combine with. (a) true (b) false
true	**20** Write the paired word for each of the following: *sed, grande, fácil, siempre.*
hambre, pequeño, difícil, nunca	
	21 When there is one consonant between two vowels, the consonant goes with the ——— vowel in syllabication.
second	**22** What usually happens when there are two consonants between two vowels?
one goes with the first vowel; one with the second	
	23 One Spanish cognate of "vicinity" is ———.
vecino	**24** *El padre de mi madre es mi* ———.
abuelo	**25** *La mujer* (wife) *de mi abuelo es mi* ———.
abuela	**26** What verb do you use when you tell time?
ser	**27** The two forms used in telling time are ———.
es ; son	**28** The Spanish speaker divides the day into three parts: *la ... , la ... ,* and *la ... .*
la mañana, la tarde, la noche	
	29 What greeting do you use in the morning?
Buenos días.	**30** Adverbs with the suffix *mente* are not stressed like other words. Divide these into syllables and underline the two stressed syllables: *finalmente, claramente.*
fi-**nal**-**men**-te, **cla**-ra-**men**-te	
	31 A word which ends in *n* or *s* is stressed on the (a) last syllable (b) next to last syllable.
next to last (Unless there is a written accent.)	
	32 A word which has no written accent and ends in any consonant (except *n* or *s*) is stressed on the ——— syllable.
last	**33** In what way are question words all spelled differently from other words?
All have a written accent mark.	
	34 When *el* becomes an adjectival residual as the object of a verb, it is changed to ———.
lo	**35** When I am taking part in a conversation, I may play four roles as subject of a verb and, so, I may have four names in Spanish. (1) When I talk, my name is ———. (2) When a close friend speaks to me, my name is ———. (3) When a stranger speaks to me, my name is ———. (4) When they talk about me (a girl), my name is ———.
(1) yo, (2) tú, (3) usted, (4) ella	
	36 Do you capitalize the names for the days of the week and the months in Spanish?
no	**37** What kind of sentences have to have a punctuation mark in front of them?
questions and exclamations	

38 You are standing at the box. Someone is moving in the direction shown by the arrow. ☐ ◄——————— ◯ What verb describes the movement?

venir

39 To locate something on a surface, you use *haber* or *estar* and the relator ⁓⁓⁓.

en

40 Give three cues that tell you to use *estar* for location.

Any one of these is correct: proper name, subject pronoun, definite article, demonstrative, or a possessive adjective.

41 You add the plural allomorph *es* to nouns which end in a ⁓⁓⁓.

consonant

42 The sound [k] may be spelled either ⁓⁓⁓.

c + a, o, u; qu + e, i

43 The letter *c* stands for [s] only before / / and / /.

/e/ and /i/

44 Write out: It is 9:45 A.M.

Son las diez menos quince (cuarto) de la mañana.

45 When you add or subtract numbers, you use the verb form ⁓⁓⁓.

son

46 You address teachers, strangers, and respected adults with (a) *tú* (b) *usted*.

usted

47 When someone knocks at your door, you answer by saying, (a) *Ya vengo* (b) *Ya voy*.

Ya voy.

48 Does Spanish have a subject pronoun equivalent to "it" or its plural "they?"

No (You just use the verb.)

49 The opposite of *anteayer* is ⁓⁓⁓.

pasado mañana (This is *el mañana*, not *la mañana*.)

50 Does *su* really mean "his, your, her, their," *etc.* to a Spanish speaker?

no (It just means possessed by the person or persons being talked about.)

51 This is the last *pregunta*. The adjective which describes it is ⁓⁓⁓.

última

Giving yourself a grade: frames missed.

0–1	A+	4	B+	7	C+	10	D+	13	F
2	A	5	B	8	C	11	D		
3	A−	6	B−	9	C−	12	D−		

No new vocabulary.

PROGRAM **72**

Review 2: Selective Self-Help

This is your last Program before your next big exam. It is not concerned with how much you know *about* Spanish. It deals, instead, with how well you can communicate *in* Spanish, and with the forms you need in order to communicate. Do the sections which deal with problems you feel you still need to review.

Part 1: Equivalents of "to be"

1 Say that the air temperature is very low.

Hace mucho frío.

2 Describe Tula as naturally very nice.

Tula es muy amable.

3 Miguel is in bed with a virus. Describe his state of health.

Miguel está enfermo.

4 Where is Asunción?

Asunción está en Paraguay.

5 Locate a pen on the chair.

Hay una pluma en la silla.

6 Marcos was born in Lima. Give his origin.

Marcos es de Lima.

7 Write out: It is 1:45 P.M.

Son las dos menos quince (cuarto) de la tarde.

8 Write out: It is 1:25 A.M.

Es la una y veinticinco de la mañana.

9 Locate Miranda in Quito.

Miranda está en Quito.

10 Write out: 23 + 8 = 31.

Veintitrés y ocho son treinta y uno.

11 Pilar has not eaten for ten hours. Describe how she feels.

Tiene hambre.   **12** You go to school. Say what you are.

Yo soy alumno or *alumna.*

13 Translate: She is eleven years old.

(Ella) tiene once años.

14 Write out: 25 − 7 = 18.

Veinticinco menos siete son dieciocho.

15 Translate: You are right. *Tú* ~~~~.

Tú tienes razón.

16 Locate *ellas* in Caracas.

Están en Caracas.

Part 2: Numbers

1 Write out the number words for *uno + diez, cinco + diez, tres + diez, diez + seis.*

once, quince, trece, dieciséis

2 Write the number words for 6, 7, 9, 20, and 30. Check your spelling.

seis, siete, nueve, veinte, treinta

3 Write out: 12 + 5 = 17.

Doce y cinco son diecisiete.

4 Write out: 12 − 5 = 7.

Doce menos cinco son siete.

5 The question word to ask for a number response is ¿ ~~~~?

¿ Cuántos ?

Part 3: Regular Verbs

1 The verb set of *viven* is ~~~~.

i.
2 So the form that goes with *nosotros* is ~~~~.

vivimos

3 The stem of *leer* is ———.

le

4 To get the *usted*-form you add ———.

e

5 And to get the *ustedes*-form you add ———.

n (ustedes leen)

6 Write the *yo*-form for *cantar, escribir, correr, subir, desear.*

canto, escribo, corro, subo, deseo

7 Make these forms match *nosotros*: *llamo, vivo, como, llego, bebo, termino.*

llamamos, vivimos, comemos, llegamos, bebemos, terminamos

8 Make these forms singular: *hablan, comen, viven, deben, esperan.*

habla, come, vive, debe, espera

9 Write the infinitive for *vives, estudio, suben, deben, escribes.*

vivir, estudiar, subir, deber, escribir

10 The *s* suffix tells you (a) the verb is plural (b) the subject is *tú.*

the subject is tú

11 Change to *tú*-forms: *necesitar, leemos, escriben, entra, subimos.*

necesitas, lees, escribes, entras, subes

12 The subject pronouns which match the second suffix *n* are ———.

ustedes, ellos, ellas

13 The infinitive form of *invitado* is ———.

invitar

Part 4: Irregular Verbs

1 Translate: I am sleepy.

Tengo sueño.   **2** She is thirsty.

Tiene sed.   **3** We are hot.

Tenemos calor.

4 They are in La Paz.

Están en La Paz.

5 I am going out. (Do not use *voy a*.)

Salgo.   **6** I make chairs.

Yo hago sillas.   **7** There they come!

¡Allí vienen!   **8** I am from Lima.

Soy de Lima.   **9** Now say a similar message with another verb: ——— *de Lima.*

Vengo de Lima.

10 *Pensar* and *empezar* each have two allomorphs of the present tense stem: ———.

pens and *piens; empez* and *empiez*

11 Translate: He is beginning to talk.

Empieza a hablar.

12 In the irregular forms of *morir* and *poder*, you change *o* to ———.

ue (puedo, muere)

13 The regular stem of these verbs appears only in the forms that go with the subject pronoun ———.

nosotros (podemos, morimos)

14 Write three different verb forms which translate "I am."

soy, estoy, tengo

15 Write the matching forms of *ser*: tú ... , ellos ... , nosotros ... .
eres, son, somos
      16 The infinitive of *seas* is ~~~~.
ser

Part 5: Adjectives

      1 The four forms of the definite article are ~~~~.
el, los, la, las   **2** Rewrite and delete the noun: *Voy a comprar el auto.*
Voy a comprarlo. (When *el* becomes the adjectival residual, you change it to
lo.)   **3** The equivalent of "good" has three singular forms: ~~~~.
bueno, buen, buena
      4 Rewrite and make all words plural: *Yo tengo el lápiz blanco.*
Nosotros tenemos los lápices blancos.
      5 Translate: I want new books.
Quiero libros nuevos.
      6 I want new pens.
Yo quiero plumas nuevas.
      7 Rewrite in the plural: *Es la idea general.*
Son las ideas generales.
      8 The speaker is a girl. Translate: I am tired.
Estoy cansada.   **9** The speaker is a boy. Translate: I am sick.
Estoy enfermo.

Part 6: Relators

      1 Translate: Why are you going?
¿Por qué vas (va)?
      2 Because I want to.
Porque quiero.
      3 Where's she going?
¿A dónde va ella?
      4 Where's he from?
¿De dónde es él?
      5 Please, sir, where is the post office?
Por favor, señor, ¿dónde está el correo?
      6 María is with me.
María está conmigo.
      7 Good-bye, until tomorrow.
Adiós, hasta mañana.
      8 Father is at home.
Papá está en casa.
      9 Father is in the house.
Papá está en la casa.
      10 They are going to work.
Van a trabajar.

Part 7: Question Words

1 Translate: How many books do you want?

¿ Cuántos libros quieres (quiere) ? (or deseas, desea)

2 How much do they have?

¿ Cuánto tienen ?

3 How is Pilar today?

¿ Cómo está Pilar hoy ?

4 What is that?

¿ Qué es eso ? **5** When do we eat?

¿ Cuándo comemos ?

6 Which of the girls is Elena?

¿ Cuál de las muchachas es Elena ?

7 Where is he coming from?

¿ De dónde viene ?

8 Where is he going to?

¿ A dónde va ? **9** Who is calling?

¿ Quién llama ?

10 (Make the last sentence plural.)

¿ Quiénes llaman ?

Part 8: Pronouns

1 Translate: Somebody is coming.

Alguien viene. **2** Make this negative.

Nadie viene. **3** The abbreviation *Vds.* stands for ———.

ustedes **4** Do they have something?

¿ Tienen algo ? **5** (Make this negative.)

¿ No tienen nada ?

6 Make this plural: *Tú tienes razón.*

Ustedes tienen razón.

7 You are a girl, speaking for a group of girls: We are hungry.

Nosotras tenemos hambre.

8 You are a girl, speaking for a group of boys and girls: We are very cold.

Nosotros tenemos mucho frío.

9 You are talking to a very small child: Are you thirsty?

¿ Tienes (tú) sed ?

10 You ask the same question of a stranger.

¿ Tiene Vd. sed ?

11 Answer this question with a negative: *¿Está la casa sucia ?*

No está sucia. **12** My name is Margarita.

Me llamo Margarita.

Part 9: Adverbs

1 Translate: She speaks clearly.

Habla claramente.

2 Here is where they live.

Aquí es donde viven.

3 Elena is well, thank you.

Elena está bien, gracias.

4 The opposite of *fuera* is ~~~~.

dentro

5 The opposite of *aquí* is ~~~~.

allí

6 The opposite of *lejos* is ~~~~.

cerca

7 What are you going to do Monday?

¿Qué vas a hacer el lunes?

8 Make this positive: *Nunca tiene sueño.*

Siempre tiene sueño.

9 It's already late.

Ya es tarde. **10** No, it's early.

No, es temprano.

11 She is still sick. (Put the adverb first.)

Todavía está enferma.

12 And, besides, it's windy.

Y, además, hace viento.

13 They work too much.

Trabajan demasiado.

14 Watch out! I work also.

¡Ojo! Yo trabajo también.

15 We are going day after tomorrow.

Vamos pasado mañana.

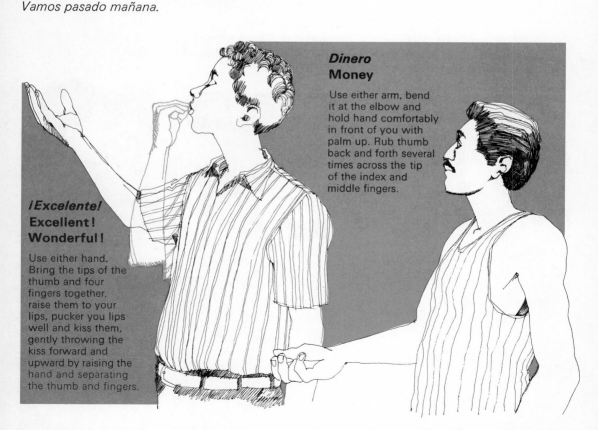

Dinero
Money

Use either arm, bend it at the elbow and hold hand comfortably in front of you with palm up. Rub thumb back and forth several times across the tip of the index and middle fingers.

¡Excelente!
Excellent!
Wonderful!

Use either hand. Bring the tips of the thumb and four fingers together, raise them to your lips, pucker you lips well and kiss them, gently throwing the kiss forward and upward by raising the hand and separating the thumb and fingers.

Ejercicio 27 | Reading Aloud

See how much you can sound like a native speaker as you read this dialog with
a classmate.

Nombres y apellidos

Lola: Tomás, la secretaria del director quiere saber cuál es tu apellido.
Tomás: Mi apellido es Martínez Sarmiento.
Lola: ¡Cómo! ¿Son necesarios dos apellidos?
Tomás: Sí, es la costumbre (*custom*) de mi país. Martínez por parte de padre
        (*on my father's side*) y Sarmiento por parte de madre.
Lola: Entonces, tu nombre completo es Tomás Martínez Sarmiento, ¿verdad?
Tomás: No, Lola, es Tomás Juan Martínez Sarmiento.
Lola: ¡Caramba! ¡Qué largo (*long*) y complicado es tu nombre!
Tomás: Largo, sí; complicado, no. Es muy fácil.
Lola: Explícamelo (*Explain it to me*), por favor.
Tomás: Tomás es por mi tío, el hermano de mi papá.
Lola: ¿Y por qué Juan? ¿Por tu abuelo?
Tomás: No, chica. Juan es por mi santo.
Lola: ¡Tu santo! No comprendo (*understand*).
Tomás: En el calendario el 24 de junio es el día de San Juan.

Lola: ¿Y qué tiene que ver eso (*what does that have to do*) con tu nombre?

Tomás: Eso es muy importante. Yo nací (*was born*) el 24 de junio, día de San Juan. Por eso me llamo Juan.

Lola: Ya comprendo. Te llamas Tomás, por tu tío; Juan, por el santo del día; y . . .

Tomás: ¡Exacto! Martínez es el apellido de la familia de mi papá y Sarmiento el de la familia de mi mamá.

Lola: ¡Tomás Juan Martínez Sarmiento! ¡Dios mío! (*Good heavens!*) ¡Cómo le explico todo esto a la secretaria!

Tomás: No hay problema. Ustedes pueden usar solamente Tomás Martínez. El nombre completo es para los documentos principalmente.

Ejercicio 28 | *ser* versus *estar*

Choose between the two verbs in parentheses:

1 Pancho y Enrique . . . (están, son) en las montañas.
2 La pobre Elena . . . (está, es) muy cansada de trabajar mucho.
3 Pancho . . . (está, es) de Caracas; . . . (está, es) venezolano, pero ahora . . . (está, es) en España.
4 ¿Cuántos . . . (están, son) diez y tres?
5 María dice que . . . (está, es) bien hoy.
6 Yo quiero . . . (estar, ser) en las montañas para las vacaciones.
7 ¡Caray! Ya . . . (es, está) la una y media.
8 Yo quiero . . . (estar, ser) profesor de español.
9 Este . . . (es, está) mi hermano José. Él . . . (es, está) en primer año.
10 ¡Caray! La alumna gorda de nuestra clase de inglés ahora . . . (es, está) muy flaca. Yo creo que ella . . . (es, está) enferma.

Ejercicio 29 | *ser* versus *estar* with Predicate Adjectives

Choose between the two verbs in parentheses:

1 Mi libro de geografía dice que en el Polo Norte el agua . . . (está, es) fría.
2 ¡Caray! El refrigerador . . . (está, es) caliente.
3 Todos saben que este señor . . . (está, es) argentino.
4 Las iglesias importantes siempre . . . (están, son) grandes.
5 Mi madre . . . (está, es) enferma hoy.
6 ¿De qué color . . . (están, son) las pizarras?
7 Yo sé que mis padres . . . (están, son) muy buenos.
8 ¡Ojo! Este chocolate . . . (está, es) muy caliente.
9 El presidente del país tiene que . . . (estar, ser) importante.
10 ¿No sabe usted que la gasolina . . . (está, es) combustible?

Ejercicio 30 | *ir* versus *venir*

Choose between the two verbs in parentheses:

1 En el banco el señor Sánchez pregunta a su amigo, el señor López, —¿ . . . (Viene, Va) usted a este banco todos los viernes?

2 El señor López contesta, —Sí, . . . (vengo, voy) aquí todos los viernes porque el viernes es el día en que recibo mi salario cada semana.

3 El director de la mina habla por teléfono a Pancho que está de vacaciones, —Por favor, . . . (venga, vaya) usted a trabajar hoy. Tenemos seis hombres ausentes porque están enfermos.

4 Pancho le responde al director, —¡Qué bueno, señor director! Necesito el dinero. . . . (Vengo, Voy) inmediatamente.

5 La mujer de Pancho le pregunta, —¿A dónde . . . (vienes, vas), Pancho?

6 Y Pancho le contesta, —. . . (Vengo, Voy) a la mina a trabajar.

7 Su mujer, ahora bastante furiosa, exclama, —¿No sabes que mis primos . . . (vienen, van) aquí a visitarnos esta tarde?

8 Pancho, muy indiferente a la reacción de su mujer, contesta, —¿Y qué? Es más importante que yo . . . (venga, vaya) a la mina a trabajar.

Ejercicio 31 | *ir* versus *venir*

Choose betweeen the two verbs in parentheses:

1 El director le dice al profesor Molina, —Señor Molina, . . . (venga, vaya) usted aquí inmediatamente.

2 El señor Molina responde, — . . . (Vengo, Voy) inmediatamente.

3 Hablo con un amigo en la escuela. —¿Sabes, Pancho, que Juan y yo . . . (venimos, vamos) al cine esta noche después de estudiar?

4 Pancho responde, —¡Qué bueno! ¿Me permiten ustedes . . . (venir, ir) también?

5 María y yo hablamos por teléfono. Ella está en casa y quiere invitarme a una fiesta allí el sábado. Dice, —¿Quieres . . . (venir, ir) a una fiesta aquí el sábado?

6 Yo le contesto, —Sí, quiero . . . (venir, ir), pero no puedo porque mis tíos . . . (vienen, van) aquí para pasar dos días de vacaciones con mi familia.

Ejercicio 32 | Adjectival Residuals

Write out the combinations which your teacher will give you.

Aquí	está	**1** el regalo.	**1** Debo poner . . . allí
		2 la invitación.	**2** Yo . . . veo bien.
	están	**3** los lápices.	**3** Yo . . . pongo en la mesa.
		4 las plumas.	**4** Voy a necesitar . . . pronto.
			5 Tú . . . necesitas, ¿verdad?
			6 Ellos quieren ver . . . .

Ejercicio 33 | Possessive Adjectives

Complete the following sentences. The subject of the sentence is the possessor.

Ejemplo: Ella tiene . . . libro. (*The answer is* su.)

   1 Yo tengo . . . lecciones.
   2 Nosotros trabajamos con . . . sobrinas.
   3 María está aquí con . . . abuelos.
   4 María y yo tenemos . . . plumas nuevas.
   5 Tú vas al cine esta noche con . . . hermana, ¿verdad?
   6 Ustedes deben tener . . . libros también.
   7 Yo voy allí con . . . tío.
   8 José tiene que hablar con . . . hermanos.
   9 Pablo y yo tenemos que trabajar con . . . prima.
10 Tú vas a hablar con . . . profesor, ¿verdad?

In the United States a couple that wishes to get married has a choice between a civil and a religious ceremony. In the Hispanic world it is customary to have both ceremonies. The couple is first married in the civil ceremony and then in church, where they receive the marriage sacrament.

In the remote rural areas and in the city slums it is not uncommon to dispense with both ceremonies. It is this tradition which gave the original meaning to *casarse con: to house oneself with.*

Ejercicio 34 | *ir* versus *venir*

Choose between the two verbs in parentheses:

1 Mi hermano está en Europa y habla con un amigo. Dice que . . . (viene, va) a casa para las vacaciones.

2 Mi mamá dice que todos estamos muy contentos porque mi hermano . . . (viene, va) a casa para las vacaciones.

3 Yo tengo que . . . (venir, ir) al banco esta noche. ¿Quieres acompañarme?

4 Pepe y Enrique viven en las montañas. Siempre me preguntan cuando me escriben, "¿Cuándo . . . (vienes, vas) aquí a pasar unos días con nosotros?"

5 Y yo siempre respondo que no puedo . . . (venir, ir) allí hasta los días de vacaciones.

6 ¿No quieres . . . (venir, ir) aquí para estudiar conmigo?

7 Sí, quiero . . . . (Vengo, Voy) dentro de quince minutos.

8 Ella nunca . . . (viene, va) a visitarme aquí en Chicago. Está demasiado lejos de donde vive ella.

Ejercicio 35 | Vocabulary of *La familia*

Write the missing word. The first sentence gives the clue.

Ejemplo: Juan es el hijo de mi padre. Juan es mi . . . . (hermano)

1 María es la hija de mi tía. Es mi . . . .

2 Mi padre tiene dos hijos: mi . . . José y yo.

3 Mis abuelos tienen, además de mi padre, siete hijas. Por eso, yo tengo siete . . . .

4 Mi hermana tiene una hija, María Luisa. Es mi . . . .

5 Juan Ramón Sánchez es el hermano de mi mamá. Es mi . . . .

6 La madre de mi padre es mi . . . .

7 ¿Qué soy yo? *(¡Ojo!)* Yo soy . . . de mis padres.

8 Cada persona tiene dos padres y cuatro . . . .

Ejercicio 36 | Adjectival Agreement

Complete the following sentences with the correct form of the adjective in the model.

Ejemplo: La señorita está *contenta*. Pancho está . . . . (contento)

1 Paco es muy *tonto*. Lola es muy . . . .

2 Mi padre es *joven*. Mis abuelos son . . . .

3 Este es *el nuevo* alumno. Estas son . . . alumnas.

4 Los muchachos son *felices*. Yo soy . . . .

5 Yo estoy *cansado*. Ellos están . . . .

6 *Mi* primo está *alegre*. . . . primas están . . . .

7 *Todas las* señoritas son *venezolanas.* . . . señores son . . . .

8 Ella es *una* chica muy *gorda.* Él es . . . chico muy . . . .

Ejercicio 37 | Adjectival Residuals

Rewrite the second sentence omitting the noun.

Ejemplo: Yo veo la iglesia. Pancho también ve la iglesia. *Pancho también la ve.*

1 Este es el libro. Pero no puedo leer el libro.

2 Aquí está la tiza. Pongo la tiza allí.

3 ¿Tienes los diálogos? Quiero leer los diálogos.

4 Roberto tiene el regalo. Voy a ver el regalo mañana.

5 Yo no tengo la hora. Él tiene la hora.

6 Esta es la pluma de que hablas. Él necesita la pluma.

7 ¿Quién tiene las invitaciones? Sara tiene las invitaciones.

8 Aquí está el ejercicio. Debo escribir el ejercicio.

9 ¿Cuáles son las lecciones? Ellos saben las lecciones.

10 ¿Sabe Pancho la fecha? No, no sabe la fecha.

Ejercicio 38 | *haber, hacer, estar, tener, ser*

First decide which of these five verbs should be used to fill the blank, then select the correct form of the verb you choose and write it.

Ejemplo: Los gauchos . . . en Nueva York, pero . . . de Argentina. (están, son)

1 ¡Caray, hombre! . . . mucho calor esta mañana.

2 Pancho . . . de Ecuador, y ahora . . . en la ciudad de Quito.

3 ¿Qué hora . . . ? . . . las cinco y media.

4 Elena dice que . . . mucha hambre.

5 ¿Cuántos lápices . . . en la mesa?

6 Juan . . . muy enfermo hoy.

7 Hoy en el desierto . . . mal tiempo y todo . . . muy húmedo.

8 Dos y cuatro . . . seis.

9 Esa muchacha nueva que se llama Lola . . . muy bonita.

10 . . . un alumno nuevo en la escuela hoy.

Ejercicio 39 | Paired Words

Match the following words.

1	subir	(a)	*nunca*
2	morir	(b)	*hombre*
3	gato	(c)	*noche*
4	caliente	(d)	*bajar*
5	día	(e)	*frío*
6	mujer	(f)	*perro*
7	amigo	(g)	*descansado*
8	mentira	(h)	*nada*
9	siempre	(i)	*vivir*
10	algo	(j)	*alguien*
		(k)	*verdad*
		(l)	*enemigo*

Ejercicio 40 | Possessive Adjectives

Complete the following sentences. The subject of the sentence is the possessor.

1 Las señoritas van al cine con . . . amigas.
2 Yo estudio en casa con . . . hermano Horacio.
3 Pancho trabaja en la mina con . . . padre.
4 Nosotros tenemos que hablar con . . . profesores.
5 Tú debes ir a la fiesta también con . . . sobrinas.
6 El profesor de inglés habla con . . . alumnos.
7 Ella y yo vamos a estudiar con . . . amigas, Carmen y Sara.
8 Yo necesito ir a la tienda con . . . primos.
9 El tigre no sale de . . . corral.
10 Nosotros vamos al cine con . . . hija.

Ejercicio 41 | Guided Conversation

The following is a conversation between Juan and Miguel or between Juanita and María. Take one of the roles and work with a partner.

J: You meet Miguel and greet him and ask him about his health.
M: You answer him and ask him what he is going to do Saturday.
J: You say that you don't know and ask him why.
M: You tell him that you are going to the beach and want to invite him.
J: You accept his invitation, tell him that he is very kind, and thank him.
M: You tell him that he is welcome and say good-by, until later.
J: You say good-by to him and wave.

Ejercicio 42 | Reading Aloud

Estudios de verano

Roberto y Miguel son estudiantes de secundaria. Durante el año escolar asisten° they attend
a una escuela muy cerca de su casa. Este año ellos van a la escuela de verano. Son
alumnos inteligentes y muy aplicados. Estudian en el verano porque tienen
mucho interés en terminar pronto sus estudios. Quieren graduarse lo más pronto
posible.

En su escuela no ofrecen cursos de verano. Por eso tienen que ir a otra escuela
bastante lejos del lugar donde viven. Está en el centro de la ciudad cerca del
Banco Nacional. Roberto va en bicicleta; Miguel tiene una motocicleta muy
buena. Todos los días los muchachos llegan a la casa sumamente° cansados. extremely
Solamente tienen clases por la mañana. Por la tarde tienen que preparar sus
lecciones para el día siguiente.

Cuando hace mucho calor es muy incómodo° estar dentro de la casa. Entonces uncomfortable
Roberto y Miguel salen a estudiar al patio. Allí hace un poco más fresco.
Además el patio es un lugar muy bonito y agradable. Pero los muchachos tienen
dificultad en concentrar su interés en sus estudios. El verano no es tiempo de
libros y tareas escolares. Es tiempo de vacaciones, de ir a las montañas y a la
playa. Allí están sus otros amigos y compañeros de escuela. Allí es donde también ellos quieren estar.

Etapa Cinco

Programs and Review of the Forms of *tener* and *venir*

Part 1: The Purpose of Programs

1 For many years there have been educators who have believed that all formal learning should take place in the school room. Some schools have even had a rule which prohibits assigning work to be done outside the classroom. Modern research has shown, however, that doing all your learning in the classroom may have serious disadvantages. For example, when all the learning takes place in the classroom, must every student try to learn as much as everyone else in the *same length of time?*

yes (This is called "lock step" learning. The teacher sets the pace and either you keep up or you get behind.)

2 This lock step learning can be avoided when you have a chance to do a great deal of learning at home, and with programed assignments you can study and learn at the speed that is most comfortable for you. Do you have to finish a Program in a fixed number of minutes?

no

3 If you are a fast learner and reader, you get through a Program in a few minutes. If not, you just take a little longer, but every day you can get to the same place as everyone else in the class. Programed assignments actually make it difficult for you to get behind in your studies. You get a small amount of work each day and you can only get behind if you fail to do your assignment regularly and on time. Did you ever stop to answer this question: Who is responsible for your doing your assignments? (a) you (b) your teacher

you are responsible (You learn only what you want to learn.)

4 Another reason programed assignments teach better than classroom learning is because the learning can be broken down into smaller steps. There is just not enough teaching time in the classroom to talk over all the fine points that can be taken up in a Program. Moreover, your teacher does not have the time to work out all the details for a course simply because it takes a great many hours to prepare, test, and rework every Program. Programed assignments attempt to make things easier for you and your teacher. If you miss a Program for any reason, should you always try to do it later?

yes

5 Here is another great difference between ordinary assignments and programed assignments. When you do an ordinary assignment, you do not find out whether you are right or wrong until your work has been corrected and handed back. When you work with a Program, do you find out whether you are right or wrong in each frame?

yes (You find out immediately.)

6 Some students complain that it is too easy to cheat when doing a Program. Nothing stops you from peeking but will power and the cover sheet. What stops you from stealing in a drugstore?

either fear of getting caught or your own personal integrity (You only hurt
yourself when you cheat doing a Program.)

7 With the exception of a few review lessons, each Program in Spanish For
Communication is designed to get you ready for something that is going to
happen in your next class. Can you expect to be really successful if you fail to
do a Program before the class meets? •

no

8 Here is something you need to know. Your Programs space out your learning
so it is easier to understand. You don't get great chunks of information at one
time. They also contain a lot of information which appears no where else in the
course. It is not in the *Ejercicios* nor is it in the *Daily Lesson Plans* your teacher
uses in class. The only place you can learn this information is in your Programs.
Do you think you can be successful in the course if you do not do your assignments? •

no

Here are some "rules" about doing your assignments properly. If you follow
them carefully, there is a 90 percent chance that you can do "A" work on every
Program.

(1) Never "read over" a Program before you are ready to study it carefully.

(2) Always work with a cover sheet and always put down or think through
an answer before you look at the answer frame. You can spoil the whole
purpose of the Program by giving up and peeking at the answer. Remember
that you are only cheating yourself when you peek.

(3) When you make a mistake, go back over the frame and try to discover
what you did wrong. Sometimes you may have to go back two or three frames
to find out why you made an error.

(4) Circle the number of each missed frame on your work sheet. When you
have completed the Program, go back to these frames and review them again.

(5) Never try to hurry through a Program. Hurried learning leads to quick
forgetting. Try always to have enough time so you can do each Program at
your most efficient learning speed. You are you, and you should learn to study
at your own rate, not in competition with other members of your class. Above
all, don't let someone "bug" you about how fast he does his assignments.
What counts is that you can learn just as much even if it takes a little longer.

(6) If you have a vacation or a long week-end, try to do your assignment
the day before the next class. You will forget less and be better prepared in
case there is a surprise quiz.

(7) If you do badly on a quiz, go back and do that Program over again.

(8) Remember that you have already learned to read, write, and speak one
language. This is all you need to prove that you can learn to do the same in a
second language. Anyone who speaks one language has all the intellectual
ability needed to learn another one. You can help yourself be successful by
working out a home-study plan in which you always save enough minutes of
every day for your Spanish assignments.

(9) Do not put off your Spanish assignments until the time of the day when
you are regularly tired. Do something mechanical when you are tired and
save your "alert" time for real study.

(10) If you think the assignments take too long or that they are too hard,

try to keep in mind that all the Programs have been tested on hundreds of students of your age and preparation. The Programs have been designed so that the majority of students can do them in 15 to 20 minutes and, at the same time, not miss more than five frames. If you are far out of line, consult your teacher for help.

Part 2: Stem-changing Verbs: *tener* and *venir*

1 How many morphemes are there in the present tense of a Spanish verb form?

three (A stem and two suffixes.)

2 When a verb is regular, the stem is the same in all forms. (a) true (b) false

true

3 The verbs *tener* and *venir* are irregular because the stem of each has more than one allomorph. The form of *tener* that goes with *yo* is ⁓.

tengo

4 The stem of *tengo* is ⁓.

teng

5 The form of *venir* that is like *tengo* is ⁓.

vengo (The stem is *veng*.)

6 The stems of the *nosotros*-form of *venir* and *tener* are (a) regular (b) irregular.

regular (They are *ven* and *ten*.)

7 The Latin form of *tener* was *tenere*. When a stressed Latin *e* became Spanish, it often changed to ⁓.

ie

8 The result is that the stems *ven* and *ten* sometimes changed to ⁓.

vien ; tien

9 You will learn more about verbs of this irregular set in your next class. This change of *e* to *ie* happened in all types of words, not just in verb forms. The air that blows through a *ventana* is a ⁓ in Spanish.

viento (The stress is on *ta* in *ventana*, but on *vien* in *viento*.)

10 The *vien* of *viento* is like the *vien* of *ellos vienen*. The other two allomorphs of the stem of *venir* are ⁓.

ven ; veng (Compare *ten* and *teng*.)

11 The adverb *bien* is like the stem of *viento* and *viene*. How would you guess it was written in Latin?

ben (The full form was actually *bene* as in "benefactor"—a "do-gooder.")

12 You already know that the Spanish adjective *dental* has the stress on *tal*. A "dentist" in Spanish is a *dentista*. He works on *dientes* which is translated by ⁓.

teeth (Did you know that the teeth of a gear wheel are called "dents" in English?)

13 When English borrowed Latin words, did stressed *e* change to *ie*?

no

No new vocabulary.

According to American etiquette, one always says "ladies first," and a speaker addressing a mixed audience begins with "Ladies and gentlemen." Many Latins are upset because American girls and women often do not wait for them to open doors or stay in a car until they get out and open the door for a female passenger. Nevertheless, when a Spanish speaker addresses a mixed audience, he begins with *Señores y señoras.*

More on Stem-changing Verbs (*e* > *ie*) and Learning Vocabulary

Part 1: Stem-changing Verbs

1 When words go from one language to another, strange things often happen to them. When the Spanish explorers first came to Florida, they discovered huge lizards, 8 to 10 feet long, which they called *el lagarto* (the lizard). When the English came to this country, they heard this name (*el lagarto*) and pronounced it very badly. As a result, today we call these huge lizards of the southern swamps ~~~~.

alligators **2** Some western cowboys still lasso a steer with a lariat without knowing that "lasso" comes from Spanish *lazo* (noose) and "lariat" from *la reata* (the strap or the rope). In the same way the modern Spanish speaker does not know that *septiembre* is a modern "mispronunciation" of Latin *september*. The change from *september* to *septiembre* exhibits a pattern which shows how Latin gradually became Spanish. The final *er* changed to ~~~~.

re (Compare *november—noviembre* and *december—diciembre*. Also *siempre* which came from *semper*.)

3 These month names have another change. The stressed *e* of *november*, etc., changes to ~~~~.

ie (This also happens in *fiesta* (festival), *desierto* (desert), *tienda* (tent), *bien* (beneficial), and in many verb forms.)

4 The form of *tener* that goes with *usted* is ~~~~.

tiene (Compare *tienda* and "tent.")

5 To make *tiene* agree with *ustedes* or *ellos*, you add only ~~~~.

n **6** There are three allomorphs of the stem of *tener*. They are ~~~~.

ten, tien, teng **7** The *ten* allomorph appears in the infinitive and in the form that goes with the subject pronoun ~~~~.

nosotros **8** The *teng* stem combines with *o* which goes with the subject pronoun ~~~~.

yo **9** Does the allomorph *tien* appear in all the other forms of the present tense?

yes **10** The infinitive is the form of the verb which appears in dictionaries. Can you tell from looking at *tener* that it is irregular?

no (So bilingual dictionaries and teaching texts have to have a system to let you know this. Most books give a number to a model and the same number to all similar verbs. Some will give the infinitive and right afterwards in parentheses the common stem change, for example, *tener* (*ie*).)

11 *Tener* is an *e*-verb and *venir* is an *i*-verb. Are they, nevertheless, very much alike in the present tense?

yes **12** To get the *yo*-form of *venir* you just change the ~~~~ of *tengo* to ~~~~.

the *t* of *tengo* to *v* (*vengo*)

13 The third allomorph of the stem of *venir* is ~~~~.

vien **14** The verb *querer* (to wish, to want, or to love) is also irregular in that the *e*

of the stem changes to *ie* when stressed. Which form will go with *yo?* (a) *quero*
(b) *quiero*

quiero (The word ends in a vowel so the stress is on **quie**-*ro*.)

15 The infinitive form *querer* is regular because the stress is on the syllable (a) *que* (b) *rer*.

rer (The word ends in the consonant *r* and so the stress is on the last syllable.)

16 The *nosotros*-form of all verb forms ends in the second suffix *mos*. Will the stress fall (a) on the stem? (b) on the first suffix?

on the first suffix (So the stem is never stressed and never irregular when the subject is *nosotros.*)

17 Write the *nosotros*-form of *querer*.

queremos

18 To change *quiero* to match *usted* you replace the first suffix *o* with ⁓⁓⁓.

e (usted quiere)

19 To make *quiere* agree with *ustedes* or *ellos* you add ⁓⁓⁓.

n (quieren)

20 Write the *tú*-form of *querer*.

tú quieres

21 Verbs like *tener* and *venir* have three allomorphs of the stem in the present tense. How many allomorphs of the stem does *querer* have?

two

22 The two allomorphs of the stem of *querer* are ⁓⁓⁓.

quer; quier

23 The verb *pensar* translates "to think" or "to intend." Although *pensar* is an *a*-verb, it has the same stem irregularities as *querer*. The *yo*-form of *querer* is *quiero*. The *yo*-form of *pensar* is ⁓⁓⁓.

pienso

24 To make *pienso* agree with *tú*, you change the *o* to *a* and add ⁓⁓⁓.

s (tú piensas)

25 Now remember what you learned about all *nosotros*-forms. The *nosotros*-form of *pensar* (we think) is ⁓⁓⁓.

pensamos (The stress is on *sa* so the *e* does not change to *ie*.)

26 The *ustedes*-form of *querer* (to want, to love) is like *pensar* (to think, to intend). The *ustedes*-form of *pensar* is ⁓⁓⁓.

piensan (The word ends in *n*, so the stress is on *pien* and *e* changes to *ie*.)

27 In your next class you are going to meet a new set of irregular verbs which had an *o* in the Latin stem. When this *o* was stressed in Spanish it changed to *ue*. The verb *envolver* (to wrap) belongs to this set. What form of *envolver* fits in the blank: *Ella* ⁓⁓⁓ *el regalo de cumpleaños?*

envuelve

28 The form *volver* translates "to return." What form would you use to say they "return" tomorrow?

vuelven

29 The *nosotros*-form of this set of verbs has no irregularity in the stem. Write the *nosotros*-form of *volver*.

volvemos

30 What you are learning about stem-changing verbs can be easily summed up in one rule. With the exception of *tengo* and *vengo*, *e* changes to *ie* and *o* changes to *ue* when the stress falls on the stem syllables. Look at this chart of *pensar* (to think). The stressed syllable is indicated.

yo	*pien*-so
nosotros	pen-*sa*-mos
tú	*pien*-sas
usted	*pien*-sa
ustedes	*pien*-san
él, ella	*pien*-sa
ellos, ellas	*pien*-san

Part 2: On Learning Vocabulary

1 With only minor exceptions, all the vocabulary you have learned so far has been presented to you in class. Moreover, each individual word has been practiced and repeated so many times that you have had to do almost nothing to memorize each new word. The real reason for all these classroom repetitions of vocabulary words has not been to teach you the words themselves but to teach their pronunciation (the phonemic system). You have now learned to pronounce words when you see them for the first time and there is not so much need for in-class practice in saying new words. Moreover, in order to learn to read and understand Spanish well, you still have to learn several thousand new words. Do you think there will be enough class time to practice each new word a great many times? ●

no

2 You will really never have the time to learn Spanish well unless you learn the meaning and pronunciation of a great many words the first time you meet them. Let us imagine, for example, that you have never seen or heard the Spanish word for island, a piece of land surrounded by water. It is just the first part of "island," that is, *isla*. Say *is-la* aloud in Spanish. Do you really need much more practice to understand the meaning of *Cuba es una isla?* ●

no

3 Translate: Puerto Rico is an island. ●

Puerto Rico es una isla.

4 You already know that you can learn and remember words better if you put them together in sets. An island (*isla*) is a geographic word like "peninsula," a piece of land that is almost an island. (The Latin for "island" is *insula*.) The word "river" is another geographic term. The big river that separates the United States and Mexico is called *el Río Grande*. The Spanish word for "river" is ﹏﹏. ●

río

5 A piece of land surrounded by water is an *isla*. A very large body of water is called an *océano* in Spanish. A small body of water which is completely surrounded by land is called *un lago* in Spanish. The English cognate of *lago* is ﹏﹏. ●

lake (Say *lago* aloud in Spanish.)

6 You now know three words for different kinds of bodies of water: *río, lago,* and *océano*. Keeping them together in a set will make them easier to remember. It also helps to notice that the Spanish words for "river," "lake," and "ocean" all begin with the same letter used in English. *Los ríos y los lagos* are geographic features of the earth or land. The Latin for "land" or "earth" is *terra*. The *e* of Latin *terra* is stressed in Spanish, so the Spanish word should be written (a) *terra* (b) *tierra*. ●

tierra (Just like *tiene* or *noviembre*. Say *tierra* aloud.)

7 *Los ríos, los lagos y los océanos son partes de la tierra* (earth). The English cognate of *partes* is ﹏﹏. ●

parts (Say *partes* aloud.)

8 You already know the definition of *isla* (island). Let's see now if you can translate this: *Las islas están rodeadas de agua* (water). ●

Islands are surrounded by water.

9 You also know that *el Río Grande* is between the United States and Mexico. Which word in the following sentence translates "between?" *El Río Grande está entre los Estados Unidos y México.* ●

entre (The English cognate is "inter" as in "inter-collegiate.")

10 In the region of *el Río Amazonas* of Brazil, there are great stretches of tropical rain forests popularly called "jungles." Which word in the following sentence translates "jungles"? *En la región del Río Amazonas de Brasil hay grandes selvas tropicales.*

selvas (The English cognate is "silvan.")

        11 The Spanish for "river" is ——.

río   **12** The cognate of "lake" is ——.

lago   **13** Spanish changes Latin *terra* to ——.

tierra (One English cognate is "territory.")

        14 In geographic terms the opposite of *montañas* is *llanuras.* The great expanse of flat territory between the Mississippi River and the Rocky Mountains is called *una gran llanura* in Spanish. The translation of *llanura* is ——.

plain (The Pampas of Argentina are *llanuras.*)

        15 Geographers talk about the earth but also about countries (*países*), the inhabitants of the countries, and their population. If you watch the cognates and use your logic, you should be able to translate this sentence: *El número de habitantes de un país es su población.*

The number of inhabitants of a country is its population.

        16 Say English "inhabitants" then Spanish *habitantes.* Spanish dislikes ending words in *nt,* so the singular of *habitantes* is ——.

habitante   **17** *Los habitantes de la tierra hablan muchas lenguas o idiomas.* Which two words above are translations of "languages?"

lenguas (literally "tongues") and *idiomas* (idioms)

        18 Translate: *Un lago está rodeado de tierra.*

A lake is surrounded by land.

        19 *Tierra* translates "land, earth, soil." Another word in English for "earth" as in "the earth is round," is ——.

world   **20** Which word in the following sentence translates "world?" *Cristóbal Colón descubrió el Nuevo Mundo en 1492.*

mundo   **21** *¿Cuál es más grande, un lago o un océano?*

un océano   **22** The big river between the United States and Mexico is called in Spanish ——.

el Río Grande (the big river)

        23 The Spanish word for "earth" is ——.

tierra (*ie*, not *ei*)

        24 The Spanish word for "jungle" is a cognate of "silvan." It is ——.

selva   **25** To get the Spanish word for "inhabitant" you drop the prefix —— and add —— to the end of the word.

you drop the prefix *in* and add *e* (*habitante*)

        26 There are two Spanish words for "language." One is *lengua,* the other is almost like "idiom." It is ——.

idioma   **27** The geographic opposite of *llanura* is a cognate of "Montana." It is ——.

montaña (With a tilde over the *n*)

        28 The translation of *llanura* is ——.

plain (You have just been presented with 16 new words in 28 frames. Have you learned them all?)

        29 You are certainly aware of the fact that you cannot learn to speak or understand Spanish very well until you have a very large vocabulary. Up until now it has been possible to keep all words "alive" by practicing them in class. However, as your vocabulary grows this will be impossible. There just will not be enough class time to keep on repeating everything. As a result, you need to develop a systematic and efficient way of learning and reviewing words. Here is a plan that works.

Set aside a section of your notebook and label it *Vocabulary*. In neat columns copy the English and Spanish for the 16 geographic terms you studied in this Program. At the top of the column write *Program 74*. Now add these words to the list:

sol	sun	**niebla**	fog
tormenta	storm	**llover (ue)**	to rain
luna	moon	**nevar (ie)**	to snow
estrella	star		

Now cover one column and see if you can say the equivalent of each word in the other. Then reverse the process, cover the other column, and do the same. If you will spend just *three* minutes every day doing this, you will gradually get to the point where you can review 100 familiar words in less than a minute, over 300 in the three minutes. This means you can review at least 1500 words each week. You will discover that some words seem harder to remember than others. Make a special list of these words and spend extra time on them until they come to your mind as fast as the others.

If you follow this procedure carefully there is no reason why you cannot learn to do "A" work on all problems involving vocabulary.

PROGRAM **75**

Stem-changing Verbs (*o* > *ue*), New Vocabulary, and the Done-to *a*

Part 1: Stem-changing Verbs: *o* > *ue*

1 You already know the verb form *puedo* (I can). The *ue* of *puedo* comes from a stressed Latin *o*. This verb is an *e*-verb. Now think carefully about what you already know about irregular verbs. The form of *puedo* that goes with *nosotros* should logically be ⌇⌇⌇⌇.

podemos (when the *o* of the stem is not stressed it does not change to *ue*.)

2 The infinitive for *puedo* and *podemos* is ⌇⌇⌇⌇.

poder

ie (quiero, vienes)

3 When Latin became Spanish, a stressed *e* often became ⌇⌇⌇⌇.

4 When Latin became Spanish, a stressed *o* often became *ue*. In comparison with *quieres* the form of *poder* that goes with *tú* should logically be ⌇⌇⌇⌇.

puedes **5** Change *puedes* so it agrees with *usted*.

puede **6** Change *puede* so it agrees with either *ustedes* or *ellos*.

pueden	**7** You now know two allomorphs of the stem of the verb that translates "can." They are ———.
pod; pued	**8** The verb *volver* (to return) has exactly the same irregularities as *poder*. The form that goes with *yo*, consequently, should logically be ———.
vuelvo	**9** Change *vuelvo* so it agrees with *usted*.
vuelve	**10** If *volver* behaves exactly like *poder*, then the form that goes with *nosotros* should logically be ———.
volvemos (The stress is on *ve* so *o* does not change to *ue*.)	
	11 The set of verbs in which stressed *o* changes to *ue* has to be memorized. Here is the pattern:

yo	*pue*-do
nosotros	po-*de*-mos
tú	*pue*-des
usted, él, ella	*pue*-de
ustedes, ellos, ellas	*pue*-den

Part 2: Review of New Vocabulary

	1 It used to be believed that too much staring at the moon could drive people crazy. Such crazy people were called "lunatics." The Spanish word for "moon" is ———.
luna	**2** When there are great explosions on the surface of the sun, there are often huge sheets of flame called "solar flares." The Spanish word for "sun" is ———.
sol	**3** A person who does "manual" labor works with (a) his brains (b) his hands.
his hands	**4** The Spanish word for "hand" is ———.
mano	**5** Which article form goes with *mano*? (a) *la* (b) *el*
la (*La mano* is an exception you have to memorize.)	
	6 On a clear night you can always see *estrellas* in the sky. The translation of *estrellas* is ———.
stars	**7** The Spanish speakers named one of our western states *Nevada* because there was a lot of snow there. The infinitive for "to snow" is ———.
nevar	**8** You know the Spanish proverb about "A bird in the hand," *etc.* The word for "bird" is ———.
pájaro	**9** The Spanish cognate of "permission" is ———.
permiso	**10** When you use *permiso* to say "Pardon me," you add the relator that translates the English "with," ———.
Con permiso.	**11** It is still possible to call a raging storm or a tempest a "torment" in English. What letter do you add to "torment" to get the common Spanish word for "storm?"
a (tormenta)	**12** A "building" in English is sometimes called an "edifice." The Spanish cognate of "edifice" translates "building." It is ———.
edificio	**13** Translate: *Una isla tiene que estar rodeada de agua.*
An island has to be surrounded by water.	
	14 Translate: *En Brasil hay muchas selvas tropicales.*
In Brazil there are many tropical jungles.	
	15 A small body of water that is completely surrounded by land is called a ——— in Spanish.
lago (Think of "lagoon" in English.)	

16 Spanish speakers write Latin *terra* (earth) as ~~~~.

tierra **17** Translate: *El español y el inglés son idiomas modernos.*
Spanish and English are modern languages.

18 Translate: *En el estado de Colorado hay una llanura grande y muchas montañas.*
In the state of Colorado there is a great plain and many mountains.

19 The English cognate of *población* is ~~~~.

population **20** Change "inhabitant" to its Spanish form.
habitante **21** When a person is pensive in English, we mean he is thinking. The infinitive cognate of "pensive" is ~~~~.

pensar **22** What word in the proverb about birds is a cognate of "value" (worth)?
vale **23** The part of the cosmos on which we live may be called either *la tierra* or *el* ~~~~.

mundo **24** Add these words to your study list and sometime before your next class spend three minutes reviewing the whole list.

pájaro	bird	**cien**	one hundred
(la) mano	hand	**¡Salud!**	health
valer	to be worth	**¡Jesús!**	Jesus
volar (ue)	to fly		used when a person sneezes

In American homes it is a fairly common practice for the members of a family to say "good morning" to each other when they meet for breakfast. For many Latins this is a strange custom, for they use *Buenos días* only to greet a person who comes in from outside or when they meet a person on the street.

Part 3: The Done-to *a*

1 You have already discovered that the patterns of Spanish and English sentences are not always alike. Some of these differences can be traced to the fact that Spanish developed from Latin (a Romance language) while English is Anglo-Saxon (a Germanic language). Some differences, however, come from the fact that each language organizes the world from an entirely different cultural point of view. In English, for example, we say, *I see the blackboard* and *I see the girl*. Which word in each sentence stands for the speaker and the doer?

I **2** I am the speaker and the one who does the seeing (the doer). Which word in *I see the blackboard* and *I see the girl* stands for the done-to (the object seen)?

blackboard; girl

3 Now, watch your linguistic logic. On the level of language, *blackboard* and *girl* are both nouns and both are the done-to in the example sentences. In actual reality, however, do *blackboard* (a thing) and *girl* (a person) belong to the same set?

no (Did you get this one wrong? Let's look carefully.)

4 Is *girl* a human being, an animate entity?

yes **5** Is *blackboard* an animate entity?
no **6** Can an animate entity and an inanimate entity belong logically to the same set in reality?

no

7 Your logic tells you that *blackboard* and *girl* do not belong to the same set. In contrast, the pattern of *I see the blackboard* and *I see the girl* tell you that the difference between *blackboard* and *girl* is not important when you make up these sentences. The Spanish speaker, however, thinks the difference should be marked in his sentences. Look at these translations:

I see the blackboard.   *Veo la pizarra.*
I see the girl.   *Veo a la muchacha.*

the person

Which entity is especially marked in Spanish? (a) the thing (b) the person

8 The Spanish language (like your logic) considers people and things to be members of a different set. Look at these translations:

He knows the country well.   *Conoce el país bien.*
He knows Ana well.   *Conoce a Ana bien.*

When the done-to of a sentence is a specific person, the word that stands for it is preceded by the marker ⌒⌒⌒.

a

9 The *a* of *Conoce a Ana bien* has no English translation. It also has no dictionary meaning in Spanish. It simply says that the done-to of the sentence is a person. Why, then, does Spanish need this *a?* Here is one good reason. The Spanish subject (the doer), unlike English, may come before or after the verb. As a result, "Pablo knows Ana well" may be translated two ways: (1) *Pablo conoce a Ana bien.* (2) *Conoce Pablo a Ana bien.* Suppose the second sentence were written *Conoce Pablo Ana bien.* Would you be able to tell which person is the doer or the done-to?

no (So the *a Ana* tells you that Ana is the done-to: the person known by Pablo.)

10 How do you translate this sentence? Watch your linguistic logic carefully: *Conoce Ana a Pablo bien.*

Ana knows Pablo well. (The *a Pablo* now tells you that Pablo is the done-to: the person known.)

11 Because the subject (doer) and the object (done-to) can come before or after the verb in Spanish, no Spanish speaker can tell what this sentence means: *Ana conoce Pablo.* Rewrite the sentence and add *a* so that it means "Ana knows Pablo."

Ana conoce a Pablo.

12 The cognate of "to comprehend" (to understand) is the regular *e*-verb *comprender.* The only translation of either *Los estudiantes comprenden* or *Comprenden los estudiantes* is ⌒⌒⌒.

The students understand.

13 The verb form *comprenden* also takes the subject pronoun *ustedes.* Now, be very careful. How do you translate "You understand the students"?

Ustedes comprenden a los estudiantes. (You need the *a* marker before *estudiantes* to show they are the done-to, not the doer. The position of the words tells you this in English.)

14 How do you translate "The students understand the lesson"?

Los estudiantes comprenden la lección. ("Lesson" is not a person and you do not use the *a* marker.)

15 Which sentence needs the *a* marker in Spanish? (a) I see the book. (b) I see the school principal.

I see the school principal. (*Yo veo al director de la escuela.*)

16 The standard translation of "to carry" is the regular *a*-verb *llevar*. Many Indian women of Latin America carry jugs on their heads. Will the Spanish speaker use *a* to say "They are carrying jugs?"

no (Jugs are things, not people.)

17 How do you translate "I see María"?

Veo a María. (With the done-to *a* for a person.)

18 How do you translate "I see the door"?

Veo la puerta. (With no *a* for a thing.)

19 Here is a summary of what you have just studied: Spanish pays more attention than English to the difference between inanimate and animate entities and, as a result, has a special marker word *a* for animate entities, especially people. This *a* has two prime functions. It says, first, that the done-to is a person or an animal being treated like a person, and, second, it clearly marks the difference between the doer and the done-to. Which question translates "Does Ana know my brother?" (a) *¿Conoce Ana mi hermano?* (b) *¿Conoce Ana a mi hermano?*

¿Conoce Ana a mi hermano?

PROGRAM 76

One Form of the Past Tense of All Verbs: the Imperfect

Part 1: *a*-Verbs

Spanish, unlike English, has two sets of past tense forms. One is called the Preterit and the other the Imperfect. In the proper context each form translates one function of the Simple English Past, *i.e., He spoke Spanish*. This Program deals with the forms of the Imperfect which are so easy to learn that you can learn to make them all in a few frames. Let's begin, then, with a review of some basic facts about Spanish verb forms.

1 How many morphemes are there in a simple Spanish verb form?

three

2 The first morpheme of a verb form gives its dictionary meaning. This part is called the ~~~~.

stem

3 All infinitive forms of all verbs end in the consonant ~~~~.

r

4 The three sets of verbs are marked by the vowels ~~~~.

a, e, i

5 In all regular forms of the Present, the stem is followed by how many suffixes?

two

6 Rewrite *cantamos* (we sing) with a dash between the morphemes (not the syllables).

cant-a-mos

7 Which suffix of a verb form always indicates person or number? (a) the first (b) the second

the second

8 In all regular verbs the stem is always the same for all tenses. In the Imperfect of all regular verbs the person-number suffixes are the same as in the Present. In view of these facts, what part of *cant-a-mos* will we have to change to make it Imperfect?

a

9 Say *aba* aloud. Which allophone of /b/ must you use? the stop [b] or the fricative [ƀ]

the fricative   **10** You will be glad to hear this: the first suffix of the Imperfect for all *a*-verbs is always *aba*. Let's say this again so you really understand and learn this fact now. The first suffix of all *a*-verbs is always *aba* in the Imperfect. This replaces the *o* or the *a* of the present tense forms. Change *canto* (I sing) to the Imperfect (I was singing).

cantaba   **11** You already know that the forms of the second suffix of the Imperfect are exactly like those of the Present. Now, think a moment. The form of *cantar* (to sing) that goes with *yo* is *cantaba*. Will the same form also go with *usted*, *él*, and *ella*?

yes (Remember: *aba* replaces the *o* of *canto* and the *a* of *canta*.)

12 To change *cantaba* to agree with *tú*, you add ⌇⌇⌇.

s (*tú cantabas*)   **13** To change *cantaba* to go with *ustedes* or *ellos*, you add ⌇⌇⌇.

n (*ustedes, ellos cantaban*)

14 There is a small problem in spelling when you write the *nosotros*-form. The second suffix is ⌇⌇⌇.

mos   **15** The stressed syllable of *can-ta-ba* is ⌇⌇⌇.

ta   **16** In the Imperfect of all *a*-verbs, the stress always falls on the first *a* of *aba*. Where will you have to put a written accent on *can-ta-ba-mos* to show this? Over the *a* of the syllable ⌇⌇⌇.

ta : *cantábamos* (Otherwise the stress would be on *ba*.)

17 Write the forms that match the new subject. *Yo miraba la montaña* (I was looking at the mountain.): *tú* ... , *ellos* ... , *nosotros* ... .

tú mirabas, ellos miraban, nosotros mirábamos (With the accent mark.)

18 Rewrite in the Imperfect: *Pedro trabaja en la mina.*

Pedro trabajaba en la mina.

19 Rewrite in the Imperfect: *¿Tú te llamas Pepita?*

¿Tú te llamabas Pepita?

20 Here is something that should make you happy. The *a*-verbs have no irregular forms in the Imperfect. Consequently, you know right now how to make the Imperfect forms of absolutely every *a*-verb in the whole Spanish language. You can even do this for verbs you have never seen or heard before. For example, *preparar*, translates "to prepare." How do you say "I was preparing"?

Yo preparaba.   **21** They were preparing.
Ellos preparaban.

Part 2: *e*- and *i*-Verbs

1 Here are two important facts about the Imperfect of *e*- and *i*-verbs. First, in the Imperfect there is no difference between the forms of all regular *e*- and *i*-verbs; they are exactly alike. Second, in the whole language, there are just three irregular verbs (*ir*, *ser*, and *ver*) in the Imperfect. The first suffix for all regular Imperfect forms of *e*- and *i*-verbs is always *ía*. This is all you have to learn to make up the Imperfect of all regular *e*- and *i*-verbs. The second suffix is the same as in the Present of all regular verbs.

You now know all you need to know to make up the Imperfect forms of all the regular *e*- and *i*-verbs in the whole Spanish language. To change *comemos* (we are eating) to the Imperfect (we were eating), you just replace the first suffix *e* with ⸺.

ía (And you have *comíamos.* Say *co-mí-a-mos* aloud.)

2 Change *ellos aprenden* (they are learning) to the Imperfect (they were learning).

ellos aprendían 3 All the irregular stems of the Present are regular in the Imperfect. So *tú duermes* (from *dormir*) becomes *tú* ⸺.

dormías 4 Write the Imperfect form of *conocer* (to know a person) that goes with *ustedes.*

conocían 5 Rewrite in the Imperfect: *Miguel come en casa.*

Miguel comía en casa.

6 The form *comía* combines with *yo,* and like *come,* with *usted,* and ⸺.

él; ella 7 To change *comía* to agree with *nosotros,* you just add the second suffix ⸺.

mos (*nosotros comíamos* = we were eating)

8 The Imperfect form of *aprender* (to learn) that goes with *tú* is ⸺.

aprendías 9 The Imperfect form of *dormir* (to sleep) that goes with *ustedes, ellos,* and *ellas* is ⸺.

dormían (Remember "dormitory.")

10 Remember that the Present irregular stems like *duerm-en* are regular in the Imperfect. Rewrite *No tengo lápiz* in the Imperfect.

No tenía lápiz. 11 Rewrite *No tiene tiza* in the Imperfect. (Remember what happens to *tien.*)

No tenía tiza. 12 The Imperfect of *vengo* is ⸺.

venía 13 The infinitive for the irregular *dice* is ⸺.

decir 14 The regular stem of *decir* is ⸺.

dec 15 To get the Imperfect form that goes with *él,* you just add ⸺ to *dec.*

ía (*él decía*) 16 The Imperfect of *viene* as in *¿De dónde viene él?* is ⸺.

venía 17 Here is a summary of what you have to remember:

(1) There are no irregular *a*-verbs in the Imperfect.

(2) The first suffix of all *a*-verbs in all forms is *aba.*

(3) In writing, the first *a* of *aba* has an accent mark in the *nosotros*-form: *hablábamos.*

(4) There are only three irregular verbs in the Imperfect: *ver, ser,* and *ir.*

(5) No stem change in the Present appears in any Imperfect form. The stem of the Imperfect is always (with three exceptions) like that of the infinitive: *dorm-ir, dorm-ía.*

(6) The first suffix of the Imperfect for all regular *e*- and *i*-verbs is *ía* in all forms.

Part 3: The Three Irregular Imperfects: *ver, ser,* and *ir*

1 Copy and underline the stem of *leo* (I read) and *veo* (I see).

leo; veo 2 The infinitive of *leo* is ⸺.

leer 3 The modern infinitive of *veo* is not *veer* but ⸺.

ver 4 Nevertheless, a long time ago *veer* was the regular infinitive of *veo* and, as a result, the Imperfect stem is still *ve.* The Imperfect of *veo,* consequently, is (a) *vía* (b) *veía.*

veía (Remember that the stem of *ve-o* is also irregular. It should be just *v,* from *v-er.*) 5 Write the Imperfect forms of *ver* (old *veer*) that match *tú* and *ellos.*

tú veías; ellos veían

6 To change *veías* so it matches *nosotros* you simply replace *s* with ⁓.

mos (veíamos)

7 The verb *ser* is irregular in almost all tenses. The Present form that goes with *tú* is ⁓.

eres

8 Like the *er* of *eres*, the stem of the Imperfect of *ser* is *er*. The first suffix for all Imperfect forms is *a*. The person-number suffixes are the same as in the Present. Write the Imperfect of *tú eres*.

tú eras

9 Change *eras* so it will go with *ellos*.

eran

10 Divide *eran* into syllables and underline the stressed syllable.

e-ran

11 The stress falls on the *e* in all the Imperfect forms of *ser*. Now, think carefully. Where will you put the written accent on *eramos*?

éramos (So the stress won't fall on *ra*.)

12 The verb *ir* (to go) is an *i*-verb. But in the Present you have forms like *vas*, *va*, *van*, and *vamos* which are like the *a*-verb forms of *dar* (to give): *das*, *da*, *dan*, and *damos*. Obviously, when Latin was becoming Spanish, people got all mixed up and began to think that *ir* was an *a*-verb. As a result, today the stem of the Imperfect of *ir* is *i*, but the first suffix for all forms is *ba* (like the *aba* of *a*-verbs). Write the Imperfect for *yo voy*.

yo iba (Remember this [b̸] is fricative in speech.)

13 The stress falls on the *i* of all imperfect forms of *ir*. Now, be careful. Write the imperfect form that goes with *nosotros*.

íbamos (The *nosotros*-form of all the Imperfects always has a written accent mark.)

Part 4: Review: A Self-test

1 Are there any irregular *a*-verbs in the Imperfect?

no

2 The first suffix for the Imperfect of all *a*-verbs is always ⁓.

aba

3 On which *a* of *aba* does the stress fall? (a) the first (b) the second

the first

4 Copy and add the written accent mark: *estudiabamos*.

estudiábamos

5 Do all regular *e*- and *i*-verbs have the same suffixes in the Imperfect?

yes

6 The first suffix of all regular *e*- and *i*-verbs is *í* plus ⁓.

a

7 The second suffix forms for all verbs in the Imperfect are the same as in the regular forms of the Present. (a) true (b) false

true

8 The only three irregular verbs in the Imperfect are ⁓.

ser, ver, ir

9 The imperfect stem of *ver* is ⁓.

ve (From old *veer*.)

10 The imperfect stem of *ser* is ⁓.

er (Remember the Present: *tú eres*.)

11 The first suffix that is added to the *ser* stem *er* is ⁓.

a

12 Copy and add the accent mark to *eramos*.

éramos

13 The Imperfect of *él va* is ⁓.

él iba

14 The /b/ of *iba* is a (a) stop (b) fricative.

fricative

15 The imperfect form of *ir* that goes with *nosotros* is ⁓.

íbamos (Remember that all forms of the Imperfect that go with *nosotros* have a written accent mark.)

16 Until linguists learned to divide words into morphemes, learning the Imperfect was a terrible job. Don't let tradition make you believe this is hard.

You have learned **all** the forms of **all** verbs in one Program because, in fact, you only had to learn *aba*, *ía*, *ve*, *iba*, and *er+a*. Here in chart form is what you have to remember. The part in dark type is new.

e- and *i-*verbs	yo vend-**ía**	(*vender*)
	yo viv- **ía**	(*vivir*)
	yo ve- **ía**	(*ver < ve-er*)
a-verbs	yo habl-**aba**	
ir	yo i-**ba**	
ser	yo er-**a**	

New Vocabulary

Add these words to your vocabulary list:

edificio	building	**población**	population
permiso	permission	**querer (ie)**	to want, love, wish
mundo	world	**pensar (ie)**	to think, intend
habitante	inhabitant	**tomar**	to drink, take
idioma (el)	language	**repasar**	to review
llanura	plain (in geography)	**rodeado de**	surrounded by
tierra	earth	**en (por) todas partes**	everywhere
río	river	**entre**	between, among
isla	island	**según**	according to
lago	lake	**desde . . . hasta**	from . . . to
selva	(rain) forest	**sin embargo**	nevertheless

PROGRAM 77

Review of the Morphemes of the Imperfect; Social Amenities and Proverbs

Part 1: The Morphology of the Imperfect

Learning a second language is very much like learning any physical skill: playing ping-pong, learning a musical instrument, or learning to swim. All these skills are acquired only by practicing the same thing over and over again until everything becomes automatic and you do not have to stop to think about either the rules of the game or what you are to do. The person who always has to stop and think what to do with his hands and feet can never learn to drive a car, but, just the same, the person who does not think about what his hands and feet are to do when he is learning to drive cannot become a successful driver. In the same way, you have to spend some more time thinking about the morphemes of the Imperfect before you reach the stage where you can talk about past events and put all your attention on the message while you produce the forms automatically. Let's review.

1 Are there any irregular *a*-verbs in the Imperfect?

no   **2** The first suffix for all forms of the *a*-verb in the Imperfect is the morpheme ～～.

aba   **3** The /b/ is (a) a stop (b) a fricative.

a fricative   **4** The stress falls on the first *a* of *aba* in all forms. This *a* takes a written accent only when the subject pronoun is ～～.

nosotros   **5** The person-number suffixes for the imperfect forms are the same as those of the Present. (a) true (b) false

true   **6** Change *yo estudio* to the Imperfect.

yo estudiaba   **7** Rewrite with the written accent mark added: *pensabamos.*

pensábamos   **8** What comes right after the stem of all regular *e*- and *i*-verbs in the Imperfect?

í (With a written accent.)

9 Write the Imperfect for *vengo.* (Remember the stem is always regular in the Imperfect.)

venía   **10** The old stem of *ver* used in the Imperfect is ～～.

ve   **11** Write the Imperfect for *ustedes ven.*

ustedes veían   **12** The imperfect stem of *ser* is ～～.

er   **13** Translate: They were from La Paz.

Ellos eran de la Paz.

14 Somewhere along the way *ir* became mixed up with *a*-verb endings. As a result, "I was going" is translated by *yo* ～～.

iba   **15** Change *iba* so it agrees with *nosotros.*

íbamos (Remember the *nosotros*-form always has a written accent mark.)

16 Translate: They were observing (*observar*) the girls.

Ellos observaban a las muchachas.

17 Change to the Imperfect: *Hace mucho frío.*

Hacía mucho frío.

18 Change to the Imperfect: *¿Tiene usted calor?*

¿Tenía usted calor?

19 Translate: *¿Tenía usted calor?*

Were you hot?

20 The form of the *Imperfect* of *conocer* that matches *ustedes* is ～～.

conocían   **21** Rewrite *Ella duerme bien* in the Imperfect.

Ella dormía bien.

22 The imperfect form of *aprender* that goes with *yo* is ～～.

aprendía   **23** Remember this: except for the three irregular verbs (*ser, ver,* and *ir*), the stem of the Imperfect is always the same as the stem of the infinitive. So the imperfect stem for *quiero* is ～～.

quer (As in *querer*)

Part 2: Social Amenities (*Fórmulas de cortesía*)

1 In every society tradition prescribes that people use certain formulas when they meet each other on the street, when they interact in a social situation, when they bump into each other, *etc*. These formulas of courtesy are used to establish and maintain friendly social relationships. What they are depends on the culture, and some may seem strange to us. In Tibet, for example, people stick out their tongue as a friendly gesture of welcome. Many formulas of courtesy have no real dictionary meaning. What do you really mean when you say *Good morning* to someone? Try to think of what this means to you.

The phrase usually means, first, you recognize the presence of the other person; second, you want to be friendly, and, often, third, you are ready to start a conversation. It no longer really means *May you have a good morning.*

2 In English *Pardon me* can have a variety of meanings. It might mean that a criminal wants a pardon for his crime so he can get out of jail. It may be used to tell another person you did not mean to step on his toe, that is, your action was unintentional and not unfriendly. It may be used to address a stranger to whom you want to ask a question (*Pardon me, sir, can you tell me where the post office is?*), to interrupt a conversation (*Pardon me, but may I ask a question?*), or to break into a conversation to announce that you have to leave (*Pardon me, folks, but I've got to go now.*) What does the Spanish speaker say when he asks for permission to leave a group?

Con permiso (Literally this means "With your permission.")

3 Suppose a Spanish speaker bumps into someone accidentally. Would it make much sense to say "With your permission"?

no   **4** So what does the Spanish speaker actually say to a stranger? (a) *Con permiso*. (b) *Perdóneme*.

Perdóneme. (This is the formula that says you did not mean to be rude or impolite.)   **5** There are two other common formulas that say the same thing. One is *Discúlpeme*. Let's see what this really means. The infinitive is *disculpar*. If we take off the negative prefix *dis*, we can see in *culpar* (to blame) the cognate of "culprit" (doer of wrong), or "culpable" (worthy of blame). If *culpar* translates "to blame," then *disculpar* must have a meaning something like "to not blame." So the real meaning of *Discúlpeme* is (a) Pardon me. (b) (Please) do not blame me (for what I've done).

The literal meaning is "Do not blame me."   **6** The third translation of "Pardon me" is *Dispénseme*. One English cognate is "dispensation" which may mean a pardon for a sin or an exemption from a civil or religious law. So *Dispénseme* translates generally the same meaning as *Discúlpeme*. (a) true (b) false

true   **7** How observant have you been? The three formulas that have *me* on the end are all based on *a*-verbs: *perdonar*, *disculpar*, and *dispensar*. The verb forms you use in these formulas are: *perdone*, *disculpe*, and *dispense*. Have you learned any *a*-verbs whose first suffix is *e*?

no (So there must be something special here.)   **8** Let's see what is going on. Are "Bring me" and "Take me" commands?

yes   **9** What is "Pardon me"? (a) a question (b) a statement (c) a kind of command

a kind of command (Like "Help me.")   **10** In the same fashion, *perdone*, *disculpe*, and *dispense* are the command forms in Spanish which are used with *usted*. What would you expect to add to *perdone* if you spoke to *ustedes*?

n (The regular plural number suffix.)

11 To make a command form of an *a*-verb with *usted*, you change the first suffix *a* to ⌇⌇⌇⌇. •

e (*perdone, disculpe, dispense*)

12 Is it likely, from what you already know, that the command form for *tú* will be the same? •

no

13 The command form for *tú* is just like the regular present tense form for *usted*, *él*, or *ella*. How would you say, using *perdonar*, "He pardons"? •

Él perdona.

14 So when you say, "Pardon me," and you are talking in *tú* you must say (a) *Perdóneme.* (b) *Perdóname.* •

Perdóname tú. (But *Perdóneme usted.*)

When a great many Americans and Spanish speakers meet for the first time, they have trouble establishing friendly relationships. The Spanish speaker thinks the American is cold and standoffish, and the American thinks the Spanish speaker is trying to be too intimate too soon. What neither realizes is that the two cultures have very fixed customs on how close two people should stand next to each other during a normal, relaxed conversation. When two Spanish speakers, either males or females, talk to each other they stand about 16 inches apart. For the average American this distance is common only for sweethearts or two persons discussing something very intimate or secret. In ordinary conversation Americans may stand two or three feet apart. Until the members of each culture understand this difference, each gets a wrong impression of the intentions of the other, and they have trouble trying to establish a friendly relationship.

Part 3: Proverbs and Sayings

1 Much of the folk wisdom of every society can be found in its proverbs and sayings. Spanish uses thousands of sayings like these, called *refranes*, very frequently. Very often you will not know what the Spanish speaker means unless you are able to translate and interpret these *refranes*. Most sayings do not mean much when they are translated word for word. They take on real meaning only when you discover an English saying that says the same thing. Let's see how this works.

Here is a common Spanish saying: *You can't walk in the procession and ring the bell in the church steeple.* What do you suppose this means? The idea is so common in the western world that the Russians say the same thing with "You can't take a bath with a dry hide." Think about these two statements. The words are not at all alike, but both say you cannot do two very different and contradictory things at the same time. Neither saying, however, seems to be something we would say in English. Can you guess what the best English equivalent would be?

Don't worry if you are stuck. Most people have to be told that the best "translation" of the Spanish and Russian sayings is "You can't have your cake and eat it too."

2 A Spanish speaker often says of another that *él tiene buenas aldabas.* The literal translation is "he has good door knockers." Let's see if you can figure out the English equivalent from this description: the Spanish speaker is saying that a person who wants to get on in the world has to know what doors to knock at to find friends who have enough influence to help him get what he wants. In English a person who has influential friends who can help him is said to have a lot of ⌒⌒⌒.

pull (He got there by the pull of his friends.)

3 As you go along in your Spanish course, you are going to learn a lot of sayings and fixed phrases. These are just as important in learning to understand the Spanish speaker and his culture as everything else you learn. Try to use them whenever it makes sense to do so.

Here is another difference between English and Spanish. When a person says something he shouldn't, we often say that he stuck his foot in his mouth. The Spanish speaker says the same thing, but instead of using *pie* (the word for the human foot) he uses *pata* (the word for the foot of an animal). Which language is more insulting?

Spanish

New Vocabulary

Add these two verbs to your vocabulary list and remember to spend three minutes before your next class in reviewing the whole list. Go from English to Spanish the first time through.

volver (ue)	to return
poder (ue)	to be able, can, may

The Nature of Events and Getting Ready to Talk about Past Events

1 In a few days, you are going to really start learning how to talk about actions or events that began or took place in the past. Learning to choose the proper verb forms and understanding their meanings can be made a great deal easier and much more interesting if everything you already know by feel (intuition) about the nature of events is first changed into conscious knowledge. Remember, however, that Spanish has *two* forms for the past tense. You may not be aware of this, but you already know by feel that all actions or events are divided into two basic sets which cue you to choose certain ways of saying things. Let's prove this. Look at this statement: *Nicolás started to walk when he was nine months old.* Is it logical to assume that Nicolás, who is now 25 years old, still walks?

yes   **2** Is it also logical to say that an action begun in the past may still be going on in the present?

yes (The earth began to revolve around the sun millions of years ago. It still does.)

3 Someone asks *When did Nicolás first walk?* Look at these answers:
(a) Nicolás started to walk when he was nine months old.
(b) Nicolás began to walk when he was nine months old.
(c) Nicolás walked when he was nine months old.
Do all three answers describe the same facts?

yes   **4** Can the past tense form *walked* have the meaning of *started* or *began to walk?*

yes   **5** Look at these three statements:
(a) He stood up and started to talk.
(b) He stood up and began to talk.
(c) He stood up and talked.
Do all three describe the same basic facts?

yes   **6** The past tense form *talked*, like *walked*, may have the meaning of *started* or *began to talk*. (a) true (b) false

true   **7** Now, be careful and watch your linguistic logic as you read these sentences:
(a) He stood up and started to open the door.
(b) He stood up and began to open the door.
(c) He stood up and opened the door.
Do all three sentences describe the same facts?

no   **8** Which sentence above tells you the action of opening the door was completed?
He stood up and opened the door.

9 Does *opened*, like *walked* or *talked*, have the meaning of *started* or *began to open?*

no   **10** The logical paired opposite of *opened* is ⁓.

closed   **11** Which statement tells you the act was completed? (a) He started to close the door. (b) He began to close the door. (c) He closed the door.

He closed the door.

12 Does *He got up and dressed* tell you the act of dressing was completed (finished)?

yes

13 Except for their stems, the past tense forms *opened, closed*, and *dressed* are exactly like *walked* and *talked*. (a) true (b) false

true

14 But *opened, closed*, and *dressed* say the actions were completed in the past while *walked* and *talked* may say that these actions merely began in the past. Now, make an educated guess. What tells you there is a difference in meaning? (a) the verb forms (b) the nature of the actions

the nature of the actions

15 You have just proved that you know by feel or intuition that *to open* and *to talk* belong to two different sets of events. Let's change this intuitive knowledge into conscious knowledge so you can use it to learn Spanish. In order to begin to talk must you say something, that is, start talking?

yes

16 Once you have begun to *talk* or *walk*, can you keep on without starting over again?

yes

17 Do *talking* and *walking* belong to a set of events which, once begun, can be kept up or extended?

yes

18 We can say that in order to begin to talk, you have to talk. Let's see if this logic applies to *to close*. In order to begin to close the door, you have to close the door completely. (a) true (b) false

false

19 The beginning of closing the door might be just taking hold of it and moving it a little bit. (a) true (b) false

true

20 To actually close the door must you push it completely shut?

yes

21 You are getting nearer and nearer to understanding the real difference between the acts of talking and closing. Can we say that talking has taken place at the very instant it begins?

yes (If you begin to hear something, somebody has said something. They have begun to talk.)

22 Can we say that *closing* has actually taken place at the very instant you start moving the door?

no (You may be just pulling the door away from the wall.)

23 Can we say that *closing* really takes place before the action is completed?

no

24 Here is another difference between *talking* and *closing the door*. Once you begin to talk, you can keep on without starting over again. Once you have closed the door, can you keep on closing it without starting over again?

no

25 *To go to bed* belongs to the same set of actions as (a) to close the door (b) to talk.

to close the door (You have not gone to bed until you are in it, and you cannot do it again without first getting up.)

26 All events like *to go to bed* and *to open* or *to close the door* have two shared or common characteristics. First, we cannot say they have taken place until the action is finished. Second, we cannot extend these events. We can keep on doing them only by going over each step again: open, close, open, close, *etc*. In many ways these events are like a wheel of a bicycle. Each time the wheel (cycle) turns around, it starts all over again. As a result, physicists call all members of this set *cyclic events*. In contrast, a *non-cyclic event* is one that once begun can be extended. There is one *non-cyclic* event in this list. It is ⌇⌇⌇⌇.

to arrive	to lock	to run
to sit down	to enter	to leave

to run (Once you begin to run you can keep on going.)

27 *To run*, like *to talk* or *to walk*, is called a *non-cyclic event*. All members of this set have two common characteristics. First, they do not have to be finished in order to take place. Second, once begun, they can be kept up without starting over again. There is one *cyclic event* in this list. It is ⌇⌇⌇⌇.

to cry	to hold	to hear
to hate	to break	to read

to break

28 Let's see now what the difference between cyclic and non-cyclic events really tells you. Pay special attention to the second verb in this sentence. It stands for a cyclic event. *He fell down and broke the window.* Does *broke* tell you the action was completed (terminated)?

yes

29 Now be careful. What does *broke* tell you in this sentence? *As he broke the window, he cut his hand.* Was the action of breaking completed and finished before he cut his hand?

no

30 He cut his hand *while he was breaking the window*, not before and not afterwards. Is it logical, then, to say that *broke* has two possible meanings?

yes

31 In the sentence *He fell down and broke the window*, the verb form *broke* says the cyclic event (a) was completed or finished at some point in the past (b) was going on at some point in the past.

was completed at some point in the past

32 In *As he broke the window, he cut his hand*, the form *broke* says the cyclic event (a) was completed at some point in the past (b) was going on at that point.

was going on at that point

33 At a point in the past, a past tense form standing for a cyclic event may describe either the event going on or the completion of that event. (a) true (b) false

true

34 Now, remember, neither *He closed the door*, nor *As he closed the door* say the same thing as *He began to close the door*. Can we, consequently, come to this logical conclusion? A past tense form standing for a cyclic event may describe either the middle of the action or its end, but never its beginning.

yes

35 Take another look at *He closed the door*. This sentence says the action was completed (terminated) at some point in the past. When we add *as* to this, *As he closed the door*, the meaning is changed to action that was going on. Is it the verb *closed* or the adverb *as* that tells you the action was going on?

as (*As* is like *while—while he closed the door*. To say the same thing with just the verb form, you must use *he was closing the door*.)

36 When a past tense form standing for a cyclic event (closed, dropped, bumped, left, *etc.*) is used all by itself, it only tells you that the action was completed at some time in the past. (a) true (b) false

true

37 Let's see now what happens when you talk about non-cyclic events. *I got up*, *picked up the microphone, and talked.* Were the first two events completed before talking began?

yes | **38** Does *talked* have the meaning of *began to talk?*

yes | **39** Let's add *as. As I talked there was suddenly a lot of static.* Does *As I talked* now describe an action that was going on when the static began?

yes | **40** Let's add something different. *I talked for ten minutes.* Does *for ten minutes* measure the length of the talking?

yes | **41** If you measure the length of an action, must you measure from its beginning to its end?

yes | **42** Is it logical, then, to say that *talked* (standing for a non-cyclic event) may say that an action began at some point in the past?

yes | **43** Is it also logical to say that a past tense form standing for a non-cyclic event (talked, walked, ran, read, *etc.*) may be used to describe the whole event: its beginning, middle, and end?

yes (I talked to him yesterday.)

44 Here, now, is a review of what, in fact, you already know intuitively about cyclic and non-cyclic events. When you talk about a cyclic event (to close, open, drop, hit, break, snap, *etc.*), the Simple Past may be used to say (a) the action was going on at a point (*As he went out the door . . .*) (b) the action was completed at a point (*He went out the door.*). To say that a cyclic event began at some point in the past, you must use a helping verb (*He started to go out the door.*).

In contrast, when you talk about a non-cyclic event (to talk, run, read, sleep, walk, *etc.*), the Simple Past may be used to say three things:

(1) the action began at some point in the past (*I heard*—began to hear—*the noise at one o'clock.*)

(2) the action was going on at some point in the past (*As I heard the noise, I began to be worried.*)

(3) the whole event took place in the past (*Yes, she heard the noise, too.*)

To say that a non-cyclic event was completed at some point in the past, you must use a helping verb. (*And, then, she* stopped *hearing the noise.*)

Why is all this knowledge important to you in learning Spanish? Because the past tense of the Spanish verb has, unlike English, two different forms. So "he talked" may be translated either by *él hablaba* or *él habló*, and "he closed" may be translated by *él cerraba* or *él cerró*. The forms *habló* and *cerró* are called preterit forms. You will study these in the near future.

What you have discovered in this Program and what you are going to learn in the next two will give you most of the cues you need to choose between the two Spanish forms: the Imperfect and the Preterit. You will find out that the choice is really easy. All native children learn to choose between the two forms without even thinking about the problem. You can too.

When a Spanish speaker joins a group of people at a table in a café or at a party, he shakes hands with each individual and greets each one personally. He also shakes hands with everyone when he leaves the group. Because of this many Spanish speakers consider Americans impolite because they often just say "Hello" or "Good-bye" to a group and do not always shake everyone's hand.

Pre-quiz Practice: Stem-changing Verbs in the Present

You will probably get more benefit from this pre-quiz review if you take a 5 or 10 minute break before you start Frame 1.

1 A stressed Latin *e* may change to ⁓⁓⁓ in Spanish.

ie

2 Here are all the verbs you have had so far in which the *e* of the stem changes to *ie* when stressed. Write the *tú*-form for each one, except *nevar: pensar, querer, venir, nevar, empezar, tener, referir.*

piensas, quieres, vienes, empiezas, tienes, refieres

3 The *yo*-form of *tener* is *tiengo* in some dialects. How do you write it in the dialect you are learning?

tengo

4 Latin *e* sometimes changes to *i*. Write the *yo*-form of *seguir, pedir, servir,* and *decir.* Don't forget what happens to *gu* of *seguir* in writing.

sigo, pido, sirvo, digo

5 When Latin *december* became Spanish there were three spelling changes. Write the Spanish form.

diciembre (One *e* became *i*, one became *ie*, and one did not change.)

6 A stressed Latin *o* may change to ⁓⁓⁓ in Spanish.

ue

7 Here are the verbs you have had so far in which this happens. Say the third person singular of each aloud. Then write each form: *dormir, poder, volver, volar, morir, llover.*

duerme, puede, vuelve, vuela, muere, llueve

8 Does *o* change to *ue* when the subject is *nosotros*?

no (dormimos, podemos, volvemos, etc.)

9 Write the *yo*-form of *salir, ver, estar,* and *saber.*

salgo, veo, estoy, sé

New Vocabulary

jarro	jug, jar	**aprender**	to learn
mirar	to look at	**llevar**	to carry
conocer	to know	**redondo**	round
pedir (i)	to order, ask	**cuadrado**	square
dormir (ue)	to sleep	**Perdóneme**	Excuse me (*usted*)

PROGRAM 79

More on the Nature of Events

In your last Program, you discovered that both you and the physicist divide all events into two great sets: cyclic and non-cyclic. This Program deals with the characteristics of these events which are going to serve as the cues which tell you to choose between the two forms of the past tense in Spanish: the Preterit and the Imperfect.

1 When an alarm clock goes off, is it possible to hear the ringing the instant it begins? •

yes (If you are asleep you may not, of course, hear it at once.)

2 Will the ringing go on until the alarm is turned off? •

yes   **3** Try this experiment. Put your hand on your knee. Now take it off. Did the action of *taking off* really take place only at the very instant the contact between your hand and knee was broken? •

yes   **4** Ringing (a non-cyclic event) can start and keep on going indefinitely: the event is extendable. Can you keep on taking your hand off your knee? •

no (You will have to put your hand back on your knee before you can take it off again. You must start over again.)

5 What kind of an event is *to take off?* (a) cyclic (b) non-cyclic •

cyclic (You cannot extend a cyclic event. You can only repeat it.)

6 The non-cyclic event *ringing* begins and keeps going on. The cyclic event *to take off* comes automatically to an end. A cyclic event can be repeated only by starting the whole process (cycle) over again. (a) true (b) false •

true   **7** Let's look at another meaning of the cyclic event *to take off*. In flying an airplane, a pilot performs three separate and distinct actions: (1) he takes off, (2) he flies, and (3) he lands. To take off, the pilot goes through a series of steps (a cycle): (a) he taxies the plane to the runway, (b) he revs up the engines, (c) he releases the brakes, (d) the plane picks up speed, and (e) the take-off is completed only at the instant the wheels leave the ground. Is it logical, then, to say that a cyclic event does not actually take place until it is completed? •

yes   **8** Is this also a logical statement? *"The pilot started* to take off at one o'clock but he actually took off at 1:03." •

yes   **9** The instant the wheels left the runway the take-off came to an end and *flying began*. Can the action of flying be extended at the pilot's will? •

yes   **10** Flying begins the instant the wheels leave the ground and it ends only when they touch down again. Now, watch your logic. Does flying, like taking off, have to be completed or finished before we can say it has taken place? •

no (Some flying takes place as soon as the wheels leave the ground.)

11 What kind of an event is flying? (a) cyclic (b) non-cyclic •

non-cyclic   **12** Is it logical to say that a non-cyclic event takes place the instant it begins? •

yes   **13** Because planes run out of gas and pilots get tired, most flying has a beginning and an end. Is it logical to suppose it also has a middle? •

yes   **14** In theory every event has three phases: (1) a beginning, (2) a middle, and (3) an end. Linguists call these phases *aspects*. What aspect is being talked about in *The plane landed?* (a) beginning (b) middle (c) end •

end (The landing does not take place until the wheels touch the ground and the action is completed.)

15 What aspect of landing are you talking about when you say *The plane was landing?* (a) beginning (b) middle (c) end •

middle (*To be+-ing* always describes something going on.)

16 Does *The plane was taking off* say the action was going on at some point in the past? •

yes

17 Both events in this sentence are cyclic: *As he was taking off, a tire blew out.* Which event was going on (in progress) when the other happened?

taking off (He was in the middle of taking off when the tire blew.)

18 *In spite of the flat tire, he took off.* Did the action of taking off come to an end?

yes

19 In *As he took off, a tire blew out*, the verb form *took off* plus *as* describes the middle of the action. In *In spite of the flat tire, he took off*, the same verb form, *took off*, describes the completion of the action. Is this a logical conclusion? In the proper English context, a simple past form standing for a cyclic event may be used to talk about two of its three aspects: the middle and the end.

yes

20 Does *He started to take off* say the same thing as *He took off*?

no

21 Think carefully about this: can *took off* and *landed* be used to say that these actions began at some point in the past?

no

22 *Took off* or *landed* may be used to describe the middle or the end of the event, but never the beginning. To talk about the beginning of a cyclic event, you have to use a helping verb such as *started* or *began*. (a) true (b) false

true

23 Let's see, now, what happens when you talk about non-cyclic events. *The pilot gunned the motor and the plane flew.* Was the plane flying before he gunned the motor?

no

24 Which aspect of flying is described by *and the plane flew?* (a) beginning (b) middle (c) end

beginning (The pilot gunned the motor and the plane *began* to fly.)

25 *As he flew past the control tower, he waved.* Which aspect of flying is now described by *flew?* (a) beginning (b) middle (c) end

middle (We can say *As he* was flying *past the control tower, he waved.*)

26 Is this a true statement: the Simple Past in English may be used to describe the beginning or middle of a non-cyclic event?

true

27 Can *flew*, all by itself, be used to describe the end (terminative) aspect of flying?

no (To state that a non-cyclic event comes to an end you have to use a helping verb such as *stopped* or *ceased*.)

28 Let's try an experiment to prove how much you already know about the aspects of events. You really know everything necessary to choose between the two past tense forms of Spanish, the Preterit and the Imperfect.

First, imagine that you are talking about some events that happened a long time ago. Second, pretend that every kind of an event can be represented by an arrow like this ———→. Third, assume that the arrow, like the event it stands for, has a beginning, a middle, and an end which we can mark by the initial letters of the aspect words. B———M———→E.

Now, let's travel back on the time line to some past point which we will mark with a big dot and a vertical line like this:

We can now show the relationship between the three aspects of events and a recalled point with a diagram like this:

Urban Life

City life means variety. Housing varies in architecture from balconied apartments in the old section of Cartegena, Colombia, to brightly painted houses in Maracaibo, Venezuela, to high-rise apartment complexes in Santiago, Chile.

City streets offer variety in means of communication. The modern telephone booth in Caracas, Venezuela serves personal communication. The sidewalk stand in Santiago, Chile offers newspapers and periodicals to communicate news of general interest.

Places to shop vary in cities from the familiar local grocery store with its wide range of products (Caracas, Venezuela) to the elegant shoe shop promoting the latest spring fashions (Santa Cruz, Bolivia).

Cities show variety in dress. While young girls in La Paz, Bolivia combine ponchos with their modern clothes, indians and a nun in Cuzco, Peru wear traditional styles.

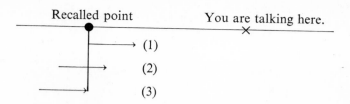

Arrow 1 shows an event that (a) began (b) was going on (c) ended at the recalled point.

began
was going on
ended

29 Arrow 2 shows an event that (a) was going on (b) ended at the recalled point.

30 Arrow 3 shows an event that ~~~~~ at the recalled point.

31 Copy the diagram below and, then, draw an arrow to represent *was pulling out* as in *It was two o'clock and the train was pulling out.*

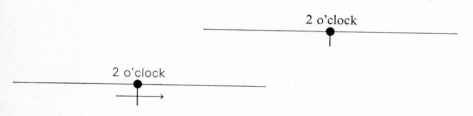

32 Copy the diagram below and draw an arrow to represent this cyclic event: *At 1:01 the boss left the office.*

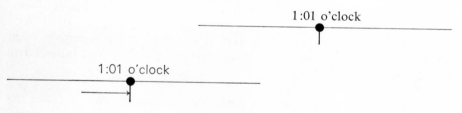

33 Copy the diagram below. The first event in this sentence is cyclic; the second is non-cyclic. Draw two arrows to represent the aspects of these events: *Then he jumped up and ran.*

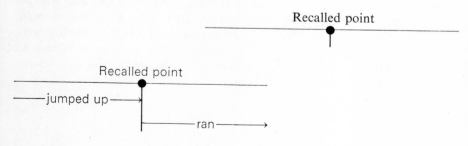

(The jumping up had to be completed before he could run. The running had to begin after he jumped up. *He jumped up and began to run.*)

34 Draw a diagram and two arrows to represent these two cyclic events: *As he went out the door, he tripped.*

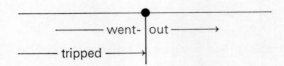

(The going out was in progress when he tripped.)

35 At a point in the past, a cyclic event may either be going on or come to an end. (a) true (b) false

true

36 At a point in the past, a non-cyclic event may either begin or be going on. (a) true (b) false

true

37 You have already started learning the forms of the past tense called the *Imperfect*. Let's see why these forms have this name. The three aspects of an event—the beginning, the middle, and the end—have technical names in linguistics which explain the meaning of *Imperfect*. The *initial* letter of a word is the letter that begins the word. (a) true (b) false

true

38 It should follow logically that the *initiative aspect* of an event should be its ‿‿‿.

beginning

39 The opposite of *to initiate* is *to terminate*. The *terminative aspect* of an event is its ‿‿‿.

end

40 The Romans used to say that a completed or finished action was *perfected*. Now, make an educated guess. The *imperfective aspect* of any event is its ‿‿‿.

middle (the on-going phase)

41 The one form of the past tense you have learned is the *Imperfect*. What aspect of any event do you expect it is always going to describe? (a) initiative (b) imperfective (c) terminative

imperfective (the middle)

42 The other form of the past tense which you will soon learn is called the *Preterit*. Now, think a moment. There are three aspects and two tense forms. The Imperfect always describes the middle (imperfective) aspect. Will the Preterit have to be used to describe two aspects?

yes (The beginning—initiative, and the end—terminative.)

43 How will you know what the Preterit is talking about? By knowing whether the event is cyclic or non-cyclic. The Preterit describes (at a point in the past) the initiative aspect of non-cyclic events and the terminative aspect of cyclic events. So, to understand Spanish you have to know the nature of events. In your next class and several that follow, you will have special practice exercises to learn how to spot each kind of event.

No new vocabulary.

PROGRAM 80

Aspect and the Order of Events

Part 1: Aspect and the Order of Events

1 In either English or Spanish the forms of the verb may be used to say an event takes place *before*, *at*, or *after* some point in time. Does *She told us a story* say the action was completed *before* the moment of speaking?

yes

2 Does *She will tell us a story* mean the action must come *after* the moment of speaking?

yes

3 Are *before* and *after* order words?

yes

4 Let's look, now, at *She is telling us a story*. Can this mean that the story telling is going on *at* the moment of speaking?

yes

5 Is it proper, then, to say that at the moment of speaking the action of telling the story is imperfective?

yes (She is in the middle of telling the story when the sentence *She is telling us a story* is said.)

6 *She told us a story* says the action is now completed. Does *As she told us a story . . .* say exactly the same thing?

no

7 *As she told us a story . . .* adds new information: the story telling was going on at some point in the past. In other words, the action was imperfective at some point in the past.

You have now discovered that the simple past form can be used to describe the order relationship of an event to the moment of speaking (*She told us a story*) or to describe the aspect of an event at some point in the past (*As she told us a story . . .*). Let's look more carefully at what happens when we talk about cyclic and non-cyclic events. Is *to run* a non-cyclic event?

yes

8 Does *He ran yesterday* say the running was completed *before* the moment of speaking?

yes

9 In *He jumped up and ran* does *ran* have the meaning of *began to run*?

yes

10 When we talk about a non-cyclic event, we can use the past tense to say that an event began at some point in the past. (a) true (b) false

true

11 Can *As he ran* in *As he ran, he tripped* have the meaning of *As he was running*?

yes

12 When we talk about a non-cyclic event, we can use the past tense to say that an event was in progress (imperfective) at some point in the past. (a) true (b) false

true

13 Let's summarize these facts. When we talk about a non-cyclic event (run, hear, walk, smell, *etc.*), we can say three different things: (1) the event began at some point in the past: He jumped up and *ran* (began to run); (2) the event was going on at some point in the past: As he *ran* (was running), *he tripped;* (3) the entire event—the .beginning, middle, and end—took place before the moment of speaking: He *ran* yesterday. Can aspect be important when we talk about the entire event?

no (There is no contrast between beginning, middle, or end.)

14 Is *to leave* a (a) cyclic or (b) a non-cyclic event?

cyclic   **15** Can *he left* in *As he left, he said* ... have the meaning of *As he was leaving?*

yes   **16** May the past tense be used to describe the imperfective aspect of either cyclic or non-cyclic events?

yes (*As he ran* and *As he left* are both imperfective.)

17 Does *He jumped up and left* say the same thing as *He jumped up and began to leave?*

no   **18** The past tense cannot be used to describe the beginning (initiative aspect) of a cyclic event. It may describe only its middle or end. There can be, consequently, no real difference between saying the action takes place before the moment of speaking (*He left yesterday*) and *at* some point in the past (*He left at one o'clock*). Is the action terminated in either sentence?

yes   **19** Let's see, now, what you have really learned about aspect. What aspect is described by "At one o'clock he was leaving?" (a) initiative (b) imperfective (c) terminative

imperfective (So you will use the Imperfect and say *A la una salía.*)

20 What aspect is described by "At one o'clock he left?" (a) initiative (b) imperfective (c) terminative

terminative (So you will use the Preterit to say *A la una salió.*)

21 What aspect is described by "At one o'clock she heard the noise"? (a) initiative (b) imperfective (c) terminative

initiative (She began to hear the noise at one o'clock.)

22 What aspect is described by *A la una ella dormía?* Do you really have to think about this one? The Imperfect always describes the ⌇⌇⌇ aspect.

imperfective (the middle)

Part 2: Pre-quiz Practice on the Done-to-*a*.

Very soon you will have a quiz like this one to find out whether you know when to use the done-to *a*. Write *a* or Ø (*nothing*) after each frame number.

         1 No puedes ver ⌇⌇⌇ Magdalena esta noche.

a   **2** No puedes ver ⌇⌇⌇ las montañas desde aquí.

Ø   **3** Yo conozco muy bien ⌇⌇⌇ este pueblo.

Ø   **4** Yo conozco muy bien ⌇⌇⌇ tu tía.

a   **5** Nunca puedo olvidar ⌇⌇⌇ mi abuela.

a   **6** Nunca puedo olvidar ⌇⌇⌇ su nombre.

Ø (The done-to is *nombre*, a name, not a person.)

7 ¿Quién busca ⌇⌇⌇ María?

a   **8** ¿Quién busca ⌇⌇⌇ este libro?

Ø   **9** Observábamos ⌇⌇⌇ los pájaros en el parque.

Ø   **10** Observábamos ⌇⌇⌇ las muchachas en el parque.

a

If you have been doing your assignments and class work properly, you should have had all of these correct.

The disappearance of the *thou* and *ye* forms of address in English reflects a change in society. Speakers of English gradually came to feel that everyone, friends and strangers, could be treated alike. The preservation of the *tú/usted* contrast in the Hispanic culture goes hand in hand with an attitude toward people in general. Although every society is divided into in- and out-groups, in the Hispanic world the in-groups tend to be much smaller and the members of the out-group are treated with much more distrust and suspicion. New friendships are formed slowly and considerable tension develops when people have to do serious business with strangers. This fact is so well known to European businessmen that their representatives often spend months in a Latin country before they attempt to do any business. During this time they arrange to meet their counterparts socially, to work on establishing confidence, and on becoming a member of some in-group. When this has been accomplished, they can do business with friends who can put them in contact with their friends. Americans, in contrast, have no hesitation in doing business with total strangers and frequently find it easy to shift to a first-name basis in a very short time. It is probably true that the great development in the United States could not have been achieved without the ability to learn to work with strangers easily. The great industrial combines, the huge research centers, and the enormous governmental agencies require close cooperation of many people who hardly know each other. Conversely, it is also probably true that one of the factors that has held back a comparable development in the Hispanic world has been the cultural tradition that makes it difficult for the people to cooperate with confidence with persons who are not close friends.

Part 3: Quiz on the Imperfect

With the exception of *ser*, *ir*, and *ver* the stems of all verbs in the Imperfect are regular. Consequently, when you want to backshift a form like *dicen* you have to remember the regular allomorph of the stem, *dec*, in order to make up *decían*. In addition, you must remember whether the verb is an *e-*, *i-*, or *a*-verb so you can choose between *ía* and *aba* as the first suffix. To do both of these things you must remember the infinitive form of every verb.

Below you see a present tense form for ten irregular verbs. Write the infinitive and the corresponding imperfect form.

1 yo pienso
pensar; pensaba

2 ellos quieren
querer; querían

3 nieva
nevar; nevaba   **4** digo
decir; decía   **5** hago
hacer; hacía   **6** vienen
venir; venían   **7** tienes
tener; tenías

morir; moría
poder; podían
empezar; empezabas

8 muere
9 pueden
10 empiezas

Aside from spelling errors, there are 20 possible mistakes. Take off 5 for each and give yourself a grade. A = 90   B = 80   C = 70   D = 60

New Vocabulary

dormir (ue)	to sleep	**seguir (i)**	to follow
aprender	to learn	**observar**	to observe

PROGRAM 81

More on Spanish Numbers

1 You have known for a long time that numbers are used in two different ways: to do problems in math and to count objects. When you do a math problem, the number word for 21 is ——.

veintiuno (It is also correct to write this as three words: *veinte y uno*.)

2 When you say there are 21 boys in the class, you change *uno* to ——.

un (Hay veintiún muchachos en la clase.)

3 If you say there are 21 girls in the class, you change *uno* to ——.

una (Hay veintiuna muchachas en la clase.)

4 It is believed that our entire numerical system came originally from people counting their fingers. Thus the word for "fingers" and the numbers from 1 to 9 is "digits." These numbers, plus zero, make up the base for all other numbers. In *trece* (13) you see the base of *tres* (3) (*trece* = 3 + 10). In *treinta* (30) you also see *tre* (3) and the form *inta* which, logically, must stand for ——.

10 (Treinta = 3 tens.)

5 Let's look at this closer. When you put 1 and 0 together in a single number, you get 10. Replace 1 with 2 and you have 20. Replace 2 with 3 and you have 30. Can we say, consequently, that the "ty" of "twenty, thirty, forty, fifty" really stands for groups of ten?

yes

6 So by the same logic we can say that the *inta* of *treinta* is like the 0 in 30 or the "ty" of "thirty." Look, now, at *cuatro* and *cuarenta*. What number do you suppose *enta* stands for?

10

7 So *cuarenta* must stand for the Arabic number ——.

40 (Literally, again, 4 tens, or in English, "fourty" = forty.)

8 If 31 is *treinta y uno*, then 41 should, if the system is logical, be ——.

cuarenta y uno (After number 29 most people write all numbers as three words: *treinta y tres, cuarenta y dos, etc.*)

9 And 47 will be ——.

cuarenta y siete

10 Look at *cinco* and *cincuenta*. The *u* of *cincu* is a variant of *o*. The *enta* stands for the number 10, so *cincuenta* is the number word for the Arabic number ~~~~.

50

11 The word *seis* looks like the first part of *sesenta* which, again logically, should be the number word for ~~~~.

60

12 In Latin *September* was the seventh month. In modern Spanish you can pronounce *septiembre* as *setiembre*, and also spell it this way. What Arabic number does *setenta* stand for?

70 (If you were to stress *sete* in *setenta*, you would get *siete*. So unstressed *siete* + *nta* = *setenta*. To keep 60 and 70 apart, remember *s-s* (**se**i**s**) = **se**senta and *s-t* (**si**ete) = **se**tenta.)

13 The first part of *ocho* appears in *ochenta* which stands for the Arabic number ~~~~.

80

14 The stressed *o* of Latin often changed to *ue* in Spanish. So *poder* becomes *puede*. What digit, consequently, can you see in *noventa*?

nueve

15 So *nueve* + *enta* = what Arabic number?

90 (But you say *noventa* today with the old Latin *o* in the unstressed position.)

16 You can now recognize in writing all the tens from 10 to 90. Let's say them aloud so you can also hear them in speech. The stressed syllable is indicated.

10	*diez*	40	cua*ren*ta	70	se*ten*ta
20	*vein*te	50	cin*cuen*ta	80	o*chen*ta
30	*trein*ta	60	se*sen*ta	90	no*ven*ta

17 Can you now write, without peeking, the number word for 60?

sesenta

18 You already know in English the base for the two Spanish words for 100. When a person borrows money from a bank, he pays some interest on each 100 dollars borrowed. One such rate is 6 per cent. This means that for every 100 dollars borrowed the person pays a rent of 6 dollars each year. Which word in *6 per cent* stands for 100?

cent (For the same reason, a *penny* is called a *cent* because there are 100 of them in a dollar.)

19 The base *cent* comes from Latin. The *e* is stressed so you can expect it to change to ~~~~ in Spanish.

ie

20 Translate: *¿Hay cien muchachos en la escuela?*

Are there 100 boys in the school?

21 Now translate this answer: *No, hay ciento dos muchachos en la escuela.*

No, there are 102 boys in the school.

22 The Latin *centum* (100) gave English "cent" and two allomorphs in Spanish, *cien* and *ciento*. You already know that when you have two allomorphs you need cues that tell you which one to choose. Here is the way a Spanish speaker counts aloud: *ochenta, noventa, cien, ciento uno, ciento dos, etc.* Which allomorph is used when another number follows?

ciento (Except in *cien mil*——100,000)

23 Which allomorph of the number word for 100 is used all by itself?

cien

24 Now look at this difference in English. Rewrite in English number words: 100 boys, 200 boys.

If you followed your "feel" (intuition), you got "*one* hundred boys" and "*two* hundred boys."

25 For the Spanish speaker, the allomorphs *cien* and *ciento* mean all by themselves "one hundred." So the Spanish translation of *"one* hundred boys" is ⌒⌒⌒.

cien muchachos

26 Write the Arabic numbers for the following: *setenta, cuarenta, noventa, cincuenta, sesenta, cien.*

70, 40, 90, 50, 60, 100

27 You see *tres* in *trece* and *treinta.* What are the Arabic numbers for *doscientos* and *trescientos?*

200 and 300 (Spanish uses *cientos* for all hundreds from 200 on.)

28 Now, use your head. The Spanish number word for 400 should logically be ⌒⌒⌒ *cientos.*

cuatrocientos **29** The base word *cinco* has an allomorph in *quince* (15). This should tell you that *quinientos* is the number word for ⌒⌒⌒.

500 **30** The number word for 600 is formed regularly. So you just put ⌒⌒⌒ in front of *cientos.*

seis (seiscientos)

31 You already know that the *ie* of *siete*, like the *ie* of *tierra*, comes from a stressed Latin ⌒⌒⌒.

e **32** Now, let's see how your linguistic logic is working. The stress on all hundred-words falls on the *cien* of *cientos: trescientos, cuatrocientos,* etc. How do you suppose, then, that Spanish writes the number word for 700? (a) *sietecientos* (b) *setecientos*

setecientos **33** By this same logic, how do you suppose Spanish writes 900? (a) *nuevecientos* (b) *novecientos*

novecientos (As in *noventa*. The *o* is unstressed and does not change to *ue.*)

34 The word for 800 is formed regularly, that is, 8 + 100. You write it ⌒⌒⌒.

ochocientos **35** Let's say the hundreds aloud the way you would say them in counting by hundreds. The stressed syllable is indicated: *cien, doscientos, trescientos, cuatrocientos, quinientos, seiscientos, setecientos, ochocientos, novecientos.*

36 A "cent" in English is one-hundredth of a dollar. A "mil" in English is one-thousandth of a dollar. English "cent" equals Spanish *cien* or *ciento.* What is your educated guess: the Spanish word for "one thousand" is ⌒⌒⌒?

mil (Now, say it aloud in Spanish. First say *mi,* then add the *l, mil.*)

37 The Spanish speaker says *cien lagos,* for "one hundred lakes," not *un cien lagos.* If he is consistent, what will he say, (a) *mil lagos?* (b) *un mil lagos?*

mil lagos (Spanish does not use the equivalent of "one" or "a" with *cien, ciento,* or *mil.*) **38** Translate: There are a thousand islands there.

Hay mil islas allí.

39 All of the numbers you have learned so far are also adjectives. You say *un muchacho, treinta y una muchachas,* or *doscientas plumas.* The number *ciento,* however, never changes to agree with its noun: *ciento dos islas.* The Spanish word for 1,000,000 is not an adjective; it is, on the contrary, a noun and takes the number word *un* with it: *un millón.* As a result, the Spanish speaker can say *mil animales* (one thousand animals), but he has to say *un millón de animales* (one million of animals). Translate: The school needs 1,000,000 books. (Use the number words.)

La escuela necesita un millón de libros.

40 The plural of *millón* is *millones*. Translate: 2,000,000 books.

dos millones de libros

41 When you see numbers written out in Spanish, you will discover that they can be punctuated in two ways. Some countries (Puerto Rico, for example) use the English system and write 1,720,640.21 while most of the others use the European system and write 1.720.640,21. In this course this latter system will be used just to get you familiar with it.

Review

1 *Cinco* (5) becomes *quince* (15) and the stem of the latter (*quin*) is used to make up the number word for 500. It is ⁓⁓.

quinientos
sete (setecientos)

2 *Siete* changes to ⁓⁓ in writing 700.

3 The word *setenta* stands for the Arabic number ⁓⁓.

70

4 The number word that gives *nove* in *novecientos* is ⁓⁓.

nueve (Latin *o* changes to *ue*.)

5 The Arabic number for *sesenta* is ⁓⁓.

60

6 When you count by tens to 100, the word for 100 is (a) *cien* (b) *ciento*.

cien
ciento (ciento diez)

7 When another number follows 100, as in 110, the word for 100 is ⁓⁓.

New Vocabulary

espacio	space	**olvidar**	to forget
servir (i)	to serve	**buscar**	to look for
empezar (ie)	to begin	**hallar**	to find (discover)
recordar (ue)	to remember	**Sí, cómo no.**	Yes, of course.

PROGRAM 82

Preparing for a Quiz

Part 1: The Morphology of the Imperfect

In your next class session, you will have a written quiz on the morphemes which make up the imperfect forms of all three sets of verbs. Here is a review.

1 The three irregular verbs which have to be learned separately are ⁓⁓.

ser, ir, ver
ve: veía (Also in *veo*.)

2 The only thing irregular about *ver* is its stem. In the Imperfect it is ⁓⁓.

3 Which present tense form of *ser* also has the stem of the Imperfect?

tú eres **4** The Imperfect of *eres* is ⏤.

eras **5** Old Spanish confused *ir* with *a*-set verbs. The present tense forms *va, vas,* and *van* have an *a*-set first suffix. The imperfect backshift of *van* is ⏤.

iban (You could, in pronunciation, put [i] in front of *va, vas,* and *van* and get the Imperfect. In writing you change the *v* to *b: iba, ibas, iban.*)

6 Aside from the three verbs just mentioned, the stem of all imperfect forms is regular. Which stem of *dormir* do you use for the Imperfect? (a) *duerm* (b) *dorm*

dorm (The stem of the Imperfect is always the same as the stem of the infinitive, except for *ir, ser,* and *ver.*)

7 Do the *e*- and *i*-verbs have different suffixes in the Imperfect?

no **8** The first suffix for all regular *e*- and *i*-verbs is always ⏤.

ía (As in *comer—comía,* and *vivir—vivía.*)

9 Is the second suffix of all verbs in the Imperfect exactly like the second suffix of the Present?

yes (Even in *ir, ser,* and *ver.*)

10 There are no irregular *a*-verbs in the Imperfect. The first suffix of all *a*-verbs in the Imperfect is ⏤.

aba **11** There is one special point you have to remember in writing the *nosotros*-forms of *a*-verbs. Write the imperfect back-shift of *hablamos.*

hablábamos (Did you remember the written accent?)

12 In your quiz on the Imperfect, you will be given 15 sentences in the Present. All you will need to do is write the imperfect back-shift of the present tense form of the verb. The infinitive will be given in parentheses to remind you of what stem to use in the back-shift. Eventually, of course, you will have to learn to do this without this aid. Here are some practice examples:

El pájaro vuela (*volar*) bien.

volaba **13** Yo quiero (*querer*) ver a Rosario pronto.

quería **14** Hace (*hacer*) mucho calor.

Hacía **15** ¿Van (*ir*) ustedes al teatro? (You change *v* to *b* and add what?)

Iban **16** No pueden (*poder*) ver bien.

podían **17** Nicanor nunca olvida (*olvidar*) a sus amigos.

olvidaba **18** ¿A qué hora comen (*comer*) ellos?

comían **19** Yo tengo (*tener*) cinco.

tenía **20** Estamos (*estar*) en Montevideo.

Estábamos (If you got the last 9 frames all correct, you are in great shape for the quiz. If you missed three or more, you are in trouble and should study the morphology of the Imperfect.)

Part 2: Review of Numbers

1 The base of *tres* appears in *trece* and the number word for 30, which is ⏤.

treinta **2** Which word, (a) *cinco* or (b) *quince*, cues you to say 500 correctly?

quince (*Quince* and *quinientos* have the same stem.)

3 What part of *setenta* is like the "ty" of "seven-ty?"

enta (*set = siete.*)

4 The *ue* of *vuelve* changes to *o* in *volver.* The *ue* of *nueve* changes to ⏤ in 900.

o

5 Write the number word for 900.

novecientos   **6** Translate: one hundred girls.

cien muchachas (You do not translate "one" and you use the allomorph *cien* when it stands alone.)

7 The other allomorph of 100 is ———.

ciento   **8** Write the number word equivalent of 110.

ciento diez   **9** Do you use the equivalent of "one" or "a" with *mil* in Spanish?

no (*Hay mil pájaros allí.*)

10 What number word in Spanish is a noun?

millón

Part 3: Review of Verb Vocabulary

1 The great mountain chain of California is called the *Sierra Nevada*. The word *sierra* means "saw" (the carpenter's cutting tool). What Spanish infinitive does *nevada* come from?

nevar (So *Sierra Nevada* means something like "the snow-covered saw.")

2 Is *nevar* a stem-changing verb?

yes   **3** What Spanish infinitive is a cognate of "value?"

valer   **4** The stem of "dormitory" gives you the stem of what infinitive?

dormir   **5** Translate the indicated portion of this sentence: "Most birds have *to learn to fly*."

aprender a volar

6 The cognate "pensive" (thoughtful) suggests what infinitive in Spanish?

pensar   **7** A "revolver" has a chamber that "revolves" and returns to its original position. What part of *revolver* is the Spanish for "to return?"

volver   **8** When one *petitions* for something in English, one is usually asking for something. Is this the same as asking a question?

no   **9** The verb for "to ask" (to petition) is ———.

pedir (Another meaning is "to order" when you order something in a restaurant.)   **10** The verb for "to ask" (a question) is ———.

preguntar   **11** Think of what you do with a *mirror*. What Spanish verb should this make you think of?

mirar (Some people "ad-mire" themselves in mirrors.)

12 The word "servant" or "serve" in English is a cognate of Spanish ———.

servir   **13** A *record* is something you keep so you will remember. The translation of "to remember" is ———.

recordar   **14** The opposite of *recordar* is ———, a cognate of "oblivion."

olvidar   **15** Here is a sentence that is something like a *refrán* (saying). Translate it: *La persona que no quiere, no puede.*

The person who does not want (to do something), can't.

16 When you *recognize* a person, you "know" him. What verb translates this meaning of "to know?"

conocer   **17** Translate *Quien busca, halla* literally.

Who seeks, finds.

18 Translate: *Yo empiezo a aprender español.*

I am beginning to learn Spanish. (And if you really did this right, you are really beginning to understand Spanish.)

It is quite customary in the United States for married couples or sweethearts to greet each other after a long absence with a hug. In the Hispanic world after similar absences, men often greet each other with a big hug, called *un abrazo* (embrace). It is also common for men friends to end a letter with *Con un abrazo* (With a hug). It is considered quite proper for grown men to hug each other. In Russia men friends sometimes hold hands when they go for a walk together. If you react negatively to these customs, the sociologist says you are suffering from "cultural shock." This means you are not ready to accept the notion that behavior patterns that are taboo in our society may be very acceptable in another culture.

Part 4: Review of the Stem of the Imperfect of Irregular Verbs

The stem-changing verbs in the Present all have regular stems in the Imperfect. This is the stem you find in the infinitive. Look at the form given below and say its infinitive aloud. Then check the answer. Go through this as fast as you can. Remember that in order to talk you must eventually be able to make these stem changes automatically.

1 tienen	6 empiezo	11 muere
tener	*empezar*	*morir*
2 vengo	7 llueve	12 pides
venir	*llover*	*pedir*
3 nieva	8 vuelvo	13 sigo
nevar	*volver*	*seguir*
4 quieres	9 puede	14 sirven
querer	*poder*	*servir*
5 pienso	10 duermo	15 digo
pensar	*dormir*	*decir*

No new vocabulary.

The Agreement of Number Adjectives

1 You already know that there are just four English adjectives that agree in number with the nouns with which they combine. These are the four demonstrative forms. Make *this dog* plural.

these dogs   **2** Make *those hats* singular.

that hat   **3** You also know that all descriptive adjectives in Spanish agree in number with their nouns. They may also have matching final phonemes as in *muchacha argentina*. The final *a* of *argentina* matches the final *a* of *muchacha*. There can, then, be two kinds of agreement in the case of descriptive adjectives: matching

number   phonemes and ⁓⁓⁓.

4 The Spanish number word for 1 is ⁓⁓⁓.

uno   **5** The number word *uno* is used only as the name for the Arabic number 1 or in doing math problems. When you say "one river" in Spanish, you say ⁓⁓⁓.

un río (The *o* of *uno* drops before any noun that can also combine with *el*:

el río.)   **6** When you say "one island" in Spanish, the *o* of *uno* is replaced by ⁓⁓⁓.

a : una isla (You use *una* with any noun that also combines with *la* : *la isla.*)

7 Translate: thirty-one islands.

treinta y una islas   **8** Translate: forty-one lakes.

cuarenta y un lagos   **9** The *una* of *treinta y una plumas* and the *un* of *cuarenta y un libros* agrees in number with *plumas* and *libros*. (a) true (b) false

false (*Plumas* and *libros* are plural; *una* and *un* are singular.)

10 In these constructions, *una* and *un* are something like *treinta plumas y una pluma* or *cuarenta libros y un libro*. The *una* and *un* agree with the omitted singular form of the noun. (a) true (b) false

true   **11** Did you ever stop to think about this? In the infinite number of possible Arabic numbers, there is only one that is numerically singular. It is the number ⁓⁓⁓.

1 (All other numbers are by their nature plural.)

12 If all numbers except 1 are plural by their nature, is there any logical reason why the number words should also have a plural suffix to mark plurality?

no (The number words *veinte, treinta, cuarenta, cincuenta, etc.* agree in meaning with plural nouns (*cuarenta estrellas*) but not, like descriptive adjectives, in form: *plumas negras, muchachos bolivianos, etc.*)

13 The hundred words from 200 through 900 all end in (a) *ciento* (b) *cientos*.

cientos   **14** Write the number word for 200.

doscientos   **15** Why does *doscientos* have a plural suffix? Let's take this compound word apart. The first word is ⁓⁓⁓.

dos   **16** *Dos* is an adjective and plural by nature. Is it logical that the word it agrees with should be also plural?

yes ("Two hundreds," then, contrast with "one hundred." This pattern

seems more logical when we think of many "hundreds" of fish or "hundreds"
of soldiers.)   **17** The number word *ochocientos* is exactly like *bolivianos*. Both have the plural
suffix *s* and the *o* which matches noun forms. How do you say "Bolivian girls?"

muchachas bolivianas (*a* matches *a*.)

18 How do you suppose, now, that you say "eight hundred girls?"

ochocientas muchachas (*a* also matches *a*.)

19 Here is a rule of usage: the number words from 200 through 900 match *o* or
a with nouns that also combine with *los* or *las*. Translate: the four hundred stars.

las cuatrocientas estrellas

20 Did you pay attention to the difference between *muchachas bolivianas* and
ochocientas muchachas? Here is another rule of usage: adjectives of nationality
follow their nouns in Spanish; number adjectives precede their nouns. Translate: six hundred Argentine girls.

seiscientas muchachas argentinas

21 There are three allomorphs of the number word for 1. They are *uno*, ⎯⎯⎯.

un; una   **22** Which allomorph do you use with a noun that also combines with *el?* (a) *uno*
(b) *un* (c) *una*

un (*el libro, un libro*)

23 Which allomorph do you use with a noun that also combines with *la?*

una (*la isla, una isla*)

24 Can the number word *uno* be used in direct combination with a noun?

no   **25** The allomorph *uno* is the mathematical word for 1. It is also used as the
adjectival residual to replace *un* when the noun is omitted. For example, someone asks, *¿Tienes un lápiz?* and you answer, "Yes, I have one." The translation
of this is ⎯⎯⎯.

Sí, tengo uno.   **26** There are two allomorphs of the number word for 100. They are ⎯⎯⎯.

cien; ciento   **27** You already know that when there are two or more allomorphs of anything,
you have to learn the cues for choice. Translate: 100 birds.

cien pájaros (You do not translate the "one" of English: "one" hundred birds.)

28 Translate: 100 islands.

cien islas   **29** The short form *cien* is used with the noun standing for anything being
counted. (a) true (b) false

true   **30** When another number (2, 10, 20, *etc.*) follows 100, which allomorph do you
use? (a) *cien* (b) *ciento*

ciento   **31** Translate: 110 buildings.

ciento diez edificios (Spanish does not say "*one* hundred and ten buildings.")

32 The literal translation of *ciento diez edificios* is ⎯⎯⎯.

hundred ten buildings

33 The Spanish word for 1,000 is ⎯⎯⎯.

mil   **34** Translate: There are a thousand inhabitants on the island.

Hay mil habitantes en la isla.

35 Have you learned this? Is there any real difference between saying "There
are *a* thousand inhabitants on the island" and "There are *one* thousand inhabitants on the island?"

no (English uses *a, an,* and *one* in much the same way. They are allomorphs
for the number word 1. Do not be confused because *a* and *an* are also called
the indefinite article. Both words come from the Anglo-Saxon word for 1.)

36 Is the word for 1,000,000 (*millón*) (a) a noun or (b) an adjective in Spanish? •

a noun   **37** Look at these two phrases: *un millón de estrellas; dos millones de estrellas.*
A plural number (*dos*) requires a plural form *millones.* (a) true (b) false •

true   **38** We can say in English "two million stars." The literal translation of *dos millones de estrellas* is ‿‿‿. •

two millions of stars

Review

un, una, uno   **1** The three allomorphs of the number word for 1 in Spanish are ‿‿‿. •

uno   **2** Which allomorph for 1 do you use when you count from 1 to 10? •

cien; ciento   **3** There are two allomorphs of the number word for 100. They are ‿‿‿. •

cien   **4** When you are just counting, 98, 99, 100, which allomorph do you use? •

ciento   **5** When you say 101, which allomorph do you use? •

doscientas tormentas (*a* must match *a*.)   **6** Translate: 200 storms. •

7 In Spanish is there any real meaning difference between *una* (the indefinite article) and *una* (the number word)? •

no (We think there should be some difference because of our English translations: a, an, one.)

New Vocabulary

héroe	hero
nacional	national

PROGRAM 84

The Preterit Forms of Regular Verbs

Part 1: The Forms of *e-* and *i*-Verbs

yes   **1** Do the *e-* and *i*-verbs all take the same suffixes in the Imperfect? •

ía   **2** The first suffix of the Imperfect for all regular *e-* and *i*-verbs is ‿‿‿. •

3 The stem of all *e-* and *i*-verbs is always followed by *i*. This combination is the past tense base. The past tense bases for *comer* and *vivir* are ‿‿‿. •

comí; viví   **4** All preterit forms of all regular *e-* and *i*-verbs are built on the past tense base. •
Here is a nice surprise for you: write the past tense base for *escribir* and *correr* •

escribí; corrí (You have just written the preterit forms that go with *yo.*)

5 *Yo escribía* says "I was writing"; *yo escribí*, in contrast, says "I wrote." To change the imperfect form *yo comía* to the Preterit, you simply drop the mark of imperfective aspect, the *a*. So the preterit form of *yo comía* is ‿‿‿. •

comí

6 The past tense base *comí* and the Preterit *comí* simply state that this non-cyclic event either began at some point in the past or was completed before the moment of speaking. (a) true (b) false

true (*Preterit* is the Latin for "gone by", past.)

7 Write the *yo*-form of the Preterit of *vivir*.

viví (The form is the same as the past tense base.)

8 Now write the *yo*-form of the Preterit of these verbs: *subir, deber, correr, escribir.*

subí, debí, corrí, escribí

9 The *nosotros*-form of the Imperfect of *comer* is ~~~~.

comíamos

10 From what you already know about *comía* (Imperfect) and *comí* (Preterit), the Preterit of *comíamos* should be ~~~~.

comimos (You don't need the written accent in this form because the stress
falls normally on the *i*.)

11 All *e* and *i* preterit *nosotros*-forms are made up of the past tense base plus *mos*. Write the Preterit *nosotros*-forms for these verbs: *escribir, beber, subir, vivir.*

escribimos, bebimos, subimos, vivimos

12 In all the forms of all the verbs you have learned so far, the second suffix that goes with *tú* has always been ~~~~.

s

13 In all forms of the Preterit of all verb sets, but in no other tense forms, the second suffix that goes with *tú* is *ste*. The *ste* is added to the past tense base of all *e*- and *i*-verbs to make up all *tú*-forms. The *i* of the base has no written accent. Change *comías* to the Preterit.

comiste

14 Change *debías, corrías,* and *subías* to the Preterit.

debiste, corriste, subiste

15 The preterit form that combines with *usted, él,* or *ella* is made by adding *ó* to the past tense base. The accent mark is now on the *ó*, not on the *i* of the base. Change *él bebía* to the Preterit.

él bebió

16 Change *escribe, sube,* and *vive* to the Preterit.

escribió, subió, vivió

17 In all tense forms of all verbs, the second suffix that goes with *ustedes, ellos,* or *ellas* is ~~~~.

n

18 Here is the *ustedes* (*ellos, ellas*)-form of the Preterit of *beber* (to drink): *bebieron.* To make up this form you put ~~~~ in between the base *bebi* and the second suffix *n*.

ero

19 Copy these bases and complete them so they agree with *ustedes: comi, volvi, aprendi, escribi.*

comieron, volvieron, aprendieron, escribieron

20 Write the preterit form of *subir* that goes with *yo*.

subí

21 Write the preterit form of *correr* that goes with *nosotros*.

corrimos

22 Write the preterit form of *volvías*.

volviste

23 Now let's see how sharp a linguistic detective you are. The present tense form of *escribir* that goes with *nosotros* is ~~~~.

escribimos

24 Will the Preterit have to be exactly the same?

yes (The *nosotros*-form for all *i*-verbs is exactly the same for the Present and
the Preterit. The meaning is fixed only by the context.)

25 You have now learned how to make up the Preterit of all regular *e*- and *i*-verbs in the whole Spanish language. Let's look at the pattern.

yo	sub	í	
nosotros	sub	i	mos
tú	sub	i	ste
usted	sub	ió	
ustedes	sub	iero	n
él	sub	ió	
ellos	sub	iero	n

The stem is regular (*sub*). There is one change in the last column (the person-number suffixes): *s* changes to *ste*. To learn all the forms you must remember the first suffix forms: *i* (*yo, nosotros, tú*), *ió* (*usted, él,* and *ella*), and *iero* (*ustedes, ellos,* and *ellas*). What is the grand total of new things you have to remember? Five!

The titles of address which you have learned (*señor, señora, señorita*) are used, like their English equivalents, with last names. They may also be used in speaking to anyone who is old enough to be addressed with a formal title and in addressing a person of any social class. In contrast, Spanish has two titles, *don* and *doña*, which are used only with first names and which originated as class titles, that is, were used only as titles of respect for the nobility. These titles are no longer reserved for just the nobility, but unlike the other titles of address, they still indicate either a difference of social class or a high degree of deference or respect. Thus, a person of a higher social class does not normally use *don* or *doña* in speaking to a person of lower class.

These titles, like *tú* and *usted*, permit a kind of inter-personal reaction which is impossible in English. They are used when two people are too intimate to interact on a last-name basis, but not intimate enough to be on a first-name basis. In general, however, only one of the two people in a conversation uses *don* or *doña* in addressing the other. Thus, a highly respected scholar may be addressed as *don Felipe* by his colleagues. Similarly, the owner of a ranch may address all his employees as *tú*, calling them by their first names, while they, in turn, use *don* and his first name, and *usted*.

One cannot get a deep understanding of Hispanic culture until one is thoroughly aware of the fact that the use of *tú, usted, don* and *doña* establish very special social relationships between people. English approaches this kind of relationship only in very special cases. For example, the nurses in a clinic may address a doctor with whom they are very friendly as "Doctor Jim."

Part 2: The Preterit Forms of *a*-Verbs

1 The *nosotros*-form of all regular *a*-verbs, like the *nosotros*-form of all *i*-verbs, is exactly the same for the Present and the Preterit. Write the Preterit of *llegar.*

llegamos

2 Change *esperábamos* to the Preterit.

esperamos

3 Write the *nosotros*-form of the Preterit for *cantar* and *necesitar.*

cantamos, necesitamos

4 To change any of these forms to the *tú*-form, you replace *mos* with (a) *s* (b) *ste*.

ste

5 Change *hablas* to the Preterit.

hablaste

6 Change *deseabas* to the Preterit.

deseaste

7 Write the preterit *tú*-form of *estudiar* and *cantar*.

estudiaste, cantaste

8 In the *i*- and *e*-verb forms, *subieron* and *comieron*, the *ie* is the set marker. What do you logically expect will replace *ie* when you make up the preterit form of *comprar*, an *a*-verb?

a (So you get *ustedes compraron*.)

9 The *ustedes*- and the *ellos*-forms are the same in all tenses. So the preterit equivalent of *ellos desean* is *ellos* ——.

ellos desearon

10 The Preterit of *ellos hablan* is *ellos* ——.

hablaron

11 There are three forms of the Preterit that have *a* right after the stem. What are they?

nosotros compr-**a**-mos; tú compr-**a**-ste; ustedes, ellos, ellas compr-**a**-ron

12 There is one form of the Preterit of *a*-verbs that has *é* right after the stem: *yo compré*. Write the *yo*-form of *llevar*.

llevé

13 Change *yo miraba* to the Preterit.

yo miré

14 There is one form of the Preterit which has *ó* as the first suffix. This *ó* goes with the same subject pronouns as the *ió* of *e*- and *i*-verbs. They are *usted*, ——.

él; ella

15 Change *usted observaba* to the Preterit.

usted observó

16 Write the *él*-form of the Preterit of *pensar*.

él pensó

17 Change these forms to the Preterit: *usted compra, él estudiaba, ella desea.*

usted compró, él estudió, ella deseó

18 When you change *desea* to the Preterit you just change the *a* to ——.

ó

19 But did you notice the problem in pronunciation? Divide these forms into syllables and underline the stressed syllable: (*yo*) *canto*, (*usted*) *cantó*.

can-to; can-**tó** (In all preterit forms, the stress falls on the vowel of the first suffix. This stress is the only thing in speech that tells you the difference between *canto* (I sing) and *cantó* (he sang). You can, of course, see the difference in writing.)

20 You are now able to make up all the forms of all regular *a*-verbs in the whole language. Let's see what you have to remember.

yo	cant	é	
nosotros	cant	a	mos
tú	cant	a	ste
usted	cant	ó	
ustedes	cant	aro	n
él	cant	ó	
ellos	cant	aro	n

Are the second suffixes the same as those for the Preterit of *e*- and *i*-verbs?

yes

21 Why don't you have to memorize the *nosotros*-form?

It's the same as the present tense form which you already know.

22 To get the first suffix you must learn that *yo* always combines with a stressed ——.

é

23 *Usted, él,* and *ella* always combine with a stressed ——.

ó

24 And the first suffix that combines with *ustedes*, *ellos*, and *ellas* is ~~~~~~. •

25 In reality you learn the Preterit of all regular *a*-verbs simply by learning the four forms of the first suffix. *é* goes with the subject pronoun ~~~~~~. •

26 *aro* goes with three subject pronouns: *ellos*, *ellas*, and ~~~~~~. •

27 *a* goes with two subject pronouns: *nosotros* and ~~~~~~. •

28 *ó* combines with three subject pronouns: *ella*, ~~~~~~. •

New Vocabulary: Numbers from 40 to 5,000,000

cuarenta	40	quinientos	500
cincuenta	50	seiscientos	600
sesenta	60	setecientos	700
setenta	70	ochocientos	800
ochenta	80	novecientos	900
noventa	90	mil	1,000
doscientos	200	dos mil	2,000
trescientos	300	un millón	1,000,000
cuatrocientos	400	cinco millones	5,000,000

You know enough to be able to supply the missing numbers.

PROGRAM **85**

Review of the Nature of Events, Order, and Aspect

In your next class session, you will have a quiz testing your ability to define events (cyclic versus non-cyclic) and your knowledge of the difference between order and aspect. This Program has been designed to help you do well on the quiz.

Part 1: Aspect and the Nature of Events

1 In theory every event may have three aspects. In non-technical terms these three aspects may be called the ~~~~~~ of the event. •

beginning, middle, end

2 Which of these three is also called the "imperfective" aspect? •

the middle

3 Every language in the world deals with aspect because knowing whether something is still going on (imperfective) or finished is important to survival. You need to know about aspects in order to choose between the Preterit and the Imperfect. At any point in the past, the Imperfect always describes (a) a completed action (b) an action in progress. •

an action in progress

4 So the Preterit must be used to describe the beginning or the end of events.

Is there anything in the form of the Preterit that can possibly tell you whether the form describes the beginning or the end of an event?

no (There is no formal marker to show this.)

5 The only way you can discover whether you are talking about the beginning of an event (initiative aspect) or the end (terminative aspect) is to know the nature of the event itself. How many basic kinds of events are there?

two

6 There is one kind of an event whose essential features can be observed the very instant it is begun. This type of event, moreover, can be extended (kept up) at the will of the doer. Does *descubrir* (to discover) belong to this set?

no (Columbus could discover the New World just once. He could not keep on discovering it.)

7 Can you recognize what event is taking place the moment someone begins to *llevar* something?

yes

8 Can the doer who is carrying something keep on doing this as long as his strength and will hold out?

yes

9 What is the technical term for events which belong to the same set as *llevar*, *querer*, *mirar*, *dormir*, *pensar*, and *observar*?

non-cyclic

10 In *He went to bed and cried* the verb *cried* says the same thing as (a) he was crying (b) he began to cry.

he began to cry

11 When a person goes to bed, is there a certain routine that is normally followed, that is, a series of steps that leads up to the end (termination) of the event?

yes

12 Ignacio is brushing his teeth. Does this tell you he is going to bed?

no

13 Ignacio is taking off his shoes. Does this tell you he is going to bed?

no

14 Ignacio is removing his shirt. Does this tell you he is going to bed?

no

15 Yet for many people, brushing the teeth, taking off their shoes and shirt are steps toward going to bed. These acts are part of the cycle that comes to an end when Ignacio actually climbs into bed. Once Ignacio has gotten into bed, can the cycle be extended?

no

16 What must Ignacio do before he can go to bed again?

He must get up.

17 Does *Ignacio went to bed* tell you that the whole cycle was completed?

yes

18 Does *cried* in *Ignacio went to bed and cried* tell you when the crying came to an end?

no

19 What kind of an event is *to sleep*? (a) cyclic (b) non-cyclic

non-cyclic (Once you are asleep the action can be extended.)

20 Which is the one non-cyclic event in this group: to open, to break, to leave, to study?

to study

21 Which is the one cyclic event in this group: to die, to read, to hear, to carry?

to die (This is one cycle that cannot be repeated.)

22 In the quiz you are going to have on the nature of events, you will be given a paragraph in English in which the verbs are in the past tense. Each verb will be numbered and you are to tell whether the event is cyclic or non-cyclic, and what aspect is being described. Practice doing this in this short pre-quiz quiz.

Do you still hear that noise? *I heard* (1) it at six o'clock while *we were eating.* (2) *I got up* (3) and *went outside.* (4)

What kind of an event is *to hear?*

non-cyclic

23 What aspect is described by *heard* in the sentence above? (a) initiative

(b) imperfective (c) terminative

initiative (One could say, *I began to hear the noise.*)

    24 What kind of an event is *to eat?*

non-cyclic (The action can be extended as long as you are hungry and there is food.)

    25 What aspect is described by *were eating?*

imperfective (The action was in progress.)

    26 What kind of an event is *to get up?*

cyclic   **27** What aspect is described by *I got up?*

terminative (The whole cycle was completed at a point in the story.)

    28 What kind of an event is *to go outside?*

cyclic   **29** What aspect is described by *I went outside?*

terminative (Again the whole cycle was completed after *I got up.*)

    If you got all these right, you should get near a perfect score on the up-coming quiz.

Part 2: The Order of Events

1 We would all become confused if we never could tell whether an event takes place *before*, *at*, or *after* the moment of speaking. Does *yesterday* mean the day before today?

yes   **2** Does *He left yesterday* mean the action of leaving is (a) at the moment of speaking? (b) before the moment of speaking?

before the moment of speaking

    3 What order relationship is expressed by *He will do it soon:* (a) before, (b) at, or (c) after the moment of speaking?

after the moment of speaking

    4 Here is something for you to remember: there can be only three order relationships between an event and a point in time. (1) The event is anterior to (before) the point, (2) the event is simultaneous with (at) the point, and (3) the event is posterior to (after) the point. You will soon learn how verb forms and adverbs give you this information.

Part 3: Review of the Preterit of Regular *a*-Verbs

In your next class, you will begin some practice drills on the Preterit of *a*-verbs. Let's see if this review can get you so well prepared that you can do the very first drill without a single mistake.

    1 The preterit form of *hablamos* is ⁓⁓⁓.

hablamos (The Present and the Preterit of the *nosotros*-forms of regular *a*-verbs are exactly alike.)

    2 The second suffix of the *tú*-form is ⁓⁓⁓ for all verbs in the Preterit.

ste   **3** Rewrite *hablas* in the Preterit.

hablaste (You just change the *s* to *ste*.)

    4 One form of the Preterit has a stressed *é* as the first suffix. The subject of this form is ⁓⁓⁓.

yo   **5** Change *yo hablaba* to the Preterit.

yo hablé (Now say *hablé* aloud with the stress on *blé: ha-blé.*)

6 *Usted*, *él*, and *ella* take the form (a) *hablo* (b) *habló*.

habló (Say **ha**-*blo* and *ha*-**bló** until you can hear the difference. Remember that stress is the only mark in speech of the difference in meaning and tense.)

7 There remains only one form of the Preterit of *hablar* to be discussed: the form that goes with *ustedes*, *ellos*, and *ellas*. The base form is *habla*. The person-number suffix is ~~~~.

n   **8** What comes between *habla* and *n*?

ro (So you have *hablaron*.)

9 Your drill tomorrow will begin with the sentence *Yo hablé de la luna*. (I spoke (talked) of the moon.) Practice saying the Spanish aloud.

10 The next drill sentence will be *Nosotros hablamos de la luna*. Its translation as Preterit is ~~~~.

We talked of (about) the moon. (Say the Spanish aloud.)

Part 4: Vocabulary Review

1 The translation of "Yes, of course" is ~~~~.

Sí, cómo no.   **2** The translation of "nevertheless" is *sin* ~~~~.

embargo   **3** Translate: *Está entre el sofá y el piano.*

It is between the sofa and the piano.

4 The meaning of *en todas partes* is "in all parts". A good translation is ~~~~.

everywhere   **5** Translate: *El edificio está rodeado de gente* (people).

The building is surrounded by people.

6 Translate the boldfaced words: *Vamos **desde** aquí **hasta** allí.*

from . . . to

New Vocabulary

boca	mouth
mosca	fly (the insect)
sentir (ie)	to regret, feel
cerrado	closed
Lo siento mucho.	I'm very sorry. (I regret it very much.)

PROGRAM 86

The Preterit and Imperfect in Contrast

Part 1: The Contrastive Functions of the Preterit and Imperfect

1 The Preterit and the Imperfect are not two different tenses. They are different forms of the same tense just as "is talking" and "talks" are different forms of the Present in English. How can we prove this? Is the past tense base the same for the Imperfect and the Preterit of *leer*?

yes (You have *leí* in *leía*—Imperfect and *leí*—Preterit.)

2 When you have to choose between two forms or two allomorphs, must you learn to spot the cues for choice?

yes (Something besides the forms must tell you when to select each.)

3 Since both the Preterit and the Imperfect deal with past events, must the contrast between the two be based on something beside pastness?

yes

4 The prime cue for choosing between the Preterit and Imperfect is aspect. Give the non-technical terms for the three aspects: initiative, imperfective, and terminative.

beginning, middle, end

5 The name Imperfect should tell you that this form always describes one aspect of an event at a point in the past. It is the ⎯⎯⎯ aspect.

imperfective or middle (the action in progress)

6 Since the Imperfect always describes the middle (imperfective) aspect and because there is only one other past tense form, is it logical to conclude that the Preterit must be used to describe two aspects?

yes

7 What two aspects does the Preterit describe?

beginning and end (initiative and terminative)

8 The Preterit may describe either the initiative or the terminative aspect of an event. There are, however, two sets of events: cyclic and non-cyclic. Is it logical to assume that the Preterit can describe either the initiative or the terminative aspect of both a cyclic and a non-cyclic event?

no

9 What kind of an event is *to close*? (a) cyclic (b) non-cyclic

cyclic

10 What aspect is described by *He closed the door*? (a) initiative (b) imperfective (c) terminative

terminative

11 Here is a very important point to remember: when the terminative aspect of a cyclic event is reached, the entire cycle must be completed. The Preterit, consequently, states that the entire cycle of any cyclic event is completed (a) before the moment of speaking (b) after the moment of speaking.

before the moment of speaking. (With a few very rare exceptions, the Preterit always describes something that happens before the moment of speaking.)

12 Look at this sentence: *I know that he closed the door*. Which event (*know* or *closed*) comes first in time?

closed (The knowing is now; the closing is past.)

13 Now look at this sentence: *I said that he closed the door*. Which event (*said* or *closed*) comes first in time?

closed (*Said* is a report on what had already happened.)

14 Let's make up a better rule on what the Preterit tells us about cyclic events.

The Preterit says that the whole cycle is completed (terminated) before the present moment of speaking. "He closed the door." *Cerró la puerta*. The Preterit can also say that the whole cycle was completed at some point in the past. "He closed the door at one o'clock." *Cerró la puerta a la una*. The Preterit can likewise say that the whole cycle was completed before some recalled report. "I said that he closed the door." *Dije que cerró la puerta*.

Can the Preterit ever say that a cyclic event began before the moment of speaking or at some recalled point?

no

15 So what do you really have to remember to always use the Preterit correctly when talking about cyclic events? The Preterit says that the entire cycle is completed either before a report on it, at some point in the past, or before the moment of speaking. Does *Yo sé que cerró la puerta a la una* (I know that he closed the door at one o'clock) give us all three kinds of information?

yes (The door is closed before I say *yo sé* (the report) and at a point in the past: *a la una.*)

16 What kind of an event is *hablar?* (a) cyclic (b) non-cyclic

non-cyclic (Once begun it can be extended.)

17 A point in time has no length (no dimension). Does it take some time to say anything?

yes

18 If it takes some time to say anything, can anything be said at a point in time which has no length?

no

19 What, then, must *habló* mean in this sentence: *Ayer a la una el presidente habló al país por radio?* (a) The president made his whole speech at precisely one o'clock. (b) The president began to speak at one o'clock.

Since nothing can be said at a point in time, the meaning must be: "The president began to speak at one o'clock."

20 Can the Preterit be used to describe the initiative aspect of a non-cyclic event?

yes (It says that a non-cyclic event began at some recalled point.)

21 Now look at this sentence: *Ayer el presidente habló al país por radio.* Is the speech now all over and completed?

yes

22 Can the Preterit be used to state that a whole non-cyclic event (the beginning, middle, and end) is completed before the moment of speaking?

yes

23 Here is a summary of what you need to know up to this point to always choose correctly between the Preterit and Imperfect:

You want to say that at some recalled point a cyclic event was going on, that is, was in progress. You choose: (a) *En ese momento él* **cerró** *la puerta.* (b) *En ese momento él* **cerraba** *la puerta.*

En ese momento él **cerraba** *la puerta.* (the Imperfect)

24 You want to say that at some recalled point a non-cyclic event was going on (was imperfective). You choose: (a) *A las seis de la tarde* **comió.** (b) *A las seis de la tarde* **comía.**

A las seis de la tarde **comía.** (the Imperfect)

25 Do you use the Imperfect to describe the imperfective aspect of either cyclic or non-cyclic events?

yes

26 You want to say that the entire cycle of a cyclic event was completed either before now or at some recalled point. You choose: (a) *A las ocho* **salía** *de la oficina.* (b) *A las ocho* **salió** *de la oficina.*

A las ocho **salió** *de la oficina.* (the Preterit)

27 You want to say that at some recalled point a non-cyclic event began. You choose: (a) *A las siete ayer* **nevaba.** (b) *A las siete ayer* **nevó.**

A las siete ayer **nevó.** (the Preterit)

28 You want to say that the entire non-cyclic event is completed before the moment of speaking. You choose: (a) *Trabajó en la mina dos días.* (b) *Trabajaba en la mina dos días.*

Trabajó en la mina dos días. (the Preterit)

29 Which verb will go into the Imperfect in Spanish? "While he *was reading,* he *heard* the noise."

was reading (The action was going on when he *began* to hear the noise.)

     30 Which verb will go into the Preterit in Spanish? "As we *talked*, I suddenly *realized* that he *was* sick."

realized (I *began* to be aware.)

Part 2: Vocabulary Review

     1 Translate: *Colón sabía que el mundo era redondo.*

Colombus knew the world was round.

     2 During *una tormenta* two kinds of precipitation may fall from the clouds. The infinitives that describe this are ⁓.

llover; nevar   **3** Translate: *Los pájaros pueden volar.*

Birds can fly.   **4** A flat area of the earth, a plain or prairie, is called *una* ⁓.

llanura   **5** Another word for *el mundo* is *la* ⁓.

tierra   **6** Translate: *En la selva hay muchos ríos, muchos lagos, y pocos habitantes.*

In the jungle there are many rivers, many lakes, and few inhabitants.

     7 What do you say? (a) *la mano* (b) *el mano*

la mano (The hand. This is an exception you should have memorized by now.)

     8 *De noche en el cielo* (sky) *podemos ver la* ⁓ *y las* ⁓.

luna; estrellas   **9** The noun cognate of "solar," as in "solar energy," is ⁓.

sol (sun)   **10** The infinitive cognate of "mirror" is ⁓.

mirar (to look at)

     11 Translate: *¡Ojo! El perro está en la calle.*

Watch out! The dog is in the street.

     12 The opposite of *recordar* is ⁓.

olvidar (to forget)

     13 The opposite of *terminar* is ⁓.

empezar (to begin)

     14 Translate: *El espacio entre las ciudades es el campo.*

The space between cities is the country.

     15 Which verb is used to ask a question? (a) *pedir* (b) *preguntar*

preguntar (*Pedir* is a cognate of "to petition" = request.)

     16 You want to say "I know him." Which verb do you use? (a) *saber* (b) *conocer*

conocer   **17** You take a drink of any liquid. Which verb do you use? (a) *tomar* (b) *llevar*

tomar   **18** Change *yo duermo* to both the Imperfect and the Preterit.

dormía; dormí (I was sleeping, I slept)

     19 Give the Present *tú*-form of *volver.*

tú vuelves (you return)

     20 The Spanish cognate of "heroes" is ⁓.

héroes (Did you remember the accent mark?)

New Vocabulary

cometa	kite
perro	dog
jugar (ue)	to play (a game)
pintar	to paint

Some Ways to Learn and Remember Words

You know from experience that learning new words or technical terms one by one is not an easy task. You have already studied enough Spanish to know that learning new words in a foreign language also takes a lot of time. At the rate you have been meeting new words up to now you will need about 180 class hours to learn some 1,200 words and approximately four years to master a vocabulary of roughly 5,000 words. Does this seem like a lot of words? You probably know from four to six times as many English words, and you are learning more every day. You can't, however, spend as many years learning Spanish as you have spent learning English, and it is highly unlikely that you will want to spend 12 years in a Spanish class just to learn some 15,000 Spanish words. All of this means that you are not going to have enough school time to learn to communicate in Spanish unless you discover short cuts to learning and remembering words. This Program talks about some of these short cuts.

1 One way to learn to understand the meaning of a word is to learn another word which is its opposite. The opposite of *morir* is ⁓⁓⁓.

vivir

2 The opposite of *noche* is ⁓⁓⁓.

día

3 When you come upon a new word, try to find out if you already have in your vocabulary an opposite which will help you remember both the word and its meaning. For example, very soon you are going to meet the verb *recibir*. It is the opposite of *dar* (to give). Now look at *recibir* and see if you know a cognate which looks like it and is the opposite of "to give." Think of this saying: "It is better to give than to ⁓⁓⁓."

receive

4 Not all words have opposites which can be used to help you remember them. There is almost no word, however, which cannot be associated with some other word which will help you learn its meaning. You know, for instance, the meaning of *hambre* and *sed*. They go together. Here is a verb which is often associated with *hambre*. It is *sufrir*. Look at this sentence: *En el mundo hay mucha gente que sufre hambre.* The translation of *sufrir* is "to ⁓⁓⁓."

suffer

5 You do not always have to associate a new word with another vocabulary item to learn and remember its meaning. There are other associations which are just as helpful. What made Columbus famous? *Descubrió el Nuevo Mundo.* You put Columbus together with the New World and you can hardly miss or forget the meaning of *descubrir*. It is "to ⁓⁓⁓."

discover

6 When you learn words in this way, you do not have to practice them over and over again in order to remember them. Look, now, at "discover" and *descubrir* and see if you can wring some more meaning out of them. Do both words begin with a negative prefix?

yes ("dis" and *des*)

7 Did you ever stop to think that "dis-cover" may mean to "un-cover" something you did not know was there? Now, look at *des-cubrir* carefully. Have you discovered that the Spanish for "to cover" is ⌇⌇⌇ ?

cubrir　**8** When you really learn what *des-cubrir* means, it is not very difficult to remember its opposite, *cubrir*. In a way, you get one word for free. You can learn to get hundreds, even thousands, of words for free once you understand how to discover meaning. And you will remember them better when you make the right association. Here is another example. Christopher Columbus got the money for his *viaje* to the New World from *la reina Isabel*. Can you make an educated guess at the translation of *viaje?*

voyage or trip　**9** Now that you know the meaning of *viaje*, you should not have too much trouble with the verb form based on it. When you take a trip, you go from one place to another. The specialized word for "going on a trip" is *viajar*. The translation of *viajar* is not "to trip"; it is "to ⌇⌇⌇."

travel (The meaning of *viajar* in Spanish is *hacer un viaje* = to make a trip.)

10 You now know *viaje* (trip) and *viajar* (to travel). Can you make this jump? *Una persona que viaja es un viajero.* What suffix do you add to "travel" to get the translation of *viajero?*

er (And you get "traveler.")

11 Let's go back, now, and look at this. *Colón recibió el dinero para su viaje al Nuevo Mundo de la reina Isabel.* Do you know enough history to guess that the translation of *reina* is ⌇⌇⌇ ?

queen　**12** The husband of Queen Isabella was *el rey Fernando*. Look at *reina* and *rey* carefully. Say *rey*, then *reina*, aloud. The word *rey* sounds exactly like the stem of *rei-na*. The translation of *rey* is ⌇⌇⌇.

king　**13** Kings and queens cannot *reinar* unless they have a *reino*. Which word translates "kingdom?"

reino　**14** With this much information, you can hardly fail to figure out that *reinar* translates "to reign." It is expected, of course, that you will make some mistakes when you try to figure out the meaning of new words. You make the same kinds of mistakes in English, but you are right most of the time. You will also be right most of the time in Spanish if you learn to use your linguistic logic carefully. By making educated guesses you can learn thousands of words all by yourself and in this way you can build up enough vocabulary to become a fluent speaker of Spanish without having to spend years in class. It may encourage you to know that a person can begin Spanish in college and in less than 1200 hours of classes get a doctor's degree in it and, believe it or not, be able to teach advanced Spanish to native speakers. All of this means that after you have mastered one language (your native English), you can be taught how to learn a second language and, as a result, you can learn the second language much faster than the first. You have, for example, learned to read Spanish aloud in less than 100 hours of class. You were probably six years old before you learned to do this in English and your school almost certainly spent more than 100 hours teaching you this complicated skill.

Another way of building up your word vocabulary is to associate words which have a similar meaning. The verb *ir* is a cover term for the specialized verb *viajar*. When Columbus set out *de España* on his famous *viaje*, he expected to be able to *regresar a España*. One opposite of *ir* is *volver*. Does *volver* have a meaning very similar to *regresar?*

yes (*Regresar* and *volver* are synonyms that have similar meanings.)

15 Once you realize that *ir, viajar, volver,* and *regresar* belong to a set of verbs which describe movement through space, you will find it easier to remember the words. What is just as important, it will be easier for you to learn other sets of words which are associated with the movement set. Let's see how this works. You come upon, for example, this sentence: *El año pasado viajamos a Europa por avión.* The context tells you that *avión* belongs to a set of words associated with travel. You might guess that it labels a means of transportation. Now look at *avión* carefully. There are several English cognates which begin with *avi* and which are associated with a means of transportation. One cognate is ⌒⌒⌒. •

You might have thought of "aviation" or "aviator."

16 You do not, of course, say, "Last year we traveled to Europe by aviation." But once you have gotten this far, you know that the word for *avión* is ⌒⌒⌒. •

plane **17** You already know that there is a big difference between the meaning of a word in Spanish and its translation in English. The translation of *Hace calor* is "It is hot." Its meaning in Spanish is ⌒⌒⌒. •

Makes heat. **18** You will remember *avión* better if you also know its real meaning. The Spanish suffix *ón* means "big." The stem *avi* appears in these cognates: aviation, aviator, aviatrix, aviculture, and aviary (the cage where birds are kept). One Spanish word for "bird" is *ave.* The original meaning of *avión* was not "plane," but ⌒⌒⌒. •

big bird (Aviators are sometimes called "bird men.")

19 In real life you only meet new words in life situations. The life situation, that is, the place where you are and the person you are talking to, plus the context in which you meet the new word help make it clear to you what in general is being talked about. What is being talked about (the subject of discourse) very frequently tells you what set the new word belongs to. Thus, for example, you are in a restaurant and someone says, *No como zanahorias.* You can guess right away that *zanahorias* belongs to the set we label as ⌒⌒⌒. •

food **20** You are in a shop which only sells vegetables. Someone says *Esas zanahorias son muy buenas.* You can be pretty sure now that *zanahorias* belongs to the subset of food labeled ⌒⌒⌒. •

vegetables **21** If you watch what the person is pointing at when he says *Esas zanahorias son muy buenas,* will you immediately learn the meaning of *zanahorias?* •

yes (You will know at once it is the word for "carrots.")

22 The subject of discourse is Christopher Columbus and his trip to the New World: *Colón viajó por barco.* What does *barco* label?

boat (The cognate is "bark.")

23 The action is *viajar.* The means of transportation is *barco.* The *viaje* is across the ocean. It is a marine voyage. The men who went with Columbus were *marineros.* Does someone have to tell you that *marineros* translates ⌒⌒⌒?

sailors (The cognate "mariners" gives the Spanish meaning.)

24 Suppose you missed the meaning of *marinero.* Should you give up? Not until you have tried this trick. You learned a little while back that the action *viajar* is based on *viaje* and that the doer of the *viaje* is a *viajero.* The Spanish suffix *ero* frequently means the doer of something associated with the meaning of the stem. The stem of *marinero* is *mar,* the word for ⌒⌒⌒. •

sea **25** The base stem *mar* is expanded in *marinero* to the long stem *marine.* A *marinero* is a person, then, who does something associated with the sea: a doer of "marine" activities. At this point you have a much better chance of guessing the meaning of *marinero*. Let's see if you can use this procedure to guess the meaning of a word you have not had.

When Columbus came back (*regresó*) to *Palos el rey Fernando y la reina Isabel estaban en Barcelona*. It was very important that the monarchs learn at once the outcome of his trip. So Columbus immediately sent a message to them by a *mensajero*. The stem of *mensajero* is the noun *mensaje*. This is a cognate of ⌇⌇⌇⌇.

message
26 The English name for the person who does something with a *mensaje* is, then, a ⌇⌇⌇⌇.

messenger
27 *Cuando el mensajero llegó a Barcelona, él les contó a los reyes la historia del viaje.* What can your logic do with *contó?* You know *contar* as "to count." Does it make much sense to say "he counted the history of the trip?"

no
28 So you know you must find a new meaning for *contar*. You can put a prefix on count which will show you the meaning: He recounted the history of the trip. A more common way of saying this is ⌇⌇⌇⌇.

told or related
29 When you know the subject of discourse (what in general is being talked about) and the set to which a word belongs, it's often very easy to figure out a new meaning for a word you already know. The *mensajero* carried a message to Ferdinand and Isabella. What, in fact, he carried was a *carta*. Can you guess the meaning of *carta?*

letter
30 The word *carta* belongs to the same set as *periódico* and *revista*. The cognate of *periódico* is a word that stands for a publication or magazine. It is "periodic" plus the suffix ⌇⌇⌇⌇.

al
31 A *carta* is a private way of sending information. A *periódico* or a *revista* is a public and commercial way of doing the same thing. Now look at *revista*. The prefix is ⌇⌇⌇⌇.

re
32 One of the common meanings of the English noun "vista" is *view*. A *revista* is a kind of magazine or periodical called a ⌇⌇⌇⌇.

review (*Vista* in Spanish has the same stem as *vió*, the Preterit of *ver*.)
33 *Periódicos* and *revistas* are published and bought because people want to read the *noticias*. The English cognate is "notices." A better translation is ⌇⌇⌇⌇.

news
34 The meaning that you know for *poner* is "to put." You are reading about Columbus and you read that he was the first to *poner pie en la isla*. The translation "to put foot on the island" gives you the meaning. A better translation for this meaning of *poner* is "to ⌇⌇⌇⌇."

set
35 This last frame is going to test almost everything you have learned in this Program. The subject of discourse is Jesus Christ and how he died. The key word you are to learn has a common English cognate. Translate: *Jesús murió en una cruz.*

Jesus died on a cross.

New Vocabulary

(la) calle	street	**tratar de**	to try to (do something)
dejar de	to stop (doing something)	**pasar**	to pass, happen
acabar de	to have just (done something)	**quedar**	to remain (stay behind)

PROGRAM 88

General Review and Vocabulary Round-up

Part 1: Vocabulary Round-up

You are going to have a major test very soon. This Program and the one that follows are designed to help you get ready to do well on the test. You can get extra help by looking again at the *Ejercicios*.

1 Here are all the regular *a*-verbs that you have had so far which are regular in the Present. Go over the list carefully and copy each verb you cannot translate into English.

acabar de	dejar (de)	hablar	mirar	preguntar
aceptar	desear	hallar	necesitar	quedar
andar	dispensar	invitar	observar	repasar
brillar	entrar	inundar	olvidar	terminar
buscar	esperar	llamar	pasar	tomar
cantar	estudiar	llegar	perdonar	trabajar
contestar	fumar	llevar	pintar	tratar

Go on to Frame 7 if you know all the meanings. If you have missed some, stop to see if you can figure out a cognate that will help you remember the meaning of the verb.

2 Here is an example: "the fume from his pipe" suggests what verb?

fumar (to smoke)

3 What you do with a "mirror" suggests which verb?

mirar (to look at)

4 Which verb is a cognate of "oblivion?"

olvidar (to forget)

5 In a Jewish temple the person who sings or chants liturgical music is called the "cantor." The verb cognate of *cantor* is ~~~~.

cantar

6 Suppose there are still some verbs whose meaning you cannot figure out. What do you do? Turn to the end of this Program where you will find a translation list. Take a small sheet of paper and write the Spanish and English side by side. Study this list until you know every verb.

7 Here are all the *e*- and *i*-verbs you have had so far which are regular in the Present. Cover the English column and see if you know their meaning.

aprender	to learn	**escribir**	to write
beber	to drink	**recibir**	to receive
comer	to eat	**cubrir**	to cover
correr	to run	**descubrir**	to discover
deber	must, ought	**vivir**	to live
responder	to answer	**subir**	to go up

8 These verbs have stem changes in the Present: *querer, pensar, tener, venir,* empezar, cerrar, nevar, and *tropezar*. The stressed *e* normally changes to ⁓ . •

ie   **9** Write the present *tú*-form of *pensar*. •

piensas   **10** Change *piensas* to the Imperfect. •

pensabas (The irregular stems are regularized in the Imperfect.)

        11 What is irregular in the present tense stem of these verbs: *volver, poder, dormir, recordar, morir, llover?* •

o changes to *ue* under stress

        12 Translate: I sleep well. •

Yo duermo bien.

        13 Rewrite *Yo duermo bien* in the Preterit. Remember the stem is regular. •

Yo dormí bien. (Many irregular present tense stems are also regularized in

the Preterit.)   **14** Give the present tense *yo*-form of *pedir* (to request, order). •

yo pido   **15** Write the present tense *yo*-form of *seguir, servir,* and *decir*. •

sigo, sirvo, digo

        16 Here is the list of all geographic terms you have had in the order in which they were presented. Go down the list slowly and copy each word whose meaning you do not remember.

país	lugar	océano	Andes	geografía	selva
ciudad	norte	mar	Amazonas	mundo	llanura
capital	sur	Pacífico	río	habitante	lago
campo	este	Caribe	desierto	tierra	población
montaña	oeste	Atlántico	pampa	isla	pueblo

If you missed any of these, look up their meaning in the end vocabulary and make yourself a study sheet.

        17 Here are some other nouns you have had recently. Translate the indicated noun: *Vivió en la **calle** Bernal Díaz.* •

street   **18** *Las indias llevan **jarros** en la cabeza* (head). •

jugs   **19** *El **espacio** entre las ciudades es el campo.* •

space   **20** *Una casa puede ser un **edificio.*** •

building   **21** *La **luna**, el **sol** y las **estrellas** están en el cielo* (sky). •

moon, sun, stars

        22 *Hay muchas **tormentas** en las selvas tropicales.* •

storms   **23** *El tigre, el **león** y el **toro** son animales.* •

lion, bull   **24** Write the number words you use in counting by tens up to 90. •

diez, veinte, treinta, cuarenta, cincuenta, sesenta, setenta, ochenta, noventa

(Check your spelling.)

        25 Write the number words you use in counting by hundreds up to 900. •

cien, doscientos, trescientos, cuatrocientos, quinientos, seiscientos, setecientos, ochocientos, novecientos

        26 The Spanish words for 1,000 and 1,000,000 are ⁓ . •

mil; millón   **27** You probably missed a few. Here is a very efficient way to learn new words. Take a 3 by 5 card, cut it in half, then write the Spanish word on one side and the English translation on the other. Mix the cards up and, then, go through them one by one. You can practice going from English to Spanish or from Spanish to English. However, each time you go through your cards, shuffle them first. This procedure is a private tutorial system which can teach you every word you have to remember.

In the United States a man standing on the street is not likely to pay compliments to a strange lady as she walks by. This is generally considered impolite. He may, however, whistle at her to let her know he thinks she is beautiful. Most women take this "wolf whistle" as a compliment and do not feel insulted. In the Hispanic world a man is permitted to compliment a woman he does not know with words. This is not considered impolite. There is even an idiom that describes this. It is *echar flores a una persona* (to throw flowers at a person).

Part 2: Review of the Past Tense Morphology

1 The first suffix of the Imperfect of all *a*-verbs is ～～.

aba
ía
volví
yo
ste (tú volviste)

2 The first suffix of the Imperfect of all regular *e*- and *i*-verbs is ～～.
3 The past tense base of *volver* is ～～.
4 What subject pronoun goes with the preterit form *volví*?
5 What do you add to *volvi* to get the *tú*-form of the Preterit?

ó (usted volvió)

6 What do you add to *volvi* to get the *usted*-form of the Preterit?

ero (ellos volvieron)

7 What goes between *volvi* and *n* to make up the *ellos*-form of the Preterit?

llevamos (The same form as the Present.)

8 The Preterit of *llevamos* is (¡Ojo!) ～～.

ste (tú llevaste)

9 To get the preterit *tú*-form, you replace the *mos* of *llevamos* with ～～.

quedé
quedó

10 The preterit *yo*-form of *quedar* is ～～.
11 Change *quedé* so it agrees with *usted* or *él*.
12 What do you put between the stem *olvid* of *olvidar* and the second suffix *n*

to get the preterit form for *ustedes* or *ellos?*

aro (ustedes olvidaron)

13 To get the right stem and past tense suffixes of *recuerdo* you have to know what verb set it is and its infinitive, which is ⁓⁓⁓.

recordar

14 In this frame, write the infinitive of the verb given.

busco	duermes	pueden
buscar	*dormir*	*poder*
empiezo	piden	vuelvo
empezar	*pedir*	*volver*
sirven	conozco	somos
servir	*conocer*	*ser*
sigo	miro	hago
seguir	*mirar*	*hacer*

Translation of *a*-Verbs: Part 1, Frame 1

to have just	to stop	to speak, talk	to look at	to ask
to accept	to want	to find, discover	to need	to stay, be left
to walk	to excuse	to invite	to observe	to review
to shine	to enter	to flood	to forget	to finish, stop
to look for	to wait	to call	to spend, pass	to take, drink
to sing	to study	to arrive	to pardon	to work
to answer	to smoke	to carry	to paint	to try

No new vocabulary.

PROGRAM 89

Preparing for a Test

In your next class, you will have a major test. You already know that great care is taken to get you ready for every test and help you avoid errors which may be made simply because you do not understand what you are supposed to do in the test. This Program covers the type of problems which will be given on the test. Use your cover sheet and go through it carefully. When you have finished, you can tell whether you need to review some *Ejercicios*.

1 In Section A of the test you will hear ten statements in Spanish. After each Spanish statement, you will hear a question about it in English. You are to answer the question very briefly in English. What you are being tested on is your ability to understand spoken Spanish. Here is an example.

Step 1: You hear: *Nuestra escuela empieza todos los días a las ocho de la mañana.*

Step 2: You now hear the question: "At what time does our school begin?"

Step 3: You write a short answer in English: ‿‿‿ .

at 8 o'clock

2 This example is a little harder: *San Diego, California, está al sur de San Francisco.* Which city is farther to the north?

San Francisco

3 *En las selvas tropicales de Sudamérica hay muchos animales y muy pocos habitantes.* What is most common in tropical jungles?

animals

4 Section B of the test will check your listening comprehension in a different way. There will be eleven pictures on display each with a letter under it. You will hear 10 statements and you are to select for each statement the letter of the picture which most logically goes with the statement. You hear, for example, *En esta parte del mundo nunca nieva.* You pick (a) a picture of Antarctica (b) a picture of a jungle.

a picture of a jungle

5 You hear: *Aquí vemos un animal feroz.* You pick the picture of (a) a mouse (b) a tiger.

a tiger

6 You hear: *Este señor va a visitar a su familia en Santiago.* You pick the picture of (a) a man with a broken leg (b) a man about to board an airplane.

The most logical choice is "a man about to board an airplane."

7 Section C of the test has been designed to check both your listening and reading comprehension. You will hear ten statements or questions. For each there will be three possible rejoinders or answers on your answer sheet. You are to choose the most logical. For example, you hear: *En los Estados Unidos hay cincuenta estados.* Which rejoinder do you pick?

(a) Sí, y también cincuenta ciudades capitales.

(b) Sí, y el más grande es Rhode Island.

(c) Sí, y todos están al oeste de Chicago.

Sí, y también cincuenta ciudades capitales.

8 You hear: *¿Cuál es más grande, el sol, la luna o la tierra?* Which answer do you pick? (a) *el sol* (b) *la luna* (c) *la tierra*

el sol

9 Section D tests your ability to understand spoken numbers. You may, for example, hear: *mil cuatrocientos noventa y dos.* You are to write the Arabic equivalent ‿‿‿ .

1492

10 You hear: *quinientos setenta y seis;* you write ‿‿‿ .

576

11 You hear: *dos millones novecientos mil;* you write ‿‿‿ .

2.900.000

12 Section E will be like a pattern drill. You will see a sentence in which the verb form is in the Preterit. You will then see a new subject. You will write the letter of the verb form that agrees with this new subject. You see: *Mis padres volvieron a casa.* You then see: *yo.* You choose (a) *volvimos* (b) *volvió* (c) *volví*

volví

13 You see: *Colón halló dos continentes nuevos.* You then see: *ellos.* You choose (a) *hallé* (b) *hallamos* (c) *hallaron.*

hallaron

14 You see: *Subí al balcón.* Then *ellos.* You choose (a) *subió* (b) *subimos* (c) *subieron.*

subieron

15 Section F is to find out if you can tell (1) whether an event is cyclic or non-cyclic and (2) which aspect is being described. There will be 10 sentences in English like this: "Columbus *discovered* the New World." The event is (a) cyclic (b) non-cyclic.

cyclic

16 The aspect described by *discovered* is (a) initiative (b) imperfective (c) terminative.

terminative   **17** Elena came in while we *were sleeping*. The event is (a) cyclic (b) non-cyclic.

non-cyclic   **18** The verb form *were sleeping* describes which aspect? (a) initiative (b) imperfective (c) terminative

imperfective   **19** The sky got black and then *it rained*. The event is (a) cyclic (b) non-cyclic.

non-cyclic   **20** The aspect is (a) initiative (b) imperfective (c) terminative.

initiative (and then it *began* to rain.)

21 Section G deals with stem-changing verbs. You will find 8 sentences with the verb in the infinitive. You are to write the present tense form of the verb. You see *Yo* ～～ *(volver) mañana.* You write ～～.

vuelvo   **22** You see: *Nosotros nunca* ～～ *(pedir) mucho.* You write ～～.

pedimos   **23** You see: *En Chile* ～～ *(nevar) mucho en el invierno.* You write ～～.

nieva   **24** Section H is to find out if you can replace present tense forms with the equivalent imperfect forms. The infinitive of each conjugated verb will be given to help you choose the right stem. You see: *Esos señores* **son** *(ser) muy amables.* In place of *son*, you write ～～.

eran   **25** You see: *Ellos* **leen** (leer) *sus lecciones.* In place of *leen*, you write ～～.

leían   **26** You see: *Sus cometas* **vuelan** *(volar) muy bien.* You write ～～.

volaban   **27** Section I deals with the done-to *a*. There will be seven sentences with a space before the done-to. You put in an *a* if it is needed. You leave the space blank if no *a* is required. What do you do in this case? *Conocí* ～～ *la señora Abreu ayer.* Do you need *a* or no *a*?

a   **28** *Buscamos* ～～ *los animales en la selva.* Do you need *a* or no *a*?

no *a*   **29** *No vimos* ～～ *la luna anoche.* Do you need *a* or no *a*?

no *a*   **30** The purpose of Section J is to evaluate your reading comprehension. You will find on your answer sheet 10 statements or questions each followed by three possible answers or rejoinders. In each item you are to select the most logical response. For example, you see: *¿Qué es un desierto?* Which response will you pick?

    (a) Es un lugar donde hay muchos republicanos.
    (b) Es un lugar donde no llueve mucho y hace calor.
    (c) Es un lugar donde hay muchos elefantes.

Es un lugar donde no llueve mucho y hace calor.

31 You see: *El león es un animal muy feroz.* Which rejoinder is most logical?

    (a) No es tan fiero como lo pintan.
    (b) Sí, es de la capital de Colorado.
    (c) Sí, es muy amable.

No es tan fiero como lo pintan.

32 You see: *La capital de un país es una ciudad muy importante.* You select:

    (a) Porque allí hay muchos vestidos nuevos.
    (b) Porque tiene muchos edificios grandes.
    (c) Porque es el centro del gobierno (*government*).

Porque es el centro del gobierno.

33 Section K also deals with reading comprehension. You will see an incomplete sentence followed by four possible endings. You pick the most logical. You see, for example: *El hermano de mi padre es* ～～ and these completions.

You pick which one? (a) *mi sobrino* (b) *mi abuelo* (c) *mi tío* (d) *mi primo*

mi tío

34 You see: *Roberto tiene mucha hambre* ⟶. Which completion is most logical?

(a) porque tiene tres tíos. (b) porque no trabajó en todo el día.

(c) porque está muy enfermo. (d) porque no comió hoy.

porque no comió hoy.

Do you want to figure out a grade for yourself? Three missed frames gives you an A—. Six missed frames a B—. Nine missed frames a C—.

New Vocabulary

león	lion	**aparecer**	to appear
dirección	address	**inundar**	to flood
	(direction)	**brillar**	to shine
avenida	avenue	**fiero**	wild (fierce)
pueblo	village, town	**tan ... como**	as ... as
toro	bull	**esta noche**	tonight
fuente (la)	fountain	**anoche**	last night
andar	to walk	**Hága(n)me**	
tropezar (ie)	to trip	**Hazme** el favor de ...	Please ...

Ejercicios

Ejercicio 43 | Silent Reading and Response

Tampa: ciudad americana y española

La ciudad norteamericana de Tampa es un centro comercial muy importante en el estado de la Florida. Está situada en la costa oeste de la península. Turistas de todos los estados de la Unión van a Tampa porque allí hace muy buen tiempo en todas las estaciones del año. La región tiene un clima ideal, ni° mucho calor, ni° mucho frío.

neither
nor

Tampa es un puerto de mar muy importante. Allí hay mucho movimiento de barcos que van y vienen del Canal de Panamá y también de otros puertos del mundo°. La bahía° de Tampa tiene mucha importancia en la historia del Golfo de México.

world/bay

En los siglos° XVI (dieciséis) y XVII (diecisiete) la bahía de Tampa fue un lugar favorito para los piratas de muchas naciones. Uno de estos piratas famosos de la historia es el capitán español José Gasparilla. En su honor, todos los años en el mes de febrero, la ciudad celebra una gran fiesta que se llama el carnaval de Gasparilla.

centuries

Estamos en el siglo veinte, pero Tampa no olvida° los primeros años de su interesante historia, los días románticos de las visitas de los piratas a la ciudad. Hay otras ciudades en los Estados Unidos que conservan la tradición española

does not forget

del pasado. Por ejemplo°, la conservan en Santa Fe, Nuevo México, en Santa   for example
Bárbara, California, y en varias más. En todas estas ciudades hoy día° viven   nowadays
muchas personas y familias enteras que hablan español.

Ejercicio 44 | Silent Reading and Response

Un problema de vocabulario

Las palabras *América* y *americano* no tienen el mismo significado en todas partes
del mundo. Las diferencias en el significado de estas dos palabras causan gran
confusión. Esta confusión no es realmente necesaria. Necesitamos eliminarla y
comprender mejor qué quieren decir las dos palabras. No hay problema si repasamos nuestras lecciones de geografía.

Un continente es una gran extensión de tierra rodeada de mar. Una isla también es una porción de tierra rodeada de agua por todas partes. En el caso de una
península, la tierra está rodeada de agua excepto en una parte. La diferencia
fundamental entre isla y continente es de tamaño°. Las islas siempre son mucho   size
más pequeñas. Hay siete grandes continentes en nuestro globo. Sus nombres son
los siguientes: África, América del Norte, América del Sur, Antártica, Asia,
Australia y Europa.

Así vemos que América, según dice la enciclopedia, es el nombre de uno de los
grandes territorios del mundo. El territorio que vemos en el mapa desde Canadá
hasta Tierra del Fuego se llama América. Incluye dos continentes y forma parte
del hemisferio occidental. Allí viven millones de personas de diferentes razas,
idiomas y culturas. Y todos los habitantes de esta enorme extensión de tierra son
americanos.

Ejercicio 45 | Silent Reading

Go through the following selection at your normal reading speed without stopping to translate into English. As soon as you finish, write the answers of the first
comprehension exercise that follows the reading. You have a limited time to go
through the entire operation.

Una noticia sensacional

Cuando un astronauta de la Tierra pone pie° en la luna, lo sabemos in-   sets foot
mediatamente. Hoy día es muy fácil y cómodo recibir° en nuestra casa las   to receive
noticias° que vienen de todas partes del mundo. Podemos oírlas° por radio,   news/hear
verlas por televisión y leerlas en periódicos° y revistas°. El telégrafo, los super-   newspapers/
aviones°, los cohetes° y los satélites permiten la comunicación rápida entre los   magazines
lugares más remotos del universo.   jet planes/
    rockets

¡Qué diferente era la situación en el siglo quince! En octubre de 1492, Cristóbal
Colón y 87 marineros° españoles bajan de sus tres barcos y ponen pie en las   sailors
playas de una pequeña isla del grupo de las Bahamas. Siguen su viaje° de una   trip
isla a otra y ponen la bandera° de España y una cruz° en las tierras que hallan.   flag/cross
Colón y sus hombres toman posesión de las nuevas tierras en nombre de su rey°   King
Fernando y de su reina° Isabel. El descubrimiento° de estos territorios es, sin   Queen/
    discovery

duda alguna°, la noticia más sensacional del momento. España y el resto de   without any doubt
Europa, sin embargo, tienen que esperar casi seis meses para recibirla.

    La sensacional noticia del descubrimiento llega a Europa por carta°. El viaje   by letter
de regreso° a España es muy difícil. Las tormentas y el mal tiempo de invierno   return trip
en el Atlántico obligan a Colón a buscar refugio en Lisboa. Antes de salir de
allí, Colón le da la carta a un mensajero°. Viajando° probablemente en mula, el   messenger/traveling
mensajero la lleva a Barcelona, en la costa este de España, donde están los reyes,
Fernando e Isabel.

    La carta de Colón cuenta° cosas muy interesantes acerca de los indios, las   tells
plantas, los animales y los minerales de las Indias. Colón creía que las islas de
Cuba y Santo Domingo eran en realidad parte de Japón y de India. Después de
tres viajes más, el 21 de mayo de 1506, Colón muere en España. Muere sin saber
nunca que había descubierto° un mundo nuevo que hoy llamamos América.   had discovered

First Comprehension Exercise: Choose the letter that corresponds to the best
completion of each statement.

1 Hoy día podemos ver las noticias en nuestra casa porque tenemos . . .
    a teléfono.   **b** telégrafo.   **c** televisión.

2 También podemos leer las noticias en nuestra casa porque tenemos . . .
    a periódicos.   **b** cohetes.   **c** barcos.

3 Los marineros trabajan generalmente en . . .
    a super-aviones.   **b** revistas.   **c** barcos.

4 En el siglo quince en Europa no tenían . . .

    a barcos.   **b** radios.   **c** cruces.

5 Los hombres que iban con Colón de isla en isla por las Antillas eran . . .

    a portugueses.   **b** ingleses.   **c** españoles.

6 La gente de Europa recibe la noticia del descubrimiento de Colón . . .

    a inmediatamente.   **b** después de seis meses.

        c después de seis años.

7 La noticia del descubrimiento de América va a Europa por . . .

    a carta.   **b** radio.   **c** televisión.

8 Colón creía que Cuba y Santo Domingo eran parte de . . .

    a África.   **b** un mundo nuevo.   **c** India y Japón.

9 Colón murió en España . . .

    a el 12 de octubre de 1492.   **b** el 14 de marzo de 1496.

        c el 21 de mayo de 1506.

Second Comprehension Exercise

1 ¿ De dónde vienen las noticias que recibimos en nuestras casas ?

    a Vienen de los barcos de Colón.

    b Vienen de todas partes del mundo.

    c Vienen de una isla en las Bahamas.

2 ¿ Por qué es fácil hoy día oír, ver y leer las noticias en la casa ?

    a Porque vivimos en un planeta.

    b Porque tenemos radio, televisión y periódico.

    c Porque estamos en el siglo diecinueve.

3 ¿ Dónde está la primera isla que descubrió Colón ?

    a En el océano Pacífico.

    b En el mar Mediterráneo.

    c En el grupo de las Bahamas.

4 ¿ Qué bandera ponía Colón en las tierras que descubría ?

    a Ponía la bandera española.

    b Ponía la bandera italiana.

    c Ponía la bandera americana.

5 ¿ Quiénes eran Isabel y Fernando ?

    a Eran dos indios de las Bahamas.

    b Eran los reyes de España.

    c Eran los reyes de Portugal.

6 ¿ Cuál fue la noticia más sensacional del siglo quince ?

    a Fue el descubrimiento de la luna.

    b Fue el descubrimiento del telégrafo.

    c Fue el descubrimiento de América.

7 ¿ Cómo fue el viaje de regreso a España ?

   a Fue magnífico.

   b Fue cómodo.

   c Fue terrible.

8 ¿ Qué animales usaban en España en el siglo quince para viajar de un lugar a otro ?

   a Usaban elefantes.

   b Usaban mulas y burros.

   c Usaban tigres.

9 ¿ Cuántos viajes en total hizo (*made*) Colón al Nuevo Mundo ?

   a Hizo cuatro viajes.

   b Hizo tres viajes.

   c Hizo solamente un viaje.

Ejercicio 46 | Pre-test Practice on Listening and Reading Comprehension

Your teacher will read a question or a statement *twice*. From the three choices given below, you are to select the most appropriate answer or rejoinder by writing the letter that corresponds to it. In your next test there will be a section exactly like this one.

1 **a** Es un insecto que corre por las montañas.

   b Es un insecto que vuela.

   c Es un insecto que tiene una boca enorme.

2 **a** Empiezan generalmente en junio (mayo).

   b Empiezan en el siglo doce.

   c Terminan generalmente en junio.

3 **a** Un período de tiempo de mil años.

   b Una estación del año muy fría.

   c Un período de tiempo de cien años.

4 **a** El descubrimiento de los Estados Unidos.

   b La independencia de los Estados Unidos.

   c La independencia de las colonias españolas en América.

5 **a** Hablaba con un amigo de mi familia.

   b Hablaba en portugués.

   c Hablaba con el descubridor del Océano Pacífico.

6 **a** Quien busca, halla.

   b ¡ Salud !

   c Lo siento mucho.

7 **a** ¡ Qué mal tiempo hace !

   b ¡ Qué mala memoria tienes !

   c Sí, cómo no.

8 a Hay mucha niebla. Yo no voy.

    b Es mejor ir cuando está nevando.

    c En el desierto hace mucho calor.

9 a Si quieres, puedes comer algo.

    b En el refrigerador hay agua fría.

    c Aquí tienes el agua caliente.

10 a ¡Caramba! No sabía que tú tenías tanto dinero.

    b ¡Caramba! No sabía que tú conocías a José.

    c ¡Caramba! No sabía que tenías una amiga millonaria.

Ejercicio 47 | Pre-test Practice on Reading Silently for Comprehension

In two and a half minutes, read the following sentences silently and select the most appropriate answer or rejoinder.

1 Los señores Rodríguez van a volver a casa a las cinco y media:

    a Sí, van a estar en el cine a esa hora.

    b Van a salir de la escuela a las seis menos veinte.

    c Porque tienen que comer temprano.

2 Dicen que va a haber mucha niebla mañana.

    a Es verdad, con un viento terrible.

    b Va a ser imposible ver nada.

    c Los aeroplanos van a poder salir sin dificultad.

3 ¿Qué es una selva tropical?

    a Es un lugar donde tienen bancos y tiendas.

    b Es un lugar donde hay muchos insectos y animales de diferentes clases.

    c Es un lugar donde nieva mucho y hace mucho frío.

4 ¿Por qué es importante mantener la boca cerrada?

    a Porque así no entran moscas.

    b Porque así no entran leones.

    c Porque tenemos un pájaro en la mano.

Ejercicio 48 | Cyclic versus Non-cyclic Events

In the following story, decide whether each indicated verb represents a cyclic (C) or a non-cyclic (NC) event.

Grandma and the Supermarket Crook

(Nancy is reporting what happened when she and her grandmother were at the supermarket waiting to be checked out.)

The man waiting in line ahead of me suddenly *took out* **1** a gun from his pocket. He *pointed* **2** it at Mrs. Jones, the clerk. She got terribly frightened and *shook* **3** like a leaf.

Mr. Smith, the manager, *came* **4** to rescue her. The thief *hit* **5** him on the head with his gun. Mr. Smith *fell* **6** to the floor and *moaned* **7**. Mrs. Jones *opened* **8** the cash register.

I was so scared, I didn't know how to act. Grandmother, however, hiding behind me, *grabbed* **9** a big ripe tomato and *threw* **10** it at the thief with all her might.

It was a direct hit between the eyes and made a big red splash! The crook *fainted* **11**. Everyone *laughed* **12**. Minutes later the police *took* him *away* **13**.

Ejercicio 49 | The Done-to *a*

Read each sentence and decide whether or not the done-to *a* is needed in the blank.

1 Nosotros tenemos . . . un cuaderno y . . . seis libros.
2 Pronto vas a olvidar . . . las dos señoritas.
3 ¿Quién puede recordar . . . el nombre del libro?
4 Vamos a mirar . . . la televisión esta noche, porque podemos ver . . . la famosa actriz Dolores del Río.
5 ¿Conoce usted . . . la señorita Álvarez?
6 Yo conozco . . . este lugar muy bien.
7 Tenemos que invitar . . . Maruja.
8 Yo miraba . . . los nuevos lápices.
9 Ellos querían aceptar . . . la invitación.

Ejercicio 50 | Discrimination of Events and Aspects

Write C or NC for cyclic or non-cyclic and B, M, or E for beginning, middle or end.

Has This Ever Happened to You?

(Larry, one of your classmates, is explaining to the attendance director why he was late for class this morning.)

Before going to bed last night, I *set* **1** the alarm. At 7:00 this morning, it *rang* **2** all right, but I *turned* it *off* **3**! I *was* so *tired* **4** that I *fell asleep* **5** again. Suddenly I *felt* **6** the sun shining on my eyes. I *jumped out* **7** of bed and *rushed* **8** as much as I could. It was 8:25 already! As I *ran* **9** on my way to school, I *remembered* **10** that I had left my books in the kitchen, and I had to go back for them. As I *entered* **11** the school grounds, the last bell for class *was ringing* **12**.

Ejercicio 51 | Forms of the Imperfect

Write the imperfect form of all the indicated verbs.

1 Vd. *quiere* estar allí mañana.
2 Todos los alumnos *empiezan* la lección.
3 No *es* posible hacerlo.
4 ¿Qué *buscas*?
5 Ella siempre *pide* un favor.

6 Este pájaro ya no *vuela*.

7 ¿Qué *piensan* hacer?

8 Pizarro *conoce* bien a Atahualpa.

9 *Trabajamos* mucho todos los días.

10 Tú *sabes* esto, ¿verdad?

11 Nunca *llueve* allí.

12 María *sigue* con sus amigas.

Ejercicio 52 | Discrimination of Events and Aspects

Indicate the type of event (cyclic or non-cyclic) by C or NC and then indicate its aspect (beginning, middle or end) by B, M, or E.

Christopher Columbus; Part I

It is generally believed that Columbus *was born* **1** in Genoa, Italy, around 1451. When they *baptized* **2** him, his parents gave him the name *Cristoforo* after the patron saint of sailors and travelers. Since they *lived* **3** in an important seaport, he had the chance to learn a great deal about boats and the sea. Throughout the entire city in those days there *circulated* **4** fabulous stories about strange lands beyond the sea.

He was poor and his life was hard, so in 1476 he *left* **5** his hometown on a ship bound for England. As they *sailed* **6** off the coast of Portugal, they were attacked by pirates. The boat *sank* **7** and many *drowned* **8**, but Columbus *swam* **9** and *reached* **10** the shore safely.

Years later in Portugal Columbus *married* **11** the daughter of a retired sea captain who had worked for Prince Henry the Navigator. Shortly after giving birth to their only son, Diego, his wife Felipa *died* **12**.

Ejercicio 53 | Discrimination of Events and Aspects

Analyze the events represented by the indicated verbs. Write C or NC for cyclic or non-cyclic and B, M, or E for aspect.

Christopher Columbus; Part II

Like other educated Europeans of the fifteenth century, Columbus *knew* **1** that the world was round. By sailing west, he *was sure* **2** that he could reach Asia and open a new route to the rich spice lands of the East. Silks, spices and other products from these lands *cost* **3** a lot in Europe in those days. Columbus *wanted* **4** to put together an expedition. He *needed* **5** a lot of money, but King John II of Portugal had refused to help him.

Discouraged, but not beaten, Columbus and Diego *left* **6** secretly for Spain in 1484. Father and son *arrived* **7** hungry and tired at a convent called La Rábida, near the southern port of Palos. Juan Pérez, confessor of Queen Isabella, *offered* **8** them food and shelter.

Some time later, leaving Diego at the convent school, Columbus *set out* **9** for court to see the rulers of Spain. People now *were calling* **10** him by his Spanish name, Cristóbal Colón. He was on his way to becoming the great "Admiral of the Ocean Sea."

Ejercicio 54 | Discrimination of Events and Aspects

First, categorize the event as cyclic or non-cyclic (C or NC) and then indicate its aspect (B, M, or E).

Christopher Columbus; Part III

Upon his arrival in Court, Colón *discussed* **1** his expedition with King Ferdinand and Queen Isabella of Spain. They *were fighting* **2** against the Moors at this time. The Queen in particular *wanted* **3** to help him, but the war *was costing* **4** them a great deal of money.

The Moors finally *surrendered* **5** in Granada, on January 2, 1492. Colón *returned* **6** to the royal castle, but this time his plan was turned down by the court experts. In despair, as he *rode* **7** away from Granada on a mule, perhaps on his way to France, a messenger from the Queen *stopped* **8** him on a bridge. Her Majesty had changed her mind and *was ready* **9** to sell her jewels in order to raise money for the voyage.

Colón *got* **10** his money, about $14,000, and the Queen's jewels did not have to be sold. The agreement papers *were signed* **11** and *sealed* **12** in April. On Friday, August 3, 1492, at 8:00 A.M., Cristóbal Colón and 87 reluctant men *sailed* **13** in three ships from Palos into history.

Ejercicio 55 | Discrimination of Events and Aspects

Mark each event as NC or C and its aspect as B, M, or E.

My Dog Doesn't Know the Days of the Week

(One of your classmates who has a dog named Taco is reporting to you what Taco did last Saturday morning.)

It was 7:00 in the morning, and I *was* fast *asleep* **1** in my bed. My dog, Taco, *came* **2** into my bedroom and *jumped* **3** on my bed. His loud barking *woke* me *up* **4**. I *glared* **5** at him, and he *got off* **6** the bed. He still *growled* **7** and *barked* **8** at me furiously and wouldn't leave the room. Finally, I *got out* **9** of bed and *chased* **10** him. I *closed* **11** the door and *went back* **12** to my warm bed. As I *lay* **13** there unable to go back to sleep, Taco *whined* **14** outside the door.

I finally *understood* **15** that my poor Taco doesn't know the days of the week.

Ejercicio 56 | Numbers and Adjectival Agreement

When necessary change the adjectives in parentheses to match the nouns.

1 Puedo contar . . . (doscientos veintiuno) estrellas ahora.

2 Tenemos . . . (veintiuno) ríos en . . . (nuestro) estado.

3 Hay muy . . . (poco) niebla hoy.

4 . . . (El) boca de . . . (el) señorita no está . . . (cerrado).

5 . . . (El) maestros . . . (chileno) están cerca del lago.

6 Es . . . (un) mosca muy . . . (bonito).

7 En . . . (su) escuela hay . . . (cuatrocientos cincuenta y uno) alumnos.

Ejercicio 57 | Present Tense Forms of Stem-changing Verbs

Write the appropriate present tense form for the infinitives given below.

1 . . . (Nevar) mucho en el invierno.
2 Yo . . . (querer) buscar una cometa más pequeña.
3 Ellos . . . (jugar) siempre con los niños de allí.
4 Pepe y Alicia . . . (seguir) a su maestro.
5 Quien mucho . . . (dormir), poco . . . (recordar).
6 Si nosotros . . . (pedir)mucho, ella . . . (servir) poco.
7 Las cometas . . . (volar) muy bien cuando hace viento.
8 ¿Qué . . . (pensar) tú hacer esta mañana?
9 Sí, señor, siempre . . . (llover) aquí en el mes de abril.
10 Él y yo . . . (empezar) los estudios a las cinco.

Ejercicio 58 | Preterit of Regular a-, e-, and i-Verbs

Write the combinations that your teacher will put on the board.

Ejemplo: 423 = Ella y yo aprendimos bastante.

1 Los habitantes	1 escribir	1 todo esto.
2 El héroe	2 aprender	2 demasiado.
3 Yo	3 recordar	3 bastante.
4 Ella y yo	4 olvidar	4 mucho.
5 Tú	5 comer	5 poco.

Ejercicio 59 | Preterit versus Imperfect

It is important that you understand what you read well enough to choose correctly between the two verb forms given in parentheses. Remember that the Imperfect is used for middle aspect, and the Preterit is used for beginning and end aspects.

El primer viaje de Colón

primer párrafo

En los últimos meses del año 1492, Colón (1 descubrió, descubría) varias islas pequeñas en la región de las Antillas. En la primera de estas islas, (2 capturó, capturaba) a varios de los nativos y los (3 llevó, llevaba) a sus barcos.° Para continuar sus exploraciones él (4 necesitó, necesitaba) guías° y estos nativos (5 pudieron, podían) ayudarle mucho. Mientras° Colón (6 viajó, viajaba) de un lugar a otro, los indios que le (7 acompañaron, acompañaban) le (8 hablaron, hablaban) constantemente de una tierra grande y rica que estaba al sur. Al° hablar de esta tierra la (9 llamaron, llamaban) siempre Cuba. (10 Pasaron, Pasaban) dos semanas y en la mañana del domingo, 28 de octubre, Colón y sus acompañantes (11 desembarcaron, desembarcaban) en la costa norte de Cuba. Inmediatamente el Almirante° (12 pensó, pensaba) que por fin ya estaba sobre el territorio del continente que él (13 buscó, buscaba).

boats
guides
While

Whenever

Admiral

Ejercicio 60 | Preterit versus Imperfect

Change the indicated verbs to past tense: either the Preterit or the Imperfect.
You are told whether each event is cyclic or non-cyclic and the aspect. You must
discover from context what the subject of the verb is, know whether it is to shift
into the Preterit or the Imperfect, and then select the appropriate verb form. The
answer to number 1 is *cambió*, the subject is Colón, it is the end of a cyclic event,
and the verb is *cambiar*, a regular *a*-verb.

El primer viaje de Colón

segundo párrafo

Colón *cambia* (1 C, E) el nombre que *tiene* (2 NC, M) la nueva tierra y la
llama (3 C, E) Juana. *Observa* (4 C, E) que los indios cubanos *viven* (5 NC, M)
en pequeños pueblos de pescadores° y que *son* (6 NC, M) muy pobres. La tierra
es (7 NC, M) extraordinariamente hermosa, un verdadero paraíso,° pero no
tiene (8 NC, M) especias° en abundancia. Tampoco *halla* (9 C, E) en ninguna
parte el oro° y las ricas ciudades de los libros de Marco Polo. *Quiere* (10 NC, M)
ver al Gran Khan, el fabuloso rey de China, porque le *trae*° (11 C, M) una carta
de los Reyes Católicos de España. Por todas estas razones, Colón no *está* (12 NC,
M) satisfecho en tierra cubana. El propósito fundamental de su viaje *es* (13 NC,
M) abrir una ruta nueva a las tierras de las especias. Aunque sus hombres *necesitan* (14 NC, M) descansar, *decide* (15 C, E) continuar el viaje por mar.

fishermen
paradise
spices
gold
is bringing

Ejercicio 61 | Preterit of Regular *a-*, *e-*, and *i*-Verbs

After reading each sentence, decide which of the four forms given is the correct
Preterit that fits the new subject. *¡Ojo!*: among the forms that you have to choose
from, some are Present, but you are asked to select the preterit form for the new
subject.

1 Los alumnos aprendieron mucho. Yo . . .

    a aprendió **b** aprendí **c** aprendiste **d** aprendo

2 La cometa voló muy bien. Las cometas . . .

    a volamos **b** vuelan **c** volaron **d** volé

3 Yo conocí a la nueva alumna. Él y yo . . .

    a conocimos **b** conocemos **c** conocen **d** conocieron

4 Las mujeres llevaron jarros. Yo . . .

    a llevé **b** llevo **c** llevó **d** llevaste

5 Usted halló el continente en el mapa. Tú . . .

    a hallé **b** hallas **c** halla **d** hallaste

6 Yo pinté un león muy feroz. Ellas . . .

    a pintan **b** pintó **c** pintamos **d** pintaron

Ejercicio 62 | Discrimination of Events and Aspects

Write C for cyclic, NC for non-cyclic and B, M, or E for aspect.

Babysitter's Nightmare

(A girl in your class is reporting what happened to her a few nights ago on her first babysitting job with the neighbor's 18-month-old son.)

When I *wasn't looking* **1**, the baby *picked up* **2** something brown that he *found* **3** on the floor and *swallowed* **4** it. I wasn't sure what it was, but immediately I thought of a pill, and I *worried* **5**.

When the baby's parents *returned* **6**, they didn't want to take any chances, so they *put* **7** him in the car, and we all rushed to the hospital. By the time we *arrived* **8** in the emergency room, I *was scared* **9** to death.

During the examination, however, the baby *seemed* **10** to be all right. The doctor *tickled* **11** him, and he *smiled* **12** happily. I *was crying*. **13**

We found out later that he had swallowed a chocolate covered peanut.

Ejercicio 63 | The Done-to *a*

If the done-to *a* is needed, write it. If not, leave a blank after the number of the corresponding sentence.

    1 Buscamos . . . los dos continentes de América en el mapa.

    2 Queremos conocer . . . la señora Gutiérrez.

    3 Pensamos comer . . . tres bananas mañana en la cafetería.

    4 Todos vimos . . . las estrellas anoche muy cerca de la luna.

    5 Primero tienen que servir . . . Juan.

    6 Debemos invitar . . . la nueva alumna a nuestra fiesta.

Ejercicio 64 | Forms of the Imperfect

Change the indicated verbs to the Imperfect. Do not change the number and person of the original sentence. Remember that only *ser*, *ver*, and *ir* are irregular in the Imperfect.

    1 Ellos siempre *vuelven* temprano.

    2 *Somos* de España.

    3 *Hay* mucha niebla y no *veo* muy bien. (Don't forget that *hay* is a verb. Do you remember what the infinitive is?)

4 En Brasil *hablan* portugués.

5 Él y yo *trabajamos* en la selva cerca de un lago.

6 Tú *vas* allí también, ¿verdad?

7 Yo *pienso* dormir hasta muy tarde mañana.

Ejercicio 65 | Present of *estar*

An irregular verb is one that does not follow the set pattern for regular verbs. Usually the irregularity is in the stem or first suffix and is not in all forms. *Estar* is an irregular *a*-verb. The *nosotros*-form is regular. There are only two other irregularities:

a The *yo*-form adds a *y* to the end with stress on the last syllable.

b The remaining forms (except *nosotros*) continue to stress the last syllable, necessitating a written accent over the *a* in the first suffix.

Yo	est	oy		Yo estoy en la clase.
Nosotros	est	a	mos	Nosotros estamos en la clase.
Tú	est	á	s	Tú estás en la clase.
Usted	est	á		Usted está en la clase.
Ustedes	est	á	n	Ustedes están en la clase.
Él	est	á		Él está en la clase.
Ellos	est	á	n	Ellos están en la clase.

Practice

A Cover the answers given to the side. As you work each problem, check your answer immediately.

1 To what verb set does *estar* belong? — *a*

2 What is irregular about the *yo*-form? — *oy* instead of *o*

3 Which form is regular? — *estamos*

4 Is the stress on the other forms on the first or last syllable? — last

5 Compare: *habla—está*. In *habla* is the stress on the first or last syllable? — first

6 In all forms of *estar* but *yo* and *nosotros* what must always be written over the first suffix? — an accent (')

B Complete the following verbs:

1 Tú est . . . en la oficina. — est*ás*

2 Tú y yo . . . mos en la oficina. — *esta*mos

3 María y Juan est . . . n bien hoy. — est*án*

4 Paco y yo est . . . bien también. — est*amos*

5 El cuaderno est . . . en el pupitre. — est*á*

6 ¿Dónde est . . . los papeles? — est*án*

7 ¿Cómo . . . usted? — *está*

8 Yo . . . y bastante bien, gracias. — *esto*y

C Write the correct form of *estar* in the Present:

1 Los profesores . . . en la oficina.   están
2 ¿Dónde . . . el señor Moreno?   está
3 Yo . . . muy bien hoy, gracias.   estoy
4 ¿Cómo . . . Paco y Lola?   están
5 Roberto y yo . . . en la clase de inglés.   estamos
6 ¿. . . ustedes en la escuela?   Están
7 Las ocho ventanas . . . allí.   están
8 Y tú, ¿cómo . . .?   estás

Ejercicio 66 | Present of *ser*

Ser is the most irregular verb in Spanish. It is an inconsistent combination of two old Latin verbs (*sedere*, to sit and *esse*, to be). Knowing that it is an *e*-verb is of little help. Although the forms are highly irregular, they are short and easy to learn because it is such a common verb. Notice that the second suffix is perfectly regular. It is necessary to combine the stem and first suffix into one because of the type of irregularities, but this makes it easier to learn.

Yo	soy		Yo soy de Colombia.
Nosotros	so	mos	Nosotros somos de Colombia.
Tú	ere	s	Tú eres de Colombia.
Usted	es		Usted es de Colombia.
Ustedes	so	n	Ustedes son de Colombia.
Él	es		Él es de Colombia.
Ellos	so	n	Ellos son de Colombia.

Practice

A Cover the answers given to the side. As you work each problem, check your answer immediately.

1 To what verb set does *ser* belong?   *e*
2 To make learning easier what is the stem combined with?   first suffix
3 Which suffix is perfectly regular?   second

B Make the following sentences plural or singular, the opposite of what is given:

Ejemplo: Soy de Argentina. = Somos de Argentina.
          Ellas son bolivianas. = Ella es boliviana.

1 Soy de Perú.   Somos de Perú.
2 Ellos son amables.   Él es amable.
3 Ella es de Lima.   Ellas son de Lima.
4 Somos chilenos.   Soy chileno.
5 Eres de aquí.   Son de aquí.

C Write the correct form of *ser* in the Present.

1	Tú . . . muy amable.	eres
2	Paco y yo . . . alumnos nuevos.	somos
3	¿Qué . . . esto?	es
4	¿Quién . . . ese señor?	es
5	Cuatro y dos . . . seis.	son
6	Yo . . . de Buenos Aires.	soy
7	Paco y Enrique . . . bolivianos.	son
8	Este . . . un lápiz.	es
9	¿De dónde . . . tú?	eres
10	Estas plumas . . . nuevas.	son
11	Nosotras . . . de la capital de Venezuela.	somos
12	Yo . . . el nuevo director de esta escuela.	soy

Ejercicio 67 | Present of *ir*

If the infinitive of this *i*-verb were *var* instead of *ir*, it would be regular in all forms except the *yo*-form that adds a *y*, the same as does *estar* and *ser* in that form. Except for the written accent in *estar*, *ir* and *estar* have the same pattern, that is, the first suffix is stressed in all forms. *Ir* does not need written accents because the forms that would take them are of only one syllable.

Yo	v	oy		Yo voy a la iglesia.
Nosotros	v	a	mos	Nosotros vamos a la iglesia.
Tú	v	a	s	Tú vas a la iglesia.
Usted	v	a		Usted va a la iglesia.
Ustedes	v	a	n	Ustedes van a la iglesia.
Él	v	a		Él va a la iglesia.
Ellos	v	a	n	Ellos van a la iglesia.

Practice

A Cover the answers; check your answer after each problem.

1	Although *ir* is an *i*-verb, what verb set do its forms resemble?	*a*
2	It is much easier to remember the forms of this verb if we think of its infinitive as being . . . instead of *ir*.	*var*
3	What is the irregular stem of *ir*?	*v*
4	What is irregular in the *yo*-form?	*a y is added*
5	Are there any irregularities in the second suffix?	*no*
6	Except for the written accent what verb has forms just like *ir*?	*estar*

B Write the present tense form of the verb in parentheses:

1	Yo . . . (estar) en las montañas, pero yo . . . (ir) a la playa.	estoy, voy
2	Paco, Lola y yo . . . (ir) al cine esta noche.	vamos
3	Este señor . . . (ir) al centro.	va
4	Elena y Mercedes . . . (ir) a comer en el café.	van

5 ¿... (Ir) usted al campo conmigo?   Va

6 Yo ... (ser) Juan Mendoza y yo ... (ir) a estudiar.   soy, voy

7 ¿De dónde ... (ser) ustedes?   son

8 Nosotros ... (ser) de Santiago, pero nosotros ... (estar) en   somos, estamos
Buenos Aires.

9 Tú ... (ir) al parque ahora, ¿verdad?   vas

10 Ella y yo ... (ir) a estudiar mañana.   vamos

11 ¿A dónde ... (ir) tú y Pepe esta tarde?   van

12 Pepe y yo ... (ir) al correo y a la tienda.   vamos

13 Tú ... (ser) el nuevo alumno.   eres

14 ¿Cuántos ... (ser) cuatro menos dos?   son

15 Tú ... (ir) a las montañas porque tú ... (estar) bastante bien   vas, estás
hoy.

Ejercicio 68 | The Pieces and Parts of the Verb

a Spanish has three sets of verbs determined by the vowel that precedes the *r* in
the infinitive or the *mos* in the Present:

Hablar is an *a*-verb (*hablamos*).
Leer is an *e*-verb (*leemos*).
Vivir is an *i*-verb (*vivimos*).

b The present tense forms of Spanish verbs consist of three parts:

1 The stem tells what the event is, *e.g.*, *habl*amos (speak), *lee*mos (read),
*viv*imos (live).

2 The first suffix tells when the event takes place, *e.g.*, *hablamos*, *leemos*,
vivimos, indicate Present.

3 The second suffix always indicates the number of the subject (singular or
plural) and in two cases the number and person. Thus *s* says the subject is *tú*
(*tú hablas*) and *mos* tells you the subject is *nosotros* (*nosotros hablamos*). The
suffix *n* indicates plural but does not tell you whether the subject is *ustedes* or
ellos (*ustedes hablan, ellos hablan*). When the second suffix is zero, the subject
is singular (*yo hablo, usted habla, ella habla, él habla*).

Practice

Cover the answers given to the side. As you work each problem, check
your answer immediately.

1 How many sets of verbs are there in Spanish?   three

2 What two verb forms indicate the set to which they belong?   infinitive and *mos*-form

3 What three vowels are used to label these three forms?   *a, e, i*

4 How many parts does each verb have in the Present?   three

5 Match the function of each part below:

   (1) Stem ...   **a** tells *when* the event occurs   **(1) b**

   (2) First suffix ...   **b** tells *what* the event is   **(2) a**

   (3) Second suffix ... **c** tells *who* performs the event **(3) c**

6 Divide this verb into its three parts: *estudian*.   *estudi-a-n*

7 What part of this verb tells that the action is "speak": *hablan*. *habl*

8 What part of this verb tells that *tú* is the subject (who performs the event): *vives*.

s

9 What part of this verb tells that the event is happening in the Present: *vives*.

e

10 What part of this verb is the stem? *hablan*

habl

11 What part of this verb is the first suffix? *hablas*

second *a*

12 What part of this verb is the second suffix? *leen*

n

13 Be careful! What part of this verb is the second suffix? *vive*

nothing (zero)

14 What part of this verb is the first suffix? *vivo*

o

Ejercicio 69 | Present of Regular *a*-Verbs

The following pattern for the Present of all regular *a*-verbs in Spanish may be used by replacing the stem of the model verb (*habl*) with the stem of any other regular *a*-verb. All that is necessary to be memorized is the first suffix (*o* and *a*) and the second suffix (*mos*, *s*, and *n*). To the right of the pattern each verb is used in a complete sentence. In actual speech the three forms *nosotros*, *él*, and *ellos* have alternate forms for females: *nosotras*, *ella*, and *ellas*.

Yo	habl	o		Yo hablo español.
Nosotros	habl	a	mos	Nosotros hablamos español.
Tú	habl	a	s	Tú hablas español.
Usted	habl	a		Usted habla español.
Ustedes	habl	a	n	Ustedes hablan español.
Él	habl	a		Él habla español.
Ellos	habl	a	n	Ellos hablan español.

Practice

A Cover the answers given to the side. As you work each problem, check your answer immediately.

1 What set verb is *hablar*, *a-*, *e-*, or *i-*?

a-

2 What part of *hablar* is the stem?

habl

3 What part of *estudiar* is the stem?

estudi

4 What set verb is *desear*?

a-

5 What part of *desear* is the stem?

dese

B Complete the following verbs:

1 Tú habl . . . inglés.

habl*as*

2 Ellas habl . . . francés.

habl*an*

3 Paco y yo . . . mos (use *hablar*) español.

*habl*amos

4 Paco y yo estudi . . . español.

estudi*amos*

5 Yo estudi . . . inglés.

estudi*o*

6 Paco estudi . . . inglés también.

estudi*a*

7 María y yo dese . . . hablar con el director.

dese*amos*

8 ¿Dese . . . tú hablar con el director?

Dese*as*

9 No, yo no . . . o (use *desear*) hablar con el director.

*dese*o

10 Paco y Lola estudi . . . mucho.

estudi*an*

C Write the present form of the verb in parentheses:

1 Ellos . . . (trabajar) en la mina.   trabajan
2 Paco y yo . . . (estudiar) mucho en la escuela.   estudiamos
3 La señorita se . . . (llamar) María Sánchez.   llama
4 Nosotras . . . (desear) estudiar aquí.   deseamos
5 ¿. . . (Necesitar) usted estudiar inglés?   Necesita
6 Sí, yo . . . (necesitar) estudiar inglés.   necesito
7 Venga con nosotros; Juan y yo . . . (trabajar) allí.   trabajamos
8 Los profesores . . . (trabajar) en la escuela.   trabajan
9 Yo me . . . (llamar) Benito Torres.   llamo
10 Ustedes . . . (hablar) mucho, ¿verdad?   hablan

Ejercicio 70 | Present of Regular *e*-Verbs

The following pattern for the Present of all regular *e*-verbs in Spanish may be
used by replacing the stem of the model verb (*le*) with the stem of any other
regular *e*-verb. All that is necessary to be memorized if you have learned the
pattern for *a*-verbs is to change *a* to *e* in the first suffix. Everything else remains
the same.

Yo	le	o		Yo leo la lección.
Nosotros	le	e	mos	Nosotros leemos la lección.
Tú	le	e	s	Tú lees la lección.
Usted	le	e		Usted lee la lección.
Ustedes	le	e	n	Ustedes leen la lección.
Él	le	e		Él lee la lección.
Ellos	le	e	n	Ellos leen la lección.

Practice

A Cover the answers given to the side. As you work each problem,
check your answer immediately.

1 What set verb is *trabajar?*   *a-*
2 What set verb is *comer?*   *e-*
3 What is the stem of *leer?*   le
4 In what suffix is there a difference between *a-* and *e-*verbs?   first suffix
5 What is the difference?   *a* becomes *e*
6 Is the rest of the pattern identical for both verbs?   yes

B Write the present tense form of the verb in parentheses:

1 Juan y Pancho . . . (comer) mucho.   comen
2 ¿. . . (Comer) tú mucho también?   Comes
3 Sí, yo . . . (comer) mucho también.   como
4 Pancho y yo . . . (leer) libros de tigres.   leemos
5 Paco . . . (comer) bastante, y Lola . . . (leer) bastante.   come, lee
6 . . . (Hacer) mucho frío hoy.   Hace
7 ¿A qué hora . . . (comer) ustedes?   comen
8 Nosotros . . . (comer) a las siete de la noche.   comemos

C This section contains *a*- and *e*-verbs and *ser* and *estar:*

1	Ellas . . . (esperar) aquí.	esperan
2	Usted . . . (deber) comer más.	debe
3	¿Cómo . . . (estar) ustedes?	están
4	Paco y yo . . . (ser) nuevos en esta escuela.	somos
5	¿En qué mina . . . (trabajar) Pancho y Enrique?	trabajan
6	María, Elena, y yo . . . (estudiar) en clase.	estudiamos
7	Tú . . . (ser) Benito, ¿verdad?	eres
8	Sí, yo . . . (ser) Benito.	soy
9	¿Tú . . . (estar) en la oficina hoy?	estás
10	Nosotras . . . (comer) aquí hoy.	comemos
11	Tú . . . (leer) la nueva lección, ¿verdad?	lees
12	Yo . . . (creer) que yo . . . (estar) bien, gracias.	creo, estoy

Ejercicio 71 | Present of Regular *i*-Verbs

The following pattern for the Present of all regular *i*-verbs in Spanish may be used by replacing the stem of the model verb (*viv*) with the stem of any other regular *i*-verb. All that is necessary to be memorized if you have learned the pattern for *e*-verbs is to change *e* to *i* only in the *nosotros*-form. Everything else remains the same.

Yo	viv	o		Yo vivo en la ciudad.
Nosotros	viv	i	mos	Nosotros vivimos en la ciudad.
Tú	viv	e	s	Tú vives en la ciudad.
Usted	viv	e		Usted vive en la ciudad.
Ustedes	viv	e	n	Ustedes viven en la ciudad.
Él	viv	e		Él vive en la ciudad.
Ellos	viv	e	n	Ellos viven en la ciudad.

Practice

A Remember to cover the answers but to check after each problem.

1	What set verb is *desear?*	*a-*
2	What set verb is *escribir?* What is the stem?	*i-, escrib*
3	What set verb is *deber?*	*e-*
4	What one form of *i*-verbs is different from *e*-verbs?	*nosotros*
5	What is the difference?	*e* becomes *i*
6	Is the rest of the pattern identical for both verbs?	yes

B Write the present form of the verb in parentheses:

1	Ellos . . . (escribir) la lección muy bien.	escriben
2	Ellos y yo . . . (escribir) con lápiz y pluma.	escribimos
3	¿. . . (Escribir) tú con lápiz o con pluma?	Escribes
4	¿Quién . . . (subir) al balcón?	sube
5	Yo . . . (vivir) en la capital.	vivo
6	¿Dónde . . . (vivir) tú?	vives

7 Y ustedes, ¿dónde . . . (vivir)?   viven

8 Nosotros . . . (subir) la montaña.   subimos

C Practice with *a-*, *e-*, and *i-*verbs:

1	Paco y yo . . . (trabajar) aquí.	trabajamos
2	Juana y yo . . . (vivir) aquí.	vivimos
3	Tú y yo . . . (comer) aquí.	comemos
4	¿Dónde . . . (vivir) ustedes?	viven
5	¿Dónde . . . (estudiar) ustedes?	estudian
6	¿Dónde . . . (leer) ustedes?	leen
7	Yo . . . (trabajar) en el banco.	trabajo
8	Yo . . . (subir) esta montaña.	subo
9	Yo . . . (correr) a la escuela.	corro
10	¿A qué hora . . . (comer) tú?	comes
11	Tú . . . (leer) y . . . (escribir) en la escuela, ¿verdad?	lees, escribes
12	Los niños . . . (entrar) en la iglesia.	entran
13	Tú . . . (hablar) muy rápido.	hablas
14	Paco y tú . . . (correr) con los animales.	corren

Ejercicio 72 | Translating "to be": *haber* and *estar* for Location

a It is necessary to learn when to use *haber* and *estar*, otherwise you may send a message you don't intend to send. They are both used in sentences that locate things and people. For example:

Hay una silla (señorita) aquí.

La silla (señorita) está aquí.

b *Hay* is from *haber*. It is frequently translated "is, are, there is, or there are." It always is used in the third person. The label for what is being located normally follows the verb.

Hay un gaucho en el rodeo.

Hay gauchos en el rodeo.

c *Haber* (*hay*) is used to locate entities that combine with

1 *un* or *una*:

Hay un muchacho en la oficina.

Hay una muchacha en la oficina.

2 nothing (zero):

Hay muchachos en la oficina.

Hay papel en la mesa.

3 public and private numbers:

Hay tres ventanas allí.

Hay muchas ventanas allí.

d *Estar* is used to locate entities when they are labeled by

1 an unmodified proper noun:

María está en España.

Pancho está en la escuela.

2 nouns that are combined with *el*, *los*, *la*, and *las*:

El señor está en Chile.

Las plumas están allí.

3 subject pronouns:

Yo estoy en Ecuador.

Ellos están en Paraguay.

e You will find some combinations of **c** and **d** above, in which case the articles (*un, una, el, los, la, las*), and zero (with plural proper nouns) take precedence. For example:

Hay tres lápices en el pupitre.   But: *Los tres lápices están en el pupitre.*

María está en la oficina.   But: *Hay una María en la oficina.*

¿Hay Marías en esta clase?

Practice

A Cover the answers on the right. Check your answers immediately after working each problem.

1 What two Spanish verbs are used to locate things and people?	estar; haber
2 Which verb is translated frequently by "there is" and "there are," *hay* or *está*?	hay
3 Which verb combines with the indefinite article (*un* or *una*) and numbers?	haber
4 Which verb combines with the definite article (*el, los, la,* and *las*)?	estar
5 When both the definite article and a number combine with a noun, which verb is used for location?	estar
6 Which verb combines with an unmodified proper noun?	estar
7 If a proper noun is preceded by *un* or *una* or if it is plural, which verb is used for location?	haber
8 Which verb combines with subject pronouns?	estar
9 Which verb combines with zero?	haber
10 Does *hay* usually precede or follow its object?	precede

B Choose *hay, está* or *están* for the following blanks:

1 Ella . . . en Ecuador.	está
2 Pancho y María . . . en España.	están
3 . . . cinco profesores en la familia.	Hay
4 ¿. . . el profesor en la oficina?	Está
5 ¿. . . una señorita en la oficina?	Hay
6 ¿. . . Pancho en la escuela?	Está
7 Sí, . . . tres Panchos en la escuela.	hay
8 En la clase . . . un profesor.	hay
9 El radio . . . en la mesa.	está
10 ¿. . . diez papeles aquí?	Hay
11 Sí, los diez papeles . . . allí en el pupitre.	están
12 Ellas no . . . aquí hoy.	están
13 . . . muchos libros en la cafetería.	Hay
14 Los tres Panchos . . . en la clase de inglés.	están

C Choose *un, una, el, los, la, las* or "zero" for the following blanks:

1 Hay . . . lápiz allí.	un
2 . . . oficina y . . . clase están allí.	La, la
3 Hay . . . pizarras en la oficina también.	zero

4 ¿Está . . . señor en la capital?	el
5 . . . reloj está en la mesa de la cafetería.	El
6 ¿Hay . . . papel en esta mesa?	un (or zero)
7 ¿Dónde hay . . . plumas?	zero
8 ¿Dónde están . . . papeles?	los

Ejercicio 73 | Translating "to be": *estar* for Health; *ser* for Origin and Equation

a Review the uses of *estar* and *haber* in Ejercicio 72. More practice is included here.

b *Estar* is used in sentences that talk about one's state of health. For example:
¿Cómo estás, Paco?
Yo estoy bien, gracias.

c *Ser* is used in sentences that tell where someone or something comes from (origin).
El libro es de España.
¿De dónde es usted?
Yo soy de Chile.

d *Ser* is used in sentences as a link between two items to show that they are equal.
Esta es una luz. (Esta = luz)
Cuatro y dos son seis. (4 + 2 = 6)
Ella es alumna. (Ella = alumna)

Practice

Cover the answers on the right. Check your answer immediately after working each problem.

A Which verb is used:

1	in sentences that locate things and people?	estar *or* haber
2	to make equations?	ser
3	when discussing one's state of health?	estar
4	when locating something that combines with the indefinite article?	haber
5	when indicating the origin of someone?	ser
6	in a sentence locating a person labeled by a subject pronoun?	estar
7	in addition and subtraction problems?	ser

B Choose *es, son, está,* or *están* for the following blanks:

1	La señorita . . . de Ecuador.	es
2	Las dos reglas . . . en el pupitre.	están
3	Este . . . el señor López.	es
4	Cinco y cinco . . . diez.	son
5	El alumno no . . . bien, hoy.	está
6	El alumno no . . . en la escuela hoy.	está

7 El alumno . . . de Argentina.	es
8 ¿Qué . . . esto?	es
9 . . . un reloj.	Es
10 Ellas . . . muy bien.	están

C Give in Spanish the infinitive of the verb that would be used in sentences pertaining to the following:

1 location with numbers	haber
2 location with "zero"	haber
3 equations	ser
4 one's state of health	estar
5 origin	ser
6 location with *el*	estar

D Choose the appropriate present tense form of *ser*, *haber* or *estar* according to the nature of the sentence:

1 Yo . . . muy bien, gracias.	estoy
2 ¿ . . . usted de Colombia?	Es
3 No, yo . . . de Brasil, pero . . . aquí ahora.	soy, estoy
4 ¿ . . . muchachos aquí de Ecuador? (*Be careful.*)	Hay
5 ¿ . . . aquí el muchacho de Ecuador?	Está
6 ¿ . . . usted de Ecuador?	Es
7 Yo . . . el nuevo profesor.	soy
8 ¿Cuántos . . . cinco menos tres?	son
9 ¿Cuántos diálogos . . . en este libro?	hay
10 . . . muchos diálogos en este libro.	Hay
11 ¿Dónde . . . María y José?	están
12 En la mesa . . . tiza.	hay
13 —¿El profesor está ausente? —Sí, no . . . bien hoy.	está
14 Ella . . . una señora muy amable.	es

Ejercicio 74 | Present of Stem-changing Verbs

Over a period of hundreds of years, when Latin was in the process of becoming Spanish, the present forms of some of the most commonly used verbs, with the exception of the first person *mos*-form, suffered three main types of changes in the stressed syllable of the stem:

1 stressed *e* became *ie*
2 stressed *o* became *ue*
3 stressed *e* became *i*

As a result of these historical changes, in present-day Spanish, three sets of verbs have stem variations (allomorphs) in the Present: one is regular (as in the infinitive) and it combines with *nosotros*, the other is irregular and it combines (with a few special exceptions) with all the other subject pronouns. The reason why the *mos*-form did not change is that the stem does not carry the stress. It falls, instead, on the vowel of the first suffix (*pen-sa-mos*).

a Set 1: *e* becomes *ie*. Model: *querer*

Yo	quier	o		Yo quiero comer algo.
Nosotros	quer	e	mos	Nosotros queremos comer algo.
Tú	quier	e	s	Tú quieres comer algo.
Usted	quier	e		Usted quiere comer algo.
Ustedes	quier	e	n	Ustedes quieren comer algo.
Él	quier	e		Él quiere comer algo.
Ellos	quier	e	n	Ellos quieren comer algo.

The chart and the sentences above show that the verb *querer* has two different stems: the regular *quer* which combines with the *nosotros*-form (*queremos*), and the irregular *quier*, where the *e* has become *ie*, which combines with all the other subject pronouns (*yo, tú, usted, ustedes, él, ella, ellos*).

b Set 2: *o* becomes *ue*. Model: *volver*

Yo	vuelv	o		Yo vuelvo a casa.
Nosotros	volv	e	mos	Nosotros volvemos a casa.
Tú	vuelv	e	s	Tú vuelves a casa.
Usted	vuelv	e		Usted vuelve a casa.
Ustedes	vuelv	e	n	Ustedes vuelven a casa.
Él	vuelv	e		Él vuelve a casa.
Ellos	vuelv	e	n	Ellos vuelven a casa.

The form *volvemos* contains the regular stem allomorph of the infinitive *volver*. In all the other forms the stem *vuelv* is irregular because the stressed *o* has changed to *ue*.

Included in this set also is the change *u* to *ue*, as in *jugar: juego, juega, juegas, juegan*, but *jugamos*. The old infinitive was *jogar*.

c Set 3: *e* becomes *i*. Model: *pedir*

Yo	pid	o		Yo pido permiso.
Nosotros	ped	i	mos	Nosotros pedimos permiso.
Tú	pid	e	s	Tú pides permiso.
Usted	pid	e		Usted pide permiso.
Ustedes	pid	e	n	Ustedes piden permiso.
Él	pid	e		Él pide permiso.
Ellos	pid	e	n	Ellos piden permiso.

Ped, the regular stem of *pedir*, occurs only in the first person plural (*pedimos*). *Pid*, the irregular stem, occurs in all the other forms because the *e* of the stem had become *i* under stress.

In all three sets above, as the name "stem-changing" indicates, the irregularities occur only in the stem. The suffixes in the last two columns are identical to those of regular *a*-, *e*-, and *i*-verbs.

Other irregular verbs are listed below according to sets, followed by their most common English translation.

	e > ie		*o > ue*		*e > i*
cerrar	to close	acostar (se)	to go to bed,	conseguir	to get
comenzar	to begin		lie down	decir	to say, tell
despertar	to wake up	almorzar	to eat lunch	despedir	to say good-by
divertir	to have fun	contar	to count, tell	impedir	to prevent, impede
empezar	to begin	costar	to cost	medir	to measure
entender	to understand	dormir	to sleep	pedir	to ask for
nevar	to snow	encontrar	to find, meet	reír	to laugh
pensar	to think, plan,	jugar	to play (games)	repetir	to repeat
	intend	llover	to rain	seguir	to follow, keep on
perder	to lose	morder	to bite	servir	to serve
preferir	to prefer	morir	to die	sonreír	to smile
quebrar	to break	mover	to move	vestir	to dress
querer	to want, love	poder	to be able, can		
sentar	to sit (down)	recordar	to remember		
sentir	to feel, regret,	volar	to fly		
	be sorry	volver	to return, come		
tener	to have		back		
tropezar	to trip				
venir	to come				

In the above verb list, it should be noted that *decir, tener* and *venir* have a third irregular stem allomorph, *dig, teng, veng*, respectively that combines with *yo*. In the case of *conseguir* and *seguir* the requirements of Spanish spelling demand the digraph *gu* before *e* and *i* but not before *o*: *sigo, seguimos, sigues, sigue, siguen.*

Practice

A Cover the answers on the right, but check your answer immediately after working each problem.

1 Do the changes *e* to *ie* or *i*, and *o* to *ue* occur in stressed or unstressed syllables?
stressed

2 In the *mos*-form of the verb, does the stress occur in the stem or in the first suffix?
first suffix

3 Does the *nosotros*-form take the regular or the irregular stem? *regular*

4 In *pensar*, is the irregular stem *pens* or *piens*? *piens*

5 Write the forms of *pensar* that combine with *tú, tú y yo*, and *ellos*.
piensas, pensamos, piensan

6 If the infinitive form is *servir* (*i*), how would you write in Spanish "I serve," "she serves," and "we serve"?
sirvo, sirve, servimos

7 Does the *e* of *sentar* become *ie* or *i* in the *ellos*-form? *ie (sientan)*

8 Does the *e* of *vestir* become *ie* or *i* in the *usted*-form? *i (viste)*

9 Does the *o* of *volar* become *ue* in the *mos*-form? *no*

10 How many irregular stems does *venir* have? *two (veng, vien)*

11 Write the irregular stem forms of *empezar, costar, reír*, and *jugar*.
empiez, cuest, rí, jueg

12 What are the regular and irregular stem variations (allomorphs) of *seguir*?
segu, sigu—sig

13 Write the Spanish translation of "I follow," "we follow," and "he follows."   *sigo, seguimos, sigue*

14 The verbs *sentar* and *sentir* have identical regular and irregular stems. What are they?   *sent, sient*

15 If 14 above is true, how can you tell the difference between the forms of *sentar* and *sentir?*   the first suffix is different

16 Which form, *sentamos* or *sentimos*, translates "we sit"?   *sentamos*

17 Write the equivalents of "I seat" and "I regret."   *siento, siento*

18 Write the equivalents of "he seats" and "he regrets."   *sienta, siente*

B Write the present tense *yo-* and *nosotros*-forms of the following verbs:

1	almorzar	almuerzo, almorzamos
2	cerrar	cierro, cerramos
3	conseguir	consigo, conseguimos
4	decir	digo, decimos
5	impedir	impido, impedimos
6	preferir	prefiero, preferimos
7	reír	río, reímos (*Note accent marks*)
8	vestir	visto, vestimos
9	jugar	juego, jugamos
10	repetir	repito, repetimos

C Write the infinitive form:

1	vuelan	volar
2	vistes	vestir
3	tropiezo	tropezar
4	sonríen	sonreír
5	sientes	sentir
6	sientas	sentar
7	sigues	seguir
8	pueden	poder
9	nieva	nevar
10	muerde	morder
11	llueve	llover
12	entienden	entender
13	divierten	divertir
14	despido	despedir
15	cuentan	contar

D Write the correct form of the Present of each infinitive given in parentheses:

1 Mi familia y yo ... (pensar) ir a México otra vez este verano.   pensamos

2 Las vacaciones ... (empezar) el 5 de junio.   empiezan

3 Mis abuelos no ... (querer) ir con nosotros.   quieren

4 Ellos ... (pensar) ir en agosto.   piensan

5 Agosto es el mes que ... (seguir) a julio.   sigue

6 Papá ... (tener) sus vacaciones en junio y él no ... (poder) esperar hasta agosto.   tiene, puede

7 En agosto . . . (llover) mucho pero no . . . (nevar). llueve, nieva

8 Nosotros no . . . (querer) estar fuera de nuestra casa en agosto. queremos

9 Cuando . . . (tener) vacaciones, nosotros . . . (dormir) hasta tenemos, dormimos
muy tarde y . . . (jugar) mucho. jugamos

10 Yo me . . . (divertir) mucho en la playa y . . . (dormir) menos divierto, duermo
que mis padres.

11 Cuando vamos a algún restaurante, mis padres . . . (pedir) piden
comida americana, pero yo . . . (pedir) algo típico de México. pido

12 Ellos y yo . . . (pedir) siempre agua mineral. pedimos

13 Los mexicanos . . . (jugar) fútbol y mis padres y yo nos . . . juegan, divertimos
(divertir) mucho viéndolos (*seeing them*).

14 En nuestra ciudad hay muchos aviones que . . . (volar) a vuelan
México.

15 Yo nunca . . . (poder) dormir en los aviones. puedo

16 Este año nosotros no . . . (poder) ir a México en avión. podemos

17 En los aviones . . . (servir) comidas deliciosas. sirven

18 Si yo no como bastante, yo me . . . (morir) de hambre. muero

19 Yo todavía . . . (recordar) la comida tan buena que comimos recuerdo
en el último viaje.

20 Cuando mis padres y yo . . . (volver) de México todos los años, volvemos
nuestros amigos y vecinos . . . (venir) a nuestra casa a ver las fotos vienen
del viaje.

21 Siempre nosotros les . . . (servir) algo de comer y de beber y servimos
todos se . . . (divertir) mucho. divierten

22 Así nosotros . . . (recordar) los momentos felices que pasamos recordamos
en nuestros viajes a México.

23 Mis amigos y yo nos . . . (morir) de risa (*laughter*) cuando morimos
vemos las fotos que mi padre sacó en la playa el año pasado.

24 Papá . . . (seguir) con el plan de salir de aquí el día 10 de junio. sigue

25 Yo . . . (seguir) observando el calendario todos los días y a sigo
veces . . . (pensar) que no es verdad que el tiempo . . . (volar). pienso, vuela
Como dice el dicho (refrán) español, "el que espera, desespera"
(*he who must wait becomes desperate*).

Ejercicio 75 | Agreement of Adjectives

a In Spanish there are two common sets of nouns:

1 One set is known as the *o*-set because nouns belonging to it combine with
the *o*-form of adjectives that have two forms, one ending in *o* and the other
in *a* (*nuevo, nueva*); e.g., *libro, cuaderno, papel*.

2 The other set is known as the *a*-set because nouns belonging to it combine
with the *a*-form of these same adjectives; e.g., *pluma, pizarra, luz*.

b There are two corresponding sets of adjectives, an *o*-set and an *a*-set; e.g.,
bueno—buena, nuevo—nueva.

c All nouns belong to one of these two sets, whether or not they end in *o* or *a*.
It is important to learn to which set each noun belongs.

d As you have already learned concerning the definite article (which is a type of adjective), when adjectives having two forms combine with nouns, they must match the nouns; *e.g., nuevo cuaderno, nueva silla, nuevo lápiz, nueva luz.*

e If nouns are plural, the adjectives that combine with them must also be plural. Adjectives ending in *o* and *a* become plural by adding *s; e.g., nuevos cuadernos, nuevas sillas, nuevos lápices, nuevas luces.*

f Study the following table:

el nuevo libro	la nueva pluma
los nuevos libros	las nuevas plumas
el nuevo papel	la nueva luz
los nuevos papeles	las nuevas luces

Practice

Cover the answers on the right. Check your answer immediately after working each problem.

A Indicate whether these nouns belong to the *o* or *a* set.

1	momentito	o
2	regla	a
3	profesor	o
4	reloj	o
5	noche	a
6	clase	a
7	pupitre	o
8	día	o
9	luz	a
10	tarde	a

B Match the adjective *argentino* (Argentinian) with the following nouns:

1	señora	argentina
2	muchachos	argentinos
3	alumnas	argentinas
4	silla	argentina
5	señores	argentinos
6	reloj	argentino
7	escuela	argentina
8	profesor	argentino

C Match the adjectives in parentheses (the singular *o*-form is given) with the nouns given in the following sentences:

1	. . . (El) . . . (nuevo) alumna es muy amable.	La nueva
2	Hay . . . (un) luz . . . (nuevo) en . . . (el) clase.	una, nueva, la
3	. . . (El) noches son . . . (bueno).	Las, buenas
4	Hay . . . (un) reloj . . . (argentino) allí.	un, argentino
5	. . . (El) muchachas son . . . (chileno).	Las, chilenas
6	Hay . . . (un) mesa en . . . (el) oficina . . . (nuevo).	una, la, nueva

7 ... (El) profesores son ... (chileno).	Los, chilenos
8 ... (Bueno) tardes, Paco.	Buenas
9 ... (Bueno) días, María.	Buenos
10 Mañana es ... (un) día ... (nuevo).	un, nuevo

Ejercicio 76 | Translating "to be": *ser* and *estar* with Predicate Adjectives

a The characteristics of everything that we talk about may be divided into two classes:

1 those characteristics that the speaker believes to be *normal* for whatever he is talking about, and

2 those characteristics that the speaker believes to be a *change from the normal*.

The grass in our lawn *is* green. (normal)

We have had no rain all summer; the grass *is* brown. (change from what is normal)

b In Spanish *ser* is used in sentences that describe a normal characteristic, and *estar* is used in sentences that describe a change from what is normal.

1 John is a good fellow; he *is* very kind. (*ser*, normal)

2 John *is* ill and grouchy today. (*estar*, change from what is normal)

c What one person considers a normal characteristic for something, another person may consider a change from what is normal, merely because each of them is accustomed to ascribing different characteristics to it. Thus, whether *ser* or *estar* is used is dependent upon what the speaker believes to be normal or a change from it.

1 Henry lives in a hot climate. To him, water *is* warm. (*ser*)

2 When he goes to northern Alaska where what is normal for water is to be cold, he will use *estar* when he says, "The water *is* cold."

3 But Bill, who lives in Alaska, when speaking of the very same water will use *ser* when he says, "The water *is* cold."

Practice

A Cover the answers on the right. Check your answer immediately after working each problem.

1 I don't want those flowers in my garden. I don't think they *are* very pretty.	ser
2 Violets *are* blue.	ser
3 With all the rain and wind storms we have had, the flowers in my garden *are* not very pretty this year.	estar
4 This particular variety of roses is supposed to be white. I wonder why they *are* so pink.	estar
5 The *ñandú*, a type of ostrich from the Argentine pampas, *is* very large.	ser
6 Although those apples *are* red, they won't ripen for several weeks yet.	estar
7 Don't pick the grapes in the patio. They *are* still quite sour.	estar
8 Don't eat the apples from that tree. They are the kind that are used for cooking only. They *are* very sour.	ser

From the capital it is a two-day journey to this Bolivian country school, one day by truck and one on foot. Many children live so far from school that it is not possible for them to attend.

Old brick sidewalks and dirt roads characterize many small towns. The tin rooftops in the Catavi mining district are evidence of Bolivia's major natural resource.

In the Andes housewives
depend on simple techniques
for such tasks as grinding flour
or doing the weekly laundry.

A family in rural Colombia gathers for the main meal in the early afternoon. Though living quarters are small, there is room for everybody at bedtime.

9 Sugar *is* sweet. — ser

10 Compared with the Mayas, the Aztecs *were* cruel and warlike. — ser

11 *Quebracho* wood from trees that grow in the Paraguayan jungles *is* very hard. — ser

12 He just saw his report card. He's very happy! — estar

13 From the very beginning he has made A's. He *is* so intelligent! — ser

14 Francisco Pizarro, conqueror of Perú, had difficulty recruiting men for his expeditions. He *was* cruel, but very brave and heroic. — ser

15 She has always been so healthy. I'm surprised she *is* so sick now. — estar

16 My bank account *is* very low now. Can you wait till the end of the month? — estar

17 Lautaro and Caupolicán, Araucanian Indian warriors from Chile, *were* very brave. — ser

18 There is a section along the Peruvian coast where it rains approximately once every ten years. That area *is* dry. — ser

19 After the defeat his troops suffered in Tenochtitlán, the Aztec capital, Cortés *was* very sad. — estar

20 Lake Titicaca on the border between Perú and Bolivia *is* the highest in the world. — ser

B Choose *es*, *está*, or *hay* to fill the blanks in the following sentences:

1 El señor Granados . . . profesor. — es

2 ¿Qué hora . . .? — es

3 Cuatro menos dos . . . dos. — son

4 ¿De dónde . . . usted, señorita? — es

5 Pancho . . . bastante bien esta mañana. — está

6 El tiempo en este país . . . terrible todo el año. — es

7 Nuestra amable maestra . . . furiosa. — está

8 Creo que . . . siete tigres en este zoológico. — hay

9 Hoy . . . lunes, ¿verdad? — es

10 Mi nuevo libro . . . sucio. — está

11 Comparado con Brasil, Paraguay . . . pequeño. — es

12 El desierto de Chile no . . . húmedo, . . . muy seco. — es, es

13 El barco . . . muy grande, y ahora . . . en el Mar Caribe, pero . . . de Valparaíso, ciudad de Chile. — es, está, es

14 Sí, . . . un tigre en el banco, pero no . . . el tigre del zoológico. — hay, es

Ejercicio 77 | English "come" and "go" versus Spanish *venir* and *ir*

a The verbs "come" (*venir*) and "go" (*ir*) have two basic meanings in both English and Spanish. "Come" (*venir*) refers to movement *toward* the person who is speaking (the speaker), and "go" (*ir*) refers to movement *away from* the the speaker.

He comes here tomorrow.   *Viene aquí mañana.*
I go there tomorrow.   *Voy allá mañana.*

b Spanish is quite rigid in following this usage. However, in English it is customary to follow it not only from the point of view of the speaker, but also from the point of view of the person spoken to. Therefore, "come" may be used to indicate movement away from the location of the speaker provided that it means movement toward the person spoken to. Spanish must continue to use "go" (*ir*) in this situation.

Come here.	*Venga usted aquí.*
I'm coming (*not* going).	*Voy* (not *Vengo*).

Therefore, *venir* may always be translated as "come," but *ir* translates both "come" and "go." It is necessary to know that English "come" indicating movement away from the speaker toward the person spoken to must be translated by *ir*, not *venir*. Spanish uses *venir* to translate the first sentence below, but *ir* in translating the second.

You are talking on the phone to a friend and ask, "Are you *coming* (*venir*) to my house tonight?"
He answers you, "No, I can't *come* (*ir*) tonight."

A Cover the answers on the right. Choose *venir* or *ir*, then check your answer immediately after working each problem.

1	*Come* here, Mary. It is time to *go* to the store.	venir, ir
2	I'm *coming*, Mother. I want to *go* with you.	ir, ir
3	John has just broken his leg. You phone the doctor and he says, "*Come* here right away."	venir
4	You answer, "I can't *come* because I don't have a car."	ir
5	He answers, "I don't have any patients right now, so I'll *come* to your house."	ir
6	You respond, just before hanging up, "Oh, thank you. Please *come* as fast as you can."	venir
7	In the evening at the dinner table Mother says, "Father is not *coming* home tonight; he has to *go* to a convention."	venir ir
8	You answer your teacher who is calling from school, "I shall *come* tomorrow if there is a test."	ir
9	She answers, "Please don't *come* unless you feel up to it."	venir
10	Your cranky aunt, listening in on the other phone, retorts, "She'll be *coming* tomorrow even if she is half dead."	ir

B Choose one of the two verbs in parentheses:

1	Hablas con un amigo en la escuela. —Pancho no . . . (viene, va) a clase hoy porque está enfermo.	viene
2	—Tú y yo debemos . . . (venir, ir) a hablar con él esta noche, ¿verdad?	ir
3	—Profesor, tengo un gran problema. . . . (Venga, Vaya) usted aquí, por favor.	Venga
4	El profesor responde, — . . . (Vengo, Voy) en un momentito. Estoy ocupado ahora.	Voy
5	Cada sábado . . . (vengo, voy) al cine. (*Speaker is at home.*)	voy
6	Paco habla con un amigo por teléfono, —¿No quieres . . . (venir, ir) aquí esta noche a estudiar?	venir
7	—Sí, quiero . . . (venir, ir) pero no puedo, —contesta su amigo.	ir

Ejercicio 78 | Negative Words and Sentences

Compare the following English-Spanish sentences. The negative words are in boldface type and the verbs are italicized.

1 I **don't** *speak*.	(Yo) **no** *hablo*.
2 **Don't** you *speak?*	¿**No** *habla* usted?
3 She **doesn't** *speak*.	(Ella) **no** *habla*.
4 She **doesn't** *wish to speak*.	(Ella) **no** *desea hablar*.
5 I *must* **not** *speak*.	(Yo) **no** *debo hablar*.
6 I *speak* **not**.	(Yo) **no** *hablo*.
7 I *speak* **no** more.	(Yo) **no** *hablo* más.
8 There *is* **no** class.	**No** *hay* clase.
9 **No** *smoking*.	**No** *fumar*.

The above patterns reveal that

a three forms of the English negative (no, not, n't) become one in Spanish (*no*).

b forms of the verb *to do* (do, does, did) frequently accompany the English negative and are needed for support (*I not speak* is not said); Spanish *no* does not need any supporting verb and when translating from English to Spanish, the equivalent of *do, does,* and *did* is zero, that is, those forms are omitted: "he doesn't speak" = *no habla*; "we don't speak" = *no hablamos*.

c the position of Spanish *no* in the sentence is fixed before the verb; it is quite variable in English—before and after the verb and between the helping and main verbs.

d *no* is an adverb in Spanish; in English *not* is an adverb (He does *not* speak), and *no* functions as an adjective (He has *no* time. He is *no* genius.)

Besides *no* you have learned the negative words *nunca, nadie* and *nada* which can also occupy the place of *no* before the verb of the sentence:

> Yo *no* escribo—Yo *nunca* escribo.
> *No* va—*Nadie* va.
> *No* tengo—*Nada* tengo.

Unlike English usage that frowns upon double negative patterns, which do not produce a positive, Spanish *no* readily combines with other negative words to form double and even triple negatives which occur frequently and are viewed as perfectly normal by Spanish speakers—the more negatives, the stronger the negation. In Spanish double negative patterns, *no* occupies its normal fixed position before the verb and other negative words have to follow it:

> Yo no escribo; Nunca escribo; Yo *no* escribo *nunca*.
> No va; Nadie va; *No* va *nadie*.
> No tengo; Nada tengo; *No* tengo *nada*.

Practice

A Cover the answers on the right. Check your answer immediately after working each problem.

1 What are the three English equivalents of Spanish *no?*   no, not, n't

2 In translating the phrases *don't, do not, doesn't, does not, didn't*
and *did not* into Spanish, which words will you delete? do, does, did

3 What is the Spanish for *He doesn't work?* (*Él*) *no trabaja*

4 Does the position of Spanish *no* change from sentence to
sentence? no

5 Where is Spanish *no* always placed in relation to the verb of
the sentence? immediately before

6 What is the Spanish for *Tom is not here?* *Tomás no está aquí.*

7 How would you translate *There is no class today?* *No hay clase hoy* or *Hoy*
no hay clase.

8 In writing compositions for your English class, are you allowed
to use double negative patterns like *I don't know nothing?* no

9 How many negatives appear in the pattern *Yo no sé nada*
nunca? three (*no, nada, nunca*)

10 When two negative words are used in the same Spanish
sentence, where does *no* always go in relation to the verb? before

B Rewrite the following sentences making them negative according to the instructions given for each group.

a Use only the negative *no:*

1	Vamos al cine.	No vamos al cine.
2	Ellos viven aquí.	Ellos no viven aquí.
3	Yo como en este café.	Yo no como en este café.
4	Él estudia siempre con Elena.	Él no estudia siempre con Elena.
5	Aquí hay muchos ecuatorianos.	Aquí no hay muchos ecuatorianos.
6	¿Tiene algo para Pepe?	¿No tiene algo para Pepe?
7	¿Vas al cine esta noche?	¿No vas al cine esta noche?

b Use *one* negative word other than *no:*

8	Alguien está en el patio.	*Nadie* está en el patio.
9	Algo tienen en el banco.	*Nada* tienen en el banco.
10	Siempre escribo a mis amigos.	*Nunca* escribo a mis amigos.
11	Todos hablan español.	*Nadie* habla español.

c Use *two* negative words one of which must be *no:*

12	Como siempre en la cafetería.	*No* como *nunca* en la cafetería.
13	Comemos algo en la escuela.	*No* comemos *nada* en la escuela.
14	En casa hay alguien.	En casa *no* hay *nadie.*
15	¿Sabe alguien la lección?	¿*No* sabe *nadie* la lección?
16	Alberto sabe mucho de música.	Alberto *no* sabe *nada* de música.

d Rewrite the following sentences making them affirmative:

17	No trabajo nunca los domingos.	Trabajo (siempre) los domingos.
18	No tiene nada en el banco.	Tiene algo en el banco.
19	¿No vas al teatro con ellos?	¿Vas al teatro con ellos?
20	Mañana no viene nadie.	Mañana viene alguien.

e Translate into Spanish using *no* and a second negative word:

21	The boy never wants to work.	El muchacho *no* desea trabajar *nunca.*

22 Lola never goes to the park.   Lola *no* va al parque *nunca*.
23 There is no one at home.   *No* hay *nadie* en casa.
24 I don't have anything.   *No* tengo *nada*.
25 I never study in the morning.   *No* estudio *nunca* por la mañana.

Ejercicio 79 | Present of *hacer, poner, saber,* and *ver*

All four of these verbs are *e*-verbs and are regular in all forms except *yo*. The *yo*-form of *hacer*, had it been regular in spelling, would have been *haco*. If the sound represented by this *c* is voiced, it becomes the present tense irregular form *hago*. To make it simple, just remember that the *c* changes to *g*.

Yo	hag	o		Yo hago esto bien.
Nosotros	hac	e	mos	Nosotros hacemos esto bien.
Tú	hac	e	s	Tú haces esto bien.
Usted	hac	e		Usted hace esto bien.
Ustedes	hac	e	n	Ustedes hacen esto bien.
Él	hac	e		Él hace esto bien.
Ellos	hac	e	n	Ellos hacen esto bien.

The only irregularity in *poner* is in the *yo*-form which adds *g* to the end of the stem, *pongo*.

Yo	pong	o		Yo pongo esto allí.
Nosotros	pon	e	mos	Nosotros ponemos esto allí.
Tú	pon	e	s	Tú pones esto allí.
Usted	pon	e		Usted pone esto allí.
Ustedes	pon	e	n	Ustedes ponen esto allí.
Él	pon	e		Él pone esto allí.
Ellos	pon	e	n	Ellos ponen esto allí.

The *yo*-form of *saber* is irregular because it uses only *s* for the stem rather than *sab*, and it substitutes *é* for the first suffix in place of *o, yo sé*.

Yo	s	é		Yo sé hablar español.
Nosotros	sab	e	mos	Nosotros sabemos hablar español.
Tú	sab	e	s	Tú sabes hablar español.
Usted	sab	e		Usted sabe hablar español.
Ustedes	sab	e	n	Ustedes saben hablar español.
Él	sab	e		Él sabe hablar español.
Ellos	sab	e	n	Ellos saben hablar español.

The old infinitive of *ver* was *veer* (like *leer*). The present tense form of *yo* still uses the stem from the old infinitive, *veo*. All other forms are built from the newer infinitive, *ver* and are regular.

Yo	ve	o		Yo veo el océano.
Nosotros	v	e	mos	Nosotros vemos el océano.
Tú	v	e	s	Tú ves el océano.
Usted	v	e		Usted ve el océano.
Ustedes	v	e	n	Ustedes ven el océano.
Él	v	e		Él ve el océano.
Ellos	v	e	n	Ellos ven el océano.

Practice

A Remember to cover the answers but to check after each problem.

1 To what set of verbs do these four belong?   *e-*
2 Which form is irregular in all of them?   *yo*
3 Are all the other forms regular?   yes
4 What does the *c* in the stem of *hacer* change to in the *yo*-form?   *g*
5 What is irregular about the stem of *poner* in the *yo*-form?   a *g* is added
6 What allomorph for the stem of *saber* is used for the *yo*-form?   *s*
7 Did you notice that *saber* has *e* in the first suffix for all forms? How does the *e* in the *yo*-form differ from the other first suffixes?   it has an accent
8 What was the old infinitive of *ver* from which comes the stem of *veo?*   *veer*

B Rewrite the following sentences substituting the new subject given following each sentence. Check your verb with the answers given.

1 Ella pone el pupitre cerca de la puerta. Yo ...   pongo
2 ¿Qué hacen ustedes a las cinco? ¿... tú ...?   haces
3 Yo pongo el radio allí. Ustedes ...   ponen
4 Paco no sabe esto. Yo ...   sé
5 ¿Ves tú el nuevo barco? ¿... ustedes ...?   Ven
6 Sí, nosotros vemos ese barco. ... yo ...   veo
7 Yo no sé qué hacer. Guillermo y Jesús ...   saben
8 Yo hago esta lección. Tú y yo ...   hacemos

C Write the present form of the verb in parentheses:

1 Yo ... (saber) que esto ... (ser) verdad.   sé, es
2 Ana ... (ver) la tiza y ella ... (poner) una tiza en la mesa del profesor.   ve, pone
3 Yo no ... (ver) la página correcta.   veo
4 El muchacho alto no ... (saber) responder.   sabe
5 Yo siempre ... (hacer) mucho trabajo el lunes.   hago
6 Bueno, ¿qué ... (hacer) nosotros?   hacemos
7 Todos los días cuando yo ... (llegar) a la escuela yo ... (poner) mi cuaderno en mi pupitre.   llego, pongo
8 Yo no ... (ser) un alumno muy inteligente, pero yo ... (escribir) todos los verbos correctamente.   soy, escribo

Ejercicio 80 | Possessive Adjectives

a This is a table of the basic possessive adjectives equated with the corresponding subject pronouns and with English translations:

yo	mi	*my*
nosotros	nuestro	*our*
tú	tu	*your (thy, thine)*
usted	su	*your*
ustedes	su	*your*
él	su	*his*
ella	su	*her*
ellos	su	*their*
ellas	su	*their*

b Possessive adjectives (besides matching the possessor, "my" = *mi*), must match in number (singular or plural) the object possessed. This is not true in English where they must only match the possessor.

mi barco (my boat)	*mis barcos* (my boats)
tu padre (your parent)	*tus padres* (your parents)
nuestro tío (our uncle)	*nuestros tíos* (our uncles)

c *Nuestro* is the only form that must also match *o* and *a* type nouns.

nuestro hermano	*nuestros hermanos*
nuestra hermana	*nuestras hermanas*

d *Su* translates "his, her, their, your, its."

su familia = his family, her family, their family, your family, its family

e The meaning of *su* must be clear in the context (surrounding information) or in the life situation. Otherwise, it may need to be clarified by *de* + the label for the possessor.

su hijo = *el hijo de Juan, el hijo de usted, or el hijo de ellos, etc.*

Practice

A Cover the answers on the right. Check your answer immediately after working each problem.

1 Possessive adjectives in Spanish have two forms, a singular form and a ... form. — plural

2 They must agree with (match) both the thing possessed as well as the .... — possessor

3 What is the plural form for *tu* and *mi?* — *tus, mis*

4 Which possessive adjective must also match *o* and *a* type nouns? — *nuestro*

5 Which possessive adjective is very ambiguous (could have several different translations)? — *su*

6 What other two translations besides "their," "your," and "his" does *su* have? — her, its

7 To clarify the meaning of *su* it may be necessary to use ... + the label for the possessor. — *de*

B Choose the appropriate possessive adjective. The subject of the sentence is also the possessor.

1	Vamos a comer en . . . casa.	nuestra
2	¿Tienes . . . libros hoy?	tus
3	Yo tengo . . . reloj aquí.	mi
4	Ellos van a . . . montañas.	sus
5	María Elena está en . . . país ahora.	su
6	El elefante tiene . . . casa en el parque.	su
7	Ella y yo tenemos que ir a . . . banco.	nuestro
8	Yo siempre trabajo con . . . primos.	mis
9	Roberto está en casa con . . . tía.	su
10	Tenemos que visitar a . . . hermanas.	nuestras
11	Ahora vivimos en . . . primera ciudad.	nuestra
12	Tú tienes que salir en . . . barco, ¿verdad?	tu
13	¿Cuándo vas a . . . clase de portugués?	tu
14	Vamos a invitar a . . . maestros a la fiesta.	nuestros

Ejercicio 81 | General Review

Try to sound like native speakers of Spanish as you ask and answer these questions.

> ¿ Cuántos son cuatro y dos?
> (*Hold up your notebook.*) ¿ Qué es esto?
> ¿ Cuántos libros tienes hoy?
> ¿ Qué día es hoy?
> ¿ Cuál es la capital de Colombia?
> ¿ Qué tiempo hace hoy?
> ¿ Comes mucho por la noche?
> ¿ A qué hora estudias tu lección de español?
> ¿ Cuántos son quince menos cinco?
> ¿ Cuántos días hay en una semana?

Ejercicio 82 | Seasons, Months, Days, and Ordinal Numbers

Work with a partner and take turns asking and answering these questions:

> ¿ Cuáles son las cuatro estaciones del año?
> ¿ Cuáles son los meses del año?
> ¿ Cuáles son los días de la semana?
> ¿ Cuál es el segundo mes del año?
> ¿ Cuál es el tercer día de la semana?
> ¿ Cuál es la cuarta estación?

Ejercicio 83 | Guided Conversation

Your partner and you should perform this dialog in Spanish following the English outline. Go through it twice reversing roles.

1 You meet a friend on the street in the morning hours and exchange greetings.
2 You ask your friend how his sister is.
3 He answers that she is not too well.
4 You ask him if he is going to school now.
5 He answers no, that it is Saturday and there is no school.
6 You answer that he is right, it is Saturday. You ask where he is going.
7 He answers that he is going to the store, and in the afternoon (*por la tarde*) he is going to the country.
8 You ask him if he is going to visit relatives (*parientes*).
9 He says no, that he has a friend that lives in the country.
10 You excuse yourself and say that you have to go to the movies.
11 He sneezes.
12 You say the appropriate thing.
13 You both say good-by until Monday (*hasta el lunes*).

Ejercicio 84 | Role-Playing the Native: Geography

Work with a partner and take turns asking and answering the following questions:

1 ¿Cuál es el idioma principal de tu país?
2 ¿Es tu país una isla?
3 ¿Hay muchas selvas o muchas llanuras en tu país?
4 ¿Hay montañas en tu país?
5 ¿Cómo se llaman las montañas principales?
6 ¿Cómo se llama el río principal?
7 ¿Hay un lago importante en tu país?

Etapa Seis

Some Pronouns for the Doer and Done-to

1 You have probably played the game of asking someone to solve a riddle. A riddle is a puzzling question that has an obvious answer which most people cannot guess. Here is a linguistic riddle. How many pronoun names may you have when you are the speaker in English? What is your guess? One? Two? Three?

The right answer is three: *me, myself,* and *I.* (The possessive *my* is excluded because it functions as an adjective.)

2 You are the person who says the following sentence and also the doer (the one who performs the action). What do you call yourself? "(a) Me (b) Myself (c) I ⁓⁓⁓ eat ice cream."

I (When you are the speaker, and the doer, your name is *I.* *I* eat ice cream; *I* play the piano; *I* saw the satellite.)

3 You speak the following sentence. This time, however, you are not the doer; you are the done-to. What is your name now? "José bumped ⁓⁓⁓."

me (This is your name when you are the speaker and someone does something to you: He hit *me;* They saw *me;* She loves *me.*)

4 You make the following statement. You are now the speaker, the doer, and the done-to. As the doer, your name is *I.* What is your done-to name? "I hurt ⁓⁓⁓."

myself

5 You are the speaker for several persons who, as a group, are the doers. What is the subject pronoun name for *you and the group?* "⁓⁓⁓ went to the beach yesterday."

We

6 What is the pronoun name for *you and the group* when all of you are the done-to? "The storm did not scare ⁓⁓⁓."

us

7 What do you say? (a) We saw us in the mirror. (b) We saw ourselves in the mirror.

We saw ourselves in the mirror.

8 When you speak for the group and something (or someone) else is the doer, the pronoun name for *you and the group* as the done-to is (a) us (b) ourselves.

us (They heard us; She saw us.)

9 When you are the speaker for yourself and the group and *you and the group* are both the doer and the done-to, your name as the doer is *we* and your name as the done-to is ⁓⁓⁓.

ourselves

10 Let's review. When I am the speaker and the doer, my subject-pronoun name is ⁓⁓⁓.

I (I hear music.)

11 When I am the speaker, the doer, and the done-to, my name as the done-to is ⁓⁓⁓.

myself (I washed myself.)

12 When I am the speaker and the done-to, but someone else is the doer, my pronoun name is ‿‿‿.

me (Can you see me?)

13 The subject of a simple sentence may be the doer. The doer in *Alberto caught a shark* is ‿‿‿.

Alberto

14 The subject and the doer in *The shark bit Alberto* is ‿‿‿.

The shark

15 What subject pronoun may be used in place of *Alberto* in *Alberto caught a shark?*

He

16 What done-to pronoun must be used to replace *Alberto* in *The shark bit Alberto?*

him

17 We may use two different pronouns to talk about Alberto, either *he* or *him*. The form *him* tells everyone that Alberto is (a) the doer (b) the done-to.

the done-to (We don't say, "Him caught a shark.")

18 *She* stands for the (a) doer (b) done-to.

doer (She grabbed the cat.)

19 The done-to pronoun that replaces *she* is ‿‿‿.

her (The cat scratched her.)

20 Do *they* and *them* seem to have the same stem?

yes

21 Which form marks the done-to? (a) they (b) them

them (They see me; I see them.)

22 The suffix *m* of *him* and *them* is the mark of the (a) doer (b) done-to.

done-to

23 Which pronoun in *Can you hear me?* stands for the doer?

you

24 Which pronoun in *Yes, I can hear you* stands for the done-to?

you

25 Do the two examples above prove that *you* may stand for either the doer or the done-to?

yes

26 There is one more English pronoun which can stand for either a doer or a done-to which is a thing. Can you guess?

it (I see it; it sees me.)

27 The subject of a simple sentence is the doer. The object on which the action is performed is the done-to. The pronouns *me, us, him, her* and *them* are (a) subject pronouns (b) object pronouns.

object pronouns

28 The subject pronoun that replaces *her* is ‿‿‿.

she

29 The subject pronouns that replace *me, us, him,* and *them* are ‿‿‿.

I, we, he, they

30 Spanish, like English, has special pronoun forms for the doer (subject) and the done-to (object). The translation of *Yo te vi* is "I saw you." Look at the form *te*. What subject pronoun form has the same stem?

tú

31 *Yo te vi* translates "I saw you." The translation of *Tú me viste* is ‿‿‿.

You saw me. (Say English "me" and Spanish *me* aloud.)

32 The doer (subject) pronoun form that matches the Spanish *me* is ‿‿‿.

yo

33 Look at *Las muchachas nos vieron.* What subject (doer) pronoun begins with *nos?*

nosotros or nosotras

34 Translate: *Las muchachas nos vieron.*

The girls saw us.

35 Let's review before you forget what you have just learned. The *tú*-form stands for (a) the doer (b) the done-to.

the doer (and subject)

36 To change *tú* to the done-to form, you replace the suffix *ú* with ———.

e (*Tú me ves; Yo te veo.*)

37 The done-to form that replaces *yo* is ———.

me

38 The done-to form of either *nosotros* or *nosotras* is the shortened form ———.

nos (*Tú nos viste ayer.*)

39 The normal English translation of *Ellos nos vieron* is (a) They us saw. (b) They saw us.

They saw us.

40 In English the done-to (object) pronoun comes *after* the verb. In Spanish the object (done-to) pronoun comes ——— the verb.

before

41 Translate: They see me.

Ellos me ven.

42 This sentence talks about *tú*. Translate: They see you.

Ellos te ven.

43 Translate: They see us.

Ellos nos ven.

44 The English cognate of *visitar* is "to ———."

visit

45 Translate: *Ellos van a visitarnos.*

They are going to visit us.

46 Translate: *Ellos van a visitarme.*

They are going to visit me.

47 The grammatical name for the forms *visitar* and "to visit" is ———.

infinitive

48 In both English and Spanish, the done-to (object) pronouns follow the infinitive. (a) true (b) false

true

49 Look at the spaces between the words in these two sentences: *Ellos van a llamarnos.* "They are going to call us." How is Spanish different from English? The Spanish done-to pronoun is ———.

attached to the infinitive form in writing (The same is true in speech. Say *Ellos van a llamarnos* aloud.)

50 The form *llamar* is called an "infinitive." In contrast, the form *llaman* is said to be "finite" (the opposite of in-finite) because it has suffixes indicating tense, person, and number. The translation of *Ellos llaman* may be ———.

They call (or are calling).

51 Now, remember what you learned earlier. Where will you put the Spanish done-to form *me*? (a) *Ellos me llaman.* (b) *Ellos llaman me.*

Ellos me llaman.

52 In Spanish, as in English, the done-to form follows a finite verb form. (a) true (b) false

false (The done-to pronoun comes immediately before the finite verb form in Spanish.)

53 Which will you say? (a) *Él nos mira.* (b) *Él mira nos.*

Él nos mira.

54 Which will you say? (a) *Yo te veo.* (b) *Yo veo te.*

Yo te veo.

55 Now, be careful. Which will you say? (a) *Voy a visitarte.* (b) *Voy a te visitar.*

Voy a visitarte. (You can say *Te voy a visitar,* but for the present follow the rule that the done-to pronoun follows and is attached to the infinitive form.)

56 Here are some facts which are going to be important for you to know. There are three sets of pronouns in English: (1) the doer or subject pronouns, (2) the done-to pronouns used when the doer is someone else, and (3) the done-to pronouns used when the doer and done-to are the same. The three done-to Spanish pronouns you have learned in this Program are *me, nos, te*. They are translated by "me, us, you." In another Program, you will discover that the same forms are used in Spanish for "myself, ourselves, yourself."

Here is a chart of these pronouns:

Doer	Done-to	
	Doer and done-to are different	Doer and done-to are the same
I	me	myself
we	us	ourselves
he	him	himself
she	her	herself
they	them	themselves
you	you	yourself, yourselves
it	it	itself

New Vocabulary

cigarro	cigar, cigarette
fumar	to smoke
desaparecer	to disappear

PROGRAM 91

The Done-to: Adjectival Residuals and Pronouns

1 The done-to pronoun that replaces *yo* is ———.

me
2 The done-to pronouns that replace *tú* and *nosotros* are ———.

te; nos (Here is a nonsense word that may help you remember these three object pronouns: menoste.)

3 Let's see, now, how English differs from Spanish when the done-to is a noun. What English done-to pronoun will replace the phrase *the house* in "They are going to buy the house?"

it
4 Can *it* replace *the large, red house* in "They are going to buy the large, red house?"

yes (You can say, "Of course, they are going to buy it.")

5 Does *it*, in the sentence above, take the place of the noun, *house*, and all its modifiers?

yes
6 Now, let's see what happens in Spanish. Copy this sentence and underline the definite article: *Ellos van a comprar la casa.*

*Ellos van a comprar **la** casa.*

7 When you say *comprar la casa* aloud, do you say it (a) as three separate words? (b) as though it were one long word: *comprarlacasa?*

as one long word

8 Now, watch what happens when the Spanish speaker says the equivalent of "They are going to buy it." He begins with *Van a comprar la casa*, he drops the noun *casa*, and just says what is left: *Van a comprarla*. In English you take out "the house" and put "it" in its place. Do you take out *la casa* in Spanish and, then, put back the *la?*

no

9 You take out "the house" in English and put "it" in its place. You just drop *casa* in Spanish and keep *la*. Does *la* actually replace the phrase *la casa?*

no (You keep *la* and drop *casa*.)

10 A pronoun is a word used in place of a noun. Is *la* a true pronoun?

no

11 *La* is an adjective in *la casa*. Is it logical, then, to say that *la* is a left-over adjective (an adjectival residual) when the noun is dropped?

yes

12 Say this sentence aloud: *Ellos van a comprar las casas*. Now say it without the noun *casas: Ellos van a comprarlas*. Translate the first sentence above.

They are going to buy the houses.

13 To get the translation of *Van a comprarlas*, you must replace "the houses" with ———.

them ("Them" is a true pronoun. It is used in place of "the houses.")

14 The translation of *Voy a leer los libros* is ———.

I'm going to read the books.

15 Complete the translation of "I'm going to read them." *Voy a* ———.

Voy a leerlos. (In both speech and writing, when you drop the noun in Spanish, you attach the adjectival residual to the infinitive.)

16 You make *libros* singular by dropping the plural suffix ———.

s

17 If you followed the same procedure, the singular of *los* would be ———.

lo

18 This *lo* is an allomorph of *el* which must be used instead of *el* when the noun is dropped. Change *Voy a leer el libro* to the translation of "I'm going to read it."

Voy a leerlo.

19 The adjectival residuals you have learned so far are *los, las, la,* and *lo*. With the exception of *lo* (which is an allomorph of *el*), they have the same forms as the (a) definite (b) indefinite article.

definite

20 The regular plural forms of the definite article are normally translated by "the." When you drop the noun from *comprar las casas* or *leer los libros*, the adjectival residuals are translated by ———.

them

21 When you drop the singular *casa* or *libro*, the adjectival residuals *la* and *lo* are translated by ———.

it

22 When you translate "to visit the girl," you must put a special marker in front of *la muchacha*. This marker of the done-to person is ———.

a (*Voy a visitar **a** la muchacha*.)

23 When the Spanish speaker drops *muchacha*, he also omits the done-to *a*. The new sentence is now *Voy a* ———.

Voy a visitarla.

24 Now, watch your linguistic logic. The *la* in *Voy a visitarla* is translated by "it." (a) true (b) false

false

25 This *la* is translated by ———.

her

26 Here is another test of your linguistic logic. You know that María is a girl. Can these two questions, consequently, be talking about the same person? (1) *¿ Vas a visitar a la muchacha?* (2) *¿ Vas a visitar a María?*

yes   **27** The phrases *a la muchacha* and *a María* may describe the same person. Can you answer either question with the same sentence?

yes   **28** To get your answer, you will drop the *a* of *a la muchacha* or *a María* and the nouns *muchacha* and *María*. The only left-over is ⁓⁓⁓.

la   **29** The answer to either *¿ Vas a visitar a la muchacha?* or to *¿ Vas a visitar a María?* may be *Sí, voy a visitarla.* Let's see why. The two sentences above can be combined into one: *¿ Vas a visitar a la muchacha María?* When the *a* and the two nouns (*muchacha* and *María*) are omitted, the adjectival residual is ⁓⁓⁓.

la (Since *María* = *la muchacha,* the Spanish speaker can use *la* to stand
for both.)   **30** What allomorph of *el* must be used when you omit *muchacho* and *a* from *¿ Vas a visitar al muchacho?*

lo (*¿ Vas a visitarlo?*)
      31 If *la* can stand for the omitted *María,* is it logical that *lo* should be able to stand for an omitted *José?*

yes (*¿ Vas a visitar a José?* can be answered by *Sí, voy a visitarlo.*)
      32 The translation of *lo* is now ⁓⁓⁓.

him   **33** This bit of linguistic history may help you remember the third person done-to forms. The third person subject pronouns and their corresponding definite article forms all come from the Latin demonstrative *ille* (that). The first part of three forms of the subject pronoun disappeared and the result was:

	el	
el	los	
el	la	> became the definite article forms
el	las	

To get the four done-to forms (the residuals) you just keep *la, las,* and *los* and change *el* to its allomorph ⁓⁓⁓.

lo (This *lo* can also be thought of as an alternate singular of *los.*)
      34 You still have to learn the done-to forms that match *usted* and *ustedes.* Can *usted* stand for either *José* or *María* when speaking to either one of them?

yes   **35** When you omit *a José* in *Quiero ver a José,* the done-to form is *lo: Quiero verlo.* Suppose one were to say, *Quiero ver a usted, José.* Can *lo* stand for both *usted* and *José* in *Quiero verlo* (I want to see you)?

yes (In many areas the pronoun is repeated redundantly: *Quiero verlo a Vd.,
José; Quiero verla a Vd., María; Quiero verlos a Vds., José y María.* Also in
some regions the *lo, la, los, las* may be replaced by *le, les.* However, this repetition is not a grammatical necessity, and either pattern may be encountered.
There is no hard and fast rule for this.)
      36 The done-to form *lo* is the singular of ⁓⁓⁓.

los   **37** Rewrite, now, *Quiero ver a ustedes* (males) using the plural done-to form *los.*

Quiero verlos.   **38** The done-to forms *lo* and *los* stand for males. Rewrite *Quiero ver a usted* (female) using the done-to form for *usted.*

Quiero verla.   **39** Can *Quiero verlas* stand for *ustedes* (females)?
yes

40 The done-to forms that came from Latin *ille* have various English translations. Write the proper translation for each adjectival residual in the following frames.

You are talking <u>about</u> a *casa. Quiero verla.*

it
her
you
it
them
him
you
them

41 You are talking <u>about</u> Josefina. *Quiero verla.*
42 You are talking <u>to</u> Josefina. *Quiero verla.*
43 You are talking <u>about</u> a book. *Voy a leerlo.*
44 You are talking <u>about</u> some books. *Es importante leerlos.*
45 You are talking <u>about</u> a *muchacho. Voy a verlo.*
46 You are talking <u>to</u> a man on the phone. *Voy a verlo.*
47 You are talking <u>about</u> some men. *Es importante verlos.*

There are many reasons why a small percentage of students do not do well on tests. Extensive testing of SFC materials among many thousands of students prior to publication has shown that the main causes of poor student performance are as follows:

(1) They do not do their assignments regularly or use the cover sheet.

(2) They do not read carefully or think about the problem enough before looking at the answer.

(3) They do not practice mentally the response to everything that goes on in class; they think that if someone else is called on they need not think through their own response. This makes them miss thousands of chances for practice.

(4) They do not practice reading aloud enough at home. This is the only practical way of learning to say new words encountered in reading.

(5) They do not take the time to review the vocabulary regularly.

Not everybody can get A's all the time, but it *is* possible to do better with just a little more effort and care. If you were dissatisfied with the results of your last exam, you should think about the above findings.

No new vocabulary.

Very few people are aware of the fact that there are about 250 American Indian dialects that are spoken in the United States. However, the number of people who speak an Indian language is small (about 300,000), and many Americans go all their life without ever meeting real Indians or hearing them speak in their own language. This situation is very different in Latin America. In Guatemala, Peru, and Bolivia more than half the population is Indian. Almost half the population of Ecuador is Indian, and more than 10 per cent of the population of Mexico, Venezuela, and Colombia is Indian. In Paraguay almost everyone speaks Spanish and Guarani, the local Indian language.

In Peru and Bolivia nearly half the people speak no Spanish at all, and in many other countries there are also people who speak no Spanish.

No one knows precisely how many Indian languages are spoken in Latin America. One author calculates that in South America alone there are 558 Indian languages. There are 52 in Mexico and 20 in Guatemala. Only one of all these languages has a literature. It is Guarani, the Indian language of Paraguay.

Preparing to Read Aloud, and More on Vocabulary

Part 1: Preparing to Read Aloud for a Grade

In your next class session you will be asked to pretend that you are a news broadcaster who reports over the radio some of the most interesting news of the New World in the 16th century. You will read aloud material you have not practiced, to demonstrate to your teacher that you have learned how to change what you see on paper into sounds that will have meaning to a native. Here is some pre-quiz practice to help you sound like a native.

1 In English we read a date like 1506 aloud as "fifteen hundred and six." In Spanish you must say the equivalent of "one thousand five hundred and six." In Spanish, however, you omit the word "one" and say just *mil*. In addition you do not translate the "and" of "five hundred and six." You say *quinientos seis*. So you read 1506 aloud as *mil quinientos seis*. Say this as though it were one long word.

2 Here are some of the dates you may have to read aloud. Say them aloud until each one sounds like one long word.

1506 mil quinientos seis
1492 mil cuatrocientos noventa y dos
1504 mil quinientos cuatro
1498 mil cuatrocientos noventa y ocho
1513 mil quinientos trece
1519 mil quinientos diecinueve
1521 mil quinientos veintiuno
1522 mil quinientos veintidós
1532 mil quinientos treinta y dos
1546 mil quinientos cuarenta y seis

3 Proper names in Spanish are read aloud just like common words. Those that are spelled the same in both languages cause the most trouble because you have to learn not to project your English habits onto Spanish. You are, for example, thoroughly conditioned to read *Cuba* as if it were *Cue-ba*. The first syllable sounds like "cue." In Spanish you must say [kuba] and with a fricative [b]. Say [kyuba] and [kuƀa] aloud.

4 Say "Florida" aloud in English. Now say in Spanish [flo-ri-ɗa] with the stress on *ri*. The name of the state in Spanish is *la Florida*.

5 When you say "Jamaica" in English, the syllable *mai* sounds like *may*. In Spanish it sounds like *my*. Say [ja-mai-ca] aloud.

6 When you say *Puerto Rico* in Spanish, the *r* of *rico* is said (a) [r] (b) [rr]
[rr] (Say *Puerto Rico* aloud.)

7 Copy *Trinidad* and divide it into syllables.
Tri-ni-dad (Now say it aloud in Spanish. Remember there is no schwa.)

8 In English you say "Bahamas" with an *h* sound. In Spanish you say [baamas]. Say the word aloud.

9 "Mississippi" becomes *Mi-si-si-pí* in Spanish. The [i] sound is the same in each syllable. Say the word aloud and be sure to stress the last syllable.

10 Say *Co-lo-ra-do* aloud in Spanish.

11 By custom most Latin Americans write *México* with an *x*. This is the old spelling. When you say the word, the *x* stands for *j*. Say [mé-ji-co].

12 Here are some names of people you should be able to read aloud without any hesitation. Say each as one long word.

Alonso del Castillo   Antonio de Mendoza   Cristóbal Colón
Andrés Dorantes   Hernando de Soto   Diego Velázquez
Franciso Pizarro   Atahualpa

13 The following names require a little more practice. Watch the accent mark and practice each until the whole name comes out like one long word.

Hernán Cortés   Juan Sebastián de Elcano
Juan Ponce de León   Álvar Núñez Cabeza de Vaca
Fernando de Magallanes   Francisco Vázquez de Coronado
Pánfilo de Narváez   García López de Cárdenas
Vasco Núñez de Balboa   Pedro Menéndez de Avilés

14 One of the ancient gods of the Mexican Indians was *Quetzalcóatl*. This name is pronounced [ket-sal-coa-tl]. Say this aloud.

15 When you are first learning to read aloud, long words sometimes cause trouble because you cannot divide them into syllables fast enough to make them sound right. In these examples say each word slowly, syllable by syllable, then say the whole word fast. The stressed syllable is indicated.

des-cu-bri-*mien*-tos > descubrimientos
go-ber-na-*dor* > gobernador
ho-rro-ri-*za*-ron > horrorizaron
des-gra-cia-da-*men*-te > desgraciadamente
in-te-re-san-*tí*-si-mo > interesantísimo
nor-te-a-me-ri-*ca*-na > norteamericana
in-te-rrum-*pi*-mos > interrumpimos
le-gen-*da*-ria > legendaria
tem-pes-*tuo*-so > tempestuoso
su-per-vi-*vien*-tes > supervivientes
im-pre-sio-*nan*-te > impresionante
ci-vi-*li*-zan > civilizan

16 You have already had enough practice in reading aloud to be able to say strange words without any hesitation. Practice on these words.

soldados (*soldiers*)   flecha (*arrow*)   alrededor (*around*)
caballos (*horses*)   venenosa (*poisonous*)   jornada (*journey*)

17 Here is a point to remember as you read aloud. Spanish, unlike English, likes to run each phrase together as one long word. You see, for example, *el Mar del Sur* but you say *elmardelsur*. Say this aloud.

18 You see *y ahora* but you say *yaora*. Say this aloud.

Part 2: More on Vocabulary

1 You have been learning the words for the parts of the body. Let's see if you have their translations memorized. Translate *cabeza* mentally. •

head   **2** *cara* •
face   **3** *frente* •
forehead   **4** *nariz* •
nose   **5** *boca* •
mouth   **6** *lengua* •
tongue   **7** *pelo* •
hair   **8** *ojo* •
eye   **9** *oreja* •
ear   **10** *labio* •
lip   **11** *diente* •
tooth   **12** Now, let's turn this around and see whether you can spell these words in Spanish. Write the translation for "head" and check your spelling. •

cabeza   **13** face •
cara   **14** forehead •
frente   **15** nose •
nariz   **16** mouth •
boca   **17** tongue •
lengua   **18** hair •
pelo   **19** eye •
ojo   **20** ear (outer) •
oreja   **21** lip •
labio   **22** tooth •
diente   **23** Words are easier to remember if you can associate them with something you already know. *Boca* and *lengua* go together. Both are used when you eat (*comer*) and talk (*hablar*). The tongue is so important in talking that *lengua* is also used to translate "language." What verb should you associate with *ojo*? •

ver (Also, *mirar.*)

No new vocabulary.

PROGRAM **93**

More Parts of the Body and the Present and Preterit of *oír*

Part 1: Parts of the Body

1 You have already discovered that English and Spanish have quite a few cognate words that name the parts of the body. Thus a person who is *bilingual* speaks two tongues or two *languages*. The Spanish cognate of "language" is ~~~~. •

lengua   **2** You learned a long time ago that a *labiodental* sound is a lip-tooth sound. The Spanish word for "lip" is ~~~~. •

labio

3 The Spanish cognate of *dental, dentist,* and *dent* which translates "tooth" is ⁓.

diente (Latin stressed *e* often becomes Spanish *ie*.)

4 The cognate of *front* which translates "forehead" (front of the head) is ⁓.

frente　　**5** Is it (a) *la frente* or (b) *el frente?*

la frente (*El frente* translates "the front" as in a war.)

6 An eye doctor is an *oculist.* The cognate of *oculist* which stands for "eye" is ⁓.

ojo (Remember this word also translates "Watch out!" or "Be careful"—use your eye. Compare English: "Keep an eye on what's going on.")

7 You have probably never heard of the English word *buccal.* It may be used to say "the tongue is a *buccal organ.*" The Spanish cognate that translates "mouth" also begins with a *b.* It is ⁓.

boca　　**8** The unvoiced Latin [p] often became a voiced Spanish [b]. Can you see the cognate word for "head" in *to decapitate* (to behead)? It is ⁓.

cabeza　　**9** The infinitive *oír* translates "to hear." The parts of your head that you hear with is your inner ear, *el oído.* What you see outside is your ⁓.

oreja　　**10** When you talk about a "nasal spray" in English, you are talking about a "nose spray." Both "nasal" and "nose" are cognates of ⁓.

nariz　　**11** Let's see, now, whether you can spell all the names of the parts of the body you have learned so far. Write the translation for "head."

cabeza　　**12** face
cara　　**13** forehead
frente　　**14** mouth
boca　　**15** tongue
lengua　　**16** hair
pelo　　**17** eye
ojo　　**18** ears (outer)
orejas　　**19** lip
labio　　**20** tooth
diente　　**21** nose

nariz　　**22** Here are some new words for other parts of the body. See if you can figure out their meaning. You already know that stressed Latin *o* sometimes changes to Spanish *ue* (*poder* > *puede*). You also know that a major proof of murder is the finding of a *corpus.* What is the common word translation of *cuerpo?*

body (So now you can say *las partes del cuerpo* in Spanish. Say this aloud.)

23 Read this aloud: *La cabeza es una parte del cuerpo.*

24 The part of the body that touches the *pedal* of a bicycle is the *pie.* The *e* of Latin *ped* changed to *ie* in Spanish. The translation of *pie* is ⁓.

foot　　**25** When you walk, you use your *pies* and your *piernas.* A good educated guess should tell you that the translation of *piernas* is ⁓.

legs (Say *pierna* aloud.)

26 A person who does "manual" labor works with his *manos.* The translation of *manos* is ⁓.

hands　　**27** On each hand you have five *dedos.* In Spanish you also have five *dedos* on each *pie.* The Spanish *dedos,* then, is translated by two English words for parts of the body. They are ⁓.

fingers; toes (You can have *veinte dedos* in Spanish.)

28 We say we have five fingers on each hand. The Spanish speaker sometimes says he has four fingers and a *pulgar*. *Pulgar* translates ⁓.

thumb (The "big toe" in Spanish is *el dedo gordo* = the fat *dedo*.)

29 How has your linguistic logic been doing? You should have gotten the last several frames right. Here is one more chance to test your ability to make an educated guess. When one person "embraces" another, he holds the other in his arms. The translation of the cognate *brazo* is ⁓.

arm **30** Let's see, now, how much of what you have just learned is sticking with you. The translation of *cuerpo* (cognate "corpus") is ⁓.

body **31** The translation of *pie* (cognate "pedal") is ⁓.

foot **32** Your *pies* are attached to the ends of your *piernas*. The translation of *piernas* is ⁓.

legs **33** The translation of *mano* (cognate "manual") is ⁓.

hand **34** Each hand has five *dedos* = ⁓.

fingers (One cognate is "digits.")

35 The translation of *brazo* (cognate "embrace") is ⁓.

arm

Part 2: The Present and Preterit of *oír* (to hear)

1 The present tense stem of *oír* has three allomorphs but the suffixes are all regular. *Yo* goes with the irregular form *oigo*. The *oi* is pronounced like *hoy* (today). Say *oigo* aloud. The irregular stem is ⁓.

oig **2** The *nosotros*-form is *oímos*. Copy and divide into syllables.

o-í-mos (Say this aloud, and remember that an accented *í* cannot be in the same syllable with another vowel.)

3 The stem of *oímos* and *oír* is regular. It is ⁓.

o (The regular stem of a verb is what you get when you remove the two infinitive suffixes: *ir, er,* or *ar.*)

4 The stem of all the other forms is *oy*, pronounced like *hoy*. What regular first suffix do you add to *oy* to get the form that goes with *usted, él,* or *ella?*

e (*Usted oye;* pronounce *oye* like *hoy-ye.*)

5 To make *oye* agree with *ustedes, ellos,* or *ellas,* you add the second suffix ⁓.

n (*Ustedes oyen;* pronounce like *hoy-yen.*)

6 Change *oyen* so it will agree with *tú.*

oyes **7** Now, let's look at some facts about spelling. The *hoy* sound of *oigo* is spelled *oi* because Spanish never writes *y* immediately before a consonant in a word. The same *hoy* sound is spelled *oy* in *oye, oyes,* and *oyen* because Spanish never writes *i* between two vowels (only *í* as in *leía*).

8 The stem of the Preterit of *oír* is regular. It is ⁓.

o **9** The past tense base of *oír* is ⁓.

oi **10** The *yo*-form is the same except that *i*, as in the preterit forms you have already learned, has a ⁓ in writing.

written accent: *oí*

11 You add *ste* to the past tense base to get the form that goes with ⁓.

tú (*Tú oíste,* with a written accent over the *i*.)

oímos
vivió
ió
y
oyó
oyeron

12 The *nosotros*-form of the Preterit of *i*-verbs is like the Present. So you write *nosotros* ～～.
13 The preterit form of *vivir* that goes with *usted* is ～～.
14 The first suffix of *vivió* is ～～.
15 Now, remember that Spanish does not write *i* between two vowels. It uses ～～ instead.
16 So the form of *oír* that is like *vivió* is written ～～.
17 By the same rule, the form of *oír* that is like *vivieron* is written ～～.
(Pronounced like *hoy-yeron*.)

New Vocabulary

mono	monkey	**te**	you
seda	silk	**¿Cómo?**	What? (Used when you do not hear something clearly.)
vestir	to dress		
me	me	**No importa.**	It doesn't matter. (It's not important.)

PROGRAM 94

Intonation

It is impossible to tell you in a Program what Spanish sounds like. You have to *hear* the spoken words and sentences to know how Spanish speech differs from English. As a result, this Program has only two purposes: to start you thinking about what you are about to learn in class and to teach you some of the technical terms your teacher will use.

1 You have often heard people say something like this: "It's not what she said that counts, but the way she said it." The "way" in this statement deals, in part, with what is called **intonation**. One important feature of intonation is stress. What syllable is stressed in *canto*?

can
2 What syllable is stressed in *cantó*?
tó
3 When we say that the *tó* of *cantó* is stressed, we mean that in speech this syllable is a little longer and a little louder than the unstressed syllable *can*. Here is the word "investigation" divided into syllables: in-ves-ti-ga-tion. Say it aloud until you are certain which syllable is longest and loudest. (Many dictionaries say it takes the primary or main stress.) This syllable is ～～.

ga
4 There is another syllable in "investigation" which carries less stress than *ga* but more than any other syllable. Say *in-ves-ti-ga-tion* aloud until you can pick out the syllable having this secondary stress. It is ～～.

ves (A dictionary might show these two stresses this way: in-ves''ti-ga'tion.)

5 Here is a major difference between English and Spanish. Most long English words have a primary and a secondary stressed syllable. In contrast, few Spanish words have a syllable which carries a secondary stress. A few compound words have two stresses but all simple Spanish words have only one stressed syllable. This difference is very important in learning how to improve your Spanish accent. All your years of training in English keep telling you (even forcing you) to put two, and sometimes three, stresses on long words. Just out of habit you are likely to pronounce the cognate *investigación* somewhat like English. This sounds very strange to the Spanish speaker, so you should try to break this habit. Divide the word into syllables. •

in-ves-ti-ga-ción

6 The only stressed syllable is 〰〰. •

ción
7 Say *ción* aloud and make the *o* sound a bit longer than the other vowels in the word. Now, let's try a backward build-up and see if you can keep any secondary stress off all the other syllables. Say aloud: ***ción; gación; tigación; vestigación; investigación.*** There is no way you can tell by yourself whether you did this correctly. But at least you now understand the problem your teacher is going to start working on in your next class.

8 Let's try one more long word. Here is "impossibility" divided into syllables: im-pos-si-bil-i-ty. Say this aloud until you are pretty certain which syllable carries the strongest (primary) stress. It is 〰〰. •

bil
9 The secondary stress falls on *pos*, and a dictionary might show the two stresses this way: im-pos''si-bil'-i-ty. The Spanish cognate is *im-po-si-bi-li-dad*. The rules for stress tell you that the stressed syllable is 〰〰. •

dad (The word ends in a consonant other than *n* or *s*, so the stress falls on the last syllable.)
10 Let's practice the backward build-up on *imposibilidad*. Say aloud and stress only *dad: **dad; li**dad; bili**dad; posibili**dad; imposibili**dad.* In your next class, your teacher will begin a drill on this problem by pairing "investigation"—*investigación* and "impossibility"—*imposibilidad.* You will learn then whether you have done this part of the Program correctly.

11 In music different notes are made long or short. In speech different syllables are also made long or short. This is called **rhythm**. In English a long syllable may be two to five times longer than a short syllable. Say, in a sort of off-hand way, "We took a long walk." Now say exactly the same sentence and make it mean "a very, very *long* walk." You do this by lengthening the word 〰〰. •

long (We took a ***long*** walk.)
12 A major difference between English and Spanish is to be found in the fact that Spanish long syllables are normally only about twice as long as the short syllables. Say aloud emphatically, "It's very *near*." Is *near* much longer in speech than *it's?* •

yes, if you said "near" emphatically
13 The translation of "It's very near," is *Está muy cerca.* The stressed, and hence, longest syllable of *cerca* is 〰〰. •

cer
14 When a Spanish speaker says *Está muy cerca* emphatically, the *cer* of *cerca* is only a little bit longer than the *tá* of *está.* Try saying *Está muy cerca* aloud in the Spanish way.

15 The length of syllables is closely tied to stress; stressed syllables are longer than unstressed syllables. From what you have just learned about the difference in stressing in English and Spanish, can you now answer this question? Which language, English or Spanish, has the greatest number of long syllables?

English (Because so many words have more than one stressed syllable.)

16 Here are two sentences in English and Spanish. The stressed syllables are indicated. Remember they are longer than the unstressed syllables.

Hablamos de la imposibilidad de verlo.
We are **talk**ing of the im**poss**i**bil**ity of **see**ing **it**.

Do you think that your Spanish would sound natural to a native if you put as many long syllables in the Spanish as in the English?

No (Your rhythm would be wrong. You would sound strangely overemphatic.)

17 In your next class, you will begin to practice saying English and Spanish sentences aloud with different rhythms, that is, with Spanish syllables all about the same length and English syllables the way you talk naturally. Here is the first pair you will practice. The bold-faced syllables are very long in English. The bold-faced syllables are much shorter in Spanish. Can you say the sentence now so you can hear the difference? "**He** is a **very old man**." *Él es un señor **muy viejo**.*

18 Another important feature of intonation is what happens when we go from sound to silence, that is, what happens when we end a sentence. The pitch can go up (↑), stay level (|), or go down (↓). Let's see if you can hear yourself make these differences. Say this question aloud: *Are you going to the beach?* Say it aloud again. At the end of the question, your voice (the pitch) (a) goes up (b) goes down.

If you asked the question the way you normally talk English, the pitch went up. Check yourself again by saying the question aloud once more. *Are you going to the beach?*↑

19 Can the question *Are you going to the beach?* be answered simply by either "yes" or "no"?

yes   **20** This type of question is called a yes-no question. Here is the Spanish for the same question: *¿ Vas a la playa?* Say it aloud in your best Spanish. Does the pitch go up as in English?

yes   **21** Here is a rule about **juncture** (the way sentences end). The pitch rises at the end of yes-no questions in both English and Spanish. Say these two sentences aloud: "Are you from Spain?" ↑ *¿ Es usted de España?* ↑ Now, listen to yourself very carefully and say these two statements: "Yes, I'm from Spain." *Sí, soy de España.* At the end of each statement, the pitch (a) goes up (b) goes down.

goes down (If you got the wrong answer, try saying the statements over until you can hear what you are doing.)

22 Here is another rule about juncture: The pitch falls at the end of statements in both languages. Now, look at these questions and say them aloud: "Where are you going?" *¿ A dónde vas?* Can they be answered by yes or no?

no (They are information questions.)

23 Say the information questions in Frame 22 aloud and listen to what happens to the pitch at the end of each. The pitch (a) falls (b) rises.

falls   **24** Here is a third rule about juncture: The pitch falls at the end of information questions. In all three examples given above, the terminal juncture (the direction of the voice at the end of an utterance) is the same in both languages. It is expected that you will recognize statements and automatically use the right terminal juncture in Spanish since it is the same as English. You will need, however, some practice in learning to spot yes-no and information questions, and in remembering how they end.

In which direction does the pitch go at the end of yes-no questions? (a) up (b) down   •

up   **25** In which direction does the pitch go at the end of information questions?   •

down   **26** What kind of a question is this: *¿ Hay muchos habitantes allí?* (a) information (b) yes-no   •

yes-no   **27** What kind of a question is this: *¿ Tienes tiza?* (a) information (b) yes-no   •
yes-no (The pitch goes up.)

28 What kind of question is this: *¿ Cómo te llamas?* (a) information (b) yes-no   •
information (You cannot logically answer it with either "yes" or "no." The
pitch goes down.)

29 What kind of question is this: *¿ Cómo está usted?* (a) information (b) yes-no   •
information (The pitch falls.)

30 There is another very important feature of intonation which you control by intuition in English but which you must learn to understand consciously before you can communicate successfully in Spanish. This is **pitch**. You understand the meaning of "pitch" in "a high pitched scream" and "a low pitched growl." You also know something about pitch in music if you understand the difference between a high and low note or tone. Pitch deals with the number of vibrations per second of a sound wave. The greater the number of vibrations, the higher the pitch. In speech, as in music or just plain noise, there are differences in pitch.

Let's see if you can hear the difference when you talk. Say aloud, in a matter-of-fact way, "It's not George; it's Henry." Now, pretend that you were expecting George, not Henry, and say with surprise and emphatically, "It's not *George;* it's *Henry!*" Say this again with strong emphasis on the *Hen* of *Henry.* Aside from the difference in loudness, the real difference between the matter-of-fact, "It's not George; it's Henry" and the excited and emphatic, "It's not *George;* it's *Henry!*" is one of pitch. Linguists say that when you say the *Hen* of *Henry* emphatically you use the *fourth* pitch level, but when you just inform someone that "It's not George; it's Henry" you say *Hen* on the *third* pitch level. Now, here is the important difference between English and Spanish. In English speech, there are *four levels of pitch*. In contrast, there are only *three levels of pitch* in Spanish.

What does this mean in communication? Pitch adds something to the meaning of the words in a message. It says you are happy, annoyed, disgusted, excited, pleased, angry, *etc.* And here's the problem. Each language uses different pitch patterns to express these different attitudes. Say in a bright, happy, and cheerful manner, "Good-bye. See you tomorrow." When you do this, the stressed syllables are all on pitch level "three" in English. Now, suppose you are very annoyed and disgusted but feel you have to say the proper formula of courtesy. You sort of growl, "Good-bye. See you tomorrow." The stressed syllables are now on pitch level two in English, and this pitch pattern is the way a Spanish speaker normally says a bright and cheerful, *Adiós, hasta mañana.* Your English intuition will tell you that it is very wrong to say *Adiós, hasta mañana* in this way, but if you use the English pattern the Spanish speaker will get the wrong message about your attitude. He will think either that you are too emphatic, over-excited or, perhaps, insincere.

From now on your teacher is going to start helping you learn to speak Spanish with Spanish pitch patterns. It will take you a long time to get used to this because your intuition will object to using patterns which, by English standards, seem to express the wrong attitudes. Gradually, however, you will learn that what sounds like a grouchy *Muchas gracias, señor* in English is, in fact, a pleasant and friendly way of saying, "Thank you, sir" in Spanish.

New Vocabulary

cabeza	head	**nariz**	nose
pelo	hair	**diente**	tooth
cara	face	**lengua**	tongue
oreja	ear	**a mí**	to me
frente (la)	forehead	**a ti**	to you
labio	lip		

You were just told that English has four pitch levels while Spanish has only three. Let's see what bearing this has on inter-cultural communication and, also, on what you still have to learn.

The vast majority of speakers of both English and Spanish do not know that the two languages have a different number of pitch levels and most teachers, as a result, teach the opposite language with the pitch levels of their own language. Here are two examples of what happens when this is not understood.

A Latin American who married an American girl lived in this country several years before he discovered why his wife insisted that he always got up grouchy. For years he protested, saying that he almost always awoke feeling very cheerful. His wife refused to believe him, and this misunderstanding was not resolved until he discovered that he always said *Good morning* with only the two pitch levels of Spanish, those used in English when you are grouchy or annoyed.

A very beautiful, talented, and highly cultured young woman from a Latin country found a job in the United States in an exclusive jewelry shop as a salesgirl. Although she knew how to deal with people most graciously in her own culture and spoke English quite fluently, she was, to the confusion of everyone, an immediate failure and had to give up the job. The explanation was eventually found in the fact that she spoke English only with the normal pitch levels of Spanish, and the customers all thought her boring and totally indifferent to their needs.

Unless you are careful, you are going to speak Spanish with the three pitch levels of English. Spanish speakers will believe that you are "pushy," over-emphatic, domineering, rude, or peculiar.

Preparing for a Quiz on the Forms of the Preterit

In your next class session you are going to have a quiz so your teacher can find out whether you can write (and spell correctly) all the forms of the Preterit that you have studied so far. This will enable (him) her to help you more. This Program is a review to get you ready for the quiz. Be sure to use your cover sheet, and don't forget to circle the number of any frame you miss.

Part 1: The Preterit Forms of Regular *a*-Verbs

1 The *nosotros*-forms of the Present and Preterit are exactly alike. Write this form for *hallar* (to find, discover).

hallamos   **2** In the quiz you will be given sentences in which the verb is in the infinitive. You are to write the preterit form. For example, *Nosotros* ～～ (*recordar*) *la calle muy bien.*

recordamos   **3** Write the Preterit of *pintar. Nosotros* ～～.

pintamos (Check your spelling carefully.)

    4 Write the Preterit of *observar. Nosotros* ～～.

observamos   **5** To get the *tú*-form of the Preterit of *tomamos*, you replace the *mos* with ～～.

ste (tú tomaste)

    6 Write the Preterit of *llevar. Tú* ～～.

llevaste   **7** Change *miramos* so it agrees with *tú.*

miraste   **8** There are two preterit forms in which *a* is the first suffix: *quedamos* and *quedaste*. This *a* also appears in the form that goes with *ustedes* and *ellos*. Write the Preterit of *quedar. Ustedes* ～～.

quedaron (The whole second suffix is *aro*.)

    9 Write the Preterit of *olvidar. Ellos* ～～.

olvidaron   **10** The suffix of the *yo*-form of the Preterit of all regular *a*-verbs is ～～.

é   **11** Translate: I found the book. (Remember the verb you learned from Frame 1.)

(Yo) hallé el libro.

    12 Write the Preterit of *pasar. Yo* ～～.

pasé   **13** To make *pasé* agree with *ella*, you replace *é* with ～～.

ó (Notice, now, that two forms of the Preterit have accent marks: *pasé* and

pasó.)   **14** Write the Preterit of *entrar. Usted* ～～.

entró   **15** Here is another example of what you are going to see in the quiz. Write in the Preterit the form of the verb in parentheses: *Él* ～～ (*quedar*) *aquí muchos meses.*

quedó (Did you remember the accent mark?)

16 Let's see, now, if you know all the preterit forms perfectly. In this and the next five frames, write the Preterit of *pintar* that matches the pronoun.
Yo ⁓⁓.

pinté   **17** Tú ⁓⁓.

pintaste   **18** Usted ⁓⁓.

pintó   **19** Él ⁓⁓.

pintó   **20** Nosotros ⁓⁓.

pintamos   **21** Ellos (ustedes) ⁓⁓.

pintaron   **22** The form *recuerda* comes from *recordar* and has a stem change (*o > ue*). Does this irregularity also appear in the Preterit?

no (All the present tense stem changes of *a-* and *e*-verbs are regularized in the Preterit.)   **23** Translate: I remembered the street.

(Yo) recordé la calle.

24 One of the common mistakes made when using the Preterit or Imperfect is to forget that the stem-changing verbs in the Present have a regular stem in the past tense forms. In this and the next four frames say the preterit equivalent of the form you see.
duermo

dormí (The stem is the same as in the infinitive *dormir*.)

25 recuerdas

recordaste   **26** empieza

empezó   **27** vuelve

volvió   **28** pienso

pensé

Part 2: The Preterit Forms of the Regular *e*- and *i*-Verbs

1 The first suffix of the Imperfect of all *e*- and *i*- verbs is ⁓⁓.

ía   **2** The *í* of *vivía* says the tense is past and the *a* says the aspect is Imperfect. The past tense base of *vivía* is ⁓⁓.

vivi (The stem plus *i*.)   **3** Change *yo vivía* to the Preterit.

yo viví (You just drop the imperfective aspect marker.)

4 The *usted*-form of the Preterit of *hablar* is *habló*. What do you add to the base *vivi* to get the preterit form for *usted*?

ó (*Usted vivió*. The accented *ó* is the mark of *usted* for the Preterit of all regular verbs.)   **5** Change *vivió* so it will agree with *tú*.

tú viviste (You just add *ste* to the past tense base.)

6 The Preterit of *vivimos* is ⁓⁓.

vivimos   **7** The Preterit of *comemos* is *comimos*. The Preterit of *aprendemos* is *aprendimos*. Now, stop and think what this tells you. In the Preterit all regular *e*-verbs behave as though they were *i*-verbs. (a) true (b) false

true   **8** There is a *ro* in the first suffix of the Preterit of all verb forms that agree with *ustedes* and *ellos*. The form of *hablar* that goes with *ustedes* is ⁓⁓.

hablaron   **9** The form of *vivir* that goes with *ustedes* is ⁓⁓.

vivieron   **10** All *e*-verbs behave just like *i*-verbs in the Preterit. So the preterit form of *correr* that goes with *ustedes* is ⁓⁓.

corrieron

11 Let's see, now, if you can give the Preterit for all the forms of *correr*.
Yo ———.

corrí   **12** Tú ———.

corriste   **13** Él ———.

corrió   **14** Ellos (*or* ustedes) ———.

corrieron **15** Nosotros ———.

corrimos   **16** Usted ———.

corrió   **17** Juan y María ———.

corrieron (*Juan y María = Ellos*)

Part 3: The Preterit of *oír*, *leer*, and *caer*

            1 *Oír* means ———.

to hear   **2** *Caer* means ———.

to fall   **3** *Leer* means ———.

to read   **4** The *nosotros*-form of *oír* in the Present is ———.

oímos   **5** The *nosotros*-form of *caer* in the Present is ———.

caemos   **6** The *nosotros*-form of *leer* in the Present is ———.

leemos   **7** The present tense form *oímos* and the preterit form *oímos* are identical. To make *caemos* and *leemos* into preterit forms you must replace the first suffix *e* with ———.

í (You get *caímos* and *leímos*.)

8 In the Preterit all *e*-verbs have the same structure as *i*-verbs. In the Imperfect all *e*-verbs also have the same structure as *i*-verbs. Write the *yo*-form of the Imperfect of *oír*, *caer*, and *leer*.

yo oía, caía, leía

9 You get the *yo*-form of the Preterit of *oía*, *caía*, and *leía* by dropping the imperfective marker *a*. So you get ———.

oí, caí, leí   **10** The past tense base of all regular *e*- and *i*-verbs has an *i* right after the stem. This *i* has a written accent in three preterit forms. Look at this chart carefully. The verb forms are divided into syllables.

yo o-í	tú o-í-ste	nosotros o-í-mos
yo ca-í	tú ca-í-ste	nosotros ca-í-mos
yo le-í	tú le-í-ste	nosotros le-í-mos

Now, hang on to this fact about Spanish spelling: when *i* immediately follows another vowel letter, the accent mark tells you that the sound it stands for is a syllable all by itself. Does *i* stand for a syllable all by itself in *oía*, *caía*, and *leía*?

yes   **11** When *i* comes between two vowel letters, the accent mark tells you it stands for a syllable all by itself. Does *i* stand for a syllable all by itself in *oigo* and *caigo*?

no   **12** Here is a second fact about Spanish spelling: when *i* immediately follows another vowel, and has no accent mark, it is always part of the same syllable as the first vowel. So what do you say? (a) *o-i-go* (b) *oi-go*

oi-go

13 A third important fact about Spanish spelling is that the letter *i*, without an accent mark, is never used between two vowel letters. Now, watch this. The preterit *usted*-form of *vivir* is made up of the stem (*viv*) and the first suffix *ió* (*viv-ió*). The preterit *usted*-form of *oír* cannot, however, be written *oió*. You must change the *i* to ⁓.

y (usted oyó)   **14** Write the Preterit of *caer* and *leer*. Usted ⁓.

cayó; leyó   **15** The preterit *ustedes*-form of *vivir* is *viv-iero-n*. You cannot write *oieron, caieron,* or *leieron.* You must write ⁓.

oyeron, cayeron, leyeron

16 Now, be careful. Change *tú oyes* to the Preterit.

tú oíste   **17** In this and the remaining frames change what you see to the Preterit. ella oye.

ella oyó   **18** ellos oyen

ellos oyeron   **19** usted lee

usted leyó   **20** ustedes caen

ustedes cayeron

New Vocabulary

Geographic names
Andes (mountains)
Atacama (desert)
Titicaca (lake)
Amazonas (river)
Pampas (plains)
Magdalena (river)

Common verbs

contar (**ue**)	to count
cerrar (**ie**)	to close
mover (**ue**)	to move
quebrar (**ie**)	to break
medir (**i**)	to measure

Expressions

Está en su casa.   Make yourself at home.

PROGRAM 96

The Done-to in Reflexive Constructions

1 Let's begin this Program by learning what a reflexive construction is. The doer in the sentence *I see the parrot* is ⁓.

I   **2** The done-to in the same sentence is ⁓.

the parrot   **3** The doer in *The parrot sees me* is ⁓.

The parrot   **4** The done-to in the same sentence is ⁓.

me   **5** The doer in *I see myself in the mirror* is ⁓.

I   **6** The done-to in the same sentence is ⁓.

myself   **7** Are the doer and the done-to the same in *The parrot sees me?*

no

8 When I am the done-to and someone or something else is the doer, my name as the done-to is (a) I (b) me.

me   **9** Are the doer and the done-to the same person in *I see myself in the mirror?*

yes   **10** When I am both the doer and the done-to, my name as the done-to is (a) I (b) me (c) myself.

myself (In proper English you don't say either "I saw I in the mirror" or "I saw me in the mirror.")

11 When the doer and the done-to in a sentence are *the same*, the construction is said to be **reflexive**. The action is not done to someone or something else but is "turned back" (reflected) onto the subject. You already know that English has a special set of pronoun forms which stand for the done-to when the doer and the done-to are the same. Let's analyze these forms.

The possessive adjective that matches *I* in "I lost ⁓⁓ pen" is ⁓⁓.

my   **12** Look at these two sentences: (1) I hurt my leg. (2) I hurt myself. Does *my* give us the same kind of information in both sentences?

yes   **13** Write the missing part: She hurt ⁓⁓self.

her   **14** Write the missing part: We hurt ⁓⁓selves.

our   **15** Write the missing part: You hurt your⁓⁓.

self   **16** The reflexive pronouns *myself, ourselves, herself,* and *yourself* are made up of the possessive adjectives (*my, our, her, your*) plus *self* or *selves*. English, however, is not consistent. Which is the proper choice? (a) He hurt himself. (b) He hurt his-self.

He hurt himself.

17 And here? (a) They hurt themselves. (b) They hurt theirselves.

They hurt themselves.

18 There remains only one reflexive pronoun to be considered, the one that matches *it*. This form is ⁓⁓.

itself   **19** English, then, has two complete sets of done-to pronouns. When the doer and the done-to are the same, all the done-to pronouns (the reflexives) end in *self* or *selves*. When the doer and done-to are different, the form that matches *I* is (a) myself (b) me.

me (The parrot bit me.)

20 What replaces *me* when *we* are the done-to? "The parrot bit ⁓⁓."

us   **21** What replaces *us* when *he* or *she* is the done-to? "The parrot bit ⁓⁓."

him or *her*   **22** Write the similar forms that match *they, you,* and *it.* "The parrot bit ⁓⁓."

them, you, it   **23** Here is a chart of the English reflexive pronouns:

I	*my*self
we	*our*selves
you (singular)	*your*self
you (plural)	*your*selves
he	*him*self
she	*her*self
they	*them*selves
it	*it*self

Spanish is very different from English and much easier to learn. The done-to forms which match *yo, nosotros,* and *tú* are, as you should already know, ⁓⁓.

me, nos, te

24 These three forms are used either when the doer and the done-to are the same or different. Compare:

She washes **me**.	*Ella **me** lava.*
I wash **myself**.	*Yo **me** lavo.*
She washes **us**.	*Ella **nos** lava.*
We wash **ourselves**.	*Nosotros **nos** lavamos.*
She washes **you**.	*Ella **te** lava.*

Rewrite *yo me lavo* so the doer (and the done-to) is *tú*.

tú te lavas   **25** Let's go back, now, to the difference between "meaning" in Spanish and "translation" into English. What does *yo me lavo* <u>mean</u> in Spanish? (a) I me wash. (b) I wash myself.

I me wash. (The proper translation is "I wash myself.")

26 Is it logical to say that Spanish, unlike English, has no special form of the reflexive pronoun that matches *yo, nosotros,* and *tú?*

yes (There is just one done-to form for each: *me, nos, te.*)

27 Spanish has only one "real" reflexive pronoun. It is *se,* and it is used to match all the other subject pronouns. Look carefully at these sentences:

She washes **herself**.	*Ella **se** lava.*
He washes **himself**.	*Él **se** lava.*
You wash **yourself**.	*Usted **se** lava.*
You wash **yourselves**.	*Ustedes **se** lavan.*
They wash **themselves**.	*Ellos **se** lavan.*

28 Does *se* in Spanish really mean "herself, himself, yourself, yourselves, themselves?"

no   **29** The Spanish speaker doesn't know English, so *se* must have a special meaning in his system. Let's see what this special meaning is. *Mamá va a lavar a la niña* can be changed to *Mamá va a lavarla.* Are the doer and the done-to the same in this sentence?

no   **30** Compare these sentences:

Mamma washes her.	*Mamá la lava.*
Mamma washes herself.	*Mamá se lava.*

Are the doer and the done-to the same in *Mamá se lava?*

yes   **31** Are the doer and the done-to the same in *Pepe se lava?*

yes   **32** Is this, then, a logical conclusion: all that *se* really says to a Spanish speaker is that the doer and the done-to are the same? (a) logical (b) illogical

logical   **33** What *se* says to a Spanish speaker does not, of course, tell you how to translate *se* into English. What key word in *Ella se lava* tells you to translate *se* as "herself?"

Ella (You translate *ella* as "she" and match this with "herself.")

34 Translate: *Pepe se lava.*

Pepe washes himself. (You replace *Pepe* with "He" and match "He" with "himself.")   **35** Let us practice what will be reviewed in your next class. What reflexive pronoun matches "we" in English?

ourselves   **36** What single done-to pronoun matches *nosotros* in Spanish?
nos

37 When the doer and done-to are different, the done-to pronoun that matches *ella* is ——.

la   **38** When the doer and the done-to are the same, the done-to or reflexive pronoun that matches *ella* is ——.

se   **39** The done-to and reflexive pronoun that matches *él, ellos, ellas, usted,* and *ustedes* is ——.

se   **40** In your next class you are going to have a drill which begins with the sentence *Yo me levanto temprano.* The form *levanto* comes from an *a*-verb. The infinitive form is ——.

levantar   **41** The meaning, not the translation, of *levantar* is "to raise" or "to lift up." So *Yo me levanto temprano* means ——.

I raise myself early. (Or, to be very literal, "I me raise early.")

42 The most likely translation of this is ——.

I get up early.   **43** Change *Yo me levanto* so the subject is *nosotros.*

Nosotros nos levantamos.

44 Translate: You (*tú*) get up early.

Tú te levantas temprano.

45 Rewrite the above so the forms match *usted.*

Usted se levanta temprano.

46 To change the above to match "you" (plural), you just add —— to *usted* and —— to *levanta.*

es to *usted* and *n* to *levanta* (The *se* remains the same.)

47 To change *Ustedes se levantan temprano* so the doer is "they" (masculine), you simply replace *ustedes* with ——.

ellos (Ellos se levantan temprano.)

48 Translate: He gets up early.

Él se levanta temprano.

49 Here is a chart of the English and Spanish pronouns used in reflexive constructions. You learn only four forms in Spanish.

I	myself	*yo*	*me*
we	ourselves	*nosotros*	*nos*
you	yourself	*tú*	*te*
you	yourself	*usted*	*se*
you	yourselves	*ustedes*	*se*
he	himself	*él*	*se*
she	herself	*ella*	*se*
they	themselves	*ellos*	*se*
it	itself	—	*se*

There is no subject pronoun for "it" in Spanish. You use zero.

New Vocabulary

cuerpo	body	**brazo**	arm
pie	foot (human)	**noticia**	news
dedo	finger, toe	**oír**	to hear
pierna	leg	**ladrar**	to bark
pulgar	thumb	**morder**	to bite
mano	hand		

In the United States a great many young people believe that persons over thirty are squares and conformists. These same young people find the social customs and mores of their elders old-fashioned or irrelevant, and they try to establish the identity of their own generation by being different and by breaking away from the old social customs.

The Spanish speaker, who places much more emphasis on individualism than the American, is simultaneously much more of a social conformist than the older generation in the United States. The grandmothers of many of the young today were the flappers of the 1920's who wore short skirts, smoked cigarettes, and scandalized their elders. There were no flappers in the Hispanic world. The mothers of these same young people made slacks popular and the fathers took to wearing loud sport shirts. Both are generally frowned on in Hispanic society.

PROGRAM 97

Preparing for a Quiz on the Uses of the Preterit and Imperfect

In your next class, you are going to be given a short passage about something that happened in the past. It will be in Spanish and all the verb forms will be in the Present. You are to replace each present tense form with either the Preterit or the Imperfect. Let's practice this in English first.

1 Put just the verb forms in the past tense: It *is* July 4, 1906, and Miguel *is working* in the country.

was; was working

2 Here is another English example: Carmen *is singing* when her friend *arrives*.

was singing; arrived

3 Do the same with this example: At that moment the dog *gets up* and *barks*.

got up; barked

4 Let's see exactly what you have to know in order to do this quiz well. The story you are going to read is told in the historical Present, that is, present tense forms are used to talk about the past. So you will see *Es el 4 de julio de 1906 y Miguel trabaja en el campo.* Will the forms *Es* and *trabaja* tell you whether the back-shifts are to be in the Preterit or the Imperfect?

no

5 You must make a logical analysis of the situation. Pretend, for example, that you are taking a movie of what is going on. What aspect of *trabajar* do you see in *Miguel trabaja en el campo?* (a) initiative (b) imperfective (c) terminative

imperfective

6 If the action is going on (imperfective), then the back-shift of *trabaja* should be (a) *trabajó* (b) *trabajaba*.

trabajaba (So the whole sentence comes out *Era el 4 de julio de 1906 y Miguel trabajaba en el campo.*)

7 Look at this sentence: *Carmen canta cuando su amigo llega.* Does the action of *llegar* come to an end while the singing is going on?

yes

8 Which form do you use to say an action came to an end in the past? (a) *llegaba* (b) *llegó*

llegó

9 If *Carmen canta* shifts to mean "Carmen was singing," then the back-shift of *canta* is ——.

cantaba (So the whole sentence is *Carmen cantaba cuando su amigo llegó.*)

10 Now look at *En ese momento el perro se levanta y ladra.* What aspect does *ladra* logically describe? (a) The dog *is barking* when he gets up. (b) The dog *stops barking* after he gets up. (c) The dog gets up and *begins to bark.*

The dog gets up and begins to bark.

11 Which past tense form is used to describe the initiative aspect of an action at some point in the past? (a) the Imperfect (b) the Preterit

the Preterit

12 So you will change *ladra* to ——.

ladró

13 Does the dog complete the action of getting up before he begins to bark?

yes

14 So you will change *se levanta* to *se* ——.

levantó (The Preterit states that the whole cycle of getting up was completed or terminated before the barking began.)

15 You need to understand that this quiz is designed to check everything you have learned about the Preterit and the Imperfect, plus all the other things you have learned about verb forms. Can you select the proper back-shift of a verb form if you do not know whether it is an *a-*, *e-*, or *i-*verb?

no (Because *a-*verbs take one set of suffixes and *e-* and *i-*verbs another set.)

16 Let's see, now, just how much you have to remember to rewrite *Es la una y María duerme* in the past tense. Is *Es* (*ser*) an irregular verb?

yes

17 The imperfect stem of *ser* is ——.

er

18 To this stem you add the first suffix ——.

a (So you have *Era la una.* Remember, clock time is always given in the Imperfect.)

19 Compare *duerme* and *come.* Do these forms tell you which verb is *e-*set and which verb is *i-*set?

no (You have to get this information from other forms like *dormimos* and *comemos.*)

20 The form *duerme* has a stem change. Do any of the present tense stem changes show up in the Preterit or Imperfect of regular *a-* and *e-*verbs?

no

21 Is *duerme* one of the three verbs that has an irregular stem in the Imperfect?

no (The three are *ser, ver,* and *ir.*)

22 Does the present tense *Es la una y María duerme* say that sleeping is in progress at one o'clock?

yes

23 Will the back-shift of *duerme,* then, be the (a) Preterit? (b) Imperfect?

Imperfect

24 The imperfect stem of *duerme* is ——.

dorm (As in "dormitory".)

25 The first suffix of the Imperfect of all regular *e-* and *i-*verbs is ——.

ía

26 You now know everything that is needed to write the past tense back-shift of *Es la una y María duerme.* It is ——.

Era la una y María dormía.

27 In the last nine frames you should have discovered that you have accumulated a lot of information about the uses of the Preterit and Imperfect, about verb forms, and about what cues the choice of the proper form. It is important that you understand that in language learning, unlike other courses, you cannot forget any of this information and still be able to communicate in the language. No native speaker can ever forget that *dormir* is a stem-changing verb or that the Preterit is used to mark the terminative aspect of cyclic events and the initiative aspect of non-cyclic events. When this does happen, doctors say that the person suffers from aphasia, a sure sign of brain damage. Just imagine what people would think of you if you suddenly could not remember that the past tense of *teach* is *taught* or that the past tense of *you are* is ⌇⌇⌇⌇.

you were **28** To be literate in a language you have to be able to read, write, and spell what you can hear or say. Write the Imperfect of *caen*.

caían **29** Copy *caían* and divide it into syllables.

ca-í-an (The accent mark over the *í* tells you it can be a syllable all by itself.)

30 Change *caían* to the Preterit. Remember what happens to plain *i* when it comes between two vowels.

cayeron **31** Write the Imperfect and Preterit of *oye*.

oía; oyó **32** Write the Imperfect of *ven*.

veían **33** To get the Imperfect of *va*, you change *v* to *b* (*ba*) and add the stem ⌇⌇⌇⌇.

i: iba (The same thing happens to *vas, vamos,* and *van.*)

34 Write the Imperfect of *vamos*. Before you do, remember what is special about all *nosotros*-forms in the Imperfect.

íbamos (The special thing is the accent mark.)

35 Remember this fact and change *recordamos* to the Imperfect.

recordábamos **36** You change only the first suffix of *eres* to get the Imperfect of *tú eres,* ⌇⌇⌇⌇.

tú eras **37** To get the Preterit of *tú oyes* you must change the *y* to ⌇⌇⌇⌇ before you add *ste*.

í (tú oíste) **38** In this and the next 9 frames, decide mentally which form of the past tense seems more logical for the context.

Entraron en la casa y después (*oían, oyeron*) los animales.

oyeron (And afterwards they began to hear the noise. Initiative aspect =
Preterit.) **39** El muchacho tropezó, (*caía, cayó*), y (*lloraba, lloró*).

cayó; lloró **40** Después Pedro (*salía, salió*) al patio y (*veía, vio*) la luna.

salió; vió **41** Ese día los niños (*comían, comieron*) en el momento que (*llegábamos, llegamos*).

comían; llegamos

42 (*Era, Fue*) el 4 de octubre y (*estábamos, estuvimos*) en Santiago.

Era; estábamos

43 En el invierno siempre (*hacía, hizo*) mucho frío y la gente (*tenía, tuvo*) hambre.

hacía; tenía **44** Y entonces (*then*) (*olvidaba, olvidó*) su lección.

olvidó **45** En 1492 Colón (*hallaba, halló*) las Américas.

halló **46** Y luego (*then*) (*entraba, entró*) en la casa y (*hablaba, habló*) con su mamá.

entró; habló **47** Y luego (*subía, subió*) al balcón mientras (*while*) nosotros (*comíamos, comimos*).

subió; comíamos

New Vocabulary

altura	height	**mulato**	mulato
indio	Indian	**dedo de la mano**	finger
mestizo	person of mixed blood: Indian and white	**dedo del pie**	toe

PROGRAM 98

Review of Spanish Spelling

The purpose of this Program is to review what you have learned about spelling Spanish words before you have a spelling quiz.

1 When you hear the Spanish word for "nose," you hear [naris]. Does what you hear tell you what letter to use for the final sound [s]? •

no

2 You have to hear and, then, see the written word for [naris] before you learn that the sound [s] in this word is spelled ———. •

z

3 Whenever Spanish uses two or more letters for the same sound, you have to either apply a rule or *see* the word before you can learn to spell it correctly. The spelling of [naris], the singular, and of the plural [narises] is an excellent example of "eye" spelling. The singular is spelled ———. •

nariz

4 But the plural is spelled *narices*. Once you see the difference between *nariz* and *narices*, you soon discover that the same thing happens in *lápiz* and *lápices*. Now you can go from "eye" spelling to "rule" spelling. Let's see how this works. When a word ends in a vowel, you make it plural by adding (a) *s* (b) *es*. •

s
labios

5 Write the plural for the word for "lips" in Spanish. •

6 When a word ends in a consonant in Spanish, you make it plural by adding the suffix ———. •

es
pulgares

7 Write the plural for "thumbs." •

8 Now look carefully at the singular and plural of the word for "nose" (noses) and "pencil" (pencils): *nariz, narices; lápiz, lápices.* Here is one rule for spelling Spanish [s]: when a word in the singular ends in the consonant z, you change z to ——— before you add the plural suffix *es*. •

c
peces

9 The word for one "fish" in Spanish is *pez*. Write the plural. •

10 The letter *c*, as just shown, can stand for the sound [s] when *c* comes right before *e*. Now write the words for "head" and "mouth." •

cabeza; boca
[k]

11 In these words the letter *c* stands for the sound (a) [s] (b) [k]. •

12 You have seen how *cabeza* and *boca* are spelled. You can now make up another rule if you observe carefully. The letter *c* stands for the sound [k] when *c* is followed by the vowel ———. •

a

13 You can now expand your rule and say that *c* stands for [s] before *e* and for [k] before *a*. Say *cien* aloud. The letter *c* in *cien* stands for the sound (a) [k] (b) [s].

[s]   **14** So you can expand your rule again and say that *c* stands for [s] before *e* and ⁓.

i (This is the complete rule on the use of *c* to stand for the sound [s].)

     15 Look at what comes after *c* in *cara*, *como*, and *disculpe*. Does *c* stand for the sound [k] in all these words?

yes   **16** There are only five vowels in Spanish: *i, e*, and *a, o, u*. With this knowledge you can make up this complete rule. The letter *c* stands for the sound [k] before the three vowels ⁓.

a, o, u   **17** You cannot always go from eye spelling to rule spelling. Let's see why. The present tense form of *ser* that goes with *nosotros* is ⁓.

somos   **18** We can now say that the sound [s] may be written *s* before *o*. The word that you hear for "arm" is [braso]. How do you spell it? (a) *braso* (b) *brazo*

brazo   **19** We can now say that the sound [s] may be written either *s* or *z* before *o*. Is it possible to make up a rule that will tell you when to write *s* or *z* before *o*?

no (So the only way you can learn to spell *somos* and *brazo* is to see the two words.)   **20** There are other cues which can tell you how to spell a word. Say *ciento* and *siento* aloud. Do they sound exactly alike?

yes   **21** Do *ciento* and *siento* have the same meaning?

no   **22** If you know the meaning of *ciento* (one hundred) and *siento* (I regret), will the meaning, once you have seen the words, tell you the way to spell each one?

yes (So you can combine eye and meaning spelling to get the correct spelling of many words.)

     23 Learning to spell is made a lot easier when you find out what letters can and cannot stand next to each other in a word. Say *pie*, *pierna*, and *diente* aloud. Now say *oye* and *oyes* aloud. Do the *ie* and the *ye* sound very much alike?

yes   **24** What you hear, then, is not going to tell you what to write. But this general rule will make spelling easier: Spanish never writes a *y* directly before or after a consonant in the same word. This fact, then, tells you to use *i*, not *y*, in *pie*, *diente*, and *pierna*. Spanish also writes only *í* between two vowels (*veía, caía*). When a sound like [i] as in *oigo*, comes between two vowels, it is written ⁓.

y (As in *oye, oyó*.)

     25 The dictionary of the Spanish Academy lists just eleven words that begin with *ze*. There are, in contrast, over fourteen pages of words that begin with *ce*. Does Spanish like to write *z* before *e*?

no   **26** There are lots of *a*-verbs in Spanish like *tropezar* (to trip) and *comenzar* (to begin) in which *z* appears before *a*. Now the *yo*-form of the Preterit of all *a*-verbs ends in the suffix ⁓.

é (*hablé, fumé, cerré*, etc.)   **27** From what you just learned in Frame 25, how would you expect the Spanish speaker to write the translation of "I tripped?" (a) *tropezé* (b) *tropecé*

tropecé   **28** You change the *z* of *nariz* to *c* in *narices*. Is this a practical rule: change *z* to *c* when it comes before *e* in another form of the same word?

yes   **29** The *yo*-form of the Preterit forces a change of letters in lots of verbs. Does the *c* of *buscar* stand for the sound of (a) [k]? (b) [s]?

[k]

30 Can *c* stand for [k] immediately before *e* (as in *centro*)?

no **31** The Spanish for "why?" is ¿ *por* ——?

qué (Did you forget the accent mark? Don't circle this frame wrong if you did.)

32 You write the sound [k] —— before *e* and *i*.

qu **33** Now, let's go back to *buscar*. In the Preterit the *yo*-form must end in the suffix ——.

é (Mark this wrong if you forgot the accent mark.)

34 How will you spell the translation of "I looked for?" (a) *buscé* (b) *busqué*

busqué **35** Most letters stand for the same phoneme (and all its allophones) all the time. Once you have learned the exceptions, you can spell all the rest of the words by ear. So you hear [lengwa] and you write ——.

lengua (Spanish, except in foreign words, always writes *u* for [w].)

36 Let's combine what you know about exceptions and what you hear and see if you can spell [kwerpo]. Say it aloud before you write.

cuerpo (You use *u* for [w]. You write [k] with *c* before *u*.)

37 You hear [frente], [pelo], [dedo], and [mano]. Do you have to use a rule or see these words to spell them?

no (Not if you know what letter stands for each phoneme in Spanish.)

38 Write the word for "he was reading."

leía **39** The accent mark in Spanish is just as much a part of spelling as the letters. Let's see why. Copy and divide *leía* and *oigo* into syllables.

le-í-a; oi-go (When [i] is the only sound in a syllable between two other vowels, it must be written *í*.)

40 Change *yo oigo* to the Imperfect. Remember the infinitive is *oír*.

yo oía **41** How many syllables are there in *oía*?

three (*o-í-a*) **42** In English we have many words which are spelled one way and pronounced in two different ways. We may enter a "contest" (pronounced *con'*-test), but we "con-*test*" a claim in court. Spanish, unlike English, uses the accent mark to tell people how to say certain words aloud. With minor exceptions, like *¿ qué?, ¿ dónde?,* etc., the accent mark is a signal which tells the reader that the word is not stressed according to rule.

When a word ends in a vowel, the stress falls (a) on the last syllable (b) on the next-to-last syllable.

on the next-to-last syllable

43 Copy and divide *hallo* into syllables.

ha-llo **44** The stressed syllable of *ha-llo* is ——.

ha **45** In the Preterit of *a*-verbs, the stress falls on the first suffix: *ha-lla-mos, ha-lla-ste*. Consequently, to write "you found" and to put the stress on the final *o*, you must write (a) *usted hallo* (b) *usted halló*.

usted halló (This tells the reader the stress does not follow the rule which says that words ending in a vowel are stressed on the next-to-the-last syllable.)

46 Words which end in *n* or *s* are also stressed on the next-to-the-last syllable. The Imperfect of *vamos* is an exception to this, so you write ——.

íbamos **47** The word for "lesson" ends in *n* and does not follow the general stress rules. So you must write ——.

lección **48** A word that ends in a consonant (except *n* or *s*) is stressed (a) on the last syllable (b) on the next-to-the-last syllable.

on the last syllable

49 The word *tunel* does not follow this rule. So it must be written ⌐⌐⌐.

túnel

50 The rules for stress say the stress falls either on the last or the next-to-last syllable. Will there have to be a written accent on every word in which the stress does not fall on one of these two syllables?

yes

úl-ti-mo; rá-pi-do

51 Copy, divide into syllables, and write the accent mark on *ultimo* and *rapido*.

52 Here are some of the words you have to see in order to spell. Look them over. The letters that may give you trouble appear in bold type. The words are arranged in the order that you met them in your lessons.

lloviendo	**h**a**b**itante	**ll**evar	**h**éroe
nevando	**ll**anura	espacio	nacional
niebla	selva	empezar	**b**oca
vale	po**b**lación	olvidar	**c**alle
volando	volver	**b**uscar	embargo
edificio	conocer	**h**allar	cigarro

New Vocabulary

teléfono	telephone	**abrazar**	to embrace, hug
besar	to kiss	**molestar**	to bother, annoy
masticar	to chew	**No se moleste.**	Don't bother.
tocar	to touch; play (a musical instrument)		

PROGRAM 99

Spelling, Done-to Pronouns, and the Reflexive Construction

Part 1: Spelling

1 Here is an important fact about cognates which will help you remember their Spanish spelling: with few exceptions, when a cognate has a sound which can be written with two letters in Spanish, the letter used will be the same as in English. So you hear [sigarro] and you write ⌐⌐⌐.

cigarro (The cognate is "cigar.")

2 Which spelling is correct for "avenue?" (a) *abenida* (b) *avenida*

avenida

3 Which spelling is correct? (a) *havitante* (b) *habitante*

habitante (Like "inhabitant.")

4 Which spelling is correct? (a) *difísil* (b) *difícil*

difícil (Like "difficult," which has *c*, not *s*.)

5 Compare *difícil* and "difficult." Do you pronounce both *f* sounds in "difficult?"

no

6 There are many double consonants in English cognates which stand for only one sound: professor, coffee, class, different, etc. Spanish writes a double consonant only when both are actually pronounced. Write the Spanish for "professor."

profesor　　　**7** In your last Program, you reviewed the four cues for spelling: (1) meaning, (2) what you hear, (3) what you see, (4) rules. What tells you to spell 100 as *ciento*, not *siento*?

meaning (*Siento* means "I'm sorry.")

　　　8 You hear [mestiso]. What tells you to write *mestizo*?

what you see　　**9** You hear [asta] and you write ⌣⌣⌣.

hasta (Because you have always seen the word with an *h*.)

　　　10 You hear [entre]. Can you trust your ear to tell you what to write?

yes

There are in the United States certain restaurants and places of public entertainment where men are not admitted without a necktie or a coat and, in general, men wear a necktie and a coat to church and other formal meetings. In these same situations sports clothes are generally considered improper.

The same customs exist in the Hispanic world, but the restrictions are much more generalized. More restaurants require coats and ties. In general, sports clothes are worn only for sporting events and, as a result, many Latins react negatively to the American tourists who wear sport shirts on the street. In some places tourists are not allowed in churches without a coat, and many people are shocked when American women tourists visit churches in slacks.

In both cultures custom usually requires women to cover their heads in Catholic churches. Many American women wear hats. This is not done in the Hispanic world. They cover their heads, instead, with a veil (*velo*), scarf (*pañuelo*), or a *mantilla*.

1 When the doer and the done-to in a sentence are the same, the construction is reflexive. The doer in *Aunque la mona se vista de seda* is ⁓⁓⁓.

la mona

2 The word for the done-to is the reflexive pronoun ⁓⁓⁓.

se

3 The *se* in Spanish merely says that the done-to is the same as the doer. The translation of *se* into English depends on who the doer is. In the proverb *la mona* is a female. So you must translate *se* as ⁓⁓⁓.

herself

4 A very precise or literal translation of the first part of the proverb goes like this: "Although the monkey may dress herself in silk." Will the meaning be changed a lot in English if *herself* is left out?

no

5 English, unlike Spanish, tends to leave out the word for the done-to when the meaning is obvious. Who gets dressed in *He got up and dressed?* (a) he (b) somebody else

he

6 Who gets washed and shaved in *I washed and shaved?* (a) myself (b) somebody else

myself

7 Would it be all right to say *I washed and shaved myself?*

yes

8 Here is a rule of usage for you to remember: when the doer and done-to are the same, Spanish regularly names the done-to. Translate: I get up at six.

Yo me levanto a las seis. (The meaning is "I get myself up at six.")

9 In the proverb about the monkey the verb form *vista* translates "may dress." This is a form you won't study for a few weeks. It is called the **subjunctive**. The translation of "The monkey dresses herself" is *La mona se viste*. The infinitive is *vestir*. Is this a stem-changing verb?

yes

10 The *e* changes to *i* in all present tense forms except the one that agrees with *nosotros*. Translate: We dress ourselves.

Nosotros nos vestimos.

11 Translate: I dress myself.

Yo me visto.

12 To change *Yo me visto* so that the doer is *tú*, you have to make three changes. First, *yo* is replaced by *tú*. Second, *me* is replaced by ⁓⁓⁓.

te (The done-to form of *tú*.)

13 You now have *Tú te* and the verb suffix of *visto* must be changed to ⁓⁓⁓.

es (*Tú te vistes*.)

14 Let's go through these three steps again so you will get used to making all the changes. To change *Tú te vistes* so the doer is "you" (plural), you replace *tú* with ⁓⁓⁓.

ustedes

15 The done-to and reflexive pronoun that matches *ustedes* is not *te;* it is ⁓⁓⁓.

se

16 You now have *Ustedes se* and the verb suffix of *vistes* must be changed to *viste* ⁓⁓⁓.

n (*Ustedes se visten.*)

17 The reflexive pronoun *se* matches *ustedes, usted, él, ella, ellos,* and *ellas*. Translate: He dresses himself.

Él se viste.

18 Change this to: They (masculine) dress themselves.

Ellos se visten.

19 Which is the more common translation of *Ellos se visten?* (a) They dress themselves. (b) They dress.

They dress (Except when the meaning is a contrast as in "Mother doesn't dress them anymore; they dress *themselves*.")

20 Here is another stem-changing verb which is common in reflexive constructions. It is *acostar*, the opposite of *levantar*. Let's see if you can figure out the translation of this sentence: *Me acuesto a las nueve de la noche y me levanto a las siete de la mañana.*

I go to bed at nine at night and get up at seven in the morning.

21 The word *costado* means the "side of a human body" and *acostarme* literally means "to put myself on my side" = to lie down on my side to sleep. The regular translation of *Me acuesto* is ⁓.

I go to bed.

22 The stem change in *acostar* is *o* to *ue*. Write the missing form: *Usted se* ⁓.

acuesta

23 To change *Usted se acuesta* so the doer is "you" (plural), you have to make two changes. Let's see if you can do this correctly.

Ustedes se acuestan. (You make the doer form and the verb plural.)

24 To change *Usted se acuesta* so the doer is "you" (intimate), you have to make three changes. Can you do this one correctly?

Tú te acuestas.

25 To change *Ustedes se acuestan* so the doer is "they" (masculine), you only have to make one change. Write the new sentence.

Ellos se acuestan.

26 In this and the next three frames, write the missing done-to form.
Nosotros ⁓ acostamos.

nos   **27** Mis hermanos y yo ⁓ acostamos.

nos   **28** Pedro ⁓ acuesta.

se   **29** Yo ⁓ acuesto.

me   **30** Here is another new verb which is commonly used in reflexive constructions. It is *desayunar*. Let's see what it means. The *des* is the negative prefix which is like "dis" in "disappear." The verb *ayunar* translates "to fast" or "to go hungry." So *desayunar* means "to break one's fast" or "to have ⁓."

breakfast (You go all night without eating. So in the morning you "break your fast," that is, you have "breakfast.")

31 *Desayunar* is a regular *a*-verb. Write the missing form: *Yo me* ⁓ *a las siete de la mañana.*

desayuno   **32** *¿ A qué hora te* ⁓ *tú?*

desayunas   **33** Translate: *¿ A qué hora te desayunas tú?* The meaning of *hora* is the same as in *¿ Qué hora es?*

At what time do you have breakfast?

34 Change *Tú te desayunas* so that the doer is "you" (formal and singular). Remember you must make three changes.

Usted se desayuna.

35 To make *Usted se desayuna* plural you keep the *se* and make *usted* and *desayuna* plural. So you get ⁓.

Ustedes se desayunan.

36 To change *Ustedes se desayunan* so the doer is "they" (feminine), you make only one change. Now you have ⁓.

Ellas se desayunan.

37 Let's review. The done-to pronoun that matches *yo* is ⁓.

me

38 The done-to pronoun that matches *nosotros* is ⁓.

nos

39 The done-to pronoun that matches *tú* is ⁓.

te

40 The only done-to and also reflexive pronoun that goes with all other doers is ⁓.

se

New Vocabulary

levantarse	to get up (from bed), to stand up
casarse	to get married
antes que	before
se	herself, himself, yourself, yourselves, themselves, itself

PROGRAM 100

More on the Done-to Pronouns and the Reflexive Construction

1 The done-to pronouns *me*, *nos*, and *te* match the doer pronouns ⁓.

yo, nosotros, tú

2 When you are the "speaker" and the "doer," your Spanish name is (a) *yo* (b) *me*.

yo

3 When you are the "speaker" and the "done-to," your Spanish name as the done-to is ⁓.

me

4 In a conversation both sets of pronouns have to be changed when you answer questions. The "yes" answer to *¿ Eres tú de España?* is *Sí,* ⁓.

Sí, yo soy de España.

5 In the question *¿ Eres tú de España?* your pronoun name is *tú*, your name as the person spoken to. When you answer you are now the speaker and your pronoun name cannot be *tú*. It must be ⁓.

yo

6 The same kind of change has to take place when you use the done-to pronouns. Let's start with a statement and see how this works. You are the speaker and you are talking to someone else. You say *Tú me ves.* The translation is ⁓.

You see me.

7 The question form of this statement is "Do you see me?" The yes answer to this question in English is "Yes, ⁓."

I see you.

8 In the original question, your name as speaker and done-to is "me." When another person answers and is the speaker, he replaces "me" with ⁓.

you ("You" is your done-to name when someone speaks to you.)

9 The same kinds of changes in the done-to names take place in Spanish. Suppose you ask *¿ Me ves tú?* The doer in this question, that is, the person seeing is ⁓.

tú

10 The done-to in *¿ Me ves tú ?* is *Me*, the speaker of the question. When someone answers the question *¿ Me ves tú ?*, that someone automatically becomes the new speaker and you become the person spoken to. Your done-to name as the person spoken to cannot be *me*. So the person answering you must change *me* to the form of direct address and say, *Sí, yo* ———— *veo.*

Sí, yo te veo.   **11** Let's look at all this more closely. Your name as the speaker and doer is *yo*. When you are the speaker, your name as the done-to is *me*. So you have three pronoun names and you have to learn when to use each one. Suppose, now, someone asks, *¿ A qué hora te acuestas ?* Your done-to name is now *te*. When you answer and are the speaker, your name as the doer must be ————.

yo   **12** Now, the matching done-to name for *yo* is ————.

me   **13** Translate: I go to bed at nine. Remember you have to change the verb form to match *yo*.

Yo me acuesto a las nueve.

14 It is easy to get mixed up when you are working with several pronoun names for the same person. So let's practice this some more. Suppose you ask someone *¿ Me recuerdas ?* The "yes" answer will be *Sí, yo* ———— *recuerdo.*

Sí, yo te recuerdo.   **15** When a close friend talks to you, your done-to name is *te*. When a stranger talks to you, your done-to name may be *se*. What will your "yes" answer be to *¿ Se levanta usted temprano ?*

Sí, yo me levanto temprano.   **16** When someone talks to you as a group, the done-to pronoun is *se* in the reflexive construction: *¿ Se levantan ustedes temprano ?* When you answer this question for the group, your doer pronoun name is ————.

nosotros   **17** The done-to pronoun that matches *nosotros* is ————.

nos   **18** Translate: We get up early. *Nosotros* ————.

Nosotros nos levantamos temprano.

19 Let's see, now, if you are learning how to handle these forms. The "yes" answer to *¿ Me conoces tú ?* is *Sí,* ————.

Sí, te conozco.   **20** The no answer to *¿ Me miras tú ?* is ————.

No, no te miro.   **21** When you answer *sí* to *¿ Te acuestas temprano ?* you say ————.

Sí, yo me acuesto temprano.

22 Suppose you are a male and someone reports what you just said to another person. You are being talked about; the reporter must use ————.

él   **23** The done-to pronoun that matches *él* is ————.

se   **24** The verb form *acuesto* must be changed to match *él*. This form is ————.

acuesta   **25** Now, translate: He goes to bed early.

Él se acuesta temprano.

26 To make this statement into a question, you merely put the doer pronoun after the verb and change the intonation: *¿ Se acuesta él temprano ?* Will the yes answer to this question be the original statement *Sí, él se acuesta temprano ?*

yes (In the third person, the done-to *se* remains the same in both the question and the answer.)

27 The Spanish verb which is a cognate of "lavatory" is ————.

lavar   **28** Can you "wash" without washing something?

no (Verbs like *lavar* always require a real or understood done-to.)

29 Remember that Spanish, unlike English, regularly says the word for the done-to. You have gotten all dirty playing and you say, "I'm going to wash now." What is the missing word in English?

myself (So you get in Spanish *Voy a lavarme ahora.*)

30 Someone is talking to you in *usted*. What must this person do to change *Voy a lavarme* into a question? The *voy* must be changed to ⁓⁓⁓.

va

31 The *me* is changed to ⁓⁓⁓, the done-to form that matches *usted*.

se (So you have *¿Va usted a lavarse?*)

32 If you make the subject *ustedes*, you change *va* to ⁓⁓⁓.

van

33 Is there a plural form of *se*?

no (So you have *¿Van ustedes a lavarse?*)

34 You are the speaker for the group addressed as *ustedes*. Your yes answer to the question *¿Van ustedes a lavarse?* must be ⁓⁓⁓.

Sí, vamos a lavarnos.

35 You are talking to a person in *tú*. Translate: Are you going to wash?

¿Vas a lavarte?

36 The other person answers, *Sí*, ⁓⁓⁓.

Sí, voy a lavarme.

37 You are a girl. Someone reports what you just said. The report is *Ella* ⁓⁓⁓.

Ella va a lavarse.

38 As a girl you have several pronoun names. As the speaker *and* doer your name is ⁓⁓⁓.

yo

39 As the person spoken *about*, your name is ⁓⁓⁓.

ella

40 As the speaker and the *done-to*, your name is ⁓⁓⁓.

me

41 As the person spoken to, you have two names in the role of the done-to. A close friend uses ⁓⁓⁓.

te

42 A stranger uses ⁓⁓⁓.

se

43 Translate: I wash at six.

Me lavo a las seis.

44 Fill in the blank on your answer sheet: *Ella dice que* (she washes herself) ⁓⁓⁓ *a las seis.*

se lava

45 Complete: *¿Es verdad que tú* ⁓⁓⁓ *a las seis?*

te lavas

46 Complete: *¿Es verdad que usted* ⁓⁓⁓ *a las seis?*

se lava

47 Answer the above question with *Sí, yo* ⁓⁓⁓ *a las seis.*

me lavo

48 When the doer and the done-to in a sentence are the same, you have a ⁓⁓⁓ construction.

reflexive

49 In the dialect of Spanish that you are learning, there are just four done-to pronouns that are used in reflexive constructions. The done-to pronoun that matches *yo* is ⁓⁓⁓.

me (*Yo me lavo.*)

50 The done-to pronoun that matches *nosotros* is the shortened form ⁓⁓⁓.

nos (*Nosotros nos lavamos.*)

51 The done-to pronoun that matches *tú* is ⁓⁓⁓.

te (*Tú te lavas.*)

52 There is just one done-to reflexive pronoun that matches *usted, ustedes, él, ella, ellos,* and *ellas.* It is ⁓⁓⁓.

se (*Usted se lava, ustedes se lavan, etc.*)

53 The answer to *¿ Vas a lavarte?* may be *Sí, voy a lavar* ———. •

me **54** Will the answer to *¿ Va usted a lavarse?* be the same? •

yes (You are still the speaker and the done-to, so you say, *Sí, voy a lavarme.*)

New Vocabulary

cartel	poster
molestia	bother
No es molestia ninguna.	It's no bother at all.

Although a great many Indians in the United States still live on reservations and preserve some features of their ancient culture, they have accepted many forms of American culture. For example, they have cars, radios, and television sets which they buy with American money. In contrast, there are many Indians in Latin America, especially in Peru, Bolivia, and Brazil, who live completely outside of the money economy. This means that they never earn any money and that they acquire whatever they have by bartering. There are no stores or shops in their villages because there is no money to buy things and, as a result, they never get many of the very common things that you take for granted. Most of them never have shoes or store-bought clothes; some use almost no clothes at all.

PROGRAM **101**

Getting Ready for a Quiz on the Done-to Pronouns, and the Preterit of Verbs Ending in *-zar*, *-gar*, and *-car*

Part 1: Done-to Pronouns

You have now a very large amount of information in and about Spanish. You know that learning a language is not like studying history, geography, or government. Most people study history and very soon afterwards start to forget many of the details. They retain only the most important facts. This is to be expected when the information learned does not have to be used every day. Learning a language, however, is very different from learning history. *You cannot use a language for communication if you forget how to make up verb forms, if you forget sentence patterns, or if you forget your name as the speaker and the done-to.* You may forget some vocabulary words, but if you forget the basic facts, patterns, and forms, you cannot talk or understand the language.

In an organized program of language teaching, you do not need to spend thousands of hours, as the native child does, in learning a language. You learned, for example, to count and tell time in Spanish in a few days and to read in a few weeks. Nevertheless, you have to have a certain minimum of practice, drill, and review or you cannot become automatic in the use of the language. So let's review once again the forms of the done-to pronouns and their position in the sentence.

1 One set of done-to pronouns is really made up of adjectival residuals: the forms of the definite article which are left over when the noun is dropped. The potential adjectival residual in *Voy a ver la casa* is ⁓⁓⁓.

la

2 Translate: I'm going to see it.

Voy a verla. (Remember: you add the residual to the end of the infinitive in writing.)

3 The done-to residual is the same in *Veo la casa*. What, however, must you do with the *la* when you translate "I see it?" Write the translation.

La veo. (The done-to pronoun comes immediately before the finite or conjugated verb form.)

4 The potential done-to residual in *Vamos a repasar las lecciones* is ⁓⁓⁓.

las

5 Translate: We are going to review them. (Watch your spelling. It will be counted on the quiz.)

Vamos a repasarlas.

6 Translate: We are reviewing them. *Nosotros* ⁓⁓⁓.

Nosotros las repasamos.

7 The potential done-to residual of *Tenemos los libros* is ⁓⁓⁓.

los

8 Translate: We have them.

(Nosotros) los tenemos.

9 The singular form of *los* has two allomorphs. As an adjectival residual the form that replaces *el* in *Tengo el libro* is the singular of *los*. It is ⁓⁓⁓.

lo (*Tengo el libro; Lo tengo.*)

10 The potential residual in *El profesor vive allí* is ⁓⁓⁓.

El

11 The article *el* becomes the doer pronoun *él* (with an accent in writing) when it is the subject of the verb. The *él*, like *el*, becomes *lo* when it stands for a male done-to. So Spanish normally does not say *Vamos a ver a él*, but *Vamos a ver* ⁓⁓⁓.

lo

12 *Vamos a ver a ellos* is changed to *Vamos a ver* ⁓⁓⁓.

los (The *los* is the second part of *el-los*.)

13 What will *Vamos a ver a ella* become? *Vamos a ver* ⁓⁓⁓.

la (This *la* is also the second part of *el-la*.)

14 If *ella* can stand for *María*, what will the done-to pronoun for *María* be?

la

15 So *Vemos a María* may be changed to ⁓⁓⁓.

La vemos.

16 Can *ellos* replace *mis amigos* in *Vamos a ver a mis amigos?*

yes

17 So the done-to pronoun for *mis amigos* will be ⁓⁓⁓.

los

18 Translate: We see them.

Los vemos.

19 The done-to forms *la, las, los,* and *lo* are used when the doer and done-to are different. *Olvidé mi libro* becomes *Lo olvidé. Recordaron a sus amigos* becomes *Los recordaron. Observó a usted* (female) becomes ⁓⁓⁓.

La observó.

20 In your quiz you will have something like this: *Papá conoce a mis amigos.* The done-to pronoun that replaces *a mis amigos* is ⁓⁓⁓.

los

21 Copy and put *los* in the right position: *Papá* ———— *conoce* ————.
Papá los conoce.

22 The other done-to pronouns are *me*, *nos*, and *te*. These are the forms that are used with the verb. So *Papá busca a nosotros* becomes *Papá* ———— *busca.*

nos

23 And *Papá busca a ti* becomes *Papá* ———— *busca.*

te

24 What will *Papá busca a él y a mí* become? *Papá* ———— *busca.*

nos

Part 2: The Preterit of Verbs Ending in *-zar*, *-gar*, and *-car*

There is nothing special about these verbs in speech. They all, however, present a problem in spelling which you already know about from writing other words. Let's see how easy, consequently, it is going to be to learn how to write these verbs.

1 The infinitive cognate of "to embrace" (hug) is ————.

abrazar

2 The first suffix of the *yo*-form of the Preterit of *a*-verbs is ————.

é (Always with the written accent.)

3 Does the Spanish speaker like to write *z* before *e*?

no

4 What letter normally replaces *z* before *e*?

c

5 So *yo abrazo* becomes *yo* ———— in the Preterit.

abracé

6 The forms *abrazar* and *abrazo* tell you that Spanish does write *z* before the vowels ————.

a; o

7 Can the letter *c* stand for the sound [s] before *a* or *o*?

no (It stands for [k] as in *casa* and *cosa*.)

8 So the Preterit of *tú abrazas* must be written *tú* ————.

abrazaste

9 The first suffix of the *usted* and *él* of the Preterit of *abrazar* is ————.

ó (With a written accent.)

10 So the Preterit of *usted abraza* is written *usted* ————.

abrazó (Remember the word for "arm" is *brazo*.)

11 The preterit form that goes with *ustedes* and *ellos* is ————.

abrazaron

12 Now you know that there is only one special spelling problem in verbs that end in *zar*. When the *a* is replaced by *é*, you write ———— instead of *z*.

c (*Yo la abracé.*)

13 Let's look, now, at *abracé* and *masticar* (to chew). The *c* before *é* stands for the sound [s]. If you write *masticé* will the *c* still stand for [s]?

yes

14 What makes a verb regular in speech is the fact that the stem has the same sound in all tenses. *Masticar* is a regular verb. Does the *c* before *a* stand for the sound [k] or [s]?

[k]

15 The sound [k] is regularly written by the digraph ———— before *e* and *i*.

qu

16 So the *yo*-form of the Preterit of *masticar* is written ————.

mastiqué

17 Write the *yo*-form of *buscar*. *Yo* ————.

busqué

18 All the other preterit forms of verbs like *buscar* and *masticar* have either *o* or *a* as the first vowel after the stem. Will there be any spelling change in these forms?

no (You write *masticaste, buscó, buscaron, etc.*)

19 Let's consider now the spelling change in the Preterit of verbs like *llegar*. Is the *g* of *llegar* pronounced like the *g* of *gato* and *gordo*?

yes

20 Is the *g* of *gente* pronounced like the *j* of *ojo?*

yes

21 The *g* before *e* and *i* is always pronounced like the *j* of *ojo* in Spanish. **Can it be used**, then, to stand for the *g* sound of *llegar* when the first suffix is *é?*

no

22 The sound [g] is the voiced equivalent of the unvoiced [k]. Remember *gato* and "cat." The [k] sound is written *qu* before the Preterit suffix *é* (*busqué*, *mastiqué*). Consequently, it should not surprise you that the *yo*-form of *llegar* is written ⁓.

llegué

23 In all other preterit forms of *llegar*, the stem is followed by either *a* or *ó*. Will there be any change in the spelling of the stem *lleg?*

no

24 The verb *jugar* has the same spelling changes as *llegar*. Write the preterit forms that go with *yo* and *él*.

yo jugué ; él jugó

25 You have been shown that only the *yo*-form of the Preterit of regular *a*-verbs has a spelling change. Eye spelling plus a rule tells you what to do. A *z* changes to ⁓ before *é*.

c

26 Write the Preterit of *yo abrazo*.

abracé

27 The *c* before *a* changes to the digraph ⁓ before *é*.

qu

28 Write the Preterit of *yo busco*.

busqué

29 The *g* before *a* or *o* changes to the digraph ⁓ before *é*.

gu

30 Write the Preterit of *yo llego*.

llegué

New Vocabulary

amarillo	yellow	**verde**	green
anaranjado	orange (color)	**verde claro**	light green
rojo	red	**verde oscuro**	dark green
rosado	rose-colored, pink	**blanco**	white
morado	purple	**negro**	black
azul	blue	**gris**	gray

PROGRAM 102

Words for Clothing, and a Vocabulary and Spelling Round-up

Part 1 : Words for Clothing

Here is a bit of history about the Spanish word for "clothes" which may help you remember the word.

In the year 409, a Germanic tribe called the Visigoths began to invade Spain. By the sixth century they had conquered most of the Peninsula and the kings in Spain continued to be of Visigothic origin until the year 711. The Visigothic conquerors spoke a form of Old German and as a result several hundred Germanic words eventually became part of modern Spanish vocabulary. The Old

German verb for "to steal" was *roubon*. The word for "booty" or "loot" was *roub*. When the Germanic tribes pillaged and looted, clothing was one of the things most highly prized. Thus, *roubon* became "to rob" in English and *robar* in Spanish. In the same way Old German *roub* became English "robe" and Spanish *ropa*, the modern Spanish word for clothes or clothing.

1 The general or cover term for clothing in Spanish is *ropa*. One important item of Spanish *ropa* is a cognate of "pantaloons," a kind of trousers worn over a hundred years ago. What men wear today is a shortened form of the word "pantaloons." This form is ⁓.

pants   **2** In English men and boys wear "pants." In Spanish these are still called *pantalones*. Say *pan-ta-lo-nes* aloud. The stress falls on the syllable ⁓.

lo   **3** A garment which males used to wear around their shoulders, over their arms, and tucked into their pantaloons used to be called a "camisole." Spanish still uses *camisa* for this garment. Our modern translation is ⁓.

shirt (Say *camisa* aloud.)

4 In Spanish a boy wears *una camisa*. A Spanish girl, however, would not wear *una camisa*. She wears, instead, *una blusa*. The cognate and translation of *blusa* is ⁓.

blouse   **5** A man's lower and outer garment is his *pantalones*. The female equivalent of this garment is *una falda*. The translation of *falda* is ⁓.

skirt   **6** A Spanish boy wears *pantalones y una* ⁓.

camisa   **7** A Spanish girl wears *una falda y una* ⁓.

blusa   **8** Inside the collar of his shirt, a man often wears a colorful piece of cloth called *una corbata*. The translation is ⁓.

necktie   **9** In English men wear "socks" and women wear "stockings." In Spanish men generally wear *calcetines* and women wear *medias*, though *medias* is frequently used as a cover term for both. Copy each, divide into syllables, and underline the stressed syllable.

*cal-ce-**ti**-nes; **me**-dias* (Now say these words aloud.)

10 The verb "to dress" in Spanish is ⁓. (Remember *la mona* and the proverb, and the English cognate "vestment.")

vestir   **11** When one has dressed (has clothes on) one *está vestido* in Spanish. The whole outfit of a person is his or her *vestido*. The most common translation for her *vestido* is ⁓.

dress (When *vestido* is used in talking of men, the best translation is "clothing." Thus in "A man's clothing tells you a lot about him," the word for "clothing" is *vestido*.)

Part 2: Vocabulary Round-up

This round-up has two purposes. It will review some vocabulary words, but, most importantly, it will deal with cues for spelling the words you have been learning recently.

1 There are four words in this set which you can spell by ear and one which you must hear and see to learn to spell: *claro, blanco, negro, azul, rojo*. The word you must see and hear is ⁓.

azul (You may write either *s* or *z* before *u: su, azul*.)

2 The sound [rr] is spelled ⌣⌣⌣ at the beginning of words.

r (But *rr* between two vowels: *perro.*)

3 You hear *rojo* (red) and *rosado* (rose-colored). Do you also have to see them to know how to spell [rr]?

no (Your ear hears [rr] but the rule says to write *r*.)

4 You hear *besar* (to kiss) and *verde* (green). Will what you hear tell you which word begins with *b* or *v*?

no (The *b* and *v* stand for the same sounds. You have to see these words before you can learn to spell them.)

5 You hear the infinitive [kebrar] (to break) and the *yo*-form of the Preterit [toké] (touched, played). What digraph will you write for [k]?

qu (*Quebrar, toqué,* like *busqué.*)

6 A spelling rule tells you to write *qu* for [k] before the two vowels ⌣⌣⌣.

e; i

7 You hear [kwerpo] (body). What letter do you write for [w]?

u

8 You hear [kwerpo], [kara] (face), and [kontar] (to count). What letter do you write for [k]?

c (Before *a, o,* and *u.*)

9 Transcribe the spoken words in Frame 8 into regular spelling.

cuerpo, cara, contar

10 There are three letters which can be used to write the sound [s]. Now watch out! Transcribe these *four* words in regular spelling: [sigarro], [naris], [siento].

cigarro, nariz, siento or *ciento*

11 You hear [siento] in context. What tells you to write *ciento* or *siento?*

the meaning

12 You hear [éroe] and [abitante]. What do you add to these words when you write them in Spanish?

h: héroe, habitante (You spell all words having *h* in them by eye.)

13 Which spelling is correct? (a) *hidioma* (b) *idioma*

idioma (You have to see all syllables that begin with a vowel in order to discover there is no *h* before the vowel. One saying in Spanish goes like this: He is so dumb he spells "love" (*amor*) with an *h* (*hamor*).

14 Say [yo], [yevar], and [oyes] aloud. Now write the word that has an *ll* in it.

llevar

15 Will anything you hear tell you when to use *ll* or *y* for [y]?

no (You have to first see these words to learn to spell them. Many poorly educated native speakers write *llo* for *yo.*)

16 Spell [yanura].

llanura

17 Except for the conjunction *y* (and), Spanish never writes *y* for a vowel sound. The translation of "island" is ⌣⌣⌣.

isla

18 Spanish also never writes *y* between a consonant and a following vowel. Translate: fog; earth.

niebla; tierra

19 Here is the spoken word for a number: [sinkwenta]. Say this aloud. The Arabic number is ⌣⌣⌣.

50

20 You write out 50 as ⌣⌣⌣.

cincuenta

21 The *h* never stands for a sound in Spanish. There are also other letters that sometimes do not stand for a sound. Does *u* stand for a sound in *querer?*

no (It is part of the digraph *qu.*)

22 You hear [reló] but you write ⌣⌣⌣.

reloj

23 The Preterit of certain verbs has a spelling change in the *yo*-form. Write the Preterit of *yo toco*.

yo toqué   **24** Write the Preterit of *yo busco*.

yo busqué   **25** The *yo*-form of the Preterit of *abrazar* is ―――― .

abracé   **26** The Preterit of *yo llego* is ―――― .

yo llegué   **27** The Preterit for *yo tropiezo* is ―――― .

yo tropecé   **28** The spelling of English cognates, as you know, helps you decide how to write Spanish words. The cognate of "avenue" is ―――― .

avenida ("Avenue" tells you to write *v* not *b*.)

29 The spelling of the cognate "telephone" is deceptive. Is there a *ph* in the Spanish alphabet?

no   **30** So the Spanish cognate is spelled ―――― .

teléfono   **31** The infinitive cognate of "dormitory" is ―――― .

dormir   **32** Let's review, once again, the cues that tell you how to spell correctly. When there is only one letter that stands for a phoneme and all its allophones, you know when you hear the sound what letter to write. This is spelling by ear. Is there any sound in [aprende] that can be written by more than one letter?

no   **33** There are some sounds which can be written by two or more letters. Thus the sound [s] can be written *s* before *o* (*sol*) or *z* before *o* (*mestizo*). Will what you hear or a spelling rule tell you which letter to use?

no (You have to see these words to learn to spell them.)

34 Can you write either *s* or *z* before the vowel *u*?

yes: *su* or *azul* (You also have to see these words to learn how to spell them.)

35 When two words having different meanings sound alike but are spelled differently, only the ―――― tells which spelling to use.

meaning   **36** When the same sound has two or more spellings, the choice can often be made by rule. Thus you spell [k] with a ―――― before *a*, *o*, and *u*.

c   **37** But you spell [k] with the digraph ―――― before *e* and *i*.

qu   **38** Here is a way to make learning how to spell a lot easier. You know that the sound of [s] can be written *s*, *c*, or *z*. It is a great waste of time to memorize the spelling of all words having the sound [s] in them. If you memorize those words spelled with *c* (*espacio, conocer, edificio, dirección, cigarro, tropecé, abracé, etc.*) and those spelled with *z* (*empezar, cabeza, nariz, brazo, mestizo, azul, abrazar, etc.*) then you can be certain that all the other words you know spell [s] with *s*. You will, of course, have to learn the spelling of new words as you meet them.

New Vocabulary

bandera	flag	**sentar(se)(ie)**	to sit down
despertar(se)(ie)	to wake up	**de prisa**	quickly, in a hurry
desayunar(se)	to have breakfast		

PROGRAM **103**

More Vocabulary for Clothing and the Preterit of Stem-changing *i*-Verbs

Part 1: Clothing Vocabulary

1 Let's begin this section with a review of the clothing words you have already had. The cognate of "pantaloon" and the word for "pants" is ⁓.

pantalones　**2** The general cover term for clothes is a cognate of "robe" and "robber." It is ⁓.

ropa (The [p] voices to [b] in *robar*—to steal.)

3 The term for one's whole outfit, for either men or women, is a form derived from the verb *vestir*. It is ⁓.

vestido (This word, however, is more commonly used for a woman's dress.)

4 The cognate of "blouse" is ⁓.

blusa (You do not have to worry about the *b* or *v* choice here. Spanish never writes *v* before another consonant.)

5 The girls' garment that regularly goes with a *blusa* is una ⁓.

falda　**6** The male equivalent of a *blusa* is una ⁓.

camisa　**7** The long, narrow strip of cloth worn with a *camisa* is una ⁓.

corbata (You have to see the *b* to learn to spell this word.)

8 A long time ago people wore long stockings which covered the leg and thigh. These were called *calzas*. A half *calza* or *media calza* came to the knee or just above it. Gradually the word *calza* was dropped and the adjectival residual, *media* became the word for a stocking. The diminutive of *calza* is *calceta* (a short stocking) and the diminutive of *calceta* is *calcetín* (a very short stocking) or ⁓.

sock (You have to see *calcetín* to learn to spell it.)

9 Here, now, are some new words for clothing which you have not seen before. Spanish borrowed *suéter* right from English. Say [swéter] aloud. The English spelling is ⁓.

sweater　**10** The part of one's outfit that people put on over *medias* or *calcetines* is called *un zapato*. This is a ⁓.

shoe (Nothing, except your eye, tells you to write *z* instead of *s*. So you must memorize that *zapato* begins with a *z*.)

11 The Spanish word for "shade" or "shadow" is *sombra*. The piece of clothing you wear on your head to shade the head and the eyes is a *sombrero*. The translation is ⁓.

hat　**12** Divide *sombrero* into syllables, underline the stressed syllable, and say the word aloud (after you have checked your division).

*som-**bre**-ro*　**13** Does Spanish ever write a *v* before another consonant?

no (So you have a rule: write *b* for /b/ before another consonant.)

14 The article of clothing that goes along with *pantalones* to make up a suit is *un saco* or a ⁓.

coat

15 The name for an outfit made up of *pantalones* and *chaqueta* (or *saco*) is *traje* or ~~~~. •

suit **16** The garment that is put on over a *saco* when it is cold is *un abrigo*. The translation is ~~~~. •

overcoat **17** When it rains, the Spanish speaker wears *un impermeable* or ~~~~. •

raincoat (When something is "impermeable" in English, water will not pass

through it.) **18** Here is *impermeable* divided into syllables: *im-per-me-a-ble*. Say it aloud in Spanish.

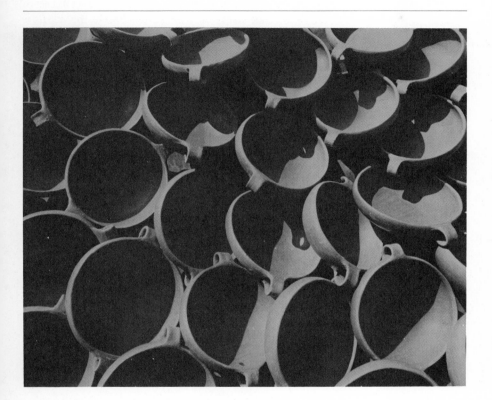

When the Spaniards took over the New World, they did not totally destroy the Indian civilization. There are still many villages which are completely Indian and some in which the people do not speak Spanish. As a result, folk traditions, customs, and art have survived. The silversmiths of Mexico and Peru are famous for their craftsmanship, and each country that has a large Indian population produces its own special artifacts: pottery, blankets, leather-work, etc. In the past, these home industries produced articles primarily for local use. With the growth of tourism, new markets opened up and modifica-tions in designs began to develop. Today many craftsmen produce imita-tion handicraft articles which sell almost exclusively to tourists. In the areas where there are ruins of ancient Indian civilizations, the craftsmen make copies of original art objects which are sometimes sold to the unsuspecting tourist as originals.

Part 2: The Preterit of Stem-Changing *i*-Verbs

1 In the Present the stressed *o* of the stem sometimes changes to *ue: yo duermo*. These same verbs have two irregular forms in the Preterit: *usted (él, ella) durmió* and *ustedes (ellos, ellas) durmieron*. The *o* of the regular stem *(dormir)* changes to ⁓⁓.

u

2 The *yo*-form of *dormir* in the Preterit is regular. It is ⁓⁓.

dormí (The past tense base of *dormía*.)

3 When you compare *dormí* and *durmió*, you see that the second syllable of each is stressed: *dor-mí, dur-mió*. Can stress be the cue to change the *o* of the stem to *u*?

no

4 Let's see if you can figure out the cue that tells you when to change *o* to *u*. The regular preterit forms of *dormir* are made up of the past tense base plus the second suffix. They are *dormí, dormimos, dormiste*. When the two irregular forms are divided into their three morphemes, you get: *durm-ió, durm-iero-n*. The cue to changing *o* to *u* is to be found in the first suffix. When it is just *i*, the stem is regular: *dorm-í, dorm-i-mos, dorm-i-ste*. When the first suffix has *i* plus ⁓⁓, the stem is irregular.

o or *e* (The combinations *io* and *ie* are called **diphthongs**.)

5 The *yo*-form of the Preterit of *dormir* is regular. It is ⁓⁓.

dormí

6 The verb *morir* belongs to the same class as *dormir*. The preterit form that matches *yo* is ⁓⁓.

morí

7 No one can use *morí* except in a figure of speech, since one can't report one's own death. You can, however, say *Casi morí de hambre*, which means "I almost ⁓⁓."

died of hunger

8 Write the form of *morir* which is like *durmió*.

murió

9 Write the form of *morir* which is like *durmieron*.

murieron

10 The *nosotros*-form of *dormir* and *morir* is regular. It is made up of the past tense base plus the second suffix ⁓⁓.

mos (dormimos, morimos)

11 Change *dormimos* and *morimos* so they match *tú*.

dormiste; moriste

12 Here is what you have to remember about this set of verbs. They are *i*-verbs. In the Present the stressed *o* of the stem changes to ⁓⁓.

ue

13 In the Preterit, the *o* changes to ⁓⁓ when the stem is followed by a diphthong (*i* plus another vowel).

u

14 The two forms of *dormir* in which this happens are *usted* ⁓⁓ and *ustedes* ⁓⁓.

usted durmió; ustedes durmieron (The same forms also go with *él* and *ellos*.)

15 There is another group of *i*-verbs which are irregular in the Present and the Preterit. These are the verbs whose stem *e* changes to *i* or *ie* in the Present: *pido, visto, siento*. Let's stop and see if you know the meaning of these verbs. The translation of *pedir*, a cognate of "petition" is ⁓⁓.

to ask, request (Sometimes very much like "to beg.")

16 The translation of *servir*, a cognate of "servant" is ⁓⁓.

to serve

17 The translations of *vestir, seguir,* and *medir* are ⁓⁓.

to dress, to follow, to measure

18 The *i*-verbs *pedir*, *medir*, *vestir*, *servir* and *seguir* change the *e* of the stem to ⌐⌐⌐⌐ in the irregular present tense forms.

i (sirvo, sirves, sirve, sirven)

19 The Preterit of all these verbs keeps the *i* in the stem when the first suffix has a diphthong (*io* or *ie*). The *usted*-form of *servir*, then, is ⌐⌐⌐⌐.

sirvió

20 The first and second suffix of the *ustedes*-form is *ieron*. So the stem of *servir* will be (a) *serv* (b) *sirv*.

sirv (sirvieron)

21 It does not make sense to memorize every single verb which has forms in the Preterit like *servir*. It is much more economical to learn one model well and to memorize what other verbs are like this model in the Preterit. So *pedir* is like *él sirvió*, and the Preterit of *él pide*, then, is *él* ⌐⌐⌐⌐.

pidió

22 The Preterit of *ellos sirven* is *ellos sirvieron*. So the Preterit of *ellos miden* is *ellos* ⌐⌐⌐⌐.

midieron (they measured)

23 Like *dormir* the *yo*-form of this set of verbs is regular in the Preterit. Write the *yo*-form of *servir* and *vestir*.

serví; vestí

24 Also like *dormir* the *nosotros*-form is regular in the Preterit. Write the *nosotros*-form of *seguir* and *pedir*.

seguimos; pedimos

25 The *tú*-form is also regular. Write the *tú*-form of *servir* and *sentir* in the Preterit.

serviste; sentiste

26 It is really easy to remember the irregular preterit forms of the *i*-verbs when you keep these facts in mind. They are, first of all, also irregular in the Present. In the Present the *o* of the stem changes to ⌐⌐⌐⌐.

ue (dormir > duermo)

27 When the *o* changes to *ue* in the Present, it also changes to ⌐⌐⌐⌐ in the Preterit when followed by a first suffix which has a diphthong.

u

28 There are just two forms in which this happens: *durmió*, *durmieron*. The *e* of the preterit stem changes to *i* in the same two forms. Change *pedí* so it agrees with *ella*.

pidió

29 Change *vestimos* so it matches *ustedes*.

vistieron

30 In your next class you will practice the Preterit of *dormir* in the reflexive. *Yo me dormí* says "I put myself to sleep" and is translated by either "I went to sleep" or "I slept." The *yo*-form *dormí* is just the past tense base with an accent mark. To get the *nosotros*- and *tú*-forms you leave off the accent mark and add ⌐⌐⌐⌐ to the base.

mos; ste (dormimos, dormiste)

31 There are two irregular stem forms. Write the forms of *dormir* for *usted* and *ustedes*.

durmió; durmieron

32 Are the first and second suffixes of these forms (a) regular? (b) irregular?

regular

33 Where *o* changes to *u* the *e* will change to ⌐⌐⌐⌐.

i

34 Write the preterit forms of *pedir* that match *usted* and *ustedes*.

pidió; pidieron

35 Translate: *Yo pedí un suéter azul.*

I asked for (ordered) a blue sweater.

No new vocabulary.

PROGRAM **104**

The Present of *decir*, Getting Ready for a Spelling Quiz, and the Preterit of *venir* and *hacer*

Part 1: The Present of *decir*

1 The Present of *decir* has only one completely regular form. It is *nosotros decimos*. In all the other forms the *e* of the stem changes to *i*. In the *yo*-form, the *c* voices and becomes *g*. The suffixes are regular, so the *yo*-form is ⁓.

digo
2 The stem is *dic* in all the other forms. Write the form that matches *tú*. Remember the present tense suffixes are regular.

tú dices
3 To get the *usted*, *él*, and *ella* form you drop the ⁓.

s (usted dice)
4 To make *dice* plural you add ⁓.

n (ustedes dicen)

5 *Decir* has three common translations: (1) to say, (2) to tell, and less commonly, (3) to speak. What is the translation of *dice* in *Papá dice que no tiene hambre.*

says
6 What is the translation of *decir* in *¿No va a decir la verdad?*

to tell (or to speak)

Part 2: Spelling

1 In your next class session, you will have a writing quiz to see how well you can manage ear and eye spelling. You can spell a word by ear whenever each sound in it is always represented by just one letter. Can you spell [luna] by ear?

yes
2 Can you spell [selba] by ear?

no
3 You hear [selba] but you write ⁓.

selva
4 Can you spell [tormenta] by ear?

yes
5 Can you spell [kaye] by ear?

no
6 You hear [kaye] but you write ⁓.

calle
7 Say *ciento* (100) and *siento* (I feel regret) aloud. Do they sound exactly alike?

yes
8 Do you have to see *ciento* and *siento* and, then, know what they mean before you spell each word correctly?

yes
9 Transcribe in regular spelling: [Está en la kaye].

Está en la calle.

10 When you use spelling rules as a help, you can spell a lot more words by ear. The preterit form [mastiké] is written ⁓.

mastiqué
11 Anyone who spells *mastiqué* wrong has forgotten that [k] is written *qu* before the two vowels ⁓.

e; i (que, quiero)

12 Say *lección* aloud. Which *c* stands for [k]? (a) the first (b) the second

the first
13 Here is a new spelling rule: the *c* cannot stand for [s] when it ends a syllable or comes before another consonant. Write the word for a piece of land that is entirely surrounded by water.

isla (You now know you cannot use *c* in this word.)

450   Etapa Seis

14 Can *c* stand for [k] in [akabar]?

yes (*acabar*)   **15** The letter *c* always stands for the sound [k] before the three vowels ⁓⁓⁓.

a, o, u (**c**alle, po**c**o, se**c**undaria)

    16 What letter do you have to see in *edificio* and *espacio* before you can spell these words?

c (You can write *c, s,* or *z* before *i*.)

    17 There are two letters in *habitante* which you have to see before you can spell the word. They are ⁓⁓⁓.

h; b   **18** Since *h* can come before any vowel, you have to see every word that begins with a vowel sound before you learn how to spell it. Here are all the words you have had that begin with an *h*. For the time being, you can memorize these and remember that all other words beginning with a vowel sound have no *h*.

haber (hay)	hambre	hola	héroe
habitante	hallar	hombre	himno
hablar	hasta	hora	historia
hacer			

    19 You can easily recognize the cognates of *habitante, hola, hora, himno,* and *historia*. Do the English cognates also have an *h*?

yes   **20** Do you pronounce the *h* in "hour?"

no (Then learning to spell *hora* is just like learning to spell "hour." You have
to see both words to learn to spell them.)

    21 Do you ever write a *v* before another consonant in Spanish?

no   **22** Translate: fog.

niebla   **23** The *yo*-form of the Preterit sometimes has a different letter than the infinitive. The *yo*-form of *buscar* is ⁓⁓⁓.

busqué   **24** The *yo*-form of the Preterit of *empezar* is ⁓⁓⁓.

empecé   **25** The *g* has the same sound as *j* before *e* or *i*. So the *yo*-form of the Preterit of *llegar* and *jugar* must be written ⁓⁓⁓.

llegué; jugué   **26** Which word in this set must you see before you can spell it: *cometa, perro, mundo, olvidar, aprender, lago?*

olvidar (After a consonant Spanish may write either *b* or *v*.)

    27 You hear the following. What do you write: [Yo yegué kom poka ambre.]?

Yo llegué con poca hambre.

Part 3: The Preterit of *venir* and *hacer*

It is a law of language that an irregular form cannot survive unless it is used a great deal. As a result, the most irregular verbs are always the most common. This is fortunate because you will use these verbs often enough to learn their irregularities by sheer repetition.

    1 The verb *venir* has two irregularities in the Present. The *yo*-form is ⁓⁓⁓.

vengo   **2** When the stem vowel *e* is stressed in all other forms, it changes to ⁓⁓⁓.

ie (*vienes, viene, vienen*)

    3 The Preterit of *venir* has three irregularities: (1) The stem of all forms is *vin*. (2) The first suffix of the *yo*-form is *e*. (3) The first suffix of the *usted, él,* and *ella* form is *o*. Write the *yo*-form.

vine

4 Write the *usted*-form.

vino
    5 The first and second suffixes of all the other forms are regular. To get the *tú*-form you add ～～～ to *vin*.

iste (tú viniste)
    6 The irregular past tense base of *viniste* is ～～～.

vini
    7 To get the *nosotros*-form you add ～～～ to *vini*.

mos (nosotros vinimos)
    8 Change *vinimos* so it agrees with *ellos*.

vinieron
    9 Here is a chart of the morphemes of all the forms. Notice there are no accent marks.

yo vin-e	tú vin-i-ste
él, usted vin-o	nosotros vin-i-mos
	ustedes, ellos vin-iero-n

Here are the same forms divided into syllables. Say them aloud. Remember the *v* sound is fricative. The stressed syllable is in bold type.

yo **vi**-ne	tú vi-**nis**-te
usted **vi**-no	nosotros vi-**ni**-mos
	ellos vi-**nie**-ron

10 The Present of *hacer* has one irregularity. The *yo*-form is ～～～.

hago
    11 The first and second suffixes of the Preterit of *hacer* are the same as for *venir*. The first suffix of the *yo*-form is ～～～.

e
    12 The first suffix of the *usted*-form is ～～～.

o
    13 The spoken stem for all forms is [is]. Do you have to see *usted hizo* in order to know that [s] is written as *z*?

yes (It could be *s*, but not *c* because *c* before *o* (*hico*) would stand for [k].)
    14 In all the other forms, the stem is written *hic*. To get the *yo*-form you add the irregular first suffix ～～～ to *hic*.

e (Say *yo hice* aloud.)
    15 To get the *él*-, *ella*-, *usted*-form you add *o* to ～～～.

hiz (All other stems are spelled *hic*.)
    16 The suffixes for all other forms are regular. Write the *tú*-form.

hiciste
    17 Change *hiciste* so it agrees with *nosotros*.

hicimos
    18 Divide *hicimos* into syllables.

hi-ci-mos (Now say it aloud.)
    19 Change *hicimos* so it matches *ellas*, *ellos*, and *ustedes*.

hicieron

New Vocabulary

Are you remembering to spend three minutes each day reviewing vocabulary?

ropa	clothing	**falda**	skirt
medias	stockings, socks	**corbata**	necktie
camisa	shirt	**vestido**	dress
blusa	blouse	**calcetines**	socks
pantalones	pants		

When the people of two different cultures first come into contact with each other, what each group usually notices first are the differences in customs and attitudes. It frequently happens that a custom which is so common in one culture that it is hardly noticed is considered to be rude, ugly, obscene, or immoral in the other. When a member of the other culture observes this custom he frequently suffers what sociologists and anthropologists call *cultural shock*. You believe, for example, that drinking milk is wholesome and proper. In contrast, for the people of one African tribe this is something filthy because they put cow's milk in the same category as urine. Similarly, most American males think nothing of showing a bit of bare leg between the top of their sock and the bottom of their trousers when they sit down and cross their legs. This is obscene in Indonesia. In the same way, many American business men do not hesitate to sit down on the edge of somebody else's desk. This is considered rude in Latin America. Kissing is a common way for couples in America to show affection. This custom shocks most Japanese and is frowned on in the Hispanic world when done in public.

You have, perhaps, suffered some cultural shock as you have read these cultural notes. You must keep in mind that you do things that are just as shocking to the Latins. They are shocked by American girl tourists who tour their churches in slacks and do not cover their heads before entering. The more religious are also shocked when these same tourists nonchalantly walk by the altar without genuflecting (bending the knees in sign of reverence).

The culturally sophisticated person quickly recovers from these shocks and rapidly learns to accept the behavior of the natives of each culture in terms of their own standards. At the same time such a person also learns not to do those things which seem natural to him, but shock the other people, when he is in their country as a guest. This is the meaning of the old saying, "When in Rome, do as the Romans do."

PROGRAM 105

More Uses of the Preterit and the Imperfect

The Present usually describes what is happening while we are talking. The past tense describes the same events when we remember them. At this very instant you *are reading* this line. A second or so ago you *were reading* the sentence before this one. All present events become past events the instant they are finished and in the same way everything we say now becomes past as soon as we say it. Thus, you say, "I'm hungry," and if I do not hear you properly, I must say, "What *did* you say?" And you must answer either with a direct quote ("I said, 'I'm hungry.'") or an indirect quote ("I said I was hungry."). All of this means that all the cues of the Preterit and Imperfect won't be completely clear until you thoroughly understand the uses of the Present.

1 One of the functions of the Present in both English and Spanish is to describe what is actually going on when a statement is made. Thus the answer to *¿Qué hace Pilar ahora?* may be *Duerme*. Is Pilar sleeping at the very instant that the speaker says *Duerme?*

yes

2 The question and answer given above have been said. They are now past. To talk about them we must recall them and back-shift them into the past tense. The question becomes *¿Qué hacía Pilar entonces?* (What was Pilar doing then?) and the answer must be (a) *Duerme.* (b) *Dormía.*

Dormía.

3 The Present does not always describe something that is actually happening at the instant something is said. Suppose, for example, that Pilar says *Yo duermo muy bien.* Is Pilar actually sleeping when she says this?

no

4 In *Yo duermo muy bien* the Present does not describe an event which is going on when the statement is made. Unless Pilar is talking in her sleep "I sleep very well" cannot describe what she is doing when she says the sentence. The statement in either language describes what Pilar (a) plans to do (b) normally does when she goes to bed.

normally does when she goes to bed

5 Can *I eat breakfast every morning* actually describe what the speaker is doing at the moment the statement is made?

No (*Now* cannot be *every morning.*)

6 Does *I eat breakfast every morning* describe what the speaker regularly does every morning?

yes

7 One of the common uses of the Present in both English and Spanish is to describe an action which is customary, habitual, or frequently repeated. You can, for example, be standing on the school steps when you say, *I watch television a lot.* Now, what you customarily do at the present time may be different from what you habitually did during some time in the past. In other words, what you regularly did in the past may be in contrast with what you are accustomed to doing in the present. Let's see how words tell us these facts.

What does "I *used to eat* a lot of candy" mean? (a) I still eat a lot of candy. (b) I no longer eat so much candy.

I no longer eat so much candy.

8 Look at these two statements: (1) He *works* in the mine. (2) He *used to work* in the mine. The verb form *works* describes what is customary now. The phrase *used to work* describes what was customary at some time in the ⁓⁓⁓.

past

9 A customary action, like any single event, can have a beginning, a middle, and an end. What aspect is described by "He works in the mine?" (a) initiative (b) imperfective (c) terminative

imperfective

10 If "works" in "He works in the mine" describes imperfective aspect, then, we can logically say that the form "works" is the Present Imperfect. In Spanish *Él trabaja en la mina* also describes the present imperfect aspect of a customary action. Which past tense form in Spanish will say the same thing about the past? (a) *trabajaba* (b) *trabajó*

trabajaba

11 English, as you know, has no Imperfect and, as a result, must use "used to" or "would" to make a contrast with the Present. Spanish has a Present Imperfect (*trabaja*) and a Past Imperfect (*trabajaba*) which contrast with each other, and thus does not need a special phrase to say "used to." This is expressed by the form of the verb. Translate: They used to eat too much.

Ellos comían demasiado.

Going Places
Doing Things

Bus and train are the principal means of transportation between rural and urban areas. People travel frequently for business and pleasure.

A short trip for a soccer match is a typical Sunday activity in Peru.

The street musician and monkey are a welcome break in the monotony of a small town in Ecuador.

Festive occasions like this variety show in La Paz bring everybody together, from the military to babies on their mothers' backs.

A procession marks the importance of present-day religious observances and an Inca festival recalls the splendors of an imperial past.

12 English contrasts the Present Imperfect with the "used to" construction: "I *live* in Los Angeles now; I *used to live* in Bogotá." Spanish contrasts Present Imperfect (*vivo*) with Past Imperfect (*vivía*) and gets exactly the same meaning. Translate: He used to talk a lot.

Él hablaba mucho.

13 English has another way of talking about customary or habitual action in the past. Which one of these statements describes something that happened regularly? (a) My father laughed when I said that. (b) My father would laugh when I said that.

My father would laugh when I said that.

14 Your intuition tells you when to use "would" and "used to" to describe customary past action. You can use this same intuition in learning to talk Spanish because "used to" and "would" (as used above) are regularly translated by the Imperfect. What you must learn is that Spanish normally lets context show this difference. As a result, the Spanish *Cuando éramos niños íbamos a las montañas con frecuencia* translates both of these sentences: (a) When we were children, we *used to go* to the mountains. (b) When we were children, we *would go* to the mountains. You will, consequently, only have troubles when you translate from Spanish to English. Which English sentence above can be used to imply that we no longer go to the mountains?

When we were children, we used to go to the mountains.

15 There are three very different uses of the Imperfect. The Imperfect is used to state that some action was in progress at a point in the past. Translate: At one o'clock I was reading.

A la una yo leía. **16** The Imperfect is used as the back-shift of the Present to describe planned action. So *Sé que ella va pronto* becomes *Sabía que ella* ⁓ *pronto.*

iba **17** The Imperfect is used for customary or habitual past action. The single translation of "He used to talk a lot" and "He would talk a lot" is ⁓.

Él hablaba mucho.

18 There are three English patterns which always cue the use of the Imperfect in Spanish: (1) *was* or *were* plus *ing* (he was talking), (2) *would*, and (3) ⁓.

used to **19** There may be just one Spanish translation for these three statements: She was singing; She used to sing; She would sing. It is ⁓.

Ella cantaba. **20** Which translation of *cantar* will you use for *Ella cantaba cuando yo entré?*

was singing **21** Translate *Cuando ella estaba muy triste no cantaba* so that you put emphasis on customary action.

When she was very sad, she would not sing. (If this use of "would" is not in your dialect, you might say, "She didn't use to sing.")

22 Translate the indicated part. You want to contrast the past with the present. *Hoy ella es muy vieja y no canta bien. Cuando era joven* **cantaba muy bien.**

she used to sing very well

23 English uses three constructions where Spanish uses only one. The context, however, tells the Spanish speaker what meaning is intended. Let's see, once more, how well you can "read" the context. Look at this statement: *Cada día antes de ir a una clase especial mi perro ladraba mucho.* What is the most logical translation of *ladraba?* (a) was barking (b) used to (would) bark

used to (would) bark ("Before going to a special class, my dog used to (would) bark a lot." The choice between "used to" and "would" depends on your dialect.)

24 You have already learned that the Preterit may describe an action that began or ended at some point in the past. What aspect is described by *corrió* in *Se levantó y corrió?* (a) initiative (b) imperfective (c) terminative

initiative (He got up and began to run.)

25 What aspect is described by *sentó* in *Él llegó a la playa y se sentó?* (a) initiative (b) imperfective (c) terminative

terminative (He arrived at the beach and sat down.)

26 The Present may say that the action is going on at the moment a statement about it is made. In other words, "I am seeing" the mountains when I say *Veo las montañas.* The Preterit, in contrast, may say that the action is completed before the statement is made. So "I am not looking" at the mountains when I say *Vi las montañas.* (I saw the mountains.)

At the moment of speaking, the Present says the action is going on: *Pedro cierra la puerta.* At the same moment the Preterit says the action was already completed. Translate: Pedro closed the door.

Pedro cerró la puerta. (Remember the stem is regular in the Preterit.)

27 The Preterit must also stand in contrast with the Imperfect. Look at these two statements: (a) *Ayer yo leía un libro.* (b) *Ayer yo leí un libro.* Which one says that you finished reading the book yesterday?

Ayer yo leí un libro.

28 *Yo leo un libro* says you have started but have not finished reading the book. You are in the process of reading it when you make the statement. *Yo leía un libro* describes what was going on at some time in the past. Does *Yo leía un libro* say that you have finished reading it?

no

29 At the moment of speaking, *Yo leo* says the action is in progress. *Yo leía* says the action was in progress at some earlier time, and *yo leí* says the action is already finished. Let's see, now, whether you can read the cues that tell you when to use the Preterit and Imperfect. Which form will you use to translate *went?* "Before we got our freezer, Mother *went* to the store every day." (a) *iba* (b) *fue*

iba

30 Keep in mind that Mother no longer goes to the store every day. You could, then, put *used to go* in place of *went:* "Before we got our freezer. Mother *used to go* to the store every day." Which form will you use to translate this *went?* "When mother was first married, she *went* to the store every day." (a) Preterit (b) Imperfect

Imperfect (She customarily went to the store every day.)

31 Which form will translate *went?* "Mother *went* to the store yesterday." (a) Preterit (b) Imperfect

Preterit (The action is over and done with.)

32 In this and the remaining frames you will see a present tense form which has an irregular stem. This stem, however, is regular in both the Preterit and Imperfect. Write the regular stem of *vuel—ve.*

volv

33 me acuest—o

acost

34 oig—o

o (As in *oí* and *oía.*)

35 cierr—an

cerr

36 muev—es

mov

empez
conoc
sal
vol

37 empiez—an
38 conozc—o
39 salg—o
40 vuel—a

You have now studied all the rules of usage of the Preterit and Imperfect. If you want to see them all in one place, turn to your *Cuaderno*. There you will find a complete summary and more examples.

New Vocabulary

saco	(suit) coat	**zapato**	shoe
traje	suit	**impermeable**	raincoat
suéter	sweater	**llevar**	to carry
sombrero	hat	**usar**	to wear, use
abrigo	overcoat	**Que te diviertas.**	Have a good time.

PROGRAM 106

Present of *dar*, *traer*, and *conocer*, and Preparing for a Quiz on Intonation

Part 1: *dar*, *traer*, and *conocer*

1 You already know the forms of the Present of *ir*. The form that goes with *yo* is ⁓.

voy

2 All the other forms take the first suffix of regular *a*-verbs. The forms that go with *usted* and *ustedes* are ⁓.

va; van

3 The present tense forms of *dar* (to give) are exactly like those for *ir*. You just put *d* in place of *v*. So the form of *dar* that goes with *yo* is ⁓.

doy

4 The form that matches *nosotros* is ⁓.

damos

5 Change *damos* so it matches *tú*.

das

6 The forms that go with *él* and *ellos* are ⁓.

da; dan

7 When *da* begins a statement, the /d/ is a (a) stop (b) fricative.

stop

8 Is the /d/ a stop in *yo doy?*

no (It's a fricative.)

9 The verbs *traer* (to bring, fetch) and *caer* (to fall) have just one irregularity. The *yo*-forms are *traigo* and *caigo*. All other forms are regular. The form of *traer* that goes with *tú* is ⁓.

traes

10 Change *traes* so it matches *nosotros*.

traemos

11 The equivalent form of *caer* is ⁓.

caemos

	12 The *ustedes*-form of *traer* is 〰.
traen	**13** To make *traen* match *usted* you drop 〰.
n	**14** The *yo*-form of *traer* is 〰.
traigo	**15** The *yo*-form of *caer* is 〰.
caigo	**16** The *yo*-form of *dar* is 〰.
doy	**17** The translation of *conocer* is 〰.
to know (In the sense of "to be acquainted with.")	

18 *Conocer*, like *dar*, *traer*, and *caer*, has only one irregular form in the Present. All others are regular. The *yo*-form is *conozco*. The form that goes with *él* is regular. It is 〰.

conoce	**19** Change *conoce* so it matches *tú*.
conoces	**20** The *nosotros*-form is 〰.
conocemos	**21** The verb *traducir* (to translate) has the same irregularity in the *yo*-form as *conocer*. The *yo*-form, then, is 〰.
traduzco	

A great many American tourists find the long, flowing skirts of the Indian women of Latin America (and the United States) to be quaint and something typically Indian. What these people do not know is that the Indian women of the New World did not wear skirts before the Discovery. When the European women came here, the Indians began to dress like them. Since all women wore long skirts at that time, the Indians did the same thing. The difference is that the Indians have kept up the custom while the city dwellers have changed their styles to match those of Paris or New York. The "typical" Indian dress, in short, is not Indian at all. It is an inheritance of the European styles of the sixteenth and seventeenth centuries.

Part 2: Preparing for a Quiz on Intonation

1 In your next class session, you are going to be asked to read some questions aloud. Your teacher will grade you on how well you deal with word stress, syllable length, and the pitch change at the end of the questions. Let's see what you remember about these features of speech. Say *bat* and *bad* aloud in English and listen to the length of the *a* sound. In which word is this sound longer?

bad   **2** Say *bad* aloud again. Now say very emphatically "He's a *bad* boy!" When you say this, do you give extra length to *bad?*

yes   **3** English can have very long syllables when they are stressed. Say *rápida* aloud in Spanish. Does Spanish speech custom permit you to make the *rá* a great deal longer than the *da?*

no (Spanish long syllables are only about twice as long as the short syllables.)

4 Say this question aloud and try to keep all the syllables about the same length: *¿ Cuántos días hay en un mes?*

5 Say very emphatically "But Juan is *my* cousin," that is, not "her" cousin. You draw out "my" for emphasis. Now say *mi* in Spanish. You can make *mi* only a tiny bit longer when you say emphatically *Pero Juan es mi primo.* Say this sentence aloud with the stress on *primo* and keep the *mi* short.

6 To overcome your English habit of saying very long and short syllables you should try to make most Spanish syllables about the same length. Say this question aloud: *¿ Es una pregunta muy importante?*

7 The second important feature of intonation is stress. How many syllables are stressed in the English word "investigation?"

two   **8** How many syllables are stressed in the Spanish word *investigación?*

one (With only minor exceptions, which you will learn later, Spanish words have only one stressed syllable.)

9 The single stress on *electricidad* falls on *dad.* Say this word aloud: *e-lec-tri-ci-dad.*

10 Say "combination" aloud. Now say *combinación* aloud with only one stressed syllable.

11 Say "impossibility" aloud. Now say *imposibilidad* with stress only on *dad: im-po-si-bi-li-dad.*

12 In the quiz your teacher will pay close attention to what happens to the pitch at the end of questions. What kind of a question is "Are you ready?" (a) yes-no (b) information

yes-no (You can answer with either "yes" or "no.")

13 What happens to the pitch level when you say *¿ Está usted listo?* At the end of the question, the pitch (a) goes up (b) goes down.

goes up (The pitch goes up at the end of yes-no questions in both English and Spanish.)   **14** What kind of a question is *¿ Fue interesante la lección?*

yes-no   **15** Say the question given above aloud. Remember: the pitch goes up.

16 What kind of a question is *¿ Cuántos años tiene usted?* (a) yes-no (b) information

information   **17** At the end of an information question, the pitch (a) goes up (b) goes down.

goes down (In both languages.)

18 Say *¿ Cuántos años tiene usted?* aloud.

19 Here is something very important to remember about the quiz you are going to have. When you talk, you know what kind of a question you are going to ask. So you know, before you start, what is going to happen to the pitch at the end of the question. In contrast, when you try to read a new question aloud, you need to recognize at once the cues that tell you what kind of question it is before you can say it aloud properly. Here is a helpful fact: any question that begins with a question word (*cuánto, cómo, dónde, qué, quién, cuál,* or *cuándo*) must be an information question and the pitch will go down at the end. So you have to be careful only with questions which do not have a question word. Most will be yes-no questions, but some may be information questions. <u>Do not start to read a question until you know for sure whether it is a yes-no or an information question.</u>

Part 3: Review of Verb Forms

This review is to let you discover whether you really learned what you studied in Part 1 of this Program. Studying is really a great waste of time if you do not remember what you studied.

	1 The Present of *dar* is like the Present of ~~~~.
ir	**2** The *yo*-form of *dar* is ~~~~.
doy	**3** Are all the other present tense forms of *dar* regular?
yes	**4** The *tú*-form of *traer* is regular. It is ~~~~.
traes	**5** The *yo*-form of *traer* is irregular. It is ~~~~.
traigo	**6** The Present of *caer* is like *traer*. The *yo*-form is ~~~~.
caigo	**7** Are all the other present tense forms of *caer* regular?
yes	**8** The verbs *conocer* and *traducir* have a peculiar irregularity in the *yo*-form of the Present. These forms are ~~~~.
conozco; traduzco	

New Vocabulary

sopa	soup
dormirse	to fall asleep
perder	to lose

PROGRAM 107

Review of the Present of Irregular Verbs and *ser* and *estar* with Predicate Adjectives

Part 1: Review of Irregular Verbs

Of the thousands of verbs in the Spanish language, there are less than 500 which are irregular. Almost all of these irregular verbs, however, are very common words which have to be learned at the beginning of any Spanish course. Many students get the impression that the majority of Spanish verbs are irregular and that the language is hard to learn. This is not true. You have already met an example of most of the sets of irregular verbs, and from now on, all you have to remember is that a new verb is like one you already know. You already know, for example, the irregular forms of *cerrar*. Now you meet *perder* (to lose) and learn that it has the same irregularities as *cerrar*. This is all the new information you need to make up the forms of *perder*.

1 The *yo*-form of *cerrar* is ⌇⌇⌇.
cierro (Latin *e* sometimes changes to *ie* under stress.)

2 *Perder* is exactly like *cerrar*, so the *yo*-form is going to be ⌇⌇⌇.
pierdo

3 The *usted*-form of *cerrar* also has the stress on the stem. It is ⌇⌇⌇.
cierra

4 Now *perder* is an *e*-verb so the *usted*-form is not going to be *pierda;* it is ⌇⌇⌇.
pierde

5 Change *pierde* so it matches *tú* and *ellos*.
tú pierdes; ellos pierden

6 The steps you have just gone through demonstrate that the whole problem of irregular verbs is greatly simplified when you memorize one model perfectly and then learn what other verbs are like it. Let's use *cerrar* again as your model. The stem is ⌇⌇⌇.
cerr

7 You know that Latin *e* sometimes changes to *ie* when stressed. There is, however, in the Present one form in which the stress does not fall on the stem. So the *e* does not change to *ie*. This form is ⌇⌇⌇.
cerramos (The stress falls on the syllable *rra: ce-**rra**-mos*.)

8 Here, then, are the facts you have to learn about this set of verbs:
(1) The stem of the infinitive has an *e* in it (*cerr-ar*).
(2) The *e* changes to *ie* under stress.
(3) There are, consequently, two allomorphs of the stem in the Present (*cierr* and *cerr*).
(4) The *cerr* allomorph appears only in the form that goes with *nosotros* (*cerramos*).
(5) The *cierr* allomorph is the stem for all other forms.
Write the forms that match *tú*, *usted*, and *ellos*.
tú cierras, usted cierra, ellos cierran

9 The irregularity of this set of verbs is in the stem. This change may happen in a-, e-, or i-verbs. So the following seven verbs are like *cerrar* in the Present: *querer, sentir, divertir, sentar, despertar, empezar*, and *pensar*. Write the *nosotros*-form for *querer, sentir*, and *sentar*.

queremos, sentimos, sentamos

10 The stem of *despertar* has two *e*'s in it. Only the stressed *e* changes to *ie*. The *yo*-form is ⁓⁓.

despierto   **11** The *yo*-form of *empezar* is ⁓⁓.

empiezo   **12** Write the *tú*-form of *pensar* and *querer*.

tú piensas ; quieres

13 The verbs *tener* and *venir* have an *e* in the stem which changes to *ie*, but they also have another irregularity which produces a third allomorph of the stem. The *yo*-forms of *tener* and *venir* are ⁓⁓.

tengo ; vengo (The *e* is stressed but no change takes place.)

14 Write the *tú*-form for *tener* and *venir*.

tienes ; vienes   **15** The Latin *o* when stressed in Spanish sometimes changes to ⁓⁓.

ue   **16** Let's use *contar* as the model. The *yo*- and the *nosotros*-forms are ⁓⁓.

yo cuento ; nosotros contamos

17 The *usted*- and *ellos*-forms of *contar* are ⁓⁓.

usted cuenta ; ellos cuentan

18 Here are all the other verbs you have had which are like *contar* in the Present: *poder, volver, recordar, morder, morir, dormir, acostar*. Write the *nosotros*-form of *poder, dormir*, and *recordar*.

podemos, dormimos, recordamos

19 Write the *yo*-form of *dormir, volver*, and *acostar*.

duermo, vuelvo, acuesto

20 Write the *tú*-form of *contar, morder*, and *poder*.

cuentas, muerdes, puedes

21 The old infinitive of *jugar* was *jogar*. This old stem is the base for the modern present tense forms having *ue*. The *yo*-form, consequently, of *jugar* is ⁓⁓.

juego (So you add *jugar* to the set of verbs whose forms are like *contar*.)

22 Old Latin *e* sometimes became *i* when stressed in Spanish. This happens, however, only in verbs of the *i*-set. Let's use *pedir* as the model. The *yo*-form is ⁓⁓.

pido   **23** The *e* does not change to *i* in the *nosotros*-form ⁓⁓.

pedimos   **24** The *usted*- and *ustedes*-forms are ⁓⁓.

pide ; piden   **25** The verbs *servir, vestir, seguir*, and *medir* belong to the same set as *pedir*. The *yo*-forms of *servir* and *medir* are ⁓⁓.

sirvo ; mido   **26** The sound [g] is written *gu* before *e* and *i*. Before *a, o*, and *u* it is written ⁓⁓.

g   **27** Write the *yo*-form of *seguir*.

sigo   **28** Change *sigo* so it matches *él*.

sigue   **29** The *nosotros*-form of all stem-changing verbs is always regular in the Present. This form of *seguir* is ⁓⁓.

seguimos   **30** Verbs which end in a vowel plus either *cer* or *cir* have just one irregularity in the Present. The *yo*-form of *conocer* is *conozco*. The *yo*-form of *traducir* is ⁓⁓.

traduzco

31 Write the *tú*-form of *traducir* and *conocer*.

tú traduces; conoces

32 The verbs *hacer, traer, caer, salir,* and *saber* have only an irregular *yo*-form in the Present. The *usted*-forms are *hace, trae, cae, sale,* and *sabe*. Change these to the *yo*-forms.

hago, traigo, caigo, salgo, sé (The written accent over *sé* just shows it is not the reflexive form *se*.)

33 Some of the most commonly used verbs have irregularities which are peculiarly their own. The *yo*-forms of *estar, ir, ser,* and *dar* are ———.

estoy, voy, soy, doy

34 Although *ir* is an *i*-verb, all its other present tense forms take the regular *a*-verb suffixes. The forms for *tú* and *ustedes* are ———.

vas; van

35 When a verb form like *habla* or *llama* ends in a vowel, the stress falls on the first syllable. *Estar* is an exception, since the stress falls on the first suffix. You do not, consequently, write *él esta* but *él* ———.

está

36 The verb *oír* has two irregularities in the Present. The *yo*-form is *oigo*. The *nosotros*-form is regular and is ———.

oímos

37 The stem of all the other forms is *oy*. Add the suffixes that go with *ustedes* and *ellos*.

oyen

38 The verb *decir* has two irregularities in the Present. The *yo*-form is ———.

digo

39 The *nosotros*-form is regular. It is ———.

decimos

40 All the other forms are like *pedir*. The *e* of the stem changes to ———.

i

41 Write the *tú*-form of *decir*.

dices

42 The present tense stem of the *yo*-form of *ver* comes from the old form *veer*. The *yo*-form is ———.

veo

Part 2: *ser* and *estar* with Predicate Adjectives

1 In "Deserts are dry," the word "dry" is a predicate adjective which describes the subject "deserts." As you know already, whenever you have a construction like this, you must choose between *ser* and *estar* in Spanish. What is your norm for deserts? (a) wet (b) dry

dry

2 When a predicate adjective gives the norm for the subject, you use (a) *ser* (b) *estar*.

*ser (Los desiertos **son** secos.)*

3 Which verb will you use to translate "Steel is stronger than iron"? (a) *ser* (b) *estar*

ser (Steel, by its nature, is normally stronger than iron.)

4 It happens, sometimes, that things are not the way they normally are supposed to be. They may change or in some way be different from the norm. They are "ab-normal." Something may, for example, go wrong in the manufacturing process and a batch of steel turns out to be soft, not hard. Which verb will you use to say "This steel is soft"? (a) *ser* (b) *estar*

estar

5 Is it normal for people to be sick?

no

6 So you say a person happens to be sick with ———.

estar (Pedro está enfermo.)

7 Each person has his own private norm for many things. Your norm for the color of grass is probably green. In some places there is a grass which is red. You are surprised to see it. You exclaim, "That grass is red!" Which verb do you use? (a) *ser* (b) *estar*

estar (Red is a deviation from your norm.)

8 You have now learned that *red* can also be the norm for grass in some places. You report this fact by saying, "In that place the grass is red." Which verb do you use?

ser

New Vocabulary

nube	cloud
decir	to say, tell, speak
planchar	to iron (clothing)

PROGRAM 108

More about Clothing and the Preterit of *ir*, *decir*, and *ser*

Part 1: More about Clothing

1 This part of your Program deals with some of the common things we do with clothing. For example, in our society, we buy and sell clothing. You have probably bought gum or candy from a *vending* machine. Is a *vending* machine a kind of "selling" machine?

yes

2 The stem of *vending* is ⌣⌣⌣⌣.

vend

3 The stem for "to sell" in Spanish is also *vend*. This verb is a regular *e*-verb. The infinitive is ⌣⌣⌣⌣.

vender (Say this aloud. The first phoneme is a stop [b]: [bender].)

4 Write the *yo*- and *usted*-forms of the Present of *vender*.

yo vendo; usted vende

5 The opposite of *vender* is *comprar*, a regular *a*-verb. Translate: *Yo compré un sombrero ayer.*

I bought a hat yesterday.

6 The Present and Preterit of the *nosotros*-form of *comprar* is ⌣⌣⌣⌣.

compramos

7 When your clothes get dirty, you have to wash them. The translation of "to wash" is a cognate of "lavatory." It is ⌣⌣⌣⌣.

lavar

8 When clothes are washed, they get wrinkled, and have to be pressed. The translation of "to press" is ⌣⌣⌣⌣.

planchar (If you missed this, it means you did not learn the vocabulary at the end of Program 107.)

9 *Planchar* is a regular *a*-verb. Translate: I ironed my shirt.

(Yo) planché mi camisa.

10 The Present and Preterit of the *nosotros*-form of *planchar* is ———— .

planchamos   **11** Can you tell, without more context, what *Planchamos las corbatas* means?

no (The statement can mean "We iron" or "We ironed the neckties.")

12 One meaning of *llevar* is "to carry." Another is "to wear." To avoid confusion, many Spanish speakers use *usar* for "to wear." Translate: She does not wear stockings.

Ella no usa medias. (The Spanish meaning is "She does not use stockings.")

13 The most common thing we do with clothes is put them on and take them off. Have you ever stopped to think about the fact that this is an odd way to talk? On *what* do we put clothes when we put them *on*? We put them (a) on the table (b) on ourselves.

on ourselves   **14** You can see this pattern better in this question: "Shall I put the hat on the doll or on myself?" English takes it for granted that "She put the hat on" ordinarily means that she put it on her own head, that is, on herself. Spanish, in contrast, always says on whom something is put. Translate: *Yo voy a ponerme el sombrero.*

I'm going to put on the hat. (You don't translate the *me*.)

15 Translate: *¿Tú vas a ponerte el sombrero?*

Are you going to put on the hat? (You don't translate the *te*.)

16 Let's stop now and analyze this pattern: *Tú vas a ponerte el sombrero.* The doer in the statement is ———— .

Tú   **17** The done-to is ———— .

el sombrero   **18** The *te*, then, stands for the person on whom the hat is put. All of this will make more sense when you consider this sentence: "I'm not going to put the hat on you; I'm going to put it on myself." English uses the reflexive "myself" only in very special constructions. Spanish uses it all the time.

     The opposite of *ponerse el sombrero* is *quitarse el sombrero.* The translation of *quitar* is "to ———— ."

take off   **19** What pronoun will you add to this sentence? *Miguel va a quitar* ———— *el sombrero.*

se   **20** The translation of "I put on the hat" is *Me pongo el sombrero.* The translation of "I take off the hat" is ———— .

Me quito el sombrero.

21 Here is another difference between English and Spanish. Carlota is wearing a heavy sweater. The sun has come out and it is very warm. She says *Voy a quitarme el suéter.* Which is the most likely translation? (a) I'm going to take off *the* sweater. (b) I'm going to take off *my* sweater.

I'm going to take off my sweater.

22 Spanish uses the definite article where English uses the possessive adjective when it is obvious who the possessor is. So the common translation of "I put on my hat" is *Me pongo el sombrero.* Translate "I take off my hat."

Me quito el sombrero.

23 Translate, using the Present: I put on my shoes.

Me pongo los zapatos.

24 When we say in English "We put on our shoes," each person puts on two shoes. How many hats does each person put on when we say, "We put on our hats?"

one hat each

25 In a certain sense, it is rather silly to say "We put on our hats" when each person only puts on one hat. It is just as silly, in contrast, to say "We put on our hat." The Spanish speaker, however, solves this problem by using the plural when two items are put on (*Nos ponemos los zapatos*), and the singular when each person puts on one item (*Nos ponemos el sombrero*). Translate: We take off our shirts.

Nos quitamos la camisa.

Part 2: The Preterit of *ir, decir,* and *ser*

1 The translation of *Ayer fue domingo* is ——.

Yesterday was Sunday.

2 When Latin was becoming Spanish, the forms for "to be" (*ser*) and "to go" (*ir*) became confused; as a result, the Preterit of *ser* and *ir* have exactly the same forms. The meaning, consequently, can only be determined by context. Translate: *¿A dónde fue usted ayer?*

Where did you go yesterday? (The *A dónde* cues motion.)

3 Translate: *La lección fue interesante.*

The lesson was interesting.

4 The plural of *fue* is *fueron*, which translates either "were" or "went." Translate: *Mis padres fueron al teatro ayer*. The cue for choice is the *a* of *al teatro*.

My parents went to the theater yesterday.

5 Translate: *Mis abuelos fueron muy amables.*

My grandparents were very kind (nice).

6 All the other preterit forms of *ser* and *ir* have *i* as the first suffix. The second suffix is regular. The form that matches *yo* is ——.

fui　　　**7** To get the *tú*-form you add —— to *fui*.

ste (And you have *fuiste*.)

8 To get the *nosotros*-form you add —— to *fui*.

mos (And you get *fuimos*.)

9 Here are all the preterit forms of *ser* and *ir:*

yo fui
nosotros fuimos
tú fuiste
usted, él, ella fue
ustedes, ellos, ellas fueron

The stem for all forms is ——.

fu　　　**10** The first suffix has three allomorphs: *i, e,* and ——.

ero (The second suffix is regular: zero, *ste, mos, n.*)

11 The Preterit of *decir* has two irregularities. First, the stem for all forms is *dij*. Second, the first suffix forms are like those of *venir*. The *yo*-form of *venir* is *vine*. The *yo*-form of *decir* is ——.

dije　　　**12** The *usted*-form of *venir* is ——.

vino　　　**13** The *usted*-form of *decir* is ——.

dijo　　　**14** The *tú*-form of *venir* has regular suffixes. It is ——.

viniste　　　**15** The *tú*-form of *decir* is ——.

dijiste

	16 Change *dijiste* so it matches *nosotros*.
dijimos	**17** The *ustedes-* and *ellos*-form of *venir* is *vinieron*. The *j* of the stem *dij* absorbs the *i* of the first suffix and the resulting form is ———.
dijeron	**18** Let's review, now, what you have just studied. You can make *fue* plural by adding ———.
ron (fue > fueron)	
	19 You can make *fui* plural by adding ———.
mos (fui > fuimos)	
	20 To get the *tú*-form you simply add the second suffix *ste* to ———.
fui > fuiste (So if you remember *fui* and *fue,* you can make up all the other	
forms.)	**21** The irregular preterit stem of *decir* is ———.
dij	**22** The *yo*-form is ———.
dije	**23** You add *ron* to *dije* to get the *ustedes*-form ———.
dijeron	**24** The *usted-* and *él*-form is ———.
dijo	**25** Two forms have *i* as the first suffix. The *tú-* and *nosotros*-forms are ———.
dijiste ; dijimos	

New Vocabulary

¡**Felicidades**!   Congratulations!

PROGRAM **109**

Review of Stem-changing Verbs, and Preparing for a Quiz on Reflexive Constructions

Part 1 : Review of Stem-changing Verbs

1 You already know that the easiest way to learn and remember stem-changing verbs is to study them by sets. One set is made up of *a-* and *e*-verbs which have either an *e* or an *o* in the stem. When the stem is stressed, these vowels may change to ———.

ie ; ue **2** Write the present tense *yo*-forms for *cerrar* and *perder*.

cierro ; pierdo **3** Write the present tense *usted*-forms for *acostar* and *morder*.

acuesta ; muerde

4 The *nosotros*-forms of this set of verbs always have the stress on the first suffix, not the stem, and they are, consequently, regular. Write the present tense *nosotros*-forms for *volver* and *contar*.

volvemos ; contamos

5 The members of this set which you have had so far are:

e > ie: *perder, despertar, cerrar, sentar, pensar, empezar, tropezar, quebrar*

o > ue: *recordar, acostar, contar, volver, morder, mover, jugar, encontrar*

In the Preterit of all of these verbs, the stress falls on the first suffix, not on the stem, and, as a result, all forms are regular. Write the *yo*-forms for *perder* and *contar*.

perdí; conté **6** Here is a summary of the facts you need to know about this set of verbs:
(1) The first and second suffixes are regular in all tenses.
(2) The irregularity appears in the stem of only the Present.
(3) The stem has two allomorphs: *cont, cuent* and *perd, pierd*.
(4) This set is made up of only *a*- and *e*-verbs.
Change *vuelvo* to the Preterit.

volví **7** There is a set of *i*-verbs which have an *e* and an *o* in the stem which also change to *ie* and *ue*. You have had four of these verbs: *divertir, sentir, dormir,* and *morir*. Write the present tense *él*-forms for all four.

divierte, siente, duerme, muere
8 All members of this set have a special irregularity in the *él*- and *ellos*-forms of the Preterit. The *e* of the stem changes to *i* and the *o* changes to *u*. Translate: They regretted (*sentir*).

Ellos sintieron. **9** Change *sintieron* so it matches *usted* or *él*.

sintió **10** Change *sintió* so it matches *yo*.

sentí **11** To make *sentí* agree with *tú* and *nosotros* you add ⌇⌇⌇ and drop the accent mark.

ste; mos (sentiste, sentimos)
12 Translate: He slept (*dormir*).

Él durmió. **13** Change *durmió* so it matches *ustedes* or *ellos*.

durmieron **14** The *yo*-form of the Preterit of *dormir* is regular. To make it you drop the *r* of *dormir* and stress the syllable (a) *dor* (b) *mi*.

mi (So you must write this form dormí.)
15 Here is a summary of the facts you need to know about this set of verbs:
(1) The set is made up of only *i*-verbs.
(2) The first and second suffixes are regular in all tenses.
(3) There are irregular stems in the Present and in the Preterit (*duerm, durm*).
(4) In the Present the stem has two allomorphs: *sent, sient,* and *dorm, duerm*.
(5) In the Preterit the stem has another allomorph: *sint* and *durm*, which is used only when the first suffix has a diphthong.
Change *divierten* and *duermen* to the Preterit.

divirtieron; durmieron
16 There is a set of *i*-verbs in which the *e* of the stem changes to *i*. This happens in the Present when the stem is stressed and in the Preterit when the first suffix has a diphthong (*ió* or *ie*). You have had five verbs of this set. They are: *pedir, despedir, servir, medir,* and *seguir*. Write the present tense *usted*-forms for *pedir* and *servir*.

pide; sirve **17** The stem of *pide* and *sirve* is the same for their preterit forms. You just change the suffix to ⌇⌇⌇ .

ió (pidió, sirvió)
18 Change *pidió* and *sirvió* so they match *ustedes*.

pidierón; sirvieron
19 In the Present of this set of verbs, only the *nosotros*-forms are regular. Write these forms for *despedir* and *seguir*.

despedimos; seguimos

20 The *nosotros*-forms of the Preterit are exactly the same as the Present. Write these forms for *pedir* and *servir*.

pedimos; servimos (You can get the meaning only from context.)

21 The *yo*-, *nosotros*-, and *tú*-forms of the Preterit are regular. To get the *yo*-forms of *pedimos* and *servimos* you drop the *mos* and stress the final syllable. Write these forms.

pedí; serví

22 Here is a summary of the facts you need to know about this set of verbs:

(1) The set is made up of only *i*-verbs.

(2) The first and second suffixes are regular in all tenses.

(3) There are irregular stems in the Present and the Preterit (*sirv, pid*).

(4) The *e* changes to *i* in the stem of both tenses.

(5) Only the *nosotros*-form is regular in the Present (*servimos, pedimos*).

(6) Only the *usted*- and *ustedes*-, *él*- and *ellos*-forms are irregular in the Preterit (*sirvió, sivieron*).

(7) The present tense *yo*-form of *seguir* has a spelling change. It is written ⎯⎯⎯.

sigo

23 The verbs *tener*, *venir*, and *decir* belong to a special set of irregular verbs. Their *yo*-forms in the Present are ⎯⎯⎯.

tengo, vengo, digo

24 In the Present, the other forms of *tener* and *venir* are like *perder*. The *e* changes to *ie* when the stem is stressed. Change *tenemos* and *venimos* so they match *ustedes*.

tienen; vienen (Remember you get the *usted*-forms by just dropping the suffix *n*.)

25 The *yo*-form of *decir* is *digo*. (It was once *dico*.) The other present tense forms of *decir* are like *servir*. The irregular stem is ⎯⎯⎯.

dic

26 Translate: They say.

Ellos dicen.

27 Change *dicen* so it matches *tú*.

dices

28 The verbs *venir* and *decir* have both an irregular stem and irregular first suffixes in the Preterit. The preterit stem of *venir* is ⎯⎯⎯.

vin

29 The preterit stem of *decir* is ⎯⎯⎯.

dij

30 The *yo*- and *usted*-forms of the Preterit have the irregular first suffix *e* and *o*. So the forms are *dije*, *vine*, *dijo*, and *vino*. The suffixes on all the other forms, with one exception, are regular. There is no *i* in *dijeron*. Write the *tú*-forms for *venir* and *decir*.

viniste; dijiste

31 Change *venimos* and *decimos* to the Preterit.

vinimos; dijimos

A good deal has been said in these cultural notes about the Indians. It should be mentioned that in Argentina and Uruguay there are almost no *pure-blooded* Indians any more. The population of most of Latin America is made up principally of mixtures of white, Indian, and Negro, with percentages varying from one region to another. This is largely dependent on factors of climate and history. Most of the population is mestizo (mixed Indian and white), and in some places the difference between mestizo and Indian is in the types of clothes worn, and occasionally the language(s) spoken.

Part 2: Preparing for a Quiz on Reflexive Constructions.

In your next class session, you will have a quiz on reflexive constructions. Your grade will depend on three things: (1) the use of the proper verb form in the Present, (2) the selection of the correct reflexive (done-to) pronoun, and (3) the placement of the pronoun in the correct position before or after the verb.

1 The *yo*-form is the name of the speaker and the doer. The done-to form that matches *yo* is ⌁.

me   **2** The done-to form that matches *nosotros* is ⌁.

nos   **3** The done-to form that goes with *tú* is ⌁.

te   **4** The done-to forms *me*, *nos*, and *te* are also used in reflexive constructions. Translate: I wash myself.

Yo me lavo.   **5** Translate: We go to bed early.

Nos acostamos temprano.

6 Translate: You (*tú*) sit down.

Tú te sientas.   **7** The reflexive pronoun and done-to form that matches *usted, ustedes, él, ella, ellos*, and *ellas* is ⌁.

se   **8** Translate: They have breakfast at seven o'clock. (The verb is *desayunar*.)

Ellos se desayunan a las siete.

9 Rewrite the above sentence with *usted* as the subject.

Usted se desayuna a las siete.

10 When the done-to pronoun is used with an infinitive it (a) comes before the infinitive (b) is attached to the end of the infinitive.

is attached to the end of the infinitive

11 Copy and fill in the proper done-to pronoun. *No queremos dormir* ⌁ *ahora.*

No queremos dormirnos ahora.

12 Translate: *No queremos dormirnos ahora.*

We don't want to go to sleep now.

13 When the done-to pronoun is used with a conjugated (finite) form of the verb, it goes (a) in front of the verb (b) after the verb.

in front of the verb

14 Translate: She goes to bed late.

Ella se acuesta tarde.

15 In your quiz you will see a cue something like this: *Yo despertarse temprano.* You will rewrite this with the three grading points in mind. The verb form in the Present must be ⌁.

despierto   **16** The *se* must be changed to match *yo*. The form is ⌁.

me   **17** You must place the *me* where?

before the verb **18** Rewrite *Yo despertarse temprano* with all the proper changes.

Yo me despierto temprano.

19 Rewrite *Nosotros ir a sentarse aquí* with the two necessary changes.

Nosotros vamos a sentarnos aquí.

New Vocabulary

dar	to give
traer	to bring
traducir	to translate

Review of Usage: *venir* versus *ir*, and the Preterit and Imperfect

Part 1: *venir* versus *ir*

1 The verbs *ir* and *venir* describe movement through space. You are the speaker and you are standing at the spot marked X. Which arrow gives the direction of movement described by *venir?*

X ⇄

X ←————— **2** *Venir* describes movement toward the position of the speaker. Pretend you are the speaker and translate: Carlota is coming here tomorrow.
Carlota viene aquí mañana.

3 The English translation of *venir* will always be "to come." When you turn this around, however, the Spanish translation of "to come" may be either *venir* or *ir*. This is because Spanish, like English, regularly uses *venir* to describe any movement toward the position of the person who says the sentence. Suppose someone phones you from his home and says, "Are you coming to my house tonight?" Which verb will be used?
venir (¿Vienes a mi casa esta noche?)

4 Suppose you answer "yes" to the question, "Are you coming to my house tonight?" When you answer, you are the speaker. You are at the spot marked X, your home. Which arrow will give the direction of your movement?

X ⇄

X ————→ (You have to move away from where you are "to go" to somebody else's house.)

5 Now complete the answer to the question: Are you coming to my house tonight? "Yes, I will ———— to your house."
come
6 When you use "come" in the answer above you are using the point of view of the person who asked the question, not your own. Spanish, in contrast, always uses the point of view of the speaker, the person who actually says the sentence. So the answer to *¿ Vienes a mi casa?* must be (a) *Sí, vengo.* (b) *Sí, voy.*
Sí, voy (You are really "going" toward the home of the person who asked the question.) **7** Let's summarize these facts. English uses *to come* (1) to describe movement toward the speaker (I see him *coming* now.) and (2) to describe movement toward the first speaker when a second speaker answers a question (Are you *coming*? Yes, I'm *coming*.) Spanish, in contrast, always uses the point of view of the speaker. In other words, you cannot *come* to where you are not, you can only *go* there. So someone knocks at your door. You are in the kitchen. You call out (a) *Ya vengo.* (b) *Ya voy.*
Ya voy. (Literally "I am already going"; you are moving away from where you were toward the door. You are, in fact, "going" to the door.)

8 Except for the differences in usage just described, Spanish uses *ir* and *venir* very much like English uses "to go" and "to come." Which verb will you use to translate "Do you want *to come* with me to the movies?"

venir

9 Which verb will you use to translate "Do you want *to go* to the movies with me?"

ir

10 Here's a short review of what you have just studied. Which verb will you use in this situation? "I can't *come* to your place today." (a) *ir* (b) *venir*

ir (You move away from where you are toward the other person.)

11 You tell someone, "*Come* here right away." (a) *ir* (b) *venir*

venir

12 This person answers, "I'm *coming*." (a) *ir* (b) *venir*

ir

13 In English when someone says, "Come here," you answer with the same verb, "I'm coming." In Spanish you must always use *ir* when you describe your movement away from where you start moving toward the position of the first speaker.

Part 2: The Preterit and the Imperfect: A Summary of Usage

1 The Preterit and Imperfect have two major functions. From one point of view these forms describe events which are over or completed at the moment of speaking. *Juan se desayuna* tells what Juan is doing as the speaker says the sentence. *Juan se desayunó* tells you the action was finished before the sentence is said.

Let's look at this another way. Compare these two sentences: (1) *Mamá dice que Juan se desayuna.* (2) *Mamá dice que Juan se desayunó.* Are *dice* and *desayuna* going on at the same time?

yes (The act of speaking (*dice*) is simultaneous with the act of breakfasting (*desayuna*).) **2** Are *dice* and *desayunó* going on at the same time?

no (The form *desayunó* says that breakfasting was finished before the act of speaking.) **3** This use of the Preterit is just like that of the Simple Past in English. Compare: (1) Mother says that Juan *is eating* breakfast. (2) Mother says that Juan *ate* breakfast.

Translate: I know (*saber*) that she bought the hat.

(*Yo*) *sé que ella compró el sombrero.*

4 Translate: Where's Carmen? She is going to the beach.

¿Dónde está Carmen? Va a la playa.

5 Now translate this answer: She went to the beach.

Fue a la playa. **6** From the point of view of the moment of speaking, the Preterit, like the simple past in English, may say the action has been completed. Translate: I lost the money.

Perdí el dinero. **7** When a habitual or customary past action is contrasted with a different but also customary present action both English and Spanish use the Present for the present action. English employs "used to" for the contrasting past action. "He used to go to bed early, now he goes to bed late." Spanish uses the Present to translate "now he goes to bed late." *ahora se acuesta tarde.* Which form do you use to translate "He used to go to bed early?" (a) *se acostó* (b) *se acostaba*

se acostaba (The "used to" construction always cues the use of the Imperfect in Spanish.)

8 Translate: We used to live in San Diego. Now we live in San Rafael.
Vivíamos en San Diego. Ahora vivimos en San Rafael. (The Past Imperfect *vivíamos* stands in contrast with the Present Imperfect *vivimos*.)

9 The major contrast between the Preterit and Imperfect shows up when you talk about events which happen at some point in the past. At a point in the past an event may begin, be going on, or come to an end. The technical terms for these three aspects are *initiative*, *imperfective*, and *terminative*. The on-going or imperfective aspect of any event is always described by the (a) Preterit (b) Imperfect.

Imperfect   **10** To state that a cyclic event was terminated at any point in the past you use the ⁓⁓⁓.

Preterit   **11** What forms of the indicated infinitives will you use to make these actions past tense? *Cuando yo llegar a la escuela hacer mucho calor.*
*Cuando yo **llegué** a la escuela, **hacía** mucho calor.*

12 To say that a non-cyclic event began at some point in the past you use the ⁓⁓⁓.

Preterit   **13** Rewrite this in the past tense: *Él se levanta y corre.*
*Él se **levantó** y **corrió**.* (The real meaning is "He got up and *began* to run.")

14 Here is another way of saying all this: you use the Imperfect to talk about the middle of an event and the Preterit to describe either end. In this and the next four frames change the indicated infinitives to the proper form of the Preterit or Imperfect.
Cuando Sabino llegar a la tienda descubrir que no tener dinero.
*Cuando Sabino **llegó** a la tienda **descubrió** que no **tenía** dinero.*

15 *Sabino estar triste porque querer comprar una camisa.*
*Sabino **estaba** triste porque **quería** comprar una camisa.*

16 *Volver Sabino a casa pero su mamá no estar allí.*
***Volvió** Sabino a casa pero su mamá no **estaba** allí.*

17 *Se quitar el sombrero y se sentar a esperar (wait for) a su mamá.*
*Se **quitó** el sombrero y se **sentó** a esperar a su mamá.*

18 *De repente (suddenly) su perro ladrar. Haber un señor a la puerta.*
*De repente su perro **ladró**. **Había** un señor a la puerta.*

19 Here is a true story. Let's see if you can figure out when to use the Preterit or Imperfect. For each frame write *P* or *I* to indicate your choice for the indicated verbs.
In 1940 a Mexican farmer by the name of Dionisio Pulido *was working* in his field.

I   **20** He suddenly *observed* that his plow animals *were behaving* in a strange way.

P, I   **21** He *walked up* to them, *bent over*, and *touched* the ground.

P, P, P   **22** The ground *was* very hot and as he *stood* there some smoke suddenly *came out* of the soil.

I, I, P   **23** Señor Pulido *did* not *know* what *was happening*.

I, I   **24** He *left* the field because he *was* afraid.

P, I   **25** In a few hours flames *shot up* from his field and huge clouds of smoke and ashes *burst* from the ground.

P, P   **26** Señor Pulido *did* not *understand* all this. He *did* not *know* that he *was watching* a volcano being born.

I, I, I

27 The volcano soon *covered* his whole farm and in a few weeks it *grew* to be several hundred feet high.

P, P **28** The whole country *was* excited, and scientists *came* from all over the world to watch the volcano grow.

I, P **29** When they *arrived*, the fields for miles around. *were* covered with ashes and dust.

P, I **30** At that time the volcano *had* no name. Finally someone *gave* it the name it still has today. It is called Paricutín.

I, P **31** There remain, now, two uses of the Imperfect which you need to remember. For some speakers of English "would" may be used as a very close equivalent of "used to." For example, "When we were living in Chile we *would go* to the beach every day." If this form is in your dialect, you will translate "would go" as (a) *íbamos* (b) *fuimos*

íbamos **32** The Imperfect is used in telling time. Translate the two verbs: It was eight o'clock when we arrived at the movies.

Eran *las ocho cuando* **llegamos** *al cine.*

33 The translation of *Ella dice que va* is "She says she is going." The past tense back-shift of "She says she is going" is ⁓⁓⁓.

She said she was going.

34 The back-shift of *Ella dice que va* is *Ella dijo que* (a) *fue* (b) *iba.*

iba (Recalled planned action is described with the Imperfect.)

Here is a summary of what you just studied:

(1) From the point of view of the moment of speaking the Preterit says that an event either began or was terminated before you say the sentence. So *Él se murió* says the event came to an end before now and *Yo lo conocí* says our acquaintanceship began before now.

(2) When you are recalling some point in the past, the Preterit says either that a cyclic event terminated at that point (*Yo llegué a casa a la una*) or that a non-cyclic event began at that point (*A la una oí el ruido* = noise).

(3) At this same recalled point the Imperfect says the action was going on (*Llovía cuando llegué a casa*). The Imperfect says the same thing about either a cyclic or non-cyclic event (*Se moría cuando llegué a casa*).

(4) From the point of view of the present time, the Imperfect is used to say that what once was customary or habitual stands in contrast with what is currently customary or habitual. The most common translation of this use of the Imperfect is "used to" plus the main verb: "I used to live in St. Louis but now I live in Los Angeles." *Vivía en San Luis pero ahora vivo en Los Angeles.*

(5) The Imperfect is used in telling time: *¿ Qué hora era? Eran las tres.*

(6) In Spanish the Simple Present is used to talk about planned future action: *Dicen que se casan en una semana.* The backshift of this use of the Present is the Imperfect: *Dijeron que se casaban en una semana.*

New Vocabulary

Dios	God
despedirse (i) de	to say good-bye to
ayudar	to help
Perdón.	Excuse me. Pardon me.

Locating Things in Space: Demonstratives, and a Vocabulary Review

Part 1: The Demonstratives

1 Here is a linguistic riddle to test your powers of observation. Why is it that *tú* and *usted* can never talk? Because the speaker is always ～～.

yo (The *tú* and *usted* are names for listeners only.)

2 The speaker *yo* is the center around which everything in the world is organized. In a speech situation, which is psychologically closer to *yo*? (a) *usted* (b) *él*

usted (*Yo* never talks to *él*, only about him.)

3 You are talking to a friend on the phone, and you say, "I can't find my Spanish book. It's not *here*." Your friend answers, "It's not *here*. You took it with you." Does *here* stand for the same space in both statements?

no (*Here* is your house when you say it, and *here* is your friend's house when he says it.)

4 The space around and near the speaker (I) is called (a) here (b) there.

here

5 The space around and near the person spoken to is ～～.

there

6 English divides space into two areas: "here" and "there." Spanish, in contrast, divides space into three areas. The space around *yo* is *aquí*. The space around *usted* is *ahí*, and the space around *él* is *allí*. This may be diagramed like this:

The space the farthest away from *yo* is ～～.

alli

7 Let's see what these areas have to do with the demonstrative adjectives. Which book is closer to the speaker? (a) this book (b) that book

this book

8 Is *this book* inside (a) here? (b) there?

here

9 Does the *that* of *that book* match *there* in distance away from the speaker?

yes

10 English has two sets of matching forms: "this here" and "that there." Spanish, as you have already seen, has an area name that matches the three persons of speech: *aquí*, *ahí*, and *allí*. Spanish also has a demonstrative that goes along with each of these three areas. You will find the demonstrative forms that go with *libro* in these circles.

The translation of *este* is ～～.

this (*este libro aquí* = this book here)

11 Since English has only two areas (here; there) and only two demonstratives to match them (this; that), there can be no neat translation for *ese* and *aquel*. The closest we can come to *aquel libro* is "that book *over* there." For most practical purposes, consequently, you have to translate both *ese* and *aquel* with ~~~~.

that (But when you put "that" back into Spanish you must always choose between *ese* and *aquel*.)

12 The two demonstratives *este* and *ese* are the only two adjectives in the Spanish language which use the final *e* as a matching phoneme. Look at these pairs:

este libro	ese libro
esta pluma	esa pluma

The *e* of *este* and *ese* combines with words which also combine with *el* and *un*. Translate: this hat

este sombrero **13** The forms *este* and *ese* cannot be made plural. The matching plurals are *estos* and *esos*. Compare these forms:

este libro	ese libro
estos libros	esos libros

The reason why *este* and *ese* are the singular of *estos* and *esos* can be found in this question. You find something strange. You do not know its name, and you ask ¿ *Qué es esto?* (What is this?) This *esto* is called the neuter form. It never agrees with a noun because it is used only to talk about something you cannot name. Translate: What is that?

¿ Qué es eso ? **14** Although many textbooks say there are no plural neuter forms, people actually use *estos*, *esos*, and *aquellos* as plural neuters. Because there is a neuter form, the Spanish demonstratives have three singular forms. The three singular forms that begin with *est* are ~~~~.

esto, este, esta **15** Let's review. The plurals of *esta* and *esa* are ~~~~.
estas ; esas **16** The plurals of *este* and *ese* are ~~~~.
estos ; esos **17** Do the neuter forms *esto* and *eso* have a plural?
yes **18** The locative adverb that goes with *yo* and *este* is ~~~~.
aquí **19** The locative adverb that goes with *usted* and *ese* is ~~~~.
ahí **20** The demonstrative adjective that goes with *él* and *allí* is *aquel* in *aquel libro allí*. You can learn the other forms of *aquel* by using *él, ellos, ella,* and *ellas* as the models. The plural of *él* is *ellos*. The plural of *aquel* is ~~~~.
aquellos **21** The plural of *aquella* is ~~~~.
aquellas **22** Here is the whole pattern:

él	ellos	ella	ellas
aquel	aquellos	aquella	aquellas

The stem of this demonstrative has two allomorphs: *aquel* and *aquell*. Now, make an educated guess. To which stem will you add the *o* to make the neuter form that matches *esto* and *eso*? (a) *aquel* (b) *aquell*

aquell (¿ Qué es aquello ?)

23 Each Spanish demonstrative has five forms. Here they are with their matching locative adverb:

aquí	*ahí*	*allí*
esto	eso	aquello
este	ese	aquel
esta	esa	aquella
estos	esos	aquellos
estas	esas	aquellas

The area farthest away from *yo* and near *él* is labelled ⁓⁓⁓. •

allí
24 Which demonstrative will you put in this space? ⁓⁓⁓ *silla cerca de él.* •

Aquella
25 ⁓⁓⁓ *animal cerca de usted.* •

Ese
26 ⁓⁓⁓ *gato que yo tengo aquí.* •

Este
27 The three Spanish demonstratives locate things near the three persons involved in a speech situation: *yo, usted,* and *él.* They are also used to point out how far an object is away from the speaker when the actual distance is in itself not important. A Spanish speaker pointing to three books laid out in a row on a table will say *este libro, ese libro, y aquel libro.* The closest book is *este.* The one farthest away is *aquel.* And the one in the middle distance is ⁓⁓⁓. •

ese
28 You were told a long time ago that all the forms of the definite article came from the Latin demonstrative *ille.* It should not surprise you to discover that the modern demonstratives can, like the article, become adjectival residuals. What is the normal way of answering *¿Vas a comprar la camisa? Sí, voy a*

⁓⁓⁓ •

comprarla
29 Any one of the three demonstratives may replace the *la* of the above question.

$$\text{¿ Vas a comprar} \left| \begin{array}{l} \text{esta} \\ \text{esa} \\ \text{aquella} \end{array} \right| \text{camisa?}$$

When the noun is dropped, the demonstrative remains as an adjectival residual, but unlike the article this residual is not attached to the infinitive. Translate these two sentences: *¿Vas a comprar la camisa? Sí, voy a comprarla.* •

Are you going to buy the shirt? Yes, I'm going to buy it. (The *la* has two English translations: "the" and "it.")

30 Now translate these two sentences: *¿Vas a comprar esa camisa? Sí, voy a comprar esa.* •

Are you going to buy that shirt? Yes, I'm going to buy that one. (When *that* becomes a residual in English, you may have to add the word "one.")

31 Translate the answer: Which book do you want? *This one.* •

Este (In most books you will see this residual written *éste.* Until 1952 the residual demonstratives had to have an accent mark on the first vowel. This is no longer required by the Spanish Academy, except in cases in which there would otherwise be confusion.)

32 There are two other locative adverbs which you will encounter in your readings and which you will learn to use later on. They are *acá* and *allá* which have a meaning very much like *aquí* and *allí.*

The custom of wearing black mourning clothes when a member of the family dies is gradually disappearing in the United States. The same thing is happening among the men in Latin countries who now often show their mourning simply by wearing a black arm band. Middle and upper-class women, in contrast, still frequently wear black; and because the death rate is high, the proportion of women in black that one sees on the street strikes many Americans as strange.

The people who are very devout and strongly traditional believe that mourning clothes should be worn for at least a year. They also believe that when a man's wife dies, he is not showing proper respect for her if he remarries before the end of the year of mourning. In reverse, it is generally considered improper for a man to pay court to a widow who is still wearing the mourning black.

Part 2: Vocabulary Review

1 The translation of *Que te diviertas* is ———.
(May you) have a good time. (The meaning is something like "I hope that you amuse yourself.")

2 Translate: Make yourself at home. (Use the *usted*-form.)
Está en su casa.

3 One way of saying "please" is *por favor*. A more formal way uses *hacer*. Translate literally: *Hágame el favor de cerrar la puerta.*
Do me the favor of closing the door. (Please close the door.)

4 Translate: *No te molestes.*
Don't bother. **5** Translate: It's no bother.
No es molestia ninguna.

6 The meaning of *Lo siento mucho* is "I feel it a lot." The translation is ———.
I'm very sorry. **7** There are three ways of saying "Pardon me" with a verb form when you address a person with *usted: Dispénseme, Discúlpeme,* and ———.
Perdóneme. **8** When someone sneezes you may say in Spanish either ———.
¡Salud! or *¡Jesús!*

9 Translate: *desde aquí hasta allí.*
from here to there

10 Translate: *Nuestra casa está rodeada de agua.*
Our house is surrounded by water.

11 The meaning of *por todas partes* is "through all parts" (You see them through all parts.). The translation is ———.
everywhere **12** The translation of *sin embargo* is ———.
nevertheless, or however

New Vocabulary

ponerse	to put on		**vender**	to sell
quitarse	to take off		**madrugar**	to get up early
comprar	to buy			

PROGRAM 112

Preparing for a Quiz on the Present of Irregular Verbs, and Vocabulary Review

Part 1: Irregular Verbs

1 In your next class you will have a quiz to find out if you can make up and write the present tense forms of irregular verbs. By now you should know that irregular verbs fall into two sets: those which have a certain pattern and those whose irregularity is not at all predictable. In the Present *despertar* has a pattern of irregularity. The second e of the stem changes to ～～～ when stressed.

ie   **2** Write the form of *despertar* that goes with *tú te* ～～～.

despiertas   **3** The only present tense form of *despertar* which does not have a stress on the stem is the *nosotros*-form. It is ～～～.

despertamos   **4** The verb *sentir* has the same patterned irregularity as *despertar*. The *yo*-form is ～～～.

siento   **5** The *usted*-form is ～～～.

siente   **6** The *nosotros*-form is regular. It is ～～～.

sentimos   **7** The verbs *pensar* and *querer* have the same patterned irregularity as *despertar* and *sentir*. Their *yo*-forms are ～～～.

pienso; quiero   **8** Change *pienso* and *quiero* so they agree with *ustedes*.
piensan; quieren

9 The verb *recordar* belongs to a set which has a patterned irregularity. The o of the stem changes to ～～～ when stressed.

ue   **10** Write the *ellos*-form of *recordar*.

recuerdan   **11** Which form goes with *nosotros*? (a) *recuerdamos* (b) *recordamos*

recordamos   **12** Change *recordamos* so it agrees with *yo*.

recuerdo   **13** Does *dormir* have the same irregularities in the Present as *recordar*?

yes   **14** Write the *yo*-form of *dormir*.

duermo   **15** The verb *servir* has a patterned irregularity. The e of the stem changes to (a) *ie* (b) *i*.

i   **16** Write the form of *servir* that goes with *él*.

sirve   **17** Change *sirve* so it matches *yo*.
sirvo

18 In the irregular verbs you have had so far the *nosotros*-forms are always regular. Write the *nosotros*-form of *servir*.

servimos   **19** A few verbs have a special irregularity in the *yo*-form of the Present. The *yo*-form of *poner* is ⁓⁓⁓.

pongo   **20** The present tense *yo*-form of *tener, decir,* and *venir* is ⁓⁓⁓.

tengo, digo, vengo

21 The verb *ver* has two stems in the Present. In the *usted*-form *ve* the stem is *v*. In the *yo*-form the stem is ⁓⁓⁓.

ve, (*Veo,* from the old infinitive *veer.*)

22 The *i*-verb *ir* has forms like the *a*-verb *dar*. The *yo*- and *usted*-forms of *ir* are ⁓⁓⁓.

voy; va   **23** To make *va* agree with *nosotros* you just add the suffix ⁓⁓⁓.

mos (*vamos*)   **24** The verb *ser* has no patterned irregularity in the Present. You have to memorize each form. Write the forms that match *yo, tú* and *ella*.

soy, eres, es   **25** In the Present the verb *saber* is regular in all forms but one. The single irregular form is ⁓⁓⁓.

yo sé   **26** Translate: I know that I am going to school tomorrow.

Yo sé que voy a la escuela mañana.

27 In the sentence you just wrote the subject of *voy* is the same as the subject of *sé*. (a) true (b) false

true   **28** When a sentence has two verb forms, the subject of the second verb does not have to be expressed if it is the same as the subject of the first verb. In English you may say, "I go home and study my lessons." You can do the same in Spanish. Translate the above sentence.

Yo voy a casa y estudio mis lecciones.

29 Let's review some more irregular forms. The present tense *yo*-form of *oír* is ⁓⁓⁓.

oigo   **30** The *yo*-form of *conocer* is ⁓⁓⁓.

conozco   **31** Translate: I dress myself.

Yo me visto   **32** Write the *yo*- and *ustedes*-forms of *estar*.

estoy; están   **33** The *tú*-form of *oír* is ⁓⁓⁓.

oyes   **34** Change *empiezo* so it agrees with *nosotros*.

empezamos   **35** In the Present the stem of *tener* has three allomorphs. Write the forms that match *yo, usted,* and *nosotros*.

yo tengo, usted tiene, nosotros tenemos

Part 2: Vocabulary Review

1 The verb for "to eat" is ⁓⁓⁓.

comer   **2** The noun *comida* is a cover term for whatever *usted come*. *Comida* translates either ⁓⁓⁓.

food or meal   **3** Look at the word *ensalada*. It has in it the English word which is its translation. This word is ⁓⁓⁓.

salad

4 People and certain animals are said to be "carnivorous." This means that they eat *carne*. The translation of *carne* is ⁓.

meat   **5** The verb *comer* gives the noun *comida*. The translation of *beber* is ⁓.

to drink   **6** The verb *beber* gives the noun *bebida*. The translation of *una bebida* is ⁓.

a drink   **7** The English cognate of *fruta* is ⁓.

fruit   **8** The main course of many meals is made up of *carne*, *fruta*, and *legumbres*. The translation of *legumbres* is ⁓.

vegetables   **9** What is "anterior" comes before something. What is "posterior" comes ⁓ something.

after   **10** What is "posterior" to the main part of a meal in Spanish is *el postre*. The cognate "posterior" does not translate *postre*. The translation is ⁓.

dessert (what comes after the main meal)

11 The vocabulary you have just been reviewing belongs to the set of words for food and drink. Not all words belong to easily defined sets. The word *aunque* is an example. You have to learn its meaning from context. In the proverb *Aunque la mona se vista de seda, mona se queda* the word *aunque* translates ⁓.

although   **12** Translate the indicated word: *La república de Panamá está situada **entre** dos océanos.*

between   **13** Translate the indicated word: *La isla de Cuba está **rodeada** de agua.*

surrounded   **14** Translate the indicated phrase: *César no está bien, **sin embargo** va con nosotros.*

nevertheless   **15** Translate: *Según mi papá hay animales por todas partes.*

According to my father, there are animals everywhere. (Add any word you missed to your special study list.)

No new vocabulary.

PROGRAM **113**

Vocabulary Round-up

Within the next few days you are going to have a major test. This Program has been specially designed to help you discover what words you still need to study before you are ready to take the test. Because there are many words, time can be saved if you do not write anything on your answer sheet. Look at each frame, *think* of the answer, and then check to see whether you are right. Jot down any words you have missed for further study. When you have finished this Program, you will have a list of the words you need to study more.

Part 1 : Verbs

In this section you will see a verb form in each frame. *Think* of its meaning or translation, then check to see if you are right. If you do not know the meaning instantly, copy the verb on your special list for more study.

1 *Está lloviendo.*

It is raining. **2** *volar*

to fly **3** La cometa *vuela* bien.

flies **4** Ellos *quieren* la comida ahora.

They want **5** ¿Qué vas a *tomar?* ¿Café o chocolate?

to have *or* to drink

6 *Pienso repasar* la lección esta noche.

I plan (intend) to review

7 Usted *no puede volver* mañana.

You cannot return

8 Yo *miro* el lago.

I am looking at

9 ¿*Conoce* usted a María?

Do you know (are you acquainted with)

10 Pablo *no duerme* bien.

does not sleep **11** Juan *pide* una ensalada.

orders (asks for)

12 El estudiante que *estudia, aprende.*

studies, learns **13** La mujer *lleva* el jarro en la cabeza.

is carrying (carries)

14 *Observo* que el pájaro *sigue* comiendo.

I observe; continues (keeps on)

15 ¿Cuándo *empieza* la lección?

does . . . begin **16** La persona que *recuerda no olvida.*

remembers, does not forget

17 Cristóbal Colón *no buscaba* un mundo nuevo.

was not looking for

18 Pero Colón *halló* un mundo nuevo.

found (discovered)

19 *Lo siento mucho.*

I regret it very much. (I'm sorry.)

20 Miguel *juega* con su perro.

plays (is playing)

21 Ellos *acaban de llegar*

have just arrived

22 El señor *terminó de hablar.*

stopped talking

23 La tormenta *pasó.*

passed (went away)

24 ¿Cuánto *queda?*

How much is left (remains)?

25 *No fumo* cigarros.

I do not smoke

	26 Aunque la mona *se vista* de seda, mona se queda.
dresses	**27** ¿*Podemos contar* las estrellas?
Can we count	**28** *cerrar*
to close	**29** *mover*
to move	**30** *quebrar*
to break	**31** *medir*
to measure	**32** *Oigo* que el perro *ladra.*
I hear, is barking	
	33 Mi perro *no muerde.*
does not bite	**34** *No se moleste.*
Don't bother.	**35** *Masticamos* con los dientes.
We chew	**36** La mamá *besa* a su hija.
kisses	**37** Los amigos *se abrazan.*
hug (embrace)	**38** ¿A qué hora *se levanta* usted?
do you get up	**39** Van a *casarse.*
to get married (to marry)	
	40 The opposite of *levantarse* is *acostarse,* "to ――――."
go to bed	**41** Voy a *lavarme.*
wash	**42** Another opposite of *levantarse* is *sentarse,* "to ――――."
sit down	**43** The action of having the first meal of the day is *desayunarse,* "to ――――."
have breakfast	**44** Yo no *uso* sombrero.
wear	**45** Mamá va a *planchar* mis pantalones.
iron	**46** Roberto *perdió* su suéter.
lost	**47** *decir*
to say	**48** *Pienso traer* la fruta.
I plan (intend) to bring	
	49 ¿Quieres *darme* la camisa?
to give me	**50** No puede *traducir* la lección.
translate	**51** Los amigos *se despiden.*
say good-by	**52** The opposite of *ponerse el sombrero* is *quitarse el sombrero.* Translate the second phrase.
to take off one's hat	

Part 2: Nouns

In the first part of this section you will be given a cognate which should help you remember the Spanish word. Think of the Spanish word before you look at the answer frame. If you do not remember the word immediately, write it down on your list for further study.

	1 *Solar energy* is energy that comes from el ――――.
sol (sun)	**2** People used to think that *lunatics* went crazy from looking at la ――――.
luna (moon)	**3** In Latin *manufactured* meant "hand made." The Spanish for "the hand" is la ――――.
mano	**4** The Spanish cognate of *edifice* is ――――.
edificio (building)	
	5 The word *territory* suggests the Spanish word for "earth." It is ――――.
tierra	**6** The part of *island* that is the Spanish word is ――――.
isla	

	7 The English *population* becomes ～～～ in Spanish.
población	**8** The cognate of *inhabitant* drops the prefix and adds *e*. The resulting word is ～～～.
habitante	**9** One meaning of *idiom* is "language." The Spanish cognate is ～～～.
idioma	**10** The cognate of *space* is ～～～.
espacio	**11** The plural of *hero* is *heroes* in English. The Spanish singular is ～～～.
héroe	**12** The Spanish word for "kite" is a cognate of our word *comet*. It is ～～～.
cometa	**13** Our word for *direction* changes to become the Spanish word for "address." It is ～～～.
dirección	**14** A person who is *bilingual* speaks two "tongues." The Spanish word for "tongue" is ～～～.
lengua	**15** The Spanish word for "tooth" is a cognate of *dentist*. The stressed *e* changes to *ie*, so the word is ～～～.
diente	**16** A "lip-tooth" sound is a *labiodental*. The Spanish for "lip" is the Latin form ～～～.
labio	**17** The cognate of *avenue* is ～～～.
avenida	**18** A raincoat is impermeable. The Spanish for "raincoat" is *un* ～～～.
impermeable	**19** A meat-eating animal is a *carnivore*. The Spanish for "meat" is ～～～.
carne	**20** In this and the next ten frames you will see an English noun. Think of its Spanish translation. The translation of "food" is ～～～.
comida	**21** fruit
fruta	**22** salad
ensalada	**23** cloud
nube	**24** soup
sopa	**25** shoes
zapatos	**26** suit
traje	**27** blouse
blusa	**28** flag
bandera	**29** foot (of a person)
pie	**30** In this and the next fifteen frames you will see a Spanish noun. Think of its English translation. Add to your study list any word you do not think of immediately or any word you miss. The translation of *pueblo* is ～～～.
town	**31** *fuente*
fountain	**32** *cabeza*
head	**33** *nariz*
nose	**34** *frente*
forehead	**35** *oreja*
ear	**36** *cuerpo*
body	**37** *pierna*
leg	**38** *dedo*
finger (toe)	**39** *brazo*
arm	**40** *altura*
height	**41** *medias*
stockings	**42** *pantalones*
pants	**43** *camisa*
shirt	**44** *camino*
road	

45 In this and the remaining frames you will find a definition of a word. Think of the word defined and say it aloud in Spanish before you look at the answer part of the frame.

The Supreme Being. •

Dios **46** The article of clothing worn on the head. •

sombrero **47** The article of clothing worn around the neck and under the shirt collar. •

corbata **48** What men wear on their feet and inside their shoes. •

calcetines **49** The male of the cow. •

toro **50** A small body of water completely surrounded by land. •

lago **51** The part of your body in which the tongue and teeth are located. •

boca **52** A domestic animal that often barks and sometimes bites. •

perro **53** A flying insect that frequently gets into the house. •

mosca

No new vocabulary.

In the American theatrical tradition, the mean and nasty villain generally has a mustache and the clean-cut hero who saves the girl is almost always smooth-shaven.

In the Hispanic world, a mustache is traditionally a mark of masculinity, the sign of a true man. As a result, the villain in Spanish movies is usually smooth shaven and the good hero wears a mustache.

Getting Ready for a Test

In your next class you will have a major test. The purpose of this Program is to make certain that you understand the test procedures and avoid making mistakes that have nothing to do with how much Spanish you actually know. Work through the Program carefully, use your cover sheet, and when you are finished, you will know how well you are prepared for the test.

1 Part A of the test will check your ability to hear and understand spoken Spanish. There will be posters on display, each identified by a capital letter. You will hear a statement and, then, you will pick the picture which is most logically associated with the statement. You might hear, for example, *Este señor trabajó mucho y ahora tiene hambre.* Which picture would you select?

A. A man wiping his brow under a desert sun.
B. A man watching a fish in a pool.
C. A man seated at a café table reading the menu.

A man seated at a café table reading the menu. (People usually do not go about ordering a meal unless they are hungry.)

2 Part B of the exam will test your ability to understand spoken Spanish and to tie what you hear with something you read. This part checks your listening and reading comprehension. You will *hear* a statement or a question and on your answer sheet you will *see* three possible reactions or responses. You pick the one that is most logical and circle the letter before it. You hear, for example, *Cuando salimos al campo ¿dónde nos ponemos el sombrero?* Which of the following is the most logical answer to the question?

(a) Ponemos el sombrero en la mesa.
(b) Lo ponemos en un río.
(c) Lo ponemos en la cabeza.

Lo ponemos en la cabeza. (The most logical place for a hat is on the head.)

3 Let's try this one again. You hear *En Paraguay hablan dos lenguas; el español y el guaraní.* Which of the following is most logically associated with this statement?

(a) Paraguay no es un país muy grande.
(b) Paraguay está al sur de Brasil.
(c) Sí, hay muchos indios en Paraguay.

Sí, hay muchos indios en Paraguay.

4 Part C deals with the Present of irregular verbs and reflexive constructions. It will be like a visual-graphic drill: you will see a verb form in the infinitive, for example, *acostarse*, and then, a possible subject such as *yo*. Change *acostarse* so it matches *yo*.

yo me acuesto **5** You see *tú*, *dormirse*, and *temprano*. Put this together with the Present of the verb.

Tú te duermes temprano.

6 You see *El muchacho*, *sentarse*, and *en la silla*. To make a present tense sentence, you write 〜〜.

El muchacho se sienta en la silla.

7 Part D of the test is designed to find out whether you know the translation of isolated words. There will be two columns of words, one in English and one in Spanish. All you have to do is match those words which translate each other. You see, for example, *traer*, *comprar*, and *vender*. Which one of the following matches *traer*? A. to sell B. to buy C. to sing D. to bring

to bring

8 Write the two words that translate each other.

medias	blouse
corbata	shirt
falda	stockings

medias, stockings

9 Write the two words that translate each other.

pelo	foot
nariz	ear
cara	nose

nariz, nose

10 In Part E of the test you prove that you know forms of the Preterit that are irregular. You see a sentence with the verb in the infinitive. You write the preterit form that matches the subject of the sentence. You see, for example, *¿ Qué . . . (hacer) tú ayer?* In place of *hacer* you write 〜〜.

hiciste

11 You see *Yo . . . (venir) al campo de noche.* In place of *venir* you write 〜〜.

vine

12 Change *muere* to the Preterit.

murió

13 Change *caen* to the Preterit.

cayeron

14 Write the Preterit of *yo decir*.

yo dije

15 Write the Preterit of *ellos ir*.

ellos fueron

16 Write the Preterit of *yo comenzar*.

yo comencé

17 Write the Preterit of *ella servir*.

ella sirvió

18 In Part F of the test you will find a short narrative in the Present. You are to read each sentence carefully and then decide which verbs should be replaced by the Preterit or the Imperfect. Let's do this in English first. Rewrite this sentence in the past tense: This morning when I wake up, it is hot.

This morning when I woke up, it was hot.

19 Now, rewrite this in the past tense: *Esta mañana cuando me despierto, hace calor.*

Esta mañana cuando me desperté hacía calor.

20 Rewrite in the past tense and show that the action of *llegar* was completed: *María está en casa cuando llega su tío.*

María estaba en casa cuando llegó su tío.

21 Rewrite in the past tense: *Aquel día mamá dice que no tiene dinero.*

Aquel día mamá dijo que no tenía dinero.

22 Rewrite in the past tense and show that the action of *acostar* was completed: *Son las diez cuando me acuesto.*

Eran las diez cuando me acosté.

23 Part G checks whether you remember all of the irregular forms of the verb in the Present. You will see ten sentences in which the verbs are in the infinitive. You then give the present tense form that matches the subject of the sentence. You see, for example, *Hoy . . . (ser) martes.* In place of *ser* you write ‿‿‿.

es
24 Write the form of *recordar* that matches *ustedes.*

recuerdan
25 Write the form of *decir* that matches *tú.*

dices
26 Write the form of *servir* that matches *él.*

sirve
27 Write the form of *saber* that matches *yo.*

sé
28 Write the form of *querer* that matches *ellos.*

quieren
29 In patterned irregular verbs a stressed *e* changes to ‿‿‿.

ie
30 A stressed *o* changes to ‿‿‿.

ue
31 In verbs like *servir*, *decir*, and *seguir* the *e* of the stem changes to ‿‿‿.

i (sirvo, digo, sigo)

32 Part H of the exam will test your reading comprehension in another way. On your exam sheet you will see an incomplete sentence followed by three ways of completing the sentence. You are to pick the most logical completion and circle the letter before it. You might see, for example, *El perro de mi tía es muy amable. Nunca . . .* Which of the following is the most logical completion?

(a) come legumbres.

(b) duerme en la mesa.

(c) muerde a nadie.

muerde a nadie
33 You see *Después de comprar la fruta, la carne, y las legumbres para la comida, mi mamá . . .* Which is the most logical completion?

(a) cuenta los dedos.

(b) se duerme en la tienda.

(c) vuelve a casa.

vuelve a casa.
34 You see *Antes de ponerse los zapatos mi abuelo siempre . . .* Which is the most logical completion?

(a) plancha sus pantalones.

(b) va a la tienda a comprar pan.

(c) se pone los calcetines.

se pone los calcetines.
35 Part I of the test deals with reading comprehension. You will see a question or a statement and three possible answers or reactions. You are to pick out the best answer from the three and circle the letter before it. For example, you may see a question like this. *¿Qué quiere un hombre que tiene sed?* Which is the most logical answer?

(a) Quiere comer sal y pimienta.

(b) Quiere hablar con el presidente.

(c) Quiere beber agua.

Quiere beber agua.
36 You may see *¿Cuándo usamos un impermeable?* Which is the most logical answer?

(a) Cuando estamos enfermos.

(b) Cuando hace mucho frío.

(c) Cuando hay una tormenta.

Cuando hay una tormenta.

37 You may see a question like this. *¿Qué ponemos en el café?* Which is the most likely answer?

    (a) Sal y pimienta.
    (b) Jugo de tomate.
    (c) Leche y azúcar.

Leche y azúcar.

New Vocabulary

comida	meal, food	**carne (la)**	meat
ensalada	salad	**camino**	road
fruta	fruit	**este**	this
bebida	drink, beverage	**ese**	that
legumbre (la)	vegetable	**aquel**	that
postre (el)	dessert	**juntos**	together

Ejercicios

Ejercicio 85 | Silent Reading

After reading this selection silently, and trying not to stop to translate into English, do the first comprehension exercise in writing.

Las cartas de Colón

Además de sus interesantes diarios de viaje,° sabemos que Colón escribió varias cartas a los reyes de España, a su hermano Bartolomé, a su hijo Diego y a otras personas importantes. Estos documentos históricos están escritos° en español antiguo° y son difíciles de comprender para los alumnos que empiezan a estudiar el idioma. Los párrafos° que siguen son un resumen° en español
    trip diaries

    written
    old
    paragraphs/ summary

moderno de las primeras impresiones que recibió Colón de la gente y la naturaleza° del Nuevo Mundo.
    nature

    "Me parece° que esta gente es muy pobre. Hombres y mujeres andan desnudos.° Tienen cuerpos° hermosos° y muy buenas caras.° Sus ojos son grandes
    It seems to me
    naked/bodies/ beautiful/faces

y muy hermosos. Son muy tímidos y creen que venimos del cielo.° Cuando nos ven, tienen miedo° y corren para la selva, porque creen que los vamos a comer. Poco a poco° pierden° el miedo y nos hacemos amigos. Son muy inocentes y
    heaven
    fear
    Little by little/ they lose

muy buenos y amables con nosotros. Vienen a nuestros barcos nadando° o en sus canoas. Nos traen agua, pescado,° papagayos,° algodón° y muchas cosas
    swimming
    fish/parrots/ cotton

de comer y de beber. No tienen muchos animales domésticos, solamente una clase de perros que no ladran.° Hablan una lengua muy dulce° y tienen costumbres° muy buenas. Creo que en el mundo no hay mejor gente. No hallamos monstruos en estas islas, pero nos dicen por señas° que cerca de aquí viven
    bark/sweet
    customs
    sign language

hombres feroces con un solo ojo y cara de perro. Dicen que esos hombres terribles comen a la gente y beben su sangre,° pero yo no lo creo. Los llaman caníbales.

    "La tierra de todas estas islas es muy fértil. En las costas hay puertos de mar que no tienen comparación con otros que yo conozco. Hay ríos muy bonitos y grandes que son una maravilla.°·Hay también sierras y montañas muy altas que parecen° llegar al cielo. Los árboles° son verdes° como los de España en primavera y no pierden las hojas° en noviembre. Hay varias clases de palmas y también pinos. Por el cielo° vuelan bandadas° de pájaros de colores brillantes que oscurecen el sol y cantan dulcemente. También hay miel° muy dulce, muchas flores lindas y frutas deliciosas. Dicen que hay minas de oro y plata° cerca de aquí . . . ¡Es la tierra más hermosa que ojos humanos han visto!"°

blood

marvel
seem/trees/
green/leaves
sky/flocks
honey
silver
have seen

First Comprehension Exercise: Select the item that best completes each statement. Indicate your choice by letter.

1 Bartolomé Colón era . . . del descubridor de América.
  a hijo
  b hermano
  c abuelo

2 Cristóbal Colón escribió su diario y sus cartas . . .
  a en español moderno.
  b en español antiguo.
  c en italiano.

3 Colón dice en sus cartas que los indios . . .
  a tenían el cuerpo desnudo.
  b usaban sombrero y suéter.
  c tenían el cuerpo torcido.

4 Los indios creían que los españoles . . .
  a venían de España.
  b venían de otro planeta.
  c venían del cielo.

5 Colón dice que los indios de las Antillas tenían . . .
  a barcos de motor.
  b canoas.
  c automóviles convertibles.

6 Los indios le traían a Colón . . .
  a toros y elefantes.
  b muchos perros y gatos.
  c papagayos, algodón y otras cosas.

7 Los perros que tenían los indios . . .
  a no ladraban.
  b no comían nada.
  c no bebían agua.

8 Llamamos "caníbales" a los hombres que comen . . .
- **a** pescado.
- **b** perros.
- **c** hombres.

9 Colón dice que la tierra de las islas que descubrió era . . .
- **a** muy mala.
- **b** un desierto.
- **c** muy fértil.

10 Colón dice que los árboles . . .
- **a** eran muy feos.
- **b** no perdían las hojas en noviembre.
- **c** eran de muchos colores.

Second Comprehension Exercise: Indicate by letter the correct answer to each question.

1 ¿A quién escribió sus cartas Cristóbal Colón?
- **a** A los indios de México.
- **b** A miembros de su familia y a los reyes de España.
- **c** A los habitantes de la luna y del sol.

2 ¿Cómo se llamaba el hijo de Colón?
- **a** Se llamaba Rodrigo.
- **b** Se llamaba Pancho.
- **c** Se llamaba Diego.

3 ¿Cómo describe Colón los cuerpos de los indios?
- **a** Dice que eran feos.
- **b** Dice que eran hermosos.
- **c** Dice que eran torcidos.

4 ¿Que dice Colón sobre (*about*) los ojos de los indios?
- **a** Dice que eran grandes y feos.
- **b** Dice que eran pequeños y feos.
- **c** Dice que eran grandes y bonitos.

5 ¿Qué creían los indios?
- **a** Creían que los españoles tenían cinco ojos.
- **b** Creían que los españoles venían del cielo.
- **c** Creían que los españoles eran monstruos con cara de perro.

6 ¿Cómo se dice en español "to be afraid?"
- **a** Se dice *tener hambre*.
- **b** Se dice *tener sed*.
- **c** Se dice *tener miedo*.

8 ¿Tenían muchos animales domésticos los indios?

   a Sí, tenían muchos.

   b Sí, tenían gatos y moscas.

   c No, tenían solamente perros que no ladraban y pájaros.

9 ¿Halló monstruos Colón en el Nuevo Mundo?

   a Sí, halló mujeres con cara de tigre.

   b No, no los halló.

   c Sí, halló caníbales con un solo ojo.

10 ¿Cómo dice Colón que cantaban los pájaros?

   a Dice que cantaban horriblemente.

   b Dice que cantaban ferozmente.

   c Dice que cantaban dulcemente.

Ejercicio 86 | Reading Aloud

Grandes noticias del siglo XVI

(Usted debe imaginar que usted es un anunciador de radio leyendo ante un micrófono las noticias del día.)

1 Valladolid, España. En este día 20 de mayo de 1506, murió en esta ciudad el gran almirante don Cristóbal Colón. Entre los años de 1492 y 1504 este gran navegante italiano hizo° cuatro viajes al Nuevo Mundo. La lista de sus descubrimientos es larga. Entre° los más importantes podemos mencionar las islas de Cuba, Santo Domingo, Jamaica, Puerto Rico, Trinidad y las Islas Vírgenes. En 1498 fue el primer europeo que vio la costa norte de América del Sur y también exploró parte de la costa de Centro América. Después del funeral su hijo Diego piensa llevar el cadáver de su famoso padre al monasterio de Santa María de las Cuevas en Sevilla.
    made
    among

2 Darién, Panamá. En el día de hoy, 29 de septiembre de 1513, el valiente explorador español Vasco Núñez de Balboa tomó° posesión de un nuevo océano en nombre de Su Majestad, el rey de España. Cuatro días antes, desde una altura del Istmo de Panamá, el joven Balboa fue el primer hombre blanco que vio esta gran masa de agua. La llamó Mar del Sur.
    took

3 Santiago, Cuba. Don Diego Velázquez, gobernador de esta isla, anunció hoy que la expedición de Hernán Cortés llegó a las costas de Nueva España. El día de Viernes Santo, 27 de abril de 1519, el joven capitán y sus setecientos hombres bajaron a tierra y fundaron la ciudad de Veracruz. Cuando los indios vieron a los soldados° en sus caballos,° se horrorizaron. Creen que es el ejército° invencible de Quetzalcóatl, el dios-rey de sus leyendas. Cortés destruyó sus barcos y ya se prepara para ir a ver a Moctezuma, el gran jefe° de los aztecas. La capital del imperio azteca está en el centro de un lago en el interior del país. Cortés piensa conquistar este gran imperio de los aztecas.
    soldiers/horses/
    army
    chief

4 La Habana, Cuba. Interrumpimos este programa de música para comunicarle al público una triste noticia. El gran capitán español don Juan Ponce de León acaba de morir en esta ciudad a los 71 años de edad. La causa de su muerte fue una flecha venenosa° de un indio seminola de la Florida. Después
    poisonous arrow

de conquistar a Puerto Rico, Ponce de León descubrió la Florida en 1513. En su segundo viaje de exploración por las Bahamas y la costa oeste de la península, el viejo capitán buscaba la legendaria fuente de la juventud.° El ataque de los indios fue tan feroz que la expedición volvió a la Habana en junio de 1521.

youth

5 Sevilla, España. Y ahora tenemos una noticia sensacional para todos ustedes. Después de un difícil viaje de tres años, la expedición de Fernando de Magallanes acaba de completar el primer viaje alrededor° del mundo. Estos valientes marineros cruzaron° un estrecho muy tempestuoso en la Patagonia y navegaron por todo el Mar del Sur. Magallanes lo llamó Océano Pacífico. Desgraciadamente,° el gran jefe portugués de la expedición murió en las Islas Filipinas antes de completar el viaje. Juan Sebastián de Elcano, uno de los oficiales que iban con él, dirigió la última parte de esta histórica jornada.° Salieron en total 239 hombres y volvieron solamente 15. Hoy, 9 de septiembre de 1522, llegaron a Sevilla los 15 supervivientes° del primer viaje alrededor del mundo.

around
crossed

Unfortunately

journey

survivors

6 Cajamarca, Perú. Después de una larga y penosa° campaña por mar, selvas, desiertos y montañas, acaba de llegar con sus valientes hombres a esta región, el explorador español don Francisco Pizarro. Atahualpa, el gran jefe de los incas, le esperaba, pero indicó que no deseaba hablar con los visitantes hasta el día de mañana, 16 de noviembre de 1532. Pizarro tiene informes fantásticos acerca de las ciudades que hay en este nuevo imperio de los incas. Los indios cuentan que los templos están adornados con cantidades° enormes de oro, plata y piedras° preciosas. Pizarro se prepara para la conquista de un imperio que es más rico que el de los aztecas.

painful

quantities
stones

7 México, Nueva España. Pasado mañana, 25 de julio, de este año de 1536, se van a celebrar en esta capital grandes fiestas en honor de Alvar Núñez Cabeza de Vaca, Andrés Dorantes, Alonso del Castillo y Estebanico. Estos cuatro supervivientes° de la expedición de Pánfilo de Narváez a la Florida en 1527, acaban de completar un increíble viaje a pie° desde la Florida hasta la costa del Pacífico. Los cuentos que hacen de sus experiencias entre los indios de la parte sur de Norte América son interesantísimos. A veces° es difícil creerlos. El gran conquistador Hernán Cortés y el virrey° Antonio de Mendoza piensan asistir° a la corrida de toros que vamos a tener en honor de estos grandes caminantes.°

survivors
on foot

At times
viceroy
attend
walkers

8 Río Misisipí, Norte América. Otra noticia triste. Nos comunican desde un lugar cerca del río Misisipí que en mayo de este año de 1542, murió el gran explorador español Hernando de Soto. El Capitán de Soto ayudó° mucho a Pizarro en la conquista de Perú y descubrió el Misisipí en la primavera del año pasado. Para no llamar la atención de los indios, un grupo de sus soldados escondieron° el cuerpo de su jefe en el tronco° de un árbol y lo depositaron en el río protegidos° por la oscuridad de la noche.

helped

hid/trunk
protected

9 Pueblo de Zuñi, Norte América. Nos comunican del territorio de los indios zuñis al norte de México que el explorador español Francisco Vázquez de Coronado llegó a las famosas "Siete Ciudades de Cíbola" el pasado mes de junio de 1540. Coronado está muy disgustado porque no halló oro. Los indios del lugar le informan que en una región más al norte está la famosa Quivira, una ciudad de oro puro. Coronado y sus hombres se preparan para continuar su viaje en dirección al noreste.

10 Río Colorado, Norte América. El capitán español García López de Cárdenas, miembro de la expedición de Coronado, acaba de descubrir una de las grandes maravillas naturales del mundo. Es un enorme cañón formado por el río Colorado que está al noroeste de la tierra de los zuñis. Podemos afirmar en este año de 1546 que este gran cañón va a ser una gran atracción turística en el futuro. El Capitán López Cárdenas tiene el honor de ser el primer hombre blanco que vio tan impresionante espectáculo de la naturaleza.°   nature

11 San Agustín, Florida. Del territorio español de la Florida nos llegó hoy una gran noticia. Don Pedro Menéndez de Avilés fundó la primera ciudad en tierra norteamericana el pasado 28 de agosto de 1565. Escogió° el nombre en   chose
honor del famoso obispo y filósofo del siglo cinco. En el calendario de la iglesia el 28 de agosto es la fiesta de San Agustín.

12 México, Nueva España. Y ahora una noticia sensacional de la ciudad de México. En este año de 1539 podemos leer con orgullo° el primer libro publicado   pride
en el Nuevo Mundo. El arzobispo Zumárraga introdujo la imprenta° en   printing press
América en 1536. Van a aparecer muy pronto libros en varias lenguas indias para las escuelas. Los españoles descubren, exploran, colonizan y conquistan los pueblos y territorios del Nuevo Mundo, pero también los civilizan.

Ejercicio 87 | Silent Reading

Read the following selection without stopping to translate into English. See if you can figure out what proverb Alfredo is going to say at the end.

Hay un refrán español que dice . . .

(primera parte)

(Lee la siguiente conversación entre Alfredo y su padre. Al fin° de la selección   end
tienen que decidir cuál es el refrán más apropiado para esta situación.)

Alfredo: Hola, papá, ¿qué tal?
Padre: Bastante cansado, hijo. ¿Ya llegó el periódico?
Alfredo: Sí, acaba de llegar. Aquí está. ¿Cómo andan las cosas por la oficina?
Padre: Bastante bien, hijo, pero en esta época° del año siempre tenemos   time
         muchísimo trabajo. Estoy muy cansado y con dolor° de cabeza.   ache
Alfredo: Si quieres, te traigo una aspirina.
Padre: No, gracias, hijo. Eres muy amable, pero no voy a necesitar ninguna
         medicina. Voy a sentarme en mi silla favorita a leer el periódico con
         calma y pronto me voy a sentir mejor.
Alfredo: Oye, papá. No quiero molestarte, pero quería pedirte un favor.
Padre: ¡Cómo no, hijo! ¿Qué deseas?
Alfredo: ¿Puedes prestarme° cincuenta dólares?   lend
Padre: ¿Cómo? Hazme el favor de repetir la pregunta. Creo que no te oí
         bien. ¿Cinco dólares, dices?

Alfredo: Cinco no, papá, cincuenta. Necesito cincuenta dólares para el baile°   dance
formal que vamos a tener en la escuela el próximo° mes. Pienso invitar   next
a mi amiga Nancy.

Padre: ¿Dónde están las aspirinas? ¡Qué barbaridad, muchacho! ¿Estás
loco? ¿Desde° cuándo cuestan° tanto dinero los bailes del colegio?   Since/cost
Cuando tu madre y yo éramos jóvenes . . .

Alfredo: Sí, sí. Ya sé qué vas a decirme. La misma° historia de siempre.   same
Cuando ustedes eran jóvenes, iban a los bailes y no les costaba ni la
tercera parte de esa cantidad.° Te olvidas que hoy día, las cosas son   amount
muy diferentes. Solamente° las flores° van a costar diez dólares.   Just/flowers

Padre: Eso es imposible. ¿Qué flores pueden costarte tanto?

Alfredo: La orquídea blanca que pienso comprarle a Nancy.

Padre: ¡Orquídeas, nada menos! Y por qué no unas rosas o claveles° ba-   carnations
ratos° . . . Tu madre tiene flores muy bonitas en su jardín y ella puede   cheap
prepararte un . . .

Alfredo: Pero, hombre, papá. ¡Cómo puedes ser tan ridículo! Todos mis
amigos van a comprar orquídeas para sus compañeras. Va a ser la
gran función social del año en un club privado° cerca del mar. Las   private
entradas° solamente cuestan quince dólares por pareja.°   tickets/couple

Padre: ¡Quince, nada más! ¡Caramba! ¡Ay, mi cabeza . . . las aspirinas,
pronto! ¿Pero tú crees que tienes un padre millonario? En mis
tiempos . . .

Alfredo: Sí, sí. Ya sé, papá. En tus tiempos los bailes eran gratis° en el gimnasio del colegio. Los tiempos cambian, pero tú no cambias. Además,° después del baile pensamos ir a comer en un restaurante de lujo.°

free
Furthermore
luxury

Padre: Y si no es indiscreción, hijo, ¿puedes decirme cuánto va a costar eso? ¿Treinta dólares para dos personas?

Alfredo: ¡Cómo exageras, papá! No va a pasar de diez dólares en total.

Padre: ¡Caramba, qué económico! No quiero saber más. Si el baile va a ser tan caro,° vas a tener que pagarlo° con tu dinero, el sueldo° que ganas° trabajando los sábados.

expensive/pay/ salary
earn

Alfredo: Es que olvidé decirte, papá, que ya no trabajo los sábados.

Padre: ¿Comó? ¿Ya no trabajas los fines de semana? ¿Cómo es eso?

Alfredo: Es que me pagaban muy poco. No vale la pena° trabajar por uno setenta y cinco la hora. Voy a buscar un trabajo mejor para ganar por lo menos° dos dólares la hora.

trouble

at least

Padre: ¿Y tú crees que un trabajo así es fácil de obtener? ¡Qué equivocado° estás, hijo! Vas a necesitar mucha suerte. Mira, Alfredo, en español hay un refrán que dice . . .

mistaken

Alfredo: Sí, sí. Ya lo sé, papá. El refrán español dice . . .

Ejercicio 88 | Silent Reading

Read silently without stopping to translate into English. Can you figure out the proverb at the end?

Hay un refrán español que dice . . .

(segunda parte)

(Después de leer esta conversación entre Alfredo y su mamá, decide cuál es el refrán más apropiado para esta situación.)

Alfredo: Hola, mamá. ¿Ya está la comida?°

supper

Madre: Todavía no, hijo. Unos minutos más. ¿Tienes hambre?

Alfredo: ¡Me muero de hambre! A mediodía° solamente comí un sandwich porque la comida de la cafetería estaba muy mala.

noon

Madre: Lo siento mucho, hijo. Pronto va a estar lista° la comida. Mira a ver si ya llegó tu padre.

ready

Alfredo: Sí, está en la sala° leyendo° el periódico. Dice que tiene dolor° de cabeza.

living room/ reading/ache

Madre: Tu pobre padre tiene un trabajo tremendo en estos días. No debemos molestarle.

Alfredo: Oye, mamá. Hablé con papá, y ¿sabes que no quiere prestarme° los cincuenta dólares que voy a necesitar para el baile? Es un tacaño.

to lend

Madre: No digas eso de tu padre, Alfredo. Es que tenemos muchos gastos° de familia—el dentista, medicinas, los pagos° del carro, la universidad de tu hermano . . . Además,° cincuenta dólares es mucho para gastar° en una noche en un baile. Tú debes comprender eso. No permito que llames tacaño a tu padre.

expenses
payments
Furthermore/ spend

Alfredo: Está bien, mamá. Perdóname. Ustedes tienen razón. Pero no voy a perderme° ese baile. Voy a empezar a buscar otro trabajo para los fines de semana.

miss

Madre:	Muy buena idea. Oye, Alfredo, ¿por qué cuestan tanto esos bailes de la escuela? Cuando tu padre y yo íbamos a bailar . . .	
Alfredo:	Sí, sí, ya sé. Papá me explicó. No costaba casi nada. Te traía° flores del jardín de su casa y los bailes eran en el gimnasio y no tenían gastos de orquesta. Un grupo de estudiantes aficionados° a la música tocaba° y . . .	brought

fans/played |
| Madre: | Exactamente. ¡Y qué bailes tan buenos teníamos! Después del baile veníamos a la casa y . . . | |
| Alfredo: | Mira, mamá. La orquesta que va a tocar° para nosotros es una de las más famosas de todo el país. Va a costar cerca de diez mil dólares. | play |
| Madre: | ¿Por tocar una noche nada más? ¡Dios mío! ¡Cómo cambian los tiempos! A propósito,° hijo, hablando de miles de dólares, ¿tienes alguna oferta° de trabajo para los fines de semana? | By the way
offer |
| Alfredo: | Mañana tengo una entrevista° con el señor de la estación donde compramos la gasolina. Dicen que necesita un muchacho trabajador,° como yo, para los sábados y los domingos. El único problema es que sólo° paga uno veinticinco la hora. | interview
hardworking

only |
Madre:	Recuerda, hijo, que más vale pájaro en mano que cien volando. ¿Te refieres al señor Fuentes?	
Alfredo:	Sí, el amigo de papá.	
Madre:	Pues, siento decirte que ya no necesita a nadie. Acabo de venir de ese garaje y vi a tu amigo Alberto trabajando allí.	
Alfredo:	¡Qué mala suerte! Bueno, no importa. Vas a ver que más tarde o más temprano consigo° algo. Si no es en un garaje, voy a ir a las tiendas, los restaurantes, las oficinas . . . Y si no es hoy, será° mañana o pasado mañana o la semana que viene, pero voy a conseguir° trabajo y voy a llevar a Nancy al baile más importante del año.	get
will be
get
Madre:	Muy bien, hijo. Con esa actitud, no dudo° que vas a tener éxito.° Tú sabes que los españoles tienen un refrán que dice . . .	doubt/success
Alfredo:	Sí, sí. No tienes que recordarme. Hay un refrán español que dice . . .	

Ejercicio 89 | Silent Reading

The following selection contains some new words, but you should be able to understand the selection without knowing the precise meaning of every word. Read it through silently and do the comprehension exercise.

El idioma español: preguntas y respuestas

(primera parte)

1 ¿De dónde viene el español?
Viene del latín, la lengua que hablaban en la antigua Roma.

2 ¿Es esta la misma° Roma que vemos frecuentemente en las películas,° y en programas de televisión?
Sí, más o menos. Hay películas que presentan la vida° de la antigua Roma con bastante exactitud; por ejemplo, *Cleopatra, Ben Hur* y *Los diez mandamientos.*°

same/movies, films

life
commandments

3 Roma tenía una civilización muy avanzada, ¿verdad?
Así es. Era la civilización más avanzada del mundo en ese tiempo. Los romanos llevaron su lengua y su cultura a muchas partes de Europa, Asia y África.

4 ¿Cuándo llegaron los romanos al territorio que hoy ocupan España y Portugal?
Las legiones de Roma invadieron la Península Hispánica en el año 218 antes de Jesucristo.

5 ¿Quién vivía en la Península antes de la invasión romana?
Vivían allí varias tribus primitivas, por ejemplo, los iberos, los celtas y los vascos. Todos hablaban lenguas diferentes.

6 ¿Estuvieron mucho tiempo los romanos en la Península Hispánica?
Sí. La dominación romana duró° varios siglos. En el año 409 grupos de bárbaros germánicos entraron en la Península por el norte.   lasted

7 ¿Quién invadió el territorio hispánico por el sur?
Los árabes o moros° cruzaron el estrecho de Gibraltar en el año 711. Hablaban la lengua árabe.   Moors

8 Entonces podemos decir que el idioma español y la cultura española son el resultado de una gran mezcla,° ¿no es cierto?   mixture
Así es. Numerosas mezclas de lenguas y culturas en diferentes momentos de la historia.

¿Sí o no?

If the statement is true, write *sí;* if it is false, write *no.*

1 El idioma español viene principalmente del ruso.

2 La antigua Roma tenía una civilización muy primitiva.

3 El cine y la televisión de nuestro tiempo nos dan (*give*) una idea aproximada de la vida en la antigua Roma.

4 Las legiones de Roma llevaron su lengua y su gran sistema de administración a la Península.

5 Las legiones de Roma entraron en la Península Hispánica en 1492.

6 Nadie vivía en la Península Hispánica cuando la invadieron las legiones de Roma.

7 Las tribus primitivas de la Península Hispánica hablaban lenguas diferentes.

8 Las tribus germánicas entraron en la Península por el sur.

9 Los bárbaros germánicos llegaron a Hispania antes que los árabes.

10 El idioma español es el resultado de la mezcla del latín que hablaban en España con las lenguas nativas y las lenguas de los diferentes grupos que vinieron (*came*) a la Península en diferentes momentos de la historia.

Ejercicio 90 | Silent Reading

After reading the following questions and answers about the Spanish language, do the comprehension exercise.

El idioma español: preguntas y respuestas

(segunda parte)

1 ¿Por qué dicen que el español es una lengua romance?
Simplemente porque tiene su origen en la lengua de Roma, de los romanos. No quiere decir que el español es una lengua "romántica".

2 ¿Es el inglés una lengua romance?
No. El inglés es una lengua germánica. El portugués, el francés y el italiano son lenguas romances.

3 ¿Qué quiere decir la palabra *España*?
Hay varias interpretaciones. Algunos creen que significa "tierra de conejos"°.   rabbits
Otros dicen que viene de la palabra *span* que quiere decir "llanura".

4 Otro nombre del idioma que estudiamos es *castellano*, ¿verdad?
Exactamente. El castellano era un dialecto romance que se hablaba solamente en la región de Castilla. En el siglo quince pasó a ser el idioma oficial de todas las provincias.

5 ¿Qué significa la palabra *Castilla*?
Castilla, el nombre de una de las regiones más importantes en la historia de la Península, quiere decir "tierra de castillos."°   castles

6 ¿Podemos usar los dos nombres, *castellano* y *español*, para hablar del idioma que estudiamos?
Sí, cómo no. Hoy día, sin embargo,° el nombre más apropiado es *español*.   nevertheless
En muchos países de América prefieren *castellano*.

7 ¿Qué lugar ocupa el español entre los idiomas del mundo?
Ocupa uno de los primeros lugares. Aproximadamente 500 millones de personas hablan chino; 300 millones hablan inglés y 180 millones hablan ruso. El español lo hablan más de 170 millones de personas.

¿Sí o no?

Write *sí*, if the statement is true; and *no*, if it is false.

1 El español es una lengua muy "bonita" y "musical" y por eso decimos que es una lengua "romance."

2 El inglés es una lengua germánica.

3 El francés y el italiano son lenguas germánicas.

4 Cuando hablamos de lenguas "romances," la palabra *romance* se refiere a Roma.

5 Algunos investigadores asocian el origen de las palabras *español* y *España* con los elefantes.

6 El idioma que estudiamos tiene dos nombres principales.
7 El idioma que hablaban en Castilla se llamaba *castellano*.
8 La palabra *Castilla* significa "tierra de conejos."
9 Entre los idiomas del mundo el español ocupa el último lugar.
10 El número de personas que hablan chino hoy día es insignificante.

Ejercicio 91 | Pre-Quiz Practice: Intonation

Your teacher will ask you to read the following sentences with the proper Spanish intonation. The next time you are asked to do this, you will be graded on it.

1 ¿ Fue una ceremonia muy bonita ?
2 ¿ Perdió la posición por su incapacidad ?
3 ¿ Crees que es desagradable la música ?
4 ¿ Por qué hablas de esa imposibilidad ?
5 ¿ Es difícil esta pronunciación ?
6 ¿ Comprendes la terminación de esta frase ?

Ejercicio 92 | Listening and Silent Reading

From the three responses given below choose the one that best corresponds to the question or statement which you will hear once. Indicate your answer by letter.

1 a Siempre me levanto muy cansado.
   b Me levanto casi siempre a las seis.
   c Me levanto siempre de mal humor.
2 a Pues, vas a tener una cara muy sucia.
   b Ella se lava los dientes cada mañana.
   c Mamá me lava la ropa los lunes.
3 a Sigue el número doscientos setenta.
   b Sigue el número trescientos sesenta y nueve.
   c Sigue el número doscientos ochenta.
4 a Pasa el Río Grande.
   b Pasa el Magdalena.
   c Pasa el Amazonas.
5 a Tenemos que masticarlo mejor.
   b Entonces ustedes están bastante lejos del parque.
   c Creo que ustedes deben ponerse los sombreros nuevos.
6 a La pobre tiene una cara muy fea.
   b Tiene unas piernas gigantescas.
   c Tiene los brazos largos como las monas.

Ejercicio 93 | Silent Reading

Select the appropriate answer or rejoinder for the following. Indicate your choice by letter.

1 ¿De qué color es la bandera de los Estados Unidos?

    a Es morada, blanca y verde.

    b Es azul, roja y amarilla.

    c Es azul, roja y blanca.

2 Generalmente, ¿cuándo nos ponemos un abrigo?

    a Nos lo ponemos cuando llueve mucho.

    b Nos lo ponemos durante el tiempo más frío.

    c Nos lo ponemos durante las últimas horas de la mañana.

3 ¿Qué significa *El niño se desayunó?*

    a Significa que el niño comió después de levantarse.

    b Significa que el niño se vistió después de levantarse.

    c Significa que el niño se lavó todo el cuerpo después de levantarse.

4 ¿Cuántas estrellas hay en el cielo esta noche?

    a La palabra *cielo* significa "back yard".

    b La palabra *cielo* significa "living room".

    c La palabra *cielo* significa "sky".

5 ¿Qué tiempo hace afuera en este momento?

    a Creo que viene una tormenta porque está lloviendo mucho.

    b Si tengo razón, son exactamente las cinco menos cuarto.

    c Pues, mire usted el reloj. Yo no sé.

6 ¿Cuántos habitantes tiene la ciudad de Pamplona?

    a Tiene treinta y nueve edificios muy grandes.

    b Yo no sé nada de la población de lugares geográficos.

    c La ciudad de Pamplona está en España y es muy linda.

7 Si salimos a ver los lugares interesantes de la ciudad esta mañana, no vamos a poder verlos bien.

    a Sí, tengo ojos azules y veo muchos programas de televisión.

    b Es verdad. El tiempo afuera es terrible; hay muchísima niebla.

    c Tienes razón. No es necesario ponerse suéter hoy.

Ejercicio 94 | Silent Reading

Read the following selections and do the multiple-choice problems that follow.

¿Sabía usted que . . .

1

. . . en la mayor parte de las escuelas privadas y públicas del mundo de habla española los estudiantes tienen que vestirse de uniforme? Las muchachas usan blusas, faldas, medias y zapatos idénticos. Los muchachos generalmente van a clase en pantalones de color oscuro, camisa blanca y corbata. Para los desfiles°   parades y otras ocasiones especiales tienen uniformes de gala que son muy vistosos° y elegantes. En los dos tipos de uniforme llevan generalmente la insignia oficial del colegio.

showy

2

... el "Cristo de los Andes" es un símbolo de paz eterna entre Argentina y Chile? Este colosal monumento está en un lugar muy elevado de la cordillera° andina que se llama Paso de Uspallata y marca la frontera° entre los dos países. En los primeros años de nuestro siglo, argentinos y chilenos se prepararon para la guerra° a causa° de las diferencias que existían entre ellos con respecto a los límites° entre las dos naciones. En 1904 resolvieron el problema pacíficamente y decidieron usar el bronce de los cañones para hacer una enorme estatua de Cristo y ponerla en la línea divisoria entre los dos países. Al pie de esta famosa estatua aparece la siguiente inscripción: "Estas montañas se convertirán° en polvo° antes que los pueblos de Argentina y Chile rompan° la paz que a los pies de este Cristo Redentor han jurado° mantener."

mountain range
border

war/because
boundaries

will turn
dust/break
have sworn

3

... en la ciudad brasileña de Rio de Janeiro también hay una estatua gigantesca del Cristo Redentor? Está en la cumbre° del monte Corcovado y desde allí podemos ver un panorama fantástico de toda la ciudad y de la bahía.

summit

1

1 ¿Comó se visten los alumnos en las escuelas del mundo de habla española?
  a Se visten de negro.
  b Se visten de uniforme.
  c Se visten de seda.

2 ¿Cuándo usan uniforme de gala?
  a Cuando hay desfiles.
  b Lo usan todos los días.
  c Lo usan solamente los domingos.

3 ¿Qué diferencia fundamental hay entre el vestido escolar de los Estados Unidos y el de los países de habla española?
  a No hay absolutamente ninguna diferencia.
  b Los colores de los uniformes son más bonitos allí.
  c En la mayoría de las escuelas públicas norteamericanas los estudiantes no usan uniformes.

4 ¿Usan uniforme los estudiantes de las universidades de América del Sur y de España?
  a Sí, todos lo usan.
  b No, lo usan solamente los alumnos de primaria.
  c El párrafo que leímos no nos dice nada sobre la ropa que usan los estudiantes universitarios.

2

5 ¿Qué hay entre Argentina y Chile?
   a Un mar y dos océanos.
   b Una alta cordillera.
   c Muchos monumentos simbólicos.

6 ¿Por qué iban a declararse en guerra los argentinos y los chilenos?
   a Porque en aquel tiempo Argentina no tenía puertos de mar.
   b Porque Chile necesitaba bronce para hacer cañones.
   c Porque existía entre ellos una gran disputa de límites.

7 ¿Está en Argentina la estatua del "Cristo de los Andes"?
   a Sí, está en territorio argentino.
   b No, está en territorio chileno.
   c Está en territorio de los dos países, en la línea que los divide.

8 ¿Qué simboliza la estatua del Paso de Uspallata?
   a El deseo (*desire*) de ir a la guerra.
   b El deseo de vivir en paz con nuestros vecinos.
   c La abundancia de cañones en dos países del sur.

3

9 ¿Hay otra estatua gigantesca de Cristo situada entre Brasil y Bolivia?
   a Sí, hay otra entre Brasil y Argentina.
   b El párrafo que leímos dice que hay dos.
   c Hay otra, pero está en Rio de Janeiro.

10 Si subimos al monte Corcovado, ¿podemos ver desde allí la ciudad de Buenos Aires?
   a Sí, cómo no, en los días en que no hay niebla.
   b No, desde Corcovado podemos ver solamente la capital de Chile.
   c Eso es absurdo. Buenos Aires está demasiado lejos de allí.

Ejercicio 95 | Silent Reading

Read the following selections and do the multiple-choice problems that follow.

¿ Sabía usted que . . .

1

. . . el lago Titicaca en la frontera entre Bolivia y Perú es el lago navegable más alto del mundo? Ocupa un área de 3.200 millas cuadradas y mide 120 millas de largo° por 40 de ancho.° Su altitud es de 12.508 pies sobre el nivel del mar° y su nombre indio significa "peña de plomo".° Toda la región del lago que incluye 25 islas es de una importancia extraordinaria para el antropólogo por sus notables tesoros arqueológicos. Alrededor° de este gran "mar" indio se formó el imperio de los incas. Según° sus mitos° y leyendas,° los fundadores de la civilización inca (Manco Cápac y Mama Ocllo) salieron de las islas del Sol y de la Luna a buscar el lugar donde debían establecer el centro de su imperio.

long/wide/
   sea level
boulder of lead

Around
According to/
   myths/legends

Por las aguas azules del Titicaca van y vienen barcos modernos y las pintorescas balsas° de los indios. Entre el puerto peruano de Puno y el boliviano de Guaqui hay servicio regular de comercio y pasajeros. Además,° la región es también un importante centro turístico. Miles de peregrinos° de los países vecinos° vienen todos los años a la iglesia de Copacabana a celebrar fiestas religiosas en honor de la Virgen del Lago.

rafts
Besides
pilgrims
neighboring

2

. . . los colores de la bandera boliviana tienen un significado° especial? El rojo representa el reino° animal, el amarillo simboliza el reino mineral y el verde es el símbolo del reino vegetal.

meaning
kingdom

1

1 ¿Cuál es el área del lago Titicaca?
  a Aproximadamente tres mil millas cuadradas.
  b Trescientas mil millas cuadradas.
  c Treinta mil millas cuadradas.
2 ¿Cuáles son las dimensiones del lago Titicaca?
  a Ciento veinte pies de largo por cuarenta de ancho.
  b Ciento veinte millas de alto por cuarenta de ancho.
  c Ciento veinte millas de largo por cuarenta de ancho.

3 ¿Cómo se llamaban los fundadores del imperio inca?

   a No tenían nombres.

   b Se llamaban Puno y Guaqui.

   c Se llamaban Manco Cápac y Mama Ocllo.

4 ¿Es posible ir de Bolivia a Perú por el lago Titicaca?

   a Sí, hay servicio regular de pasajeros.

   b Sí, pero solamente en balsas y canoas.

   c No, es necesario nadar o ir por tierra.

5 ¿Por qué es importante para el antropólogo la región del lago Titicaca?

   a Porque allí vivieron los aztecas.

   b Porque allí hay muchas ruinas de civilizaciones antiguas.

   c Porque los indios que viven allí hoy día no tienen pelo en la cabeza.

6 ¿Hay mucho movimiento de barcos en el lago Titicaca?

   a No, el clima no lo permite.

   b No, el lago Titicaca no es navegable.

   c Sí, hay bastante movimiento de balsas y barcos.

7 ¿Por qué van miles de peregrinos de muchos países a Copacabana?

   a Porque su propósito (*purpose*) es inspeccionar las minas.

   b Porque allí hay un santuario muy famoso.

   c Porque creen que el sol y la luna son dioses.

2

8 ¿Tienen algún significado especial los colores de la bandera de Bolivia?

   a Sí, son unos colores muy bonitos.

   b Sí, representan los tres reinos naturales.

   c Sí, el azul representa el color del agua del lago Titicaca.

9 ¿Qué simboliza el color amarillo en la bandera de Bolivia?

   a La abundancia de fruta en el país, por ejemplo, bananas.

   b Los animales de ese color que viven en las selvas del país.

   c El oro, la plata y otros productos minerales semejantes (*similar*).

Ejercicio 96 | Intonation and Linkage

When you read Spanish, the spaces between words on the page do not tell you
to pause. Read the sentences below, linking words into groups the way Spanish
speakers do.

1 Voy a hacer un viaje a Argentina.

2 Una carta a Alicia llegó ayer.

3 Su elefante es grande.

4 Duda hay, si no lo cree él.

5 Ella usa una blusa azul.

6 El rey encuentra a la reina.

7 La revista está allí.

8 Regresó a ese hotel.

9 Si ese alumno va, también voy yo.

10 Yo toqué el diente inferior.

Ejercicio 97 | Intonation and Linkage

Read the following sentences, joining the words together the way Spanish speakers do.

1 Toda esta comida es buena.
2 Esta ensalada es deliciosa.
3 Regreso o vuelvo; todo es igual.
4 Sin embargo Ofelia le ayuda.
5 Esto es para ojos, no es para orejas.

6 La carne está en el plato.
7 El postre está allí.
8 Recibí y abrí esa carta ayer.
9 La nube es aquella allí.
10 Enrique está en su auto.

Ejercicio 98 | Pre-Test Practice: Reading Comprehension

Read the following sentences and select the most logical completion for each.

1 Los colores de la bandera de los Estados Unidos son . . .
   a azul, verde y blanco.
   b blanco, azul y rojo.
   c blanco, rosado y azul.
2 Después de lavar nuestra ropa, generalmente mi mamá . . .
   a la plancha.
   b la vende.
   c la compra.
3 Nos ponemos los calcetines . . .
   a en las orejas.
   b en los pies.
   c en los brazos.
4 Yo tengo la costumbre de leer las noticias del mundo . . .
   a antes de despertarme en la mañana.
   b en el periódico que viene todos los días.
   c en cartas de mi hija de siete años.
5 Cada mañana cuando la niña sale para la escuela, se despide de su mamá y . . .
   a la besa.
   b se acuesta.
   c se duerme inmediatamente.

Ejercicio 99 | Pre-Test Practice: Reading Comprehension

After reading each problem, indicate your choice by letter. The choices are responses or rejoinders (not completions) to the first sentence.

1 Pero, hombre, no te molestes con todo esto.
   a Te digo que no es ninguna molestia.
   b Hay pantalones en la mesa y calcetines en la silla.
   c Espera. Tengo que ponerme el abrigo.

2 ¿Cuándo es una buena idea planchar la ropa?

  a Después de venderla.

  b Después de lavarla y secarla.

  c Mientras uno se divierte en una fiesta.

3 ¿Quién fue el primero en despertarse?

  a Luisa no llegó anoche hasta las doce.

  b No sé, pero Miguel se desayunó antes que los otros.

  c No había luna anoche.

4 "Antes que te cases, mira lo que haces."

  a ¿Te vas a casar muy pronto?

  b Es una buena idea casarse en junio.

  c Es tarde decir eso porque el pobre muchacho se casó anteayer.

5 ¿Qué vestido vas a ponerte para ir al banco?

  a Ese que tiene un lugar especial para los pies.

  b Mi nueva camisa está muy sucia.

  c Uno que tiene los colores, verde, amarillo y negro.

6 "A quien madruga, Dios le ayuda".

  a Sí, "Quien mucho duerme, poco aprende".

  b Sí, "No es tan fiero el león como lo pintan".

  c Es verdad, "En boca cerrada no entran moscas."

7 ¿Cuál de las siguientes frases es verdad?

  a La cabeza está conectada a la mano.

  b El pie está conectado a la pierna.

  c La nariz está conectada al brazo.

Ejercicio 100 | Pre-Test Practice: Listening and Reading Comprehension

One of the three responses given below is a logical reaction to a question or statement that you will hear *once*. Indicate your choice by letter.

1 a Tiene cinco en cada mano y en cada pie, veinte en total.

  b No tiene dedos porque es un profesor de biología.

  c Tiene catorce dedos y dos pulgares.

2 a Vuela como un pájaro.

  b Tropieza y cae en la fuente.

  c Anuncia a la gente que no muerde.

3 a Muerde a la gente mala, pero no a la buena.

  b No muerde a nadie.

  c Hace un viaje por mar.

4 a La tenemos en medio de la cara.

  b No tenemos nariz; en lugar de la nariz, usamos los dientes.

  c No tenemos nariz porque hace tanto calor.

5 **a** Y los toros tenían mucha sed.

   b Y el río inundó el pueblo.

   c Y toda la tierra estaba muy seca.

6 **a** Era cierto, pero los perdimos en el cine.

   b No, no es cierto, porque no andamos mucho estos días.

   c Sí, señor, yo creo que usted tiene razón.

7 **a** Son blancas y muy secas.

   b Nunca hay nubes durante una tormenta.

   c Son negras y oscuras.

8 **a** Que una persona plancha la ropa inmediatamente después de lavarla.

   b Que alguien pasa unos momentos muy agradables.

   c Significa comer por la mañana después de despertarse.

Ejercicio 101 | Preterit versus Imperfect

Select one of the two forms in parentheses according to the meaning of the context.

El primer viaje de Colón

(tercer párrafo)

Colón y sus marineros (1 volvieron, volvían) a sus barcos y (2 navegaron, navegaban) de nuevo en dirección a la isla que llamamos hoy día Santo Domingo. Después de varias semanas de navegación (3 llegaron, llegaban) a la costa norte de la isla. El aspecto general de esta nueva tierra les (4 recordó, recordaba) inmediatamente a España. Por esta razón la (5 llamaron, llamaban) *La Española*. Era el 25 de diciembre, día de Navidad.° Colón (6 paró, paraba)° allí los barcos y (7 bajó, bajaba) a tierra. Los indios del lugar (8 parecieron, parecían) muy amables y el Almirante (9 vio, veía) que muchos de ellos (10 usaron, usaban) adornos de oro y plata en diferentes partes del cuerpo. El lugar (11 pareció, parecía) ideal para la construcción de un fuerte.

Christmas/
stopped

Ejercicio 102 | Preterit versus Imperfect

Change the indicated verbs to the past tense. Choose either the Preterit or the Imperfect according to the meaning within the paragraph and using the added information in parentheses.

El primer viaje de Colón

(cuarto párrafo)

A poca distancia de la costa dominicana el barco principal de la expedición se *encalla*° (1 C, E) una noche en un banco de arena.° Con gran disgusto Colón *abandona* (2 C, E) a la *Santa María* y *usa* (3 C, E) muchos de sus materiales en la construcción del fuerte° *La Navidad*. *Llega* (4 C, E) el mes de enero y el Almirante ya *está* (5 NC, M) muy cansado de tanto explorar. *Tiene* (6 NC, M)

goes aground/
sand

fort

grandes deseos de volver a España con la sensacional noticia de sus descubrimientos. En el fuerte *La Navidad deja°* (7 C, E) a un pequeño grupo de sus   leaves
hombres y *sale* (8 C, E) para España en la *Niña.* Después de muchos problemas
y tormentas terribles de invierno, el primer viaje a las Indias *termina* (9 C, E)
en Palos, el 15 de marzo de 1493. *Son* (10 NC, M) más o menos las doce del
día cuando Colón y sus marineros *entran* (11 C, E) en el puerto.°   port

Ejercicio 103 | Preterit versus Imperfect

Select one of the two forms in parentheses according to the meaning of the
context.

El primer viaje de Colón

(párrafo cinco)

Cuando los residentes de Palos (1 vieron, veían) que una de las tres carabelas°   ships
de Colón venía en dirección al muelle,° se (2 alegraron, alegraban) muchísimo.   dock
(3 Tocaron, Tocaban) las campanas de la iglesia y (4 corrieron, corrían) al
muelle a recibirlo. Alegres y felices, después de una larga ausencia de seis meses
y medio, los marineros (5 bajaron, bajaban) rápidamente del barco. Al pisar
tierra española, muchos de ellos (6 lloraron, lloraban) de felicidad, mientras
toda la gente del pueblo (7 miró, miraba) el impresionante espectáculo con
gran emoción y curiosidad. Mientras Colón y sus hombres (8 caminaron,
caminaban)° por la calle en dirección a la iglesia para darle gracias a Dios,   walked
todos los habitantes del pueblo (9 gritaron, gritaban),° locos de alegría, y   shouted
(10 aplaudieron, aplaudían) con entusiasmo. (11 Desearon, Deseaban) saludar°   greet
y abrazar a los primeros hombres que el 12 de octubre de 1492 (12 pisaron,
pisaban) la tierra de las Antillas.

Ejercicio 104 | Preterit versus Imperfect

Change the indicated verbs to the past tense. Choose either the Preterit or the
Imperfect according to the meaning within the paragraph and using the added
information in parentheses.

El primer viaje de Colón

(párrafo seis)

Sin perder mucho tiempo con sus amigos en Palos, el grupo de Colón *sale*
(1 C, E) por tierra para Barcelona. Allí *están* (2 NC, M) entonces los Reyes
Católicos. Miles de personas los *esperan* (3 NC, M) ansiosos° en las calles de   anxiously
la ciudad. Todos *miran* (4 NC, M) a los indios con asombro.° Por primera vez   astonishment
ven (5 NC, B) los papagayos° y otros regalos extraños° de las nuevas tierras   parrots/strange
que los indios *llevan* (6 NC, M) para los reyes. Cuando *aparece* (7 C, E) Colón en
la puerta del enorme salón real,° la reina Isabel y el rey Fernando se *emocionan°*   royal hall/
(8 NC, B). Rodeado de sus compañeros y del pequeño grupo de nativos, el   became excited

Almirante se *sienta* (9 C, E) ante los reyes y les *cuenta* (10 NC, B) las maravi-
llosas aventuras de su viaje. Nadie se *imagina* (11 NC, M) en aquel momento
que las nuevas tierras de que *habla* (12 NC, M) el descubridor no *son* (13 NC,
M) realmente parte de las Indias sino° un mundo nuevo.   but

Ejercicio 105 | Intonation

Match the items in the column on the right with the appropriate words in the
column on the left:

1 Rhythm	a going up and down in speech as in singing
2 Terminal	b only three pitch levels
3 Spanish	c the voice goes up at the end
4 Pitch	d the voice goes down at the end
5 Information questions	e the degree of loudness of a syllable in speech
6 English	
7 Stress	f four pitch levels
8 Yes-no question	g the variation in length of syllables in speech
	h the direction of the voice at the end of an utterance

Ejercicio 106 | Done-to Pronouns and Preterit Forms

Don't do the next combination on the list until after you have checked your
work against what is on the board. Remember that the verb form from the
middle column must be in the Preterit.

Ejemplo: 314 = Julia y Pilar me oyeron.

1 Rodolfo	1 oír	1 a nosotros.
2 Yo	2 ver	2 a usted (f).
3 Julia y Pilar	3 mirar	3 a ti.
4 Tú	4 tratar de olvidar	4 a mí.
5 Toña y yo		5 a ustedes (m).

Ejercicio 107 | Preterit Morphology

Write the correct preterit form of all the infinitives in parentheses.

1 Yo . . . (cerrar) la puerta y . . . (salir).
2 Los leones no me . . . (mirar), gracias a Dios.
3 Primero nosotros . . . (ver) la noticia, y entonces ellos . . . (escribir) el
párrafo.
4 Tú no me . . . (olvidar) nunca, ¿verdad?

5 El perro ... (morder) el nuevo cuaderno.

6 Sí, Jorge y yo ... (cerrar) esa ventana.

7 Tú ... (medir) todos los jarros y yo los ... (llevar) a la tienda.

8 El pobre turista no ... (llegar).

Ejercicio 108 | Done-to Pronouns

Answer each question affirmatively using a done-to pronoun.

1 ¿ Conoces a Beatriz ?

2 ¿ Conoces a Fernando ?

3 ¿ Quieres conocer a Luisa y a Manuela ?

4 ¿ Quieres conocer a estos muchachos ?

5 ¿ Quieres invitarme a la fiesta ?

6 ¿ Puedo invitarte a la fiesta ?

7 ¿ Puedo invitarlos a ustedes a la fiesta ?

Ejercicio 109 | Preterit versus Imperfect

Select one of the two forms in parentheses according to the meaning of the context.

La serpiente que quería aprender inglés

(La siguiente narración no es un cuento.° Es una historia verdadera que ocurrió en una escuela secundaria del estado de Arizona. Esta es la primera parte. En la próxima clase ustedes van a tener un examen sobre el uso del pretérito y el imperfecto. El examen es la segunda parte de esta historia.) — fiction

Estábamos en la clase de inglés. El segundo timbre° (1 sonó, sonaba),° como siempre a las 2:30, pero varios de los estudiantes (2 hablaron, hablaban) en voz alta y no lo (3 oyeron, oían). La señora Willoughby, nuestra profesora, (4 esperó, esperaba) impaciente, con una cara muy seria, para empezar la lección. Por fin, se (5 sentaron, sentaban) todos y (6 empezamos, empezábamos) a leer un cuento sobre las aventuras de un famoso detective inglés en que aparece una víbora.° — bell/rang / snake

Todos (7 leímos, leíamos) en silencio acerca de la víbora, mientras la profesora (8 escribió, escribía) en la pizarra. De repente, mi amiga Ester, sentada° cerca de la puerta abierta, se (9 levantó, levantaba) y (10 gritó, gritaba) como una loca. Yo me preocupé muchísimo. De pronto todos (11 vimos, veíamos) horrorizados que una enorme serpiente se (12 movió, movía) sigilosa y descaradamente° en dirección a la mesa de la profesora ... — seated / silently and impertinently

(Continúa en la próxima lección.)

Ejercicio 110 | Done-to Pronouns and Reflexive Constructions

The teacher will give you the combinations which you are to write one at a time. Column three tells you which pronoun to use, and if you think the construction is reflexive, indicate it with R.

Ejemplo: 212 = Tú te acuestas. (R)

1 Yo	1 acostar (ue)	1 a mí.
2 Tú	2 despertar (ie)	2 a ti.
3 El niño	3 servir (i)	3 al niño.
4 Las niñas	4 acabar de mirar	4 a las niñas.
5 Nosotros		5 a nosotros.

Ejercicio 111 | Done-to Pronouns

Write the combinations that your teacher will give you one at a time. In the next class session you will have a quiz similar to this.

Ejemplo: 24 = Mamá acaba de servirte.

		1 a los invitados.
		2 a mí.
	1 sirve	3 a usted y a mí.
Mamá		4 a ti.
	2 acaba de servir	5 a usted (f).
		6 a mi tía.

Ejercicio 112 | Preterit Forms

Write the appropriate preterit form of each infinitive. Correct your work by the board.

1 El pobre viejo . . . (morir).
2 Yo . . . (venir) después que ella.
3 Ellos no . . . (sentir) nada.
4 Usted lo . . . (hacer) también, ¿ verdad ?
5 Creo que yo me . . . (dormir) a las nueve más o menos.
6 ¿ Cuándo se . . . (dormir) ustedes ?
7 ¿ . . . (Oír) ustedes el tigre en el corral ?
8 No, nosotros no . . . (oír) absolutamente nada.
9 ¿ Qué . . . (hacer) tú ayer ?
10 Te digo verdaderamente que yo no . . . (hacer) nada.

Ejercicio 113 | Irregular Preterits

Your teacher will give you the combinations one at a time.

Ejemplo 112: Gilda y yo nos divertimos en la playa.

1 Gilda y yo	**1** divertirse en	
2 Tú	**2** venir de	**1** la fiesta.
3 Las monas	**3** hacer esto en	**2** la playa.
4 Usted	**4** dormir en	**3** (e)l cine.
5 Yo	**5** oír la música en	

Ejercicio 114 | Preterit versus Imperfect

After reading the complete sentence, indicate whether the Spanish equivalent for each indicated verb will be expressed in the Preterit (P) or in the Imperfect (I).

My First Experience on Skis

Although I *was* **1** only seven at the time, I will never forget my first experience on skis. One Friday afternoon on the way home from work, Dad *heard* **2** the news about the season's first snowfall over the car radio. He ran into the house and *ordered* **3** everyone to get ready for the trip to the ski area in the northern part of the state. My father *loved* **4** winter sports more than any other human being I know, and he *was* **5** terribly excited.

We left in such a hurry that Dad *forgot* **6** to make reservations at the lodge where we *were going* **7** to spend the night. Fortunately, the season *was* barely *getting started* **8** and we *were able* **9** to get rooms without difficulty. We were all exhausted when we arrived at the lodge, so everyone *went* **10** to bed without delay. We were going to need a good rest before morning.

After eating a hearty breakfast, the entire family headed for the snow. The weather was beautiful and skiing conditions perfect. Everyone already *knew* **11** how to ski well except me. Dad *stayed* **12** in the children's area to give me the first lessons. After several hours of patient tutoring and much encouragement from my father, I began to hold my own on the snow, so he *left* **13** me alone in the beginner's area.

It wasn't very long before the inevitable had to happen. I *fell* **14** down and couldn't get on my feet again. When my older brother came to my rescue, my left leg *hurt* **15** terribly. Fortunately, it *did* not *break* **16**.

After many more experiences of this type and many more trips to the mountains, I, too, became an expert on the slopes. My older brother *used to brag* **17** constantly about being the champion skier in the family, but the day soon came when his awkward, fumbling little brother gave him stiff competition and eventually took away his title.

Ejercicio 115 | Vocabulary Matching

Match the column of Spanish words with their English equivalents.

1	sin embargo	a	*lips*
2	llanura	b	*to find*
3	moscas	c	*nevertheless*
4	seguir	d	*to play*
5	hallar	e	*thumb*
6	jugar	f	*plain*
7	calle	g	*flies*
8	labios	h	*street*
9	seda	i	*silk*
10	morder	j	*purple*
11	molestia	k	*bother*
12	morado	l	*to follow*
		m	*to bite*

Ejercicio 116 | Preterit Forms and Their Spelling

Change each infinitive to the required finite form. Make sure that you have spelled each form correctly.

1 ¿Qué . . . (hacer) tú anoche? ¿. . . (Estudiar) tus lecciones para hoy?
2 Ellos . . . (salir) de allí a las cinco y . . . (llegar) aquí a las seis.
3 Primero yo . . . (buscar) mi cuaderno y después yo . . . (empezar) el trabajo.
4 ¿A qué hora . . . (venir) tú anteayer?
5 Usted . . . (aceptar) las cartas que ella me . . . (regalar).
6 Yo me . . . (levantar) a las siete y cuarto y . . . (jugar) con mis hermanos.
7 Todos ellos se . . . (divertir) y entonces se . . . (dormir).

Ejercicio 117 | Reflexive Constructions

Write the pronouns that are needed to complete the following reflexive constructions.

1 Todos nosotros . . . divertimos mucho en la fiesta.
2 ¿Van ustedes a levantar . . . temprano mañana?
3 El niño . . . durmió porque estaba tan cansado.
4 Yo voy a lavar . . . antes de vestir . . . .
5 No . . . molestes, Lola.
6 Antes que usted . . . case, mire lo que hace.
7 Mi familia y yo vamos a acostar . . . porque ya es muy tarde.
8 ¿A qué hora . . . desayunan ustedes?

Ejercicio 118 | Preterit versus Imperfect

Read each complete sentence in the story, and change each indicated verb form from the Present to the past tense. The meaning will tell you which past tense form to use, the Preterit or the Imperfect.

Hernán Cortés: un muchacho problema

El hombre que va (iba) a ser en 1519 la figura central de la invasión y conquista de México no es (fue) en sus primeros años de vida° un niño modelo. Hoy día lo llamaríamos° un joven problema. Primero por razones de salud y más tarde por su conducta, desde el momento en que *ve* **1** la primera luz del día, Hernán Cortés le *causa* **2** muchos dolores° de cabeza a su familia.

life
would call

aches

Nace° **3** en el año de 1485 en un pequeño pueblo° español de la región de Extremadura que se *llama* **4** Medellín. Sus padres, Martín Cortés Monroy y Catalina Pizarro Altamirano, *son* **5** de familia noble, pero no rica. Cuando su hijo *tiene* **6** catorce años lo *mandan*° **7** a estudiar para abogado° en la ciudad de Salamanca donde *hay* **8** una famosa universidad que todavía existe en nuestros días. Después de dos años el inquieto muchacho se *cansa* **9** de estudiar y *vuelve* **10** a la casa de sus padres.

He is born/town

send/lawyer

Por toda la provincia donde *vive* **11**, se *oyen*° **12** noticias y rumores exagerados de los viajes al Nuevo Mundo. El joven Hernán o Hernando *empieza* **13** a imaginar grandes aventuras. *Hace* **14** planes para buscar trabajo de marinero en alguna de las expediciones que *salen* **15** de Sevilla frecuentemente para las Indias. *Quiere* **16** buscar fortuna y fama en las nuevas tierras.

there are heard

Por fin,° a los diecinueve años, *viene* **17** a la isla de Santo Domingo a vivir de la agricultura y de las minas. Dos años más tarde *sale* **18** a colonizar la isla de Cuba con Diego Velázquez, el futuro gobernador de la isla. Durante varios años *sirve* **19** a su amigo don Diego de secretario y también en capacidad de alcalde° de Santiago, la capital de la isla. En 1518 el gobernador Velázquez *nombra* **20** a Cortés jefe° de la tercera expedición a la tierra llamada por los indios Culúa o México.

At last

mayor
chief

Ejercicio 119 | Preterit versus Imperfect

Change all indicated verbs to the past tense.

El oro° de Culúa

gold

Durante los primeros años del siglo XVI (dieciséis), miles de emigrantes españoles *vienen* **1** a organizar colonias en las islas de Santo Domingo y Cuba. Aunque *tienen* **2** tierras fértiles en abundancia y esclavos° indios para cultivar los campos y trabajar en las minas, muchos de los nuevos habitantes no *están* **3** contentos con ese tipo de vida.° Además,° el clima de las islas y los mosquitos les *molestan* **4** mucho. Por muchas razones no se *sienten* **5** satisfechos.° La mayoría° de ellos *son* **6** hombres de acción. El deseo de obtener gloria y riquezas° y su gran espíritu aventurero *demandan* **7** otra cosa—nuevos descubrimientos, más viajes de exploración y la conquista° de nuevos territorios. No

slaves

life/Furthermore
satisfied
majority
riches
conquest

pueden **8** vivir en paz porque constantemente *oyen* **9** hablar a los indios de grandes y ricas ciudades donde *hay* **10** gran abundancia de oro, plata° y piedras° preciosas.   silver/stones

En 1517 Francisco Hernández de Córdoba, un español residente en Cuba, *hace* **11** un viaje de exploración a la península de Yucatán y *descubre* **12** las costas de México. Un año más tarde le *sigue* **13** Juan de Grijalva con una segunda expedición que *explora* **14** nuevas partes de la costa, pero sin poder penetrar en el interior del país. Los miembros de estas dos expediciones *ven* **15** templos magníficos de piedra y *oyen* **16** las palabras mágicas de boca de los indios: ¡Culúa, México! De la región de ese nombre dicen (decían) ellos que *vienen* **17** los objetos de oro que les *dan* **18** unas veces como regalo y otras para cambiar° por las cuentas° de vidrio° de Castilla.   exchange/ beads/glass

Cuando Grijalva y sus expedicionarios *vuelven* **19** a Cuba con las noticias de Culúa, el gobernador Velázquez *organiza* **20** sin perder tiempo una tercera expedición capitaneada por Hernán Cortés.

Ejercicio 120 | Preterit versus Imperfect

Change all indicated verbs to the Preterit or the Imperfect.

Dioses blancos a caballo

En un libro de historia titulado *Los exploradores españoles del siglo XVI* (dieciséis) el escritor° norteamericano Carlos F. Lummis *hace* **1** la siguiente   writer
comparación: "El desembarco° de los españoles en México *causa* **2** tanta sen-   landing
sación como causaría° hoy la llegada° a Nueva York de un ejército° procedente   would cause/
del planeta Marte.°" Cuando *aparecen* **3** los once barcos de Cortés con sus 508   arrival/army
soldados, 105 marineros y 16 caballos,° los primitivos habitantes de México   Mars
que *viven* **4** en los pueblos de la costa *abandonan* **5** sus casas y *corren* **6** ho-   horses
rrorizados para los bosques.°   woods

El soldado Bernal Díaz del Castillo nos cuenta° en un libro que *escribe* **7** sobre   tells
la conquista de México que al ver° a los soldados a caballo,° los indios "*creen* **8**   upon seeing/
que el caballo y el caballero° *son* **9** todo uno". Más tarde cuando *oyen* **10** el   on horseback
ruido° de los cañones y otras armas de fuego° se *convencen* **11** de que los   rider
españoles *son* **12** dioses° que según una de sus leyendas vienen (venían) a   noise/fire
destruirlos.   gods

Por medio° de un intérprete indio de Yucatán, en todas partes Cortés siem-   By means
pre les *explica* **13** a los nativos que no *va* **14** a hacerles ningún mal y que
quiere **15** hacerse su amigo para cambiar cuentas° azules y verdes de cristal por   beads
agua y comida.° Un día *vienen* **16** al campamento de Cortés cuarenta caciques°   food/chiefs
importantes de la región a traerle regalos muy finos—objetos de oro y plata,
plumas° de colores brillantes, mantas° y ropa de algodón,° incienso y comida.°   feathers/
Cortés se *sienta* **17** en una silla y los jefes indios se *sientan* **18** en petates° a su   blankets/
alrededor.° El capitán español les *dice* **19** que *piensa* **20** hacerle una visita a su   cotton/food
gran señor° Moctezuma para saludarle° en nombre de su emperador Carlos V   rugs
(quinto) y hablarle de las cosas de Dios.   around him
                                                                                  Lord/greet him

Ejercicio 121 | Preterit versus Imperfect

Change all indicated verbs to the Preterit or the Imperfect.

Los periodistas de Moctezuma

Cuando leemos los viejos documentos que nos *dejan*° **1** varios de los partici-   leave
pantes en la conquista de México es muy interesante notar los métodos aztecas
para la transmisión de las noticias del día. El emperador Moctezuma no *va* **2**
nunca a la costa para conferenciar con Cortés. La capital de su imperio, Tenochtitlán, *está* **3** en el interior del país a una distancia considerable del mar.
Sin embargo, mientras Cortés y sus hombres *exploran* **4** las diferentes regiones
del Golfo de México, en el palacio real° de la capital, Moctezuma y sus caciques°   royal/chiefs
no solamente *oyen* **5** las noticias que *traen* **6** diariamente° sus mensajeros,°   daily/messen-
sino que° también las *ven* **7** con sus propios° ojos. Bernal Díaz del Castillo, el   gers
soldado cronista de las tres expediciones a México, nos cuenta° en su *Historia*   but/own
verdadera de la conquista de la Nueva España que él *ve* **8** a pintores indios   tells
haciendo dibujos° de los barcos, el vestido de los españoles, sus armas, sus   drawings
caballos y hasta el perro de uno de los marineros.

Los mensajeros de Moctezuma que hoy llamaríamos° "periodistas" o "re-   would call
porteros" *ven* **9** y *pintan* **10** acontecimientos° de gran importancia para su señor   happenings
Moctezuma y para la historia de América. Por ejemplo, la destrucción de los
ídolos en los templos mayas de la costa, los pactos y alianzas que Cortés *hace* **11**
con varias de las tribus, la fundación de la ciudad de Veracruz y la división que
existe **12** en aquel momento entre los soldados del campamento español.

Cuando Cortés les *dice* **13** a sus hombres que *siente* **14** grandes deseos de
empezar la marcha al interior de México, sus partidarios° *aplauden* **15** la idea.   followers
Los amigos del gobernador Velázquez, sin embargo, le *dicen* **16** que ellos *van* **17**
a volver a Cuba. Para resolver el problema, Cortés da (dio) órdenes de destruir
los barcos. No los quema° (quemó), como dice la leyenda; los hunde° (hundió)   burns/sinks
en las aguas del Golfo.

Cuando Cortés *llega* **18** a la capital meses más tarde, Moctezuma *sabe* **19**
todas las cosas que ocurren (ocurrieron) en la costa. Las había visto° en las   had seen
pinturas que *hacen* **20** sus magníficos reporteros.

Ejercicio 122 | Preterit versus Imperfect

Change the indicated verbs to the Preterit or Imperfect.

Los intérpretes de Cortés

En las playas de Guanahaní, en octubre de 1492, Colón y sus hombres *sienten* **1**
por primera vez la necesidad de comunicarse oralmente con los nativos. En
los viajes de exploración y conquista que *siguen* **2** al primer desembarco,° los   landing
españoles se *encuentran* **3** con varias tribus indias que *hablan* **4** lenguas diferentes. Para resolver este serio problema, cuando *visitan* **5** algún lugar nuevo, su
costumbre° era reclutar a algunos indios y enseñarles el castellano con la mayor   custom
rapidez posible. En los documentos de la exploración y conquista de México

encontramos los nombres de varios individuos que *sirven* **6** de intérpretes o traductores; por ejemplo, Julianillo, Melchorejo, Juan de Aguilar y doña Marina.

Julianillo y Melchorejo, dos indios que el explorador Hernández de Córdoba *captura* **7** en Yucatán, *aprenden* **8** algo de español en Cuba y *van* **9** en las expediciones a México.

En 1511, el español Juan de Aguilar *va* **10** de Panamá a Santo Domingo cuando una fuerte tormenta *hunde* **11** el barco. Diez de los pasajeros pueden (pudieron) llegar a las playas de Yucatán donde varios de ellos *mueren* **12** de hambre y sed. Los otros *caen* **13** en manos de los indios y todos, excepto Aguilar y un compañero, fueron sacrificados en los altares de los dioses. Aguilar *vive* **14** como esclavo entre los indios por ocho años y *aprende* **15** muy bien el maya. Cortés lo rescata° (rescató) en la isla de Cozumel.

Doña Marina, hija de un cacique° indio, aparece también en la historia y las leyendas con los nombres de Malinali, Malintzín y Malinche. Cuando la *llevan* **16** de regalo con otras muchachas indias al campamento de Cortés, *sabe* **17** hablar varios idiomas indios. Siempre le *explica* **18** las cosas a Aguilar en maya y él las *traduce* **19** al castellano. Estos dos intérpretes *ayudan* **20** mucho a Cortés en todas sus campañas por México.

rescues
chief

Ejercicio 123 | Preterit versus Imperfect

Change the indicated verbs to the Preterit or the Imperfect.

El encuentro con Moctezuma

Después de la destrucción de sus barcos, Cortés se *despide* **1** del pequeño grupo de sus hombres que *van* **2** a quedarse en las tierras calientes de la costa. Con su valiente ejército° de menos de 500 soldados *empieza* **3** la marcha hacia° Tenochtitlán, la capital de los aztecas, que *está* **4** en las tierras frías de la alta meseta° central. La histórica jornada duró° casi dos meses y los españoles *sufren* **5** mucho a causa del° calor, el frío, el hambre, la sed y las heridas° recibidas en varias batallas° muy feroces y sangrientas.° Los indios *defienden* **6** su tierra valientemente contra los ataques del invasor. Tenían un número mucho mayor de tropas, pero la superioridad de la artillería española fue demasiado para ellos. Además,° muchos pueblos indios *son* **7** enemigos de los aztecas y se alían (aliaron) a Cortés.

En el otoño de 1519, Cortés y sus tropas *llegan* **8** a Tenochtitlán (ciudad de México), la ciudad de sus sueños.° La "Venecia de América" estaba construida sobre pequeñas islas en el lago Texcoco. Es (Era) una ciudad limpia y muy hermosa con templos y palacios impresionantes, jardines, mercados° y hasta un parque zoológico. *Tiene* **9** calles muy anchas° y puentes° que *comunican* **10** con la tierra firme. Por el agua salada° del lago y los canales iban y venían cientos de canoas llenas° de gente. Desde los balcones, terrazas y azoteas° de los edificios, miles de indios *miran* **11** admirados el encuentro de su rey con los extraños dioses blancos de ojos azules y largas barbas° negras.

army/toward

plateau/lasted
because of the/
wounds
battles/bloody

Besides

dreams

markets
wide/bridges
salty
full/roof tops

beards

The Land and its Products

Mining is a major industry in much of the Andes — silver from Peru and copper from Chile. At Chuquicamata, one of the world's largest copper-producing facilities, copper is mined and prepared for industry.

Tin household wares are an important product from Bolivia's vast mining industry.

Using the clay soil the people make bricks, build houses, and shape pottery.

Sugar from Bolivia, coffee from Colombia, and wine from Chile are known throughout the world.

Argentinean wool makes colorful blankets. Some textiles are handwoven, others are manufactured.

Cortés se *baja* **12** de su caballo y *va* **13** a saludar° a Moctezuma con un abrazo° a la manera española. Uno de los caciques que *acompañan* **14** al gran señor° *hace* **15** un gesto de oposición y Cortés no lo *abraza.* **16** Entonces el capitán español se *quita* **17** un collar° de cuentas verdes y perlas° y lo pone° (puso) en el cuello° del rey de los aztecas. Después del cambio° de regalos Cortés y sus capitanes *siguen* **18** a Moctezuma hasta uno de los palacios. Con mucha ceremonia el emperador les *dice* **19** que estaban en su casa.

Las expresiones de amistad,° cortesía y buena voluntad° no parecen° (parecían) muy sinceras. Las mentes° de los dos líderes enemigos *están* **20** llenas° de dudas, sospecha° y sentimientos mutuos de desconfianza° y temor.°

greet/embrace
lord

necklace/pearls/ put
neck/exchange

friendship/will/ did not seem
minds/filled
suspicion/ mistrust/fear

Ejercicio 124 | Irregular Preterits

Your teacher will give the combinations one at a time. All verbs in the middle column must be Preterit.

Ejemplo: 111 = Tú llegaste a las nueve.

1 Tú	**1** llegar	**1** a las nueve.
2 Usted y yo	**2** venir	**2** en diciembre.
3 Claudia	**3** hacerlo	**3** durante el otoño.
4 Yo	**4** caerse	**4** en la primavera.
5 Tú y Jorge	**5** pedirlo	**5** durante el invierno.

Ejercicio 125 | *ser* versus *estar*

Choose between *ser* and *estar* and make the verb Imperfect.

1 Antes de venir a América Cristóbal Colón sabía que la tierra . . . redonda.

2 Caperucita Roja fue (*went*) a ver a su abuelita porque . . . muy enferma.

3 Cuando nos llamaron por teléfono del aeropuerto, mamá y yo no . . . en casa.

4 Cuando tu padre y yo . . . soldados, no había guerra (*war*).

5 Todo el mundo sabía que la serpiente no . . . venenosa (*poisonous*).

6 Los vikingos . . . del norte de Europa.

7 ¡ Qué bonita . . . Anita anoche con su traje largo antes de ir a la fiesta !

8 ¡ Qué fría . . . la noche cuando salimos a cantar villancicos (*carols*) de Navidad (*Christmas*) !

9 Pedimos chocolate caliente en el café porque hacía mucho frío, pero cuando lo sirvieron . . . frío.

10 En ese tiempo Pancho . . . el mejor amigo que yo tenía.

Ejercicio 126 | **Reflexive Constructions**

In writing the combinations that your teacher gives you, do the following three things: select the proper present tense form of the verbs in the center column, decide which done-to pronoun is needed for the reflexive construction, and determine whether the pronoun should precede or follow the verb. You will have a quiz like this in the next class session.

Ejemplo: 24 = Yo me siento a la mesa a las siete.

1 Federico	**1** querer levantarse.	
2 Yo	**2** ir a vestirse	
3 Nosotras	**3** acostarse	a las siete.
4 Tú	**4** sentarse a la mesa	
5 Bartolo y Tomás	**5** despedirse	

Ejercicio 127 | *venir* versus *ir*

Choose the verb that fits the situation described in each sentence.

1 El verano pasado mi hermano mayor (fue, vino) a estudiar español en la universidad de Guadalajara.

2 Mis abuelos (fueron, vinieron) de México a pasar un mes de vacaciones en los Estados Unidos con nosotros.

3 Cristóbal Colón (fue, vino) a América cuatro veces.

4 De la isla de Santo Domingo, Colón (fue, vino) a la costa norte de América del Sur.

5 Cuando yo (fui, vine) a Europa con mis padres, vi muchos lugares de gran interés histórico.

6 Los Peregrinos del *Mayflower* que fundaron nuestro país (fueron, vinieron) a Nueva Inglaterra en 1620.

7 Adela y yo no (fuimos, vinimos) a la fiesta en casa de Margarita porque ella vive muy lejos de aquí.

8 Estoy aquí en la oficina del director porque no (fui, vine) a la escuela ayer.

9 Lola y Cristina están en la playa. Cristina le pregunta a Lola, — ¿ (Fuiste, Viniste) aquí ayer?

10 En la clase de inglés Ernesto le pregunta a un amigo, — ¿ (Fuiste, Viniste) al cine el sábado por la noche?

Ejercicio 128 | Present of Irregular Verbs

The quiz in the next session of the class will be very much like this exercise. Write the appropriate form of the Present for each infinitive given in parentheses.

Son las siete de la mañana cuando yo me . . . (1 despertar). Mi mamá me . . . (2 decir) que es muy tarde, pero yo . . . (3 saber) que . . . (4 tener) bastante tiempo para prepararme sin prisa.° Yo me . . . (5 vestir) y me lavo la cara antes de desayunar. Son las siete y media cuando . . . (6 salir) de mi casa y . . . (7 ir) a la casa de mi amigo José. Él y yo siempre . . . (8 ir) juntos° a la escuela. A las ocho menos diez yo ya . . . (9 estar) en casa de José y por la ventana yo . . . (10 ver) que nuestro amigo Enrique . . . (11 venir) a acompañarnos hoy. Enrique, José y yo nos . . . (12 despedir) de la mamá de José y . . . (13 empezar) a caminar° hacia el colegio. José me pregunta que si yo . . . (14 conocer) al muchacho nuevo que hay en su clase de historia. Yo le . . . (15 decir) que sí y que yo . . . (16 oír) decir siempre que es un muchacho muy simpático.° Cuando llegamos a la escuela ya es un poco tarde y vamos directamente a la clase de inglés. Yo . . . (17 poner) los libros en el pupitre y me preparo para aprender la primera lección del día.

hurry

together

walk

nice

Ejercicio 129 | Preterit of Irregular Verbs

Select and copy from the alternatives given the appropriate preterit form of the verbs in parentheses.

1 Los alumnos . . . (hacer) una pequeña casa para el pájaro. *hacen, hacían, hicieron, hacíamos*

2 El pobre pájaro . . . (morir). *murió, moría, muere, morí*

3 Yo . . . (oír) decir que el nuevo director . . . (venir) ayer. *oí, oía, oye, oigo; venía, viene, vine, vino*

4 Cuando yo . . . (llegar), yo . . . (comenzar) a buscarlo por todas partes. *llegó, llegué, llego, llegaba; comenzaba, comienzo, comencé, comenzó*

5 Pancho me . . . (decir) que ellos . . . (ir) al centro. *dije, dijo, digo, decía; fueron, iban, fuimos, íbamos*

6 Ella es la señorita que nos . . . (servir). *sirvió, sirve, servía, serví*

7 El señor del suéter azul . . . (tropezar) y . . . (caer) en la fuente. *tropecé, tropieza, tropezó, tropezaba; caía, cayeron, caigo, cayó*

Ejercicio 130 | Present of Irregular Verbs in Reflexive Constructions

Write the combinations that your teacher will give you one at a time and correct your work by the example on the board. Several steps are involved:
(1) select the form of the verb that goes with the doer.
(2) select the appropriate done-to pronoun.
(3) decide whether the pronoun should be placed before or after the verb.

Ejemplo: 55 = Tú y yo nos vestimos en casa.

1 Yo	1 sentarse
2 Los niños	2 ir a acostarse
3 Tú	3 dormirse en casa.
4 Pepe	4 venir a desayunarse
5 Tú y yo	5 vestirse

Ejercicio 131 | Vocabulary Matching

Match each Spanish word with its English equivalent.

1 ayudar		a	to eat breakfast
2 divertirse		b	to say good-by
3 ponerse		c	raincoat
4 despedirse		d	feet
5 madrugar		e	to help
6 impermeable		f	to have a good time
7 bandera		g	bother
8 molestia		h	to put on (clothing)
9 altura		i	town
10 antes (de) que		j	flag
11 pueblo		k	to trip
12 tropezar		l	before
13 cerrar		m	to get up early
14 medir		n	height
		o	to close
		p	to measure

Ejercicio 132 | Adjectival Residuals: *lo, los, la,* and *las*

a In one type of sentence, the subject (the doer) does something (the verb) to something or someone (the done-to).

Pizarro (the doer) ordered assassinated (the verb) Atahualpa (the done-to).

They (the doer) took (the verb) his hat (the done-to).

b Frequently there is need for a string of sentences that talk about what is done to one single thing (done-to). So rather than label the done-to repeatedly (be redundant),

I got a book from the library. I read the book last night. I took the book back today. I told my friend to read the book.

a pronoun is substituted in English for the label of the done-to.

I got a book from the library. I read it last night. I took it back today. I told my friend to read it.

c This redundancy (repetition of the done-to) is avoided in Spanish also. However, rather than having to learn a whole new set of pronouns, the articles are used with one minor change, *el* becomes *lo*. They are called "adjectival residuals."

d When an infinitive precedes the done-to in Spanish, and the speaker does not wish to repeat the label for the done-to, all that is necessary is to omit the noun.

Quiero ver la capital. → *Quiero ver la ~~capital~~.* → *Quiero ver la.*

e However, in writing, the Spanish speaker never permits an article to end a sentence, so it is attached to the infinitive, forming one written word.

Quiero ver la capital. → *Quiero ver la ~~capital~~.* → *Quiero ver la.* → *Quiero verla.*

Deseo terminar las lecciones. → *Deseo terminar las ~~lecciones~~.* → *Deseo terminar las.* → *Deseo terminarlas.*

f Remember that *el* becomes *lo*, the singular of *los*.

Quiero leer el libro. Quiero leer el. (el > lo) Quiero leerlo.

Mañana voy a tener el reloj. Mañana voy a tenerlo.

g If the verb is finite (not an infinitive), the adjectival residual must change position in the sentence, moving to directly in front of the verb. (You will learn two exceptions later.)

Tengo el reloj. (el > lo) Tengo lo. Lo tengo.

Yo veo la capital. Yo la veo.

Termino las lecciones. Las termino.

Yo no tengo el reloj. Yo no lo tengo.

Practice

A Cover the answers on the right. Check your answer immediately after working each problem.

1 What word is the done-to in this sentence? *Columbus discovered America.*

America

2 Which word is redundant in this sentence? *She **bakes** the pie and eats the pie.*

(the) pie

3 In Spanish the adjectival residuals are the same as the . . . .

definite article

4 When *el* becomes an adjectival residual, it changes to . . . .

lo

5 When the verb is an infinitive, where does the adjectival residual go in the sentence?

after the verb

6 In writing, the adjectival residual must be attached to the end of the . . . .

infinitive

7 In relation to finite verbs, where does the adjectival residual go in the sentence?   in front of the verb

8 What would be the adjectival residuals for the following?
   a el estudiante   *lo*
   b las abuelas   *las*
   c los tíos   *los*
   d la sobrina   *la*

9 Select the correct adjectival residual and place it in the proper place in relation to the verb.
   a saber los apellidos   *saberlos*
   b yo sé los apellidos   *yo los sé*
   c ver la familia   *verla*
   d vemos la familia   *la vemos*
   e poner el dinero   *ponerlo*
   f ponen el dinero   *lo ponen*
   g hago las lecciones   *las hago*
   h hacer las lecciones   *hacerlas*

B Rewrite the second sentence by deleting the done-to noun and placing the adjectival residual in the proper location in the sentence:

   1 Esta es la pregunta.
       Quiero contestar la pregunta.   Quiero contestarla.

   2 No sé el apellido.
       Quiero saber el apellido.   Quiero saberlo.

   3 Necesito el tiempo.
       Tengo el tiempo.   Lo tengo.

   4 Allí están los gatos.
       No quiero los gatos.   No los quiero.

   5 La lección es difícil.
       Necesitamos estudiar la lección.   Necesitamos estudiarla.

   6 Las montañas son altas.
       Nosotros subimos las montañas.   Nosotros las subimos.

   7 Toda la gente está en el campo.
       Veo la gente allí.   La veo allí.

   8 El libro es muy grande.
       Empezamos el libro esta noche.   Lo empezamos esta noche.

   9 La playa es muy linda.
       No puedo resistir la playa.   No puedo resistirla.

  10 El café está caliente.
       No podemos beber el café.   No podemos beberlo.

Ejercicio 133 | Possessive Adjectives

a This is a table of the basic possessive adjectives equated with the corresponding subject pronouns and with English translations:

yo	mi	*my*
nosotros	nuestro	*our*
tú	tu	*your* (*thy, thine*)
usted	su	*your*
ustedes	su	*your*
él	su	*his*
ella	su	*her*
ellos	su	*their*

b Possessive adjectives (besides matching the possessor, "my" = *mi*) must match in number (singular or plural) the object possessed. This is not true in English where they must only match the possessor.

mi barco (my boat) *mis barcos* (my boats)
tu padre (your father) *tus padres* (your parents)
nuestro tío (our uncle) *nuestros tíos* (our uncles)

c *Nuestro* is the only form that must also match *o* and *a* set nouns.

nuestro hermano *nuestros hermanos*
nuestra hermana *nuestras hermanas*

d *Su* translates "his, her, their, your, its."

su familia = his family, her family, their family, your family, its family.

e The meaning of *su* must be clear in the context (surrounding information) or in the life situation. Otherwise, it may need to be clarified by *de* + the label for the possessor.

su hijo = *el hijo de Juan, el hijo de usted,* or *el hijo de ellos, etc.*

Practice

A Cover the answers on the right. Check your answer immediately after working each problem.

1 Possessive adjectives in Spanish have two forms, a singular form and a ... form. plural

2 They must agree with (match) both the thing possessed as well as the .... possessor

3 What is the plural form for *tu* and *mi*? *tus, mis*

4 Which possessive adjective must also match *o* and *a* set nouns? *nuestro*

5 Which possessive adjective is very ambiguous (could have several different translations)? *su*

6 What other two translations besides "their," "your," and "his" does *su* have? her, its

7 To clarify the meaning of *su* it may be necessary to use ... + the label for the possessor. *de*

B Fill in the blank with the appropriate possessive adjective. The subject of the sentence is also the possessor.

1	Vamos a comer en . . . casa.	nuestra
2	¿Tienes . . . libros hoy?	tus
3	Yo tengo . . . reloj aquí.	mi
4	Ellos van a . . . montañas.	sus
5	María Elena está en . . . país ahora.	su
6	El elefante tiene . . . casa en el parque.	su
7	Ella y yo tenemos que ir a . . . banco.	nuestro
8	Yo siempre trabajo con . . . primos.	mis
9	Roberto está en casa con . . . tía.	su
10	Tenemos que visitar a . . . hermanas.	nuestras
11	Ahora vivimos en . . . primera ciudad.	nuestra
12	Tú tienes que salir en . . . barco, ¿verdad?	tu
13	¿Cuándo vas a . . . clase de portugués?	tu
14	Vamos a invitar a . . . maestros a la fiesta.	nuestros

Ejercicio 134 | Role-Playing the Native: Geography

Work with a partner and take turns asking and answering the following questions:

1 ¿Cuál es la capital de tu país?

2 ¿A qué altura (*height*) está? (La capital está a . . . pies de altura.)

3 ¿En qué parte del país está la capital? (Está en el norte, en la parte central, *etc.*)

4 ¿Cuántos habitantes tiene tu país?

5 ¿Qué son los habitantes? (Son indios, mestizos, *etc.*)

6 ¿Quién es el héroe nacional?

7 ¿Cuáles son dos puntos geográficos de interés? (Uno es el río . . . Otro es . . . .)

Ejercicio 135 | Role-Playing the Native: Geography

Work with a partner. Ask and answer the following questions:

1 ¿Cuál es la capital de tu país?

2 ¿En qué parte del país está la capital?

3 ¿A qué altura está? (La capital está a . . . pies de altura.)

4 ¿Cuántos habitantes tiene el país?

5 ¿Qué son los habitantes? (Son indios, mestizos, *etc.*)

Ejercicio 136 | Role-Playing the Native

Choose a partner and ask each other the following questions about your adopted country:

        1 ¿De qué país eres?
        2 ¿Cuántos habitantes tiene tu país?
        3 ¿A qué altura está la capital?
        4 ¿En qué parte del país está la capital?

Etapa Siete

PROGRAM 115

The Present Perfect in English and Spanish

1 In your Programs on the Preterit and Imperfect you learned that all events fall into two sets: cyclic and non-cyclic. *To fall*, in the sense of *to fall down*, is a ⌒⌒⌒ event.

cyclic   **2** You have also learned that events have three aspects: a beginning, a middle, and an end. Which aspect does the form *falling* describe? (a) initiative (b) imperfective (c) terminative

imperfective (Therefore, "falling" is called the *imperfect participle*.)

3 Which aspect does *fallen* describe? (a) initiative (b) imperfective (c) terminative

terminative   **4** Formerly, grammars listed the opposite of "imperfective" as "perfective," that is, completed or finished. As a result, the form "fallen" is still called the *perfect participle*. This word *perfect* appears in the name of the tense you are studying: the **Present Perfect**. Let's see what is present in the Present Perfect. Which form is Present? (a) has (b) had

has   **5** A "fallen tree" is one that *has fallen*. (a) true (b) false

true   **6** The tense of *has* is Present. The form *fallen* is the perfect participle. The tense name for *has fallen* is ⌒⌒⌒.

Present Perfect   **7** Your intuition tells you when to use the Present Perfect in English. Let's bring this knowledge to the surface so you can use it to learn how to use the Present Perfect in Spanish. Compare these two statements: (1) The tree is falling. (2) The tree has fallen. Which one says the action has come to an end?

The tree has fallen.

8 The Present Perfect, *has fallen*, stands in contrast with the Present Imperfect, *is falling*. The form *is falling* says the action is going on, is imperfect, at the moment of speaking: "Watch out! The tree is falling." The form *has fallen* says that the cyclic event came to an end, was perfected, *before* the moment of speaking: "Look! The tree has fallen." Let's look more carefully at this form. It is made up, really, of two verbs. The action is actually described or defined by (a) has (b) fallen.

fallen   **9** The form *has* is called a "helping" or **auxiliary** verb. The tense of *has* is Present. This tells you the action, *fallen*, was completed (perfected) before the moment of speaking. "The tree had fallen" would tell you that the action was completed *before some point in the past*.

In terms of the moment of speaking there are just three things we can say about a single cyclic event: (1) it has yet to take place (*The tree will fall*), (2) it is taking place (*The tree is falling*), or (3) it is already completed (*The tree has fallen*). The Present Perfect, *has fallen*, contrasts with the Present Imperfect, *is falling*. It must also stand in contrast with the past tense. What do you say? (a) The tree has fallen yesterday. (b) The tree fell yesterday.

The tree fell yesterday.

10 Is it proper to say "They have visited him last year"?

no

11 The Present Perfect does not combine with adverbs which stand for past intervals of time: *last year, yesterday, in 1916, etc.* The Present Perfect, then, is not a past tense. It simply says that a cyclic event is completed *before* the moment of speaking, that is, the action is not going on now. Let's see what the Present Perfect tells us when the action is non-cyclic. Is *to work* a non-cyclic event?

yes

12 Which of the following sentences tells you that Peter is still working in the factory? (a) Peter worked in the factory all his life. (b) Peter has worked in the factory all his life.

Peter has worked in the factory all his life.

13 When we talk about a non-cyclic event, the Present Perfect may describe an action which began in the past and is still going on in the present. Peter *began* to work in the factory a long time ago. He *has worked* there ever since. Does *He has always believed in ghosts* imply that he still believes in ghosts?

yes

14 Let's see, now, what the difference is between the simple past and the Present Perfect: "We came here, saw the beach, the mountains, and the house. We loved it." Does *We loved it* describe an event that (a) came to an end at some point in the past? (b) began at some point in the past?

began at some point in the past

15 *We loved it* states that the action of loving began at some point in the past. Does *We loved it* also say that the action is going on now?

no

16 Let's prove this by adding to the story above: "We came here, saw the beach, the mountains, and the house. We loved it and bought the house. Then the oil wells came and spoiled everything. Now we hate the place." The statement *We loved it* means only that the action began at some point in the past. This story, however, could have another ending: "We came here, saw the beach, the mountains, and the house. We loved it and bought the house. We *have loved* it ever since." Do we still love the house?

yes

17 Here is another example of this usage. Which sentence says that I still have confidence in Walter? (a) I believed Walter for many years. (b) I have believed Walter for many years.

I have believed Walter for many years. (And I see no reason not to continue believing him.)

18 Which sentence do you consider to be proper English? (a) Up to this moment we have seen ten planes. (b) Up to this moment we saw ten planes.

Up to this moment we have seen ten planes. (The looking for planes is still going on, so we use the Present Perfect.)

19 Which sentence implies that we are no longer on duty as plane spotters? (a) We have seen ten planes today, captain. (b) We saw ten planes today, captain.

We saw ten planes today, captain.

20 *We saw ten planes today* describes an action that came to an end at some time in the past. We are no longer looking for planes. *We have seen ten planes today*, in contrast, implies that we are still watching out for them. Here is another example of this contrast: (a) I have not seen him for a week. (b) I did not see him for a week. In which sentence does *a week* include yesterday and today?

I have not seen him for a week. (The week is measured back from the moment of speaking.)

21 Which tense relates events more closely to the moment of speaking? (a) the Past (b) the Present Perfect

the Present Perfect

22 Non-cyclic events may begin in the past and continue to the moment of speaking: *She has lived here since 1961.* Is this possible with a single cyclic event?

no

23 The Present Perfect says that a single cyclic event is completed *before* the moment of speaking. Someone asks, *Where's Miguel?* Are both of the following answers acceptable English? (1) He has gone out for a coke. (2) He went out for a coke.

yes

24 When we are talking about a single cyclic event, the past tense, *went out*, also says the event is completed *before* the moment of speaking. May you say either *He just went out* or *He has just gone out?*

yes

25 Which verb phrase is the least complex? (a) went out (b) has gone out.

went out

26 When we have a choice, which form do you expect we are likely to use more often? (a) the simpler (b) the more complex

the simpler

27 Spanish uses the Present Perfect to say the same things it does in English. However, when a choice between the Preterit and the Present Perfect exists, the Preterit is most frequently used. Which form will be used to translate "He went out" (He has gone out)? (a) *Salió.* (b) *Salía.* (c) *Ha salido.*

Salió.

28 In your next Program you will learn the Spanish forms of the Present Perfect. The Spanish Present Perfect is morphologically very much like English. So let's review the English now.

The Present Perfect is made up of two verb forms. The main verb describes the action being talked about. The main verb in *He has closed the door* is ⁓⁓⁓.

closed

29 The form *closed* is called a **participle.** It contrasts with *closing.* Which form is the perfect participle? (a) closed (b) closing

closed

30 In the Present Perfect of both languages the main verb always has the form of the perfect participle. What is the tense of the auxiliary verb forms *has* and *have* in *He has gone* and *They have gone?* (a) Present (b) Past

Present (Just as in "He *has* a dog," "They *have* cats.")

31 In the Present Perfect the tense of the helping or auxiliary verb is always Present in both languages. Now, look at *He has gone* and *They have gone.* Does the perfect participle have the same form in both statements?

yes

32 In both English and Spanish the same form of the perfect participle is used with all subject pronouns. Only the auxiliary verb changes to agree with the different subjects. English writes the auxiliary verb in two different ways. What is the full form of *He's* in *He's sleeping?*

He is

33 What is the full form of *He's* in *He's eaten the pie?*

He has

34 There are two possible full forms of *He's gone.* They are ⁓⁓⁓.

He is gone; He has gone.

35 In your next Program you will discover that Spanish *always* writes the auxiliary verb form in just one way. In English we use *has* in *He has gone* and *He has a dog.* Translate: He has a dog.

Tiene un perro.

36 Spanish uses *tener* to express possession. In contrast, it uses forms of *haber* to make up the Present Perfect.

New Vocabulary

sal (la)	salt	**pan**	bread
pimienta	pepper	**mantequilla**	butter
crema	cream	**queso**	cheese
azúcar (el)	sugar	**huevo**	egg

In many American homes the children are trained to eat everything that is put on their plate. When Americans carry this custom over into the Hispanic society, they give some people the impression of being gluttons. A guest in a Hispanic home is often expected to leave a little portion of something on the plate. This is considered proper etiquette and does not insult the hostess.

PROGRAM 116

The Forms of The Present Perfect and Vocabulary for Food

Part 1: The Forms of the Present Perfect

1 In your last Program you learned that the Present Perfect in both English and Spanish is made up of two verbs: the Present of the auxiliary verb and the perfect participle of the main verb. The perfect participle of all regular *a*-verbs is made up by replacing the infinitive *r* with *do*. So the perfect participle of *hablar*, which will translate "spoken," is ⌢⌢⌢.

hablado
estudiado

2 The perfect participle of *estudiar* is ⌢⌢⌢.

3 The verb which serves as the auxiliary in Spanish is not *tener*. It is *haber*. Does the *h* of *haber* stand for a sound?

no (The letter *h* never stands for a sound in Spanish.)

4 The translation of "I have spoken" is *yo he hablado*. The present tense form *he* comes from *haber*. Is it regular?

no (To be regular it should be *habo*.)

5 In writing, the *h* of *he* is all that is left of the stem of *haber*. In speech, however, the stem is lost and you say [yo e ablado]. Say this aloud. Now make an educated guess. What will you add to *he* to say "we have spoken"?

mos (So you get *hemos hablado*.)

6 Remember that the perfect participle *hablado* stays the same in all forms: *yo he hablado, nosotros hemos hablado*. You have to learn just three more forms of *haber* to know how to make up all the forms of the Present Perfect. The form that goes with *usted*, *él*, and *ella* is *ha*. The translation, then, of "she has sung" is ⌢⌢⌢.

ella ha cantado

7 In all verb forms of the Present the second suffix that matches *ustedes, ellos,* and *ellas* is ⌢⌢⌢.

n

8 Since the perfect participle (*hablado, cantado, estudiado*) never changes, the person-number suffixes are added to the auxiliary. Change *ella ha hablado* so the form matches *ellas*.

ellas han hablado

9 In all verb forms of the Present the second suffix that matches *tú* is ⁓．

s

10 Change *han hablado* so it matches *tú*.

tú has hablado **11** Translate: you (*tú*) have invited.

tú has invitado **12** Change *has invitado* so it matches *usted*.

usted ha invitado

13 You have now seen all the forms of the Present Perfect of *a*-verbs. They are:

yo he hablado

nosotros hemos hablado

tú has hablado

usted, él, ella ha hablado

ustedes, ellos, ellas han hablado

Does the auxiliary have a stem in speech?

no (The written *h* is all that is left of the stem of *haber*.)

14 The auxiliary is made up of just the first and second suffix. Is the second suffix regular?

yes (You must remember *e* and *a* as the first suffix.)

15 The perfect participles of *e*- and *i*-verbs do not have different suffixes. To the stem of the infinitive you add *ido*. So the perfect participle of *tener* and *venir* is ⁓．

tenido; venido **16** There is no change in the auxiliary with *e*- and *i*-verbs. Translate: He has learned.

Él ha aprendido.

17 Translate: They have served.

Ellos han servido.

18 Translate: *Yo he aprendido las formas del presente perfecto en español.*

I have learned the forms of the Present Perfect in Spanish. (There are some irregular forms of the perfect participle which you will learn in later lessons.)

Part 2: Vocabulary for Food

This part of your Program is designed to help you discover whether you are being efficient in your learning of vocabulary. In the next 28 frames you will be given a chance to study vocabulary for food. Go through each frame carefully, stop and think about any word you may miss, then say it aloud twice. After frame 28 there is a short self-test which will tell you how much you have really learned and whether you need to study more.

1 In your last class session you came across the Spanish word *banana*. Both English and Spanish took this word from a South American Indian language. It will become part of your Spanish vocabulary as soon as you can say it with the correct Spanish sounds. Words like *banana* are called *identical cognates*. Most cognates are not identical and when you study them, you must put your attention on how they differ from each other. How do you change "tomato" to get the Spanish cognate?

Change the final *o* to *e: tomate*. (Say *tomate* aloud in Spanish.)

2 The Spanish word for "juice" begins with *ju*, but otherwise does not look very much like its cognate. The full form is ⁀⁀.

jugo (If you missed this word, stop a moment and look at it carefully, then say *jugo* aloud. You'll remember better too if you think of tomato juice: *jugo de tomate.*)

3 When coffee was first introduced into Europe there were shops which only sold this drink. A shop of this kind was called a coffee shop or a *café*. The Spanish word for a café and for "coffee" is still ⁀⁀.

café

4 In the United States coffee is commonly flavored with *crema y azúcar*. These words are translated ⁀⁀.

cream and sugar (You'll remember words like this better if you learn them in pairs.)

5 In much of the Hispanic world a favorite drink is hot *leche* which is flavored with very strong coffee. This is called *café con leche*. The translation of this phrase is ⁀⁀.

coffee with milk

6 It sometimes happens that the same spelling stands for two very different words in English and Spanish. Thus the English word "pie" stands for a dessert while the Spanish word *pie* stands for "foot." Words like these are hard to learn and remember until you thoroughly understand their differences. The English word "pan" stands for a metal dish. The Spanish word *pan* translates ⁀⁀.

bread

7 You already know that it is easier to remember words when you learn them in associated pairs. *Crema y azúcar* go together and both are used in *café*. In the same way bread and butter go together. The Spanish is *pan y* ⁀⁀.

mantequilla (In some areas *manteca* translates "butter." When this happens, the common word for "lard" is *grasa*, the cognate of "grease.")

8 What is the English paired word that goes with "salt"?

pepper

9 What part of *salt* is the Spanish word for "salt"?

sal

10 The English word "pimento" stands for a sweet pepper often used to stuff olives. Change *pimento* to the Spanish word for "pepper."

pimienta

11 Inside of a hen there is a special organ called the "ovary" which produces eggs. The Spanish word for "egg" came from the Latin *ovum*. When Latin **o** was stressed, it often changed to ⁀⁀.

ue

12 The Spanish word for "egg" is a cognate of *ovary* and *oval* (egg-shaped). This word is ⁀⁀.

huevo

13 A very common sandwich in this country is made with *pan y queso*. The translation of *queso* is ⁀⁀.

cheese

14 The Spanish word for "dessert" is a cognate of *posterior* (after). It is ⁀⁀.

postre (What you have *after* the main meal.)

15 One meaning of *carnival* is a festival in which meat is eaten. Think also of the word *carnivorous*, meaning "meat-eating." The Spanish word for "meat" is ⁀⁀.

carne

16 The word *salad* appears in the Spanish cognate which is ⁀⁀.

ensalada

17 If you drop the *b* from *vegetables*, you get the Spanish spelling of the cognate. It is ⁀⁀.

vegetales (But the word you have learned for "vegetable" is *legumbre*.)

18 The Spanish cognate of *fruit* is ⁀⁀.

fruta

19 From the verbs *comer* and *beber* the Spanish speakers get the nouns for "food" and "drink." They are ⁀⁀.

comida; bebida

20 Many people drink *agua* with their meals. Let's see why the Spanish speaker says *el agua* instead of *la agua*. In late Latin "the water" was *illa acua*. When you say this fast, the *a* of *illa* and the first *a* of *acua* run together and you hear [illacua]. This became *el agua* and, as a result, this *el* is now an allomorph of *la*. It is used when the noun begins with a stressed *a* or *ha*. This should tell you that the plural of *el agua* is (a) *los aguas* (b) *las aguas*.

las aguas   **21** Now be careful and translate "good water." Put the adjective after the noun. •
agua buena (The *a* of *buena* matches the final *a* of *agua*.)

22 In your last class session you met some new words for food. Let's see if you remember them. The translation of *manzana* is ⁓. •

apple   **23** *Naranja* is ⁓. •
orange   **24** The cognate of *patata* is ⁓. •
potato (The more common translation of "potato" is *papa*.)

25 *Frijoles* is ⁓. •
beans   **26** *Arroz* is ⁓. •
rice   **27** Very soon you are going to meet the word *pescado*. This is the perfect partici- •
ple of the verb ⁓.

pescar   **28** The verb *pescar* translates "to fish." You eat what you have fished, so the noun *pescado* stands for ⁓. •
fish (The live fish in the water is *un pez*.)

29 In this and the remaining frames you can test yourself on how well you have learned the vocabulary for food. You will see an English word or a pair of words. Think of the Spanish equivalent, say it aloud, and then check yourself. If you miss a word, copy it on your answer sheet. The word for "food" or "meal" is ⁓. •

comida   **30** *Beber* is "to drink". "A drink" is ⁓. •
una bebida   **31** salad •
ensalada   **32** fruit •
fruta   **33** vegetables •
legumbres (or *vegetales*)

34 meat •
carne   **35** dessert •
postre   **36** salt and pepper •
sal y pimienta   **37** cream and sugar •
crema y azúcar   **38** bread and butter •
pan y mantequilla

39 egg •
huevo   **40** cheese •
queso   **41** water •
agua   **42** milk •
leche   **43** coffee •
café   **44** tomato juice •
jugo de tomate   **45** banana •
banana (Another kind of banana is a *plátano*.)

46 fish (that has been caught). The verb is *pescar*. •
pescado (Spend some time now on the words you missed. You are not being efficient in learning vocabulary if you missed more than three.)

New Vocabulary

agua (el)	water	**jugo**	juice
leche (la)	milk	**tomate (el)**	tomato
café (el)	coffee, café		

Americans usually have only three meals a day: breakfast, lunch, and dinner. For most people lunch is at noon and dinner is around six o'clock in the evening. A great many Spanish speakers, in contrast, regularly have four meals a day: breakfast, lunch, *merienda,* and dinner. The reason for the fourth meal (*merienda*) is that dinner is served very late in the evening (sometimes as late as 10 o'clock) and the *merienda* is something like an after-school snack or our five o'clock tea. The Spanish breakfast and *merienda* are light meals. Their lunch and dinner are both heavy meals. The American custom of having just a sandwich for lunch seems strange to the Spanish speaker, and only restaurants that cater to tourists normally have sandwiches on their menus.

The heavy noon meal makes people sleepy, and this helps explain the Spanish habit of taking a *siesta.* And, of course, having an afternoon nap explains why so many people stay up later at night than most Americans.

PROGRAM 117

More on Demonstratives, the Present Perfect, and Vocabulary for Food

Part 1: More on Demonstratives

1 Which demonstrative does the speaker use to point out something near him? (a) *este* (b) *ese* (c) *aquel*

este (*Este libro que yo tengo es rojo.*)

2 Which demonstrative does the speaker use to point out something near the person spoken to?

ese

3 Which demonstrative does the speaker use to point out something that is some distance from the speaker and the person spoken to?

aquel

4 Now, let's put this logic to work. Suppose I ask you, *¿ De qué color es este libro?* When you answer will the book be (a) near you as the speaker? (b) near me as the person spoken to?

near me as the person spoken to

5 Which demonstrative do you use to point out something near the person spoken to? (a) *este* (b) *ese*

ese

6 So your answer to the question *¿ De qué color es este libro?* should be (a) *Este libro es rojo.* (b) *Ese libro es rojo.*

Ese libro es rojo.

7 This should not confuse you. You do the same thing in English. Suppose your teacher asks a question. What should your answer be to "What color is this book"? (a) This book is red. (b) That book is red.

That book is red.

8 Now, be careful. You have a book in your hand. Someone asks, *¿ De qué color es ese libro?* You answer, ⁓⁓⁓ *libro es rojo.*

Este libro es rojo. (It is near you, so you say *este*.)

9 Here is one more example to test your linguistic logic. Someone asks, *¿ De qué color es aquel libro?* The book is at some distance from both you and the speaker. Your answer is: ⁓⁓⁓ *libro es rojo.*

Aquel libro es rojo.

Part 2: The Spelling of Certain Forms of the Perfect Participle

1 You already know that a simple Spanish verb form has three parts: a stem and two suffixes. Recently you learned that the suffixes of the perfect participle of *e*- and *i*-verbs are *i* plus *do*. Write the perfect participle forms of *vivir* and *comer*.

vivido; comido **2** Copy the two participles above and divide them into syllables.

vi-vi-do; co-mi-do

3 In these forms the *i*-suffix serves as the vowel of a syllable. However, in ordinary speech when an *i* follows *a*, *e*, or *o* it runs together with these sounds and makes what is called a "diphthong." You can see this in *veinte* which has only two syllables: *vein-te*. To show that an *i* after *a*, *e*, or *o* belongs to another syllable, Spanish uses a written accent on the *i*; for example: *oír* (to hear). How many syllables are there in *oír*?

two (You say *o-ír*)

4 The *i* of the perfect participle is a suffix and always stands as the vowel of a syllable. Consequently, it should have a written accent on it when it is preceded by *a*, *e*, or *o*. The perfect participle of *oír* is written ⁓⁓⁓.

oído (And you pronounce it *o-í-do*.)

5 Write the perfect participle for *creer* and *leer*, and say them aloud.

creído; leído (You pronounce these *cre-í-do* and *le-í-do*.)

6 Write and pronounce the perfect participle of *traer* and *caer*.

traído; caído (*tra-í-do; ca-í-do*)

7 Let's be sure you understand this spelling problem. One word for "alligator" is *caimán*. Copy and divide it into syllables.

cai-mán (When *i* has no accent, it stays in the same syllable as a preceding *a*, *e*, or *o*.) **8** The Spanish name for the Biblical character "Cain" is *Caín*. Copy this word and divide it into syllables.

Ca-ín (When *i* after *a*, *e*, or *o* has a written accent it belongs to the following syllable.) **9** Translate: I have heard.

Yo he oído.

	10 Translate: They have believed (*creer*).	●
Ellos han creído.		
	11 Translate: She has read.	●
Ella ha leído.		

Part 3: Vocabulary for Food

	1 When you say "banana" aloud in English the first and last *a* becomes a schwa sound. Is there a schwa in Spanish?	
no	**2** When you say *banana* aloud in Spanish are all three *a* sounds said exactly alike?	●
yes	**3** When you say *banana* as a citation form (all by itself) the /b/ is (a) a stop (b) a fricative.	●
a stop	**4** When you say *una banana* the /b/ is (a) a stop (b) a fricative.	●
a fricative	**5** The potato is a New World vegetable. It was unknown in Europe until after the discovery of the New World. The word is Indian and the Spanish cognate is ﹌﹌.	●
patata (However, you are to learn to use the more common form, *papa*.)		
	6 The cognate of "orange," the fruit, is ﹌﹌.	●
naranja (An orange tree is *un naranjo*.)		
	7 In the Hispanic world corn, rice, and beans are food staples. The word for "corn" is *maíz*. The English cognate is "maize." The words for "rice" and "beans" are ﹌﹌.	●
arroz; frijoles	**8** A very common Spanish dish is *arroz con pollo*. The translation of *pollo* is ﹌﹌.	●
chicken	**9** The cognate of *naranja* is ﹌﹌.	●
orange	**10** The cognate of *jamón* is ﹌﹌.	●
ham	**11** The perfect participle of *pescar* is ﹌﹌.	●
pescado	**12** *Un pescado* is (a) a fish in the water (b) a caught fish.	●
a caught fish (The live fish is *un pez*.)		
	13 *Naranja* and *manzana* are tree fruits. The translation of *manzana* is ﹌﹌.	●
apple	**14** Here is a quick review of what you have just studied. Look at the Spanish word, say it aloud carefully, and *think* of the English translation. Then check to see if you are right.	
	frijoles	●
beans	**15** *arroz*	●
rice	**16** *patata*	●
potato	**17** *naranja*	●
orange	**18** *manzana*	●
apple	**19** *pollo*	●
chicken	**20** *pescado*	●
fish	**21** What form of the definite article do you use with *agua*? (a) *la* (b) *el*	●
el	**22** Write the plural of *el agua*.	●
las aguas	**23** What word commonly pairs with *sal*?	●
pimienta	**24** What word pairs with *crema*?	●
azúcar	**25** What pairs with *pan*?	●
mantequilla	**26** The perfect participle of *comer* is ﹌﹌.	●
comido		

comida
bebido
bebida
sopa

27 Change *comido* so it stands for "food."
28 The perfect participle of *beber* is ~~~~.
29 Change *bebido* so it stands for a "drink."
30 The cognate of "soup" is ~~~~.

No new vocabulary.

PROGRAM **118**

Irregular Perfect Participles, and Vocabulary for Food and Eating

Part 1: Irregular Perfect Participles

1 The regular perfect participles have two suffixes. The *a* and *i* are verb set markers; the *do* is the morpheme which says the action is perfected. In the irregular perfect participles the *do* is replaced by *to* or *cho*. The stem may also have a change. Can you guess the infinitive for *escrito?*

escribir (One cognate of *escrito* is "script.")

2 In the perfect participles the *o* of the stem frequently changes under stress to *ue*. The stem of *muerto* is *muer*. The regular stem of this form is ~~~~.

mor (As in *morir*.)

3 The translation of *Él ha muerto* is ~~~~.

He has died.

4 Can you guess the infinitive for *vuelto?* Remember that *to* is the perfective mark. The regular form of *vuel* is *vol*. What infinitive that you know begins with *vol?*

volver

5 The preterit backshift of *pone* is *puso*. Translate: *Ella puso la mesa.*

She set the table.

6 The *puso*-form of *poner* should help you recognize the perfect participle, *puesto*. Translate: *Ella ha puesto la mesa.*

She has set the table.

7 You know two meanings for *poner*. One is "to set" and the other is "to ~~~~."

put

8 Translate: *Ella ha puesto el libro en la mesa.*

She has put the book on the table.

9 In English a "vista" is a "view." Both of these words are cognates of the perfect participle *visto*. The infinitive for *visto* is ~~~~.

ver

10 Translate: *Lo he visto.*

I have seen it.

11 The two participles *dicho* and *hecho* give you very little clue as to what their infinitives are. Nevertheless, you should be able to guess which comes from *decir* and which from *hacer*. The perfect participle of *decir* (remember *dice*) is ~~~~.

dicho
hecho

12 The perfect participle of *hacer* is ~~~~.

	13 Let's review what you have just studied. The infinitive of *escrito* is ———. ●
escribir	**14** In this and the next five frames write the infinitive for the participle given. ●
	puesto ●
poner	**15** visto ●
ver	**16** vuelto ●
volver	**17** muerto ●
morir	**18** hecho ●
hacer	**19** dicho ●
decir	**20** Translate: They have returned. ●
Ellos han vuelto.	
	21 Translate: I have written. ●
Yo he escrito.	**22** Translate: She has said. ●
Ella ha dicho.	**23** Translate: *¿ Lo has hecho tú?* ●
Have you done it ?	

In the United States children and many adults drink milk with their meals.
Adults often drink coffee or tea with their meals. In the Hispanic world, coffee
and milk are not regularly served with the meal. Coffee is drunk after the meal.
During the meal the common drink is water or a table wine. In some families
the children are allowed to have wine with their meals. Many children are also
allowed to drink *café con leche,* that is, hot milk which is flavored with very
strong coffee, and most people drink this at breakfast.

Part 2:

           1 The cover term for food and all meals is 〰.

comida   **2** The verb from which *comida* comes is 〰.

comer   **3** The noun "breakfast" is translated by 〰.

desayuno   **4** To make *desayuno* into the infinitive verb form you replace *o* with *a* and add 〰.

r   **5** This form is usually reflexive: *desayunarse*. There are two common translations: "to have breakfast," "to eat breakfast." Translate: I eat breakfast.

Yo me desayuno.

           6 The word for "lunch" is *almuerzo*. The stressed syllable is *muer* which also appears in the irregular verb form *yo almuerzo*. In the infinitive the irregular stem *almuerz* is changed to 〰.

almorz (So the infinitive is *almorzar.*)

           7 Translate: We have had lunch.

(Nosotros) hemos almorzado. (The literal meaning is "We have lunched.")

           8 The last meal of the day is *la cena*. To make *cena* into the infinitive form you just add 〰.

r (*cenar*)   **9** Translate: She has had dinner.

Ella ha cenado. (The literal meaning is "She has dinnered.")

           10 Write the noun that matches *desayunar*.

desayuno (The word for "fast" is *ayuno*. The negative prefix *des* gives *des-ayuno* the literal meaning of "not fasting" = breaking the fast = breakfast.)

           11 Write the noun that matches *almorzar*. Remember what happens to the *o*.

almuerzo   **12** Write the nouns that match *cenar* and *comer*.

cena ; comida **13** The rest of this Program is a self-test to find out (1) whether you have learned all the words for food and (2) whether you can now spell these words correctly. In each frame you will see the English word. You write the Spanish equivalent. Remember your cover sheet. Circle the frame number on your work sheet if you do not remember the word. Put a bar through the circle if you spell it incorrectly. This will tell you how to grade yourself when you are finished. Here's the first word: soup.

sopa   **14** salad

ensalada   **15** fruit

fruta   **16** drinks

bebidas   **17** vegetables

legumbres or *vegetales*

           18 dessert

postre   **19** meat

carne   **20** salt

sal   **21** pepper

pimienta (Check your spelling carefully.)

           22 cream

crema   **23** sugar

azúcar   **24** bread

pan   **25** butter

mantequilla **26** cheese

queso

	27 egg
huevo	**28** the water
el agua	**29** milk
leche	**30** coffee
café	**31** juice
jugo	**32** tomato
tomate	**33** banana
banana	**34** apple
manzana	**35** orange
naranja	**36** potato

papa (Do not mark this wrong if you wrote *patata.*)

	37 rice
arroz	**38** beans
frijoles	**39** chicken
pollo	**40** ham
jamón	**41** fish (which has been caught)
pescado	

There are 29 words in the test you just finished. Take off two points if you did not remember a word and one point if you spelled it incorrectly. Add these up and get your grade from this chart:

0–1 mistakes = A+	7 mistakes = C
2 = A	8 = C−
3 = A−	9 = D+
4 = B	10 = D−
5 = B−	11 = F
6 = C+	

If you do not like your grade, study the words you missed.

New Vocabulary

banana	banana
trecho	while, interval
a veces	at times, sometimes

gustar and the Forms of the Involved Entity

1 Let's begin the Program by finding out what is meant by the *involved entity*. Compare these two statements: (1) That noise annoyed me. (2) That dog bit me. On the surface both sentences seem to be alike. Each has a doer (noise, dog) and it looks like each has a done-to (me). However, your intuition tells you that the first sentence can be changed to *That noise was annoying to me*. Can you also change *That dog bit me* to *That dog was biting to me*?

no **2** So now you know for sure that the relationship between *annoyed* and *me* and the relationship between *bit* and *me* are not the same. *That dog bit me* says the dog did something to me directly, but there is no information in the sentence which tells you what I did. In contrast, *That noise was annoying to me* really describes how I reacted to the noise. There was a stimulus (a noise) which produced a response (annoyance) and I happened to be the person who reacted to the stimulus. Do we get just about the same information if we change *That noise was annoying to me* to *I disliked that noise*?

yes **3** Can we now say that *That noise annoyed me* really means that I was actively involved because I reacted to the noise?

yes **4** Let's do this comparison over once again so you will be sure you understand what is going on. Which sentence says that I reacted, not just was acted upon? (a) That dog scared me. (b) That dog bit me.

That dog scared me. (My response to the dog was fear. I was involved in the event because I did something.)

5 Does *That dog bit me* say that I also did something?

no (the dog just did something to me.)

6 When we say that very loud noises are annoying, we do not specify who is annoyed by loud noises. What we say is that a loud noise is a *stimulus* (a cause) which produces the *reponse* (reaction) of annoyance. When we specify who responds to the stimulus, we are actually stating who is involved, that is, who is reacting to loud noises. Who is the involved entity in *Juana irritates me*?

me (I am the one who responds to what Juana does. I react and am involved in some way.) **7** Which word stands for the stimulus in *That noise frightens me*?

noise **8** Suppose I say, *I don't like that noise*. What am I reporting? (a) I am doing something to the noise. (b) The noise causes me to react in a negative fashion because I consider it unpleasant.

The noise stimulates my response. (It does something to *me*.)

9 I could respond in a stronger fashion and say, *That noise disgusts me*. Will this change (transformation) say just about the same thing? *That noise is disgusting to me*.

yes (So the rewording tells you I am the involved entity. I react.)

10 In the word *disgusts*, the prefix *dis.* is (a) negative (b) positive.

negative

11 What does *disgusts* mean? (a) is pleasing to (b) is not pleasing to

is not pleasing to

12 The Spanish cognate of "to disgust" is *disgustar*. The translation of "That disgusts me" is *Eso me disgusta*. Which form, *nos* or *nosotros*, will you use to translate "That disgusts us"?

nos (*Eso nos disgusta.*)

13 In this example the person who is disgusted is *tú*. However, the *tú*-form is the label for the person as the doer, not as the involved entity. So be careful and translate "That disgusts you." *Eso ⌇⌇⌇ disgusta.*

Eso te disgusta.

14 The involved entity pronouns which match *yo*, *nosotros*, and *tú* are ⌇⌇⌇.

me, nos, te (These are the same forms as the pronouns for the done-to.)

15 The form of the involved entity pronoun which matches *usted*, *él*, and *ella* shows us that the Latin also recognizes that the involved entity is different from the done-to. This form is *le*. Since *le* stands for either *usted*, *él*, or *ella*, you must tell from the context which person is meant. For example, we are talking about María. Translate: That disgusts her. *Eso ⌇⌇⌇ disgusta.*

Eso le disgusta.

16 Your previous experience with singular and plural forms should tell you that the plural of *le* ought to be ⌇⌇⌇.

les (This is the involved entity form that matches *ustedes*, *ellos*, and *ellas*.)

17 Translate: That disgusts them.

Eso les disgusta.

18 Here is a summary of the involved entity forms, plus the matching subject forms:

Eso *me* disgusta.	(yo)
Eso *nos* disgusta.	(nosotros)
Eso *te* disgusta.	(tú)
Eso *le* disgusta.	(usted, él, ella)
Eso *les* disgusta.	(ustedes, ellos, ellas)

The verb *disgustar*, like "disgust," has a negative prefix. Does English have the positive equivalent of "to disgust," that is, "to gust"?

no

19 Let's pretend for a moment that English does have a form "to gust." Now translate these two sentences: *Eso me disgusta. Eso me gusta.*

That disgusts me. That gusts me.

20 Spanish, as you have just seen, has both the negative form *disgustar* and the positive opposite *gustar*. However, since English lacks the cognate of *gustar* (to gust), we have to translate the opposite of "to disgust" with "to please." In other words, instead of using a cognate of *gustar*, you must translate the meaning. The regular translation, then, of *Eso me gusta* is not "That gusts me" but ⌇⌇⌇.

That pleases me.

21 Let's prove, now, that *me* is the involved entity. Do we have the same meaning when we transform "That pleases me" into "That is pleasing to me"?

yes

22 Many people who start to learn Spanish have real trouble with *disgustar* and *gustar* because one of the common translations of *gustar* is also "to like." Let's see, now, if you can avoid this trouble. In the sentence "I eat the apples," the doer is ⁓.

I
23 The done-to in the same sentence is ⁓.

the apples
24 Many students become confused because the sentence *I eat the apples* seems, on the surface, to be exactly like *I like the apples*. By now you should know better. Remember the notions of stimulus and response. When I say, *I like the apples*, (a) am I doing something to the apples? (b) are the apples doing something to me, that is, causing me to react?

The apples are doing something to me, that is, causing me to react.

25 The apples (that is, their taste) stimulate me in a pleasant fashion. I react pleasantly to the apples. The word in *I like the apples* which describes my pleasant reaction is ⁓.

like
26 The Spanish translation of "I like the apples" is *Me gustan las manzanas*. In the Spanish sentence the doer or stimulus is ⁓.

las manzanas
27 Now look at this. The doer or stimulus is *las manzanas*. The verb form *gustan* is plural. It agrees with (a) the involved entity, *me* (b) the doer or stimulus, *las manzanas*.

the doer or stimulus, *las manzanas*

28 The same thing happens in English with "disgust." Compare:

That **disgusts** me.	*Eso me **disgusta**.*
Those **disgust** me.	*Esos me **disgustan**.*

In both languages the verb agrees in number with the stimulus or doer. Spanish uses the same pattern with *gustar*. Compare: *Eso me gusta; Esos me gustan.* This agreement is lost when *gustar* is translated by "to like." Translate *Esos me gustan* using "like."

I like them.
29 In the English translation of *Esos me gustan*, that is, "I like them," the involved entity in Spanish (*me*) becomes the subject of the English sentence. You should now begin to understand why so many speakers of English have trouble with *gustar*. They can translate *Me disgustan esas palabras* as "Those words disgust me" because we have the cognate "disgust." They get confused when they try to translate *No me gustan esas palabras* because we do not say "Those words do not gust me." They now have to translate the meaning. One meaning is "Those words do not please me." The more common translation is with "like." It is ⁓.

I do not like those words.

30 In *Me gustan esas palabras* the plural verb form *gustan* agrees in number with the subject (stimulus) *esas palabras*. What will you put in place of *me* to get the equivalent of "We like these words"? (a) *nosotros* (b) *nos*

nos (*Nos gustan estas palabras.* Remember this is like "Those words disgust us"—*Nos disgustan esas palabras.*)

31 To rewrite *Nos gustan estas palabras* so that the involved entity is "you" (familiar), you replace *nos* with ⁓.

Te *gustan estas palabras.*

32 Look at the following examples and think of the translations of the involved entity pronouns:

<table>
<tr><td>Me disgustan esas palabras.</td><td>Me gustan esas palabras.</td></tr>
<tr><td>Nos disgustan esas palabras.</td><td>Nos gustan esas palabras.</td></tr>
<tr><td>Te disgustan esas palabras.</td><td>Te gustan esas palabras.</td></tr>
</table>

There are two translations of *me*, *nos*, and *te*. In the first column with *disgustan* they are translated by "me, us, you." In the second column *te* is also translated by "you" (You like those words), but the translation of *me* and *nos* is changed from "me" and "us" to ‿‿‿.

I; we (I like those words; We like those words.)

33 Translate: *Me gusta la sopa.*

I like the soup (The soup gusts me.)

34 Translate: I like the meal.

Me gusta la comida.

35 Translate: We like the meal.

Nos gusta la comida ("The meal gusts us." The meal is still the stimulus, the doer, and the subject of the sentence in Spanish. *We* are involved because we respond to the stimulus.)

36 Let's check to see whether you really understand this Spanish pattern and its English translation. Look at *Tú me gustas.* The subject of the verb *gustas* is the doer or stimulus. This subject is (a) *tú* (b) *me*.

tú

37 In other words *tú* causes *me* to respond in a pleasant fashion. The meaning translation of *gustar* is "to like." Now, use your linguistic logic. The meaning translation of *Tú me gustas* is (a) I like you. (b) You like me.

I like you (You are pleasing to me = You cause me to respond pleasantly = You gust me.)

38 Let's turn this around and ask *¿Yo te gusto?* Who is the doer or stimulus? (a) *Yo* (b) *te*

Yo

39 Who is the involved entity?

te

40 What is the translation of *¿Yo te gusto?* (a) Do you like me? (b) Do I like you?

Do you like me? (Do I gust you? = Am I pleasing to you?)

41 The involved entity pronoun form which matches the singular forms *usted*, *él*, and *ella* is ‿‿‿.

le

42 Translate: She likes the beans. ("The beans gust her." The stimulus or subject more commonly comes after the verb in Spanish.)

Le gustan los frijoles.

43 The involved entity pronoun form which matches the plural forms *ustedes*, *ellos*, and *ellas* is ‿‿‿.

les

44 Translate: They like the beans. (The beans gust them.)

Les gustan los frijoles. (You will learn later that this also translates "They like beans.")

45 Translate: They like the soup.

Les gusta la sopa. (The soup gusts them.)

46 Let's do a pattern drill on paper. The model sentence is *Me gusta la sopa.* The new cue is *nosotros.* The matching involved entity form is ‿‿‿.

nos (So your new sentence is *Nos gusta la sopa.*)

47 Write the new sentence that makes *tú* the involved entity.

Te gusta la sopa.

48 Do the same for *usted*.

Le gusta la sopa.

49 Change the stimulus (subject) to *tus amigos*.

Le gustan tus amigos.

50 Change the involved entity to *nosotros*.

Nos gustan tus amigos.

51 Translate: Your friends disgust us.

Nos disgustan tus amigos.

52 Rewrite and omit the negative prefix.

Nos gustan tus amigos.

53 The common translation of this last sentence is _____.

We like your friends.

New Vocabulary

pollo	chicken (what is eaten)
jamón (el)	ham
pescado	fish (caught)

PROGRAM 120

More Practice with *gustar*, and Preparing for a Quiz on the Demonstratives

Part 1: More Practice with *gustar*

You already know that almost everything you learn has to be practiced and re-practiced many times before you master the problem. The purpose, consequently, of this part of the Program is to let you discover whether you remember what you studied in Program 119.

1 The forms of the involved entity pronouns which match *yo, tú,* and *nosotros* are _____.

me, te, nos

2 The form of the involved entity pronoun which matches *usted, él* and *ella* is _____.

le

3 The plural of *le* is _____.

les

4 The form *les* matches the subject pronouns _____.

ustedes, ellos, ellas

5 The positive opposite of *disgustar* is _____.

gustar

6 English has a cognate to translate *disgustar*. Is there a cognate to translate *gustar*?

no

7 If we had an English opposite of "to disgust," it would be "to gust." Translate: That gusts me.

Eso me gusta

8 One equivalent of "That gusts me" is "That pleases me." The more common translation of *Eso me gusta* is ———. ●

I like that.
9 When I say, "I like your hat," (a) am I doing something to your hat? (b) am I reacting to your hat? ●

I am reacting to your hat.
10 What will be the subject of the Spanish translation of "I like your hat"? (a) *yo* (b) *su sombrero* ●

su sombrero **11** Where will you put *su sombrero?* (a) before the verb (b) after the verb ●
after the verb **12** Translate: I like your hat. (Your hat gusts me.) ●
Me gusta su sombrero.

13 Make *su sombrero* plural and rewrite the sentence. ●
Me gustan sus sombreros.

14 Things can give you pleasure, cause you to react pleasantly. So can events or actions. Translate: *Me gusta leer.* ●

I like to read. (Notice that the infinitive *leer* takes the singular verb form *gusta.*)
15 Translate: We like to eat. ●
Nos gusta comer.

16 The form of *gustar* always agrees in number and person with the stimulus— the doer and subject, not with the involved entity. Translate: We like the eggs. ●
Nos gustan los huevos. (*Gustan* is plural to agree with *los huevos.*)
17 Rewrite changing the subject to *el huevo.* ●
Nos gusta el huevo. (*Gusta* is now singular to agree with *el huevo.*)
18 Rewrite changing the involved entity to "you" (formal and plural). ●
Les gusta el huevo.

19 In this and the next six frames translate the sentence given into Spanish. She likes to talk. ●
Le gusta hablar.

20 We like the meat. ●
Nos gusta la carne.

21 We like the mountains. ●
Nos gustan las montañas.

22 I like Chile. ●
Me gusta Chile.

23 She likes the skirts. ●
Le gustan las faldas.

24 I like you (*tú*). (You gust me.) ●
Tú me gustas. (or *Me gustas tú.*)

25 You like me. (I gust you.) ●
Yo te gusto.

In the United States electric companies frequently try to get more business by advertising to the housewife that she no longer needs to cook over an open flame, that is, with a gas stove. In 1969 there was being sold in Spain a special pan for cooking a common dish called *paella*. With the pan came a recipe in several languages. At the end of the recipe was the statement: cook over an open wood fire.

Part 2: Preparing for a Quiz on the Demonstratives

1 In English just two demonstratives are used to show distances from the speaker. The forms *this* and *these* say the object or objects pointed out are (a) near the speaker (b) at some distance from the speaker.

near the speaker

2 The forms that match *this* and *these* but point out something farther away are ⌇⌇⌇.

that; those

3 Spanish divides distance into three parts and has three demonstrative forms. The form that translates "this shirt" (near me) is ⌇⌇⌇.

esta camisa

4 The English demonstratives have suffixes which indicate number. The plural of "this" and "that" are ⌇⌇⌇.

these; those

5 The Spanish demonstratives also have plural forms. The plural of *esta camisa* is ⌇⌇⌇.

estas camisas

6 The final phoneme of the singular form of the Spanish demonstrative matches the final phoneme of the noun with which it agrees. Thus the /a/ of *esta* matches the final /a/ of *camisa*. Change *esta* so it will match *sombrero*.

este

7 The plural of *esta* is *estas*. The plural of *este* is not *estes*, but ⌇⌇⌇.

estos

8 The forms *este, estos, esta*, and *estas* point out objects near the speaker. The matching forms which point out something near the person spoken to are ⌇⌇⌇.

ese, esos, esa, esas

9 Which of the above forms will you use to translate "What is *that* book you have in your hand"?

ese

10 You are reading a book. You say *Me gusta este libro*. A friend who is visiting you says, "I also like ⌇⌇⌇ book." What demonstrative in English goes into the blank?

that

11 Which Spanish demonstrative will translate "that" in this context?

ese

12 You and a friend are looking at a mountain off in the distance. Your friend says, "I like that mountain." What would he say in Spanish? *Me gusta* ⌇⌇⌇ *montaña*.

aquella

13 The form of *aquella* that matches *camino* is ⌇⌇⌇.

aquel

14 The plural of *aquella* is ⌇⌇⌇.

aquellas

15 The plural of *aquel* is ⌇⌇⌇.

aquellos

16 In the quiz that you will have in your next class you will be graded on two grammatical points: (1) do you select the right demonstrative to show the distance of the object from the speaker, the person spoken to, or both, and (2) does the form agree properly with the noun used with it? The following frames have sentences like those you will see on your quiz. Translate only the words indicated: I like *those stockings* you are wearing.

esas medias

17 Do you see *that house* on the mountain top?

aquella casa

18 *This skirt* that I just bought is too long.

Esta falda

19 *That dog* of yours is very friendly.

Ese perro

20 I can't hear *those animals* way over there.

aquellos animales

21 Will you please open *that window* near you.

esa ventana

22 He broke *that window* up there.

aquella ventana

23 Do you like *these neckties?*

estas corbatas **24** Yes, I like *those neckties.*

esas corbatas **25** Look way over there, what are *those gauchos* doing?

aquellos gauchos

26 On your quiz the demonstrative will be given in English; for example, *No me gustan* (these) *camisas.* The proper form to translate "these" is ⁓⁓⁓.

estas

New Vocabulary

lechuga	lettuce
zanahoria	carrot

---

1 Let's pretend you are eating a steak. To cut off a piece you use your knife and fork. In which hand do you normally hold the fork? (1) right (2) left.

left **2** You have now cut off a bite size piece of the steak. What do you normally do now? (1) You pick up the piece with the fork in your left hand and put it in your mouth. (2) You put down your knife, shift the fork to your right hand, then pick up the meat with the fork and put it in your mouth.

If you are a typical American, you shift the fork to the right hand and then pick up the meat.

3 A great many Spanish speakers follow the European custom of not changing the fork to the right hand. They cut whatever they are eating while holding the fork in the left hand and, then, with the fork (still in the left hand) they put the food in their mouth. The opposite custom is so typically American that during World War II an American spy was caught in Germany by a counter agent who observed him eating in the American fashion.

PROGRAM 121

Stress and Accentuation; Review of Vocabulary for Food and Eating

Part 1: Stress and Accentuation

This review of what you have already studied will help you find out whether you have missed or forgotten some things that you should know.

1 The smallest possible syllable is made up of (a) a single vowel (b) a single consonant.

a single vowel (Linguists say that the nucleus of a syllable must be a vowel.)

2 Since the smallest possible syllable is made up of a vowel, it follows logically that the nucleus or core of every syllable must be a vowel. You can, consequently, find out the number of syllables in a word by counting the pure vowels. How many syllables are there in *contábamos?*

four

3 When a syllable is stressed, the stress falls on the nucleus or vowel. When you put a written accent on a syllable, you write it over (a) the vowel (b) the consonant.

the vowel

4 Write the Spanish for "sugar."

azúcar

5 When you learn a word by hearing and imitating it, you automatically learn to stress the right syllable. When you read a strange word aloud, however, you need to have rules that tell you which syllable to stress. Copy the following words, divide them into syllables, and underline the stressed syllable: *hablas, hablan.*

ha-blas; ha-blan

6 When a word ends in the consonant *n* or *s* the stress falls on (a) the last syllable (b) the next-to-last syllable.

the next-to-last syllable

7 Copy, divide into syllables, and underline the stressed syllable: *papeles.* (Watch out! The plural suffix becomes part of a syllable in speech.)

pa-pe-les

8 Copy, divide into syllables, and underline the stressed syllable: *tormenta, tomate.*

tor-men-ta; to-ma-te

9 When a word ends in a vowel, the stress falls on (a) the last syllable (b) the next-to-last syllable.

the next-to-last syllable

10 You can now put the two rules you have just reviewed into one: when a word ends in a vowel or *n* or *s*, the stress falls on the next-to-last syllable. Copy, divide into syllables, and underline the stressed syllable: *tenedor, animal.*

te-ne-dor; a-ni-mal

11 The words you just wrote end in (a) a vowel (b) a consonant.

a consonant

12 When a word ends in a consonant, except *n* or *s*, the stress falls on (a) the next-to-last syllable (b) the last syllable.

the last syllable

552   Etapa Siete

13 There are four kinds of exceptions to the two rules above. Some words that end in *n* or *s* have the stress on the last syllable. Write the present tense *tú*-form of *estar* and the word for "ham."

estás; jamón　**14** When a word ends in *n* or *s* and is stressed on the last syllable, it must have ⌇⌇⌇⌇.

an accent mark in writing

15 Copy these words and add the accent mark: *millon, direccion, ingles.*

millón, dirección, inglés

16 Some words which end in a vowel have the stress on the last syllable. Translate: I sold (Preterit) the coffee.

(Yo) vendí el café. (When a word ends in a vowel and is stressed on the last syllable, it must have a written accent mark on the final vowel.)

17 According to the rules given above the vast majority of words have the stress on the last or next-to-last syllable. There are, however, some exceptions which have the stress on earlier syllables. All these must have a written accent on the stressed syllable. Write the word for "telephone" and "bird."

teléfono; pájaro

18 There are some words which have only one syllable and also have a written accent mark. The definite article *el* has no mark; the pronoun *él* has a mark. Similarly the subject pronoun *tú* has a mark but the possessive adjective *tu* does not. Now, figure out the rule for accenting. Say the following two questions aloud and stress the subject of each: (1) *¿Dónde está él?* (2) *¿Dónde está el libro?* In the first question you stressed *él*. In the second question you stressed (a) *el* (b) *libro*.

libro　**19** When a word having one syllable actually has two functions, the form which can be stressed usually (a) has an accent mark (b) has no accent mark.

has an accent mark

20 Let's see exactly how the above rules help you learn to say strange words aloud with the stress on the right syllable. If a strange word has an accent mark, you know immediately what syllable to stress. If the word has no accent mark, you must look at the last phoneme to find out whether it is a vowel, *n* or *s*, or any other consonant. Now apply the two base rules. If the word ends in a vowel or *n* or *s*, the stress falls on the ⌇⌇⌇⌇ syllable.

next-to-last　**21** If the word ends in a consonant, except *n* or *s*, the stress falls on the ⌇⌇⌇⌇ syllable.

last　**22** You learned above that the pronoun *él* (which can be stressed) has an accent mark while the definite article *el* (which is not stressed) has no accent mark. Aside from stress, do you pronounce *él* and *el* exactly alike?

yes　**23** Say the following sentence aloud: *El pueblo donde yo vivo.* Now say this question aloud: *¿Dónde vive usted?* In which sentence did you stress *donde*, the first or the second?

the second　**24** Will the stress normally fall on the *don* of *donde?*

yes　**25** You have just discovered that when *donde, que, como, quien, cuanto, cuantos, etc.* are used as question words they have a written accent mark on the stressed vowel (a) to show which vowel is stressed (b) to show that the question word is stressed.

to show that the question word is stressed (*¿ **Cómo** está usted? ¿ **Qué** tiene usted?, ¿ **Cuántos** años tiene usted?*)

Part 2: Review of Vocabulary for Food and Eating

1 It has been suggested that learning words can be made much easier if you learn them in sets or learn those words which are associated with each other. Write the infinitive form of the verbs that match *desayuno, almuerzo,* and *cena.* •

desayunar, almorzar, cenar

2 The three utensils you normally use in eating are *cuchillo, tenedor,* and *cuchara.* Their English equivalents are ———. •

knife, fork, spoon

3 Let's see if you have been watching for all the associations which can help you remember words. What verb does *tenedor* come from? •

tener (Tener means "to have" and "to hold." A *tenedor* is a holder.)

4 The three common objects in which you put food and drink are "cup, glass, plate." The Spanish cognates of "plate" and "vase" (glass) are ———. •

plato; vaso   **5** The translation of "cup" is ———.

taza   **6** The names for *legumbres* that you know in Spanish are *lechuga, zanahoria, papa, frijol,* and *tomate.* Which words stand for "carrot" and "potato"? •

zanahoria; papa

7 You know the Spanish words for three *frutas.* They are ———. •

manzana, naranja, banana

8 What grain is frequently used to make a dish with *pollo?* •

arroz (con pollo)

9 The cover term for *jamón* and *pollo* is ———. •

carne   **10** For a long time Catholics were not supposed to eat *carne* on Friday. They were, however, permitted to eat ——— in place of it. (Give the word in Spanish.) •

pescado   **11** The three most common drinks that go with meals are "water, milk, coffee." In Spanish they are ———. •

agua, leche, café

12 When you squeeze tomatoes to make a drink, you get ———. •

jugo de tomate **13** The paired word that goes with *pimienta* is ———. •

sal   **14** The paired word that goes with *crema* is ———. •

azúcar   **15** The most common spread used on *pan* is ———. •

mantequilla **16** A dish made up of a mixture of fresh *legumbres* is called una ———. •

ensalada   **17** When many *legumbres* are cooked together you get *una* ——— *de legumbres.* •

sopa   **18** A hen produces a food called *un* ———. •

huevo   **19** According to legend the favorite food of mice is ———. •

queso   **20** The last course in a meal is el ———. •

postre   **21** The nouns derived from *comer* and *beber* are ———. •

comida; bebida

22 *Una coca-cola es una* ———. •

bebida

New Vocabulary

cuchillo	knife	plato	plate
cuchara	spoon	taza	cup
tenedor (el)	fork (holder, from *tener*)		

PROGRAM **122**

Street Addresses; the Preterit of *dar* and *poner*

Part 1: Giving Your Address in Spanish

1 In both American and Spanish culture there are special names for the passage ways along which one travels. In English we talk of roads and highways in the country. The Spanish equivalent of "road" is *camino*. In the old days a *camino* was a path or trail along which one could *caminar* (walk). A pathway big enough for a wagon or cart (*carreta*) was called a *carretera* and today this is the common word for a "highway." In a town or city the common word for "street" is a word you already know. It is ———.

calle
2 In both English and Spanish the width and elegance of a street help to determine whether it will be called a street, an avenue, or a boulevard. In general, a boulevard is the most pretentious and many have center strips with plants, trees, grass, and flowers. You already know the Spanish cognate of "avenue." It is ———.

avenida
3 English borrowed "boulevard" from the French. So did Spanish, but in Spanish the word is spelled *bulevar*. Spanish also has its own word for an elegant street like a boulevard. It is *paseo*. One of the famous streets of Mexico City is El Paseo de la Reforma.

When a house or building on *una calle*, *una avenida*, *un bulevar*, or *un paseo* has a number, the name of the street plus the number is an "address." The Spanish word for "address" is the cognate of "direction." It is ———.

dirección (From the direction one follows to get there.)
4 In the following frames there are common questions used in asking about an address. Let's see if you can translate them. *¿ En qué calle vives?*

On what street do you live?
5 *¿ Cuál es su dirección?* (A variation is *¿ Cuál es la dirección de su casa?*)

What is your address?
6 *¿ Cuál es el número de su casa?* (A variation is *¿ Qué número tiene su casa?*)

What is your house number?
7 When you answer the question *¿ Cuál es su dirección?*, you first give the name of your street (*Calle Corrientes, Avenida España*), then the number of your house. Thus, *Calle Real 28*. In writing, a comma may or may not be used between the street name and the house number. Translate this address into Spanish: 1921 Columbia Avenue.

Avenida Columbia 1921
8 When you count, the number 1921 comes out as *mil novecientos veintiuno*. However, when you give a house number you may say either *diecinueve, veintiuno* or even *uno, nueve, dos, uno*. This makes it easier for people to remember or write down the house number. Using the first system above, translate: My address is 1718 Laborde Street.

Mi dirección es Calle Laborde diecisiete, dieciocho.

9 When the house number has five digits, the numbers may be given in several ways. For example, 73945 may be said like this: 7-39-45, or 73-94-5, or even 739-45. To make learning easier for you, all such numbers will be practiced by dividing them into two digit groups with the single odd number coming first: 5-22-43. Write this number in words as in counting. ·

cinco, veintidós, cuarenta y tres

10 When you say what your address is, it is common but not necessary to use the word *número* before the house number. For example, you might say, *Mi dirección es Paseo de la Reforma número nueve, setenta y seis*. As a return address on an envelope, you just give the street and the number in Arabic numerals. Write out the above address in this fashion.

Paseo de la Reforma 976

11 Which form of the definite article do you use with *paseo* and *bulevar?* (a) *el* (b) *la*

el

12 Which form of the indefinite article do you use with *calle* and *avenida?* (a) *un* (b) *una*

una

13 Some day you may want to write to someone in the Hispanic world. When you put the return address on the envelope, remember that the letter you get back will be handled by American mailmen. Will you write your return home address (a) according to the English or (b) the Spanish system?

according to the English system

14 This letter will also be handled by a Spanish-speaking mailman and he needs to know that it is supposed to go to the United States. So you will have to add to your return address the Spanish equivalent of U.S.A. One abbreviation for *Estados Unidos* in Spanish is *EE.UU*. Spanish uses two E's and two U's to show that the original words are plural. Another common abbreviation is *E.U.A.*

In your next class session your teacher will ask ¿*Cuál es tú dirección?* Can you give your real address in Spanish? Write it out now the way you would say it.

The manufacturers of breakfast cereals in the United States spend a lot of money suggesting that fruit mixed with cereal makes a delicious breakfast. Many Americans put slices of banana in their cereal or eat banana with sugar and cream. This would horrify most Cubans who firmly believe that eating bananas with milk or cream will make one sick.

The bananas that you eat are not tree-ripened. When the stalks are taken from the trees the bananas are a deep green. They "ripen" to their yellow color in the warehouse.

In the tropical countries of Latin America there is a common type of banana plant called plantain which is rarely seen in the United States. This banana is more angular than the one you are accustomed to and, when ripe, it is a yellowish green. This is a staple item of diet for many people. In contrast with American custom, this banana is not eaten raw. It is usually fried or cooked.

Part 2: The Preterit of *dar* and *poner*

1 The early Spanish speakers used *e*-verb suffixes for the *a*-verb *dar* in the Preterit. If you remember this, then the Preterit of *dar* is very easy to learn. The stem is *d* and the suffixes are the same as those for *vender*. Write the *yo*-form of the Preterit of *vender* and *dar*.

vendí; di (You omit the written accent in modern Spanish: *di*.)

2 The *tú*-form of *vender* is *vendiste*. The *tú*-form of *dar* is ———.

diste　　**3** The *nosotros*-form of *vender* is ———.

vendimos　　**4** The *nosotros*-form of *dar* is ———.

dimos　　**5** The *usted*-, *él*-, and *ella*-form of *vender* is ———.

vendió　　**6** The *usted*-, *él*-, and *ella*-form of *dar* is ———.

dio (Some books still write this as *dió*. The accent mark is no longer needed.)

7 You now know enough about *dar* to be able to write the *ustedes*-, *ellos*-, and *ellas*-form without any help: ———.

dieron (As in *vendieron*.)

8 Let's review this. The preterit *yo*-form of *dar* is ———. (If you remember the Preterit of *vender*, you can't forget the Preterit of *dar*. You just delete *ven* and what is left is the Preterit of *dar*.)

di　　**9** The *nosotros*-form is ———.

dimos　　**10** The *tú*-form is ———.

diste　　**11** The *usted*-form is ———.

dio　　**12** The *ellos*-form is ———.

dieron　　**13** The verb *poner* has a very irregular stem in the Preterit. It is *pus*. The suffixes of it are the same as those for *venir* or *hacer*. The *tú* suffixes are regular. Write the *tú*-form: *pus* ———.

pusiste　　**14** The *nosotros*-suffixes are regular. Write this form: *pus* ———.

pusimos　　**15** The suffixes that match *ustedes*, *ellos*, and *ellas* are also regular. Add them to *pus* ———.

pusieron　　**16** The suffix that matches *usted*, *él*, and *ella* is irregular. Write the Preterit of *venir* that matches these subjects.

vino　　**17** Replace *vin* with *pus* and you have ———.

puso　　**18** The preterit *yo*-form of *venir* is *vine*. The preterit *yo*-form of *poner* is ———.

puse　　**19** Let's review these forms. Write the Preterit of *poner* that matches *tú*.

pusiste　　**20** nosotros

pusimos　　**21** ustedes

pusieron　　**22** yo

puse　　**23** él

puso

New Vocabulary

desayuno	breakfast	**almorzar**	to lunch, have lunch
almuerzo	lunch	**le, les**	him, her, you, them
cena	dinner	**avenida**	avenue
concordancia	agreement	**carretera**	highway
gustar	to like, please	**direccion**	address, direction
disgustar	to disgust	**paseo**	drive
cenar	to have dinner		

More on Stress and Accentuation, and Spelling Words for Food and Eating

Part 1: Stress and Accentuation

1 The word for "days" is *días*. The word for "stockings" is *medias*. Say *días* aloud twice. Do you say *días* with one or two syllables? (a) *días* (b) *dí-as*

You say *dí-as* with the stress on *i*.

2 Now, say *medias* aloud. What do you say? (a) *me-dias* (b) *me-di-as*

me-dias   **3** Say *traigo* aloud. What do you say? (a) *tra-i-go* (b) *trai-go*

trai-go   **4** The perfect participle of *traer* is *traído*. Say this word aloud. What do you say? (a) *tra-í-do* (b) *trai-do*

tra-í-do   **5** Let's see how writing tells you what to say. You say *días* with two syllables (*dí-as*) and you say the *-dias* of *medias* with just one syllable (*me-dias*). You say *traigo* with two syllables (*trai-go*) but *traído* with three syllables (*tra-í-do*). When *i* comes before *a*, and has <u>no written accent mark</u> (*me-dias*), the *i* sound is part of the same syllable as the *a*. (a) true (b) false

true   **6** When *i* comes before *a*, and has <u>a written accent mark</u> (*días*), the *i* is the nucleus of another syllable. (a) true (b) false

true   **7** When *i* follows *a*, and has <u>no written accent mark</u> (*trai-go*), the *i* (a) belongs to the same syllable as *a* (b) is the nucleus of another syllable.

belongs to the same syllable as *a*

8 When *i* follows *a*, and has <u>a written accent mark</u> (*tra-í-do*), the *i* (a) belongs to the same syllable as *a* (b) is the nucleus of another syllable.

is the nucleus of another syllable

9 Let's say what you have just learned in a different way. When *i* all by itself is preceded or followed by a consonant (*comida, mina, cuchillo*), it is always the nucleus of a syllable. Copy and divide the three words just given into syllables.

co-mi-da, mi-na, cu-chi-llo

10 When *i* (without an accent mark) precedes or follows *a*, the nucleus of the syllable is *a*, and *i* is part of the syllable. Divide *caigo* and *estudiar* into syllables.

cai-go; es-tu-diar

11 When *i* has an accent mark (*í*), it either serves as the nucleus of a syllable (*Martín*) or stands all by itself as a syllable. Copy *policía* and *caía* and divide into syllables.

po-li-cí-a; ca-í-a

12 The rules that you have just learned also describe what happens to *i* when it precedes or follows any other vowel letter. Copy *patio* and *tío* and divide into syllables.

pa-tio; tí-o   **13** How many syllables are there in either *veinte* or *diente*?

two (*vein-te; dien-te*)

14 Does *bien* have one or two syllables? ●

15 Copy and divide *ciudad* into syllables. ●

16 Here is a summary of what you have just studied. When *i* has no accent mark, it serves as a syllable nucleus only when preceded or followed by a consonant (*di-go, si-lla, ci-ne*). When *i* has no accent mark and is preceded or followed by another vowel, except *u*, the other vowel is the syllable nucleus and the *i* is part of the syllable:

(1) *a + i*: *trai-go, cai-go*
(2) *i + a*: *me-dia, fa-mi-lia*
(3) *e + i*: *vein-te, rei-na* (queen)
(4) *i + e*: *sie-te, di-ciem-bre*
(5) *i + o*: *lim-pio, su-cio*
(6) *o + i*: *oi-go, hoy* (*i* becomes *y* in word final position)
(7) *u + i*: *cui-da-do* (the *u* is pronounced [w] and *i* is the syllable nucleus)
(8) *i + u*: *ciu-dad* (the *u* is pronounced [u])

Here are most of the words you have had in which *i* has an accent mark and, therefore, stands either as the syllable nucleus or as a syllable all by itself. The words are divided into syllables to show how they are pronounced. Say them aloud:

dí-a	rí-o	o-í-do	tra-í-do	le-í-do
pa-ís	tí-o	ca-í	cre-ís-te	le-í-mos
frí-o	po-li-cí-a	o-ír	ca-í-do	cre-í-mos

To this list you must add the imperfect of all regular *e*- and *i*-verbs, that is, the forms like *co-mí-a, ven-dí-as, dor-mí-an,* etc.

17 When *i* is preceded or followed by a consonant, it may also have an accent mark. This mark merely tells you what syllable to stress when you read aloud. Thus in *a-llí* and *a-quí* you stress (a) the first syllable (b) the last syllable. ●

18 The accent mark on *sí* has an entirely different function. It marks the difference between *sí* (yes) and *si* (if). The mark now shows a difference in meaning in writing. The two words sound exactly alike in speech.

Part 2: Getting Ready for a Dictation Quiz on the Vocabulary for Food and Eating

The four ways of learning how words are spelled are: (1) by rule, (2) by hearing, (3) by seeing, and (4) by meaning. This part of your Program is designed to call your attention to these facts once more and to get you ready to write the words for food when they are dictated. (You will actually write whole sentences in which the words appear.)

1 The sound [s] can be written *s, z,* or *c.* Can *c* stand for [s] when it comes directly before *a, o,* or *u?* ●

2 Can either *s* or *z* stand for [s] before any vowel (*a, e, i, o, u*)? ●

3 Must you, consequently, see *sopa* before you can learn how it is spelled? ●

4 What letter in *bebida* must you see before you can learn to spell the word correctly?

b (You would read *vevida* and *bebida* aloud in exactly the same way.)

5 Which word stands for "glass"? (a) *baso* (b) *vaso*

vaso (*Baso* sounds exactly like *vaso*, but it is the *yo*-form of the verb *basar*— "to base.")

6 Why must you see *cena* before you can learn to spell the word? Because the sound [s] can also be written either ⁓⁓⁓ before *e*.

s or *z*

7 There are three letters in *servilleta* which you have to see before you can learn to spell the word. They are ⁓⁓⁓.

s, v, ll

8 Here are all the words for food and eating which you have to see in order to learn to spell them. The letters you have to watch are indicated. Study the list to be sure you can spell each word.

sopa	huevo	arroz	taza	cena
ensalada	banana	frijoles	*v*aso	almuerzo
sal	manzana	pol*l*o	*s*ervilleta	pescado
azúcar		zanahoria	desayuno	

9 In this and the next 9 frames you have a self-test to see whether you now know for certain how to spell these words. You will see the English word. Say the translation aloud and, then, write the Spanish word. The first word is "sugar."

azúcar   **10** rice

arroz   **11** carrot

zanahoria   **12** apple

manzana   **13** lunch (from *almorzar*)

almuerzo   **14** cup

taza   **15** dinner

cena   **16** egg

huevo   **17** napkin

servilleta   **18** breakfast

desayuno (If you missed more than three words, you need to study some more.)

19 You learn to spell [keso] by learning a spelling rule. (Remember the Spanish alphabet has no letter *k*, except in foreign words.) The sound [k] is spelled ⁓⁓⁓ before *e* or *i*.

qu   **20** The sound [k] is spelled ⁓⁓⁓ before *a*, *o*, *u*, and other consonants.

c   **21** Here are the words which require the use of the above rules to be spelled correctly. Study them. The letters you have to watch are indicated.

cuchillo	pescado	**qu**eso	azúcar	carne
cuchara	café	mante**qu**illa	crema	comida

Let's see now, if you can spell all of them correctly. Translate "sugar."

azúcar   **22** food

comida   **23** cream

crema   **24** meat

carne   **25** butter

mantequilla   **26** cheese

queso

27 coffee

café (You misspelled it if you left off the accent mark.)

28 fish (after it is caught)

pescado   **29** knife

cuchillo   **30** spoon

cuchara

Special Review of Vocabulary

This little review is to let you find out whether you are really learning new words the first time you meet them. You met the following words in your last class session. Can you translate them?

     1 *muñeca*

doll   **2** *romper*

to break   **3** *quitar*

to take away   **4** *arreglar*

to fix

New Vocabulary

Buen provecho.   *No real English equivalent.* (May you) enjoy your meal.

acompañado   accompanied

sólo   only

The Hispano and the American tend to exhibit very different habits when they eat a meal. In the average American home all the food for a meal, except dessert, is commonly put on the table at once, and a person helps himself to a little of everything and begins to eat. For elegant meals, especially when there are guests, an appetizer is served before the meal, then there is a soup or a salad, followed by the main meal, and, finally, dessert. A great many people in the Hispanic world tend to follow this second pattern regularly, that is, each dish is eaten separately or in a rather strict combination with other dishes. What may be eaten along with something else reveals a marked contrast in eating habits. In both cultures meat, fish, vegetables, rice, and bread are frequently eaten together. In both cultures fruit and other sweet things are served as a dessert. It is, indeed, a rare American, however, who eats apple pie along with meat and potatoes. A great many Latins, as well as other people in parts of Europe, carry this tradition farther. They eat nothing sweet with their meat. Many Americans, in contrast, eat jelly along with meat, use sugar on rice that is eaten with the meat, or put honey on their bread. This is as strange to many Latins (and certain Germans) as eating meat and apple pie simultaneously is to the average American.

PROGRAM **124**

Review of the Preterit and Imperfect

You have been working for some time with the Preterit and the Imperfect and know all the uses of these two forms of the past tense. This Program, consequently, is like a self-test to find out if there is something you need to study more. Keep track of any frames you miss and look up the problem in your *Cuaderno*.

1 When you report the clock time at which some event in the past began, was going on, or came to an end, you use the (a) Imperfect (b) Preterit.

Imperfect   **2** Rewrite in the past tense: *Son las doce cuando, por primera vez, vemos el avión.*

Eran las doce cuando, por primera vez, vimos el avión.

3 Look at the sentence above. The phrase *por primera vez* translates "for the first time." Did the action described by *vimos* begin at 12 o'clock?

yes (The implication is that we began to see the plane at 12 o'clock and we continued to look at it for some time.)

4 The event labeled *ver* is (a) cyclic (b) non-cyclic.

non-cyclic   **5** The Preterit is used to describe the initiative aspect of a non-cyclic event. (a) true (b) false

true   **6** Translate: *Era la una cuando llegó la tormenta y llovió.*

It was one o'clock when the storm arrived and it rained.

7 Did the rain *begin* after the storm arrived?

yes   **8** Would this be a possible translation? "It was one o'clock when the storm arrived and it began to rain."

yes (When you are uncertain about whether to use the Preterit or Imperfect with non-cyclic events use "began" with the verb. If this makes good sense, you can be certain the Preterit is correct.)

9 Translate the indicated words: *It was three* in the morning when suddenly *we heard* this terrible noise in the corral.

Eran las tres . . . oímos (In place of "we heard," you could say "we began to hear.")

10 Non-cyclic events like *ver* or *oír* can begin at some point in the past. (a) true (b) false

true   **11** The verb for "to cry" is the regular *a*-verb *llorar*. Do you remember the poster pictures? The young man recalled what happened when he began to walk. He said, "I fell down and cried." Is "to cry" a non-cyclic event?

yes (It can begin and be extended.)

12 Did the crying *begin* after he fell down?

yes   **13** Translate: I fell down and cried. "To fall down" in this context is *caerse*.

Me caí y lloré.   **14** When you fall down, must you get up before you can fall again?

yes

15 "To fall down" is a (a) non-cyclic (b) cyclic event.

cyclic event **16** The Preterit tells you that the whole cycle of a cyclic event was completed in the past. Is *llegar* a cyclic event?

yes **17** Rewrite in the past tense: *Son las once de la noche cuando al fin* (finally) *llegan a casa.*

Eran las once de la noche cuando al fin llegaron a casa.

18 All non-cyclic events can have a beginning, a middle, and an end. The Preterit can be used to say the whole action was completed at some time *before* the moment of speaking. Translate: It rained a lot yesterday.

Llovió mucho ayer. (The rain began, went on, and came to an end sometime yesterday.) **19** Translate: *Eran las cuatro de la tarde y llovía.*

It was four in the afternoon and it was raining.

20 The Imperfect *llovía* says that a non-cyclic event was going on (was imperfect) at some point in the past. Translate the indicated clause: *Eran las cuatro de la tarde **cuando llegábamos a casa.***

when we were arriving home **21** The Imperfect *llegábamos* says that a cyclic event was going on (was imperfect) at some point in the past. Translate: When I was in Bogotá, I lost my raincoat.

Cuando estaba en Bogotá perdí mi (or *el*) *impermeable.* **22** Being in a place (a non-cyclic event) was going on when a cyclic event (lost) was completed. Translate: I was sleeping when you (*tú*) returned home.

Yo dormía cuando volviste a casa.

23 Here is a summary of what you have just reviewed. Notice that the facts are very simple and easy to understand and remember. When you talk about clock time in the past tense, you use *ser* in the (a) Preterit (b) Imperfect.

Imperfect (*Eran las ocho cuando salimos del cine.*)

24 When you want to say that a whole event (either cyclic or non-cyclic) was completed before the moment of speaking, you use the (a) Preterit (b) Imperfect.

Preterit (*Ayer el niño se cayó tres veces y lloró mucho.*)

25 When you say that a non-cyclic event began at some point in the past, you use the (a) Preterit (b) Imperfect.

Preterit (*Hacía un sol brillante toda la mañana y, luego, a la una llovió.* "And then, at one o'clock it began to rain.")

26 When you say that a cyclic event was completed at some point in the past, you use the (a) Preterit (b) Imperfect

Preterit (*En ese momento salimos de la selva.*)

27 When you want to say that any event, either cyclic or non-cyclic, was going on (was imperfect) at some point in the past, you use the (a) Preterit (b) Imperfect

Imperfect (*Llovía cuando salíamos de la selva.*)

Here is the same summary stated positively:

(1) When you talk about past clock time you use the Imperfect: *Eran las dos.*
(2) To say that a whole event, either cyclic or non-cyclic, was completed <u>before</u> the moment of speaking, you use the Preterit: *Entré y hablé con ellos.*
(3) To say that a non-cyclic event <u>began</u> either at some point in the past or <u>before</u> the moment of speaking, you use the Preterit: *Él habló a la una; Lo conocí ayer.*

(4) To say that a cyclic event was completed either <u>at</u> some point in the past or <u>before</u> the moment of speaking, you use the Preterit: *Llegó a la una; Llegó anoche.*

28 Three uses of the past tense remain to be reviewed. You use the simple Present in Spanish to describe what you are planning to do in the future. Translate: *Mi hermana se casa en una semana.*

My sister is getting married in a week. (But you use the Progressive in English for planned action.)

29 Translate: *Yo sabía que mi hermana se casaba en una semana.*

I knew that my sister was getting married in a week.

30 When you back-shift planned action to the past tense, you use the (a) Preterit (b) Imperfect.

Imperfect   **31** Rewrite in the past tense: *Y luego dicen que van a comprar la casa.*

Y luego dijeron que iban a comprar la casa. (The present planned action *van a comprar* becomes the recalled planned action *iban a comprar.*)

32 When we say "He used to work in the store but now he works in the bank," we compare what is customary now with what was customary before now. Is it logical, then, to say that "he works in the bank" describes an action which, in general, is going on in the present?

yes   **33** Spanish has no commonly used word for "used to." The same idea, however, can be expressed by the tense form normally used to say that an action was going on in the past. This form is the (a) Preterit (b) Imperfect.

Imperfect   **34** Translate: He used to work in the store but now he works in the bank.

Él trabajaba en la tienda pero ahora trabaja en el banco.

35 Does "They used to be married to each other" tell you that they are no longer married?

yes   **36** In certain contexts *used to* clearly says that what was customary or habitual in the past is no longer so. Is this also true for the following statement? "She told me that when she worked with him he would always say no when she asked him to do that."

no (Because one may add, "Does he still do it?")

37 Spanish has no commonly used special way to show the difference between *used to* and *would*. As a result, there is only one translation for both of these statements: (a) When I was a child, I *used to wake up* at 5 o'clock every morning. (b) When I was a child, I *would wake up* at 5 o'clock every morning. The translation of the verb phrase is ⌁⌁⌁.

me despertaba   **38** Here is a summary of the uses of the past tense forms that you have just reviewed. The Imperfect is used (1) as the back-shift of the Present to recall planned action, and (2) to translate either *used to* or *would* when talking about customary or habitual past actions.

See if you can put into practice what you have just reviewed. In this and the next nine frames you can test your knowledge. Give yourself a grade by taking off ten points for each frame you miss. 90 is an A, 80 a B, 70 a C, and 60 a D.

In this sentence you want to say that one event (a non-cyclic action) was going on when a cyclic event was terminated. Translate: Mother was ironing the clothes when I returned from school.

Mamá planchaba la ropa cuando yo volví de la escuela. (Take off 10 points if you got both verb forms wrong. Take off 5 if you got one wrong.)

39 In this sentence you want to say that one event was completed before another event began. Translate: We went out to the street and we saw the airplane. ●

Salimos a la calle y vimos el avión. (In this test do not take off points for spelling errors.)

40 You want to say that two events were completed before the moment of speaking. Rewrite in the past tense: *Ayer me levanto temprano y trabajo diez horas.* ●

Ayer me levanté temprano y trabajé diez horas.

41 In this sentence you give the time when a cyclic event was terminated. Translate: It was nine o'clock when I went to bed. ●

Eran las nueve cuando me acosté.

42 This sentence describes a present customary action which contrasts with what you used to do in the past. Translate: We used to have dinner at six, now we have dinner at eight. (The verb is *cenar*.) ●

Cenábamos a las seis, ahora cenamos a las ocho.

43 This sentence describes one action which was going on and one which was customary at the same time in the past. Translate: When he lived in the country, he would get up at five o'clock. ●

Cuando él vivía en el campo se levantaba a las cinco.

44 Let's see, now, if you can do four sentences without any help. Translate: I lived in San Diego four years. ●

(Yo) viví en San Diego cuatro años.

45 It was raining when I arrived at the beach. ●

Llovía cuando llegué a la playa.

46 I saw the word and it disgusted me. ●

Vi la palabra y me disgustó.

47 I was a child when my father died. ●

Yo era un niño cuando mi papá (padre) murió.

If you do not like your grade, you can get more practice in your *Cuaderno.*

No new vocabulary.

It is a commonly accepted social custom for Americans to invite friends and even mere acquaintances to dinner in their homes. The Basques of Spain almost never do this, and many Hispanic families often invite only the most intimate of friends. Americans who are unaware of this custom often feel hurt because they are not invited to dinner by Latins whom they appear to know really well. An American may know Latins and Spanish people well enough to talk to them in tú, yet never be invited for dinner in their homes.

Getting Ready for a Quiz on the Present Perfect, and Vocabulary Review

Part 1: Getting Ready for a Quiz on the Present Perfect

The quiz in your next class session will show whether you have learned both the regular and irregular forms of the Present Perfect in Spanish. This Program will give you a chance to study any forms which you have not yet memorized perfectly. Remember that the grade you are going to get on the test depends entirely on how much *you* study. Your teacher cannot teach you these forms; *you have to learn them by studying.*

1 The Present Perfect in Spanish has the same structure as the Present Perfect in English. In both languages there is an auxiliary (helping) verb. The auxiliary verb in English is "to have." The Spanish auxiliary is (a) *tener* (b) *haber.*

haber   **2** The tense of the auxiliary verb in both languages is (a) Past (b) Present.

Present   **3** The main verb (the one that stands for the action being talked about) appears in both languages in the form of the perfect participle. The perfect participle of "to look" in English is ⁓⁓⁓.

looked   **4** The perfect participle of *mirar* is ⁓⁓⁓.

mirado   **5** In speech the auxiliary verb *haber* has lost its stem in all the forms you are now learning. In writing, however, this stem is represented by *h. Haber* has two irregular forms (vowels) for the first suffix. What do you add to *h* to get the written form that matches *yo?*

e   **6** Translate: I have looked.

Yo he mirado.   **7** What do you add to *he* to get the regular written form that matches *nosotros?*

mos   **8** Translate: We have talked.

(Nosotros) hemos hablado.

    9 The second suffix of the Present of *haber* is regular. The morpheme /s/ matches the subject ⁓⁓⁓.

tú   **10** The second suffix which matches *ustedes, ellos,* and *ellas* is ⁓⁓⁓.

n   **11** The first suffix that goes with *yo* and *nosotros* is *e.* In all the other forms of the Present of *haber* the irregular first suffix is ⁓⁓⁓.

a   **12** Translate: You (*tú*) have talked.

Tú has hablado.

    13 Change the subject to *ustedes.*

Ustedes han hablado.

    14 Rewrite in the singular.

Usted ha hablado.

    15 In all the forms of the Present Perfect, the perfect participle of *hablar* always has the same form. (a) true (b) false

true (The hablado stays the same regardless of the subject.)

16 To make the perfect participle of all regular *a*-verbs, you **add *a*** to the stem and **add** the perfective marker ~~~.

do (You replace the *r* of the infinitive with *do*.)

17 Write the perfect participle for *llamé* and *estudió*.

llamado; estudiado

18 To make the perfect participle of all regular *e*- and *i*-verbs, you add ~~~ to the stem and add the perfective marker *do*.

i　　**19** Write the perfect participle for *comer* and *vivieron*.

comido; vivido **20** There are a number of irregular perfect participles in Spanish which end in either *to* or *cho*. Let's see if you remember all those you have studied. Write the perfect participle of *decir*.

dicho　　**21** romper

roto　　**22** poner

puesto　　**23** hacer

hecho　　**24** ver

visto　　**25** morir

muerto　　**26** volver

vuelto　　**27** escribir

escrito　　**28** The verb *ir* has no stem, so for the perfect participle you write ~~~.

ido　　**29** There is a special spelling problem when you write the perfect participle of verbs like *caer*, *leer*, *traer*, and *oír*. The stress falls on the *i* of the ending and this *i* stands as a syllable all by itself. To show this in writing, you must do what?

write an accent mark over the *i*

30 Write the perfect participle for *caer*, *leer*, *traer*, and *oír*.

caído, leído, traído, oído

31 When the construction is reflexive, the reflexive pronoun immediately precedes the auxiliary verb in Spanish. Translate: Abelardo has eaten breakfast.

Abelardo se ha desayunado.

Part 2: Vocabulary Review

This review deals with a special class of words whose meaning generally can't be figured out from the context. You have to learn each word one by one and memorize each meaning. Let's see how well you have been doing. Translate mentally each sentence and check the translation for the indicated word in each of the following frames. If you miss a word, add it to your special study list.

1 *Ya* lo he visto.

I have *already* seen it.

2 Comemos y *luego* estudiamos.

We eat and *then* we study.

3 Pablo no ha llegado *todavía*.

Pablo *still* hasn't arrived. (Or, "Pablo hasn't arrived *yet*.")

4 ¿*Por qué* dices eso?

Why do you say that?

5 Lo digo *porque* es importante.

I say it *because* it is important.

6 Lo hacemos *después de* cenar.

We do it *after* eating dinner.

7 The opposite of the above is: Lo hacemos *antes de* cenar.
We do it *before* eating dinner.

8 What comes between *antes* and *después* is expressed by *mientras:* Lo hacemos *mientras* cenamos.
We do it *while* we are eating dinner.

9 Colón llegó a la isla. *Entonces* descubrió que había indios allí.
Colombus arrived at the island. *Then* he discovered that there were Indians there.

10 Nuestra casa está *entre* el río y la montaña.
Our house is *between* the river and the mountain.

11 Be careful with this one. There is a different meaning for *entre: Entre* todas las cosas que tenemos que hacer, no hay nada importante.
Among all the things we have to do, there is nothing important.

12 *Según* mi padre, no tenemos tiempo.
According to my father, we don't have time.

13 Pensamos ir *desde* Buenos Aires *hasta* Córdoba.
We plan to go *from* Buenos Aires *to* Córdoba.

14 Él no habla mucho, *sin embargo* sabe mucho.
He does not talk a lot, *nevertheless* he knows a lot.

15 *Aunque* es muy interesante, no voy a leerlo.
Although it is very interesting, I'm not going to read it.

16 No es *tan* grande *como* tú dices.
It is not *as* big *as* you say.

17 Lo hacemos *a veces.*
We do it *sometimes* (now and then).

18 No quiero ir. *Además* no tengo el dinero.
I don't want to go. *Besides* I don't have the money.

19 No era *ni* gato *ni* león. Era un burro.
It was *neither* a cat *nor* a lion. It was a burro.

20 Let's turn this around in a few frames and see if you can give the Spanish for the indicated words: We went there *before* one o'clock.
Fuimos allí **antes de** *la una.*

21 We *sometimes* go to the beach.
A veces *vamos a la playa.*

22 We study *while* we eat.
Estudiamos **mientras** *comemos.*

23 *Although* it is cold, I'm going to the mountains.
Aunque *hace frío, voy a las montañas.*

No new vocabulary.

Visitors from Latin America who come to the United States are often bothered and upset by the fact that a great many restaurants and cafes in this country do not have tablecloths on their tables. Some have bare tables; others just use place mats. In contrast, a tablecloth is used in most respectable restaurants of Latin America, and it is a *must* of etiquette when guests are invited for dinner in Spanish homes.

PROGRAM **126**

Review of Vocabulary and Idioms

Part 1: Vocabulary Review

In your last Program you were asked to translate a special set of words from Spanish into English. In this Program you are to reverse the process and translate from English to Spanish. Look at the English sentence in each frame, translate the whole sentence *mentally*, then write the Spanish equivalent of the indicated word. The number of words you miss will tell you how much more you need to review your vocabulary.

1 I have *already* seen it.

Ya lo he visto. **2** We eat and *then* we study. (then = next)

*Comemos y **luego** estudiamos.*

3 Pablo *still* has not arrived.

*Pablo no ha llegado **todavía.***

4 *Why* did you (*tú*) say that?

*¿**Por qué** dijiste eso?* (Notice that *por qué* (why) is two separate words in writing, and is stressed *por* **qué**.)

5 I said it *because* it is important.

*Lo dije **porque** es important.* (Note that *porque* (because) is one word in writing, and is stressed ***por**que.*)

6 We did it *after* eating.

*Lo hicimos **después de** cenar.*

7 We did it *before* eating dinner.

*Lo hicimos **antes de** comer.*

8 We did it *while* we were eating.

*Lo hicimos **mientras** cenábamos.*

9 Colombus arrived at the island. *Then* (at that time) he discovered that there were Indians there.

*Colón llegó a la isla. **Entonces** descubrió que había indios allí.*

10 Our house is *between* the river and the mountain.

*Nuestra casa está **entre** el río y la montaña.*

11 *Among* all the things we have to do, there is nothing important.

Entre todas las cosas que tenemos que hacer, no hay nada importante.

12 *According to* my father, we don't have the time.

Según mi padre, no tenemos tiempo.

13 We plan to work *from* 6 *to* 12.

Pensamos trabajar *desde* las seis *hasta* las doce.

14 He does not talk a lot; *nevertheless*, he knows a lot.

Él no habla mucho, *sin embargo* sabe mucho.

15 *Although* it is very interesting, I'm not going to read it.

Aunque es muy interesante, no voy a leerlo.

16 It is not *as* big *as* you (tú) say.

No es *tan* grande *como* tú dices.

17 We do it *sometimes*.

Lo hacemos *a veces*.

18 I don't want to go. *Besides* I don't have the money.

No quiero ir. *Además* no tengo el dinero.

19 It was *neither* a cat *nor* a lion. It was a burro. (You begin the sentence with *No* in Spanish.)

No era *ni* gato *ni* león. Era un burro.

Part 2: Review of Idioms

1 When either the literal meaning or translation of a phrase does not give you a hint as to the meaning of the phrase, then you have an idiom (something peculiar to the language). The literal translation of *Sí, cómo no* is the meaningless phrase "Yes, how no." The proper translation keeps "Yes" and replaces "how no" with ⸺.

of course

2 The meaning of *tener prisa* is "to have haste" (to be in a hurry) and in this pattern *prisa* is a noun. To make a noun describe an action, Spanish normally requires the addition of a relator which merely indicates that the noun is to be treated as a modifier. Since this relator may have only a syntactic function, it frequently has no real meaning and, as a result, often disappears in the English translation. Translate the indicated phrase: *Ella siempre come de prisa.*

quickly (hurriedly)

3 The "by" in "surrounded by" has two meanings in English. In one context it marks the agent in a passive voice construction: "The wagon train was surrounded by the Indians." In another context it merely indicates the locative relationship between entities: "Our house is surrounded by trees." Spanish uses *rodeado* and either *por* or *de* to translate "by." Which relator should be used to translate the second sentence above?

de (*Nuestra casa está rodeada de árboles.*)

4 The translations of *noche, anoche,* and *esta noche* are ⸺.

night, last night, tonight

5 You have already learned a lot of fixed phrases without actually knowing that they are, in fact, idioms. You use the phrase "What such?" as a greeting when you ask another person how things are going. The Spanish is ¿ ⸺ ?

¿Qué tal?

6 The phrase "of nothing" is used to translate "You are welcome." The Spanish is ——.

De nada.   **7** One equivalent of "please" is "for favor." The Spanish is ——.

por favor   **8** You know when to use "nevertheless" in English but no one really knows what "never the less" actually says. This English idiom is translated by the Spanish idiom "without embargo." The Spanish is ——.

sin embargo (Which also translates "however.")

9 The phrase *en todas partes* means to the Spanish speaker "in all parts." So the meaning of *Hay animales en todas partes* is "There are animals in all parts." English, however, says this in a different way. In place of "in all parts" we say ——.

everywhere (We understand, however, the meaning of "in all parts," so *en todas partes* is not an idiom. The two languages just say the same thing in different ways.)

No new vocabulary.

Many American entertainers are astonished and upset when they first play before a Latin American audience. The audience frequently whistles at them noisily and, often, this is interpreted as a sign of displeasure. In actuality, this means that they liked the performance. Both whistling and clapping of hands are ways of showing approval.

PROGRAM **127**

Review of Verb Morphology: a Self-test

There will be a major test very soon and the purpose of this self-test Program is to let you find out whether you need to work more on verb morphology before the test. Go through the Program as rapidly as possible, write each form, check your spelling, and at the end count the number of mistakes. You can then give yourself a grade on the following basis: 3 mistakes = A, 6 = B, 9 = C, 12 = D. If you do not like your grade, go through the *Ejercicios* and *Cuaderno* for more review and practice.

In each frame the indicated infinitive is to be changed to match the subject.

Part 1: Change the infinitive to the Present

1 Yo no *venir* aquí con mucha frecuencia.

vengo   **2** Si yo *salir* ahora llegaré a tiempo.

salgo   **3** Ella no sabe que yo lo *saber* también.

sé

	4 Si yo te lo *dar*, ¿estarás satisfecha?
doy	5 Yo siempre me *poner* furioso al oír eso.
pongo	6 Yo no *ver* nada aquí.
veo	7 He perdido mi dinero. ¿Qué *hacer* ahora?
hago	8 Hay poco viento y las cometas no *volar* bien.
vuelan	9 Ella nunca *volver* a casa antes de las cinco.
vuelve	10 ¿Por qué no *dormir* Vd. bien?
duerme	11 Esta cosa no *servir* para nada.
sirve	12 Mi perro me *seguir* por todas partes.
sigue	13 ¡Cuidado! *Empezar* a llover.
Empieza	

Part 2: Change the infinitive to the Imperfect

	1 Nunca supe lo que ellos *buscar*.
buscaban	2 Nos casamos cuando *tener* 22 años.
teníamos	3 Ella *medir* la tela cuando esto pasó.
medía	4 En aquel tiempo se *ver* muchos indios en este pueblo.
veían	5 Todo el mundo creía que *ser* imposible.
era	6 Yo te dije que *ir* la semana siguiente.
iba	

In a great many homes in the United States, it is considered very impolite to eat with both hands on the table. According to high etiquette, you are supposed to keep one hand on your lap while you eat. In the Hispanic world, keeping one hand hidden while you eat is very impolite. To be polite you must keep both hands on the table, resting your wrists on the edge.

Part 3: Change the infinitive to the Preterit

	1 Y en aquel momento él *oír* una explosión tremenda.
oyó	2 Ellos se asustaron tanto que nunca *volver* a ese lugar.
volvieron	3 Me dijeron que casi se *morir* ellos de miedo.
murieron	4 Después de la tormenta todo *seguir* como antes.
siguió	5 Ella nunca *sentir* lo que hizo.
sintió	6 Él la *conocer* anoche en el baile.
conoció	7 Los dos no se *mirar* durante toda la conversación.
miraron	8 ¿Qué *pensar* ellas?
pensaron	9 Luego salí, lo *buscar* por todas partes, pero no lo encontré.
busqué	10 Eran las tres de la mañana cuando yo *llegar* a casa.
llegué	11 Tenía yo tanto miedo que no *empezar* a hacerlo.
empecé	12 Yo se lo *pedir* varias veces pero nunca me lo dieron.
pedí	13 Cuando yo era joven nunca *aprender* a nadar.
aprendí	

Part 4: Change the infinitive to the Present Perfect

han escrito
ha vuelto
he puesto
hemos dicho

1 Ellos me *escribir* que no pueden visitarnos este año.
2 ¿No *volver* él todavía?
3 Yo nunca lo *poner* en la mesa.
4 Nosotros te *decir* muchas veces que es imposible.

No new vocabulary.

Most Americans consider the bullfight to be a national sport in the Hispanic world. This impression, however, is created primarily by just two countries, Spain and Mexico, although bullfights are also staged regularly in Colombia and Peru and, occasionally in other countries.

What most Americans do not know is that soccer attracts more attention than bullfighting and that cockfights, which are illegal in the United States, are very popular.

PROGRAM **128**

Vocabulary Round-up

The purpose of this Program is to remind you of the things you need to remember about words and help you discover whether you need to do more special vocabulary studying. As you do the Program make a list of those words whose meaning you do not remember. When you are finished, look them up in the end vocabulary and study them.

1 You will make fewer mistakes in Spanish if you classify each word according to what you have to do with it in communication. You need to learn the "meaning" and the "translation" of each word. The meaning of a word is what it tells a Spanish speaker. Thus the meaning of *calor* in *Hace calor* is ――――.

heat
It is hot.
2 The translation of *Hace calor* is not "Makes heat" but ――――.
3 To the Spanish speaker the meaning of *gustar* is the opposite of *disgustar*. The meaning and the translation of *disgustar* are the same, that is, ――――.

to disgust
4 To the Spanish speaker the meaning of *gustar* is "to gust." The most common translation of *gustar*, however, is ――――.

to like
5 Translate: I like this island.
Me gusta esta isla.

6 You also need to know what changes a word may have when you use it to send different messages. For example, any noun which stands for something which can be counted can have two forms in Spanish, a singular and a plural. Which noun in the following list is normally not plural: *huevo, frijol, comida, azúcar, legumbre*?

azúcar (You can talk about eggs, beans, or meals, but not normally about "sugars.")

7 The number word *cien* has an alternate form when it is followed by a smaller number. This form is ~~~~.

ciento

8 The adjective *lindo* can have four forms, *lindo, linda, lindos,* and *lindas*, but the adjective *alegre* can have only two forms. The only other possible form of *alegre* is ~~~~.

alegres

9 How many forms may *difícil* have?

two (The other form is the plural, *difíciles*.)

10 Here are the adjectives you have had which can have only two forms, a singular and a plural. Look them over carefully.

presente	terrible	nacional	alegre	difícil
mi	excelente	popular	grande	inteligente
triste	joven	feliz	amable	caliente
azul	gris	verde	su	fácil
	tu		cruel	

Have you ever paid attention to these facts? With the single exception of *este* and *ese*, adjectives which end in the vowel *e*, *i*, and *u* have only two forms, a singular and a plural. An adjective can have four forms only when one form ends in *a* (*fría*) and another ends in *o* (*frío*) or certain consonants (*español, españoles, española, españolas*).

11 Here are most of the adjectives you have had which can have four forms. Check the list to be sure you know the meaning of each one. Note these all end in *o*.

bueno	tacaño	brasileño	seco	lindo
gordo	paraguayo	bonito	chico	fiero
peruano	bajo	viejo	cuadrado	claro
mucho	cansado	torcido	morado	descansado
alto	recto	redondo	solo	fresco
perfecto	bruto	rosado	malo	último
enfermo	rojo	junto	chileno	pequeño
tonto	negro	ecuatoriano	inmenso	colombiano
anaranjado	frío	nuevo	todo	feo
blanco	limpio	flaco	uruguayo	nuestro
boliviano	magnífico	venezolano	sucio	amarillo
húmedo		argentino		oscuro

Write the three other forms of *blanco*.

blanca, blancos, blancas

12 When you meet a new verb you must, in addition to learning its meaning, memorize its set (*a*, *e*, or *i*) and whether it is regular or irregular. If the verb is irregular, you must also learn what is irregular and in which tense. Here is the list of all the regular *a*-verbs you have had. If there are any whose translation you have forgotten, look them up in the end vocabulary.

abrazar	comprar	hablar	masticar	quebrar
acabar	contestar	hallar	mirar	quedar
arreglar	dejar	invitar	molestar	quitar
ayudar	desayunar	ladrar	nadar	repasar
bailar	desear	lavar	necesitar	terminar
besar	disgustar	levantar	observar	tocar
buscar	entrar	llamar	olvidar	tomar
cantar	esperar	llegar	pasar	trabajar
casar	estudiar	llevar	pintar	tratar
cenar	fumar	madrugar	planchar	usar
	gustar		preguntar	

All of these verbs have two predictable irregularities. The *yo*-form of the Present always has a first suffix which is ⁓.

o

13 The second suffix of the *tú*-form of the Preterit is ⁓.

ste

14 In all other tenses the second suffix of the *tú*-form is ⁓.

s (bailas, bailabas, has bailado, etc.)

15 Here are all the *a*-verbs you have had which are irregular in some way. Look at each verb and try to remember one form that is irregular.

estar	empezar	nevar	recordar	despertar
dar	pensar	llover	cerrar	acostar
sentar	almorzar	jugar	contar	

Write the Preterit of the *ellos*-form of *dar*.

dieron

16 Write the Present of the *yo*-form of *recordar*.

recuerdo

17 Here is the complete list of the regular *e*- and *i*-verbs you have had. Check the meaning of each.

comer	correr	aprender	vivir
beber	responder	vender	subir
deber			

Write the preterit *yo*-form of *aprender* and *escribir*.

aprendí; escribí

18 Here are all the irregular *e*- and *i*-verbs you have had. Try to think of one form of each which is irregular.

ser	morir	pedir	volver	venir
seguir	querer	poner	despedir	conocer
poder	dormir	sentir	traducir	ir
salir	perder	traer	ver	tener
morder	tener	hacer	medir	decir
haber	romper	servir	escribir	mover

Write the *yo*-form of the Present of *tener*, *hacer*, *poner*, *traer*, and *decir*.

tengo, hago, pongo, traigo, digo

19 Because you are learning to write and spell in Spanish, you need to remember what tells you how to spell each word. The sound [s] may be written *s*, *c*, *x*, or *z* in Spanish. Must you remember what you *have seen* in order to spell the words having this sound?

*yes (What you hear will not tell you to write *vez* with a *z* and *veces* with a *c*.)*

20 Here is a helpful fact: when you make a noun or an adjective plural the sound [s] of the plural suffix is always written ⁓⁓.

s

21 Remember this also: when the sound [s] comes directly before another consonant, it is almost always written *s*. Translate: star, island, dress.

estrella, isla, vestido (The exception is *x* as in *explicar.*)

22 Do *b* and *v* stand for the same sounds?

yes

23 What you hear will not tell you whether to write *b* or *v*. Here is a helpful hint: only *b* is used immediately before another consonant. Below are the nouns you have had in which *b* comes directly before another consonant. Notice that in all these words this consonant is either *l* or *r*.

octubre	noviembre	sobrino	libro	población
septiembre	hambre	nombre	broma	impermeable
abril	hombre	sombrero	niebla	blusa
diciembre				

24 Cognates are usually spelled like the English. Look at these words and try to think of an English cognate for each.

vaso	banco	balcón	habitante
banana	brazo	ventana	barco
verdad	avenida	viento	invitación

25 You have to see a word with an *h* in it to learn to spell it. Here are all the words you have had which have an *h*.

hasta	haber	hambre	hermano	héroe
hola	himno	húmedo	historia	hallar
hablar	hora	hijo	habitante	zanahoria
hacer	hombre			

26 The words which are hardest to remember are the little ones such as adverbs and relators. In the remaining frames you will see a single English word. *Think* of its translation and, then, look at the answer. Write any word that you miss on your answer sheet. Here is the first word: already.

ya
27 then (next)

luego
28 still

todavía
29 Why?

¿Por qué?
30 because

porque
31 after

después (de)
32 before

antes (de)
33 while

mientras
34 then (at that time, not *luego* which translates "then" = next.)

entonces
35 between

entre
36 among

entre
37 according to

según
38 nevertheless

sin embargo
39 although

aunque
40 besides

además

No new vocabulary.

It is well-known that each culture has its own favorite foods and dishes. Although Americans eat pizza, wieners, and Chinese food, the traditional dishes are meat, potatos, apple pie, chicken, turkey, hamburger, bread, butter, etc. In Spain butter is quite uncommon. They much prefer olive oil. In Cuba the traditional meat for Christmas dinner is pork. In many parts of the Hispanic world, kids (young goats) are considered a delicacy. In tropical countries the natives eat monkeys. Corn is not a staple in the Peninsular (Spain) diet; it is replaced by rice or potatoes. Rice, corn, beans, and potatoes are common in most of Latin America. The tortillas of Mexico are made from corn flour.

What each group considers a delicacy is often surprising to the other. Ice cream and coca cola are found in every country, but many people drink their cokes *de tiempo* (at air temperature). Cokes and cookies are so foreign in some places that there are no words for them in Spanish. A favorite dessert is like a rich custard called *flan*, something for which we have no word. The same is true for *paella,* a dish made of rice and different meats and fish. In Mexico there is a rather large worm which grows on the *maguey* plant. These worms are harvested, fried crisp, and are sold by street vendors as a special delicacy. The vendors stand on street corners with the worms in a small paper bag tied with a loop of string attached to each finger. They hawk their wares by calling out *gusanillos* (the diminutive of *gusanos* which means "worms.")

When most Americans think of Spanish food they are usually thinking of the extremely hot, spicy food of Mexico. This is not typical for the rest of the Hispanic world.

PROGRAM **129**

Getting Ready for a Major Test

In your next class session you are going to have an important test. This Program, like others you have had before major tests, is designed to give you pre-test practice so you will not make errors. Work through the Program carefully. Use your cover sheet, and if you make a mistake try to figure out why.

1 Part A (10 points) tests your listening comprehension. You will see a number of pictures each with a letter under it. You will hear a statement. For example, you may see a picture of a man on a horse and another of a lady in a shoe shop. Which picture is more logically associated with *La persona que usted ve está en el campo?*

the man on the horse (The lady in the shoe shop is clearly not in the country.)

2 You see three pictures: a desert, a green plain, and a snow-covered mountain. Which one is most logically associated with *Aquí tenemos que usar mucha ropa porque hace mucho frío?*

the snow-covered mountain

3 Part B (8 points) will test your listening and reading comprehension. You will hear eight questions. For each question there will be on your answer sheet three possible responses. You are to pick the most logical one. You may hear, for example, *¿A qué hora llegas a la escuela todos los días?* Which is the most likely answer? On the test you circle the letter of the best response.

    (a) A las cuatro de la madrugada.
    (b) A las ocho de la mañana.
    (c) A las diez de la noche.

A las ocho de la mañana.

4 You hear *¿Por qué fuiste al campo ayer?* Which is the most likely answer?

    (a) Porque era importante hablar con el director de mi escuela.
    (b) Porque tenía mucha hambre y no había pan en casa.
    (c) Porque me gusta caminar.

Porque me gusta caminar.

5 You hear *¿Cuál es el día de la independencia de los Estados Unidos?* Which is the only possible answer?

    (a) El veinticinco de diciembre.
    (b) El catorce de febrero
    (c) El cuatro de julio

El cuatro de julio.

6 In Part C (12 points) you will see two columns of words. One column will be in English, the other in Spanish. You are to match the words that translate each other. You see, for example, *tenedor.* Which word is its translation?
(a) tenant (b) tenor (c) fork

fork

7 You see the Spanish noun *impermeable*. The translation you have learned for this word is (a) impermeable (b) raincoat (c) table cloth.   •

raincoat

8 Part D (12 points) deals with the verb *gustar* and the forms of the involved entity pronouns. The pronouns that match *yo*, *nosotros*, and *tú* are ﹏﹏.   •

me, nos, te

9 The involved entity pronoun that matches *usted*, *él*, and *ella* is ﹏﹏.   •

le

10 The plural of this form is ﹏﹏. It matches *ustedes*, *ellos*, and *ellas*.   •

les

11 In the test you will translate English sentences. Translate: I like to swim.   •

Me gusta nadar.

12 They like to swim.   •

Les gusta nadar. (The infinitive always goes with a singular form of *gustar*.)

13 Translate: We like the shirts.   •

Nos gustan las camisas. (Remember the meaning is "The shirts gust us.")

14 Rewrite the above sentence and make the subject *la camisa*.   •

Nos gusta la camisa.

15 Translate: She likes the car.   •

Le gusta el carro (*coche*).

16 There are three main things you have to remember when you use *gustar*. Here they are:

(1) the involved entity pronouns: *me, nos, te, le, les*
(2) The stimulus and subject of the sentence usually comes after the verb: *Nos gusta **la sopa.***
(3) The verb agrees in number with the subject (the stimulus). Translate: I like the roads.   •

Me gustan los caminos.

17 Here's one last frame to check what you know about *gustar*. Translate: *¿Te gusto yo?*   •

Do you like me? (In Spanish the doer, stimulus, and subject is *yo*. The *te* stands for the involved entity, the person who reacts. The positive response to the above question is *Sí, me gustas tú*—Yes, I like you.)

18 Part E (14 points) of the test deals with the Preterit of irregular verbs. There will be a sentence with an infinitive in parentheses. You are to write the Preterit of this infinitive. For example: *Ellos los . . .* (*poner*) *en el avión.*   •

pusieron

19 No me . . . (decir) tú la verdad.   •

dijiste

20 ¿Qué . . . (hacer) usted ayer?   •

hizo

21 Here is a list of all the verbs you have had which have irregular preterit forms. Check each verb and be certain you know how to spell the forms.

poner	dar	dormir	seguir	venir
despedir	ser	sentir	pedir	morir
ir	decir	servir	creer	hacer

22 Part F (14 points) is going to test your ability to make up the forms of the Present Perfect. You have to remember (1) the present tense forms of *haber*, (2) whether the perfect participle is regular or irregular, and (3) how to make up the participle. In the test you will see a sentence in Spanish. The verb will be in the Present. You write the equivalent of the verb in the Present Perfect. For example: *Alfredo escribe la lección.*   •

ha escrito
han vendido

23 Ellos venden su carro.

24 No leo la carta.

he leído 25 ¿Lo compra usted?

ha comprado 26 Part G (14 points) deals with the demonstratives. You have to select the one that indicates the proper distance from the speaker and you have to make it agree with its noun. You will see a Spanish sentence with the demonstrative in English. You write the correct Spanish equivalent. For example: ¿De quién es (*this*) pluma que tengo en la mano?

esta 27 ¿No ves (*that*) edificio allí en la montaña?

aquel 28 Por favor, déme (*those*) libros que están en la mesa cerca de usted.

esos 29 Me gustan (*these*) camisas que acabo de comprar.

estas 30 Me gusta (*that*) vestido que tienes puesto.

ese 31 Part H (8 points) will test your reading comprehension. You will read a part of a sentence and, then, three possible completions. You are to select the best or most likely completion. You see, for example, *No puedo ir al cine esta noche* ... Which is the best completion? Remember, on the test you circle the letter before the best completion.

   (a) porque tengo tres tíos.

   (b) porque tengo mucha hambre.

   (c) porque tengo poco dinero.

porque tengo poco dinero

32 Here is the way this part will look on the exam:
Cuando como lechuga yo uso ...

   (a) una cuchara.

   (b) un cuchillo.

   (c) un tenedor.

un tenedor 33 Me gusta mucho ir al centro porque hay ...

   (a) muchos animales feroces allí.

   (b) mucho dinero en el banco.

   (c) muchas cosas interesantes allí.

muchas cosas interesantes allí

34 El país de Sudamérica donde hablan portugués es ...

   (a) Uruguay.

   (b) Brasil.

   (c) Paraguay.

Brasil 35 Part I, the last part of the exam (8 points), also measures your reading comprehension. You will see a statement or a question and three possible responses. You are to pick the most likely or logical response. You see, for example, *Yo tengo muchos amigos en México*. Which is the most likely response?

   (a) Nosotros somos de Chile.

   (b) ¿Has viajado en México?

   (c) Eres un hombre muy inteligente.

¿Has viajado en México?

36 Mis tíos viven en una casa pequeña de Santa Fe.

   (a) ¡Felicidades! Es importante tener tíos.

   (b) ¿Cuántos años tienen ellos ahora?

   (c) Me gustan mucho las islas del Mar Caribe.

¿Cuántos años tienen ellos ahora?

No new vocabulary.

In most American small towns or villages the streets have names. There is Main Street or First Street, etc., and, usually, signs on the street corners which give these names. In many Latin American small towns and villages (and even in some larger towns) the streets are not named. As a result, when a stranger wants to find somebody's home he has to be directed by landmarks such as "go to the church, turn left to the banana grove, then cross the bridge to the right, and stop at the house with a broken green shutter on the left upper window."

Ejercicios

Ejercicio 137 | Silent Reading

Read the following selections without stopping to translate into English. Then answer *sí* or *no* to the questions at the end.

¿ Sabía usted . . .

1

. . . que el arroz con pollo es un plato° típico de España y muy popular en Hispanoamérica? Lo preparan generalmente en ocasiones especiales, por ejemplo, la comida de los domingos, los días de fiesta, reuniones de familia o cuando tienen invitados. Además de° los ingredientes básicos, arroz y pollo, la receta° incluye también pimienta, sal, ajo,° cebolla,° aceite de oliva, laurel, pimientos y huevo. Para darle color amarillo al arroz usan un poco de azafrán.° Mucha gente le pone también pedazos° de jamón y un poco de vino° seco. La preparación de este delicioso plato requiere experiencia y mucho cuidado. Si no se hace bien, los resultados pueden ser desastrosos. En los principales hoteles y restaurantes sirven con frecuencia el arroz con pollo.

°dish

°Besides
recipe/garlic/
onion
saffron
pieces/wine

2

. . . que cuando vinieron los españoles a Ecuador, Perú y Bolivia, los incas ya conocían el sistema de secar° las papas? Las papas secas que las amas de casa° modernas pueden preparar casi instantáneamente no son un invento reciente. El chuño que los indios de la región andina todavía comen en nuestros días son papas secas. La papa o patata, como se llama en España, es originaria de la región del lago Titicaca. Los españoles la llevaron a España en el siglo XVI (dieciséis) para alimentar° a los animales. Como alimento humano, el uso de la papa no se generalizó en Europa hasta cien años más tarde. Ya en el siglo XIX (diecinueve) la papa era considerada como un alimento de primera importancia en muchos países europeos. En 1846, por ejemplo, cuando una epidemia destruyó la cosecha° de papas en Irlanda, más de 600.000 personas murieron de hambre.

°to dry/
housewives

°to feed

°crop

¿ Sí o no?

1

1 En los países de habla española nunca comen arroz.

2 Algunas personas ponen pedazos de jamón en el arroz con pollo.

3 En Argentina las amas de casa preparan arroz con pollo por lo menos (*at least*) dos veces al día.

4 El arroz con pan es un plato típico muy común en Hispanoamérica y en España.

5 En los países de habla española el arroz con pollo **es un** plato típico para los días de invierno.

6 El azafrán es una sustancia que le da color amarillo a la comida.

2

7 Los incas de Perú podían comer papas durante todo el año.

8 En el siglo XIX (diecinueve) los irlandeses (habitantes de Irlanda) no conocían las papas.

9 Los incas secaban las papas para poder comerlas durante todo el año.

10 Los indios de Perú y Bolivia preparan un alimento de maíz que se llama chuño.

Ejercicio 138 | Silent Reading

Read the selections and answer the following questions with *sí* or *no*.

¿ Sabía usted . . .

1

. . . que en Brasil hay una montaña que se llama Pan de Azúcar? El nombre en portugués es Pão de Açucar.

. . . que en España el maíz° es principalmente un alimento° para los animales? En América, sin embargo, es el ingrediente básico de cientos de platos típicos.

corn/food

. . . que en los supermercados° de nuestro país venden carne en lata° que viene de la América del Sur? La carne es uno de los productos principales de Argentina, Brasil, Uruguay y Paraguay. La procesan en plantas enormes que se llaman frigoríficos.

supermarkets/ can

2

. . . que antes del siglo XIX en Europa solamente la gente rica podía tomar chocolate? El ingrediente básico del chocolate es el cacao, el fruto de un árbol° originario de México. Hoy día hay grandes plantaciones de cacao en Ecuador, Brasil, Colombia y muchas otras regiones tropicales del mundo. El árbol de cacao es pequeño y muy delicado. Requiere un clima caliente, tierra rica, lluvias abundantes y protección contra el viento. Los aztecas creían que el cacao era de origen divino. Según sus leyendas, el dios Quetzalcóatl lo trajo° a México y les enseñó° a cultivarlo. Además de utilizar los granos° de cacao como moneda,° los indios mexicanos lo usaban también para hacer chocolate, una bebida

tree

brought
taught/grains
money

amarga° que servían fría al fin de las comidas. La receta° para preparar la bebida favorita de Moctezuma incluye cacao molido,° agua, chile y especias.° Desde que° Hernán Cortés llevó el cacao a España en 1529, la fórmula para la preparación del chocolate ha cambiado mucho a través de° los años. El gusto° español lo hizo dulce y los ingleses lo hicieron más nutritivo usando leche en su preparación en lugar de agua.

bitter/recipe
ground/spices
Since
through/taste

¿ Sí o no ?

1

1 En algunos mercados (*markets*) de los Estados Unidos es posible comprar carne paraguaya.
2 Los habitantes del norte de España comen maíz casi todos los días.
3 Una montaña de Brasil tiene el nombre de una sustancia muy dulce.
4 Las plantas donde preparan la carne en algunos países latinoamericanos se llaman frigoríficos.

2

5 El chocolate que bebían los aztecas era demasiado dulce.
6 En las regiones ecuatoriales donde llueve mucho y hace calor hay grandes plantaciones de cacao.
7 Los aztecas tomaban chocolate muy caliente antes de las comidas.
8 Cuando los españoles llevaron el cacao a Europa, inmediatamente millones de personas en Roma, París y Londres empezaron a desayunarse con chocolate.
9 El viento y la nieve favorecen el cultivo de los árboles de cacao.
10 La manera de preparar el chocolate no ha cambiado nada a través de los siglos.

Ejercicio 139 | Silent Reading

Read the following selection and do the true-false comprehension exercise following it.

El nombre de este personaje histórico es . . .

(primera parte)

Este gran hombre de acción era del pequeño e insignificante pueblo de Trujillo que está en la provincia de Extremadura. De esta región de España salieron muchos de los exploradores y conquistadores que vinieron al Nuevo Mundo.

Los expertos no han podido determinar todavía el año exacto en que nació. Casi todos han dicho que fue entre los años de 1471 y 1478.

Los historiadores que han escrito biografías de este famoso personaje dicen que durante su infancia vivió en la pobreza y la ignorancia. Pasó° muchos trabajos° y mucha hambre.

He underwent
hardships

Su padre era oficial de infantería y su madre una mujer del pueblo de baja condición. No estaban casados. Dicen algunos libros que la madre abandonó a su hijo en el portal de una iglesia cuando era muy pequeño.

Este hombre que llegó a ser gobernador de un vasto territorio en la América del Sur y que recibió del rey el título de marqués fue analfabeto durante toda su vida. (La palabra "analfabeto" quiere decir que no sabía leer ni escribir.) Cuentan° las leyendas que en vez de° asistir° a la escuela, el pobre muchachito tenía que ir a los campos todos los días a cuidar° puercos.°

Cuando tenía que firmar° algún documento importante, lo hacía con una cruz. Otras veces su secretario le escribía el nombre, y él ponía la rúbrica:

Su nombre de pila (primer nombre) es igual que° la segunda parte de una ciudad muy bonita en la costa norte de California. Comienza con la letra *F*.

say/instead of/ attending take care of/ pigs sign

the same as

¿ Sí o no ?

Ejercicio: ¿Comprendió usted lo que leyó? Indique la respuesta escribiendo *sí* o *no* después de cada número.

1 El hombre famoso de quien hablamos era de una ciudad española muy populosa e importante.

2 Gran número de los conquistadores que vinieron a América en el siglo XVI (dieciséis) eran de Extremadura.

3 Los expertos dicen que es casi seguro (*sure*) que este hombre nació en 1267.

4 Una biografía es la historia de la vida de una persona.

5 La frase "pasó muchos trabajos" quiere decir que tuvo muchos problemas y dificultades.

6 Su padre era militar.

7 Su madre era una señora muy rica y de una familia noble y distinguida.

8 La madre lo abandonó cuando era niño en el portal de un hotel muy elegante.

9 La palabra "marqués" se refiere a un título de nobleza. También los príncipes, las princesas y los condes son personas nobles.

10 Las personas que saben leer y escribir las letras del alfabeto son analfabetos.

11 Una rúbrica no es un nombre. Llamamos rúbrica a las líneas que acompañan la firma (*signature*) de una persona.

12 El nombre de pila de este hombre famoso es Antonio.

Ejercicio 140 | Silent Reading

Read the following selection once without stopping to translate every word. As soon as you finish, answer the multiple-choice comprehension questions that follow.

El apellido de este personaje histórico es . . .

(segunda parte)

Antes de salir para La Española (Isla de Santo Domingo) en la primera década del siglo XVI (dieciséis), este personaje cuyo° nombre de pila empieza con *F* tomó parte en las campañas del ejército° español en Italia. Fue un excelente soldado que demostró tener una energía fantástica y extraordinario valor.°

whose

army

bravery

En Santo Domingo se encontró° con su primo Hernán Cortés, el futuro con-   met
quistador de México. En 1509 pasó a la colonia española que se llamaba entonces Castilla del Oro en el territorio que es hoy Panamá. Cortés iba a salir
en el mismo barco, pero a última hora se enfermó y tuvo que° quedarse atrás.°   had to/behind

En Panamá este capitán español cruzó el istmo en compañía de Vasco Núñez
de Balboa y fue uno de los primeros europeos que vieron el Océano Pacífico.
También presenció° en 1517 la trágica muerte de Balboa que fue decapitado   witnessed
por orden de Pedrarias Dávila, uno de los gobernadores más ambiciosos y per-
versos que ha tenido el continente. ("Decapitar" significa cortarle la cabeza a
una persona.)

La vida de nuestro personaje en su finca (rancho) de Panamá era relativa-
mente tranquila y bastante cómoda. No era rico, pero tenía las tierras que
necesitaba y suficientes indios para trabajarlas. Sin embargo, los años pasaban
rápidamente y le molestaba no ser más que un humilde° agricultor (ranchero).   humble

Un día llegaron a Panamá las noticias de la conquista de México. Su primo
Hernán, mucho más joven que él, era el gran héroe del día. Aunque ya tenía
casi cincuenta años, el viejo soldado sintió nuevamente el deseo de buscar fama
y fortuna y salió a explorar la costa oeste de la América del Sur por la parte que
es hoy Colombia, Ecuador y Perú.

En lecciones futuras vamos a leer otras cosas interesantes que hizo el conquistador del Birú o Pirú. Si todavía algunos de ustedes no saben cuál fue su
apellido, este último detalle les va a ayudar a recordarlo. Piensen en la palabra
española que indica el lugar de la clase donde podemos escribir con tiza.
Empieza con la letra *P*.

Ejercicio: ¿Entendió usted la selección que acaba de leer? Vamos a ver si puede
demostrarlo seleccionando la letra que corresponde a la respuesta correcta.

1 El nombre de pila del conquistador de quien hablamos en las dos últimas
lecciones de lectura (*reading*) es . . .
   a Faustino.
   b Francisco.
   c Felipe.

2 En este momento todos los alumnos de la clase deben saber ya que su
apellido era . . .
   a Pizarra.
   b Pirú.
   c Pizarro.

3 Un ejército se compone de . . .
   a gobernadores.
   b rancheros o agricultores.
   c soldados.

4 Hernán Cortés Pizarro, el conquistador de los aztecas, y Francisco Pizarro
Morales, el conquistador de los incas, eran . . .
   a primos.
   b enemigos.
   c hermanos.

5 Cortés no fue a Panamá en la misma expedición en que fue Pizarro porque . . .

    a le gustaba más vivir en La Española.

    b estaba enfermo a la hora de salir.

    c tenía que arreglar un barco que se rompió la noche antes.

6 Cerca del lugar donde está hoy la ciudad de Panamá, Pizarro trabajó varios años en . . .

    a una mina de oro.

    b una finca que le dieron por servir al rey.

    c la oficina del gobernador Pedrarias Dávila.

7 Balboa, el descubridor del Mar del Sur (Pacífico), murió de una manera muy trágica en . . .

    a España.

    b la isla de Santo Domingo.

    c la región del istmo de Panamá.

8 Los adjetivos que mejor describen el carácter y la personalidad del gobernador Pedrarias Dávila son . . .

    a dulce y sensitivo.

    b cruel y sanguinario.

    c inteligente y honorable.

9 Los adjetivos que mejor describen a Francisco Pizarro son . . .

    a tímido y cobarde.

    b enfermizo y delicado.

    c enérgico y valiente.

Ejercicio 141 | Pre-Test Practice: Listening and Reading Comprehension

Your teacher will read a question *once*. From the three choices below, select the letter corresponding to the answer.

    1 **a** De la mano a la boca se pierde la sopa.

        b Más vale estar solo que mal acompañado.

        c Antes que te cases, mira lo que haces.

    2 **a** ¿Cómo te va?

        b Que te vaya bien.

        c Buen provecho.

    3 **a** El desayuno.

        b El almuerzo.

        c La cena.

4 **a** Es mucho mejor estar solo.

   b Es mejor estar solo y también mal acompañado.

   c Más vale estar mal acompañado.

5 **a** Primero puse el mantel.

   b Primero puse leche en los vasos.

   c Primero puse zanahorias en los platos para ensalada.

6 **a** Un poco de postre.

   b Un poco de sal y pimienta.

   c Lechuga fresca.

7 **a** Sí, Adriana me rompió el reloj.

   b Sí, jugué todo el día con mis amigos.

   c Sí, comí demasiado y me enfermé.

Ejercicio 142 | Pre-Test Practice: Reading Comprehension

Read the following sentences and select the most logical completion for each.

1 Para el desayuno yo siempre tomo café con crema y . . .
   a zanahorias.
   b una ensalada de legumbres.
   c dos huevos.

2 Más vale estar solo que . . .
   a con una persona que vive lejos.
   b con gente de mala influencia.
   c con parientes de otro país.

3 No tengo mi traje de baño; por eso no puedo . . .
   a romper el reloj del invitado.
   b tener más hambre que Tomás.
   c nadar en el lago.

4 Los muchachos no bailan con ella porque . . .
   a es muy gorda y tiene los pies gigantescos.
   b siempre usa un vestido muy lindo en los bailes.
   c tiene solamente cinco dedos en cada mano.

5 Pancho me dijo que no se divirtió en el baile el sábado pasado porque . . .
   a se cayó y se rompió los pantalones.
   b tenía que bailar con una muchacha muy bonita.
   c sirvieron solamente los postres que a él le gustaban.

6 Páseme usted la crema.
   a Me gusta mucho el azúcar.
   b No me gusta el café negro.
   c Me gusta la leche caliente.

Ejercicio 143 | Pre-Test Practice: Reading Comprehension

Read the following sentences and select the most logical response or rejoinder for each.

1 Yo vivo en la calle Almendro, número 43321.
   a Que te vaya muy bien, amigo.
   b Eso debe estar bastante lejos de aquí.
   c El hombre que maneja el autobús está muy cansado.

2 ¿Vas a cruzar la calle aquí?
   a Sí, voy a tener mucho cuidado.
   b Sí, el agua está muy alta en aquel río.
   c No, el gato viejo se ha muerto.

3 Dígame usted, ¿le gusta bailar con Antonio?
   a Sí, él es un niño tan pequeño que no ha aprendido a caminar todavía.
   b Sí, porque él trata de aprender todos los bailes modernos.
   c ¿Cómo le puedo contestar si no sé la fecha?

4 Ellos siempre sirven una bebida deliciosa para la cena los domingos.
   a Creo que la hacen con huevos, leche y azúcar.
   b Este jugo de jamón está delicioso.
   c Crema, azúcar, jugo de tomate, todos se venden en aquella tienda.

5 Hombre, no te pongas esos pantalones viejos.
   a Tengo que buscar el menú para el almuerzo.
   b La bandera de su tierra nativa está a una altura de veinte pies.
   c ¿Por qué me dices eso?

Ejercicio 144 | Agreement of Demonstratives

Write the combinations that your teacher will give you one at a time and correct your work by the example on the board.

Ejemplo: 355 = Aquel es un suéter rojo.

1 Est-´		**1** corbatas	**1** amarill-.	
2 Es-	es	**2** un traje	**2** blanc- y negr-.	
3 Aquel(l)-	son	**3** vestidos	**3** azul.	
		4 una camisa	**4** verde.	
		5 un suéter	**5** roj-.	

Ejercicio 145 | Present Perfect

Write the combinations that your teacher will give you one at a time and correct your work by the example on the board. Change the first infinitive in the second column to the Present Perfect.

Ejemplo: 55 = Esos señores se han levantado temprano.

1 Yo	**1** traer zanahorias.
2 Pepe y yo	**2** creer en Dios.

3 Usted	**3** tratar de hacerlo.
4 Tú	**4** dormirse.
5 Esos señores	**5** levantarse temprano.

Ejercicio 146 | Present Perfect

Write the combinations that your teacher will give you one at a time and correct your work by the example on the board. All verbs in the second column should be Present Perfect.

Ejemplo: 122 = Graciela ha traído estas blusas amarillas.

1 Graciela	**1** ver	
2 Nosotras	**2** traer	**1** ese sombrero azul.
3 Graciela y tú	**3** ponerse	**2** estas blusas amarillas.
4 Tú	**4** hacer	**3** aquel suéter verde.
5 Yo	**5** quitarse	**4** aquellos zapatos grises.

Ejercicio 147 | Preterit versus Imperfect

After reading the following letter from Pilar to her cousin Lola, imagine that you are telling somebody about its content by completing the blanks in the exercise with the appropriate form of the Preterit or the Imperfect.

> Avenida del Sol 168
> Albuquerque, Nuevo México
> Enero 16 de 1972

Querida prima Lola,

El martes pasado recibí tu carta. ¡Qué bueno que vas a poder venir a visitarme en las próximas vacaciones de primavera!

El viernes, gracias a Dios, terminé mi último examen del primer semestre. Estudié muchísimo y recibí notas° excelentes en todas mis asignaturas.° Mis padres están muy contentos conmigo.   grades/subjects

El próximo° fin de semana pensamos ir a esquiar° en las montañas. Papá tiene un poco de gripe en estos días y no se siente muy bien, pero mamá y yo creemos que muy pronto va a estar completamente bien. Ya tenemos reservaciones en el hotel para el viernes y el sábado.   next/ski

¿Te dije que durante las vacaciones de Navidad pasamos tres días con tío Eugenio en Guadalajara? No te puedes imaginar cómo nos divertimos. Una noche fuimos todos a comer en un restaurante muy elegante. Papá y mamá pidieron arroz con pollo, pero yo pedí comida típica mexicana. ¡Qué platos tan deliciosos hacen en México!

Escríbeme pronto. Muchos besos y abrazos para todos.

Sabes te quiere, tu prima,

Pilar

Ejercicio: Pilar le dijo a su prima Lola en la carta . . .

    1 que el martes pasado ella . . . (recibir) su carta.
    2 que el viernes pasado, ella . . . (terminar) sus exámenes de semestre.

3 que ella . . . (estudiar) muchísimo para sus exámenes.

4 que sus padres . . . (estar) muy contentos.

5 que ella y su familia . . . (pensar) ir a esquiar en las montañas.

6 que su papá . . . (tener) un poco de gripe.

7 que él no se . . . (sentir) bien.

8 que ella y su mamá . . . (creer) que el papá . . . (ir) a estar completamente bien muy pronto.

9 que ella y su familia . . . (tener) reservaciones en el hotel.

10 que durante las vacaciones de Navidad ella y su familia . . . (pasar) tres días en Guadalajara en casa de su tío Eugenio.

11 que todos se . . . (divertir) mucho en México.

12 que una noche todos . . . (ir) a comer en un restaurante.

13 que los padres de ella pidieron arroz con pollo, pero ella . . . (pedir) comida mexicana.

Ejercicio 148 | Demonstratives

Write the translation of the demonstratives one at a time. Do not start on the next one until after you have corrected your work by the example on the board.

1 (*This*) comida está deliciosa.

2 ¿ De quién son (*these*) blusas ?

3 (*That*) suéter que usted usa es muy lindo.

4 Vamos por (*this*) camino.

5 ¡ Qué amarillos son (*those*) plátanos allí !

6 (*Those*) manzanas que tú tienes deben ser muy buenas.

7 ¿ No quieres traerme (*that*) periódico que está allí cerca de la ventana ?

8 Todavía no he visto (*that*) revista que tienes.

9 Es muy fácil leer (*those*) palabras allí en la pizarra.

10 (*Those*) zapatos nuevos que ustedes tienen son muy feos.

Ejercicio 149 | Demonstratives

Translate the demonstratives into Spanish.

1 Aquí en (*this*) casa grande vivo yo con mis padres; ahí en (*that*) apartamento detrás del garaje viven mis abuelos; y allí en (*that*) edificio alto que puedes ver en la distancia tienen su apartamento mis tíos.

2 ¿ Por qué no lees tú (*this*) libro que tengo aquí, y yo leo (*that*) novela corta que tienes en tu bolsillo (*pocket*) ?

3 (*Those*) corbatas que tienes en la mano son muy finas.

4 (*These*) papeles que tengo aquí en mi mesa son muy importantes.

5 (*Those*) aviones que vuelan allá muy lejos por las nubes van muy rápido.

6 (*Those*) huevos que comes no tienen sal.

7 (*Those*) montañas allá muy lejos en el horizonte que casi no podemos ver son los Andes.

Ejercicio 150 | *Gustar* with Involved Entity Pronouns

Write the combinations that your teacher will give you one at a time. Correct your work by the example on the board.

Ejemplo: 12 = A Cristina le gusta el postre.

1 A Cristina		**1** las legumbres.
2 A mí		**2** el postre.
3 A ti	gusta(n)	**3** los huevos.
4 A Alfredo y a mí		**4** el queso.
5 A ustedes		**5** la crema y el azúcar.

Ejercicio 151 | Present Perfect

Change the indicated verbs to the Present Perfect.

Ejemplo: ¿A dónde *va* ella? → ¿A dónde *ha ido* ella?

1 *Voy* a la tienda.
2 *Trabajan* dos horas.
3 *Vemos* la televisión juntos.
4 ¿*Vuelves* a la escuela hoy?
5 ¿Quién lo *rompe*?
6 *Leen* la carta.
7 *Venimos* con ellos.
8 No lo *hago* bien.
9 Pero, hermano, ¿qué me *dices*?
10 Nadie lo *sabe.*

Ejercicio 152 | Present Perfect

Change the indicated verbs to the Present Perfect.

Ejemplo: Tomás *nada* mucho. → Tomás *ha nadado* mucho.

1 Me *disgusta* todo esto.
2 *Cenamos* bastante tarde.
3 Me *dicen* muchas cosas.
4 María *baila* conmigo.
5 ¿*Hablas* con Manuel?
6 Yo lo *leo* también.
7 El pobre se *muere.*
8 ¿Qué *haces*, hombre?
9 Yo *pongo* la mesa.
10 María y yo lo *vemos* desde aquí.

Ejercicio 153 | Preterit versus Imperfect

After reading the complete sentence in which the numbered verb appears, decide whether it should be changed to the Preterit or to the Imperfect.

Un perro que ladra y sí muerde

Es cierto que el refrán español dice que un "perro que ladra no muerde." Pero también hay otro refrán que dice: "No hay regla sin excepción."

Entre° los perros que ha tenido mi familia recuerdo a Pepito ... un simpático° chihuahua que *ladra* (1) mucho y, cada vez° que tiene (tenía) la oportunidad, también *muerde* (2). Es (Era) el enemigo público número uno del lechero, el cartero, el basurero° y de todas las personas que *vienen* (3) a nuestra casa a arreglar° o vender algo.

    Among

    cute/whenever

    garbage man

    fix

Un día *viene* (4) un hombre de la compañía de teléfonos a investigar un problema que *tenemos* (5) en la extensión de mi papá. Cuando Pepito lo *ve* (6), *empieza* (7) a ladrar como un loco. Aunque es (era) un animal muy pequeño, hace (hacía) tanto ruido,° que el pobre señor del teléfono está (estaba) bastante nervioso y le *dice* (8) a mi mamá que a él no le *gustan* (9) los perros. Inmediatamente, mamá *pone* (10) a Pepito en el patio y le *da* (11) un poco de agua para calmarlo. Unos minutos más tarde, accidentalmente, mi hermanito abre (abrió) la puerta del patio. Pepito entra (entró) en la casa como una flecha,° *va* (12) a donde está (estaba) el antipático intruso° y le *muerde* (13) una pierna. Afortunadamente, sus pequeños dientes no penetran (penetraron) el fuerte material de los pantalones.

    noise

    arrow

    hated intruder

Después de este incidente, mi mamá deja (dejó) de creer en refranes. Cada vez° que viene (venía) alguien que no es (era) de la familia a la casa, *pone* (14) a Pepito en su jaula.° Allí el furioso y feroz guardián de nuestros intereses ladra (ladraba) incansablemente hasta que se van (iban), pero no *puede* (15) salir a morderlos.

    time

    cage

Ejercicio 154 | Preterit versus Imperfect

Change the indicated verbs to the Preterit or the Imperfect.

Sola° en la casa

    Alone

Cada vez° que sus padres *salen* (1) de noche y la *dejan* (2) sola° en la casa, Lola *cierra* (3) todas las puertas y las ventanas. Aunque ya *tiene* (4) 15 años, es (era) una muchacha muy miedosa.°

    time/alone

    fearful

Son (5) las once y media de un martes por la noche y Lola está (estaba) sola en la casa. Cuando menos° lo espera (esperaba), *oye* (6) un ruido° en el garaje.

    least/noise

—¿Quién está ahí? —pregunta (preguntó) Lola.

No contesta (contestó) nadie.

—¡Qué tonta soy! Debe ser el gato. —piensa (pensó).

Se sienta (7) en el sofá a leer una revista. Otra vez° ruidos en el garaje.   Again
Alguien quiere (quería) abrir la puerta. Lola se *levanta* (8) del sofá y *pone°* (9)   turns on
el televisor.

"Interrumpimos este programa para dar una noticia importante. Acaba de escapar del hospital del estado un loco . . ."

¡Qué desesperación! ¡El teléfono! ¡La policía! ¡Los vecinos! ¿Qué hacer? En el momento en que vienen (venían) todas estas ideas a la mente° de la histérica   mind
muchacha, alguien *llama* (10) a la puerta.

—¿Quién es? —*grita* (gritó) desesperada.

—Abre, hija. Somos nosotros—*contesta* (contestó) una voz desde afuera.

Lola *reconoce* (reconoció) la voz de su padre y le *da* (dio) gracias a Dios.

Ejercicio 155 | Irregular Preterits

Write the preterit form of the infinitive in parentheses.

1 ¿Quién . . . (poner) la mesa anoche?
2 Yo la . . . (poner).
3 ¿A dónde . . . (ir) tú anoche?
4 Yo . . . (ir) a la estación de ferrocarril.
5 Abelardo te . . . (decir) eso, ¿verdad?
6 No, Abelardo y su amiga Adriana me lo . . . (decir).
7 Primero ellos . . . (venir) y luego ellos nos . . . (dar) el regalo.
8 Genoveva . . . (hacer) un viaje a Asunción.
9 Cuando usted me lo . . . (decir), yo no . . . (hacer) nada.

Ejercicio 156 | Present Perfect

Back-shift the indicated verbs to the Present Perfect.

1 El pobre gato *muere*.
2 Sí, yo·*vuelvo*.
3 Usted *hace* una ensalada magnífica.
4 Todos *decimos* que no *vemos* nada.
5 Tú *escribes* bastante.
6 ¿*Viven* ustedes en la calle Estancia?
7 ¿Quiénes *leen* las revistas?
8 No *oigo* absolutamente nada.
9 No lo *rompes* frecuentemente.
10 Él y yo no *recordamos* nada.

Ejercicio 157 | Demonstratives

Translate the demonstratives into Spanish.

1 ¿De quién es (*this*) leche?
2 (*This*) es mi amigo Alberto Gómez.
3 ¿Ves (*that*) avión allí?
4 ¿De quién es (*that*) dirección que tienes ahí?
5 (*These*) papas son las mejores.
6 Hazme el favor de darme uno de (*those*) tenedores que tienes.
7 (*Those*) huevos allí son malos.
8 Vamos a comprar (*those*) calcetines que vimos ayer en (*that*) tienda allá en el centro.

Ejercicio 158 | Vocabulary Matching

Match each Spanish word with its corresponding English equivalent.

1 provecho		a	he fixes
2 impermeable		b	necktie
3 dirección		c	socks
4 almuerzo		d	cloud
5 acompaña		e	profit
6 arregla		f	he irons
7 nube		g	carrot
8 corbata		h	he accompanies
9 huevo		i	cup
10 zanahoria		j	lunch
11 taza		k	raincoat
12 plancha		l	egg
		m	address

Ejercicio 159 | Present Perfect

Change the indicated verbs to the Present Perfect.

1 *Escribimos* la carta en español.
2 Ellos la *leen*.
3 Me *dicen* muchas cosas.
4 María *baila* conmigo.
5 ¿*Hablas* con Manuel?
6 Yo lo *leo* también.
7 El pobre se *muere*.
8 ¿Qué *haces*, hombre?
9 Yo *pongo* la mesa.
10 María y yo la *vemos* desde aquí.

Ejercicio 160 | General Review

Select a partner and perform twice the following dialog in Spanish. Change roles the second time.

1 You tell your brother (or sister) that you are going downtown.
2 He asks you why (*por qué*) you are going downtown.
3 You answer that you are going to buy new shoes.
4 He says that he wants to go with you (*contigo*).
5 You say that you are going to the show afterwards (*después*).
6 He says, fine, that he still (*todavía*) wants to go with you.
7 You ask him if he has money.
8 He answers, yes, a little; enough to go (*para ir*) to the show.
9 You say that you have to find your sweater.
10 He says that he is going to help you.

Ejercicio 161 | General Review

Work with a partner and take turns asking and answering the following questions.

¿ Cuál es la fecha de hoy ?
¿ A qué hora te levantaste esta mañana ?
¿ Te desayunaste ?
¿ Viniste a la escuela con un amigo ?
¿ Fuiste al cine anoche ?
¿ De qué color son los pantalones de ... (nombre de un muchacho de tu clase) ?
¿ De qué color es la blusa de ... (nombre de una muchacha de tu clase) ?

Ejercicio 162 | General Review

Work with a partner. Ask and answer the following questions.

¿ A qué hora te despertaste esta mañana ?
¿ Comiste mucho para el desayuno ?
¿ Cuándo llegaste a la escuela ?
¿ Qué día es hoy ?
¿ Qué tiempo hace ahora ?
¿ Cuántos dedos tienes en los pies ?
¿ De qué color es la camisa de ... (nombre de un muchacho en tu clase) ?
¿ De qué color es el vestido de ... (nombre de una muchacha en tu clase) ?
¿ Quién llegó tarde a clase hoy ?

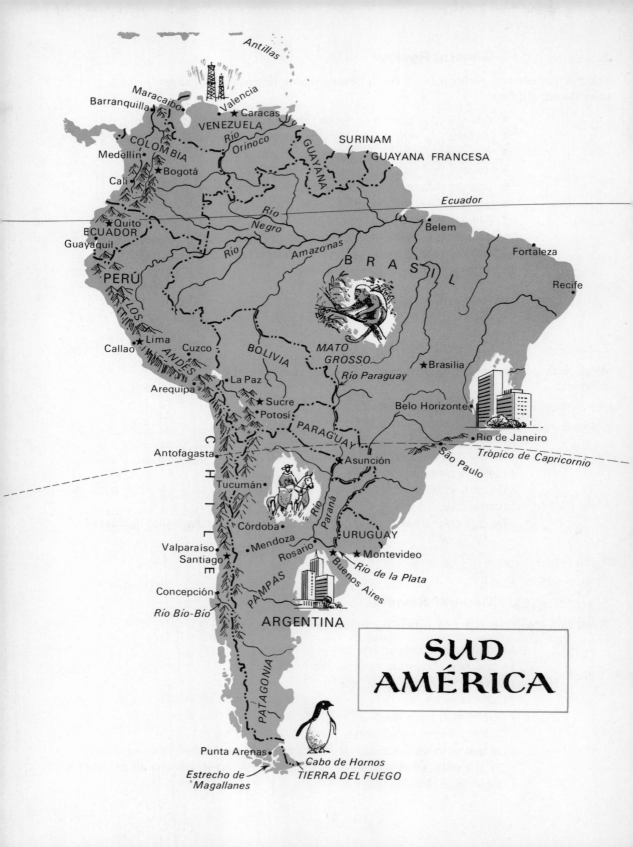

APPENDIX I: NOTAS CULTURALES

Learning Spanish involves more than mastering the skills of hearing and saying new sounds or studying new and often conflicting ways of arranging words into sentences. To understand, appreciate, and enjoy Spanish, you need to learn as much as you can about the people who speak this language, their way of life, and the varied nations and regions of the world they live in.

These "Notas Culturales" are an outline of basic information about each of the major countries of South America. Because of its importance in the Pan-American family, Portuguese-speaking Brazil has also been included.

The "Notas Culturales" are used with the classroom map activities and general reviews of information about South America. You will be asked to refer to this section from time to time when you role-play the native from your "adopted" country. The nations are grouped as follows: Venezuela and Colombia; Ecuador, Bolivia, and Perú; Chile, Argentina, Uruguay, and Paraguay; and Brazil.

Venezuela

Nombre oficial: República de Venezuela

Población: 9.686.000 habitantes. El 69 por ciento son mestizos; el 9 por ciento negros; el 2 por ciento indios y el 20 por ciento son blancos. Después de la segunda guerra mundial, Venezuela abrió sus puertas a emigrantes europeos y vinieron italianos, españoles, portugueses y austriacos.

Capital: Caracas. Tiene cerca de dos millones de habitantes y está a una altura de 3.000 pies. En 1755 y 1812 fue casi totalmente destruída por terremotos (earthquakes). Entre la costa del mar Caribe y el valle donde está la ciudad se encuentra el monte Ávila.

Ciudades principales: Maracaibo, Barquisimeto y Valencia.

Topografía: El territorio venezolano incluye tierras muy altas, llanuras parecidas (resembling) a las pampas argentinas, tierras muy bajas y grandes selvas tropicales.

Montañas: Las montañas venezolanas de mayor altura forman parte del sistema de los Andes. Los picos más altos son el Bolívar (16.411 pies) y el Humboldt.

Volcanes: No tiene volcanes de gran importancia.

Desiertos: No tiene ningún desierto de importancia.

Islas: Venezuela posee más de 70 islas. La más importante es la Isla Margarita que fue descubierta por Colón en su tercer viaje y es muy famosa por la pesca (fishing) de perlas.

Ríos: El río Orinoco, tercero en importancia en la América del Sur, atraviesa (crosses) la parte central del territorio venezolano y va a desembocar en el Atlántico. Es un río muy famoso en la historia y en las leyendas. Cuando Cristóbal Colón lo descubrió en su tercer viaje lo describió como un "gran mar de agua dulce" y creyó que estaba en el Paraíso Terrenal. Es navegable en gran parte de su curso y tiene gran importancia como medio de comunicación.

Lagos: El lago Maracaibo contiene los depósitos petrolíferos más ricos de América del Sur y es la principal fuente de riqueza del país. Se comunica con el mar Caribe por un corto canal. El lago Valencia también es importante.

Cataratas (falls): Cerca de la frontera con Guayana están las cataratas o salto de Ángel que son las más altas del mundo. El aviador norteamericano Jimmy Angel las vio por primera vez desde su avión en 1937.

Héroe nacional y Libertador de cinco países: Simón Bolívar.

Clima: El clima venezolano depende de la altura y varía desde los extremos más fríos en las alturas hasta los más calientes en las tierras bajas. La estación de las lluvias es de junio a noviembre y la seca es de diciembre a mayo. La capital tiene un clima agradable con variaciones de temperatura entre 54 y 84 grados **F**.

Productos principales: Venezuela es el tercer productor mundial de petróleo y productor muy importante de hierro. También produce en menor escala café, azúcar, cacao, bananas, carne, diamantes y perlas.

Idioma oficial: Español.

Día de la Independencia: 5 de julio.

Colombia

Nombre oficial: República de Colombia.

Población: 19.825.000 habitantes. El 20 por ciento son blancos; el 57 por ciento son mestizos; el 14 por ciento son mulatos; el 4 por ciento son negros; el 3 por ciento son zambos (mezcla de indios y negros); y solamente el 1 por ciento son indios chibchas.

Capital: Bogotá, con cerca de dos millones de habitantes, está a una altura de 8.600 pies sobre el nivel del mar.

Ciudades principales: Cali, Medellín y Barranquilla.

Topografía: El territorio colombiano está dividido por tres cordilleras que son parte de los Andes: la Occidental, la Central y la Oriental. Al pie de la Cordillera Oriental está la región de los Llanos, grandes llanuras cruzadas por gran número de ríos y arroyos (streams) que hacen imposibles las comunicaciones en la época (time) de lluvias. Al sur de los Llanos, en dirección a las fronteras con Brasil, Perú y Ecuador se encuentran inmensas selvas vírgenes tropicales habitadas por tribus salvajes o semisalvajes. Hay también valles y mesetas muy fértiles.

Montañas: Los picos más altos son: Cristóbal Colón, Simón Bolívar, Huila y Tolima.

Volcanes: Tiene muchos volcanes. Los principales son Puracé, Cumbal, Sotará, Chiles y Pan de Azúcar.

Ríos: Cauca y Magdalena. El río Cauca corre entre las cordilleras Central y Occidental y va a unirse cerca del mar Caribe con el río Magdalena que corre por el territorio que está entre las cordilleras Central y Oriental. Hay muchos otros ríos que son tributarios del Amazonas y del Orinoco (Venezuela).

Lagos: No tiene lagos de importancia.

Clima: El viajero (traveller) que va de un extremo a otro del país encuentra gran variedad de climas según la altitud: "Tierras calientes" muy húmedas en las zonas bajas de la costa; "tierras templadas" en los valles que están a menos de 6.000 pies de altura; y "tierras frías" en las zonas más altas. Los picos que tienen más de 14.000 pies sobre el nivel del mar están cubiertos de nieve durante la mayor parte del año.

Héroe nacional: Francisco de Paula Santander.

Productos principales: Ocupa el primer lugar del mundo en la producción de esmeraldas y el tercero en la producción de bananas. También produce oro y platino (platinum). El café de Colombia es de muy buena calidad y es una de sus fuentes (sources) principales de riqueza. Su industria petrolera ocupa el cuarto lugar entre los países latinoamericanos.

Idioma oficial: Español.

Día de la Independencia: 20 de julio.

Ecuador

Nombre oficial: República del Ecuador

Población: 5.695.000 habitantes. Solamente el 10 por ciento son blancos. La mayoría son indios (40 por ciento) y mestizos (40 por ciento). El grupo de negros no es muy numeroso (5 por ciento) y habita principalmente en la costa.

Capital: Quito. Tiene cerca de medio millón de habitantes. Está situada casi en la línea ecuatorial, a una altura de 9.248 pies. El sol sale todos los días a las 6:00 de la mañana y se pone a las 6:00 de la tarde. La temperatura media de todo el año es de 55 grados. La ciudad está rodeada de montañas y al pie del Pichincha, hay un volcán apagado (extinto).

Ciudades principales: Guayaquil, Cuenca y Ambato.

Topografía: La cordillera de los Andes pasa por el centro del país y lo divide en tres zonas: la Costa, la Sierra o Interior y el Oriente o región de selvas amazónicas.

Montañas: En los Andes ecuatorianos hay más de 22 picos que se elevan a una altura que varía entre 14.000 y más de 20.000 pies sobre el nivel del mar. Los más importantes son el Chimborazo, el Cotopaxi y el Cayambe.

Volcanes: La mayoría de los picos en el centro del país son volcánicos. Un científico alemán, el Barón Alejandro Von Humboldt, llamó a esta región "Avenida de los Volcanes." El Chimborazo es el más alto de la avenida con una altura de 20.577 pies. El Cotopaxi es el volcán activo más alto del mundo (19.344 pies). La erupción más reciente de este volcán fue en 1911. Otros volcanes activos son el Tungurahua y el Sangay.

Islas: Entre las islas que pertenecen (belong) a Ecuador las más importantes son las Islas Galápagos o Archipiélago de Colón que están en el Pacífico a una distancia de 500 millas de la costa. La palabra "galápagos" es el nombre de unas tortugas gigantescas que pueden pesar (weigh) hasta 400 libras (pounds) y pueden vivir hasta los 300 o 400 años. Hay pájaros y peces (fish) muy raros de gran interés científico. El naturalista inglés, Darwin, visitó las islas en 1835 e hizo allí investigaciones para su libro *El origen de las especies* que es la base de la famosa teoría de la evolución. Casi todas las islas del grupo tienen dos nombres, uno inglés y otro español, por ejemplo, Isabela (Albemarle), Rábida (Jarvis), Pinta (Abingdon), San Cristóbal (Chatham), etc. Durante muchos años las islas sirvieron de refugio a los piratas y aventureros de muchas naciones.

Ríos: En la región de la costa hay dos ríos principales: el Guayas y el río Esmeraldas. En la región oriental hay muchos tributarios del Amazonas.

Héroe nacional: Eugenio de Santa Cruz y Espejo.

Lagos: Los lagos de Ecuador son pequeños y no tienen gran importancia.

Clima: Aunque el país, como indica su nombre, está dentro de la zona tórrida, el clima es muy variado por las grandes diferencias de altitud. En las tierras bajas del Oriente y de la costa el clima es caliente y húmedo. En la sierra central el clima depende de la altura.

Productos principales: Ecuador es gran productor de bananas, café, cacao, arroz, caña de azúcar, vainilla y maderas (wood) finas. Además tiene depósitos de petróleo y de sal. En las selvas ecuatorianas hay gran abundancia de árboles y plantas que tienen valor industrial y medicinal. Por ejemplo, el palo de balsa (balsa wood) y la corteza (bark) del quino, fuente (source) principal en un tiempo de la quinina.

Idioma oficial: Español. Se hablan también lenguas indias, principalmente el quechua.

Día de la Independencia: 10 de agosto.

Bolivia

Nombre oficial: República de Bolivia.

Población: 4.439.000 habitantes. Solamente el 15 por ciento son blancos y el resto son indios (principalmente quechuas y aimarás) y mestizos.

Capital: La capital legal es Sucre, pero la mayoría de las oficinas del gobierno están en La Paz que está a una altura de más de 12.000 pies sobre el nivel del mar y es el centro de la industria, el comercio, la cultura y la política del país. Tiene cerca de 400.000 habitantes.

Ciudades principales: Cochabamba, Oruro, Santa Cruz y Potosí.

Topografía: Es uno de los países más montañosos de América del Sur. En los Andes bolivianos se encuentran varias de las montañas más altas del continente, por ejemplo, los picos de Illampú, Illimani y Sajama de más de 20.000 pies de altura. Abundan los volcanes, algunos de ellos en actividad. El territorio está dividido en tres regiones: el altiplano, una de las regiones habitadas más altas del mundo; la región de las yungas (hot valleys) donde hay valles muy fértiles; y los llanos o llanuras que están en la zona tropical.

Ríos: Desaguadero, Beni, Mamoré y Madre de Dios.

Lagos: Titicaca, el lago navegable más alto del mundo, en la frontera con Perú. El lago Poopó de agua salada está conectado con el Titicaca por el río Desaguadero.

Clima: Depende principalmente de la altitud. Se distinguen tres zonas: la "tierra fría" del altiplano con una temperatura media de 50 grados, la "tierra templada" de los valles andinos, y la "tierra caliente" de los llanos. Las montañas del altiplano tienen nieve todo el año. La temperatura en La Paz varía entre 26 grados en junio y 76 en noviembre.

Productos principales: Tiene grandes depósitos minerales: estaño (tin), oro, plata, plomo (lead), cobre, cinc, etc. También produce petróleo y productos agrícolas y forestales.

Héroe nacional: Antonio José Sucre.

Idioma oficial: Español. La población india habla el quechua y el aimará. Solamente el 36 por ciento de la población habla el idioma oficial.

Día de la Independencia: 6 de agosto.

Perú

Nombre oficial: República de Perú.

Población: 12.772.000 habitantes. La mitad aproximadamente son indios de las tribus aimará y quechua, descendientes de los incas. Los blancos son descendientes principalmente de españoles y de inmigrantes recientes de Alemania e Italia y constituyen el 13 por ciento de la población. Mestizos y un pequeño grupo de negros y de asiáticos completan el total.

Capital: Lima, "la Ciudad de los Reyes." En tiempos del imperio español fue la ciudad más rica y célebre de América del Sur. Está situada a ocho millas del mar, a una altura de 500 pies, y tiene más de un millón de habitantes. Tiene un clima agradable. La temperatura media anual es de 66 grados. En Lima no llueve casi nunca, pero en los meses de invierno (de junio a octubre) hay un tipo de niebla casi constante que los limeños llaman *garúa*.

Ciudades principales: Arequipa, El Callao y Trujillo.

Topografía: El territorio peruano está dividido en tres regiones naturales: la costa o región de los llanos, la sierra o región andina donde están las grandes montañas y valles; y la selva o Amazonia que tiene tierras bajas.

Montañas: Los picos más altos de los Andes peruanos son el Huascarán (22.205 pies), el Yerupajá y el Coropuna.

Volcanes: *El Misti* es un volcán activo cerca de la ciudad de Arequipa en el sur del país. La región alrededor de Lima es afectada por la actividad volcánica.

Desiertos: La costa peruana es una región desértica.

Islas: A poca distancia de la costa hay unas 40 islas donde depositan su guano o excremento millones de pájaros. Este guano es muy rico en nitrógeno y es un excelente fertilizante. Los depósitos de guano hoy día están casi agotados (exhausted) pero en un tiempo constituyeron una de las riquezas principales de Perú.

Ríos: El Rímac y el Pisco desembocan (end) en el Pacífico. El Marañón y sus afluentes se unen al Amazonas.

Lagos: El gran lago Titicaca pertenece (belongs) en parte a Perú. El resto de los lagos en comparación son pequeños, por ejemplo, el de Junín.

Puertos: Callao y Mollendo en el Pacífico; Puno en el lago Titicaca; Iquitos en el Amazonas conecta a Perú con el Atlántico.

Clima: Todo el país está dentro del trópico, pero el clima depende de la altura y de la influencia de las corrientes oceánicas. El clima de la costa es templado y seco gracias a la corriente oceánica fría de Humboldt. En las sierras el clima varía con la altura de fresco a frío glacial, con una estación de lluvias de octubre a abril. En las selvas el clima es caliente y húmedo con abundantes lluvias.

Productos principales: Tiene grandes riquezas minerales. Es el primer productor mundial de bismuto y el segundo de plata. Además tiene depósitos de petróleo, cobre, carbón y hierro. En los últimos años la industria pesquera (fishing) ha adquirido importancia considerable.

Héroe nacional: José de San Martín, Simón Bolívar y Antonio José de Sucre ayudaron a los peruanos a independizarse de España.

Idioma oficial: Español. También se hablan mucho el quechua y el aimará.

Días de la Independencia: 28, 29, y 30 de julio.

Chile

Nombre oficial: República de Chile.

Población: 9.351.000 habitantes. El 75 por ciento son blancos de origen español; el 20 por ciento son de otras extracciones europeas; y solamente el 5 por ciento son indios araucanos, famosos en la historia porque los españoles no pudieron (could) conquistarlos por la fuerza. En 1850, por invitación del gobierno, varios miles de alemanes vinieron a establecerse en la región del sur. La influencia alemana se nota en la arquitectura y el modo de vivir en esa parte del país.

Capital: Santiago con una población de más de dos millones y medio de habitantes. Está a una altura de 1.860 pies sobre el nivel del mar.

Ciudades principales: Valparaíso, el puerto de mar más importante del país. Los ingleses la llaman "Valpo" y los chilenos la llaman "Pancho." Concepción, en el sur, es la tercera ciudad del país y ha sido destruída varias veces por terremotos (earthquakes). Viña del Mar es un lugar de veraneo (summer resort) de fama internacional. Antofagasta es el centro de la industria minera en el norte. Punta Arenas está en el Estrecho de Magallanes y es el centro de la industria de la lana (wool).

Topografía: Chile es un país largo, estrecho (narrow) y extraordinariamente montañoso. Solamente el 20 por ciento de su superficie son tierras planas. Tiene dos cadenas (chains) principales de montañas: los Andes y la Cordillera de la Costa. En la región andina hay grandes depósitos minerales.

Montañas: Los picos principales de los Andes chilenos son Ojos de Salado (22.500 pies), Mercedario (22.000 pies) y varios otros que pasan de 20.000 pies de altura.

Volcanes: Hay más de mil volcanes, algunos de ellos activos.

Desiertos: El famoso desierto de Atacama está en el norte y es uno de los más secos y áridos del mundo. En algunos lugares no se ha registrado lluvia nunca y en otros con frecuencia pasan años sin llover. Este desierto tiene los depósitos de salitre (nitrate) más grandes del mundo. También hay en la región importantes minas de cobre (copper). En algunas partes del desierto hay pequeños oasis dedicados a la agricultura. En el siglo dieciséis el conquistador de Chile, Pedro de Valdivia, tardó (took) seis meses en cruzar la región, y su expedición sufrió allí mucha hambre y sed.

Islas: Parte del territorio chileno lo forman varios archipiélagos en los que hay varias islas de importancia. La famosa Isla de Pascua (Easter) es un monumento nacional, centro de antiguas civilizaciones que construyeron enormes y misteriosas cabezas de piedra. Una de las islas del archipiélago de Juan Fernández es famosa en la literatura porque allí pasó cuatro años el marinero escocés (Scottish) Alexander Selkirk que sirvió de modelo al escritor Daniel Defoe para su famosa novela *Robinsón Crusoe.*

Ríos: Los ríos chilenos son cortos y muy rápidos. Aunque no tienen gran volumen de agua, el Bío Bío, el Valdivia y el Maule tienen pequeñas partes que son navegables.

Lagos: Los lagos principales están en el sur en una región muy importante para el turismo internacional que tiene el nombre de "La Suiza de América." No son grandes, pero en sus aguas de color verde esmeralda se reflejan las cumbres nevadas de los volcanes. Los lagos más importantes son: Todos los Santos, San Martín y Buenos Aires.

Clima: Las diferencias de altitud, la proximidad del mar y la influencia moderadora de la corriente de Humboldt producen grandes contrastes climáticos, pero el clima templado predomina en la mayor parte del territorio chileno. En los desiertos del norte el clima es muy seco, pero la temperatura no sube demasiado. En el sur el clima varía de fresco a frío, pero temperaturas extremadamente bajas se registran solamente en las grandes alturas. En la Patagonia llueve con mucha frecuencia durante todo el año. El verano comienza en el mes de enero y el invierno en junio.

Productos principales: El salitre (nitrate) que se usa como fertilizante en muchos países del mundo. Una de las minas más ricas de cobre (copper) se llama Chuquicamata. En la zona central se produce trigo (wheat), uvas y otros productos agrícolas. En Patagonia tiene mucha importancia la cría (raising) de ovejas (sheep) y la industria de la lana (wool) y de la carne. En los últimos años la industria del pescado ha adquirido gran importancia para Chile.

Héroe nacional: Bernardo O'Higgins.

Idioma oficial: Español.

Día de la Independencia: 18 de septiembre.

Argentina

Nombre oficial: República Argentina.

Población: 23.617.000 habitantes. El 97 por ciento son de ascendencia europea, principalmente españoles e italianos.

Capital: Buenos Aires (Distrito Federal). Tiene una población de más de seis millones de habitantes.

Ciudades principales: Rosario, Córdoba, Mendoza.

Topografía: Montañas cubiertas perennemente de nieve separan a Chile de Argentina. La más alta es el pico de Aconcagua que tiene una altura de 23.035 pies sobre el nivel del mar. En el norte hay selvas tropicales y en el centro del país están las inmensas llanuras de las pampas.

Ríos: Los tres ríos principales son el Paraná, el Uruguay y el Río de la Plata que son navegables en la mayor parte de su extensión.

Lagos: En la región del sur hay más de 400 lagos que tienen gran importancia como centros turísticos.

Clima: A causa de la larga extensión del territorio y de las diferencias de altura hay gran diversidad de clima. La región del norte tiene un clima tropical con una estación de lluvias y otra de seca. En Tierra del Fuego el clima es muy frío, con mucha niebla y fuertes vientos. Allí también nieva y llueve frecuentemente. En la región central el clima es templado y saludable.

Productos principales: carne, cueros, lana, productos agrícolas y petróleo. De la yerba mate se hace una clase de té que es la bebida nacional del país. El quebracho es un tipo de madera muy dura.

Héroe nacional: El General José de San Martín.

Idioma oficial: Español.

Día de la Independencia: 9 de julio.

Uruguay

Nombre oficial: República Oriental del Uruguay.

Población: Cerca de tres millones de habitantes. Son casi en su totalidad blancos de origen europeo, principalmente descendientes de españoles e italianos. La mayoría de los uruguayos son de clase media.

Capital: Montevideo, "la ciudad de las rosas". El nombre de la ciudad viene del portugués "Monte vide eu", la exclamación de uno de los marineros de la expedición de Magallanes que significa, "Yo veo un monte."

Ciudades principales: Paysandú, Salto y Punta del Este.

Topografía: El territorio uruguayo no está dividido en diferentes regiones naturales. Es una gran llanura de hierba (grass) con ondulaciones (rolling hills) de poca elevación. Hay pocos árboles y en el verano los llanos están cubiertos de verbena, una flor de color purpúrea y un perfume muy agradable. Por eso han llamado al Uruguay, "la tierra purpúrea."

Montañas: Uruguay no tiene grandes montañas.

Volcanes: Uruguay no tiene volcanes.

Desiertos: En Uruguay no hay desiertos.

Islas: Uruguay tiene varias islas pequeñas en el Atlántico. Las principales son Gorriti y Lobos.

Ríos: El río Uruguay nace en Brasil y recibe el agua de numerosos afluentes en territorio uruguayo. El río Yaguarón separa a Uruguay de Brasil. El río Negro corre de este a oeste y termina en el río Uruguay. Son todos ríos navegables.

Lagos: No hay grandes lagos en el Uruguay.

Clima: Tiene un clima ideal: templado (ni muy frío ni muy caliente) y muy saludable. En el mes más frío, julio, la temperatura media es de 50 grados F. y en enero, el mes más caliente, la temperatura media es de 74 grados F. Cuando sopla (blows) el viento pampero se registran cambios bruscos (abrupt) de temperatura.

Productos principales: Carne, lana (wool), cueros (leather) y productos agrícolas.

Héroe nacional: José Gervasio Artigas.

Idioma oficial: Español.

Día de la Independencia: 25 de agosto.

Paraguay

Nombre oficial: República del Paraguay.

Población: Cerca de dos millones de habitantes. El 97 por ciento de los paraguayos son descendientes de españoles y de los indios nativos de la región que se llaman guaraníes. Solamente el 3 por ciento son indios puros. La mayoría de los habitantes viven al este del río Paraguay. En la región del Chaco, al oeste del río Paraguay, viven solamente unas 90.000 personas.

Capital: Asunción, situada a orillas del Río Paraguay a una distancia de mil millas del océano Atlántico. Su población es de cerca de medio millón de habitantes.

Ciudades principales: Concepción, Villarrica y Encarnación.

Topografía: No es un país montañoso. Tiene solamente cerros (hills) de poca altura. Predominan las llanuras en casi todo el territorio que está dividido en dos regiones principales por el río Paraguay: la región oriental es la más desarrollada, la región occidental o Chaco Boreal tiene pocos habitantes que son principalmente indios y colonias de extranjeros como la secta religiosa de los Menonitas de Estados Unidos y Canadá.

Montañas: Paraguay no tiene grandes montañas.

Ríos: Los ríos paraguayos tienen gran importancia como medios (means) de comunicación. Son tres: el Paraguay, el Alto (upper) Paraná y el Pilcomayo. Son navegables en gran parte de su extensión.

Lagos: No hay lagos de gran importancia.

Clima: Tiene un clima subtropical muy parecido (similar) al del estado de la Florida. En el verano (de diciembre a febrero) puede hacer bastante calor; en el invierno (de junio a agosto) el tiempo es muy agradable y saludable.

Productos principales: En la región del Chaco hay grandes bosques (woods) de quebracho, de donde se obtiene el tanino que se emplea en medicina y en la industria de cueros (leather). La madera de quebracho es muy dura (hard) y se hunde (sinks) fácilmente en el agua. El nombre viene de *quebrar* (break) y *hacha* (ax) y quiere decir en inglés *axbreaker*.

La hierba mate o té (tea) paraguayo es una bebida muy popular en los países del sur.

El ñandutí es un encaje (lace) muy delicado que hacen los indios. Paraguay también produce muchas naranjas, algodón y productos de carne.

Idiomas oficiales: Español y guaraní. La mayoría de los paraguayos hablan los dos idiomas.

Día de la Independencia: 14 de mayo.

Héroe nacional: Paraguay se declaró independiente de España en 1814 sin tener que luchar (fight). No tiene un gran héroe nacional. Tiene una historia trágica de dictaduras y disputas territoriales contra Bolivia, Argentina, Uruguay y Brasil en que murieron miles de sus habitantes. Hay varios héroes de estas guerras.

Brasil

Nombre oficial: República de los Estados Unidos del Brasil (el nombre portugués es República dos Estados Unidos do Brasil).

Población: 88.209.000 habitantes: el 62 por ciento son blancos, el 26 por ciento mestizos, y el 11 por ciento son negros. En Brasil se han mezclado (mixed) muchas razas y nacionalidades: indios, negros, europeos y orientales. Entre 1821 y 1945, más de cinco millones de inmigrantes entraron en Brasil. Eran principalmente portugueses, españoles, italianos, alemanes (Germans) y japoneses.

Capital: Brasilia con una población de casi 348.000 habitantes y a una altura sobre el nivel del mar de casi cuatro mil pies. Hasta el año 1960 la capital fue Río de Janeiro.

Ciudades principales: São Paulo, gran centro industrial y cultural con casi cinco millones de habitantes; Río de Janeiro, una de las ciudades más bellas del mundo; Recife, Belo Horizonte.

Topografía: En comparación con sus vecinos Brasil no tiene montañas de gran importancia. No es una nación montañosa. Los picos más elevados no tienen más de 10.000 pies de altura. Es un territorio de grandes llanuras y selvas tropicales.

Ríos: El Amazonas es el río más grande del mundo. Nace en los Andes peruanos y va a morir al océano Atlántico. Más que un río es un gran "mar" interior con más de mil tributarios. En total Brasil tiene un gran sistema de ríos que son navegables por una extensión de 27.000 millas. Siguen en importancia al Amazonas el río San Francisco, el Paraná y el Uruguay que terminan en el Río de la Plata en Argentina.

Lagos: No hay lagos de gran importancia.

Clima: El clima de las diferentes regiones depende de la altura, los vientos, las lluvias y la distancia del mar. En las selvas amazónicas el clima es muy húmedo y caliente. En el nordeste hay una región también caliente, pero muy seca. En el sur y en las costas de la región central el clima es templado y muy agradable. En muchas regiones hay solamente dos estaciones: la seca (de junio a octubre) y la lluviosa (de noviembre a mayo).

Productos principales: Ocupa el primer lugar en el mundo en la producción y exportación de café. También produce algodón, azúcar, plátanos, cacao, carne, petróleo, hierro (iron), piedras preciosas y semipreciosas.

Héroe nacional: José Bonifacio de Andrada e Silva.

Idioma oficial: Portugués.

Día de la Independencia: 7 de septiembre.

APPENDIX II: REFRANES

In the cosmopolitan-oriented culture of modern America, the folk wisdom expressed in the proverb has lost much of its meaning and more of its prestige. The Spanish culture is still closer to the land, its folk wisdom is still legal tender among the educated, and the proverb is a key to understanding the people. The proverbs that you learn in class are given below. They are some of the most commonly heard ones in the language. You will learn more vocabulary and structures from them besides getting to understand the people better. After you learn a proverb, try to use it whenever appropriate. Your teacher will help you learn when it is appropriate to use them.

1. ***Más vale pájaro en mano que cien volando.*** *A bird in the hand is worth two in the bush.* (Literally, *A bird in hand is worth more than a hundred flying.*)

2. ***Quien mucho duerme poco aprende.*** *He who sleeps much, learns little.*

3. ***Quien busca halla.*** *He who seeks, finds.*

4. ***En boca cerrada no entran moscas.*** *Flies do not enter a closed mouth.*

5. ***No es tan fiero el león como lo pintan.*** *The lion is not as ferocious as they paint him.*

6. ***Aunque la mona se vista de seda, mona se queda.*** *Although the monkey may dress in silk, she remains a monkey.*

7. **Perro que ladra no muerde.** *Barking dogs don't bite.* (Literally, *Dog that barks does not bite.*)

8. **Antes que te cases, mira lo que haces.** *Look before you leap.* (Literally, *Before you get married, look at what you are doing.*)

9. **De la mano a la boca se pierde la sopa.** *'Twixt the cup and the lip there's many a slip.* (Literally, *From the hand to the mouth the soup is lost.*)

10. **A quien madruga Dios le ayuda.** *The early bird gets the worm* or *God helps those who help themselves.* (Literally, *God helps him who gets up early.*)

11. **Del dicho al hecho hay gran trecho.** *From the said* (*word*) *to the done* (*act*) *there is a great gap.* (Similar to, *More easily said than done.*)

12. **Más vale estar solo que mal acompañado.** *It is better to be alone than in bad company* (*poorly accompanied*).

13. **Vísteme despacio que estoy de prisa.** *Haste makes waste.* (Literally, *Dress me slowly, for I'm in a hurry.*)

14. **No dejes para mañana lo que puedas hacer hoy.** *Don't leave for tomorrow what you can do today.*

15. **Si le viene el saco, póngaselo.** *If the coat fits, put it on* (*wear it*). (In English we usually speak of a shoe rather than a coat.)

APPENDIX III: FÓRMULAS DE CORTESÍA

The non-native remains a stranger in an alien land until he learns the culture's social graces and becomes accustomed to using them with both the sincerity and sophistication of the native. Some of the most common and most generally used fixed expressions of social amenity appear below. As you learn them in class, try to use them as often as you can.

1. **Salud.** *Health.* or **Jesús.** *Jesus.* (These are the two most common expressions used when someone sneezes. They are equivalent to "God bless you.")

2. **Con permiso.** *Pardon me.* (This is used to ask permission to do something which might otherwise be interpreted as rude or impolite; e.g., to

walk in front of someone, to get out of a crowded elevator, to leave a group, etc.)

3. ***Perdóneme usted.*** or ***Perdóname (tú).***
   Dispénseme usted. or ***Dispénsame (tú).*** *Pardon me.*
   Discúlpeme usted. or ***Discúlpame (tú).***

   (These are interchangeable and may be made plural (for addressing more than one person) by using the *usted* form and adding *n* to it, e.g., *Perdónenme ustedes.* In contrast with number 2 above, these are used to ask a person to forgive you or pardon you for having done something that you regret or did not do intentionally.)

4. ***Sí, cómo no.*** *Yes, of course.* or *Yes, why not* (literally). (This is used as a response to a person who says any one of the expressions in number 2 or 3 above.)

5. ***Lo siento mucho.*** *I'm very sorry.* (The verb is *sentir* (*ie, i*) and may be used in any person.)

6. ***Hágame (usted) el favor de . . .*** or ***Hazme (tú) el favor de . . .*** *Please . . .* (Fill the blank with the infinitive of whatever you are asking to be done; e.g., *Please come here = Hágame (Hazme) el favor de venir aquí.*)

7. ***¿ Cómo ?*** *What?* (This is used when you don't hear what was said and want it repeated.)

8. ***No importa.*** *It doesn't matter.* (Literally, *It is not important.*)

9. ***Está(s) en su (tu) casa.*** *Make yourself at home.* (Literally, *You are in your home.*)

10. ***No se (te) moleste(s).*** *Don't bother.*

11. ***No es molestia ninguna.*** *It's no bother.*

12. ***Que se (te) divierta(s, n).*** *Have a good time.* (Used only with *tú, usted,* and *ustedes.*)

13. ***¡Felicidades!*** *Congratulations!*

14. ***Perdón.*** *Pardon me.* (This is a shortened form for any expression in number 3 above.)

15. ***Usted lo tiene.*** *Yes, of course.* or *Certainly.* (Literally, *You have it.* The familiar equivalent would be *Lo tienes.* This is a common response to *Con permiso,* number 2 above.)

16. ***¿Cómo te (le, les) va ?*** *How goes it?* or *How are you?* **Bien, gracias, ¿ y a ti (usted)?** *Fine thanks, and (with) you?*

17. ***Buen provecho.*** *Good appetite.* (Literally, *Good profit.* This is used whenever one wishes to express a desire that something contribute to the health or general welfare of another person. It is especially used when taking leave of or coming upon a person who is eating.)

18. ***Que te (le, les) vaya bien.*** *Good-by.* (Literally, *May it go well to you.*)

19. **_Quiero presentarle(te) al señor Fulano._**   *I want you to meet Mr.*
                                                                     So-and-So.

       Mucho (Tanto) gusto.   *Pleased to meet you.*

       Igualmente. Gracias.   *Same here. Thank you.*

20. **_¡Qué lástima!_** *What a pity!*

       ¡Qué formidable! *How wonderful!* (Literally, *How formidable!*)

SPANISH-ENGLISH VOCABULARY

In Spanish for Communication you learn to spell any Spanish word that you hear spoken unless that word belongs to the category of "eye-spelling words" or—in few cases—to the category of "meaning-spelling words". In the following list letters that you need to see in order to spell are indicated; for example the **z** in **abrazar.**

1) The sound [s] is represented in writing by various letters or letter combinations. Since the majority are spelled with the letter *s*, when this sound is represented by the letter *s* it is not indicated. In this way you only need to memorize the spelling of this sound when it is spelled with a *c*, *x*, *z*, or *ps*.

2) All *b*'s and *v*'s are indicated except when followed immediately by another consonant. When [b] or [ʋ] is followed by another consonant, it is *always* spelled *b*. But these sounds may be written *b* or *v* in all other cases, and it is necessary for you to memorize which letter is used in each word.

3) All *h*'s are indicated since this letter represents no sound.

4) The [x] (jota) sound may be spelled by either *g* or *j* before *e* or *i*. Therefore, all such instances are indicated.

5) As consonants, both *ll* and *y* represent the same sound. Therefore, they are always indicated.

6) Words that bear a written accent mark, the function of which is to distinguish meaning rather than to mark the stressed syllable in speech, fall into the "eye-spelling" as well as the "meaning-spelling" categories. The vowel over which the accent is written is indicated; e.g., **mí, dónde, sólo.**

7) All *n*'s and *m*'s preceding bilabials (*m, p, v, b*) are indicated since they stand for [m] in such combinations; e.g., **inmediatamente, también, invierno.**

A

a   at, by, from, on, to
abierta, –o   open, opened
abrazar   to hug, embrace
abrigo   overcoat, top coat
abril   April
abrir   to open
abuela   grandmother
abuelo   grandfather
abuelos   grandfathers, grandparents
acabar   to finish, complete, end
acabar de + inf.   to have just ... , to finish ... –ing
aceptar   to accept
acompañar   to accompany, join
acostar (ue)   to put to bed
acostarse (ue)   to go to bed
además   besides
adentro   inside

adiós   good-by
afuera   outside
agosto   August
agradable   pleasant
agua   water
ahí   there (not distant)
ahora   now
al = a + el   to the
alegre   glad, cheerful, happy
algo   something
alguien   someone, somebody
allí   there (distant)
almorzar (ue)   to eat lunch
almuerzo   lunch
alta, –o   tall, high; loud
altura   height
alumna, –o   pupil, student
amable   kind, friendly
amarilla, –o   yellow
americana, –o   American

amiga, –o friend
anaranjada, –o orange-colored
andar to walk, go, to run (clock)
anteayer day-before-yesterday
año year
aparecer to appear
apellido surname, last name
aprender to learn
aquel, aquella that (distant)
aquellas, –os those
aquello that (neuter form)
aquí here
árbol (el) tree
arena sand
argentina, –o Argentinian
arreglar to fix, repair, arrange
arroz (el) rice
así so, thus, like that
aunque although, even though
ausente absent
autobús (el) bus
automóvil (el) car
avenida avenue
avión (el) airplane
¡ay! oh!, ouch!
ayer yesterday
ayudar to help
azúcar (el) sugar
azul blue

B

bailar to dance
bajar to come or go down, lower
bajo, –a short, low; under
balcón (el) balcony
banco bank, bench
bandera flag
bañar(se) to bathe, take a bath
barco boat, ship
bastante enough; quite, fairly
beber to drink
bebida drink, beverage
besar to kiss
bicicleta bicycle
bien well, fine
blanca, –o white
blusa blouse
boca mouth
boliviana, –o Bolivian
boliviano Bolivian, monetary unit
bonita, –o pretty, beautiful
brasileña, –o Brazilian
brazo arm
brillante shining, brilliant
brillar to shine
broma joke
bruta, –o dumb, stupid
buen good
buena, –o good, O.K.
burro donkey, burro
buscar to look for

C

cabeza head
cada each, every
caer(se) to fall (down)
café (el) coffee; restaurant
calcetines (los) socks
calendario calendar
caliente hot
calor (el) heat
calle (la) street
cambiar to change
caminar to walk
camino road, way
camisa shirt
campo field, country
cansada, –o tired
cantar to sing
cara face
¡caramba! gosh!
¡caray! golly!
carne (la) meat; flesh
carretera highway
carro car
carta letter (mail)
cartel (el) poster
casa house, home
casar(se) to marry, get married
castellano, –a Castilian, Spanish
catorce fourteen
celebrar to celebrate
cena supper, dinner
cenar to eat supper, have dinner
centro center, downtown
cerca near
cero zero
cerrar(ie) to close
cesta basket
cielo sky, heaven
cien(to) a (one) hundred
cigarro cigarette, cigar
cinco five
cincuenta fifty
cine (el) movie
ciudad (la) city
clara, –o light, clear
¡claro! sure! of course!
clase (la) class, kind, (type), classroom
colombiana, –o Colombian
comer to eat
cometa kite
como like, as, how
¡Cómo!, ¿Cómo? What? How?
cómoda, –o comfortable
compañera, –o companion
complicada, –o complicated
comprar to buy, purchase
comprender to understand, comprehend
común common
con with
conejo rabbit
conmigo with me

conocer to know, be acquainted with

contar (ue) to tell; to count

contestar to answer

corbata necktie

correo post office; mail

correr to run (on foot)

cortar to cut

cortesía courtesy (politeness)

costumbre (la) custom

creer to believe

crema cream

cruzar to cross

cuaderno notebook

cuadrada, –o square

¿Cuál? Which? What?

cuando when

¿Cuándo? When?

¿Cuánta, –o? How much?

¿Cuántas, –os? How many?

cuarenta forty

cuarta, –o fourth

cuarto room

cuatro four

cuatrocientos four hundred

cuchara spoon

cuchillo knife

cuerpo body

cuidado care (careful)

cumpleaños (el) birthday

Ch

chica, –o small; girl, boy

chilena, –o Chilean

D

dar to give

de of, from, about, by

deber ought, must (or untranslatable)

decir to say, tell

dedo finger, toe

del = de + el of the

demasiado too much; too

desayunar(se) to eat breakfast

desayuno breakfast

descansada, –o rested

desear to desire, wish

desierto desert

despacio slowly

despedir(se) (i) to dismiss, say good-by

despertar(se) (ie) to awaken, wake up

después (de) afterward, later, after

diálogo dialog

día (el) day

dicho said; a saying

diciembre December

diecinueve nineteen, nineteenth

dieciocho eighteen, eighteenth

dieciséis sixteen, sixteenth

diecisiete seventeen, seventeenth

diente (el) tooth

diez ten

diferente different

difícil hard, difficult

dificultad (la) difficulty

dinero money

Dios God

dioses (los) gods

dirección (la) address, direction

director (el) principal, director

disculpar to excuse, pardon

disgustar(se) to disgust, get upset

dispensar to excuse, pardon

divertirse (ie) to have a good time

doblar to turn (a corner)

doce twelve

domingo Sunday

donde where

¿Dónde? Where?

dormir (ue, u) to sleep

dos two

doscientos, –as two hundred

duda doubt

durante during

E

e and

ecuador (el) equator

ecuatoriana, –o Ecuadorian

edificio building

ejemplo example

ejercicio exercise

el the

él he, him

elefante (el) elephant

ella she, her

ellas they, them

ellos they, them

empezar (ie) to begin

en in, on, at, into

encontrar (ue) to find, meet

enemigo enemy

enero January

enferma, –o sick, ill

ensalada salad

entender (ie) to understand

entonces then (interval of time)

entrar (en) to come in, enter

entre between, among

escribir to write

escrita, –o written

escuela school

esa, ese that (not distant)

esas, esos those

eso that

espada sword

español, –ola Spanish, Spaniard

¡Espera! Wait! Hold it!

esta, estas this, these

estación (la) season, station

estado state

Estados Unidos (E.U. or E.E. U.U.)
    United States (U.S.)
estar   to be
este (el)   east
este, estos   this, these
esto   this
estrella   star
estudiante   student
estudiar   to study
estudios   studies
exacta, –o   exact, exactly
exagerar   to exaggerate
examen (el)   examination
excelente   excellent
excepto   except
explicar   to explain

F

fácil   easy
fácilmente   easily
falda   skirt
familia   family
famosa, –o   famous
febrero   February
fecha   date
¡Felicidades!   Congratulations!
feliz   happy
fea, –o   ugly
feroz   fierce, ferocious
fiera, –o   fierce, wild
fiesta   party, holiday
flaca, –o   thin, skinny
flor (la)   flower
francés, –esa   French
frase (la)   phrase, sentence
(con) frecuencia   frequently
frecuente   frequent
frecuentemente   frequently
frente (la)   forehead
fresca, –o   fresh, cool
frijol (el)   bean
fría, –o   cold
frío (el)   cold
fruta   fruit
fuente (la)   fountain
furiosa, –o   furious

G

garaje (el)   garage
gata, –o   cat
generalmente   generally
gente (la)   people
geografía   geography
gesto   gesture
gorda, –o   fat
gracias   thanks
gran   great, big, large
grande   big, large, great
gris   gray
gustar   to be pleasing; to like
gusto   pleasure

H

haber   to have; to be
habitante (el)   inhabitant
hablar   to speak
hacer   to do, make; to be
hallar   to find (discover)
hambre   hunger
hasta   until; even
hay   there is, there are
hecha, –o   done, made; fact
hemisferio   hemisphere
hermana   sister
hermano   brother
hermanos   brothers, brothers and
    sisters
héroe (el)   hero
hija   daughter
hijo   son, child
hijos   sons, children
himno   hymn
historia   history, story
hola   hi, hello
hombre   man
hora   hour, time
hoy   today
hoy día   nowadays
huevo   egg
húmeda, –o   humid, damp
hundir   to sink

I

idioma (el)   language
iglesia   church
igual   equal, same
igualmente   same to you, equally
imitar   to imitate
impermeable (el)   raincoat
importar   to matter, be important
incómoda, –o   uncomfortable
independencia   independence
india, –o   Indian
inglés, –esa   English
ingleses, –esas   English
inmediatamente   immediately
inteligente   intelligent
interés (el)   interest
interesante   interesting
intérprete (el)   interpreter
inundar   to flood
invierno   winter
invitación (la)   invitation
invitadas, –os   guests
invitar   to invite
ir   to go, to come
isla   island
italiana, –o   Italian

J

jamón (el)   ham
jardín (el)   garden
joven   young
juego   game

jueves Thursday
jugar (ue) to play (a game)
jugo juice
julio July
junio June
junta, –o, together

L

la the, her, you, it
labio lip
ladrar to bark
lago lake
lápiz (el) pencil
larga, –o long
las the, them, you
lástima shame, pity
latinoamericana, –o Latin American
lavar(se) to wash
le him, you; to him, her, you, it
lección (la) lesson
leche (la) milk
lechuga lettuce
leer to read
lejos far, far away
lengua tongue, language
león (el) lion
les to them, to you, them, you
levantar(se) to get up; to raise
libro book
limón (el) lemon
limpiar to clean
limpia, –o clean
linda, –o pretty, beautiful
lista list, roll
lista, –o ready
lo the, it, him, you
los the, them, you
luego then, later
lugar (el) place
luna moon
lunes Monday
luz (la) light

Ll

llamar to call; to knock; to name
llamarse to be called, named
llanura plain (flat land)
llegar to arrive
llevar to carry, take, wear
llover (ue) to rain
lluvia rain

M

madre (la) mother
madrugar to get up early
maestra, –o teacher
magnífica, –o great, wonderful
mal bad, badly; (el) evil
mala, –o bad; sick, ill
mamá mother, mom

mano (la) hand
mantel (el) tablecloth
mantequilla butter
manzana apple
mañana (la) morning; (el) tomorrow
mapa (el) map
mar (el) sea
marinero sailor
martes Tuesday
marzo March
más more, most
masticar to chew, masticate
mayo May
me me, to me
media, –o half
medianoche (la) midnight
medias socks, hose
mediodía (el) noon
medir (i) to measure
menos minus, less
mentira lie
mes (el) month
mesa table
mi my
mí me
mientras while
miércoles Wednesday
mil thousand
millón (el) million
mina mine (iron, coal, etc.)
minuto minute
mirar to look (at)
misma, –o same
molestar(se) to bother
molestia bother, trouble
momento, –ito moment, minute
montaña mountain
morada, –o purple
morder (ue) to bite
morir (ue, u) to die
mosca fly
motocicleta motorcycle
mover (ue) to move
mucha, –o much, a lot
muchacha, –o girl, boy
muchachos boys, boys and girls
muchísimo a great deal, very much
mujer (la) woman
mundo world
muñeca doll, wrist
música music
muy very

N

nación (la) nation
nacional national, Arg. coin
nada nothing, anything
nadar to swim
nadie nobody, no one, anybody
naranja orange (fruit)
nariz (la) nose
necesaria, –o necessary
necesitar to need
negra, –o black; Negro

nerviosa, –o nervous
nevar (ie) to snow
ni . . . ni neither . . . nor
nido nest
niebla fog
nieve (la) snow
ningún none, any, no
ninguna, –o none, any, no
niña, –o girl, boy
niños children, boys and girls
no no, not
noche (la) night
nombre (el) name
norte (el) north
nos us, to us, ourselves
nosotras, –os we, us
notar to note, notice
noticia (item of) news
novecientas, –os nine hundred
noventa ninety
noviembre November
nube (la) cloud
nuestra, –o our, ours
nueve nine
nueva, –o new
número number
nunca never

O

o or
observar to observe
océano ocean
ochenta eighty
ocho eight
ochocientas, –os eight hundred
octubre October
oeste (el) west
oficina office
oído (inner) ear, hearing
oír to hear
ojo eye
¡Ojo! Look out! Be careful!
oler (ue) to smell
olvidar(se) to forget
once eleven
oreja (outer) ear
oscura, –o dark, obscure
otoño fall, autumn
otra, –o other, another

P

padre (el) father; priest
padres parents, fathers
página page (in a book)
país (el) country, nation
pájaro bird
palabra word
pan (el) bread
pantalones (los) pants, trousers
papa (la) potato
papá (el) father, dad

papel (el) paper
para to, for, toward, in order to
paraguaya, –o Paraguayan
parecer to seem, appear (to be)
parque (el) park
parte (la) part
pasada, –o past
pasar to pass; to spend (time); to happen
paseo drive (Morningside Drive)
pedir (i) to order, ask for, request
pelo hair
pensar (ie) to think; intend, plan
pequeña, –o small, little
perder (ie) to lose, spoil
perdón (el) pardon
¡Perdón! Pardon me! Excuse me!
perdonar to pardon
perfecta, –o perfect
periódico newspaper
periodista (el) reporter
permiso permission, permit
permitir to permit, allow
pero but
perro dog
persona person
peruana, –o Peruvian
pescado fish (caught)
peso monetary unit
pie (el) foot
piedra stone
pierna leg
pimienta pepper
pino pine
pintar to paint, color
pizarra blackboard
plancha iron (for clothing)
planchar to iron
plátano banana
plato plate, dish
playa beach
pluma pen, feather
población (la) population
pobre poor
poca, –o little, few, a little
poder (ue) to be able, can, may
policía (el) policeman; ∼(la) police force
Polo Norte North Pole
pollo chicken
poner to place, put, set; turn on
ponerse to put on, become
poquito a little bit
por through, by, per, for
por because of
¿por qué? why?
porque because
portugués, -esa Portuguese
postre (el) dessert
practicar to practice
pregunta question
preguntar to ask (questions)
preparar to prepare

presentar to introduce, present
presente present
prima, –o cousin
primavera spring (season)
primer first
primera, –o first
principal main
principalmente mainly, chiefly
prisa hurry, haste
privada, –o private
problema (el) problem
profesor, –ora teacher, professor
prohibir to prohibit
pronto soon, fast
pronunciar to pronounce
provecho profit, benefit
pública, –o public
pueblo people; town, village
puerta door
puerto sea (river) port
puesta, –o put
puesto job, position
pulgar (el) thumb
pupitre (el) (school) desk

Q

que what, that, which, who
¿Qué? What? How?
quedar(se) to remain, stay
querer (ie) to want, wish; to love
queso cheese
¿Quién? Who? Whom?
quince fifteen, fifteenth
quinientas, –os five hundred
quinta, –o fifth
quitar(se) to take off, take away

R

rancho ranch, farm
rápida, –o fast, rapid
rápidamente rapidly, fast
razón (la) reason; right
recibir to receive
recordar (ue) to remember, recall
recta, –o straight
redonda, –o round
refrán (el) proverb, saying
regalo gift, present
regla ruler (for measuring)
regresar to return, come or go
  back
regular fair
reina queen
reloj (el) clock, watch
repetir (i) to repeat
responder to answer, respond
respuesta answer
resto rest, remainder
revista magazine, review
rey (el) king
rica, –o rich

río river
roja, –o red
romper to break
ropa clothes
rota, –o broken
rosa rose
rosada, –o pink

S

sábado Saturday
saber to know
sacar to take out
saco coat
sal (la) salt
salario salary, wages
salir to go out, leave
salud (la) health
¡Salud! Bless you!
san saint (San Patricio)
santa, –o saint, holy
santo Saint's Day
se self; to him, her, them, you
seca, –o dry
secretaria, –o secretary
secundaria, –o secondary
sed (la) thirst
seda silk
seguir (i) to continue, follow
según according to
segunda, –o second
seis six
seiscientas, –os six hundred
selva jungle
semana week
semestre (el) semester
sentada, –o seated
sentarse (ie) to sit down
sentir (ie, i) to feel, regret, be
  sorry
señor (el) Mr., sir, man, gentleman
señora Mrs., lady, wife
señorita Miss, young lady
septiembre September
ser to be; (el) being
servilleta napkin
servir (i) to serve, help
sesenta sixty
setecientas, –os seven hundred
setenta seventy
si if, whether
sí yes
siempre always
siesta nap
siete seven
siglo century
significar to mean, signify
siguiente following, next
silla chair
sin without
sistema (el) system
sobre on, over, about
sobrina niece
sobrino nephew

sobrinos nephews *or* nephews and nieces
sol (el) sun
sola, –o alone, single
solamente only
sólo only
sombrero hat
sopa soup
su his, her, its, their, your
subir to climb, go *or* come up
sucia, –o dirty
sucre (el) monetary unit of Ecuador
Sud south
sueño sleep, dream
suéter (el) sweater
sumamente exceedingly
superficie (la) area, surface
sur (el) south

T

tabaco tobacco
tacaña, –o stingy, tightwad
tal such, such a
también also, too
tampoco neither
tan so
tanta, –o so (as) much
tarde (la) afternoon, evening
tarde late
tarea task, homework
taza cup
te you, to you, yourself
té (el) tea
teléfono telephone
temprano early
tenedor (el) fork
tener to have, possess; to be
tener que + *inf.* to have to
tercer third
tercera, –o third
terminar (de) to finish, terminate, end
ti you
tía aunt
tiempo time; weather
tienda store; tent
tierra earth, land
tigre (el) tiger, cougar, mountain lion
tío uncle
tíos uncles, aunt(s) and uncle(s)
tipo type, kind
título title
tiza chalk
toda, –o all, every, whole
todavía still, yet
todo everything
tomar to take; to drink, eat
tonta, –o foolish, fool, silly
torcida, –o crooked, twisted
tormenta storm
toro bull
total (el) total

trabajar to work (*not* to function)
trabajo job, work
tradición (la) tradition
traducir to translate
traer to bring
traje (el) suit
tranvía (el) streetcar
tratar (de) to try to
trece thirteen, thirteenth
trecho stretch (distance)
treinta thirty
tremenda, –o tremendous
tren (el) train
tres three
trescientos three hundred
triste sad
tropezar (ie) to trip, stumble
tu your
tú you
túnel (el) tunnel

U

u or
Ud., Uds., abr. of **usted, ustedes**
última, –o last, final
un a, an, one
una, –o a, an, one
universidad (la) university
uruguaya, –o Uruguayan
usar to use; to wear (clothes)
usted(es) you

V

vacaciones (las) vacation
valer to be worth
valiente brave, valiant
vamos a + *inf.* let's
varias, –os various, several
vaso glass (for water, milk, etc.)
vecino, –a neighbor
vegetales (los) vegetables
veinte twenty, twentieth
veintiuno twenty-one
veintidós twenty-two
veintitrés twenty-three
veinticuatro twenty-four
veinticinco twenty-five
veintiséis twenty-six
veintisiete twenty-seven
veintiocho twenty-eight
veintinueve twenty-nine
velocidad (la) speed, velocity
vender to sell
venezolana, –o Venezuelan
venir to come
ventana window
ver to see
verano summer
verdad (la) truth
¿verdad? true? right?
verdadero true, real
verde green

vestida, –o dressed
vestido dress, clothes
vestir(se) **(i)** to dress, get dressed
vez **(la)** time (instance)
viajar to travel
viaje **(el)** trip
vida life
vieja, –o old
viento wind
viernes Friday
vino wine
violenta, –o violent
virgen **(la)** virgin
virrey **(el)** viceroy
visita visit
visitar to visit
vivir to live

vocabulario vocabulary
volar **(ue)** to fly
volver **(ue)** to return, come back
voz **(la)** voice
vuelta, –o returned

Y

y and
ya already
yo I

Z

zanahoria carrot
zapato shoe
zoológico zoo

A

a un, una, –o
about de
absent ausente
to accept aceptar
to accompany acompañar
according to según
ache dolor (el)
address dirección (la)
after después (de)
afternoon tarde (la)
afterward después
airplane avión (el)
all toda, –o
to allow permitir
alone sola, –o
already ya
also también
although aunque
always siempre
American americana, –o
among entre
an un, una, –o
and y, e
another otra, –o
to answer contestar, responder
any ningún, ninguna, –o
to appear aparecer
apple manzana
April abril
area superficie (la)
Argentinian argentina, –o
arm brazo
to arrange arreglar
to arrive llegar
as como
to ask (questions) preguntar
to ask for pedir
at a, en
to attend (a meeting, etc.) asistir
August agosto
aunt tía
autumn otoño
avenue avenida
to awaken despertar(se) (ie)

B

bad, badly mal
bad mala, –o
bag bolsa
balcony balcón (el)
banana banana, plátano
bank banco
to bark ladrar
basket cesta
to bathe bañar(se)
to be estar, ser, haber, hacer, tener
to be able poder (ue)
beach playa
bean frijol (el)
to be born nacer
beautiful bonita, –o; linda, –o

because porque
because of por
to begin empezar (ie)
to believe creer
bench banco
besides además
between entre
beverage bebida
bicycle bicicleta
big gran, grande
bird pájaro
birthday cumpleaños (el)
to bite morder (ue)
black negra, –o
blackboard pizarra
Bless you! ¡Salud! ¡Jesús!
blood sangre (la)
blouse blusa
blue azul
boat barco
body cuerpo
Bolivian boliviana, –o
book libro
bother molestia
to bother molestar(se)
boy muchacho, chico, niño
boys, boys and girls muchachos, chicos, niños
brave valiente
Brazilian brasileña, –o
bread pan (el)
to break romper
breakfast desayuno
bridge puente (el)
brilliant brillante
to bring traer
broken rota, –o
brother hermano
brothers, brothers and sisters hermanos
building edificio
bull toro
to burn quemar
bus autobús (el)
but pero, sino
butter mantequilla
to buy comprar
by a, por, de

C

calendar calendario
to call llamar
can poder (ue)
car automóvil (el), coche (el), carro
care cuidado
careful cuidado
carrot zanahoria
to carry llevar
Castilian castellana, –o
cat gato
to catch coger
to celebrate celebrar

center centro
century siglo
chair silla
chalk tiza
to change cambiar
cheap barata, –o
cheerful alegre
cheese queso
to chew masticar
chicken pollo
chiefly principalmente
Chilean chilena, –o
child hijo, hija, niño, niña
children hijos, niños
to choose escoger
church iglesia
cigar cigarro
cigarette cigarro
city ciudad (la)
class clase (la)
classroom clase (la)
clean limpia, –o
to clean limpiar
clear clara, –o
to climb subir
clock reloj (el)
to close cerrar (ie)
clothes ropa, vestido
cloud nube (la)
coat saco
coffee café (el)
cold fría, –o; frío (el)
Colombian colombiana, –o
to color pintar
to come venir; ir
to come back regresar, volver (ue)
to come down bajar
to come in entrar (en)
comfortable cómoda, –o
common común
companion compañera, –o
complicated complicada, –o
to comprehend comprender
Congratulations! ¡Felicidades!
to continue seguir (i)
cool fresca, –o
cougar tigre (el)
to count contar (ue)
country campo, país (el)
couple pareja
courtesy cortesía
cousin prima, –o
cream crema
crooked torcida, –o
to cross cruzar
cup taza
custom costumbre (la)
to cut cortar

D

dad papá (el)
daily diaria, –o
damp húmeda, –o

to dance bailar
dark oscura, –o
date (calendar) fecha
daughter hija
day día (el)
day-before-yesterday anteayer
December diciembre
desert desierto
to desire desear
desk (school) pupitre (el)
dessert postre (el)
dialog diálogo
to die morir (ue, u)
different diferente
difficult difícil
difficulty dificultad (la)
direction dirección
director director (el)
dirty sucia, –o
to disgust disgustar
dish plato
to dismiss despedir (i)
to do hacer
dog perro
doll muñeca
done hecha, –o
donkey burro
door puerta
doubt duda
to doubt dudar
downtown centro
dream sueño
dress vestido
to dress vestir(se) (i)
dressed vestida, –o
drink bebida
to drink beber, tomar
drive (street) paseo
to drive (a car) manejar
dry seca, –o
during durante

E

each cada
ear (inner) oído, (outer) oreja
early temprano
earth tierra
east este (el)
easy fácil
easily fácilmente
to eat comer, tomar
to eat breakfast desayunar(se)
to eat lunch almorzar (ue)
to eat supper cenar
Ecuadorian ecuatoriana, –o
egg huevo
eight ocho
eighteen dieciocho
eighteenth dieciocho
eight hundred ochocientas, –os
eighty ochenta
elephant elefante (el)
eleven once

to embrace abrazar
empty vacía, –o
to end acabar, terminar
enemy enemigo
English inglés, -esa
enough bastante
to enter entrar
equal igual
equally igualmente
equator ecuador (el)
even hasta
evening tarde (la)
even though aunque
every cada, todas, –os
everything todo
evil mal (el)
exact(ly) exacta, –o
to exaggerate exagerar
exam(ination) examen (el)
example ejemplo
exceedingly sumamente
excellent excelente
except excepto
to excuse disculpar, perdonar, dispensar
Excuse me. Perdón.
exercise ejercicio
expensive cara, –o
to explain explicar
eye ojo

F

face cara
fact hecho
fair (health) regular
fairly (quite) bastante
fall (season) otoño
to fall (down) caer(se)
family familia
famous famosa, –o
far, far away lejos (de)
farm rancho
fast rápida, –o; pronto
fat gorda, –o
father padre, papá (el)
feather pluma
February febrero
to feel sentir (ie, i)
ferocious feroz
few poca, –o
field campo
fierce feroz, fiera, –o
fifteen quince
fifteenth quince
fifth quinta, –o
fifty cincuenta
film película
final última, –o
to find encontrar (ue), hallar
finger dedo
to finish acabar, terminar
fire fuego
fireman bombero

first primer, primera, –o
fish (caught) pescado
five cinco
five hundred quinientas, –os
to fix (repair) arreglar
flag bandera
flesh carne (la)
to flood inundar
flower flor (la)
fly mosca
to fly · volar (ue)
fog niebla
to follow seguir (i)
following siguiente
fool, foolish tonta, –o
foot pie (el)
for por, para
forbid prohibir
forehead frente (la)
to forget olvidar
fork tenedor (el)
forty cuarenta
fountain fuente (la)
four cuatro
four hundred cuatrocientas, –os
fourteen catorce
fourth cuarta, –o
free (of charge) gratis
French francés, -esa
frequent frecuente
frequently con frecuencia, frecuentemente
fresh fresca, –o
Friday viernes
friend amiga, –o
friendly amable
from de, a
fruit fruta
full llena, –o
furious furiosa, –o

G

game juego
garage garaje (el)
garden jardín (el)
generally generalmente
geography geografía
gesture gesto
to get conseguir (i)
to get married casar(se)
to get up levantar(se)
gift regalo
girl muchacha, chica, niña
to give dar
glad alegre
glass vaso (drinking)
to go ir
God Dios
gods dioses (los)
to go down bajar
gold oro
golly! ¡caray!
to go to bed acostarse (ue)

good *b*uen, *b*uena, –o
good-by adiós
Gosh! ¡Cara*mb*a!
grandfather a*b*uelo
grandfathers, grandparents a*b*uelos
grandmother a*b*uela
gray gris
great magnífica, –o, gran, grande
a great deal muchísima, –o
green *v*erde
grief dolor
guest in*v*itada, –o

H

hair pelo
half media, –o
ham jamón (el)
hand mano (la)
to happen pasar
happy feliz
hard difícil, duro
haste prisa
hat so*m*brero
to have *h*a*b*er, tener
to have a good time di*v*ertirse
  (ie, i)
to have just aca*b*ar de + *inf.*
to have to tener que + *inf.*
he, him *é*l
head ca*b*eza
health salud (la)
to hear oír
hearing oído
hello *h*ola
to help a*y*udar, ser*v*ir (i)
hemisphere *h*emisferio
her la
to her se, le
here aquí
hero *h*éroe (el)
to hide esconder
highway carretera
him, to him lo, le, se
his su
history *h*istoria
holiday fiesta
home casa
homework tarea
to hope esperar
horse ca*b*a*ll*o
hose (footwear) medias
hot caliente
hour *h*ora
house casa
how c*ó*mo
how many cu*á*ntas, -os
how much cu*á*nta, –o
to hug abrazar
humid *h*úmeda, –o
a (one) hundred *c*ien(to)
hunger *h*a*m*bre
hurry prisa
hymn *h*imno

I

I *y*o
if si
ill enferma, –o, mala, –o
to imitate imitar
immediately i*n*mediatamente
in en
independence independen*c*ia
Indian india, –o
inexpensive *b*arata, –o
inhabitant *h*a*b*itante (el)
in order to para
inside adentro, dentro
intelligent inteligente
to intend pensar (ie)
interest interés (el)
interesting interesante
interpreter intérprete
into en
to introduce (a person) presentar
invitation in*v*itación (la)
to invite in*v*itar
iron (for clothes) plancha
to iron planchar
island isla
it la, lo, le
Italian italiana, –o
its su

J

January enero
job tra*b*ajo, puesto
to join (someone) aco*m*pañar
joke broma
juice jugo
July julio
to jump saltar
June junio
jungle sel*v*a

K

kind clase (la), tipo
king rey (el)
to kiss *b*esar
kite cometa
knife cuchi*ll*o
to knock (at a door) *ll*amar
to know cono*c*er; sa*b*er

L

lake lago
land tierra
language idioma (el), lengua
last última, –o
last name ape*ll*ido
late tarde
later después, luego
to laugh reír(se)
leaf *h*oja
to learn aprender

to leave salir
left (left hand) izquierda, –o
leg pierna
lemon limón (el)
lesson lección (la)
let's vamos
letter (mail) carta
lettuce lechuga
lie (falsehood) mentira
life vida
light clara, –o; luz (la)
like como
to like (please) gustar
like that así
lip labio
list lista
little pequeña, –o; poca, –o
a little bit poquito
to live vivir
long larga, –o
to look (at) mirar
to look for buscar
Look out! ¡Ojo!
a lot mucha, –o
loud alta, –o
to love querer (ie)
low baja, –o
to lower bajar
lunch almuerzo

M

magazine revista
mail correo
main principal
mainly principalmente
to make hacer
man hombre
many muchas, –os
map mapa (el)
March marzo
to marry casar(se)
to masticate masticar
to matter importar
May mayo
me, to me me, mi
to mean significar
to measure medir (i)
meat carne (la)
to meet (come upon) encontrar (ue)
midnight medianoche (la)
milk leche (la)
million millón (el)
mine (mineral) mina
minus menos
minute minuto
miss señorita
mistaken equivocada, –o
mom mamá
moment momento, momentito
Monday lunes
money dinero
month mes (el)
moon luna

more más
morning mañana (la)
most más
mother madre
motorcycle motocicleta
mountain montaña
mountain lion tigre (el)
mouth boca
to move mover (ue)
movies cine
Mr. señor
Mrs. señora
much mucha, –o
music música
must deber
my mi

N

name nombre (el)
to name llamar(se)
nap siesta
napkin servilleta
nation nación (la), país (el)
national nacional
near cerca (de)
necessary necesaria, –o
necktie corbata
to need necesitar, faltar
Negro negra, –o
neither tampoco
neither . . . nor ni . . . ni
nephew sobrino
nephews, nephew(s) and niece(s)
  sobrinos
nervous nerviosa, –o
nest nido
never nunca
new nueva, –o
news (item of) noticia
newspaper diario, periódico
niece sobrina
night noche (la)
nine nueve
nine hundred novecientas, –os
nineteen, nineteenth diecinueve
ninety noventa
no no, ninguna, –o
nobody nadie
none ninguna, –o
noon mediodía (el)
no one nadie
north norte (el)
North Pole Polo Norte
nose nariz (la)
not no
to note notar
notebook cuaderno
nothing nada
to notice notar
November noviembre
now ahora
nowadays hoy día
number número

O

obscure oscura, –o
to observe observar
ocean océano
October octubre
Of course! ¡Claro!
Oh! ¡Ay!
old vieja, –o
on en, a
one una, –o, un
only sólo, solamente
only (one) única, –o
open, opened abierta, –o
to open abrir
or o, u
orange naranja (fruit)
orange-colored anaranjada, –o
to order mandar; pedir (i)
other otra, –o
Ouch! ¡Ay!
ought deber
our, ours nuestra, –o
ourselves nos
outside afuera
over (above) sobre
overcoat abrigo
own (one's own) propia, –o

P

page página
pain dolor (el)
to paint pintar
pair (persons) pareja
pants pantalones (los)
Paraguayan paraguaya, –o
paper papel (el)
to pardon disculpar, perdonar, dispensar
pardon, pardon me perdón
parents padres (los)
park parque (el)
part parte (la)
party fiesta
to pass pasar
past pasada, –o
pen pluma
pencil lápiz (el)
people gente (la), pueblo
pepper pimienta
per por
perfect perfecta, –o
permission permiso
to permit dejar, permitir
person persona
Peruvian peruana, –o
phrase frase (la)
to pick out escoger
pine pino
pink rosada, –o
pity lástima
place lugar (el)
plate plato

to play (a game) jugar (ue)
to play (musical instrument) tocar
pleasant agradable
to please gustar
pleasure gusto
pocket bolsillo
police force policía (la)
policeman policía (el)
politeness cortesía
poor pobre
population población (la)
Portuguese portugués, -esa
position puesto
to possess tener
poster cartel (el)
post office correo
potato papa (la), patata
practice practicar
to prepare preparar
present (adj.) presente
present (gift) regalo
to present (introduce) presentar
pretty bonita, –o, linda, –o
principal director (el); principal
private privada, –o
problem problema (el)
professor profesor (el), profesora (la)
profit provecho
to prohibit prohibir
to pronounce pronunciar
proverb refrán (el)
public pública, –o
pupil alumna, –o
to purchase comprar
purple morada, –o
purse bolsa
put puesta, –o
to put poner
to put on poner(se)

Q

quarter cuarto
question pregunta
quite bastante

R

railroad ferrocarril (el)
rain lluvia
to rain llover (ue)
raincoat impermeable (el)
to raise levantar(se)
ranch rancho
rapid rápida, –o
rapidly rápidamente
to read leer
ready lista, –o
real verdadera, –o
reason razón (la)
to recall recordar (ue)
to receive recibir
red roja, –o

to regret sentir (ie, i)
to remain quedar(se)
remainder resto
to remember recordar (ue)
to repair arreglar
to repeat repetir (i)
reporter periodista (el)
to request pedir (i)
to respond responder
rest (remainder) resto
restaurant café (el)
rested descansada, –o
to return regresar, volver (ue)
returned vuelta, –o
review revista
rice arroz (el)
rich rica, –o
right razón; derecha, –o
Right? ¿Verdad?
river río
river port puerto
road camino
roll (list of names) lista
room cuarto
rose rosa
round redonda, –o
ruler regla
to run (on foot) correr

S

sad triste
sailor marinero
saint san, santa, –o
Saint's Day santo
salad ensalada
salary salario
salt sal (la)
same misma, –o, igual
same to you igualmente
sand arena
Saturday sábado
to say decir
to say good-by despedir(se) (i)
　(de)
saying refrán (el)
school escuela
sea mar (el)
seaport puerto
season estación
seated sentada, –o
second segunda, –o
secondary secundaria, –o
secretary secretaria, –o
to see ver
to seem parecer
to select escoger
to sell vender
semester semestre (el)
sentence frase (la)
September septiembre
to serve servir (i)
to set (the table) poner

seven siete
seven hundred setecientas, –os
seventeen, seventeenth diecisiete
seventy setenta
several varias, –os
shame lástima
she ella
sheet (of paper) hoja
to shine brillar
shining brillante
ship barco
shirt camisa
shoe zapato
short baja, –o
to shout gritar
sick enferma, –o, mala, –o
to signify significar
silk seda
silver plata
to sing cantar
single sola, –o
to sink hundir
sir señor
sister hermana
to sit down sentarse (ie)
six seis
six hundred seiscientas, –os
sixteen, sixteenth dieciséis
sixty sesenta
skinny flaca, –o
skirt falda
sky cielo
sleep sueño
to sleep dormir (ue)
slowly despacio
small pequeña, –o, chica, –o
to smell oler (ue)
to smile sonreír (i)
snow nieve (la)
to snow nevar (ie)
so tan; así
so much tanta, –o
socks calcetines (los), medias
somebody alguien
someone alguien
something algo
son hijo
sons, sons and daughters hijos
soon pronto
soup sopa
south sud, sur (el)
Spaniard español, -ola
Spanish español; español, -ola
to speak hablar
speed velocidad
to spend (time) pasar
spoon cuchara
spring (season) primavera
square cuadrada, –o
star estrella
state estado
station estación (la)
to stay quedar(se)

still toda*v*ía
stingy tacaña, –o
stone piedra
to stop terminar (de), dejar de
store tienda
storm tormenta
story *h*istoria
straight recta, –o, derecha, –o
strait estrecho
street ca*ll*e (la)
streetcar tra*nv*ía (el)
stretch trecho
student estudiante, alumna, –o
studies estudios
to study estudiar
stumble trope*z*ar (ie)
stupid bruta, –o
success éxito
such, such a tal
sugar a*z*úcar (el *or* la)
suit tra*j*e (el)
summer *v*erano
sun sol (el)
Sunday domingo
supper *c*ena
Sure! ¡Claro!
surface super*f*icie (la)
surname ape*ll*ido
sweater suéter (el)
to swim nadar
sword espada
system sistema (el)

T

table mesa
tablecloth mantel (el)
to take *ll*e*v*ar, tomar
to take a bath *b*añar(se)
to take off quitar(se)
to take out sacar
tall alta, –o
task tarea
tea t*é* (el)
teacher maestra, –o, profesor, -ora
telephone teléfono
to tell contar (ue), de*c*ir
ten die*z*
to terminate terminar (de)
that que; eso, ese, esa; aque*ll*o,
aquel, aque*ll*a
the el, la, los, las
their su
them e*ll*os, -as; los, las, les
then enton*c*es, luego
there a*h*í, a*ll*í
there is, there are *h*ay
these estas, –os
they e*ll*os, -as
thin flaca, –o
to think pensar (ie)
thirst sed (la)
third ter*c*er, ter*c*era, –o

thirteen, thirteenth tre*c*e
thirty treinta
this esto, este, esta
those esas, –os; aque*ll*as, –os
thousand mil
three tres
three hundred tres*c*ientas, –os
through por
thumb pulgar (el)
Thursday jue*v*es
thus así
tigre tigre (el)
tightwad tacaña, –o
time *h*ora; tiempo; *v*ez
tired cansada, –o
title título
to turn on (electricity) poner
to a
tobacco to*b*aco
today *h*oy
toe dedo
together junta, –o
tomorrow mañana (el)
tongue lengua
too; too much demasiado
too (also) ta*mb*ién
tooth diente (el)
top coat abrigo
total total (el)
to touch tocar
toward ha*c*ia, para
town pueblo
tradition tradi*c*ión (la)
train tren (el)
to translate tradu*c*ir
translator intérprete (el)
to travel *v*iajar
tree ár*b*ol (el)
tremendous tremenda, –o
trip *v*ia*j*e (el)
to trip trope*z*ar (ie)
trouble molestia, dificultad (la)
trousers pantalones (los)
truck camión (el)
true *v*erdadera, –o
True? ¿ *V*erdad?
truth *v*erdad (la)
Tuesday martes
tunnel túnel (el)
to turn (a corner) doblar
twenty, twentieth *v*einte
twenty-eight *v*eintiocho
twenty-five *v*einticinco
twenty-four *v*einticuatro
twenty-nine *v*eintinue*v*e
twenty-one *v*eintiuna, –o, *v*eintiún
twenty-seven *v*eintisiete
twenty-six *v*eintiséis
twenty-three *v*eintitrés
twenty-two *v*eintidós
twisted tor*c*ida, –o
two dos
two hundred dos*c*ientas, –os

U

ugly   fea, –o
uncle   tío
uncles, uncle(s) and aunt(s)   tíos
uncomfortable   incómoda, –o
to understand   comprender
unfortunate   desgraciada, –o
unique   única, –o
university   universidad (la)
until   hasta
Uruguayan   uruguaya, –o
us   nosotras, –os, nos
to use   usar

V

vacation   vacaciones (las)
valiant   valiente
various   varias, –os
vegetables   vegetales (los)
velocity   velocidad (la)
Venezuelan   venezolana, –o
very   muy
viceroy   virrey (el)
village   pueblo
violent   violenta, –o
virgin   virgen (la)
visit   visita
to visit   visitar
vocabulary   vocabulario
voice   voz (la)

W

wages   salario
Wait!   ¡Espera!
to wake up   despertar(se) (ie)
to walk   andar, caminar
to want   querer (ie), desear
to wash   lavar(se)
watch   reloj (el)
water   agua
way (road)   camino
we   nosotras, –os
to wear   llevar, usar
weather   tiempo
Wednesday   miércoles
week   semana
well   bien

west   oeste (el)
what   cuál, cómo, qué, que
when   cuándo, cuando
where   dónde, donde
which   qué, cuál, que
whether   si
while   mientras
white   blanca, –o
who, whom   quién(es), quien(es), que
whole   toda, –o
why   por qué
wide   ancha, –o
wild   fiera, –o
wind   viento
window   ventana
wine   vino
winter   invierno
to wish   querer (ie), desear
with   con
without   sin
woman   mujer (la)
wonderful   magnífica, –o
word   palabra
work   trabajo
to work   trabajar
to be worth   valer
wrist   muñeca
to write   escribir
written   escrita, –o

Y

year   año
yellow   amarilla, –o
yesterday   ayer
yes   sí
yet   todavía
you   tú, te, ti; usted, ustedes
   (Abrev: Ud., Uds., Vd., Vds.),
   la, lo, le, las, los, les
to you   te, le, les, se
young   joven
young lady   señorita
your   tu, su

Z

zero   cero
zoo   zoológico

Acknowledgments

Illustrations by George Ulrich
Detailed map by Ernest Sawtelle

Black and White Photographs

p. 22, Donald Wright Patterson; p. 34, Paul Conklin; p. 48, Donald Wright Patterson; p. 88 Allan Cash, Rapho Guillumette; p. 100, Owen Franken; p. 113, Marie Mattson, Black Star; p. 122, Carol Ginandes; p. 122 center, Marion Patterson; p. 122 right, Carol Ginandes; p. 153, Constantine Manos, Magnum; p. 169, United Nations; p. 203, P. Anderson, Black Star; p. 248, Nicholas Sapieha, Rapho Guillumette; p. 293, Wayne Miller, Magnum; p. 318, Carol Ginandes; p. 338, René Burri, Magnum; p. 358, Jesse Fernandez, Nancy Palmer; p. 433, Wayne Miller, Magnum; p. 447, Carol Ginandes; p. 458, Shari Riff Kessler; p. 485, Azteca Films; p. 504, Fenno Jacobs, Black Star; p. 551, John Urban; p. 577, Marion Patterson.

Color Photographs

Insert 1   My Land, Your Land, Our Land

p. 1: top—Jan Lukas/Black Star; bot—Alan D. Hewitt; p. 2: top—Marc St. Gil, Black Star; bot—Marc St. Gil, Black Star; p. 3: top—Charles Moore, Black Star; bot—Charles Moore, Black Star; p. 4: top—Josef Muench; bot—Josef Muench.

Insert 2   Colombia, Venezuela, Ecuador

p. 1: top—Editorial Photocolor Archives/NY; bot—Editorial Photocolor Archives/NY; p. 2: top—Weston Kemp; cen—Weston Kemp; bot—Weston Kemp; p. 3: Pan American World Airways; p. 4: top—Thomas Höpker, Black Star; bot—Weston Kemp.

Insert 3   Peru, Bolivia

p. 1: top—Editorial Photocolor Archives/NY; bot—Pan American World Airways; p. 2: top—Editorial Photocolor Archives/NY; bot—Editorial Photocolor Archives/NY; p. 3: top—Claus Meyer, Black Star; bot—Lee Boltin; p. 4: top—Editorial Photocolor Archives/NY; bot lt—Bill Parsons, Nancy Palmer; bot rt—Jacques Jangoux.

Insert 4   Argentina, Chile

p. 1: top—Pan American World Airways; bot—Jacques Jangoux; p. 2: top—Editorial Photocolor Archives/NY; bot—Sergio Larrain, Magnum; p. 3: top—Editorial Photocolor Archives/NY; bot lt—Paul Conklin; bot rt—René Burri, Magnum; p. 4: top—Richard Wilkie, Black Star; bot—Weston Kemp.

Insert 5   Urban Life

p. 1: top—Oscar Buitrago, Black Star; cen—Weston Kemp; bot—Ernest Manewal, Black Star; p. 2: top—Weston Kemp; bot—Frederic Ohringer, Nancy Palmer; p. 3: top—Weston Kemp; bot—Bill Parsons, Nancy Palmer; p. 4: top—Claus Meyer, Black Star; bot—Reichman, International Foto File.

Insert 6   Rural Life

p. 1: top—Ernest Manewal, Black Star; bot—Ernest Manewal, Black Star; p. 2: top—Bill Parsons, Nancy Palmer; bot—Charles Harbutt, Magnum; p. 3: top—Bill Parsons, Nancy Palmer; bot—René Burri, Magnum; p. 4: top—Cornell Capa, Magnum; bot—Cornell Capa, Magnum.

Insert 7   Going Places, Doing Things

p. 1: top—Editorial Photocolor Archives/NY; bot—Lee Boltin; p. 2: Editorial Photocolor Archives/NY; p. 3: top—Reichman, International Foto File; bot—Bill Parsons, Nancy Palmer; p. 4: top—Robert Bobrow, Black Star; bot—Claus Meyer, Black Star.

Insert 8 The Land and Its Products

p. 1: top lt—Claus Meyer, Black Star; top rt—Ernest Manewal, Black Star; bot—Jacques Jangoux; p. 2: top—Bill Parsons, Nancy Palmer; bot—Ernest Manewal, Black Star; p. 3: top—Claus Meyer, Black Star; bot lt—Ernest Manewal, Black Star; bot rt—Jacques Jangoux; p. 4: top—Bill Parsons, Nancy Palmer; bot—Paul Conklin.

Symbols used in Etapas 1–7: 1—detail from Peruvian cloak; 2—head of Peruvian mace found at Vicus; 3—detail from Peruvian tapestry; 4—design on Ecuadorian bowl; 5—detail from Bolivian tapestry; 6—design from woven belt, Chile; 7—detail from Chancay pottery, Peru.